Oxford Dictionary of

Humorous
Quotations

FOURTH EDITION

Edited by
Ned Sherrin

with a Foreword by
Alistair Beaton

OXFORD
UNIVERSITY PRESS

OXFORD
UNIVERSITY PRESS

Great Clarendon Street, Oxford OX2 6DP

Oxford University Press is a department of the University of Oxford.
It furthers the University's objective of excellence in research, scholarship,
and education by publishing worldwide in

Oxford New York

Auckland Cape Town Dar es Salaam Hong Kong
Karachi Kuala Lumpur Madrid Melbourne Mexico City Nairobi
New Delhi Shanghai Taipei Toronto

With offices in

Argentina Austria Brazil Chile Czech Republic France Greece
Guatemala Hungary Italy Japan Poland Portugal
Singapore South Korea Switzerland Thailand Turkey Ukraine Vietnam

Oxford is a registered trade mark of Oxford University Press
in the UK and in certain other countries

Published in the United States
by Oxford University Press Inc., New York

Selection and arrangement © Ned Sherrin, Oxford University Press 1995, 2001, 2005, 2008, 2009
Introduction © Ned Sherrin 1995, 2001, 2005
Foreword to the fourth edition © Alistair Beaton 2008, 2009

British Library Cataloguing in Publication Data
Data available

Library of Congress Cataloging-in-Publication Data
Data available

ISBN 978-0-19-923716-6 (Hbk)
ISBN 978-0-19-957006-5 (Pbk)

10 9 8 7 6 5 4 3 2 1

Typeset in Photina and Frutiger
Printed in Great Britain
by Clays Ltd, St Ives plc

In memory of
NED SHERRIN
1931–2007

Contents

Project *Team*

Commissioning Editor	Ben Harris
Associate Editor	Susan Ratcliffe
Reading Programme	Jean Harker Verity Mason Richard Ramage
Library Research	Ralph Bates Russell Inglis
Data Capture	Susanne Charlett
Proofreading	Carolyn Garwes

Foreword to the
Fourth Edition

Compiling a dictionary—any kind of dictionary—is not usually thought of as
a glamorous activity. Compilers need to be precise, thorough, and obsessively
accurate. They must have a compendious knowledge of the subject and be at
ease with the material. Without diligent attention to detail, they will get lost in a
jungle of words (in which case a desperate publisher will have to send in rescue
teams to save the project from chaos). In short, I imagine the perfect compiler of
dictionaries to be a polite, reclusive, bookish, mild-mannered, professorial sort
of person; the sort of person whom one can admire at a distance but whom one
doesn't necessarily want to invite round for dinner, on the grounds that an evening
of Rabelaisian pleasure is unlikely to ensue.

This is, of course, all rank prejudice. I know it is rank prejudice because the
compiler of this particular dictionary was a man who combined the most enormous
erudition with a relentless joie de vivre. Ned Sherrin, who died in 2007 at the age
of 76, brought a boundless brio to the art of living. His encyclopedic knowledge of
theatre, books, and popular music went hand in hand with a fearless wit and an
irreverent, almost childlike sense of fun. It is this mixture of fun and erudition that
makes the *Oxford Dictionary of Humorous Quotations* such a glorious volume.

The concept of 'humour' is a broad one. It covers everything from the gently
arresting to the laugh-out-loud funny, on the way taking in the amusing, the
witty, the provocative, the vicious, and the scabrous. Thus when we read George
Orwell's claim, 'Advertising is the rattling of a stick inside a swill bucket', it is not
likely to make us laugh. It is, however, a vigorously provocative and entertaining
statement (unless you're an advertising executive, I suppose) and therefore earns its
keep in this dictionary.

At the other end of the spectrum there is the tale of actor Richard Harris, dying
of cancer, who was carried out of the Savoy to a waiting ambulance. As he passed
fellow diners he shouted out:

> It was the food. It was the food.

This makes me laugh out loud, even though it skates on morbidly thin ice—or
perhaps *because* it skates on morbidly thin ice. In its cheeky disrespect for death it
echoes Peter O' Toole's ringing declaration a few years earlier that:

> The only exercise I take is walking behind the coffins of friends who took exercise.

Sherrin, of course, had the advantage of knowing both Harris and O'Toole in
person. In fact, to go out to the theatre or to a restaurant with Sherrin was to
gain the impression that he knew everybody in Britain. By this I don't mean only
actors, singers, writers, directors, and producers. He seemed equally at home with
politicians, poets, bankers, restaurateurs, newsreaders, musicians, cricketers,
footballers, hookers, vicars, priests, archbishops, accountants, taxi drivers, and
perfectly ordinary members of the public. His familiarity with some of the great

wits of the age, combined with his extraordinary ability to recall funny lines (what he called his 'magpie memory'), most certainly gave him a head start in putting together this collection, here in the lovingly revised and updated version on which he worked in the last year of his life.

Naturally, any dictionary of quotations worth its name is obliged to include the greatest funny lines of all time. Some of these may now be a little threadbare through familiarity, but they have become part of the culture, and must have their place. Thus the great Oscar Wilde is represented by over ninety entries, and quite right too. These include such classics as:

> There is only one thing in the world worse than being talked about and that is not being talked about;

and:

> To lose one parent, Mr Worthing, may be regarded as a misfortune; to lose both looks like carelessness;

and:

> One must have a heart of stone to read the death of Little Nell without laughing;

and of course:

> I have nothing to declare except my genius.

Where Sherrin includes quotations from the very famous, however, he does not restrict himself to the obvious. Thus, one may be familiar with the work of Noël Coward, be able even to recite 'Mad Dogs and Englishmen' by heart, yet not have come across this lesser-known gem:

> We must all be very kind to Auntie Jessie,
> For she's never been a Mother or a Wife,
> You mustn't throw your toys at her
> Or make a vulgar noise at her,
> She hasn't led a very happy life.

Some quotations have been so absorbed into the culture that it is useful to be reminded that they really are quotations. Thus, when Clare Booth Luce stood aside for Dorothy Parker saying, 'Age before Beauty,' Parker replied with, 'Pearls before swine'. This is so familiar now that it probably no longer raises a smile. All humour needs an element of surprise. That, however, is almost the only generalization about humour that I would confidently make. As Sherrin himself observed in his introduction to the 1995 edition of this dictionary, it is impossible to be objective about humour. This is why one person's collection of humorous quotations is in the end a very personal affair. It is partly a question of taste, partly a matter of circumstance.

A witty rejoinder witnessed personally is always a great joy. To read it later in a compilation is perhaps less joyful, but becomes dazzling again if we allow our fantasy free rein, and imagine we might have been there at the time. There is always something more awesome about a spontaneous moment of wit than one crafted carefully for the page. So I wish I'd been there when Groucho Marx was asked if Groucho were his real name and he replied, 'No, I'm breaking it in for a friend.' I wish I'd been there when somebody enquired of Billy Wilder, 'What's an associate producer?' and Wilder replied, 'Anyone who's prepared to associate with a producer.' And I certainly wish I'd been there when Sir John Gielgud, urged by Peter Brook to dig deeper into his emotions by thinking of something terrifying, replied, 'We open in two weeks.'

Sherrin was too much the professional to attempt to include any of his own quotations in a dictionary of which he himself was editor. But since he was no mean wit himself, I think it is only right that this introduction should include a line from the great man himself. A few weeks before his death I went to see him in his Chelsea flat and was hardly through the door before he barked, 'Champagne, please! Large one for you, small one for me.' I poured as requested. He raised himself from the pillows, screwed up his eyes, stared at his glass, and said 'Not *that* fucking small.'

ALISTAIR BEATON

April 2008

Preface to *Third Edition*

A new edition of this dictionary inspires mixed emotions in the editor's breast. There is the business of welcoming new friends and saying farewell to old ones who have already served through two editions. However, some are waved goodbye with relief, while some new entries are welcomed with apprehension. The editor may love his new babies, but can he be sure that they will find favour with his readers?

Take the very first themes, *Acting* and *Actors*. Five of those severe and perhaps too clever verdicts on Shakespearean performances have gone: Agate on Balliol Holloway's Othello, Tynan on Margaret Leighton's Rosalind, Cardus on Forbes Robertson's Hamlet, and Darlington on Richard Briers's Dane. But newly arrived is Tynan on Yvonne Furneaux in *Ondine*, 'A buxom temptress . . . more impressive in silhouette than in action.' (So much more restrained than John Simon on Diana Rigg as a naked Heloïse, 'built like a brick mausoleum with insufficient flying buttresses'.) And plenty of the harsh old excoriations remain, Alan Brien on Michael Hordern's Macbeth, Noël Coward on Anna Neagle's Queen Victoria ('Albert must have married beneath him'), Nancy Banks Smith on John Hannah's Inspector Rebus ('He could also play John Knox, the teenage years'), and Tynan again on Claire Bloom's Virgilia ('she yearns so hungrily that I longed to throw her a fish').

To Ralph Richardson's splendid summing up of acting, 'the art of keeping a large group of people from coughing', we now add Patrick Troughton's even sharper definition, 'Acting is shouting in the evening', and Katharine Hepburn's dismissive, 'Acting is the most minor of gifts and not a very high-class way to earn a living. Shirley Temple could do it at the age of four.' The late Miss Hepburn is backed up by another new (and contemporary) entry from Johnny Depp, 'There's nothing worse than actors who give the impression that they've taken on the priesthood. Acting is really about lying and, in my case, drinking coffee.' Give the last new word to Joanne Woodward, 'Acting is like sex. You should do it, not talk about it.'

An editor required to find the space for well over 600 new quotations and nearly 30 new themes can luxuriate in a sigh of relief when he spots a candidate for rejection. It may have truth, it may be pertinent, it may be strongly expressed— but why did he ever think it was funny? An example, from Osbert Lancaster, 'The aristocracy and landed gentry, although Nationally Entrusted and sadly Thirkellised, are still thank goodness, for all their constant complainings of extinction, visibly and abundantly there.' This reads as well past its sell-by date, and plenty of Osbert Lancaster's wit survives alongside the newcomers.

Alan Bennett is guaranteed to set the armchair on a roar. Now we have room to add up-to-date Bennett from his latest play, *The History Boys*, 'History is a commentary on the various and continuing incapabilities of men. What is history? History is women following behind with the buckets.' And that wonderful mute, inglorious Mrs or Ms Milton who found her anonymous voice when she queued to see the Prime Minister at the Hutton Enquiry: 'I want to see the hand of history on his collar.' Sadly her wish was not granted.

In choosing new quotations we have leaned towards the contemporary across a variety of fields. Nigella Lawson defended toad-in-the-hole to an American audience: 'This is nothing to do with frogs' legs. No amphibian is harmed in making this dish.' On the football field, Liverpool fans serenaded West Ham supporters to the tune of *La Donna e Mobile*, 'You've got DiCanio, We've nicked your stereo.' From *The Simpsons*, Groundskeeper Willie's opinion of the French was a classic cliché, 'Bonjour, you cheese-eating surrender monkeys.' (Woody Allen had a more liberal comment, 'I don't want to have to refer to my French fry potatoes as freedom fries, and I don't want to have to freedom kiss my wife.') According to Christina Onassis's deadly phrase, Teddy Kennedy arrived at her father's funeral, 'Looking like a priestly hustler peddling indulgences.'

Alastair Campbell's unconsciously hilarious, 'We don't do God', when Tony Blair was asked about his faith, jostles with a line from Monty Python's *Life of Brian*, the more artful, 'He's not the Messiah, he's a very naughty boy!' A book published in 2004 (Bevis Hillier's *The Bonus of Laughter*) reminded us, just in time, of John Betjeman's comment when he saw a commemorative stone engraved, 'Laid by the Poet Laureate' and murmured, 'Every nice girl's ambition.'

Few comments are as succinct as Hugh Dyson's protest at the appearance of yet another elf when he was listening to a reading from Tolkien's *The Lord of the Rings* (Mrs Patrick Campbell might have warned that its strength could 'frighten the horses'). And it was high time that the traditional BBC management cry was included, 'Assistant heads must roll!'

A dictionary of quotations can acquaint a phrase-maker with strange bedfellows. How happy would Baden-Powell be to be crammed between the covers alongside Lord Rochester? How shocked would he have been by the latter Lord's account of precisely how he expressed a fit of rage. Imagine Rochester's contempt for Baden-Powell's mistrust of 'men with waxed moustaches'—'It often means vanity and sometimes drink.'

Lord Melbourne is a world away from Miss Janet Jackson, but both find a place: Melbourne with his reasons for not reading *Oliver Twist*, 'It's all among workhouses and Coffin Makers and Pickpockets . . . I wish to avoid them'; Ms Jackson with the excuse for her sartorial comeuppance while duetting with young Mr Timberlake, 'A wardrobe malfunction.' The globetrotting Peter Ustinov, of whom his Army Selection Board reported 'On no account is this man to be put in charge of others' has little in common with the reluctant traveller Philip Larkin, 'I wouldn't mind seeing China if I could come back the same day.'

Three new women contributors are more in sympathy. Barbara Skelton and Elizabeth Arden would probably both sympathize with Lynn Fontanne, mystified by baseball, 'Finally I realized that the gentleman holding the bat is antagonistic to the man throwing the ball.' Fontanne and Arden would understand Skelton's keenly felt disappointment, 'My birthday. No adequate fuss made.' So would the other two appreciate Arden's reaction to the Wall Street Crash, 'Our clients are coping with the stress of financial loss by soaking in a hot bath scented with my Rose Geranium bath crystals.'

From a different generation Johnny Depp is vivid about his two small children, 'It's like hanging out with two miniature drunks.'

But all my choices remain subjective. For anyone who turns the pages with a long face I can only offer my apologies. Let me rather point you to some felicities. To Sydney Smith on Brighton Pavilion, 'As if St Paul's had come down and littered', I have added Keith Waterhouse's exact verdict on the recently elevated city, 'Brighton looks like a town that is constantly helping the police with their enquiries.'

'Regrets, I've had a few . . . ' as that appalling song puts it; but my regrets for the third time are the quotations which came too late into my ken. They repeated the 1980s *Arena* Profile of Mel Brooks with the funny title *I Thought I Was Taller*, to celebrate the opening of *The Producers* at the end of 2004. It reminded me of his line in the earlier interview, 'What's going on? I have meetings with important gentiles.' Jimmy Carr, suddenly a favourite comedian, vouchsafed his favourite joke—black as they get, 'Throwing acid is wrong—in some people's eyes.' Petronella Wyatt, no stranger to romance in Doughty Street herself, summed up the luncheon at which she introduced Mr David Blunkett to Mrs Kimberly Quinn, 'David and I ate Dover sole, Kimberly ate Mr Blunkett.'

Talking of Doughty Street, it was also too late when I remembered Mrs Leo Hunter's immortal poem in *The Pickwick Papers*:

> . . . Can I unmoved see thee dying
> On a log
> Expiring frog!

'Finely expressed' as Mr Pickwick put it. Perhaps we can have it *all* next time.

Sometimes a new quip arrived too late to be subjected to the strict standard of OUP verification. Sitting in the stalls on the first night of the new, stage, musical version of *Mary Poppins*, I joined in the laughter when the boy child describes the Nasty Nanny who had terrified his father a generation earlier, 'She looks like someone who would eat her own young.' Is that a line from one of P. L. Travers's original books (unlikely) or the screenplay of the 1964 film, or did it spring from Julian Fellowes' fertile mind when he worked on the book of the stage show? Then we must enquire if the writer concerned knew of Harry Champion, the great turn-of-the-century music-hall star (sadly neither 'Boiled beef and carrots' nor 'Any old iron' have found a place in the book). Asked about unfriendly audiences in a Glasgow hall he said, 'They eat their own young.'

Perhaps we can resolve it before a 4th edition. There might even be room for, 'This is my Jerry Springer moment!'

NED SHERRIN

January 2005

Preface to *Second Edition*

This edition of the *Oxford Dictionary of Humorous Quotations*, like its predecessor, attempts to ensure that 'the liveliest effusions of wit and humour are conveyed to the world in the best chosen language' (Jane Austen, *Northanger Abbey*). In pursuit of this aim, over 800 new quotations have been added, some material has (regretfully but firmly) been cut, and over 30 completely new themes (from **Baseball** to **Secrecy**) have been added.

Canvassing readers' opinions confirmed the importance of contemporary resonance, and underlined (as a critic of the first edition pointed out) that we are now so blest with living humorists. Among welcome new arrivals to the *Dictionary* are Dick Vosburgh ('I'm aghast! if there ever was one') and David Mamet ('They say the definition of ambivalence is watching your mother-in-law drive over a cliff in your new Cadillac'). Some older quotations have had to go, but earlier periods still make fresh contributions, as with Lady Mary Wortley Montagu's view of Queen Caroline and her maids-of-honour dressed in pink:

> Superior to her waiting nymphs,
> As lobster to attendant shrimps.

Inadvertent humour can also make an insistent claim, as with the rebuke to Zero Mostel when appearing before the House Un-American Activities Committee: 'If your interpretation of a butterfly at rest brought any money into the coffers of the Communist Party, you contributed directly to the propaganda effort of the Communist Party.'

In reviewing another dictionary, the same critic, Mr Bevis Hillier, took issue with the recycling of quotations: 'As a child I would politely decline the gobstopper that three other kids had already sucked.' The problem here is that a dictionary is a reference book, and if its proud purchaser wishing to check a famous quotation dimly recalled goes to his *Humorous Quotations* and does not find it there, he feels short changed. Again, some wiseacres opening the book will discover that a quotation the editor has rejected is absent, and conclude gleefully that ignorance is the explanation. And what if this Mr Know-All has less self-awareness than the character in Edward Albee's *Who's Afraid of Virginia Woolf*: 'I have a fine sense of the ridiculous but no sense of humour'?

Mr Hillier's advice is to 'buy a large hard-backed notebook, read books and newspapers for ten years, writing down the things that make you smile or laugh, then organize them into a book'. This is very much the method I have employed for both these editions, augmenting my own finds from the Oxford University Press's vast store of quotations. Items which I have been pleased to add range from Gore Vidal's response to his novel *Lincoln* being described as 'meretricious' ('Really? Well, meretricious and a happy New Year to you!') to Lord Runcie's comment after appearing on Loose Ends with Diana Rigg in the last months of his life: 'Being hugged by Diana Rigg is worth three sessions of chemotherapy.' Despite the risk of contagion from a second suck at the gobstopper, I have included those quotations which amused me from lists of omissions in reviews: two welcome additions of this kind are Mary Anne Disraeli's assessment of her husband ('I wish you could only see Dizzy in his bath, then you would know what a white skin is') and Else Mendl on her dislike of soup: 'I do not believe in building a meal on a lake.'

It is not only a fisherman who laments the one that got away. One quotation found just too late was Peter Nichols' comment on Harold Hobson's assessment of Tom Stoppard: 'Last time Hobson compared him favourably with Shakespeare. This time he puts him in the scales with God and finds the older man a bit lightweight.' And only as the Dictionary goes to press have I remembered that Arlington Stringham's jokes were filched (on Clovis's evidence) from Lady Isabel, 'who slept in a hammock and understood Yeats's poems'. Eleanor Stringham took an overdose on discovering this. When the story was first published in a Saki collection in 1912, the *New Age* complained, 'Why, oh why, can we see no humour in these stories?' John Lane published the criticism in the midst of universal raves to advertise the book, but the sole voice of dissent reminds us of the eternal problem of humour— its unassailable subjectivity.

Another wonderful item, which also surfaced just too late, was a couplet by H. F. Ellis, quoted by Miles Kington in his *Guardian* obituary of Ellis in December 2000:

> Mine eyes have missed the glory of the coming of the Lord
> Through searching through my pockets where my optic aids are stored . . .

Here I hope to have included 'the Quip Modest, the Reproof Valiant and the Countercheck Quarelsome' in sufficient measure to satisfy the reader. At least the Quips, Reproofs and Counterchecks are offered without analysis. 'Humour can be dissected in the same way a frog can—but the thing dies in the process' (E. B. White).

As a tiny envoi to this preface, here is a story that does not fit the main text. Sir Michael Gambon told me the other day that he had once played Oscar Wilde. A civilian had asked him, 'Was it hard playing a homosexual?'

'Oh, no,' said the great Gambon, whimsically leading him on. 'You see, I used to be one.'

'Why did you stop?'

'It made my eyes water.'

On reflection, I think 'It made my eyes water' might slip into the literature to do duty for a multitude of excuses.

NED SHERRIN

November 2000

Introduction to the
First Edition

Wittgenstein claimed that his ambition to write a philosophical work constructed entirely of jokes was frustrated when he realized that he had no sense of humour. The editor of a dictionary of humorous quotations, looking back on his final selection, must wonder how many of his choices will convince the reader that he shares Wittgenstein's disability. For the philosopher there was comfort in the thought that no-one *completely* devoid of a sense of humour would be so aware of his limitations. There is also the suspicion, supported by diligent research, that many jokes are indeed fashioned by people who have no sense of humour.

These reassurances are denied to an editor. He is accountable for deciding that every one of roughly 5,000 quotations in this collection is likely to set the table on a roar. His paranoia is increased by the spectrum of attitudes to humour. 'Humour's a funny thing,' says a character in Terry Johnson's play *Dead Funny*. But an old lady coming out of one of Victoria Wood's shows complained within earshot of the star, 'I don't find humour funny.'

'The joy of simple laughter' is another of Terry Johnson's deftly deployed clichés. Laughter is not invariably joyous and what produces it is rarely simple. I make this disclaimer because I have been encouraged by the publishers to make a more personal selection than the compilers of the fourth edition of the *Oxford Dictionary of Quotations* and the *Oxford Dictionary of Modern Quotations*. These were assembled in the former case by recruiting 'a team of distinguished advisers, united by scholarship in particular literary periods and subject fields' who picked their way through 'the *embarras de richesses*' offered by earlier editions; and in the latter by reducing 'a collection of more than 200,000 citations assembled by combing books, magazines, and newspapers'. Both books are 'an objective selection of quotations which are most widely known and used'.

It is impossible to be objective about humour. Therefore although I have combed both dictionaries because they contain so many quotations which are humorous as well as well-known, I have also sought to admit many which gain entrance not because they are well-known but because they are amusing and deserve our better acquaintance.

Chronologically the spread is from the earliest quotations; but I have justified the inclusion of antique saws solely on the grounds that they raise a smile today. Paul Johnson recently suggested in the *Spectator* that the first recorded laughter occurred at the end of the Early Bronze Age, about 2000 BC:

> Significantly it was a woman who laughed. The Book of Genesis tells us (xviii. 10 ff.) that, when Sarah overheard the Lord inform her husband Abraham she was to have a son, 'Sarah laughed within herself, saying, after I am waxed old shall I have pleasure, my lord being old also?'

Johnson's conclusion is that the first joke was female and was about sex. Sarah tried to keep it to herself; but the men accused her of laughing. She denied it, 'for she was afraid'. It may have seemed a good joke to Sarah in 2000 BC but that does not justify its inclusion today. On the other hand some 3,600 years later, Shakespeare's stage direction 'Exit, pursued by a bear' in *The Winter's Tale*, now a mellow 400 years old, still makes me smile—whether he intended it or not. However, there is no room for all the smiles in Shakespeare. I mourn the passing of 'Nay, faith, let me not play a woman: I have a beard coming,' from the *Dream*, which is warm, funny, and well observed; however, it is preserved in the *Oxford Dictionary of Quotations*.

I have not thought it necessary to reopen the ever-raging debate fought over the boundaries between wit and humour. In introducing his *Anthology of Wit*, Guy Boas derives humour from the supposition that human nature was once held to be determined by the physical 'humours' and fluids which make up the body. Imbalance of these fluids produces (as in Ben Jonson's plays) conduct which was freakish, absurd, or whimsical—provoking laughter at the recognizably humorous situation. The word 'wit', however, stems from the Old English *witan* to know, which lent itself flatteringly to the Anglo-Saxon approximation to Parliament, and implied optimistically the exercise there of the intellect. So wit is associated with the mind's contribution to what is amusing. 'Humour', to Boas, 'is the funny situation or object; wit is the fun which a particular mind subjectively perceives on the situation or object.' There is room in this book for both. So what were the criteria for the quotations which survive?

No such book can afford to ignore perennials like Wilde, Mencken, Coward, Parker, Kaufman, and Shaw; Johnny Speight, the creator of *Till Death Do Us Part* (and therefore, in America, of *All in the Family*) grew up reading collections of quotations and concluded that Bernard Shaw was a gag-writer, which fuelled his own ambitions in the field of comedy. Among phrase-makers in recent years Gore Vidal, Tom Stoppard, Alan Bennett, Russell Baker, P. J. O'Rourke, Stephen Fry, and Craig Brown demand inclusion as new hardy annuals. Some writers are consistently witty, some have a happy inspiration. The former earn more entries than the latter. I did not consider it useful to operate a quota system.

The unintentionally humorous can be as diverting and must also be found a place. With its 'Colemanballs' feature *Private Eye* magazine spotlighted for our superior pleasure the pressure under which sports commentators try and sometimes fail to find the right word—though who can be sure whether 'the batsman's Holding, the bowler's Willey' was Brian Johnston's accidental comment or the result of a confrontation for which he had long been lying in wait. In America there is the famous Phil Rizzuto remark when his commentary was interrupted by the news of the Pope's death: 'that puts a damper, even on a Yankee win.' Dan Quayle and George Bush are modern political stars on the unconscious humour circuit. It is hard to do better than Quayle's alleged hesitation on visiting Latin America, 'not having studied Latin', or his insistence on the 'e' at the end of 'potato'.

Political correctness throws up a shoal of examples of unconscious humour, some of which have found a place. I might have found room for excerpts from the reported BBC *Woman's Hour* directive to new presenters in the early 1990s:

> 3. Do not be surprised that a woman has achieved something . . . 4. Do not be surprised that an older person has achieved something . . . 5. Do not be surprised that a black person has achieved something . . .

but there is a leaden mind behind that directive which does not deserve to be included.

The pronouncements of censors are another rich vein of unconscious humour. In the 1920s Nina Shortt, a daughter of a film censor and ex-Home Secretary, Sir Edward Shortt, refused a certificate to Jean Cocteau's avant-garde movie *The Seashell and the Clergyman*:

> [This film] is so cryptic as to be almost meaningless. If there is a meaning, it is doubtless objectionable.

Lord Tyrell, who succeeded Shortt, went one better in 1937:

> We take pride in observing that there is not a single film showing in London today that deals with any of the burning issues of the hour.

The sublimely named Major de Fonblanque Cox combined censorship with dogbreeding. On his appointment he declared:

> No, my boy, let us show clean films in the old country! I shall judge film stories as I would horseflesh, or a dog. I shall look for clean lines everywhere.

There may be less art in this than in the words which the Grossmiths put into Mr Pooter's mouth, 'I left the room with silent dignity but caught my foot in the mat,' but there is no less humour.

Another *Private Eye* feature, 'Pseud's Corner', is based on yet another sort of unconscious humour. I do not think Professor Karl Miller's verdict on the footballer Paul Gascoigne for *The London Review of Books* found its way there, but it deserved to:

> He was a highly charged spectacle on the field of play: fierce and comic, formidable and vulnerable, urchin-like and waiflike, a strong head and torso with comparatively breakable legs, strange-eyed, pink-faced, fair-haired, tense and upright, a priapic monolith in the Mediterranean sun . . . he is magic, and fairy-tale magic at that.

Of them all, the late Lord Massereene and Ferrard emerges as a new star provider of unintentional amusement, recommending the warning notice, 'Beware of the Agapanthus'.

Quotations are taken from novels, plays, poems, essays, letters, speeches, films, radio and television broadcasts, songs, popular jokes, graffiti, and advertisements, accurately attributed where possible. Some have had to fall by the wayside for reasons for space, or because I could not legitimize them. Under the firm but patient guidance of the Dictionary Department at Oxford University Press, I have endeavoured to help their devoted detectives to verify the quotations chosen in original or authoritative sources.

I have found space for some of the best-known catchphrases which have sprung from radio or television programmes, but sources are so prolific that a general anthology can only hint at the richness—from the inventive conceits of Frank Muir and Denis Norden in *Take It From Here* to the anachronistic whimsies of Ben Elton and Richard Curtis in *Blackadder*. In *Take It From Here* the puns were elaborate, the plotting devious:

> [SILAS THE PURITAN] Thou art spending all the royal coffers on this female person [Nell Gwynne]. But yesterday you sold the Crown Jewels . . . to buy her a sedan chair with a sunshine roof!
> [KING CHARLES II] So I blued a couple of baubles? 'Tis of no account.
> [SILAS] (reproachfully) But you're forever blueing baubles.

In *Blackadder* the humour is starker:

> The Germans are a cruel race. Their operas last for six hours and they have no word for fluffy.

Some catchphrases demand to be included, such as the Chief Whip's notorious response in Michael Dobbs' *House of Cards*:

> You might very well think that. I couldn't possibly comment.

Formula jokes are also generally too plentiful and often too unfunny to earn a place—sick jokes, light-bulb jokes, elephant jokes, and drummer jokes are excluded. I have also resisted the temptation to follow a 1994 trend with the latest fashionable American joke craze, 'Doing the Dozens', allegedly a venerable Afro-American habit of trading insults—preferably about the opponent's mother. For example, 'Your mother is so ugly, when she walks into the bank they turn off the camera,' or 'Your mother is so dumb, she went to the movies and the sign said, "Under 17 not admitted", so she came back with 18 friends.' 'Doing the Dozens' can wait for the slim paperback volume in which these ripostes will doubtless one day be collected by another publisher.

At the moment when I identified a mass-multiplying reproach 'like turkeys voting for Christmas', a scholarly commentator in the *Independent Magazine* traced the birth of this death-wish simile to the late David Penhaligon who used it to highlight his distaste for the British Lib-Lab pact (1977–8). For Penhaligon it emphasized the Prime Minister's (James Callaghan's) certainty that the Liberals would never vote to bring him down. Callaghan himself plundered it the next year to slight the weak position of Scottish Nationalists. It crossed the Irish Sea when a Fianna Fáil member of the Dáil said that, 'a woman voting for divorce is like turkeys . . .' Both the Bruges Group of Conservative MPs and Michael Heseltine rented the phrase for their own ends in 1991. Paddy Ashdown, the leader of Penhaligon's old party, grabbed it to pour scorn on rebel Tories during the Maastricht debate. The Tory Party, he said, would not be defeated by its place-preserving backbenchers. For them to bring the Government down, 'would be like turkeys . . .' he said, 'etc.' The apotheosis of this witfest came when the French awarded a special 'foreign political humour prize' to the British MP Teresa Gorman for trotting out the same rubric, once again in the context of Maastricht. If anyone deserves to accept the prize it is the Widow Penhaligon.

Topicality admitted the inclusion of a borderline case, a version of another cliché-ridden humorous quip which is custom-made for hand-me-down insults. John Major was not being witty or original when he called some of his backbenchers 'a few apples short of a picnic', but the phrase caught the public fancy. I can't remember whether the ex-chairman of Test Selectors, Ted Dexter, said of someone or was described by someone as being, 'a few roos loose in the top paddock'. 'One brick short of a load' and 'One slice short of a sandwich' are in the same vein: but none of them earns inclusion. Victor Lewis-Smith, describing Lord Rees-Mogg as 'two coupons short of a pop-up toaster', gets nearer with a vivid variation but is still disqualified by the curse of formula. Had he been Prime Minister he might have made it.

The files of the OUP Dictionary Department have inevitably provided a mass of material, all providentially sourced. Sadly many of the contributions derived from my own serendipitizing were lodged solely in the mind which failed to remember where I had found them. However, perhaps I should have let stand more of those remarks at whose birth I was present. One example is Anthony Quinton's impromptu comment as solemn music flooded a BBC studio when we were taken off the air for a news bulletin during the Falklands War. 'I know that tune,' he said, 'it's Sibelius' "You Can't Win 'Em All".' I can't think of a better authority.

In culling the new material the decision to organize the book thematically and not to arrange quotations under author headings was often revealing. In the section on **Wealth**, for example, some fun is to be had by the witty at the expense of the wealthy; but I relish the petulant note that invades the voices of the rich from Lord Durham (who in the nineteenth century was known as 'King Jog' because he could 'jog along' on £40,000 a year) through Lord Northcliffe (who said that when he wanted a peerage he would 'buy it like an honest man') and Chips Channon (who found it difficult in 1934 to go out shopping and spend less than £200) to Alan Clark (moaning in his diary in 1987 of the £700,000 in his Abbey National Crazy-High-Interest account, 'but what's the use?'). Sadly I could not confirm the Duke of Marlborough's bleat when urged to sack one of his many Viennese pastry-cooks, 'May not a man have a biscuit?'

Looking at other collections, I was frustrated by innumerable headings which yield very few quotations. Here we have a total of 149 classifications, some of which represent the combination of related headings. For example, **Truth** is linked with **Lies** rather than sitting unhappily in separate beds, while on the other hand the stage is such a productive source that I have separated **Actors and Acting** from **The Theatre**. Appropriate cross-reference entries are supplied, and keyword and author indexes further facilitate the chasing of references. (For a more detailed account, see 'How to Use the Dictionary'.)

I have introduced a large number of quotations from popular songs—so much wit is crammed into the discipline which a lyric writer observes. My selection cannot be comprehensive but it aims to point the road to a Samarkand of riches. Which do you choose from a Sondheim lyric? Look at 'Now', a song from *A Little Night Music*, in which a literary-minded middle-aged husband is trying to decide which gem will turn on his reluctant young wife. I sacrificed:

> The Brontes are grander
> But not very gay.
> Her taste is much blander
> I'm sorry to say,
> But is Hans Christian Ander-
> sen ever risqué?

in favour of:

> And Stendhal would ruin
> The plan of attack,
> As there isn't much blue in
> The Red and the Black.

But the whole score is laced with wit.

To backtrack, I was tempted to include the current Professor of Poetry at Oxford's review of Sondheim's *Sweeney Todd* in the *Sunday Times*, 'the worst rhymes in London', along with Dan Quayle's contributions to unconscious humour; but it got away. Coward, Porter, and Hart are dinosaurs in the field but other British and American lyric writers from E. Y. Harburg to Raymond Douglas Davis (The Kinks) deserve a more detailed examination than this book can afford. I hope enough creeps in to point the reader in the right direction.

Songs are easy to source, but an arrangement in themes prompted all sorts of quotations that dance tantalizingly in my magpie memory and have eluded our keenest detectives. Some of recollection's children I cannot legitimize. Some I have had to omit for others more favoured. Here are some of those I mourn:

Lord Thorneycroft's reply to Lord Houghton's letter, 'outlining his massive campaign to put animals into politics':

> Dear Douglas, Thank you for your letter about animals. I do think that the poor creatures have enough to put up with without being put into politics. Yours sincerely . . .

Nietzsche and Michael Frayn on books:

> Books for general reading always smell badly. The odour of the common people hangs about them. (Nietzsche)

> There is something about a blurb-writer paying his respects to a funny book which puts one in mind of a short-sighted Lord Mayor raising his hat to a hippopotamus. (Frayn)

Robert Altman on children:

> If you have a child who is seven feet tall, you don't cut off his head or his legs. You buy him a bigger bed and hope he plays basketball.

Evelyn Waugh on class:

> No writer before the middle of the nineteenth century wrote about the working-class other than as grotesques or as pastoral decorations. Then when they were given the vote, certain writers started to suck up to them.

Ronald Firbank on the country:

> I'd like to spank the white walls of (that shepherd's) cottage.

Antonia Fraser on death:

> Once there was a Drag Hunt Ball, just outside Oxford, to which I had unaccountably failed to be asked. I asked God to do something about it, and God recklessly killed poor King George, as a result of which the Hunt Ball was cancelled.

Mickey Rose on dress-sense:

> Nobody would wear beige to rob a bank.

Lord Rosebery's advice to Queen Victoria:

> There is much exaggeration about the attainments required for a speaker. All Speakers are highly successful, all Speakers are deeply regretted, and are generally announced to be irreplaceable. But a Speaker is soon found, and found, almost invariably, among the mediocrities of the House.

Bernard Levin on Barbara Cartland's grasp of history:

> Miss Cartland insists that Earl Mountbatten helped her with the writing . . . All that expert help, however, has still not managed to correct her apparent belief that Trafalgar came very shortly after Waterloo; perhaps she has confused English history with the London Underground system.

Lily Tomlin on love:

> If love is the answer, could you rephrase the question?

Chekhov on marriage:

> If you're afraid of loneliness, don't marry.

Carl Sandburg on murder:

> Papa loved Mamma
> Mamma loved men
> Mamma's in the graveyard
> Papa's in the pen.

Thomas Beecham on a fellow-musician:

> Sir Adrian Boult came to see me this morning—positively reeking of Horlicks.

J. G. Saxe on the newspaper world:

> Who would not be an Editor? To write
> The magic 'we' of such enormous might.
> To be so great beyond the common span
> It takes the plural to express the Man.

Senator Wyche Fowler on being asked whether, in 'those permissive sixties', he had smoked a marijuana cigarette:

> Only when committing adultery.

Norman Douglas on Suffolk:

> Land of uncomfortable beds, brown sherry, and Perpendicular Gothic.

The Duke of Devonshire on President Nasser and Anthony Eden:

> The camel that broke the straw's back.

P. G. Wodehouse's Sir Roderick Glossop on religion:

> A lay interest in matters to do with liturgical procedure is invariably a prelude to insanity.

Horace Walpole on Queen Charlotte in her later years:

> I do think the bloom of her ugliness is going off.

The Prince of Conti, a noted rake, when he at last became aware of his failing sexual prowess:

> It is time for me to retire. Formerly my civilities were taken for declarations of love. Now my declarations of love are taken for civilities.

W. G. Grace, apologizing for his bad fielding in old age:

> It's the ground. It's too far away.

The President of Cornell University on a proposed sporting fixture:

> I shall not permit thirty men to travel four hundred miles (to Michigan) to agitate a ball of wind.

William Faulkner on Henry James:

> One of the nicest old ladies I ever met.

Edith Sitwell and Herman Mankiewicz on modern writers:

> A lot of people writing poetry today would be better employed keeping rabbits. (Sitwell)

> 'Tell me, do you know any 75 dollar-a-week writers?'
> 'Yes, I know lots of them. But they're all making 1500 dollars a week.' (Mankiewicz)

I found one aspect of the arrangement of previous dictionaries unsympathetic to humorous quotations. It has been customary to print the quote and follow it with the contextual explanation. This is often like giving the punchline of a joke and then adding the premise. Where appropriate I have put the explanation first, for example this quotation from Thomas Gainsborough:

> On attempting to paint two actors, David Garrick and Samuel Foote:
> Rot them for a couple of rogues, they have everybody's faces but their own.

The learned editor of the *Oxford Dictionary of Quotations* has wisely written, 'Ideally, a quotation should be able to float free from its moorings, remaining detached from its original context.' However, one could compare two extracts from a page opened at random in the fourth edition; while the Wolcott Gibbs quote 'Backward ran sentences until reeled the mind' is arresting enough to stand with the subsequent note ('satirizing the style of *Time* magazine'), André Gide's sigh, '*Hugo—hélas!*' would read more entertainingly if the explanation, 'When asked who was the greatest 19th-century poet' preceded it.

I have tried to resist the temptation to admit anecdote where quotation is the brief. Lord Albemarle might have found a place in the unconscious humour section, but the preamble to his striking sentence is too long and involved:

> The dancer Maude Allen had been accused of lesbianism in an article entitled 'The Cult of the Clitoris', and Miss Allen sued for libel in a much publicized lawsuit which caught the puzzled attention of Lord Albemarle, who complained:
> I've never heard of this Greek chap Clitoris they're talking about.

However vivid the phrase may be its context is overpoweringly anecdotal. While Lord Macaulay's riposte, aged four, having had hot coffee spilt over his legs, 'Thank you, Madam, the agony is abated,' is a splendid quote preceded to its advantage by a succinct explanation.

I hope that this collection gathers together a vast number of old friends whom it would be disloyal to exclude—conscious that they will still surprise some. I am often astonished at the way an audience can pounce on an over-familiar quip by Coward or Wilde and welcome it as new-minted. It proved particularly enjoyable to hunt for less well-known quotations from established wits. Noël Coward's chestnuts are included, but also his vivid vignette (in spite of Lord Byron's warning, 'Damn description, it is always disgusting'):

> Edith Sitwell, in that great Risorgimento cape of hers, looks as though she were covering a teapot or a telephone.

Less familiar Oscar Wilde contributions include his admonishment to a waiter:

> When I ask for a watercress sandwich, I do not mean a loaf with a field in the middle of it;

his judgement on publishers:

> I suppose all publishers are untrustworthy. They certainly always look it;

and his request to his examiners in his viva at Oxford when he was asked to stop his brilliant translation of the Greek version of the New Testament:

> Oh, do let me go on, I want to see how it ends.

Sydney Smith is sharp on the incongruity of oratorio, 'How absurd to see 500 people fiddling like madmen about Israelites in the Red Sea,' and playful on two Edinburgh women hurling insults at one another across an alleyway, 'Those two women will never agree; they are arguing from different premises.' There is

Whistler on the picture of his mother, 'Yes, one does like to make one's mummy just as nice as possible', and Gore Vidal on ex-President Eisenhower, 'reading a speech with his usual sense of discovery'.

Among the modern phrase-makers I enjoy Jonathan Lynn and Antony Jay in *Yes Minister*:

> I think it will be a clash between the political will and the administrative won't.

Richard Curtis and Ben Elton in *Blackadder*:

> To you, Baldrick, the Renaissance was just something that happened to other people, wasn't it?

Keith Waterhouse in his play *Bookends*:

> Should not the Society of Indexers be known as Indexers, Society of, The?

Joseph O'Connor in his novel *Cowboys and Indians*:

> Buckingham Palace looked like a vast doll's house that some bullying skinhead brother had kicked down the Mall.

Clive James writes of John McEnroe that he 'did his complete Krakatoa number', and John Osborne says of his American producer David Merrick that he 'liked writers in the way a snake likes live rabbits'.

Unlikely candidates include: Lord Tennyson's brother, introducing himself to Dante Gabriel Rossetti:

> I am Septimus, the most morbid of the Tennysons.

Rupert Murdoch, asked to explain Page 3:

> I don't know. The editor did it while I was away.

T. E. Lawrence on reading *Lady Chatterley's Lover*:

> Surely the sex business isn't worth all this damned fuss? I've met only a handful of people who cared a biscuit for it.

Samuel Beckett encouraging an actor who lamented, 'I'm failing':

> Go on failing. Only next time, try to fail better.

C. S. Lewis on desire:

> He that but looketh on a plate of ham and eggs to lust after it, hath already committed breakfast with it in his heart.

There are some new Royal quotes, often falling into the category of unconscious humour. 'Aren't we due a royalty statement?' (Charles, Prince of Wales), 'I know no person so perfectly disagreeable and even dangerous as an author' (William IV), and George V, asked which film he would like to see while convalescing, 'Anything except that damned Mouse,' which makes a change from 'Bugger Bognor.' Furthermore, I have tried to add to the files of the OUP some quotations which are less familiar. This has meant casting a wider net over, for instance, North American sources, and again I have tried to balance the quotations which demand inclusion on account of the fame of their authors—Dorothy Parker, Robert Benchley, Mark Twain, Sam Goldwyn, and S. J. Perelman ('God, whom you doubtless remember as that quaint old subordinate of General Douglas MacArthur'), with the words of modern masters. I have taken pleasure in adding:

Mary McGrory on Watergate:

> Haldeman is the only man in America in this generation who let his hair grow for a courtroom appearance.

P. J. O'Rourke on certainty:

> That happy sense of purpose people have when they are standing up for a principle they haven't really been knocked down for yet.

Bill Bryson on childhood:

> I had always thought that once you grew up you could do anything you wanted—stay up all night or eat ice-cream straight out of the container.

The film critic James Agee on *Tycoon*:

> Several tons of dynamite are set off in this picture: none of it under the right people.

Jackie Mason on the English:

> If an Englishman gets run down by a truck he apologizes to the truck.

Woody Allen, Neil Simon, Fran Lebowitz, and Russell Baker appear *passim*, and for a British angle on America, Anthony Burgess supplies, 'the US Presidency is a Tudor monarchy with telephones.' George Bush ('What's wrong with being a boring kind of guy?') and Dan Quayle supply generous helpings of unconscious humour, such as 'Space is almost infinite. As a matter of fact, we think it is infinite' (Quayle), and are convenient targets, as in 'Poor George [Bush], he can't help it—he was born with a silver foot in his mouth' (Ann Richards). Sports writers like Jimmy Cannon are rewarding on their own craft, 'Let's face it, sports writers, we're not hanging around with brain surgeons'; so, sometimes, can sportsmen be, 'If people don't want to come out to the ball park, nobody's going to stop 'em' (Yogi Berra). Canada supplies both the unconscious humour of Brian Mulroney's 'I am not denying anything I did not say,' and, at the other extreme, Robertson Davies:

> I see Canada as a country torn between a very northern, rather extraordinary, mystical spirit which it fears and its desire to present itself to the world as a Scotch banker.

Australia under Paul Keating has been developing a rich vein of humorous invective like the exchange between the Prime Minister and his opponent John Hewson. Keating's comment:

> [John Hewson] is simply a shiver looking for a spine to run up,

is countered by Hewson with:

> I decided the worst thing you could call Paul Keating, quite frankly, is Paul Keating.

Reflecting on the insularity of his homeland, Clive James has written:

> A broad school of Australian writing has based itself on the assumption that Australia not only has a history worth bothering about, but that all the history worth bothering about happened in Australia.

To verify this range of information would not have been possible without the diligent and imaginative work of the Oxford Dictionary Department researchers. However, the responsibility for the taste and the accuracy must be mine, the only caveat being Simon Strunsky's 'Famous remarks are very seldom quoted correctly.' Above all it is my sense of humour which conditions the final choice and my regret if your favourite humorous quotation is not recorded here or if you pass too many entries without amusement.

NED SHERRIN

August 1994

How to Use the *Dictionary*

The *Oxford Dictionary of Humorous Quotations* is organized by themes, such as **Actors, The Family, Food, Love, Travel and Exploration, The Weather**, and **Writing**. The themes are placed in alphabetical order, and within each theme the quotations are arranged alphabetically according to author.

The themes have been chosen to reflect as wide a range of subjects as possible. Themes such as **Death, Life**, and **Success** emphasize the general rather than the particular, but categories such as **Description, Last Words, People and Personalities**, and **Towns and Cities** have a wider coverage of quotations relevant to specific people, places, and events.

Related topics may be covered by a single theme, such as **Nature and the Environment** and **Sleep and Dreams**, and linked opposites may also be grouped in a single antithetical theme, such as **Heaven and Hell** and **Trust and Treachery**. A cross-reference from the second element of the pair appears in the appropriate place in the alphabetic sequence both in the main text and in the List of Themes. Where themes are closely related, 'See also' references are given at the head of a section, immediately following the theme title and preceding the quotations. The heading **The Family** is thus followed by See also **Children, Parents**.

Each quotation has a marginal note giving the name of the author to whom the quotation is attributed; dates of birth and death (where known) are given. In general, the authors' names are given in the form by which they are best known, so that we have **Saki** rather than 'H. H. Munro'. If the authorship is unknown, 'Anonymous' appears.

A source note, usually including the specific date of the quotation, follows the author information. Quotations which are in general currency but which are not at present traceable to a specific source are indicated by 'attributed' in the source note; quotations which are popularly attributed to an author but whose authenticity is doubted are indicated by a note such as 'perhaps apocryphal'.

Contextual information regarded as essential to a full appreciation of the quotation precedes the relevant text in an italicized note; information seen as providing helpful amplification follows in an italicized note.

Allocation of a quotation to an individual theme is inevitably subjective, but the keyword index makes provision for tracing specific items other than by theme titles. Citations by named authors may similarly be traced via the author index. In each case, references show the theme name, sometimes in a shortened form (**Satisfaction** for **Satisfaction and Discontent; Theatre** for **The Theatre**), followed by the number of the quotation within the theme: '**Travel** 7' therefore means the seventh quotation within the theme **Travel and Exploration**.

List of *Themes*

A

Acting
Actors
Advertising
America
Anger
Animals
Appearance
Architecture
Argument
The Aristocracy
The Armed Forces
Art
Australia
Autobiography
Awards and Prizes

B

Baseball
Behaviour
Betting
The Bible
Biography
Birds
The Body
Books
Bores
Boxing
Broadcasting
Bureaucracy
Business

C

Canada
Catchphrases *see Comedy
    Routines and Catchphrases*
Censorship
Certainty and Doubt
Character
Children
Choice
Christmas

The Cinema
Cities *see Towns and Cities*
Civil Servants
Class
The Clergy
Colours
Comedy Routines and
    Catchphrases
Computers
Conversation
Cookery
Countries and Peoples
The Country
Cricket
Crime
Critics

D

Dance
Death
Debt
Democracy
Description
Despair *see Hope and Despair*
Diaries
Dictionaries
Diets
Diplomacy
Discontent *see Satisfaction
    and Discontent*
Dogs
Doubt *see Certainty and
    Doubt*
Dreams *see Sleep and Dreams*
Dress
Drink
Drugs

E

Economics
Education
Enemies

England
Environment *see Nature and
    the Environment*
Epitaphs
Examinations
Exploration *see Travel and
    Exploration*

F

Faces
Failure
Fame
The Family
Fashion
Film
Film Producers and
    Directors
Film Stars
Fishing
Flattery *see Praise and
    Flattery*
Food
Foolishness
Football
France
Friends
Funerals
The Future

G

Gambling
Games *see Sports and Games*
Gardens
The Generation Gap
God
Golf
Gossip
Government
Grammar

H

Handwriting
Happiness

Quotations

Acting
See also **Actors, The Theatre**

> **❝** *Don't put your daughter on the stage, Mrs Worthington.* **❞**
> **Noël Coward**

1 This Iago was obviously an intellectual, and refreshingly unlike the usual furtive dog-stealer who would not impose upon the most trustful old lady, not to mention an experienced man of affairs like Othello.
of Neil Porter's Iago in 1927

James Agate 1877–1947: *Brief Chronicles* (1943)

2 *Shakespeare is trying to make a start on* Love's Labour Won, *but Burbage interrupts him:*
'I've been thinking,' he said, 'I'd like to play a Dane—young, intellectual—I see him pale, vacillating, but above everything sad and prone to soliloquy.' 'I know,' said Shakespeare. 'Introspective.'

Caryl Brahms 1901–82 and **S. J. Simon** 1904–48: *No Bed for Bacon* (1941)

3 This Thane of Cawdor would be unnerved by Banquo's valet, never mind Banquo's ghost.
of Michael Hordern in Macbeth *in 1959*

Alan Brien 1925– : Diana Rigg *No Turn Unstoned* (1982)

4 When I read 'Be real, don't get caught acting,' I thought, 'How the hell do you do that?'

Billy Connolly 1942– : John Miller *Judi Dench: With a Crack in Her Voice* (1998)

5 Don't put your daughter on the stage, Mrs Worthington,
Don't put your daughter on the stage,
One look at her bandy legs should prove
She hasn't got a chance,
In addition to which
The son of a bitch
Can neither sing nor dance.

Noël Coward 1899–1973: 'Mrs Worthington' (1935)

6 CLAUDETTE COLBERT: I knew these lines backwards last night.
NOËL COWARD: And that's just the way you're saying them this morning.

Noël Coward 1899–1973: Cole Lesley *The Life of Noel Coward* (1976)

7 Anna Neagle playing Queen Victoria always made me think that Albert must have married beneath him.

Noël Coward 1899–1973: Sheridan Morley *The Quotable Noël Coward* (1999)

8 There's nothing worse than actors who give the impression that they've taken on the priesthood. Acting is really about lying and, in my case, drinking coffee.

Johnny Depp 1963– : in *Radio Times* 18 May 2002

9 She's the only sylph I ever saw, who could stand upon one leg, and play the tambourine on her other knee, like a sylph.

Charles Dickens 1812–70: *Nicholas Nickleby* (1839)

10 I found out that acting was hell. You spend all your time trying to do what they put people in asylums for.

Jane Fonda 1937– : attributed; J. R. Colombo *Wit and Wisdom of the Moviemakers* (1979)

11 *when asked to say something terrifying during rehearsals for Peter Brook's* Oedipus *in 1968:*
We open in two weeks.

John Gielgud 1904–2000: Peter Hay *Theatrical Anecdotes* (1987)

12 *when asked by Michael Hordern for advice before playing Lear for the first time:*
All I can tell you is, get a light Cordelia.

John Gielgud 1904–2000: attributed, in *New York Times* 4 May 1995

13 I made a great hit in *Macbeth* as the messenger because I took the precaution of running three times round the playground before I made my entrance so that I could deliver the news in a state of exhaustion.
on a school production

Alec Guinness 1914–2000: John Mortimer *Character Parts* (1986)

14 I acted so tragic the house rose like magic,
The audience yelled 'You're sublime.'
They made me a present of Mornington Crescent
They threw it a brick at a time.

W. F. Hargreaves 1846–1919: 'The Night I Appeared as Macbeth' (1922)

15 Acting is the most minor of gifts and not a very high-class way to earn a living. Shirley Temple could do it at the age of four.

Katharine Hepburn 1907–2003: attributed; Nigel Rees *Cassell's Movie Quotations* (2000)

16 If your interpretation of a butterfly at rest brought any money into the coffers of the Communist Party, you contributed directly to the propaganda effort of the Communist Party.
to Zero Mostel, appearing before the House Un-American Activities Committee (HUAC)

Donald L. Jackson: at a hearing of HUAC, 14 October 1955

17 Shakespeare is so tiring. You never get a chance to sit down unless you're a king.

George S. Kaufman 1889–1961 and **Howard Teichmann** 1916–87: *The Solid Gold Cadillac* (1953); spoken by Josephine Hull

18 *watching Spencer Tracy on the set of* Dr Jekyll and Mr Hyde *(1941):*
Which is he playing now?

W. Somerset Maugham 1874–1965: attributed; Leslie Halliwell *The Filmgoer's Book of Quotes* (1978 edn)

19 When you do Shakespeare they think you must be intelligent because they *think* you understand what you're saying.

Helen Mirren 1945– : interviewed on *Ruby Wax Meets . . .* ; in *Mail on Sunday* 16 February 1997 'Night and Day'

20 The only thing wrong with performing was that you couldn't phone it in.

Robert Mitchum 1917–97: attributed; in *Sunday Times* (Magazine section) 11 May 1980

21 I used to work for a living, then I became an actor.

Roger Moore 1927– : in *Independent* 1 July 1989

22 Left eyebrow raised, right eyebrow raised.
summary of his acting range

Roger Moore 1927– : David Brown *Star Billing* (1985)

23 *on the part of Lear:*
When you've the strength for it, you're too young; when you've the age you're too old. It's a bugger, isn't it?

Laurence Olivier 1907–89: in *Sunday Telegraph* 4 May 1986

24 But I have a go, lady, don't I? I 'ave a go. I do.

John Osborne 1929–94: *The Entertainer* (1957)

25 Let me know where you are next week! I'll come and see you.

John Osborne 1929–94: *The Entertainer* (1957); last lines

26 The difference between being a director and being an actor is the difference between being the carpenter banging the nails into the wood, and being the piece of wood the nails are being banged into.

Sean Penn 1960– : in *Guardian* 28 November 1991

27 Acting is merely the art of keeping a large group of people from coughing.

Ralph Richardson 1902–83: in *New York Herald Tribune* 19 May 1946

28 I don't care for Lady Macbeth in the streetwalking scene.

Edward Linley Sambourne 1844–1910: R. G. C. Price *A History of Punch* (1957)

29 The best actors in the world, either for tragedy, comedy, history, pastoral, pastoral-comical, historical-pastoral, tragical-historical, tragical-comical-historical-pastoral, scene individable, or poem unlimited.

William Shakespeare 1564–1616: *Hamlet* (1601)

30 I could play Ercles rarely, or a part to tear a cat in, to make all split.

William Shakespeare 1564–1616: *A Midsummer Night's Dream* (1595–6)

31 I wish sir, you would practise this without me. I can't stay dying here all night.

Richard Brinsley Sheridan 1751–1816: *The Critic* (1779)

32 I told Mad Frankie Fraser 'I'm doing Hamlet'—he said, 'I'll do him for you.'

Arthur Smith 1954– : *Arthur Smith's Hamlet*

33 *to an over-genteel actress in an Egyptian drama:*
Oh my God! Remember you're in Egypt. The *skay* is only seen in Kensington.

Herbert Beerbohm Tree 1852–1917: M. Peters *Mrs Pat* (1984)

34 *to a motley collection of American females, assembled to play ladies-in-waiting to a queen:*
Ladies, just a little more virginity, if you don't mind.

Herbert Beerbohm Tree 1852–1917: Alexander Woollcott *Shouts and Murmurs* (1923)

35 *definition of acting:*
Shouting in the evenings.

Patrick Troughton 1920–87: recalled as heard in a radio interview; Michael Simkins *What's My Motivation?* (2004)

36 Talk low, talk slow, and don't say much.

John Wayne 1907–79: attributed

37 Acting is like sex. You should do it, not talk about it.

Joanne Woodward 1930– : attributed, 1987; in Nigel Rees *Cassell's Movie Quotations* (2000)

Actors

See also **Film Stars**

❝ We're actors—we're the opposite of people! ❞
Tom Stoppard

1 John Hannah has the high cheekbones and low spirits for Inspector Rebus, a man under a cloud. He could also play John Knox, the teenage years.

Nancy Banks-Smith: in *Guardian* 27 April 2000

2 For an actress to be a success, she must have the face of a Venus, the brains of a Minerva, the grace of Terpsichore, the memory of a Macaulay, the figure of Juno, and the hide of a rhinoceros.

Ethel Barrymore 1879–1959: George Jean Nathan *The Theatre in the Fifties* (1953)

3 My only regret in the theatre is that I could never sit out front and watch me.

John Barrymore 1882–1942: Eddie Cantor *The Way I See It* (1959)

4 Nobody thought Mel Gibson could play a Scot but look at him now! Alcoholic and a racist!

Frankie Boyle 1972– : at the Edinburgh Festival, 2006, in *Independent* 26 August 2006

5 Every actor has a natural animosity towards every other actor, present or absent, living or dead.

Louise Brooks 1906–85: *Lulu in Hollywood* (1982)

6 Tallulah Bankhead barged down the Nile last night as Cleopatra—and sank.

John Mason Brown 1900–69: in *New York Post* 11 November 1937

7 Like acting with 210 pounds of condemned veal.
of a dull actor

Coral Browne 1913–91: attributed

8 Like a rat up a rope.
of an over-busy actor

Coral Browne 1913–91: attributed

9 Tallulah [Bankhead] is always skating on thin ice. Everyone wants to be there when it breaks.

Mrs Patrick Campbell 1865–1940: in *Times* 13 December 1968

10 She's such a nice woman. If you knew her you'd even admire her acting.
of another actress

Mrs Patrick Campbell 1865–1940: James Agate diary, 6 May 1937

11 *the daughter of Sybil Thorndike and Lewis Casson explaining to a telephone enquiry why neither of her charitably inclined parents was at home:*
Daddy is reading Shakespeare Sonnets to the blind and Mummy's playing Shakespeare to the lepers.

Anne Casson: recounted by Emlyn Williams; James Harding *Emlyn Williams* (1987)

12 She [Edith Evans] took her curtain calls as though she had just been un-nailed from the cross.

Noël Coward 1899–1973: diary, 25 October 1964

13 *seeing a poster for 'Michael Redgrave and Dirk Bogarde in* The Sea Shall Not Have Them*':*
I fail to see why not; everyone else has.

Noël Coward 1899–1973: Sheridan Morley *The Quotable Noël Coward* (1999)

14 Language was not powerful enough to describe the infant phenomenon.

Charles Dickens 1812–70: *Nicholas Nickleby* (1839)

15 Is it Colman's smile
That makes life worth while
Or Crawford's significant form?
Is it Lombard's lips
Or Mae West's hips
That carry you through the storm?

Gavin Ewart 1916–95: 'Verse from an Opera' (1939)

16 *of Creston Clarke as King Lear:*
He played the King as though under momentary apprehension that someone else was about to play the ace.

Eugene Field 1850–95: review attributed to Field; in *Denver Tribune* c.1880

17 Dear Ingrid—speaks five languages and can't act in any of them.
of Ingrid Bergman

John Gielgud 1904–2000: Ronald Harwood *The Ages of Gielgud* (1984); attributed

18 People like to hear me say 'shit' in my gorgeous voice.
of his popularity in America

John Gielgud 1904–2000: in *New Yorker* 10 July 2000; attributed

19 My dear fellow, I never saw anything so funny in my life, and yet it was not in the least bit vulgar.
of Beerbohm Tree's Hamlet (1892)

W. S. Gilbert 1836–1911: D. Bispham *A Quaker Singer's Recollections* (1920)

20 An actor is a kind of a guy who if you ain't talking about him ain't listening.

George Glass 1910–84: Bob Thomas *Brando* (1973); said to be quoted frequently by Marlon Brando

21 On the stage he was natural, simple, affecting;
'Twas only that when he was off he was acting.
of David Garrick

Oliver Goldsmith 1730–74: *Retaliation* (1774)

22 Many actors want to play Hamlet and Macbeth, and ever since I became an actor from the very beginning, I just wanted to play a Shetland pony. I can't explain why.

Dustin Hoffman 1937– : in *Observer* 30 January 2005

23 *of Irving as Mephistopheles in Goethe's* Faust:
The actor, of course, at moments presents to the eye a remarkably sinister figure. He strikes us, however, as superficial—a terrible fault for an archfiend.

Henry James 1843–1916: *The Scenic Art* (1948)

24 Massey won't be satisfied until he's assassinated.
on Raymond Massey's success in playing Lincoln

George S. Kaufman 1889–1961: Howard Teichmann *George S. Kaufman* (1973)

25 I'd like to work with her again in something appropriate. Perhaps Macbeth.
after starring opposite Barbra Streisand in Hello, Dolly!

Walter Matthau 1920–2000: Anne Edwards *Streisand: It Only Happens Once* (1996)

26 *on being refused membership of an exclusive golf-club:*
I'm *not* an actor, and I enclose my press cuttings to prove it.

Victor Mature 1915–99: Ned Sherrin *Cutting Edge* (1984)

27 I have worked with more submarines than leading ladies.

John Mills 1908–2005: in *Times* 12 February 2000 'Quotes of the Week'

28 *of Katharine Hepburn at the first night of* The Lake (*1933*):
She ran the whole gamut of the emotions from A to B, and put some distance between herself and a more experienced colleague [Alison Skipworth] lest she catch acting from her.

Dorothy Parker 1893–1967: attributed

29 It is greatly to Mrs Patrick Campbell's credit that, bad as the play was, her acting was worse.
review of Sardou Fedora *1 June 1895*

George Bernard Shaw 1856–1950: *Our Theatre in the Nineties* (1932)

30 We're *actors*—we're the opposite of people! . . . Think, in your head, *now*, think of the most . . . *private* . . . *secret* . . . *intimate* thing you have ever done secure in the knowledge of its privacy . . . Are you thinking of it? . . . *Well, I saw you do it!*

Tom Stoppard 1937– : *Rosencrantz and Guildenstern Are Dead* (1967)

31 As Virgilia in *Coriolanus* she yearns so hungrily that I longed to throw her a fish.
of Claire Bloom in 1955

Kenneth Tynan 1927–80: *Curtains* (1961)

32 A buxom temptress . . . more impressive in silhouette than in action.
of Yvonne Furneaux in Giraudoux's Ondine

Kenneth Tynan 1927–80: in *Observer* 23 October 1955

33 ALISON SKIPWORTH: You forget I've been an actress for forty years.
MAE WEST: Don't worry, dear. I'll keep your secret.

Mae West 1892–1980: G. Eells and S. Musgrove *Mae West* (1989)

34 *on the Burton-Taylor* Private Lives *in 1964:*
He's miscast and she's Miss Taylor.

Emlyn Williams 1905–87: James Harding *Emlyn Williams* (1987)

35 They say an actor is only as good as his parts. Well, my parts have done me pretty well, darling.

Barbara Windsor 1937– : in *Times* 13 February 1999

36 She was like a sinking ship firing on the rescuers.
of Mrs Patrick Campbell in her later years

Alexander Woollcott 1887–1943: *While Rome Burns* (1944) 'The First Mrs Tanqueray'

Advertising

❝ *The most fun you can have with your clothes on.* **❞**
Jerry Della Femina

1 While you were out your exterminator called.
heading of leaflet left in a New York letter-box

Anonymous: Sylvia Townsend Warner letter to David Garnett, 12 May 1967

2 The cheap contractions and revised spellings of the advertising world which have made the beauty of the written word almost unrecognizable—surely any society that permits the substitution of 'kwik' for 'quick' and 'e.z.' for 'easy' does not deserve Shakespeare, Eliot or Michener.

Russell Baker 1925– : column in *New York Times*; Ned Sherrin *Cutting Edge* (1984)

3 Advertising is the most fun you can have with your clothes on.

Jerry Della Femina 1936– : *From Those Wonderful Folks Who Gave You Pearl Harbor* (1971)

4 It is far easier to write ten passably effective sonnets, good enough to take in the not too enquiring critic, than one effective advertisement that will take in a few thousand of the uncritical buying public.

Aldous Huxley 1894–1963: *On the Margin* (1923) 'Advertisement'

5 Advertising may be described as the science of arresting human intelligence long enough to get money from it.

Stephen Leacock 1869–1944: *Garden of Folly* (1924)

6 Good wine needs no bush,
And perhaps products that people really want need no
    hard-sell or soft-sell TV push.
Why not?
Look at pot.

Ogden Nash 1902–71: 'Most Doctors Recommend or Yours For Fast, Fast, Fast Relief' (1972)

7 I think that I shall never see
A billboard lovely as a tree.
Perhaps, unless the billboards fall,
I'll never see a tree at all.

Ogden Nash 1902–71: 'Song of the Open Road' (1933)

8 The consumer isn't a moron; she is your wife.

David Ogilvy 1911– : *Confessions of an Advertising Man* (1963)

9 Advertising is the rattling of a stick inside a swill-bucket.

George Orwell 1903–50: *Keep the Aspidistra Flying* (1936)

10 If the client moans and sighs,
Make his logo twice the size.

John Trench 1920–2003: attributed, perhaps apocryphal; in *Times* 14 March 2003 (obituary)

11 *asked why he had made a commercial for American Express:*
To pay for my American Express.

Peter Ustinov 1921–2004: in *Ned Sherrin in his Anecdotage* (1993)

America

See also **Countries and Peoples, Places**

❝ The youth of America is their oldest tradition. ❞
Oscar Wilde

1 California is a fine place to live—if you happen to be an orange.

Fred Allen 1894–1956: in *American Magazine* December 1945

2 He held, too, in his enlightened way, that Americans have a perfect right to exist. But he did often find himself wishing Mr Rhodes had not enabled them to exercise that right in Oxford.

Max Beerbohm 1872–1956: *Zuleika Dobson* (1911)

3 They're the experts where personality is concerned, the Americans; they've got it down to a fine art.

Alan Bennett 1934– : *Talking Heads* (1988)

4 America is a model of force and freedom and moderation—with all the coarseness and rudeness of its people.

Lord Byron 1788–1824: letter, 12 October 1821

5 Your eyes are like the prairie flowers
When they're refreshed by sudden showers,
Next to Texas I love you.

Sammy Cahn 1913– : 'Next to Texas I Love You' (1947)

6 I have always liked Americans, and the sort of man that likes Americans is liable to like Russians.

Claud Cockburn 1904–81: *Crossing the Line* (1958)

7 Father's name was Hezikiah,
Mother's name was Anna Maria,
Yanks, through and through!
Red White and Blue.

George M. Cohan 1878–1942: 'Yankee Doodle Dandy' (1904)

8 I like America . . .
All delegates
From Southern States
Are nervy and distraught.
In New Orleans
The wrought-iron screens
Are dreadfully overwrought . . .
But—I like America,
Every scrap of it,
All the sentimental crap of it.

Noël Coward 1899–1973: 'I like America' (1949)

9 When I was a boy I was told that anybody could become President. I'm beginning to believe it.

Clarence Darrow 1857–1938: Irving Stone *Clarence Darrow for the Defence* (1941)

10 The thing that impresses me most about America is the way parents obey their children.

Edward VIII 1894–1972: in *Look* 5 March 1957

11 Molasses to
Rum to
Slaves!
'Tisn't morals, 'tis money that saves!
Shall we dance to the sound
Of the profitable pound, in
Molasses and

Sherman Edwards: 'Molasses to Rum' (1969)

Rum and
Slaves?

12 When J. P. Morgan bows, I just nod;
Green Pastures wanted me to play God.
But you've got me down hearted
'Cause I can't get started with you.

Ira Gershwin 1896–1983: 'I Can't Get Started' (1936)

13 I'm as corny as Kansas in August
I'm as normal as blueberry pie . . .
. . . High as a flag on the fourth of July.

Oscar Hammerstein II 1895–1960: 'I'm in Love with a Wonderful Guy' (1949)

14 Once we had a Roosevelt
Praise the Lord!
Now we're stuck with Nixon, Agnew, Ford
Brother, can you spare a rope!

E. Y. Harburg 1898–1981: parody of 'Brother Can You Spare a Dime?', written for the *New York Times* at the time of Watergate

15 *Gilbert Harding, applying for a US visa, was irritated by having to fill in a long form with many questions, including 'Is it your intention to overthrow the Government of the United States by force?':*
Sole purpose of visit.

Gilbert Harding 1907–60: W. Reyburn *Gilbert Harding* (1978)

16 I could come back to America . . . to die—but never, never to live.

Henry James 1843–1916: letter to Mrs William James, 1 April 1913

17 To Americans, English manners are far more frightening than none at all.

Randall Jarrell 1914–65: *Pictures from an Institution* (1954)

18 Never criticize Americans. They have the best taste that money can buy.

Miles Kington 1941–2008: *Welcome to Kington* (1989)

19 *the universal philosophy of young America:*
I can do that.

Ed Kleban 1939–87: song-title (1975)

20 So I really think that American gentlemen are the best after all, because kissing your hand may make you feel very very good but a diamond and safire bracelet lasts forever.

Anita Loos 1893–1981: *Gentlemen Prefer Blondes* (1925)

21 I like to be in America!
O.K. by me in America!
Ev'rything free in America
For a small fee in America!

Stephen Sondheim 1930– : 'America' (1957)

22 In the United States there is more space where nobody is than where anybody is. That is what makes America what it is.

Gertrude Stein 1874–1946: *The Geographical History of America* (1936)

23 In America any boy may become President and I suppose it's just one of the risks he takes!

Adlai Stevenson 1900–65: speech in Detroit, 7 October 1952

24 America is a vast conspiracy to make you happy.

John Updike 1932–2009: *Problems* (1980) 'How to love America and Leave it at the Same Time'

25 The land of the dull and the home of the literal.

Gore Vidal 1925– : *Reflections upon a Sinking Ship* (1969)

26 The goal of white Americans has always been shining cities on the hill, with converted Indians and imported African slaves to do the heavy lifting.

Gore Vidal 1925– : *Inventing a Nation: Washington* (2003)

27 MRS ALLONBY: They say, Lady Hunstanton, that when good Americans die they go to Paris.
LADY HUNSTANTON: Indeed? And when bad Americans die, where do they go to?
LORD ILLINGWORTH: Oh, they go to America.

Oscar Wilde 1854–1900: *A Woman of No Importance* (1893)

28 The youth of America is their oldest tradition. It has been going on now for three hundred years.

Oscar Wilde 1854–1900: *A Woman of No Importance* (1893)

Anger

❝ *McEnroe . . . did his complete Krakatoa number.* **❞**
Clive James

1 Anger makes dull men witty, but it keeps them poor.

Francis Bacon 1561–1626: *Works* (1859) 'Baconiana'

2 I expect to pass through this world but once and therefore if there is anybody that I want to kick in the crutch I had better kick them in the crutch *now*, for I do not expect to pass this way again.
while lunching at the Reform Club with a bishop at the next table

Maurice Bowra 1898–1971: Arthur Marshall *Life's Rich Pageant* (1984)

3 When you get angry, they tell you, count to five before you reply. Why should I count to five? It's what happens *before* you count to five which makes life interesting.

David Hare 1947– : *The Secret Rapture* (1988)

4 McEnroe . . . did his complete Krakatoa number.
of John McEnroe disputing a line call at Wimbledon

Clive James 1939– : in *Observer* 5 July 1981

5 It's my rule never to lose me temper till it would be dethrimental to keep it.

Sean O'Casey 1880–1964: *The Plough and the Stars* (1926)

6 I storm and I roar, and I fall in a rage,
And missing my whore, I bugger my page.

Charles Sackville 1638–1706: 'Regime d'vivre' (often attributed to Lord Rochester, but probably not by him)

7 Whereat, with blade, with bloody blameful blade,
He bravely broached his boiling bloody breast.

William Shakespeare 1564–1616: *A Midsummer Night's Dream* (1595–6)

8 John Major's self-control in cabinet was rigid. The most angry thing he would ever do was to throw down his pencil.

Gillian Shephard 1940– : in November 1999

9 He never let the sun go down on his wrath, though there were some colourful sunsets while it lasted.
of W. G. Grace

A. A. Thomson: Alan Gibson *The Cricket Captains of England* (1979)

10 When angry, count four; when very angry, swear.

Mark Twain 1835–1910: *Pudd'nhead Wilson* (1894)

11 The adjective 'cross' as a description of his Jovelike wrath . . . jarred upon Derek profoundly. It was as though Prometheus, with the vultures tearing his liver, had been asked if he were piqued.

P. G. Wodehouse 1881–1975: *Jill the Reckless* (1922)

Animals

See also **Birds, Dogs**

66 *One end is moo, the other, milk.* 99

Ogden Nash

1 The lion and the calf shall lie down together but the calf won't get much sleep.

Woody Allen 1935– : in *New Republic* 31 August 1974

2 *during his time in the Lords the eighth Earl of Arran was concerned with measures for homosexual reform and the protection of badgers, interests concisely summed up by a fellow peer:*
Teaching people not to bugger badgers and not to badger buggers.

Anonymous: in *Ned Sherrin in his Anecdotage* (1993)

3 The rabbit has a charming face:
Its private life is a disgrace.
I really dare not name to you
The awful things that rabbits do.

Anonymous: *The Week-End Book* (1925) 'The Rabbit'

4 *Puella Rigensis ridebat*
Quam tigris in tergo vehebat;
Externa profecta,
Interna revecta,
Risusque cum tigre manebat.

There was a young lady of Riga
Who went for a ride on a tiger;
They returned from the ride
With the lady inside,
And a smile on the face of the tiger.

Anonymous: R. L. Green (ed.) *A Century of Humorous Verse* (1959)

5 I shoot the Hippopotamus
With bullets made of platinum,
Because if I use leaden ones
His hide is sure to flatten 'em.

Hilaire Belloc 1870–1953: 'The Hippopotamus' (1896)

6 The Tiger, on the other hand, is kittenish and mild,
He makes a pretty play fellow for any little child;
And mothers of large families (who claim to common sense)
Will find a Tiger well repay the trouble and expense.

Hilaire Belloc 1870–1953: 'The Tiger' (1896)

7 I had an Aunt in Yucatan
Who bought a Python from a man
And kept it for a pet.
She died, because she never knew
These simple little rules and few;—
The Snake is living yet.

Hilaire Belloc 1870–1953: 'The Python' (1897)

8 It's awf'lly bad luck on Diana,
Her ponies have swallowed their bits;
She fished down their throats with a spanner
And frightened them all into fits.

John Betjeman 1906–84: 'Hunter Trials' (1954)

9 To my mind, the only possible pet is a cow. Cows love you
. . . They will listen to your problems and never ask a thing in return. They will be your friends for ever. And when you get tired of them, you can kill and eat them. Perfect.

Bill Bryson 1951– : *Neither Here Nor There* (1991)

10 I am fond of pigs. Dogs look up to us. Cats look down on us. Pigs treat us as equal.

Winston Churchill 1874–1965: M. Gilbert *Never Despair* (1988); attributed

11 *after an operation to remove a fishbone stuck in her throat:*
After all these years of fishing, the fish are having their revenge.

Queen Elizabeth, the Queen Mother 1900–2002: in November 1982, attributed; Christopher Dobson (ed.) *Queen Elizabeth the Queen Mother: Chronicle of a Remarkable Life* (2000)

12 The great thing about racehorses is you don't need to take them for walks.

Albert Finney 1936– : in *Mail on Sunday* 9 April 2000

13 My God . . . The hero is a bee!
  on reading the synopsis of a story by Maurice Maeterlinck in 1920

Sam Goldwyn 1882–1974: Michael Freedland *The Goldwyn Touch* (1986)

14 Even the rabbits
Inhibit their habits
On Sunday at Cicero Falls.

E. Y. Harburg 1898–1981: 'Sunday at Cicero Falls' (1944)

15 Tar-baby ain't sayin' nuthin', en Brer Fox, he lay low.

Joel Chandler Harris 1848–1908: *Uncle Remus and His Legends of the Old Plantation* (1881) 'The Wonderful Tar-Baby Story'

16 I live in a colony
I like to get all polleny.

John Hegley 1953– : 'Bees' (2002)

17 Honey bees are amazing creatures. I mean, think about it, do earwigs make chutney?

Eddie Izzard 1962– : *Unrepeatable* (1994)

18 What the horse is to the Arab, or the dog is to the Greenlander, the pig is to the Irishman.

J. G. Kohl 1808–78: *Ireland, Scotland and England* (1844)

19 Arabs of means rode none but she-camels, since they . . . were patient and would endure to march long after they were worn out, indeed until they tottered with exhaustion and fell in their tracks and died: whereas the coarser males grew angry, flung themselves down when tired, and from sheer rage would die there unnecessarily.

T. E. Lawrence 1888–1935: *Seven Pillars of Wisdom* (1926)

20 Its tail was a plume of such magnificence that it almost wore the cat.

Hugh Leonard 1926– : *Rover and Other Cats* (1992)

21 Where are you going
With your fetlocks blowing in the . . . wind
I want to shower you with sugar lumps
And ride you over . . . fences
I want to polish your hooves every single day
And bring you to the horse . . . dentist.
  'My Lovely Horse' as sung by Fathers Ted and Dougal

Graham Linehan and **Arthur Mathews**: 'A Song for Europe' (1996), episode from *Father Ted* (Channel 4 TV, 1995–8)

22 A
water bison
is what
yer wash
yer face in.

Roger McGough 1937– : *An Imaginary Menagerie* (1988)

23 Rudolph, the Red-Nosed Reindeer
Had a very shiny nose,
And if you ever saw it,
You would even say it glows.

Johnny Marks 1909–85: 'Rudolph, the Red-Nosed Reindeer' (1949)

24 Outside of a dog, a book is a man's best friend. Inside of a dog, it's too dark to read.

Groucho Marx 1890–1977: Groucho Marx and Stefan Kanfer *The Essential Groucho* (2000)

25 Slow but sure the turtle
Enormously fert'le
Lays her eggs by the dozens,
Maybe some are her cousins,
Even the catamount is nonplussed by that amount
It's Spring, Spring, Spring!

Johnny Mercer 1909–76: 'Spring, Spring, Spring' (1954)

26 Eeyore, the old grey Donkey, stood by the side of the stream, and looked at himself in the water. 'Pathetic,' he said. 'That's what it is. Pathetic.'

A. A. Milne 1882–1956: *Winnie-the-Pooh* (1926)

27 Pooh began to feel a little more comfortable, because when you are a Bear of Very Little Brain, and you Think of Things, you find sometimes that a Thing which seemed very Thingish inside you is quite different when it gets out into the open and has other people looking at it.

A. A. Milne 1882–1956: *The House at Pooh Corner* (1928)

28 One disadvantage of being a hog is that at any moment some blundering fool may try to make a silk purse out of your wife's ear.

J. B. Morton 1893–1975: *By the Way* (1931)

29 God in His wisdom made the fly
And then forgot to tell us why.

Ogden Nash 1902–71: 'The Fly' (1942)

30 The turtle lives 'twixt plated decks
Which practically conceal its sex.
I think it clever of the turtle
In such a fix to be so fertile.

Ogden Nash 1902–71: 'Autres Bêtes, Autres Moeurs' (1931)

31 The cow is of the bovine ilk;
One end is moo, the other, milk.

Ogden Nash 1902–71: 'The Cow' (1931)

32 Four legs good, two legs bad.

George Orwell 1903–50: *Animal Farm* (1945)

33 Your elephant seal . . . is not a natural self-starter. Start him, however, and he goes, not like a rocket, but a sort of turbo-charged mega-caterpillar.

Matthew Parris 1949– : in *Spectator* 17 June 2000

34 Don't go into Mr McGregor's garden: your father had an accident there, he was put into a pie by Mrs McGregor.

Beatrix Potter 1866–1943: *The Tale of Peter Rabbit* (1902)

35 There was one poor tiger that hadn't *got* a Christian.

Punch 1841–1992: vol. 68 (1875)

36 Oh how the family affections combat
Within this heart, and each hour flings a bomb at
My burning soul! Neither from owl or from bat
Can peace be gained until I clasp my wombat.
   on the loss of his pet wombat, and his other pets

Dante Gabriel Rossetti 1828–82: 'The Wombat' (1849)

37 I know two things about the horse
And one of them is rather coarse.

Naomi Royde-Smith c.1875–1964: in *Weekend Book* (1928)

38 So, naturalists observe, a flea
Hath smaller fleas that on him prey;
And these have smaller fleas to bite 'em,
And so proceed *ad infinitum*.

Jonathan Swift 1667–1745: 'On Poetry' (1733)

Appearance

See also **Faces**

❝ My beauty am faded. ❞
Rudolf Nureyev

1 It often means vanity and sometimes drink.
   explaining his mistrust of 'men with waxed moustaches'

Lord Baden-Powell 1857–1941: *Scouting for Boys* (1908)

2 *question as the notably tanned Robert Kilroy-Silk launched his new political party, 'Veritas':*
   Is your tan veritas?

Tom Baldwin: in *Mail on Sunday* 6 February 2005

3 He had a thin vague beard—or rather, he had a chin on which a large number of hairs weakly curled and clustered to cover its retreat.

Max Beerbohm 1872–1956: 'Enoch Soames' (1912)

4 I know I looked awful because my mother phoned and said I looked lovely.
   after getting a makeover on television

Jo Brand 1957– : in *Sunday Telegraph* 28 December 2003

5 Men who are too good looking are never good in bed because they never had to be.

Cindy Chupack: *Sex and the City* 'Unoriginal Sin' (2002), spoken by Carrie (Sarah Jessica Parker)

6 Glamour is on a life-support machine and not expected to live.

Joan Collins 1933– : in *Independent* 24 April 1999

7 Edith Sitwell, in that great Risorgimento cape of hers, looks as though she were covering a teapot or a telephone.

Noël Coward 1899–1973: William Marchant *The Pleasure of his Company* (1975)

8 I guess a drag queen's like an oil painting: You gotta stand back from it to get the full effect.

Harvey Fierstein 1954– : *Torch Song Trilogy* (1979)

9 I don't trust photographers. I'm now a relaxed, contented 60-year-old, but look at my pictures and you see a crazy, bug-eyed serial killer.
   on a photograph accompanying an Independent *article to mark his 60th birthday*

Richard Ingrams 1937– : in *Observer* 24 August 1997

10 I'm tired of all this nonsense about beauty being only skin-deep. That's deep enough. What do you want—an adorable pancreas?

Jean Kerr 1923–2003: *The Snake has all the Lines* (1958)

11 Her ugliness was destined to bloom late, hidden first by the unformed gawkiness of youth, budding to plainness in young womanhood and now flowering to slow maturity in her early forties.

Brian Moore 1921– : *The Lonely Passion of Judith Hearne* (1955)

12 No power on earth, however, can abolish the merciless class distinction between those who are physically desirable and the lonely, pallid, spotted, silent, unfancied majority.

John Mortimer 1923–2009: *Clinging to the Wreckage* (1982)

13 Sure, deck your lower limbs in pants;
   Yours are the limbs, my sweeting.
   You look divine as you advance—
   Have you seen yourself retreating?

Ogden Nash 1902–71: 'What's the Use?' (1940)

14 My beauty am faded.
   on being rejected by a young man he had tried to pick up

Rudolf Nureyev 1939–93: in *Ned Sherrin in his Anecdotage* (1993)

15 In Los Angeles everyone has perfect teeth. It's crocodile land.

Gwyneth Paltrow 1972– : in *Sunday Times* 3 February 2002

16 I always say beauty is only sin deep.

Saki 1870–1916: *Reginald* (1904)

17 You're welcome to take a bath. You look like the second week of the garbage strike.

Neil Simon 1927– : *The Gingerbread Lady* (1970)

18 Women never look so well as when one comes in wet and dirty from hunting.

R. S. Surtees 1805–64: *Mr. Sponge's Sporting Tour* (1853)

19 If beauty is truth, why don't women go to the library to have their hair done?

Lily Tomlin 1939– : Sally Feldman (ed.) *Woman's Hour Book of Humour* (1993)

20 By the time you hit 50, I reckon you've earned your wrinkles, so why not be proud of them?

Twiggy 1949– : in *Observer* 8 September 2002

21 A man who can part the Red Sea but apparently not his own hairpiece.
of Charlton Heston

Dick Vosburgh 1929–2007 and **Denis King**: *Beauty and the Beards* (2001)

22 It is better to be beautiful than to be good. But . . . it is better to be good than to be ugly.

Oscar Wilde 1854–1900: *The Picture of Dorian Gray* (1891)

23 The Right Hon. was a tubby little chap who looked as if he had been poured into his clothes and had forgotten to say 'When!'

P. G. Wodehouse 1881–1975: *Very Good, Jeeves* (1930)

24 I was so ugly when I was born, the doctor slapped my mother.

Henny Youngman 1906–98: in *Times* 26 February 1998; obituary

Architecture

❝ *A monstrous carbuncle.* **❞**

Charles, Prince of Wales

1 The floozie in the jacuzzi.
popular description of the monument in O'Connell Street, Dublin

Anonymous: comment, c.1988

2 *of the cramped office he shared with Dorothy Parker:*
One square foot less and it would be adulterous.

Robert Benchley 1889–1945: in *New Yorker* 5 January 1946

3 Sir Christopher Wren
Said, 'I am going to dine with some men.
If anybody calls
Say I am designing St Paul's.'

Edmund Clerihew Bentley 1875–1956: 'Sir Christopher Wren' (1905)

4 Ghastly good taste, or a depressing story of the rise and fall of English architecture.

John Betjeman 1906–84: title of book (1933)

5 The existence of St Sophia is atmospheric; that of St Peter's, overpoweringly, imminently substantial. One is a church to God: the other a salon for his agents. One is consecrated to reality, the other, to illusion. St Sophia in fact is large, and St Peter's is vilely, tragically small.

Robert Byron 1905–41: *The Road to Oxiana* (1937)

6 A monstrous carbuncle on the face of a much-loved and elegant friend.

Charles, Prince of Wales 1948– : speech on the proposed extension to the National Gallery, London, 30 May 1984

7 The Pavilion
Cost a million
As a monument to Art,
And the wits here
Say it sits here
Like an Oriental tart!

Noël Coward 1899–1973: on Brighton Pavilion; 'There was Once a Little Village' (1934)

8 My client—God—is in no hurry.
of the church of the Sagrada Familia in Barcelona (begun 1884)

Antonio Gaudi 1853–1926: attributed

9 O Dome gigantic, Dome immense
Built in defiance of common sense.

P. D. James 1920– : attributed in *Daily Telegraph* 18 May 2000

10 A taste for the grandiose, like a taste for morphia, is, once it has been fully acquired, difficult to keep within limits.

Osbert Lancaster 1908–86: *Homes Sweet Homes* (1939)

11 A lot of nuns in a rugger scrum.
on the Sydney Opera House

George Molnar 1910–98: attributed

12 I am proud to be an Eskimo, but I think we can improve on the igloo as a permanent dwelling.

Abraham Okpik d. 1997: in *Northern Affairs Bulletin* March 1960

13 A singularly dreary street. What I would term Victorian Varicose.

Peter Shaffer 1926– : *Lettice and Lovage* (rev. ed. 1989)

14 *on Brighton Pavilion:*
As if St Paul's had come down and pupped.

Sydney Smith 1771–1845: Peter Virgin *Sydney Smith* (1994)

15 Whatever may be said in favour of the Victorians, it is pretty generally admitted that few of them were to be trusted within reach of a trowel and a pile of bricks.

P. G. Wodehouse 1881–1975: *Summer Moonshine* (1938)

16 The physician can bury his mistakes, but the architect can only advise his client to plant vines.

Frank Lloyd Wright 1867–1959: in *New York Times* 4 October 1953

Argument

❝ A clash between the political will and the administrative won't. ❞
Jonathan Lynn and Antony Jay

1 Sir Roger told them, with the air of a man who would not give his judgement rashly, that much might be said on both sides.

Joseph Addison 1672–1719: *The Spectator* 20 July 1711

2 Jimmy [Connors] was such an out-and-out 'personality' that he managed to get into a legal dispute with the president of his own fan club.

Martin Amis 1949– : in *New Yorker* 5 September 1994

3 I've never won an argument with her; and the only times I thought I had I found out the argument wasn't over yet.
of his wife Rosalynn

Jimmy Carter 1924– : in *Reader's Digest* March 1979

4 You can't turn a thing upside down if there's no theory about it being the right way up.

G. K. Chesterton 1874–1936: attributed

5 'My idea of an agreeable person,' said Hugo Bohun, 'is a person who agrees with me.'

Benjamin Disraeli 1804–81: *Lothair* (1870)

6 I'll not listen to reason . . . Reason always means what someone else has got to say.

Elizabeth Gaskell 1810–65: *Cranford* (1853)

7 Those who in quarrels interpose,
Must often wipe a bloody nose.

John Gay 1685–1732: *Fables* (1727)
'The Mastiffs'

8 There is no arguing with Johnson; for when his pistol
misses fire, he knocks you down with the butt end of it.

Oliver Goldsmith 1730–74: James
Boswell *Life of Samuel Johnson* (1934
ed.) 26 October 1769

9 Any stigma, as the old saying is, will serve to beat a
dogma.

Philip Guedalla 1889–1944: *Masters
and Men* (1923)

10 The concept of two people living together for 25 years
without having a cross word suggests a lack of spirit only
to be admired in sheep.

A. P. Herbert 1890–1971: in *News
Chronicle*, 1940

11 Several excuses are always less convincing than one.

Aldous Huxley 1894–1963: *Point
Counter Point* (1928)

12 The only person who listens to both sides of a husband
and wife argument is the woman in the next apartment.

Sam Levenson 1911–80: *You Can
Say That Again, Sam!* (1975)

13 I think it will be a clash between the political will and the
administrative won't.

Jonathan Lynn 1943– and **Antony
Jay** 1930– : *Yes Prime Minister* vol. 2
(1987)

14 The first obligation of the demonstrator is to be legible.
Miss Manners cannot sympathize with a cause whose
signs she cannot make out even with her glasses on.

Judith Martin 1938– : 'Advice from
Miss Manners', column in
Washington Post 1979–82

15 I had inherited what my father called the art of the
advocate, or the irritating habit of looking for the flaw in
any argument.

John Mortimer 1923–2009: *Clinging
to the Wreckage* (1982)

16 Why, i'faith, I believe I am between *both*.
*when two royal dukes walking on either side of him told him
that they were trying to decide if he was a greater fool or
rogue*

Richard Brinsley Sheridan
1751–1816: Walter Jerrold *Bon-Mots*
(1893)

17 JUDGE: What do you suppose I am on the Bench for, Mr
Smith?
SMITH: It is not for me, Your Honour, to attempt to fathom
the inscrutable workings of Providence.

F. E. Smith 1872–1930: Lord
Birkenhead *F. E.* (1959 ed.)

18 *on seeing two Edinburgh women hurling insults at one another
across an alleyway:*
Those two women will never agree; they are arguing from
different premises.

Sydney Smith 1771–1845: Peter
Virgin *Sydney Smith* (1994)

19 And who are you? said he.—Don't puzzle me, said I.

Laurence Sterne 1713–68: *Tristram
Shandy* (1759–67)

20 My uncle Toby would never offer to answer this by any
other kind of argument, than that of whistling half a
dozen bars of Lillabullero.

Laurence Sterne 1713–68: *Tristram
Shandy* (1759–67)

21 I don't take orders from you, you're just a figure-head and
I've seen better ones on the sharp end of a dredger.

Tom Stoppard 1937– : *The Dog It
Was That Died* (1983)

22 When two strong men stand face to face, each claiming to
be Major Brabazon-Plank, it is inevitable that there will be
a sense of strain, resulting in a momentary silence.

P. G. Wodehouse 1881–1975: *Uncle
Dynamite* (1948)

The Aristocracy

See also **Class**

"There's a lot to be said for the Lords."
A. P. Herbert

1 The young Sahib shot divinely, but God was very merciful to the birds.

Anonymous: G. W. E. Russell *Collections and Recollections* (1898)

2 *the much-married Duke of Westminster had died the previous day:*
There was a bad fire next door; lots of smoke, but it turned out *not* to be the four bereaved Duchesses of Westminster committing suttee.

Chips Channon 1897–1958: diary, 21 July 1953

3 The Stately Homes of England,
How beautiful they stand,
To prove the upper classes
Have still the upper hand.

Noël Coward 1899–1973: 'The Stately Homes of England' (1938)

4 Spurn not the nobly born
With love affected,
Nor treat with virtuous scorn
The well-connected.

W. S. Gilbert 1836–1911: *Iolanthe* (1882)

5 I can trace my ancestry back to a protoplasmal primordial atomic globule. Consequently, my family pride is something in-conceivable. I can't help it. I was born sneering.

W. S. Gilbert 1836–1911: *The Mikado* (1885)

6 Hearts just as pure and fair
May beat in Belgrave Square
As in the lowly air
Of Seven Dials.

W. S. Gilbert 1836–1911: *Iolanthe* (1882)

7 There never was a Churchill from John of Marlborough down that had either morals or principles.

W. E. Gladstone 1809–98: in conversation in 1882, recorded by Captain R. V. Briscoe; R. F. Foster *Lord Randolph Churchill* (1981)

8 I am a well-known élitist. I don't even own a pair of trainers. If I did, I am sure they would be very fragrant.

Lord Gowrie 1939– : in *Independent* 24 January 1998

9 We don't represent anybody, it's true,
But that's not a thing to regret;
We can say what we think—and I know one or two
Who've never said anything yet.
While the Commons must bray like an ass every day
To appease their electoral hordes,
We don't say a thing till we've something to say—
There's a lot to be said for the Lords.

A. P. Herbert 1890–1971: *Big Ben* (1946)

10 *replying to Harold Wilson's remark (on Home's leading the Conservatives to victory in the 1963 election) that 'the whole [democratic] process has ground to a halt with a fourteenth Earl':*
As far as the fourteenth earl is concerned, I suppose Mr Wilson, when you come to think of it, is the fourteenth Mr Wilson.

Lord Home 1903–95: in *Daily Telegraph* 22 October 1963

11 I am an ancestor.
*reply when taunted on his lack of ancestry, having been
made Duke of Abrantes, 1807*

Marshal Junot 1771–1813: attributed

12 We always feel kindly disposed towards noble authors.

Lord Macaulay 1800–59: in
Edinburgh Review January 1833

13 An aristocracy in a republic is like a chicken whose head
has been cut off: it may run about in a lively way, but in
fact it is dead.

Nancy Mitford 1904–73: *Noblesse
Oblige* (1956) 'The English
Aristocracy'

14 We are here only as a pustule on the rump of the body
politic to remind the Government of their honour pledge to
do something proper with this House.

Lord Onslow 1938– : speaking in the
House of Lords, 2 December 2003

15 I'll purge, and leave sack, and live cleanly, as a nobleman
should do.

William Shakespeare 1564–1616:
Henry IV, Part 1 (1597)

16 At the palace of the Duke of Ferrara,
Who was prematurely deaf but a dear,
At the palace of the Duke of Ferrara
I acquired some position
Plus a tiny Titian . . .
Liaisons! What's happened to them?

Stephen Sondheim 1930– : 'Liaisons'
(1972)

17 LORD ILLINGWORTH: A title is really rather a nuisance in
these democratic days. As George Harford I had everything
I wanted. Now I have merely everything that other people
want.

Oscar Wilde 1854–1900: *A Woman
of No Importance* (1893)

The Armed Forces
See also **War**

❝ *Nothing but rum, sodomy, and the lash.* **❞**
Winston Churchill

1 On no account is this man to be put in charge of others.
Army selection board on the young Peter Ustinov, c.1942

Anonymous: quoted in *Daily
Telegraph* 30 March 2004

2 My home at my uncle's brought me acquainted with a
circle of admirals. Of *Rears* and *Vices*, I saw enough. No, do
not be suspecting me of a pun, I entreat.
Mary Crawford to a disapproving Edmund

Jane Austen 1775–1817: *Mansfield
Park* (1814)

3 What would your great grandfather who
Was aide-de-camp to General Brue,
And lost a leg at Waterloo,
And Quatre-Bras and Ligny too!
And died at Trafalgar!

Hilaire Belloc 1870–1953:
'Hildebrand' (1907)

4 We joined the Navy to see the world,
And what did we see? We saw the sea.

Irving Berlin 1888–1989: 'We Saw
the Sea' in *Follow the Fleet* (1936)

5 Don't talk to me about naval tradition. It's nothing but
rum, sodomy, and the lash.

Winston Churchill 1874–1965: Peter
Gretton *Former Naval Person* (1968)

6 I can always guarantee that the Irish Citizen Army will
fight, but I cannot guarantee that it will be on time.

James Connolly 1868–1916: Diana
Norman *Terrible Beauty* (1987)

7 Have you had any word
Of that bloke in the 'Third',
Was it Southerby, Sedgwick or Sim?
They had him thrown out of the club in Bombay
For, apart from his mess bills exceeding his pay,
He took to pig-sticking in *quite* the wrong way.
I wonder what happened to him!

Noël Coward 1899–1973: 'I Wonder What Happened to Him' (1945)

8 Has anybody seen our ship?
The H.M.S. Peculiar
We've been on shore
For a month or more,
And when we see the Captain we shall get 'what for'.

Noël Coward 1899–1973: 'Has Anybody Seen Our Ship' (1935)

9 For a soldier I listed, to grow great in fame,
And be shot at for sixpence a-day.

Charles Dibdin 1745–1814: 'Charity' (1791)

10 *to the Duke of Newcastle, who had complained that General Wolfe was a madman:*
Mad, is he? Then I hope he will *bite* some of my other generals.

George II 1683–1760: Henry Beckles Willson *Life and Letters of James Wolfe* (1909)

11 Stick close to your desks and never go to sea,
And you all may be Rulers of the Queen's Navee!

W. S. Gilbert 1836–1911: *HMS Pinafore* (1878)

12 I'm very good at integral and differential calculus,
I know the scientific names of beings animalculous;
In short, in matters vegetable, animal, and mineral,
I am the very model of a modern Major-General.

W. S. Gilbert 1836–1911: *The Pirates of Penzance* (1879)

13 Fortunately, the army has had much practice at ignoring impossible instructions.

Michael Green 1927– : *The Boy Who Shot Down an Airship* (1988)

14 I had examined myself pretty thoroughly and discovered that I was unfit for military service.

Joseph Heller 1923–99: *Catch-22* (1961)

15 Ben Battle was a soldier bold,
And used to war's alarms:
But a cannon-ball took off his legs,
So he laid down his arms!

Thomas Hood 1799–1845: 'Faithless Nelly Gray' (1826)

16 For here I leave my second leg,
And the Forty-second Foot!

Thomas Hood 1799–1845: 'Faithless Nelly Gray' (1826)

17 My parents were very pleased that I was in the army. The fact that I hated it somehow pleased them even more.

Barry Humphries 1934– : *More Please* (1992)

18 No man will be a sailor who has contrivance enough to get himself into a jail; for being in a ship is being in a jail, with the chance of being drowned . . . A man in a jail has more room, better food, and commonly better company.

Samuel Johnson 1709–84: James Boswell *Life of Samuel Johnson* (1791) 16 March 1759

19 The uniform 'e wore
Was nothin' much before,
An' rather less than 'arf o' that be'ind.

Rudyard Kipling 1865–1936: 'Gunga Din' (1892)

20 Though I've belted you and flayed you,
By the livin' Gawd that made you,
You're a better man than I am, Gunga Din!

Rudyard Kipling 1865–1936: 'Gunga Din' (1892)

21 *as young army musician, having composed a march for his regiment:*
GENERAL: Isn't it a little fast, Korngold? The men can't march to that.
KORNGOLD: Ah yes, well, you see Sir, this was composed for the retreat!

Erich Korngold 1897–1957: Brendan G. Carroll *The Last Prodigy* (1997)

22 *to a general who sent his dispatches from 'Headquarters in the Saddle':*
The trouble with Hooker is that he's got his headquarters where his hindquarters ought to be.

Abraham Lincoln 1809–65: P. M. Zall *Abe Lincoln Laughing* (1982)

23 [Haig is] brilliant—to the top of his boots.

David Lloyd George 1863–1945: Paul Johnson (ed.) *The Oxford Book of Political Anecdotes* (1986); attributed

24 If these gentlemen had their way, they would soon be asking me to defend the moon against a possible attack from Mars.
of his senior military advisers, and their tendency to see threats which did not exist

Lord Salisbury 1830–1903: Robert Taylor *Lord Salisbury* (1975)

25 'He's a cheery old card,' grunted Harry to Jack
As they slogged up to Arras with rifle and pack.
But he did for them both by his plan of attack.

Siegfried Sassoon 1886–1967: 'The General' (1918)

26 I don't consider myself dovish and I certainly don't consider myself hawkish. Maybe I would describe myself as owlish—that is, wise enough to understand that you want to do everything possible to avoid war.

H. Norman Schwarzkopf III 1934– : in *New York Times* 28 January 1991

27 Napoleon's armies always used to march on their stomachs shouting: 'Vive l'Intérieur!'

W. C. Sellar 1898–1951 and **R. J. Yeatman** 1898–1968: *1066 and All That* (1930)

28 Your friend the British soldier can stand up to anything except the British War Office.

George Bernard Shaw 1856–1950: *The Devil's Disciple* (1901)

29 When the military man approaches, the world locks up its spoons and packs off its womankind.

George Bernard Shaw 1856–1950: *Man and Superman* (1903)

30 As for being a General, well at the age of four with paper hats and wooden swords we're all Generals. Only some of us never grow out of it.

Peter Ustinov 1921–2004: *Romanoff and Juliet* (1956)

31 The General was essentially a man of peace, except in his domestic life.

Oscar Wilde 1854–1900: *The Importance of Being Earnest* (1895)

Art

❝ Two out of death, sex and jewels. ❞
Roy Strong

1 I'm a guy who can't function well in life, but I can in art.

Woody Allen 1935– : *Deconstructing Harry* (1997 film)

2 A cow and calf are cut in half
And placed in separate cases
To call it art, however smart
Casts doubt on art's whole basis.

Anonymous: unattributed; in
Spectator 5 July 2003

3 *an old lady on Epstein's controversial* Christ in Majesty:
I can never forgive Mr Epstein for his representation of Our Lord. So very un-English!

Anonymous: in *Ned Sherrin in his Anecdotage* (1993)

4 Oh, I wish I could draw. I've always wanted to draw. I'd give my right arm to be able to draw. It must be very relaxing.

Alan Ayckbourn 1939– : *Joking Apart* (1979)

5 All the arts in America are a gigantic racket run by unscrupulous men for unhealthy women.

Thomas Beecham 1879–1961: in *Observer* 5 May 1946

6 Of course he [William Morris] was a wonderful all-round man, but the act of walking round him has always tired me.

Max Beerbohm 1872–1956: letter to S. N. Behrman c.1953; *Conversations with Max* (1960)

7 The artistic temperament is a disease that afflicts amateurs. It is a disease which arises from men not having sufficient power of expression to utter and get rid of the element of art in their being.

G. K. Chesterton 1874–1936: *Heretics* (1905)

8 There are only two styles of portrait painting; the serious and the smirk.

Charles Dickens 1812–70: *Nicholas Nickleby* (1839)

9 If I were alive in Rubens's time, I'd be celebrated as a model. Kate Moss would be used as a paint brush.

Dawn French 1957– : in *Sunday Times* 13 August 2006

10 *to a lawyer who had asked him why he laid such stress on 'the painter's eye':*
The painter's eye is to him what the lawyer's tongue is to you.

Thomas Gainsborough 1727–88: William Hazlitt *Conversations of James Northcote* (1830)

11 *on attempting to paint two actors, David Garrick and Samuel Foote:*
Rot them for a couple of rogues, they have everybody's faces but their own.

Thomas Gainsborough 1727–88: Allan Cunningham *The Lives of the Most Eminent Painters, Sculptors and Architects* (1829)

12 Then a sentimental passion of a vegetable fashion must
    excite your languid spleen,
An attachment à la Plato for a bashful young potato, or a
    not too French French bean!
Though the Philistines may jostle, you will rank as an
    apostle in the high aesthetic band,
If you walk down Piccadilly with a poppy or a lily in your
    medieval hand.

W. S. Gilbert 1836–1911: *Patience* (1881)

13 *a few days after the funeral of Sir William Orpen:*
Our painter! He never got under the surface till he got under the sod.

Oliver St John Gogarty 1878–1957: Ulick O'Connor *Oliver St John Gogarty* (1964)

14 Yes, Frances [his wife] has the most beautiful hands in the world—and someday I'm going to have a bust made of them.

Sam Goldwyn 1882–1974: Michael Freedland *The Goldwyn Touch* (1986)

15 As my poor father used to say
In 1863,
Once people start on all this Art
Goodbye, moralitee!

A. P. Herbert 1890–1971: 'Lines for a Worthy Person' (1930)

16 It's amazing what you can do with an E in A-level art, twisted imagination and a chainsaw

Damien Hirst 1965– : in *Observer* 3 December 1995 'Sayings of the Week'

17 There is, perhaps, no more dangerous man in the world than the man with the sensibilities of an artist but without creative talent. With luck such men make wonderful theatrical impresarios and interior decorators, or else they become mass murderers or critics.

Barry Humphries 1934– : *More Please* (1992)

18 It is a symbol of Irish art. The cracked lookingglass of a servant.

James Joyce 1882–1941: *Ulysses* (1922)

19 *of Art Nouveau:*
Certainly no style seems at first glance to provide a richer field for the investigations of Herr Freud.

Osbert Lancaster 1908–86: *Homes Sweet Homes* (1939)

20 Mr Landseer whose only merit as a painter was the tireless accuracy with which he recorded the more revoltingly sentimental aspects of the woollier mammals.

Osbert Lancaster 1908–86: *Homes Sweet Homes* (1939)

21 *when Carl André's* Equivalent VIII *consisting of 120 bricks was exhibited at the Tate Gallery in 1976:*
I think the fellow needs to have his hod examined.

Osbert Lancaster 1908–86: attributed

22 The adjective 'modern', when applied to any branch of art, means 'designed to evoke incomprehension, anger, boredom or laughter'.

Philip Larkin 1922–85: *All What Jazz* (1985)

23 Dali is the only painter of LSD without LSD.

Timothy Leary 1920–96: Salvador Dali *Dali by Dali* (1970)

24 If a scientist were to cut his ear off, no one would take it as evidence of a heightened sensibility.

Peter Medawar 1915–87: 'J. B. S.' (1968)

25 Monet began by imitating Manet, and Manet ended by imitating Monet.

George Moore 1852–1933: *Vale* (1914)

26 The perfect aesthete logically feels that the artist is strictly a turkish bath attendant.

Flann O'Brien 1911–66: *The Best of Myles* (1968)

27 *on a South African statue of the Voortrekkers:*
Patriotism is the last refuge of the sculptor.

William Plomer 1903–73: Rupert Hart-Davis letter to George Lyttelton, 13 October 1956

28 My art belongs to Dada.

Cole Porter 1891–1964: attributed

29 Epstein is a great sculptor. I wish he would wash, but I believe Michelangelo *never* did, so I suppose it is part of the tradition.

Ezra Pound 1885–1972: Charles Norman *The Case of Ezra Pound* (1948)

30 He didn't like heads, did he?

John Prescott 1938– : opening a Henry Moore exhibition in Beijing, in *Sunday Times* 22 October 2000

31 If you want art to be like ovaltine, then clearly some art is not for you.

Peter Reading 1946– : in *Critics' Forum*, Radio 3, 22 November 1986; attributed

32 I don't think rock'n'roll songwriters should worry about Art . . . As far as I'm concerned, Art is just short for Arthur.

Keith Richards 1943– : *Keith Richards: in His Own Words* (1994)

33 *on the probable reaction to the painting of the subjects of
Turner's Girls Surprised while Bathing:*
I should think devilish surprised to see what Turner has
made of them.

34 I don't know what art is, but I do know what it isn't. And
it isn't someone walking around with a salmon over his
shoulder, or embroidering the name of everyone they have
slept with on the inside of a tent.

35 I always ask the sitter if they want truth or flattery. They
always ask for truth, and I always give them flattery.

36 I doubt that art needed Ruskin any more than a moving
train needs one of its passengers to shove it.

37 *the ingredients for a successful exhibition:*
You've got to have two out of death, sex and jewels.

38 There is only one position for an artist anywhere: and that
is, upright.

39 A genius with the IQ of a moron.
of Andy Warhol

40 Painters are so bitchy. Magritte told Miró that Kandinsky
had feet of Klee.

41 *on a Constable painting of the Thames:*
It is as though Constable had taken a long steady
appraising stare at Canaletto and then charged straight
through him.

42 Mrs Ballinger is one of the ladies who pursue Culture in
bands, as though it were dangerous to meet it alone.

43 Yes—one does like to make one's mummy just as nice as
possible!
on his portrait of his mother

44 *in his case against Ruskin, replying to the question: 'For two
days' labour, you ask two hundred guineas?':*
No, I ask it for the knowledge of a lifetime.

45 *to a lady who had been reminded of his work by an 'exquisite
haze in the atmosphere':*
Yes madam, Nature is creeping up.

46 All that I desire to point out is the general principle that
Life imitates Art far more than Art imitates Life.

47 *after the death of the outlaw Jesse James relics of his house
were sold:*
His sole work of art, a chromo-lithograph of the most
dreadful kind, of course was sold at a price which in
Europe only a Mantegna or an undoubted Titian can
command!

48 The Sheridan stands in the heart of New York's Bohemian
and artistic quarter. If you threw a brick from any of its
windows, you would be certain to brain some rising young
interior decorator, some Vorticist sculptor or a writer of
revolutionary *vers libre*.

Dante Gabriel Rossetti 1828–82: O.
Doughty *A Victorian Romantic* (1960)

Brian Sewell: in *Independent* 26 April
1999

Ruskin Spear 1911–90: attributed; in
Sunday Times (Letters) 4 January 2004

Tom Stoppard 1937– : in *Times
Literary Supplement* 3 June 1977

Roy Strong 1935– : in *Sunday Times*
23 January 1994

Dylan Thomas 1914–53: *Quite Early
One Morning* (1954)

Gore Vidal 1925– : in *Observer* 18
June 1989

Dick Vosburgh 1929–2007: told to
the Editor

Sylvia Townsend Warner
1893–1978: letter, 6 February 1969

Edith Wharton 1862–1937: *Xingu
and Other Stories* (1916)

James McNeill Whistler 1834–1903:
E. R. and J. Pennell *The Life of James
McNeill Whistler* (1908)

James McNeill Whistler 1834–1903:
D. C. Seitz *Whistler Stories* (1913)

James McNeill Whistler 1834–1903:
D. C. Seitz *Whistler Stories* (1913)

Oscar Wilde 1854–1900: *Intentions*
(1891) 'The Decay of Lying'

Oscar Wilde 1854–1900: letter 25
April 1882

P. G. Wodehouse 1881–1975: *The
Small Bachelor* (1927)

Australia

❝By God what a site! By man what a mess!❞
Clough Williams-Ellis

1 Australia is a huge rest home, where no unwelcome news is ever wafted on to the pages of the worst newspapers in the world.

Germaine Greer 1939– : in *Observer* 1 August 1982

2 Earth is here so kind, that just tickle her with a hoe and she laughs with a harvest.

Douglas Jerrold 1803–57: *The Wit and Opinions of Douglas Jerrold* (1859) 'A Land of Plenty' (Australia)

3 When New Zealanders emigrate to Australia, it raises the average IQ of both countries.

Robert Muldoon 1921–92: attributed

4 In Australia,
Inter alia,
Mediocrities
Think they're Socrates.

Peter Porter 1929– : unpublished clerihew; Stephen Murray-Smith (ed.) *The Dictionary of Australian Quotations* (1984)

5 By God what a site! By man what a mess!
of Sydney

Clough Williams-Ellis 1883–1978: *Architect Errant* (1971)

Autobiography

See also **Biography**

❝To speak ill of everybody except oneself.❞
Henri Philippe Pétain

1 Every time somebody's Autobiography comes out I turn to the Index to see if my name occurs, and of course it never does.

James Agate 1877–1947: diary 16 September 1932

2 I used to think I was an interesting person, but I must tell you how sobering a thought it is to realize your life's story fills about thirty-five pages and you have, actually, not much to say.

Roseanne Arnold 1953– : *Roseanne* (1990)

3 *on James Agate's autobiography:*
I did so enjoy your book. Everything that everybody writes in it is so good.

Mrs Patrick Campbell 1865–1940: James Agate diary 6 May 1937

4 Reformers are always finally neglected, while the memoirs of the frivolous will always eagerly be read.

Chips Channon 1897–1958: diary, 7 July 1936

5 An autobiography should give the reader opportunity to point out the author's follies and misconceptions.

Claud Cockburn 1904–81: *Crossing the Line* (1958)

6 An autobiography is an obituary in serial form with the last instalment missing.

Quentin Crisp 1908–99: *The Naked Civil Servant* (1968)

7 *Giles Gordon's father had criticized the length of his son's entry in Who's Who:*
I've just measured it, with a ruler; it's exactly the same length as my male organ, which I've also just measured.

Giles Gordon 1940– : *Aren't We Due a Royalty Statement?* (1993)

8 Autobiography is now as common as adultery and hardly less reprehensible.

John Grigg 1924– : in *Sunday Times* 28 February 1962

9 Next to the writer of real estate advertisements, the autobiographer is the most suspect of prose artists.

Donal Henahan: in *New York Times* 1977

10 The purpose of the Presidential Office is not power, or leadership of the Western World, but reminiscence, best-selling reminiscence.

Roger Jellinek 1938– : in *New York Times Book Review* 1969

11 If a man is to write *A Panegyric* he may keep vices out of sight; but if he professes to write *A Life*, he must represent it as it really was.

Samuel Johnson 1709–84: James Boswell *Life of Samuel Johnson* (1791) 1777

12 I am being frank about myself in this book. I tell of my first mistake on page 850.
of his autobiography Years of Upheaval

Henry Kissinger 1923– : in *Observer* 2 January 1983

13 The reminiscences of Mrs Humphrey Ward . . . convinced me that autobiography is a sin.

Harold Laski 1893–1950: letter to Oliver Wendell Holmes, 1 December 1918

14 *on Margot Asquith's forthcoming memoirs:*
As scandal is the second breath of life my name is down for an early copy.

Harold Laski 1893–1950: letter to Oliver Wendell Holmes, 6 March 1920

15 Like all good memoirs it has not been emasculated by considerations of good taste.

Peter Medawar 1915–87: review of James D. Watson *The Double Helix* (1968)

16 Every autobiography . . . becomes an absorbing work of fiction, with something of the charm of a cryptogram.

H. L. Mencken 1880–1956: *Minority Report* (1956)

17 Even when Micheál [MacLíammoir] took in later life to autobiographies, they were about as reliable as his hairpieces.

Sheridan Morley 1941–2007: in *Sunday Times* 6 February 1994

18 To write one's memoirs is to speak ill of everybody except oneself.

Henri Philippe Pétain 1856–1951: in *Observer* 26 May 1946

19 If you really want to hear about it, the first thing you'll probably want to know is where I was born, and what my lousy childhood was like, and how my parents were occupied and all before they had me, and all that David Copperfield kind of crap, but I don't feel like going into it.

J. D. Salinger 1919– : *The Catcher in the Rye* (1951)

20 My problem is that I am not frightfully interested in anything, except myself. And of all forms of fiction autobiography is the most gratuitous.

Tom Stoppard 1937– : *Lord Malquist and Mr Moon* (1966)

21 Only when one has lost all curiosity about the future has one reached the age to write an autobiography.

Evelyn Waugh 1903–66: *A Little Learning* (1964)

22 I shall not say why and how I became, at the age of fifteen, the mistress of the Earl of Craven.

Harriette Wilson 1789–1846: opening words of *Memoirs* (1825)

23 *of political memoirists:*
It is an exceptionally inadequate ex-minister who fails to secure a six-figure sum for his work, serialization included.

Hugo Young 1938–2003: in *Guardian* 20 September 1990

Awards and Prizes
See also **Honours**

❝ *Like piles. Sooner or later, every bum gets one.* ❞
Maureen Lipman

1 Prizes are like sashes, you can wear them and be Miss World for a bit . . . I've been royally dissed by prizes.

Martin Amis 1949– : in *Observer* 10 March 1996 'Sayings of the Week'

2 My career must be slipping. This is the first time I've been available to pick up an award.

Michael Caine 1933– : at the Golden Globe awards, Beverly Hills, California, 24 January 1999

3 Oscar night at my house is called Passover.

Bob Hope 1903–2003: in *Daily Telegraph* 29 May 2003 (online edition)

4 *suggestion for a winning poem for the competition for Bard of Humberside:*
I put my luncheon in the fridge
and go and look at Humber Bridge.

Philip Larkin 1922–85: in conversation with Andrew Motion; quoted in *Sunday Times* 23 May 1999

5 Awards are like piles. Sooner or later, every bum gets one.

Maureen Lipman 1946– : in *Independent* 31 July 1999

6 It's about time a transvestite potter won the Turner Prize.
accepting the prize, 7 December 2003

Grayson Perry 1960– : in *Daily Telegraph* 8 December 2003 (online edition)

7 The award for travel-writing was for 'people who've been somewhere and written about it.' . . . Veni, vidi, velcro; I came, I saw, I stuck around.

Sandi Toksvig 1959– : in *Daily Telegraph* 20 March 2004

Baseball
See also **Sports and Games**

❝ *If people don't want to come out to the ball park, nobody's going to stop 'em.* ❞
Yogi Berra

1 One of the chief duties of the fan is to engage in arguments with the man behind him. This department of the game has been allowed to run down fearfully.

Robert Benchley 1889–1945: Ralph S. Graben *The Baseball Reader* (1951)

2 Think! How the hell are you gonna think and hit at the same time?

Yogi Berra 1925– : *Nice Guys Finish Seventh* (1976)

3 If people don't want to come out to the ball park, nobody's going to stop 'em.

Yogi Berra 1925– : attributed

4 For those of us who are baseball fans and agnostics, the [Baseball] Hall of Fame is as close to a religious experience as we may ever get.

Bill Bryson 1951– : *The Lost Continent* (1989)

5 If baseball goes for pay television, shouldn't the viewers be given a bonus for watching a ball game between Baltimore and Kansas City?

Jimmy Cannon 1910–73: in *New York Post* 1951–54 'Nobody Asked Me, But . . . '

6 Finally I realized that the gentleman holding the bat is antagonistic to the man throwing the ball.

Lynn Fontanne 1887–1983: Margot Peters *Design for Living* (2003)

7 Baseball is very big with my people. It figures. It's the only way we can get to shake a bat at a white man without starting a riot.

Dick Gregory 1932– : D. H. Nathan (ed.) *Baseball Quotations* (1991)

8 *after leaving his sick-bed in October 1935 to attend the World Baseball Series in Detroit, and betting on the losers:*
I should of stood in bed.

Joe Jacobs 1896–1940: John Lardner *Strong Cigars* (1951)

9 Although he is a bad fielder he is also a poor hitter.
of a baseball player

Ring Lardner 1885–1933: R. E. Drennan *Wit's End* (1973)

10 Take me out to the ball game,
Take me out with the crowd.
Buy me some peanuts and cracker-jack—
I don't care if I never get back.

Jack Norworth 1879–1959: 'Take Me Out to the Ball Game' (1908 song)

11 Don't look back. Something may be gaining on you.
a baseball pitcher's advice

Leroy ('Satchel') Paige 1906–82: in *Collier's* 13 June 1953

12 All you have to do is keep the five players who hate your guts away from the five who are undecided.
a baseball manager's view in 1974

Casey Stengel 1891–1975: John Samuel (ed.) *The Guardian Book of Sports Quotes* (1985)

13 I don't think I can be expected to take seriously any game which takes less than three days to reach its conclusion.
a cricket enthusiast on baseball

Tom Stoppard 1937– : in *Guardian* 24 December 1984 'Sports Quotes of the Year'

14 Baseball, it is said, is only a game. True. And the Grand Canyon is only a hole in Arizona. Not all holes, or games, are created equal.

George F. Will 1941– : *Men At Work: The Craft of Baseball* (1990)

Behaviour

66*Manners are especially the need of the plain.*99
Evelyn Waugh

1 Thank you for the most *marvellous* interview, darling, you're quite the politest lesbian I've ever met.
calling out in a crowded lobby after a self-righteous reporter

Tallulah Bankhead 1903–68: Bryony Lavery *Tallulah Bankhead* (1999)

2 My grandmother took a bath every year, whether she was dirty or not.

Brendan Behan 1923–64: *Brendan Behan's Island* (1962)

3 It looked bad when the Duke of Fife
Left off using a knife;
But people began to talk
When he left off using a fork.

Edmund Clerihew Bentley 1875–1956: 'The Duke of Fife' (1905)

4 You know what charm is: a way of getting the answer yes without having asked any clear question.

Albert Camus 1913–60: *La Chute* (1956)

5 It isn't etiquette to cut any one you've been introduced to. Remove the joint.

Lewis Carroll 1832–98: *Through the Looking-Glass* (1872)

6 Curtsey while you're thinking what to say. It saves time.

Lewis Carroll 1832–98: *Through the Looking-Glass* (1872)

7 I always take blushing either for a sign of guilt, or of ill breeding.

William Congreve 1670–1729: *The Way of the World* (1700)

8 Don't let us be familiar or fond, nor kiss before folks, like my Lady Fadler and Sir Francis . . . Let us be very strange and well-bred: Let us be as strange as if we had been married a great while, and as well-bred as if we were not married at all.

William Congreve 1670–1729: *The Way of the World* (1700)

9 HECKLER: We expected a better play.
COWARD: I expected better manners.
to a heckler in the audience after Sirocco (1927) *was booed*

Noël Coward 1899–1973: Sheridan Morley *A Talent to Amuse* (1969)

10 How would I like to be remembered? By my charm, you silly bugger.

Noël Coward 1899–1973: Sheridan Morley *The Quotable Noël Coward* (1999)

11 I tried to keep in mind the essential rules of British conduct which the Major had carefully instilled in me:
1. The English never speak to anyone unless they have been properly introduced (except in case of shipwreck).
2. You must never talk about God or your stomach.

Pierre Daninos: *Major Thompson and I* (1957)

12 He'd say 'Par'n my glove', politely
When he shook my hand.
And he'd pass me the evening paper
When his soup was fanned.
He only used four-letter words
I didn't understand.
He had refinement.

Dorothy Fields 1905–74: 'He Had Refinement' (in *A Tree Grows in Brooklyn*, 1951 musical)

13 You children must be extra polite to strangers because your father's an actor.

Mrs Fields: Dorothy Fields' mother; taped lecture in Caryl Brahms and Ned Sherrin *Song by Song* (1984)

14 Suspect all extraordinary and groundless civilities.

Thomas Fuller 1654–1734: *Gnomologia* (1734)

15 I get too hungry for dinner at eight.
I like the theatre, but never come late.
I never bother with people I hate.
That's why the lady is a tramp.

Lorenz Hart 1895–1943: 'The Lady is a Tramp' (1937)

16 *on Harold Wilson's 'Lavender List' (the honours list he drew up on resigning the British premiership in 1976):*
Such a graceful exit. And then he had to go and do this on the doorstep.

John Junor 1919–97: in *Observer* 23 December 1990

17 'What are you doing for dinner tonight?'
'Digesting it.'
to a dinner invitation arriving at 8.30 pm

George S. Kaufman 1889–1961: Howard Teichmann *George S. Kaufman* (1973)

18 Eccentricity, to be socially acceptable, had still to have at least four or five generations of inbreeding behind it.

Osbert Lancaster 1908–86: *All Done From Memory* (1953)

19 The mayor gave no other answer than that deep guttural grunt which is technically known in municipal interviews as refusing to commit oneself.

Stephen Leacock 1869–1944: *Arcadian Adventures with the Idle Rich* (1914)

20 I have noticed that the people who are late are often so much jollier than the people who have to wait for them.

E. V. Lucas 1868–1938: *365 Days and One More* (1926)

21 *aged four, having had hot coffee spilt over his legs:*
Thank you, madam, the agony is abated.

Lord Macaulay 1800–59: G. O. Trevelyan *Life and Letters of Lord Macaulay* (1876)

22 Etiquette, sacred subject of, 1–389.

Judith Martin 1938– : *Miss Manners' Guide to Rearing Perfect Children* (1985); index entry

23 Good manners are a combination of intelligence, education, taste, and style mixed together so that you don't need any of those things.

P. J. O'Rourke 1947– : *Modern Manners* (1984)

24 Do you suppose I could buy back my introduction to you?

S. J. Perelman 1904–79 et al.: in *Monkey Business* (1931 film)

25 Miss Otis regrets she's unable to lunch today, Madam.

Cole Porter 1891–1964: 'Miss Otis Regrets' (1934)

26 In olden days, a glimpse of stocking
Was looked on as something shocking,
But now, God knows,
Anything goes.

Cole Porter 1891–1964: 'Anything Goes' (1934)

27 One of those telegrams of which M. de Guermantes had wittily fixed the formula: 'Cannot come, lie follows'.

Marcel Proust 1871–1922: *Le Temps retrouvé* (Time Regained, 1926)

28 I am a woman of the world, Hector; and I can assure you that if you will only take the trouble always to do the perfectly correct thing, and to say the perfectly correct thing, you can do just what you like.

George Bernard Shaw 1856–1950: *Heartbreak House* (1919)

29 These sort of boobies think that people come to balls to do nothing but dance; whereas everyone knows that the real business of a ball is either to look out for a wife, to look after a wife, or to look after somebody else's wife.

R. S. Surtees 1805–64: *Mr Facey Romford's Hounds* (1865)

30 *Somerset Maugham excused his leaving early when dining with Lady Tree by saying, 'I must look after my youth':*
Next time do bring him. We adore those sort of people.

Lady Tree 1863–1937: in *Ned Sherrin in his Anecdotage* (1993); a similar story is told of Maugham and Lady Cunard

31 This is a free country, madam. We have a right to share your privacy in a public place.

Peter Ustinov 1921–2004: *Romanoff and Juliet* (1956)

32 Orthodoxy is my doxy; heterodoxy is another man's doxy.

William Warburton 1698–1779: to Lord Sandwich; Joseph Priestley *Memoirs* (1807)

33 Manners are especially the need of the plain. The pretty can get away with anything.

Evelyn Waugh 1903–66: in *Observer* 15 April 1962

34 I am very sorry to hear that Duff [Cooper] was surprised and grieved to hear that I had detested him for 23 years. I must have nicer manners than people normally credit me with.

Evelyn Waugh 1903–66: letter to Lady Diana Cooper, 29 August 1953

35 *hearing someone object that the good manners of the French were all on the surface:*
Well, you know, a very good place to have them.

James McNeill Whistler 1834–1903: E. R. and J. Pennell *The Life of James McNeill Whistler* (1908)

36 It is very vulgar to talk like a dentist when one isn't a dentist. It produces a false impression.

Oscar Wilde 1854–1900: *The Importance of Being Earnest* (1895)

37 Duty is what one expects from others, it is not what one does oneself.

Oscar Wilde 1854–1900: *A Woman of No Importance* (1893)

38 It is a good rule in life never to apologize. The right sort of people do not want apologies, and the wrong sort take a mean advantage of them.

P. G. Wodehouse 1881–1975: *The Man Upstairs* (1914)

39 The confessions of error, as jocular as they are suspect, which the upper class have always associated with good manners.

Hugo Young 1938–2003: in *Guardian* 20 September 1990

Betting

See also **Gambling**

66 *Horse sense is a good judgement which keeps horses from betting on people.* 99
W. C. Fields

1 Lord Hippo suffered fearful loss
By putting money on a horse
Which he believed, if it were pressed,
Would run far faster than the rest.

Hilaire Belloc 1870–1953: 'Lord Hippo' (1911)

2 It's one thing to ask your bank manager for an overdraft to buy 500 begonias for the borders in Haslemere, but quite another to seek financial succour to avail oneself of some of the 5–2 they're offering on Isle de Bourbon for the St Leger.

Jeffrey Bernard 1932–97: in *Guardian* 23 December 1978 'Sports Quotes of the Year'

3 Horse sense is a good judgement which keeps horses from betting on people.

W. C. Fields 1880–1946: attributed; Nigel Rees *Cassell Dictionary of Humorous Quotations* (1999)

4 Don't let's go to the dogs tonight,
For mother will be there.

A. P. Herbert 1890–1971: 'Don't Let's Go to the Dogs Tonight' (1926)

5 I got a horse right here,
The name is Paul Revere,
And here's a guy that says if the weather's clear,
Can do, can do, this guy says the horse can do.

Frank Loesser 1910–69: 'Fugue for Tinhorns' (1950)

6 Not for good old reliable Nathan for it's always just a short walk,
To the oldest established permanent floating crap game in New York.

Frank Loesser 1910–69: 'The Oldest Established' (1950)

7 It may be that the race is not always to the swift, nor the battle to the strong—but that's the way to bet.

Damon Runyon 1884–1946: attributed

8 'You are snatching a hard guy when you snatch Bookie Bob. A very hard guy, indeed. In fact,' I say, 'I hear the softest thing about him is his front teeth.'

Damon Runyon 1884–1946: in *Collier's* 26 September 1931, 'The Snatching of Bookie Bob'

9 There are two times in a man's life when he should not speculate: when he can't afford it and when he can.

Mark Twain 1835–1910: *Following the Equator* (1897)

10 My immediate reward for increasing the tax on bookmaking was major vilification. It was confidently asserted in the bookmakers' circles that my mother and father met only once and then for a very brief period.
in 1972, when Chairman of the British Betting Levy Board

George Wigg 1900–83: Jonathon Green and Don Atyeo (eds.) *The Book of Sports Quotes* (1979)

The Bible

❝ *A wonderful book, but there are some very queer things in it.* **❞**
George V

1 There's a great text in Galatians,
Once you trip on it, entails
Twenty-nine distinct damnations,
One sure, if another fails.

Robert Browning 1812–89: 'Soliloquy of the Spanish Cloister' (1842)

2 *on Moses and the reason why there are only ten commandments:*
He probably said to himself, 'Must stop or I shall be getting silly.'

Mrs Patrick Campbell 1865–1940: James Agate diary, 6 May 1937

3 The Bible . . . is a lesson in how not to write for the movies.

Raymond Chandler 1888–1959: letter to Edgar Carter, 28 March 1947

4 A wonderful book, but there are some very queer things in it.

George V 1865–1936: K. Rose *King George V* (1983)

5 It ain't necessarily so,
It ain't necessarily so—
De t'ings that yo' li'ble
To read in de Bible—
It ain't necessarily so.

Ira Gershwin 1896–1983: 'It Ain't Necessarily So' (1935)

6 The number one book of the ages was written by a committee, and it was called the Bible.

Louis B. Mayer 1885–1957: attributed

7 The Ten Commandments should be treated like an examination. Only six need to be attempted.

Bertrand Russell 1872–1970: attributed, perhaps apocryphal

8 LORD ILLINGWORTH: The Book of Life begins with a man and a woman in a garden.
MRS ALLONBY: It ends with Revelations.

Oscar Wilde 1854–1900: *A Woman of No Importance* (1893)

9 I read the book of Job last night. I don't think God comes well out of it.

Virginia Woolf 1882–1941: letter to Lady Robert Cecil, 12 November 1922

10 It's just called 'The Bible' now. We dropped the word 'Holy' to give it a more mass-market appeal.
a publisher's view

Judith Young: attributed, 1989

Biography

See also **Autobiography**

❝ *It is always Judas who writes the biography.* **❞**
Oscar Wilde

1 *to the biographer Richard Holmes, arriving to speak in a tent at the Hay on Wye Literary Festival on a particularly muddy day:*
Perfect biographer's weather. Feet of clay everywhere.

Anonymous: in *Daily Telegraph* 8 March 2003

2 Biography should be written by an acute enemy.

Arthur James Balfour 1848–1930: in *Observer* 30 January 1927

3 Nobody likes being written about in their lifetime, it's as though the FBI and the CIA were suddenly to splash your files in the paper.
   on his forthcoming biography

Saul Bellow 1915–2005: in *Guardian* 10 September 1997

4 The Art of Biography
Is different from Geography.
Geography is about Maps,
But Biography is about Chaps.

Edmund Clerihew Bentley 1875–1956: *Biography for Beginners* (1905) introduction

5 *reason for shelving a planned biography of L. P. Hartley:*
I was told I had to track one butler down to a male brothel in Norway.

Penelope Fitzgerald 1916–2000: in *Daily Telegraph* 6 May 2000; obituary

6 Biography, like big game hunting, is one of the recognized forms of sport, and it is as unfair as only sport can be.

Philip Guedalla 1889–1944: *Supers and Supermen* (1920)

7 Do not send me your manuscript. Worse than the practice of writing books about living men is the conduct of living men in supervising such books.
   to his would-be biographer Houston Martin

A. E. Housman 1859–1936: letter, 22 March 1936

8 *on hearing that Arthur Benson was to write the life of Rossetti:*
No, no, no, it won't do. *Dear* Arthur, we know just what he can, so beautifully, do, but no, oh no, this is to have the story of a purple man written by a white, or at the most, a pale green man.

Henry James 1843–1916: George Lyttelton letter to Rupert Hart-Davis, 28 February 1957

9 I never read the life of any important person without discovering that he knew more and could do more than I could ever hope to know or to do in half a dozen lifetimes.

J. B. Priestley 1894–1984: *Apes and Angels* (1928)

10 I have done my best to die before this book is published. It now seems possible that I may not succeed . . . I shall try to keep my sense of humour and the perspective of eternity.
   letter to his biographer, Humphrey Carpenter, shortly before publication

Robert Runcie 1921–2000: H. Carpenter *Robert Runcie* (1996)

11 Biography is the mesh through which real life escapes.

Tom Stoppard 1937– : *The Invention of Love* (1997)

12 He's written me a rather plaintive letter, saying will you at least read the typescript to correct any factual errors and I've replied no, I want it to be as inaccurate as possible.
   of his response to a would-be and unwanted biographer

Tom Stoppard 1937– : in *Daily Telegraph* 27 February 1999

13 Discretion is not the better part of biography.

Lytton Strachey 1880–1932: Michael Holroyd *Lytton Strachey* (1967)

14 I have a good track record with larger-than-life iron ladies.
   on writing the story of the liner QEII

Carol Thatcher 1953– : in *Sunday Times* 19 March 2000 'Talking Heads'

15 Blamelessness runs riot through six hundred pages.
   review of Kenneth Harris's biography of Attlee

John Vincent 1937– : in *Sunday Times* 26 September 1982

16 Then there is my noble and biographical friend who has added a new terror to death.
   on Lord Campbell's Lives of the Lord Chancellors *being written without the consent of heirs or executors*

Charles Wetherell 1770–1846: also attributed to Lord Lyndhurst (1772–1863)

17 Every great man nowadays has his disciples, and it is always Judas who writes the biography.

Oscar Wilde 1854–1900: *Intentions* (1891) 'The Critic as Artist'

Birds
See also **Animals**

❝ *I told you to stick to ducks.* ❞
Marlene Dietrich

1 I am a sundial. Ordinary words
Cannot express my thoughts on Birds.

Hilaire Belloc 1870–1953: 'On Another' (1954)

2 Ornithology used to be an arcane hobby for embittered schoolmasters, dotty spinsters and lonely little boys, but now it is as normal a weekend occupation as rug-making or wife-swapping.

Kyril Bonfiglioli 1928–85: *Don't Point that Thing at Me* (1972)

3 A hen is only an egg's way of making other eggs.

Samuel Butler 1835–1902: *Life and Habit* (1877)

4 *to her husband, a chicken farmer in California, after a flash flood had wiped out his entire flock:*
I told you to stick to ducks.

Marlene Dietrich 1901–92: attributed; Richard Eyre *Diaries* 14 May 1992

5 Get out of town!
And he went, with a quack and a waddle and a quack,
In a flurry of eiderdown.

Frank Loesser 1910–69: 'The Ugly Duckling' (1952)

6 This woodcock, by a happy fluke,
Might have avoided either duke.
Had it the commoner preferred,
It would have been a wiser bird.
Alas, its fate became a cert,
Betwixt Duke Bobo and Duke Bert.

Harold Macmillan 1894–1986: 'Ode to a woodcock which, on emerging from the covert, was fired on simultaneously by the Dukes of Roxburghe and Marlborough'; collected by Peter Fleming from an unidentified gamebook, and quoted by Duff Hart-Davis in *Sunday Telegraph* 6 August 2000

7 Oh, a wondrous bird is the pelican!
His beak holds more than his belican.
He takes in his beak
Food enough for a week.
But I'll be darned if I know how the helican.

Dixon Lanier Merritt 1879–1972: in *Nashville Banner* 22 April 1913

8 Canaries, caged in the house, do it,
When they're out of season, grouse do it.

Cole Porter 1891–1964: 'Let's Do It, Let's Fall in Love' (1928)

9 I live in a city. I know sparrows from starlings. After that everything's a duck as far as I'm concerned.

Terry Pratchett 1948– : *Monstrous Regiment* (2003)

10 Phoney-rustic bards,
Spare us your thoughts about birds.

Peter Reading 1946– : 'Nips' in *Collected Poems 1970–1984* (1995)

11 If I were a cassowary
On the plains of Timbuctoo,
I would eat a missionary,
Cassock, band, and hymn-book too.

Samuel Wilberforce 1805–73: impromptu verse, attributed

The Body

See also **Appearance, Description, Faces**

❝ *I could do with sharing my bottom and thighs with at least two other people.* **❞**
Christine Hamilton

1 My brain? It's my second favourite organ.

Woody Allen 1935– and **Marshall Brickman** 1941– : *Sleeper* (1973 film)

2 The verandah over the toy shop.
Australian term for a beer belly.

Anonymous: Richard Eyre *National Service: Diary of a Decade* (2003)

3 If I had the use of my body I would throw it out of the window.

Samuel Beckett 1906–89: *Malone Dies* (1988)

4 Your private parts have become public property.

Alan Bennett 1934– : *Kafka's Dick* (1987)

5 All legs leave something to be desired, do they not? That is part of their function and all of their charm.

Alan Bennett 1934– : attributed

6 Hello boys, have a good night's rest? . . . I missed you.
Governor Le Petomane facing his secretary's cleavage

Andrew Bergman 1945– and **Mel Brooks** 1926– : *Blazing Saddles* (1974 film), spoken by Mel Brooks

7 And our carcases, which are to rise again, are they worth raising? I hope, if mine is, that I shall have a better pair of legs than I have moved on these two-and-twenty years, or I shall be sadly behind in the squeeze into Paradise.

Lord Byron 1788–1824: letter, 13 September 1811

8 I've got difficult feet. They're almost round, like an elephant's. Lengthways they're size ten and sideways size twelve.

Patrick Campbell 1913–80: *Gullible Travels* (1969)

9 I'm the female equivalent of a counterfeit $20 bill. Half of what you see is a pretty good reproduction, the rest is a fraud.

Cher 1946– : Doug McClelland *Star Speak: Hollywood on Everything* (1987)

10 I keep on having my hair cut, but it keeps on growing again.

G. K. Chesterton 1874–1936: *The Napoleon of Notting Hill* (1904)

11 Imprisoned in every fat man a thin one is wildly signalling to be let out.

Cyril Connolly 1903–74: *The Unquiet Grave* (1944)

12 I didn't pay three pounds fifty just to see half a dozen acorns and a chipolata.

Noël Coward 1899–1973: on David Storey's *The Changing Room*; attributed

13 He had but one eye, and the popular prejudice runs in favour of two.

Charles Dickens 1812–70: *Nicholas Nickleby* (1839)

14 If you could see my legs when I take my boots off, you'd form some idea of what unrequited affection is.

Charles Dickens 1812–70: *Dombey and Son* (1848)

15 What is man, when you come to think upon him, but a minutely set, ingenious machine for turning, with infinite artfulness, the red wine of Shiraz into urine?

Isak Dinesen 1885–1962: *Seven Gothic Tales* (1934) 'The Dreamers'

16 I wish you could only see Dizzy in his bath, then you would know what a white skin is.
of her husband

Mary Anne Disraeli d. 1872: attributed; William Gregory *An Autobiography* (1894)

17 If you walk down the street and you've got a disabled leg, people look at you, they can't help it . . . Paul McCartney once said that if he gets recognised in Soho, he walks brusquely away. But if I walk brusquely away I fall over.

Ian Dury 1942–2000: Richard Balls *Sex & Drugs & Rock'n'roll: the life of Ian Dury* (2001)

18 *to William Cecil, who suffered from gout:*
My lord, we make use of you, not for your bad legs, but for your good head.

Elizabeth I 1533–1603: F. Chamberlin *Sayings of Queen Elizabeth* (1923)

19 Being a woman is worse than being a farmer—There is so much harvesting and crop spraying to be done: legs to be waxed, underarms shaved, eyebrows plucked, feet pumiced, skin exfoliated and moisturized, spots cleansed, roots dyed, eyelashes tinted, nails filed, cellulite massaged, stomach muscles exercised . . . Is it any wonder girls have no confidence?

Helen Fielding 1958– : *Bridget Jones's Diary* (1996)

20 I travel light; as light,
That is, as a man can travel who will
Still carry his body around because
Of its sentimental value.

Christopher Fry 1907–2005: *The Lady's not for Burning* (1949)

21 My body, on the move, resembles in sight and sound nothing so much as a bin-liner full of yoghurt.

Stephen Fry 1957– : *The Hippopotamus* (1995)

22 My complexion owes much to my Franco-Slavic mamma and little to my British papa. My waist is my own work.

Mark Gatiss 1966– : *The Vesuvius Club* (2004)

23 I have a left shoulder-blade that is a miracle of loveliness. People come miles to see it. My right elbow has a fascination that few can resist.

W. S. Gilbert 1836–1911: *The Mikado* (1885)

24 There is something between us.

Donald Hall 1928– : 'Breasts' (a one-line poem, 1971)

25 I wouldn't change anything but I could do with sharing my bottom and thighs with at least two other people.

Christine Hamilton: in *Observer* 4 April 2004

26 Lydia, oh Lydia—Say, have you met Lydia?
Oh, Lydia, the tattooed lady?
When she stands, her lap grows littler,
When she sits, she sits on Hitler!

E. Y. Harburg 1898–1981: 'Lydia, the Tattooed Lady' (*A Day at the Circus*, 1939 film)

27 [Alfred Hitchcock] thought of himself as looking like Cary Grant. That's tough, to think of yourself one way and look another.

Tippi Hedren 1930– : interview in California, 1982; P. F. Boller and R. L. Davis *Hollywood Anecdotes* (1988)

28 What they call 'heart' lies much lower than the fourth waistcoat button.

Georg Christoph Lichtenberg 1742–99: notebook (1776–79) in *Aphorisms* (1990)

29 VICKY POLLARD (MATT LUCAS): No but yeah but no but yeah but no but yeah but no because I'm not even going on the pill because Nadine reckons they stop you from getting pregnant.

Matt Lucas 1974– and **David Walliams** 1971– : *Little Britain* (series 1, episode 1) 16 September 2003

30 If your mother had married a proper decent Limerickman you wouldn't have this standing up, North of Ireland, Presbyterian hair.

Frank McCourt 1930– : *Angela's Ashes* (1996)

31 *seaside postcard showing a very fat man whose stomach obscures the small boy at his feet:*
Can't see my little Willy.

Donald McGill 1875–1962: caption, c.1910; in 'Quote Unquote Newsletter', July 1994

32 I'd like to borrow his body for just 48 hours. There are three guys I'd like to beat up and four women I'd like to make love to.

Jim Murray: of Muhammad Ali; attributed

33 A bit of talcum
Is always walcum.

Ogden Nash 1902–71: 'The Baby' (1931)

34 In an advanced state of nudity.

Joe Orton 1933–67: *Up Against It*, screenplay written for the Beatles but never filmed

35 If I see something sagging, dragging or bagging, I'm going to have the stuff tucked or plucked.

Dolly Parton 1946– : interview with Larry King, 12 July 2003

36 *a gay friend, patting her bottom, had commented that it was flabby:*
FRIEND: You should feel mine. It's all taut.
JENNIFER PATERSON: Oh really? And who taut it?

Jennifer Paterson 1928–99: in *Times* 11 August 1999, obituary

37 I'm deeply honoured, but a bit confused. I was only ever a B-cup.
on being voted the sexiest television star 'of all time' by Americans

Diana Rigg 1938– : in *Times* 3 May 1999

38 I don't really like knees.

Yves Saint Laurent 1936–2008: in *Observer* 3 August 1958

39 It's hard to be naked and not be upstaged by your nipples.

Susan Sarandon 1946– : in *Independent* 28 December 2002

40 Thou seest I have more flesh than another man, and therefore more frailty.

William Shakespeare 1564–1616: *Henry IV, Part 1* (1597)

41 The body of a young woman is God's greatest achievement . . . Of course, He could have built it to last longer but you can't have everything.

Neil Simon 1927– : *The Gingerbread Lady* (1970)

42 *on seeing her son Toby Stephens appear naked in the television adaptation of* The Camomile Lawn:
I hadn't see Toby's willy since he was about two, so you can imagine the terrible shock of it all!

Maggie Smith 1934– : attributed (told to the Editor)

43 Mrs Bennett . . . had but two back teeth in her head, but, thank God, they still met.

Edith Œ. Somerville 1858–1949 and **Martin Ross** 1862–1915: *Some Experiences of an Irish R.M.* (1899)

44 Big breasts à la Pamela Anderson are one thing but ones that look more like old socks with tangerines dropped in the bottom are an entirely different kettle du poisson.

Arabella Weir: *Does My Bum Look Big in This?* (1997)

45 Bah! the thing is not a nose at all, but a bit of primordial chaos clapped on to my face.

H. G. Wells 1866–1946: *Select Conversations with an Uncle* (1895) 'The Man with a Nose'

46 Let's forget the six feet and talk about the seven inches.

Mae West 1892–1980: G. Eells and S. Musgrove *Mae West* (1989)

47 Look how she moves! It's like Jell-O on springs!
watching Marilyn Monroe

Billy Wilder 1906–2002 and **I. A. L. Diamond** 1915–88: *Some Like It Hot* (1959 film), spoken by Jack Lemmon as Jerry

48 A lot of people are very critical of modern reproductive processes without understanding all the ins and outs.

Lord Winston 1940– : attributed in *Private Eye*, 6 February 2004

49 He was built on large lines, and seemed to fill the room to overflowing. In physique he was not unlike what Primo Carnera would have been if Carnera hadn't stunted his growth by smoking cigarettes when a boy.

P. G. Wodehouse 1881–1975: *Mulliner Nights* (1933)

50 You're a man, and that's a bonus
'Cause when you're swinging your cojones
You'll show 'em what testosterone is.

David Yazbek: 'Man' in *The Full Monty* (musical, 2000)

Books

See also **Dictionaries, Indexes, Libraries, Literature, Reading, Publishing**

> ❝ *Book—what they make a movie out of for television.* ❞
> **Leonard Louis Levinson**

1 My desire is . . . that mine adversary had written a book.

Bible: *Job*

2 If Louisa May Alcott had really been sound, she'd have written a trilogy, and called the last one *Divorced Lesbian Sluts*.

Julie Burchill 1960– : in *Independent* 30 December 1995

3 Take care not to understand editions and title-pages too well. It always smells of pedantry, and not always of learning . . . Beware of the *bibliomanie*.

Lord Chesterfield 1694–1773: *Letters to his Son* (1774)

4 *on hearing that a fellow guest was 'writing a book':*
Neither am I.

Peter Cook 1937–95: attributed (disclaimed as original by Cook); Nigel Rees *Cassell Dictionary of Humorous Quotations* (1999)

5 PETER BOGDANOVICH: I'm giving John Wayne a book as a birthday present.
JOHN FORD: He's *got* a book.

John Ford 1895–1973: Peter Bogdanovich *Who the Hell's in It?* (2004)

6 When the [Supreme] Court moved to Washington in 1800, it was provided with no books, which probably accounts for the high quality of early opinions.

Robert H. Jackson 1892–1954: *The Supreme Court in the American System of Government* (1955)

7 One man is as good as another until he has written a book.

Benjamin Jowett 1817–93: Evelyn Abbott and Lewis Campbell (eds.) *Life and Letters of Benjamin Jowett* (1897)

8 This is primarily a picture-book and the letterpress is intended to do no more than provide a small mass of information leavened by a large dose of personal prejudice.

Osbert Lancaster 1908–86: *Pillar to Post* (1938)

9 Synopsis of Previous Chapters: There are no Previous Chapters.

Stephen Leacock 1869–1944: *Nonsense Novels* (1911) 'Gertrude the Governess'

10 Book—what they make a movie out of for television.

Leonard Louis Levinson: Laurence J. Peter (ed.) *Quotations for our Time* (1977)

11 I opened it at page 96—the secret page on which I write my name to catch out borrowers and book-sharks.

Flann O'Brien 1911–66: *Myles Away from Dublin* (1990)

12 Some savage faculty for observation told him that most respectable and estimable people usually had a lot of books in their houses.

Flann O'Brien 1911–66: *The Best of Myles* (1968)

13 This is not a novel to be tossed aside lightly. It should be thrown with great force.

Dorothy Parker 1893–1967: R. E. Drennan *Wit's End* (1973)

14 I hate books; they only teach us to talk about things we know nothing about.

Jean-Jacques Rousseau 1712–78: *Émile* (1762)

15 A best-seller is the gilded tomb of a mediocre talent.

Logan Pearsall Smith 1865–1946: *Afterthoughts* (1931) 'Art and Letters'

16 No furniture so charming as books.

Sydney Smith 1771–1845: Lady Holland *Memoir* (1855)

17 A. L. ROWSE: You don't read my books, John. Do you know *Tudor Cornwall?*
   JOHN SPARROW: Do you know Stuart Hampshire?

John Sparrow 1906–92: Noel Annan *The Dons* (1999)

18 Digressions, incontestably, are the sunshine;—they are the life, the soul of reading;—take them out of this book for instance,—you might as well take the book along with them.

Laurence Sterne 1713–68: *Tristram Shandy* (1759–67)

19 'Pilgrim's Progress', about a man that left his family it didn't say why . . . The statements was interesting, but tough.

Mark Twain 1835–1910: *The Adventures of Huckleberry Finn* (1884)

20 I haven't been so happy since the day Reader's Digest lost my address.

Dick Vosburgh 1929–2007: *A Saint She Ain't* (1999)

21 In every first novel the hero is the author as Christ or Faust.

Oscar Wilde 1854–1900: attributed

22 There is no such thing as a moral or an immoral book. Books are well written, or badly written.

Oscar Wilde 1854–1900: *The Picture of Dorian Gray* (1891)

23 The good ended happily, and the bad unhappily. That is what fiction means.

Oscar Wilde 1854–1900: *The Importance of Being Earnest* (1895)

24 The scratching of pimples on the body of the bootboy at Claridges.
   of James Joyce's Ulysses

Virginia Woolf 1882–1941: letter to Lytton Strachey, 24 April 1922

Bores

66 *Even the grave yawns for him.* **99**
Herbert Beerbohm Tree

1 He really is terribly heavy going. Like running up hill in roller skates.

Alan Ayckbourn 1939– : *Living Together* (1975)

2 A person who talks when you wish him to listen.

Ambrose Bierce 1842–c.1914: definition of a bore; *Cynic's Word Book* (1906)

3 What's wrong with being a boring kind of guy?

George Bush 1924– : during the campaign for the Republican nomination; in *Daily Telegraph* 28 April 1988

4 Dullness is so much stronger than genius because there is so much more of it, and it is better organized and more naturally cohesive *inter se*. So the arctic volcano can do nothing against arctic ice.

Samuel Butler 1835–1902: *Notebooks* (1912)

5 VISITOR TO ETON: I hope that I am not boring you.
PROVOST: Not yet.

Lord Hugh Cecil 1869–1956: attributed; in *Dictionary of National Biography* (1917–)

6 He is not only dull in himself, but the cause of dullness in others.
    on a dull law lord

Samuel Foote 1720–77: James Boswell *Life of Samuel Johnson* (1934 ed.) 1783

7 Most of my contemporaries at school entered the World of Business, the logical destiny of bores.

Barry Humphries 1934– : *More Please* (1992)

8 He was dull in a new way, and that made many people think him *great*.

Samuel Johnson 1709–84: of Thomas Gray; James Boswell *Life of Samuel Johnson* (1791) 28 March 1775

9 The boredom occasioned by too much restraint is always preferable to that produced by an uncontrolled enthusiasm for a pointless variety.

Osbert Lancaster 1908–86: *Pillar to Post* (1938)

10 I freely confess that there have been times recently when almost anything—the shape of a patch on the ceiling, a recipe for rhubarb jam read upside down in the paper—has seemed to me more interesting than the passionless creep of a Miles Davis trumpet solo.

Philip Larkin 1922–85: *All What Jazz* (1985)

11 A bore is simply a nonentity who resents his humble lot in life, and seeks satisfaction for his wounded ego by forcing himself on his betters.

H. L. Mencken 1880–1956: *Minority Report* (1956)

12 The only rule I have found to have any validity in writing is not to bore yourself.

John Mortimer 1923–2009: *Clinging to the Wreckage* (1982)

13 He was not only a bore; he bored for England.

Malcolm Muggeridge 1903–90: of Anthony Eden; *Tread Softly* (1966)

14 It is to be noted that when any part of this paper appears dull there is a design in it.

Richard Steele 1672–1729: *The Tatler* 7 July 1709

15 A bore is a man who, when you ask him how he is, tells you.

Bert Leston Taylor 1866–1901: *The So-Called Human Race* (1922)

16 Dylan talked copiously, then stopped. 'Somebody's boring me,' he said, 'I think it's me.'

Dylan Thomas 1914–53: Rayner Heppenstall *Four Absentees* (1960)

17 He is an old bore. Even the grave yawns for him.
    of the actor Israel Zangwill

Herbert Beerbohm Tree 1852–1917: Max Beerbohm *Herbert Beerbohm Tree* (1920)

18 In England people actually try to be brilliant at breakfast. That is so dreadful of them! Only dull people are brilliant at breakfast.

Oscar Wilde 1854–1900: *An Ideal Husband* (1895)

Boxing
See also **Sports and Games**

66 *Only connect.* **99**
Philip Larkin

---

1 I figure I'll be champ for about ten years and then I'll let my brother take over—like the Kennedys down in Washington.
before becoming world heavyweight champion in 1964

Muhammad Ali 1942– : attributed, 1979

2 It's gonna be a thrilla, a chilla, and a killa,
When I get the gorilla in Manila.

Muhammad Ali 1942– : in 1975; attributed

3 Boxing is show-business with blood.

David Belasco: in 1915; Michael Parkinson *Sporting Lives* (1993); later also used by Frank Bruno

4 Tall men come down to my height when I hit 'em in the body.

Jack Dempsey 1895–1983: in 1920, attributed

5 The bigger they are, the further they have to fall.

Robert Fitzsimmons 1862–1917: prior to a fight, in *Brooklyn Daily Eagle* 11 August 1900 (similar forms found in proverbs since the 15th century)

6 I want to keep fighting because it is the only thing that keeps me out of the hamburger joints. If I don't fight, I'll eat this planet.

George Foreman 1948– : in *Times* 17 January 1990

7 Putting a fighter in the business world is like putting silk stockings on a pig.
in 1961, a boxing promoter's view

Jack Hurley: attributed, 1979

8 *after Jack Sharkey beat Max Schmeling (of whom Jacobs was manager) in the heavyweight title fight, 21 June 1932:*
We was robbed!

Joe Jacobs 1896–1940: Peter Heller *In This Corner* (1975)

9 *borrowing E. M. Forster's literary maxim during a bad amateur boxing match:*
Only connect.

Philip Larkin 1922–85: attributed; in *Guardian* 3 December 1985 (online edition, obituary by Craig Raine)

10 We're all endowed with God-given talents. Mine happens to be hitting people in the head.

Sugar Ray Leonard 1956– : Thomas Hauser *The Black Lights* (1986)

11 I miss the things like the cameraderie in the gym. I don't miss being smacked in the mouth every day.
on retirement from the ring

Barry McGuigan 1961– : in *Irish Times* 18 April 1998 'This Week They Said'

12 They're selling video cassettes of the Ali–Spinks fight for $89.95. Hell, for that money Spinks will come to your house.

Ferdie Pacheco: in *Guardian* 23 December 1978 'Sports Quotes of the Year'

13 *when asked by the coroner if he had intended to 'get Doyle in trouble':*
Mister, it's my *business* to get him in trouble.
following the death of Jimmy Doyle from his injuries after fighting Robinson, June 1947

Sugar Ray Robinson 1920–89: *Sugar Ray* (1970, with Dave Anderson)

14 In boxing the right cross-counter is distinctly one of those things it is more blessed to give than to receive.

P. G. Wodehouse 1881–1975: *The Pothunters* (1902)

Broadcasting

See also **Television**

❝ To goad the BBC is a rewarding sport in itself. ❞

Clive James

1 Adams' first law of television: the weight of the backside is greater than the force of the intellect.

Phillip Adams 1939– : in 1970; attributed

2 A nice enough bunch, big breasted women and tired looking men who smiled a lot. Was there a connection between them? Was that why the department was so named?
on the BBC religious affairs department

David Benedictus 1938– : *Dropping Names* (2005)

3 We hope to amuse the customers with music and with rhyme
But ninety minutes is a long, long time.

Noël Coward 1899–1973: '90 Minutes is a Long, Long Time' (1955); opening song for a CBS television live special starring Noël Coward and Mary Martin

4 IAN ST JOHN: Is he speaking to you yet?
JIMMY GREAVES: Not yet, but I hope to be incommunicado with him in a very short space of time.

Jimmy Greaves 1940– : Barry Fantoni (ed.) *Private Eye's Colemanballs 2* (1984)

5 When the late Roy Plomley swooped down on me with all those screeching seagulls . . . He made me feel like discarded offal thrown over the stern of a ship.
of appearing on Desert Island Discs

Alec Guinness 1914–2000: *My Name Escapes Me* (1996)

6 Every time I think that Ned Sherrin is dead I switch on the television and see him in some dreadful, off-colour programme which brings home all too painfully the fact that he is still alive.

Ian Hamilton 1938– : Ned Sherrin *Cutting Edge* (1984); attributed

7 To goad the BBC is a rewarding sport in itself. It makes a tabloid feel like a heavyweight.

Clive James 1939– : *The Dreaming Swimmer* (1992)

8 The media. It sounds like a convention of spiritualists.

Tom Stoppard 1937– : *Night and Day* (1978)

Bureaucracy

See also **Civil Servants, Management**

❝ We pay more taxes, but the hospitals don't kill you. ❞

Kristin Scott Thomas

1 A memorandum is written not to inform the reader but to protect the writer.

Dean Acheson 1893–1971: in *Wall Street Journal* 8 September 1977

2 MAM: Opportunities calling for devoted self-sacrifice don't turn up every day of the week.
MS CRAIG: Quite. Any really first-rate chance of improving the soul gets snapped up by the social services department.

Alan Bennett 1934– : *Enjoy* (1980)

3 This island is made mainly of coal and surrounded by fish. Only an organizing genius could produce a shortage of coal and fish at the same time.

Aneurin Bevan 1897–1960: speech at Blackpool 24 May 1945

4 Whatever was required to be done, the Circumlocution Office was beforehand with all the public departments in the art of perceiving—HOW NOT TO DO IT.

Charles Dickens 1812–70: *Little Dorrit* (1857)

5 The Pentagon, that immense monument to modern man's subservience to the desk.

Oliver Franks 1905–92: in *Observer* 30 November 1952

6 *his secretary had suggested throwing away out-of-date files:* A good idea, only be sure to make a copy of everything before getting rid of it.

Sam Goldwyn 1882–1974: Michael Freedland *The Goldwyn Touch* (1986)

7 Official dignity tends to increase in inverse ratio to the importance of the country in which the office is held.

Aldous Huxley 1894–1963: *Beyond the Mexique Bay* (1934)

8 *on his dislike of working in teams:* A camel is a horse designed by a committee.

Alec Issigonis 1906–88: in *Guardian* 14 January 1991 'Notes and Queries' (attributed)

9 The truth in these matters may be stated as a scientific law: 'The persistence of public officials varies inversely with the importance of the matter on which they are persisting.'

Bernard Levin 1928–2004: *In These Times* (1986)

10 It is characteristic of committee discussions and decisions that every member has a vivid recollection of them and that every member's recollection differs violently from every other member's recollection.

Jonathan Lynn 1943– and **Antony Jay** 1930– : *Yes Prime Minister* vol. 2 (1987)

11 Perfection of planned layout is achieved only by institutions on the point of collapse.

C. Northcote Parkinson 1909–93: *Parkinson's Law* (1958)

12 Everything is easier in France. We pay more taxes, but the hospitals don't kill you.

Kristin Scott Thomas 1960– : in *Daily Telegraph* 17 January 2005

13 Underneath runs the main current of preoccupation, which is keeping one's nose clean at all times. This means that when things go wrong you have to pass the blame along the line, like pass-the-parcel, till the music stops.

Tom Stoppard 1937– : *Neutral Ground* (1983)

Business
See also **Management**

❝ Doing well that which should not be done at all. ❞
Gore Vidal

1 Our clients are coping with the stress of financial loss by soaking in a hot bath scented with my Rose Geranium bath crystals.
on the Wall Street crash

Elizabeth Arden c.1880–1966: attributed

2 My first rule of consumerism is never to buy anything you can't make your children carry.

Bill Bryson 1951– : *The Lost Continent* (1989)

3 I always invest in companies an idiot could run, because one day one will.

Warren Buffett 1930– : in *Mail on Sunday* 18 March 2007 'Quotes of the Week'

4 Some accountants are comedians, but comedians are
never accountants.
  defending Ken Dodd on the charge of tax evasion

George Carman 1930– : in *Times* 30
August 2000; attributed

5 Accountants are the witch-doctors of the modern world
and willing to turn their hands to any kind of magic.

Lord Justice Harman 1894–1970:
speech, February 1964

6 The last stage of fitting the product to the market is fitting
the market to the product.

Clive James 1939– : in *Observer* 16
October 1989

7 As a simple countryman, he distrusted the use of money
and, finding barter cumbersome, preferred to steal.

Miles Kington 1941–2008: *Welcome
to Kington* (1989)

8 Doing well by doing good.
  later the slogan of Monsanto

Tom Lehrer 1928– : 'The Old Dope
Peddler' (1953 song)

9 A: I play it the company way
Where the company puts me, there I'll stay.
B: But what is your point of view?
A: I have no point of view!
Supposing the company thinks . . . I think so too!

Frank Loesser 1910–69: 'The
Company Way' (1962)

10 *asked if there were signs of a depression in London:*
If you mean that one could fire a gun across the Savoy
Grill without hitting either a diner or an Italian waiter the
answer is 'No'

David Montague: attributed, 1963

11 We even sell a pair of earrings for under £1, which is
cheaper than a prawn sandwich from Marks & Spencers.
But I have to say the earrings probably won't last as long.

Gerald Ratner 1949– : speech to the
Institute of Directors, Albert Hall, 23
April 1991

12 I think I was the first person at Motown to ask where the
money was going. And that made me an enemy. Did I find
out? Honey, I found my way out the door.

Martha Reeves 1941– : Gerri Hirshey
*Nowhere to Run: the story of soul
music* (1985)

13 Running a company on market research is like driving
while looking in the rear view mirror.

Anita Roddick 1942–2007: in
Independent 22 August 1997

14 *the daughter of the Body Shop's founders on her sex
emporium:*
We employ Muslim women refugees, use unionised
factories, run a 'fair trade' project in Brazil and our
wooden dildos are made from naturally felled trees.

Sam Roddick: attributed; in *Times* 3
June 2003

15 Whenever I feel in the least tempted to be methodical or
business-like or even decently industrious, I go to Kensal
Green and look at the graves of those who died in
business.

Saki 1870–1916: *The Square Egg*
(1924)

16 *definition of insider trading:*
Stealing too fast.

Calvin Trillin 1935– : 'The Inside on
Insider Trading' (1987)

17 It's a recession when your neighbour loses his job; it's a
depression when you lose yours.

Harry S. Truman 1884–1972: in
Observer 13 April 1958

18 Put all your eggs in one basket—and WATCH THAT BASKET.

Mark Twain 1835–1910: *Pudd'nhead
Wilson* (1894)

19 The public be damned! I'm working for my stockholders.

William H. Vanderbilt 1821–85:
comment to a news reporter, 2
October 1882

20 [Commercialism is] doing well that which should not be
done at all.

Gore Vidal 1925– : in *Listener* 7
August 1975

21 Go to your business, I say, pleasure, whilst I go to my pleasure, business.

William Wycherley c. 1640–1716: *The Country Wife* (1675)

22 Nothing is illegal if one hundred well-placed business men decide to do it.

Andrew Young 1932– : Morris K. Udall *Too Funny to be President* (1988)

Canada

66 *Climb every Mountie.* 99
Dick Vosburgh and Denis King

1 Canada is a country so square that even the female impersonators are women.

Richard Benner: *Outrageous* (1977)

2 *definition of a Canadian:*
Somebody who knows how to make love in a canoe.

Pierre Berton 1920–2004: in *Toronto Star* 22 December 1973

3 I see Canada as a country torn between a very northern, rather extraordinary, mystical spirit which it fears and its desire to present itself to the world as a Scotch banker.

Robertson Davies 1913–95: *The Enthusiasms of Robertson Davies* (1990)

4 In Pierre Elliott Trudeau, Canada has at last produced a political leader worthy of assassination.

Irving Layton 1912–2006: *The Whole Bloody Bird* (1969)

5 Canadians are Americans with no Disneyland.

Margaret Mahy 1937– : *The Changeover* (1984)

6 *asked about Canadian sovereignty over the Arctic:*
That's ours—lock, stock and iceberg.

Brian Mulroney 1939– : speaking to reporters, Ottawa, 5 April 1987

7 I have to spend so much time explaining to Americans that I am not English and to Englishmen that I am not American that I have little time left to be Canadian . . . (On second thought, I am a true cosmopolitan—unhappy anywhere.)

Laurence J. Peter 1919–90: *Quotations for our Time* (1977)

8 I'm world famous, Dr Parks said, all over Canada.

Mordecai Richler 1931–2001: *The Incomparable Atuk* (1963)

9 Climb every Mountie.

Dick Vosburgh 1929–2007 and **Denis King**: *Beauty and the Beards* (2001)

Catchphrases See Comedy Routines and Catchphrases

Censorship

66 *Think what you could get away with in Japanese!* 99
George Devine

1 She insists on all these torrid romances . . . I have to wrap them round with copies of *Country Life* to carry them home.

Alan Ayckbourn 1939– : *Round and Round the Garden* (1975)

2 There are no alternatives to 'bastard' agreeable to me. Nevertheless I have offered them 'swine' in its place.
on changes to the text of Endgame *required by the Lord Chamberlain for the London production, summer 1958*

Samuel Beckett 1906–89: James Knowlson *Damned to Fame* (1996)

3 I'm all in favour of free expression provided it's kept rigidly under control.

Alan Bennett 1934– : *Forty Years On* (1969)

4 Everybody favours free speech in the slack moments when no axes are being ground.

Heywood Broun 1888–1939: in *New York World* 23 October 1926

5 It's because it's in English, you can get away with much more in French. Think what you could get away with in Japanese!
on the refusal of the Lord Chamberlain to grant a licence to Samuel Beckett's Endgame, *February 1958*

George Devine 1910–66: Irving Wardle *The Theatres of George Devine* (1978)

6 I dislike censorship. Like an appendix it is useless when inert and dangerous when active.

Maurice Edelman 1911–75: Jonathon Green (ed.) *A Dictionary of Contemporary Quotations* (1982)

7 It's red hot, mate. I hate to think of this sort of book getting into the wrong hands. As soon as I've finished this, I shall recommend they ban it.

Ray Galton 1930– and **Alan Simpson** 1929– : *The Missing Page* (1960 BBC television programme) words spoken by Tony Hancock

8 No less than twenty-two publishers and printers read the manuscript of *Dubliners* and when at last it was printed some very kind person bought out the entire edition and had it burnt in Dublin.

James Joyce 1882–1941: letter, 2 April 1932

9 Freedom of the press is guaranteed only to those who own one.

A. J. Liebling 1904–63: 'The Wayward Press: Do you belong in Journalism?' (1960)

10 Careful now!
placard alerting Craggy Island to a banned film

Graham Linehan and **Arthur Mathews**: 'The Passion of St Tibulus' (1995), episode from *Father Ted* (Channel 4 TV, 1995–8)

11 She sits among the cabbages and leeks.
substitution for 'she sits among the cabbages and peas', which was supposedly forbidden by a local watch committee

Marie Lloyd 1870–1922: attributed; Nigel Rees *Cassell Dictionary of Humorous Quotations* (1999)

12 Censorship, like charity, should begin at home, but, unlike charity, it should end there.

Clare Boothe Luce 1903–87: attributed, 1982

13 We have long passed the Victorian Era when asterisks were followed after a certain interval by a baby.

W. Somerset Maugham 1874–1965: *The Constant Wife* (1926)

14 *on being appointed Irish film censor:*
I am between the devil and the Holy See . . . [My task is to prevent] the Californication of Ireland.

James Montgomery: Ulick O'Connor *Oliver St John Gogarty* (1964)

15 I suppose that writers should, in a way, feel flattered by the censorship laws. They show a primitive fear and dread at the fearful magic of print.

John Mortimer 1923–2009: *Clinging to the Wreckage* (1982)

16 Mr de Valera, like Mr Cosgrave, regarded literary censorship as part of our freedom to achieve fuller freedom.

Brendan Ó hEithir 1930– : *The Begrudger's Guide to Irish Politics*

17 A censor is a man who knows more than he thinks you ought to.

Laurence J. Peter 1919–90: Jonathon Green (ed.) *A Dictionary of Contemporary Quotations* (1982)

18 Assassination is the extreme form of censorship.

George Bernard Shaw 1856–1950: *The Showing-Up of Blanco Posnet* (1911) 'Limits to Toleration'

19 We are paid to have dirty minds.

John Trevelyan 1903–86: when British Film Censor; in *Observer* 15 November 1959 'Sayings of the Week'

Certainty and Doubt
See also **Religion**

❝ *I'll give you a definite maybe.* **❞**
Sam Goldwyn

1 He used to be fairly indecisive, but now he's not so certain.

Peter Alliss 1931– : Barry Fantoni (ed.) *Private Eye's Colemanballs 3* (1986)

2 The Flying Scotsman is no less splendid a sight when it travels north to Edinburgh than when it travels south to London. Mr Baldwin denouncing sanctions was as dignified as Mr Baldwin imposing them.

Lord Beaverbrook 1879–1964: in *Daily Express* 29 May 1937

3 Often undecided whether to desert a sinking ship for one that might not float, he would make up his mind to sit on the wharf for a day.
  of Lord Curzon

Lord Beaverbrook 1879–1964: *Men and Power* (1956)

4 ESTRAGON: Charming spot. Inspiring prospects. Let's go.
VLADIMIR: We can't.
ESTRAGON: Why not?
VLADIMIR: We're waiting for Godot.

Samuel Beckett 1906–89: *Waiting for Godot* (1955)

5 Oh! let us never, never doubt
What nobody is sure about!

Hilaire Belloc 1870–1953: 'The Microbe' (1897)

6 You can put up a sign on the door, 'beware of the dog', without having a dog.

Hans Blix 1928– : in *Guardian* (online edition) 18 September 2003

7 *when asked whether he really believed a horseshoe hanging over his door would bring him luck:*
Of course not, but I am told it works even if you don't believe in it.

Niels Bohr 1885–1962: A. Pais *Inward Bound* (1986)

8 There is something pagan in me that I cannot shake off. In short, I deny nothing, but doubt everything.

Lord Byron 1788–1824: letter, 4 December 1811

9 We can dance on pinheads till the cows come home.

Alastair Campbell 1957– : in *Times* 10 January 2004

10 I don't believe in astrology; I'm a Sagittarius and we're sceptical.

Arthur C. Clarke 1917–2008: attributed; Nigel Rees *Cassell Dictionary of Humorous Quotations* (1999)

11 *of Thomas Arnold, son of Dr Arnold of Rugby, a notable and frequent nineteenth-century convert:*
Poor Tom Arnold has lost his faith *again.*

Eliza Conybeare 1820–1903: Rose Macaulay letter to Father Johnson, 8 April 1951

12 The archbishop [Archbishop Runcie] is usually to be found nailing his colours to the fence.

Frank Field 1942– : attributed in *Crockfords 1987/88* (1987); Geoffrey Madan records in his *Notebooks* that Harry Cust made a similar comment on A. J. Balfour, *c.*1904.

13 I'll give you a definite maybe.

Sam Goldwyn 1882–1974: attributed

14 PHILIP: I'm sorry. (Pause.) I suppose I'm indecisive. (Pause). My trouble is, I'm a man of no convictions. (Longish pause.) At least, I think I am.

Christopher Hampton 1946– : *The Philanthropist* (1970)

15 At this moment in time I did not say them things.

Glenn Hoddle 1957– : in *Daily Telegraph* 2 February 1999

16 Certitude is not the test of certainty. We have been cocksure of many things that were not so.

Oliver Wendell Holmes Jr. 1841–1935: 'Natural Law' (1918)

17 A young man who wishes to remain a sound atheist cannot be too careful of his reading.

C. S. Lewis 1898–1963: *Surprised by Joy* (1955)

18 Like all weak men he laid an exaggerated stress on not changing one's mind.

W. Somerset Maugham 1874–1965: *Of Human Bondage* (1915)

19 I wish I was as cocksure of anything as Tom Macaulay is of everything.

Lord Melbourne 1779–1848: Lord Cowper *Preface to Lord Melbourne's Papers* (1889)

20 I am not denying anything I did not say.

Brian Mulroney 1939– : in *The Globe and Mail* 18 September 1986

21 That happy sense of purpose people have when they are standing up for a principle they haven't really been knocked down for yet.

P. J. O'Rourke 1947– : *Give War a Chance* (1992)

22 Well, sir, you never can tell. That's a principle in life with me, sir, if you'll excuse my having such a thing, sir.

George Bernard Shaw 1856–1950: *You Never Can Tell* (1898)

23 All right, have it your own way—you heard a seal bark!

James Thurber 1894–1961: cartoon caption; in *New Yorker* 30 January 1932

24 I would earnestly warn you against trying to find out the reason for and explanation of everything . . . To try and find out the reason for everything is very dangerous and leads to nothing but disappointment and dissatisfaction, unsettling your mind and in the end making you miserable.

Queen Victoria 1819–1901: letter to Princess Victoria of Hesse, 22 August 1883

25 A mind not so much open as vulnerable to a succession of opposing certainties.
    on David Howell

Hugo Young 1938–2003: Matthew Parris *Scorn with Extra Bile* (1998)

26 To convince Cézanne of anything is like teaching the towers of Notre Dame to dance.

Émile Zola 1840–1902: Lawrence Gowing 'The Great Transformation'

Character

See also **Self-Knowledge and Self-Deception**

> ❝ *I've met a lot of hardboiled eggs in my time, but you're twenty minutes.* ❞
> **Billy Wilder**

1 He never failed to seek a peaceful solution of a problem when all other possibilities had failed.

Anonymous: Cecil Roth 'Joseph Herman Hertz' (1959) in *The Dictionary of National Biography*

2 Though [Lucia was] essentially autocratic, her subjects were allowed and even encouraged to develop their own minds on their own lines, provided always that those lines met at the junction where she was station-master.

E. F. Benson 1867–1940: *Queen Lucia* (1920)

3 Take care not to be the kind of person for whom the band is always playing in the other room.

Quentin Crisp 1908–99: in *Spectator* 20 November 1999

4 I am so sorry. We have to stop there. I have just come to the end of my personality.
closing down an interview

Quentin Crisp 1908–99: attributed, in *Times* 26 October 2002

5 We never knows wot's hidden in each other's hearts; and if we had glass winders there, we'd need keep the shutters up, some on us, I do assure you!

Charles Dickens 1812–70: *Martin Chuzzlewit* (1844)

6 Claudia's the sort of person who goes through life holding on to the sides.

Alice Thomas Ellis 1932–2005: *The Other Side of the Fire* (1983)

7 Clevinger was one of those people with lots of intelligence and no brains, and everyone knew it except those who soon found it out. In short, he was a dope.

Joseph Heller 1923–99: *Catch-22* (1961)

8 Nice guys, when we turn nasty, can make a terrible mess of it, usually because we've had so little practice, and have bottled it up for too long.

Matthew Parris 1949– : in *The Spectator* 27 February 1993

9 He's so wet you could shoot snipe off him.

Anthony Powell 1905–2000: *A Question of Upbringing* (1951)

10 You can tell a lot about a fellow's character by his way of eating jellybeans.

Ronald Reagan 1911–2004: in *New York Times* 15 January 1981

11 My father named me Autolycus; who being, as I am, littered under Mercury, was likewise a snapper-up of unconsidered trifles.

William Shakespeare 1564–1616: *The Winter's Tale* (1610–11)

12 An unforgiving eye, and a damned disinheriting countenance!

Richard Brinsley Sheridan 1751–1816: *The School for Scandal* (1777)

13 He's too nervous to kill himself. He wears his seat belt in a drive-in movie.

Neil Simon 1927– : *The Odd Couple* (1966)

14 Felix? Playing around? Are you crazy? He wears a vest and galoshes.

Neil Simon 1927– : *The Odd Couple* (1966)

15 I'm told he's [a] decent sort when you get to know him, but no one ever has, so his decency is sort of secret.

Tom Stoppard 1937– : *Neutral Ground* (1983)

16 Then, with that faint fleeting smile playing about his lips, he faced the firing squad; erect and motionless, proud and disdainful, Walter Mitty, the undefeated, inscrutable to the last.

James Thurber 1894–1961: in *New Yorker* 18 March 1939 'The Secret Life of Walter Mitty'

17 Few things are harder to put up with than the annoyance of a good example.

Mark Twain 1835–1910: *Pudd'nhead Wilson* (1894)

18 There, standing at the piano, was the original good time who had been had by all.

Kenneth Tynan 1927–80: at an Oxford Union Debate, while an undergraduate; attributed (also attributed to Bette Davis of a passing starlet)

19 CECIL GRAHAM: What is a cynic?
LORD DARLINGTON: A man who knows the price of everything and the value of nothing.

Oscar Wilde 1854–1900: *Lady Windermere's Fan* (1892)

20 I am afraid that he has one of those terribly weak natures that are not susceptible to influence.

Oscar Wilde 1854–1900: *An Ideal Husband* (1895)

21 I've met a lot of hardboiled eggs in my time, but you're twenty minutes.

Billy Wilder 1906–2002: *Ace in the Hole* (1951 film, co-written with Lesser Samuels and Walter Newman)

22 Slice him where you like, a hellhound is always a hellhound.

P. G. Wodehouse 1881–1975: *The Code of the Woosters* (1938)

Children

See also **The Family, Parents, Youth**

❞ *It seems to me to go on like the rabbits in Windsor Park!* ❞

Queen Victoria

1 I was very relieved when the child was born at the Chelsea and Westminster hospital. I had thought he would be born in a manger.
on the birth of Leo Blair

Leo Abse 1917– : in *Observer* 28 May 2000 'They said what . . . ?'

2 I sometimes think, Mary, that it is a mistake to have a dog for a nurse.
Mr Darling, of Nana

J. M. Barrie 1860–1937: *Peter Pan* (1928)

3 A Trick that everyone abhors
In Little Girls is slamming Doors.

Hilaire Belloc 1870–1953: 'Rebecca' (1907)

4 And always keep a-hold of Nurse
For fear of finding something worse.

Hilaire Belloc 1870–1953: 'Jim' (1907)

5 I had always thought that once you grew up you could do anything you wanted—stay up all night or eat ice-cream straight out of the container.

Bill Bryson 1951– : *The Lost Continent* (1989)

6 I don't know what Scrope Davies meant by telling you I liked children, I abominate the sight of them so much that I have always had the greatest respect for the character of Herod.

Lord Byron 1788–1824: letter 30 August 1811

7 The place is very well and quiet and the children only scream in a low voice.

Lord Byron 1788–1824: letter 21 September 1813

8 Speak roughly to your little boy,
And beat him when he sneezes;
He only does it to annoy,
Because he knows it teases.

Lewis Carroll 1832–98: *Alice's Adventures in Wonderland* (1865)

9 I am fond of children (except boys).

Lewis Carroll 1832–98: letter to Kathleen Eschwege, 24 October 1879

10 Timothy Winters comes to school
With eyes as wide as a football-pool,
Ears like bombs and teeth like splinters:
A blitz of a boy is Timothy Winters.

Charles Causley 1917– : 'Timothy Winters' (1957)

11 *on being asked what sort of child he was:*
When paid constant attention, extremely lovable. When not, a pig.

Noël Coward 1899–1973: interview with David Frost in 1969

12 I'll thcream and thcream and thcream till I'm thick. And I *can.*
Violet Elizabeth Bott's habitual threat

Richmal Crompton 1890–1969: *Still—William* (1925)

13 It's like hanging out with two miniature drunks.
on his two small children

Johnny Depp 1963– : in *Independent* 16 August 2003

14 If men had to have babies, they would only ever have one each.
while in late pregnancy

Diana, Princess of Wales 1961–97: in *Observer* 29 July 1984 'Sayings of the Week'

15 I only know two sorts of boys. Mealy boys, and beef-faced boys.

Charles Dickens 1812–70: *Oliver Twist* (1838)

16 It is only rarely that one can see in a little boy the promise of a man, but one can almost always see in a little girl the threat of a woman.

Alexandre Dumas 1824–95: attributed remark, 1895

17 There never was a child so lovely but his mother was glad to get asleep.

Ralph Waldo Emerson 1803–82: *Journal* 1836

18 She looks like someone who would eat her young.
Michael Banks on his father's old Nanny

Julian Fellowes 1949– : *Mary Poppins* (2004); see **The Theatre** 13

19 O'er the rugged mountain's brow
Clara threw the twins she nursed,
And remarked, 'I wonder now
Which will reach the bottom first?'

Harry Graham 1874–1936: 'Calculating Clara' (1899)

20 When Baby's cries grew hard to bear
I popped him in the Frigidaire.
I never would have done so if
I'd known that he'd be frozen stiff.
My wife said, 'George, I'm so unhappé!
Our darling's now completely *frappé*!

Harry Graham 1874–1936: *Ruthless Rhymes for Heartless Homes* (1899) 'L'Enfant glacé'

21 Kids are the best, Apu. You can teach them to hate the things you hate. And they practically raise themselves, what with the Internet and all.
Homer Simpson

Matt Groening 1954– : *The Simpsons* 'Eight Misbehavin'' (1999) written by Matt Selman

22 *at the first night of J. M. Barrie's* Peter Pan*:*
Oh, for an hour of Herod!

Anthony Hope 1863–1933: Denis Mackail *The Story of JMB* (1941)

23 *definition of a baby:*
A loud noise at one end and no sense of responsibility at the other.

Ronald Knox 1888–1957: attributed

24 The realization that it was not people I disliked but children was for me one of those celebrated moments of revelation.
   on growing up

Philip Larkin 1922–85: *Required Writing* (1983) 'The Savage Seventh'

25 The parent who could see his boy as he really is, would shake his head and say: 'Willie is no good; I'll sell him.'

Stephen Leacock 1869–1944: *Essays and Literary Studies* (1916)

26 Don't bother discussing sex with small children. They rarely have anything to add.

Fran Lebowitz 1946– : *Social Studies* (1981)

27 *Jack Llewelyn-Davies, stuffing himself with cakes at tea, was warned by his mother Sylvia, 'You'll be sick tomorrow':*
   I'll be sick tonight.

Jack Llewelyn-Davies 1894–1959: Andrew Birkin *J. M. Barrie and the Lost Boys* (1979); Barrie used the line in *Little Mary* (1903)

28 Having a baby is like trying to push a grand piano through a transom.

Alice Roosevelt Longworth 1884–1980: Michael Teague *Mrs L* (1981)

29 *a nurse, excusing her illegitimate baby:*
   If you please, ma'am, it was a very little one.

Frederick Marryat 1792–1848: *Mr Midshipman Easy* (1836)

30 All bachelors love dogs, and we would love children just as much if they could be taught to retrieve.

P. J. O'Rourke 1947– : *The Bachelor Home Companion* (1987)

31 Every luxury was lavished on you—atheism, breast-feeding, circumcision.

Joe Orton 1933–67: *Loot* (1967)

32 As yet a child, nor yet a fool to fame,
   I lisped in numbers, for the numbers came.

Alexander Pope 1688–1744: 'An Epistle to Dr Arbuthnot' (1735)

33 Parents—especially step-parents—are sometimes a bit of a disappointment to their children. They don't fulfil the promise of their early years.

Anthony Powell 1905–2000: *A Buyer's Market* (1952)

34 Go directly—see what she's doing, and tell her she mustn't.

Punch 1841–1992: vol. 63 (1872)

35 The fat greedy owl of the Remove.

Frank Richards 1876–1961: 'Billy Bunter' in *Magnet* (1909)

36 I'm in that benign form of house arrest that is looking after a baby.

J. K. Rowling 1965– : in *Sunday Times* 12 June 2005

37 Children with Hyacinth's temperament don't know better as they grow older; they merely know more.

Saki 1870–1916: *Toys of Peace and Other Papers* (1919)

38 Children are given us to discourage our better emotions.

Saki 1870–1916: *Reginald* (1904)

39 Childhood is Last Chance Gulch for happiness. After that, you know too much.

Tom Stoppard 1937– : *Where Are They Now?* (1973)

40 I s'pect I growed. Don't think nobody never made me.

Harriet Beecher Stowe 1811–96: *Uncle Tom's Cabin* (1852)

41 Children can be awe-inspiringly horrible; manipulative, aggressive, rude, and unfeeling to a point where I often think that, if armed, they would make up the most terrifying fighting force the world has ever seen.

Jill Tweedie 1936–93: *It's Only Me* (1980)

42 You will find as the children grow up that as a rule children are a bitter disappointment—their greatest object being to do precisely what their parents do not wish and have anxiously tried to prevent.

Queen Victoria 1819–1901: letter to the Crown Princess of Prussia, 5 January 1876

43 I fear the seventh granddaughter and fourteenth grandchild becomes a very uninteresting thing—for it seems to me to go on like the rabbits in Windsor Park!

Queen Victoria 1819–1901: letter to the Crown Princess of Prussia, 10 July 1868

44 [The baby] romped on my lap like a short stout salmon.

Sylvia Townsend Warner 1893–1978: diary, 13 October 1929

45 I love my children . . . I'm delighted to see them come and delighted to see them go.

Mary Wesley 1912–2002: attributed

46 Children begin by loving their parents; after a time they judge them; rarely, if ever, do they forgive them.

Oscar Wilde 1854–1900: *A Woman of No Importance* (1893)

47 Like so many infants of tender years he presented to the eye the aspect of a mass murderer suffering from an ingrowing toenail.

P. G. Wodehouse 1881–1975: *A Few Quick Ones* (1959)

Choice

> ❝*Anything except that damned Mouse.*❞
> **George V**

1 More than any other time in history, mankind faces a crossroads. One path leads to despair and utter hopelessness. The other, to total extinction. Let us pray we have the wisdom to choose correctly.

Woody Allen 1935– : *Side Effects* (1980)

2 That's a bit like asking a man crawling across the Sahara whether he would prefer Perrier or Malvern Water.
replying to a question by Ian McKellen on his sexual orientation

Alan Bennett 1934– : attributed

3 I would rather have my tongue beaten wafer-thin by a snake tenderiser and then stapled to the floor with a croquet hoop.

Richard Curtis 1956– and **Ben Elton** 1959– : *Blackadder Goes Forth* (1989) 'Major Star'

4 I'll have what she's having.
woman to waiter, seeing Sally acting an orgasm

Nora Ephron 1941– : *When Harry Met Sally* (1989 film)

5 He had polyester sheets and I wanted to get cotton sheets. He discussed it with his shrink many times before he made the switch.

Mia Farrow 1945– : in *Independent* 8 February 1997 'Quote Unquote'

6 *on the contrast between Alec Douglas-Home and Harold Wilson:*
Dull Alec versus Smart Alec.

David Frost 1939– : in *That Was The Week That Was* in 1963

7 *George V was asked which film he would like to see while convalescing:*
Anything except that damned Mouse.

George V 1865–1936: George Lyttelton letter to Rupert Hart-Davis, 12 November 1959

8 'You oughtn't to yield to temptation.' 'Well, somebody must, or the thing becomes absurd,' said I.

Anthony Hope 1863–1933: *The Dolly Dialogues* (1894)

9 Economy is going without something you do want in case you should, some day, want something you probably won't want.

Anthony Hope 1863–1933: *The Dolly Dialogues* (1894)

10 Too rich and you lose sight of reality; too thin and you end up dead.

Shazia Mirza 1976– : in *Times* 5 February 2004

11 A compromise in the sense that being bitten in half by a shark is a compromise with being swallowed whole.

P. J. O'Rourke 1947– : *Parliament of Whores*

12 *a restaurateur asked for his most unusual request from a customer:*
The table next to Michael Winner, please.

Simon Slater: in *Evening Standard* 27 May 1999

13 *in the post office, pointing at the centre of a sheet of stamps:*
I'll take that one.

Herbert Beerbohm Tree 1852–1917: Hesketh Pearson *Beerbohm Tree* (1956)

Christmas

❝ *I'm walking backwards for Christmas.* **❞**
Spike Milligan

1 I have often thought, says Sir Roger, it happens very well that Christmas should fall out in the Middle of Winter.

Joseph Addison 1672–1719: *The Spectator* 8 January 1712

2 There are six evacuated children in our house. My wife and I hate them so much that we have decided to *take away* something from them for Christmas!

Anonymous: letter from a friend in the country; James Agate diary 22 December 1939

3 Christmas Eve can be hell on earth . . . Everyone running round doing their last-minute shopping. It's as if Christmas comes on people by surprise, as if they hadn't known for weeks it was on its way.

Maeve Binchy 1940– : *The Glass Lake* (1994)

4 If the Three Wise Men arrived here tonight, the likelihood is that they would be deported.
advocating an amnesty for asylum-seekers

Proinsias de Rossa: in *Irish Times* 20 December 1997 'This Week They Said'

5 A Merry Christmas to all my friends except two.

W. C. Fields 1880–1946: attributed

6 *confessing she takes pretend baths to get away from it all:*
Sometimes I get in with no water and just lie there. I've been known to have five 'baths' on Christmas Day.

Dawn French 1957– : in *Sunday Times* 5 December 2004

7 I am a poor man, but I would gladly give ten shillings to find out who sent me the insulting Christmas card I received this morning.

George Grossmith 1847–1912 and **Weedon Grossmith** 1854–1919: *The Diary of a Nobody* (1894)

8 DRIFTWOOD (Groucho Marx): It's all right. That's—that's in every contract. That's—that's what they call a sanity clause.
FIORELLO (Chico Marx): You can't fool me. There ain't no Sanity Claus.

George S. Kaufman 1889–1961 and **Morrie Ryskind** 1895–1985: *Night at the Opera* (1935 film)

9 A lovely thing about Christmas is that it's compulsory, like a thunderstorm, and we all go through it together.

Garrison Keillor 1942– : *Leaving Home* (1987) 'Exiles'

10 I'm walking backwards for Christmas
Across the Irish Sea.

Spike Milligan 1918–2002: 'I'm Walking Backwards for Christmas' (1956)

11 Christmas begins about the first of December with an office party and ends when you finally realize what you spent, around April fifteenth of the next year.

P. J. O'Rourke 1947– : *Modern Manners* (1984)

12 Christmas, that time of year when people descend into the bunker of the family.

Byron Rogers: in *Daily Telegraph* 27 December 1993

13 Be nice to yu turkeys dis christmas,
Don't eat it, keep it alive,
It could be yu mate an not on yu plate
Say, Yo! Turkey I'm on your side.

Benjamin Zephaniah 1958– :
'Talking Turkeys!!' (1994)

The Cinema
See also **Acting, Actors, Film, Film Producers, Film Stars, Hollywood**

66 *A story that starts with an earthquake and works its way up to a climax.* 99
Samuel Goldwyn

1 *an assistant director trying to encourage some uninspired extras during the filming of* Julius Caesar (1953):
All right, kids. It's Rome, it's hot and here comes Julius!

Anonymous: recounted by John Gielgud; in *Ned Sherrin in his Anecdotage* (1993)

2 There are no rules in filmmaking. Only sins. And the cardinal sin is dullness.

Frank Capra 1897–1991: in *People* 16 September 1991

3 Bring on the empty horses!
said while directing the 1936 film The Charge of the Light Brigade

Michael Curtiz 1888–1962: David Niven *Bring on the Empty Horses* (1975)

4 It might be a fight like you see on the screen
A swain getting slain for the love of a Queen,
Some great Shakespearean scene
Where a ghost and a prince meet
And everyone ends as mince-meat . . .

Howard Dietz 1896–1983: 'That's Entertainment' (1953)

5 'She reads at such a pace,' she complained, 'and when I asked her *where* she had learnt to read so quickly, she replied "On the screens at cinemas."'

Ronald Firbank 1886–1926: *The Flower Beneath the Foot* (1923)

6 The movies are the only court where the judge goes to the lawyer for advice.

F. Scott Fitzgerald 1896–1940: *The Crack-up* (1945)

7 Will Hays is my shepherd, I shall not want, He maketh me to lie down in clean postures.
on the establishment of the 'Hays Office' in 1922 to monitor the Hollywood film industry

Gene Fowler 1890–1960: Clive Marsh and Gaye Ortiz (eds.) *Explorations in Theology and Film* (1997)

8 GEORGES FRANJU: Movies should have a beginning, a middle and an end.
JEAN-LUC GODARD: Certainly. But not necessarily in that order.

Jean-Luc Godard 1930– : in *Time* 14 September 1981

9 *told that he could not film Radclyffe Hall's* The Well of Loneliness *as it dealt with lesbians:*
So, make them Latvians.

Sam Goldwyn 1882–1974: attributed; Topol *A Treasury of Jewish Wit, Wisdom and Humour* (1999)

10 The trouble with this business is the dearth of bad pictures.

Sam Goldwyn 1882–1974: after making *The Goldwyn Follies* in 1937; Michael Freedland *The Goldwyn Touch* (1986)

11 Our comedies are not to be laughed at.

Sam Goldwyn 1882–1974: N. Zierold *Hollywood Tycoons* (1969)

12 Pictures are for entertainment, messages should be delivered by Western Union.

Sam Goldwyn 1882–1974: Arthur Marx *Goldwyn* (1976)

13 This business is dog eat dog and nobody is gonna eat me.

Sam Goldwyn 1882–1974: Michael Freedland *The Goldwyn Touch* (1986)

14 Let's have some new clichés.

Sam Goldwyn 1882–1974: attributed, perhaps apocryphal

15 A verbal contract isn't worth the paper it is written on.

Sam Goldwyn 1882–1974: Alva Johnston *The Great Goldwyn* (1937)

16 What we need is a story that starts with an earthquake and works its way up to a climax.

Sam Goldwyn 1882–1974: attributed, perhaps apocryphal

17 'Do you have a leading lady for your film?'
'We're trying for the Queen, she sells.'

George Harrison 1943–2001: at a press conference in the 1960s; Ned Sherrin *Cutting Edge* (1984)

18 Porn? That's films where the plot doesn't thicken.

Sean Lock: *No Flatley! I am Lord of the Dance* (Edinburgh Festival, August 2000)

19 Life in the movies is like the beginning of a love affair. It's full of surprises and you're constantly getting —ed.

David Mamet 1947– : *Speed-the-Plow* (1988)

20 This might have been good for a picture—except it has too many characters in it.
    to Jack Warner, on the LA telephone directory

Wilson Mizner 1876–1933: Max Wilk *The Wit and Wisdom of Hollywood* (1972)

21 The writer, in the eyes of many film producers, still seems to occupy a position of importance somewhere between the wardrobe lady and the tea boy, with this difference: it's often quite difficult to replace the wardrobe lady.

John Mortimer 1923–2009: *Clinging to the Wreckage* (1982)

22 Oh come, my love, and join with me
The oldest infant industry.
Come seek the bourne of palm and pearl
The lovely land of Boy-Meets-Girl.
Come grace this lotus-laden shore,
This Isle of Do-What's-Done-Before.
Come, curb the new, and watch the old win,
Out where the streets are paved with Goldwyn.

Dorothy Parker 1893–1967: 'The Passionate Screen Writer to His Love' (1937)

23 STUDIO EXECUTIVE: Where would you say the centre of your script was?
    JACK ROSENTHAL: Somewhere in the middle.

Jack Rosenthal 1931–2004: in *Independent Review* 9 September 2004

24 *on the take-over of United Artists by Charles Chaplin, Mary Pickford, Douglas Fairbanks and D. W. Griffith:*
The lunatics have taken charge of the asylum.

Richard Rowland c. 1881–1947: Terry Ramsaye *A Million and One Nights* (1926)

25 The trouble, Mr Goldwyn, is that you are only interested in art and I am only interested in money.
    telegraphed version of the outcome of a conversation between Shaw and Sam Goldwyn

George Bernard Shaw 1856–1950: Alva Johnson *The Great Goldwyn* (1937)

26 I wouldn't say when you've seen one Western you've seen the lot; but when you've seen the lot you get the feeling you've seen one.

Katharine Whitehorn 1928– : *Sunday Best* (1976) 'Decoding the West'

Cities See **Towns and Cities**

Civil Servants

66 *Civil servants are human beings, and must be treated as such.* 99
J. B. Morton

1 Going about persecuting civil servants.
   assessment by one unidentified senator of how politicians spend their time

Anonymous: R. F. Foster *Modern Ireland* (1988)

2 I confidently expect that we [civil servants] shall continue to be grouped with mothers-in-law and Wigan Pier as one of the recognized objects of ridicule.

Edward Bridges 1892–1969: *Portrait of a Profession* (1950)

3 Give a civil servant a good case and he'll wreck it with clichés, bad punctuation, double negatives and convoluted apology.

Alan Clark 1928–99: diary 22 July 1983

4 A civil servant doesn't make jokes.

Eugène Ionesco 1912–94: *Tueur sans gages* (The Killer, 1958)

5 May I hasten to support Mrs McGurgle's contention that civil servants are human beings, and must be treated as such?

J. B. Morton 1893–1975: M. Frayn (ed.) *The Best of Beachcomber* (1963)

6 By the time the civil service has finished drafting a document to give effect to a principle, there may be little of the principle left.

Lord Reith 1889–1971: *Into the Wind* (1949)

7 Here lies a civil servant. He was civil
   To everyone, and servant to the devil.

C. H. Sisson 1914–2003: *The London Zoo* (1961)

Class

See also **The Aristocracy, Snobbery**

66 *If the lower orders don't set us a good example, what on earth is the use of them?* 99
Oscar Wilde

1 A gentleman never eats. He breakfasts, he lunches, he dines, but he *never* eats!

Anonymous: Cole Porter's headmaster, c.1910; Caryl Brahms and Ned Sherrin *Song by Song* (1984)

2 His lordship may compel us to be equal upstairs, but there will never be equality in the servants' hall.

J. M. Barrie 1860–1937: *The Admirable Crichton* (performed 1902)

3 Mankind is divisible into two great classes: hosts and guests.

Max Beerbohm 1872–1956: *And Even Now* (1920)

4 Like many of the Upper Class
   He liked the Sound of Broken Glass.

Hilaire Belloc 1870–1953: 'About John' (1930)

5 *when asked by interviewer Sandra Harris on the* Today
*programme whether she thought British class barriers had
come down:*
Of course they have, or I wouldn't be sitting here talking
to someone like you.

Barbara Cartland 1901–2000: Jilly
Cooper *Class* (1979)

6 If you bed people of below-stairs class, they will go to the
papers.

Jane Clark: in *Daily Telegraph* 31 May
1994

7 A branch of one of your antediluvian families, fellows that
the flood could not wash away.

William Congreve 1670–1729: *Love
for Love* (1695)

8 I came upstairs into the world; for I was born in a cellar.

William Congreve 1670–1729: *Love
for Love* (1695)

9 Today it may be three white feathers,
But yesterday it was three brass balls.

Noël Coward 1899–1973: 'Three
White Feathers' (1932)

10 Dear me, I never knew that the lower classes had such
white skins.

Lord Curzon 1859–1925: K. Rose
Superior Person (1969)

11 Gentlemen do not take soup at luncheon.

Lord Curzon 1859–1925: E. L.
Woodward *Short Journey* (1942)

12 He [Lord Home] is used to dealing with estate workers. I
cannot see how anyone can say he is out of touch.
comment on her father's becoming Prime Minister

Caroline Douglas-Home 1937– : in
Daily Herald 21 October 1963

13 If they could see me now,
My little dusty group,
Traipsing 'round this
Million-dollar chicken coop!
I'd hear those thrift shop cats say:
'Brother! Get her!'
Draped on a bedspread made from
Three kinds of fur.

Dorothy Fields 1905–74: 'If my
Friends could See Me Now' (1966)

14 We are all Adam's children but silk makes the difference.

Thomas Fuller 1654–1734:
Gnomologia (1732)

15 Boston social zones
Are changing social habits,
And I hear the Cohns
Are taking up the Cabots.

Ira Gershwin 1896–1983: 'Love is
Sweeping the Country' (1931)

16 The Earl, the Marquis, and the Dook,
The Groom, the Butler, and the Cook— . . .
The Aristocrat who banks with Coutts . . .
The Aristocrat who cleans our boots—
They all shall equal be.

W. S. Gilbert 1836–1911: *The
Gondoliers* (1889)

17 Bow, bow, ye lower middle classes!
Bow, bow, ye tradesmen, bow, ye masses.

W. S. Gilbert 1836–1911: *Iolanthe*
(1882)

18 When every one is somebodee,
Then no one's anybody.

W. S. Gilbert 1836–1911: *The
Gondoliers* (1889)

19 When the idle poor become the idle rich
You'll never know just who is who or who is which.

E. Y. Harburg 1898–1981: 'When the
Idle Poor become the Idle Rich' (1947)

20 Finer things are for the finer folk
Thus society began
Caviar for peasants is a joke
It's too good for the average man.

Lorenz Hart 1895–1943: 'Too Good
for the Average Man' (1936)

21 There are those who think that Britain is a class-ridden society, and those who think it doesn't matter either way as long as you know your place in the set-up.

Miles Kington 1941–2008: *Welcome to Kington* (1989)

22 Will the people in the cheaper seats clap your hands? All the rest of you, if you'll just rattle your jewellery.

John Lennon 1940–80: at the Royal Variety Performance, 4 November 1963

23 Of all the hokum with which this country [America] is riddled the most odd is the common notion that it is free of class distinctions.

W. Somerset Maugham 1874–1965: *A Writer's Notebook* (1949) written in 1941

24 I no longer keep the coal in the bath. I keep it in the bidet.

John Prescott 1938– : in *Independent* 3 July 1999

25 'She's leaving her present house and going to Lower Seymour Street.' 'I dare say she will, if she stays there long enough.'

Saki 1870–1916: *The Toys of Peace* (1919)

26 I don't want to talk grammar, I want to talk like a lady.

George Bernard Shaw 1856–1950: *Pygmalion* (1916)

27 He's a gentleman: look at his boots.

George Bernard Shaw 1856–1950: preface to *Pygmalion* (1916)

28 Mr Knox . . . was a fair, spare young man, who looked like a stableboy among gentlemen, and a gentleman among stableboys.

Edith Œ. Somerville 1858–1949 and **Martin Ross** 1862–1915: *Some Experiences of an Irish R.M.* (1899)

29 She sits
At The Ritz
With her splits
Of Mum's
And starts to pine
For a Stein
With her Village chums.
But with a Schlitz
In her mitts
Down in Fitz—
Roy's Bar,
She thinks of the Ritz—oh,
It's so
Schizo.

Stephen Sondheim 1930– : 'Uptown Downtown', song rejected from *Follies* (1971); composer's archive

30 The only infallible rule we know is, that the man who is always talking about being a gentleman never is one.

R. S. Surtees 1805–64: *Ask Mamma* (1858)

31 The so called immorality of the lower classes is not to be named on the same day with that of the higher and highest. This is a thing which makes my blood boil, and they will pay for it.

Queen Victoria 1819–1901: letter to the Crown Princess of Prussia, 26 June 1872

32 I expect you'll be becoming a schoolmaster, sir. That's what most of the gentlemen does, sir, that gets sent down for indecent behaviour.

Evelyn Waugh 1903–66: *Decline and Fall* (1928)

33 Really, if the lower orders don't set us a good example, what on earth is the use of them?

Oscar Wilde 1854–1900: *The Importance of Being Earnest* (1895)

34 I think factories would close down, actually, if it wasn't for working-class people.

Victoria Wood 1953– : *Victoria Wood—As Seen on TV* BBC2 January 1985

The Clergy

See also **Religion**

66 *There are three sexes—men, women, and clergymen.* **99**
Sydney Smith

1 A priest is a man who is called Father by everyone except his own children who are obliged to call him Uncle.

Anonymous: said to be an Italian saying found in a French novel; Rupert Hart-Davis letter to George Lyttelton, 15 July 1956

2 As for the British churchman, he goes to church as he goes to the bathroom, with the minimum of fuss and with no explanation if he can help it.

Ronald Blythe 1922– : *The Age of Illusion* (1963)

3 Don't like bishops. Fishy lot. Blessed are the meek my foot! They're all on the climb. Ever heard of meekness stopping a bishop from becoming a bishop? Nor have I.

Maurice Bowra 1898–1971: in conversation while lunching at the Reform Club with a bishop at the next table; Arthur Marshall *Life's Rich Pageant* (1984)

4 Poor Uncle Harry
Having become a missionary
Found the natives' morals rather crude.
He and Aunt Mary
Quickly imposed an arbitrary
Ban upon them shopping in the nude.
They all considered this silly and they didn't take it well,
They burnt his boots and several suits and wrecked the
    Mission Hotel,
They also burnt his mackintosh, which made a disgusting
    smell . . .
Uncle Harry's not a missionary now.

Noël Coward 1899–1973: 'Uncle Harry' (1946)

5 The parson knows enough who knows a duke.

William Cowper 1731–1800: 'Tirocinium' (1785)

6 Mr Doctor, that loose gown becomes you so well I wonder your notions should be so narrow.
to the Puritan Dr Humphreys, as he was about to kiss her hand on her visit to Oxford in 1566

Elizabeth I 1533–1603: F. Chamberlin *Sayings of Queen Elizabeth* (1923)

7 I remember the average curate at home as something between a eunuch and a snigger.

Ronald Firbank 1886–1926: *The Flower Beneath the Foot* (1923)

8 I was a pale young curate then.

W. S. Gilbert 1836–1911: *The Sorcerer* (1877)

9 As I take my shoes from the shoemaker, and my coat from the tailor, so I take my religion from the priest.

Oliver Goldsmith 1730–74: James Boswell *Life of Samuel Johnson* (1934 ed.) 9 April 1773

10 The crisis of the Church of England is that too many of its bishops, and some would say of its archbishops, don't quite realise that they are atheists, but have begun to suspect it.

Clive James 1939– : *The Dreaming Swimmer* (1992)

11 This merriment of parsons is mighty offensive.

Samuel Johnson 1709–84: James Boswell *Life of Samuel Johnson* (1791) March 1781

12 Evangelical vicar, in want of a portable, second-hand font, would dispose, for the same, of a portrait, in frame, of the Bishop, elect, of Vermont.
   advertisement placed in a newspaper

Ronald Knox 1888–1957: W. S. Baring-Gould *The Lure of the Limerick* (1968)

13 It's great being a priest, isn't it, Ted?

Graham Linehan and **Arthur Mathews**: 'Good Luck, Father Ted' (1995), episode from *Father Ted* (Channel 4 TV, 1995–8)

14 *on the appointment of Michael Ramsey to succeed Geoffrey Fisher as Archbishop of Canterbury:*
   We have had enough of Martha and it is time for some Mary.

Harold Macmillan 1894–1986: attributed

15 *to a clergyman who thanked him for the enjoyment he'd given the world:*
   And I want to thank you for all the enjoyment you've taken out of it.

Groucho Marx 1890–1977: Joe Adamson *Groucho, Harpo, Chico and sometimes Zeppo* (1973)

16 As the French say, there are three sexes—men, women, and clergymen.

Sydney Smith 1771–1845: Lady Holland *Memoir* (1855)

17 I have seen nobody since I saw you, but persons in orders. My only varieties are vicars, rectors, curates, and every now and then (by way of turbot) an archdeacon.

Sydney Smith 1771–1845: letter to Miss Berry, 28 January 1843

18 A Curate—there is something which excites compassion in the very name of a Curate!!!

Sydney Smith 1771–1845: *Edinburgh Review* (1822) 'Persecuting Bishops'

19 There is a species of person called a 'Modern Churchman' who draws the full salary of a beneficed clergyman and need not commit himself to any religious belief.

Evelyn Waugh 1903–66: *Decline and Fall* (1928)

20 *Merit*, indeed! . . . We are come to a pretty pass if they talk of *merit* for a bishopric.

Lord Westmorland 1759–1841: Lady Salisbury, diary, 9 December 1835

21 The Bishop . . . was talking to the local Master of Hounds about the difficulty he had in keeping his vicars off the incense.

P. G. Wodehouse 1881–1975: *Mr. Mulliner Speaking* (1929)

Colours

❝ *If I could find anything blacker than black, I'd use it.* ❞
J. M. W. Turner

1 She has perfected the art of answering questions at length and saying absolutely nothing. She would never, even under torture, admit that pink was her favourite colour for fear of offending orange and mauve.
   of Margot Fonteyn

Richard Buckle 1916– : in *Sunday Times* 30 March 1969

2 I was shown round Tutankhamun's tomb in the 1920s. I saw all this wonderful pink on the walls and the artefacts. I was so impressed that I vowed to wear it for the rest of my life.

Barbara Cartland 1901–2000: in *Irish Times* 28 March 1998 'This Week They Said'

3 I cannot pretend to feel impartial about the colours. I rejoice with the brilliant ones, and am genuinely sorry for the poor browns.

Winston Churchill 1874–1965: *Thoughts and Adventures* (1932)

4 Gentlemen never wear brown in London.

Lord Curzon 1859–1925: attributed; Nigel Rees *Cassell Dictionary of Humorous Quotations* (1999)

5 *on the choice of colour for the Model T Ford:*
Any colour—so long as it's black.

Henry Ford 1863–1947: Allan Nevins *Ford* (1957)

6 It's just my colour: it's *beige*!
a fashionable interior decorator's first view of the Parthenon

Elsie Mendl 1865–1950: Osbert Sitwell *Rat Week: An Essay on the Abdication* (1986)

7 A brilliant blue garment that was an offence alike to her convictions and her complexion.

Edith Œ. Somerville 1858–1949 and **Martin Ross** 1862–1915: *Further Experiences of an Irish R.M.* (1908)

8 If I could find anything blacker than black, I'd use it.

J. M. W. Turner 1775–1851: remark, 1844

9 Pink is the navy blue of India.

Diana Vreeland 1903–89: attributed, 1977

10 I think it pisses God off if you walk by the colour purple in a field somewhere and don't notice it.

Alice Walker 1944– : *The Colour Purple* (1982)

Comedy Routines and Catchphrases

66 *George—don't do that.* 99
Joyce Grenfell

1 CECIL: After you, Claude.
CLAUDE: No, after you, Cecil.

Ted Kavanagh 1892–1958: catchphrase in *ITMA* (BBC radio programme, 1939–49)

2 Am I bovvered?

Catherine Tate 1968– : teenager Lauren, in *The Catherine Tate Show* (BBC TV, 2004–)

3 Can I do you now, sir?
spoken by 'Mrs Mopp'

Ted Kavanagh 1892–1958: catchphrase in *ITMA* (BBC radio programme, 1939–49)

4 Collapse of Stout Party.
supposed standard dénouement in Victorian humour

Anonymous: R. Pearsall *Collapse of Stout Party* (1975) introduction

5 D'oh!
Homer J. Simpson's habitual expression of annoyance

Matt Groening 1954– : *The Simpsons* (American TV series, 1990–)

6 Don't have a cow, man.
catchphrase associated with Bart Simpson

Matt Groening 1954– : *The Simpsons* (American TV series, 1990–)

7 Drink! Drink!
habitual cry of Father Jack

Graham Linehan and **Arthur Mathews**: 'New Jack City' (1996), episode from *Father Ted* (Channel 4 TV, 1995–8)

8 Eat my shorts!
catchphrase associated with Bart Simpson

Matt Groening 1954– : *The Simpsons* (American TV series, 1990–)

9 Ee, it was agony, Ivy.

Ted Ray 1906–77: catchphrase in *Ray's a Laugh* (BBC radio programme, 1949–61)

10 'Er indoors.
used by Arthur Daley (played by George Cole) to refer to his wife

Leon Griffiths 1928–92: ITV television series *Minder* (1979 onwards)

11 Fact.
David Brent's favourite assurance

Ricky Gervais 1961– and **Stephen Merchant**: *The Office* (2001–3)

12 George—don't do that.

Joyce Grenfell 1910–79: used as a recurring line in monologues about a nursery school, from the 1950s

13 A good idea—son.

Eric Sykes and **Max Bygraves** 1922– : *Educating Archie*, 1950–3 BBC radio comedy series

14 Good morning, sir—was there something?
catchphrase used by Sam Costa

Richard Murdoch 1907–90 and **Kenneth Horne** 1900–69: radio comedy series *Much-Binding-in-the-Marsh* (started 2 January 1947)

15 BURNS: Say goodnight, Gracie.
ALLEN: Goodnight, Gracie.

George Burns 1896–1996: said to be customary conclusion to *The George Burns and Gracie Allen Show* (1950–58), although Burns in *Gracie: a Love Story* (1990) described this as a showbusiness myth

16 Have you read any good books lately?
catchphrase used by Richard Murdoch

Richard Murdoch 1907–90 and **Kenneth Horne** 1900–69: radio comedy series *Much-Binding-in-the-Marsh* (started 2 January 1947)

17 Heeere's . . . Johnny!

Ed McMahon: introducing Johnny Carson on the NBC TV *Tonight Show* (1962–92); catchphrase later used by Jack Nicholson in the *The Shining* (1980 horror film)

18 Hello, I'm Julian and this is my friend, Sandy.

Barry Took 1928–2002 and **Marty Feldman** 1933–83: catchphrase in *Round the Horne* (BBC radio series, 1965–8)

19 Hello possums!
Dame Edna's habitual greeting to her fans

Barry Humphries 1934– : *The Barry Humphries Show: Dame Edna Everage*

20 I 'ate you, Butler.
Inspector Blake (Stephen Lewis) to Stan Butler (Reg Varney)

Ronald Wolfe and **Ronald Chesney**: *On the Buses* (1969–73).

21 I didn't get where I am today without —.
habitual boast of Reggie Perrin's boss CJ

David Nobbs 1935– : BBC television series *The Fall and Rise of Reginald Perrin*, 1976–80

22 I don't mind if I do.
catchphrase spoken by 'Colonel Chinstrap'

Ted Kavanagh 1892–1958: *ITMA* (BBC radio programme, 1939–49)

23 If you've got it, flaunt it!

Mel Brooks 1926– : *The Producers* (1967 film)

24 I go—I come back.
catchphrase spoken by 'Ali Oop'

Ted Kavanagh 1892–1958: *ITMA* (BBC radio programme, 1939–49)

25 I have a cunning plan.
Baldrick's habitual overoptimistic promise

Richard Curtis 1956– and **Ben Elton** 1959– : *Blackadder II* (1987) television series

26 I'm free!
cry of 'Mr Humphries' (played by John Inman) of Grace Brothers

David Croft 1922– and **Jeremy Lloyd**: in *Are You Being Served?* (1973–83).

27 It's being so cheerful as keeps me going.
catchphrase spoken by 'Mona Lott'

Ted Kavanagh 1892–1958: *ITMA* (BBC radio programme, 1939–49)

28 CORBETT: It's goodnight from me.
BARKER: And it's goodnight from him.

Ronnie Barker 1929–2005 and **Ronnie Corbett** 1930– : in *The Two Ronnies*, 1971–87 BBC television series

29 It's *sooo* unfair!
habitual plaint of Kevin the Teenager

Harry Enfield 1961– : *Harry Enfield and Chums* (BBC TV, 1994)

30 I've arrived and to prove it I'm here!

Eric Sykes and **Max Bygraves** 1922– : *Educating Archie*, 1950–3 BBC radio comedy series

31 Just like that!

Tommy Cooper 1921–84: catchphrase

32 Mind my bike!

Jack Warner 1895–1981: catchphrase used in the BBC radio series *Garrison Theatre*, 1939 onwards

33 My arse!
Jim Royle's usual sceptical comment on people or circumstances

Caroline Aherne 1963– , **Craig Cash**, and **Henry Normal**: *The Royle Family* (BBC television series, 1998–2000); spoken by Ricky Tomlinson

34 Nobody expects the Spanish Inquisition! Our chief weapon is surprise—surprise and fear . . . fear and surprise . . . our two weapons are fear and surprise—and ruthless efficiency . . . our *three* weapons are fear and surprise and ruthless efficiency and an almost fanatical devotion to the Pope . . . our *four* . . . no . . . *Amongst* our weapons—amongst our weaponry—are such elements as fear, surprise . . . I'll come in again.

Graham Chapman 1941–89, **John Cleese** 1939– , et al.: *Monty Python's Flying Circus* (BBC TV programme, 1970)

35 No sex, please—we're British.

Anthony Marriott 1931– and **Alistair Foot**: title of play (1971)

36 Oh, calamity!

Robertson Hare 1891–1979: catchphrase in *Yours Indubitably* (1956)

37 Oh, groovy baby, yeah!

Mike Myers 1963– : Austin Powers (Mike Myers) in *Austin Powers—International Man of Mystery* (1996 film)

38 Ohhh, I don't *believe* it!
Victor Meldrew (Richard Wilson)

David Renwick 1951– : *One Foot in the Grave* (BBC television series, 1989–)

39 Oh, titter ye not.

Frankie Howerd 1922–92 : habitual adjuration to his audience, first introduced in *The Frankie Howerd Variety Show* 1978

40 Pass the sick bag, Alice.
referring to a canteen lady at the old Express *building in Fleet Street, who conveyed plates of egg and chips to journalists at their desks*

John Junor 1919–97: in *Sunday Express* 28 December 1980

41 Respect!
Ali G acknowledges quality

Ali G (Sacha Baron Cohen) 1970– : *Da Ali G Show* (2000–1)

42 Shoulders back, lovely boy!
Sergeant-Major Williams (Windsor Davies) to his concert party

Jimmy Perry 1923– and **David Croft** 1922– : *It Ain't Half Hot, Mum* (1974–81)

43 So Harry says, 'You don't like me any more. Why not?' And he says, 'Because you've got so terribly pretentious.' And Harry says, 'Pretentious? *Moi?*'

John Cleese 1939– and **Connie Booth**: *Fawlty Towers* (BBC TV programme, 1979)

44 Seriously, though, he's doing a grand job!

David Frost 1939– : catchphrase written by Waterhouse and Hall for Roy Kinnear's sketch 'The Safe Comedian', and adopted by David Frost for 'That Was The Week That Was', on BBC Television, 1962–3

45 Shome mishtake, shurely?

Anonymous: catchphrase in *Private Eye* magazine, 1980s

46 Stop messing about!
protest of Snide (Kenneth Williams)

Ray Galton 1930– and **Alan Simpson** 1929– : *Hancock's Half Hour* (1954–9).

47 STRIKER: Surely you can't be serious.
DR RUMACK: I am serious. And don't call me Shirley.

Jim Abrahams, **David Zucker**, and **Jerry Zucker**: *Airplane!* (1980 film)

48 Take my wife—please!

Henny Youngman 1906–98: in *Times* 26 February 1998; obituary

49 ABBOTT: Now, on the St Louis team we have Who's on first, What's on second, I Don't Know is on third.
COSTELLO: That's what I want to find out.

Bud Abbott 1895–1974 and **Lou Costello** 1906–59: *Naughty Nineties* (1945)

50 They don't like it up 'em!
Lance-Corporal Jones (Clive Dunn)

Jimmy Perry 1923– and **David Croft** 1922– : *Dad's Army* (1968–77).

51 Very interesting . . . but stupid.

Dan Rowan 1922–87 and **Dick Martin** 1923–2008: catchphrase in *Rowan and Martin's Laugh-In* (American television series, 1967–73)

52 What do you think of the show so far? Rubbish!

Eric Morecambe 1926–84: on *The Morecambe and Wise Show* (BBC Television, 1968–78; Thames Television, 1978–83)

53 Yeah but no but yeah but no.
Vicky Pollard's habitual protest

Matt Lucas 1974– and **David Walliams** 1971– : spoken by Matt Lucas, in the BBC comedy *Little Britain* (2003–)

54 SEAGOON: Ying tong iddle I po.

Spike Milligan 1918–2002: *The Dreaded Batter Pudding Hurler* in *The Goon Show* (BBC radio series) 12 October 1954; catchphrase also used in *The Ying Tong Song* (1956)

55 You can't get the wood, you know.

Spike Milligan 1918–2002: *The Goon Show* (BBC radio, 1951–61)

56 You dirty old man!
Harold Steptoe (Harry H. Corbett) to his father Albert

Ray Galton 1930– and **Alan Simpson** 1929– : *Steptoe and Son* (1962–5 and 1970–4).

57 You might very well think that. I couldn't possibly comment.
the Chief Whip's habitual response to questioning

Michael Dobbs 1948– : *House of Cards* (televised 1990)

58 You plonker!
Del Boy Trotter (David Jason) to his brother Rodney (Nicholas Lyndhurst)

John Sullivan: *Only Fools and Horses* (1987–)

59 You stupid boy!
Captain Mainwaring (Arthur Lowe) to Private Pike (Ian Lavender)

Jimmy Perry 1923– and **David Croft** 1922– : *Dad's Army* (1968–77).

Computers
See also **Science, Technology**

> **❝ The email of the species is deadlier than the mail. ❞**
> **Stephen Fry**

1 To err is human but to really foul things up requires a computer.

Anonymous: in *Farmers' Almanac for 1978*

2 *Charles Babbage, inventor of the first mechanical computer, had sacrificed some very precious time to a lady, on the supposition that she understood as much as she thought she did:*
Now, Mr Babbage, there is only one thing that I want to know. If you put the question in wrong, will the answer come out right?

Anonymous: Harriet Martineau *Autobiography* (1877)

3 A modern computer hovers between the obsolescent and the nonexistent.

Sydney Brenner 1927– : in *Science* 5 January 1990; attributed

4 I am afraid it is a non-starter. I cannot even use a bicycle pump.
when asked whether she uses e-mail

Judi Dench 1934– : in *Times* 13 February 1999

5 The email of the species is deadlier than the mail.

Stephen Fry 1957– : in *Sunday Telegraph* 23 December 2001

6 This Ken Starr report is now posted on the Internet. I'll bet Clinton's glad he put a computer in every classroom.

Jay Leno 1950– : in *Sunday Times* 20 September 1998

7 Computer says No.
Matt Lucas as 'Carol'

Matt Lucas 1974– and **David Walliams** 1971– : *Little Britain* (series 2, episode 1) 19 October 2004

8 We've all heard that a million monkeys banging on a million typewriters will eventually reproduce the entire works of Shakespeare. Now, thanks to the Internet, we know this is not true.

Robert Wilensky 1951– : in *Mail on Sunday* 16 February 1997 'Quotes of the Week'

Conversation
See also **Speeches**

66 *Faith, that's as well said, as if I had said it myself.* 99
Jonathan Swift

1 It was such a voice as icebergs might be supposed to use to speak to each other as they passed by night in the Arctic Sea.

E. F. Benson 1867–1940: *Miss Mapp* (1922)

2 Although there exist many thousand subjects for elegant conversation, there are persons who cannot meet a cripple without talking about feet.

Ernest Bramah 1868–1942: *The Wallet of Kai Lung* (1900)

3 You'll interrupt yourself in a minute.
being interviewed by John Humphrys on the Today *programme, BBC Radio 4, 1 March 2006*

David Cameron 1966– : in *Mail on Sunday* 5 March 2006

4 When you were quite a little boy somebody ought to have said 'hush' just once!

Mrs Patrick Campbell 1865–1940: letter to George Bernard Shaw, 1 November 1912

5 'Then you should say what you mean,' the March Hare went on. 'I do,' Alice hastily replied; 'at least—at least I mean what I say—that's the same thing, you know.' 'Not the same thing a bit!' said the Hatter. 'Why, you might just as well say that "I see what I eat" is the same thing as "I eat what I see!" '

Lewis Carroll 1832–98: *Alice's Adventures in Wonderland* (1865)

6 *on visiting Lord Alfred Douglas:*
We had resolved not to mention Oscar Wilde, prison, Winston, Robbie Ross or Frank Harris, but we were soon well embarked on all five subjects, though not at once.

Chips Channon 1897–1958: diary, 10 October 1942

7 It makes a change from talking to plants.
being photographed with penguins in the Falklands

Charles, Prince of Wales 1948– : in *Sunday Times* 21 March 1999 'Talking Heads'

8 Too much agreement kills a chat.

Eldridge Cleaver 1935– : *Soul on Ice* (1968)

9 Is it possible to cultivate the art of conversation when living in the country all the year round?

E. M. Delafield 1890–1943: *The Diary of a Provincial Lady* (1930)

10 The fun of talk is to find what a man really thinks, and then contrast it with the enormous lies he has been telling all dinner, and, perhaps, all his life.

Benjamin Disraeli 1804–81: *Lothair* (1870)

11 Blessed is the man who, having nothing to say, abstains from giving us wordy evidence of the fact.

George Eliot 1819–80: *Impressions of Theoprastus Such* (1879)

12 How time flies when you's doin' all the talking.

Harvey Fierstein 1954– : *Torch Song Trilogy* (1979)

13 If you are ever at a loss to support a flagging conversation, introduce the subject of eating.

Leigh Hunt 1784–1859: J. A. Gere and John Sparrow (eds.) *Geoffrey Madan's Notebooks* (1981); attributed

14 I've just spent an hour talking to Tallulah for a few minutes.

Fred Keating: Denis Brian *Tallulah, Darling* (1980)

15 My ear is open like a greedy shark
To catch the tunings of a voice divine.

John Keats 1795–1821: *Poems* (1817) 'Woman! when I behold thee'

16 There are two things in ordinary conversation which ordinary people dislike—information and wit.

Stephen Leacock 1869–1944: *The Boy I Left Behind Me* (1947)

17 The opposite of talking isn't listening. The opposite of talking is waiting.

Fran Lebowitz 1946– : *Social Studies* (1981)

18 Considering how foolishly people act and how pleasantly they prattle, perhaps it would be better for the world if they talked more and did less.

W. Somerset Maugham 1874–1965: *A Writer's Notebook* (1949) written in 1892

19 She plunged into a sea of platitudes, and with the powerful breast stroke of a channel swimmer made her confident way towards the white cliffs of the obvious.

W. Somerset Maugham 1874–1965: *A Writer's Notebook* (1949) written in 1919

20 It is clear enough that you are making some distinction in what you said, that there is some nicety of terminology in your words. I can't quite follow you.

Flann O'Brien 1911–66: *The Dalkey Archive* (1964)

21 *inviting George Galloway to be interviewed on* Newsnight, *after his eviction from the Big Brother house:*
Whenever you are ready . . . with or without your leotard.

Jeremy Paxman 1950– : in *Times* 26 January 2006

22 With first-rate sherry flowing into second-rate whores,
And third-rate conversation without one single pause:
Just like a young couple
Between the wars.

William Plomer 1903–73: 'Father and Son: 1939' (1945)

23 If you have nothing to say, or, rather, something extremely stupid and obvious, say it, but in a 'plonking' tone of voice—i.e. roundly, but hollowly and dogmatically.

Stephen Potter 1900–69: *Lifemanship* (1950)

24 He never knew what to say. If life was a party, he wasn't even in the kitchen.

Terry Pratchett 1948– : *Thief of Time* (2001)

25 *commenting that George Bernard Shaw's wife was a good listener:*
God knows she had plenty of practice.

J. B. Priestley 1894–1984: *Margin Released* (1962)

26 You talkin' to me?

Paul Schrader 1946– : *Taxi Driver* (1976 film); spoken by Robert de Niro as Travis Bickle

27 [Macaulay] has occasional flashes of silence, that make his conversation perfectly delightful.

Sydney Smith 1771–1845: Lady Holland *Memoir* (1855)

28 —d! said my mother, 'what is all this story about?'— 'A Cock and a Bull,' said Yorick.

Laurence Sterne 1713–68: *Tristram Shandy* (1759–67)

29 *You* talked animatedly for some time about language being the aniseed trail that draws the hounds of heaven when the metaphysical fox has gone to earth; he must have thought you were barmy.

Tom Stoppard 1937– : *Jumpers* (rev. ed. 1986)

30 Faith, that's as well said, as if I had said it myself.

Jonathan Swift 1667–1745: *Polite Conversation* (1738)

31 I re-iterate. You remember, I iterated before.

Dick Vosburgh 1929–2007: *A Saint She Ain't* (1999)

32 If one plays good music, people don't listen and if one plays bad music people don't talk.

Oscar Wilde 1854–1900: *The Importance of Being Earnest* (1895)

33 If one could only teach the English how to talk, and the Irish how to listen, society here would be quite civilized.

Oscar Wilde 1854–1900: *An Ideal Husband* (1895)

34 'What ho!' I said.
'What ho!' said Motty.
'What ho! What ho!'
'What ho! What ho! What ho!'
After that it seemed rather difficult to go on with the conversation.

P. G. Wodehouse 1881–1975: *My Man Jeeves* (1919)

Cookery

See also **Diets, Food**

❝ For 30 years she served nothing but leftovers. The original meal was never found. ❞
Tracey Ullman

1 Anyone who tells a lie has not a pure heart, and cannot make a good soup.

Ludwig van Beethoven 1770–1827: Ludwig Nohl *Beethoven Depicted by his Contemporaries* (1880)

2 Be content to remember that those who can make omelettes properly can do nothing else.

Hilaire Belloc 1870–1953: *A Conversation with a Cat* (1931)

3 My mother tells me she's worn out pouring tinned sauce over the frozen chicken.

Maeve Binchy 1940– : *Evening Class* (1996)

4 The discovery of a new dish does more for the happiness of mankind than the discovery of a new star.

Anthelme Brillat-Savarin 1755–1826: *Physiologie du Goût* (1826)

5 He said, 'I look for butterflies
That sleep among the wheat:
I make them into mutton-pies,
And sell them in the street.'

Lewis Carroll 1832–98: *Through the Looking-Glass* (1872)

6 You cannot trust people who have such bad cuisine. It is the country with the worst food after Finland.
on the British

Jacques Chirac 1932– : in *Times* 5 July 2005

7 Great cookery is making doughnuts like Fanny's.
comment on one of his wife Fanny Cradock's televised cookery programmes; David Coleman is said to have introduced the following 'Match of the Day' with the words, 'For those of you who watched the last programme, I hope all your doughnuts turn out like Fanny's.'

Johnny Cradock c.1904–87: attributed, perhaps apocryphal

8 Heaven sends us good meat, but the Devil sends cooks.

David Garrick 1717–79: 'On Doctor Goldsmith's Characteristical Cookery' (1777)

9 The difference between a chef and a cook is the difference between a wife and a prostitute. Cooks do meals for people they know and love. Chefs do it anonymously for anyone who's got the price.

A. A. Gill 1954– : in *Independent* 4 November 1998

10 We could not have had a better dinner had there been a *Synod of Cooks*.

Samuel Johnson 1709–84: James Boswell *Life of Samuel Johnson* (1791) 5 August 1763

11 A cucumber should be well sliced, and dressed with pepper and vinegar, and then thrown out, as good for nothing.

Samuel Johnson 1709–84: James Boswell *Journal of a Tour to the Hebrides* (1785) 5 October 1773

12 *watching the TV chef Michael Barry prepare a venison dish:* Bambi—see the movie! Eat the cast!

Henry Kelly: in *Daily Telegraph* 26 February 1994

13 Sorry, I don't do offal.
invited to help improve the food in the Westminster kitchens

Jamie Oliver 1975– : in *Mail on Sunday* 15 June 2003

14 The vulgar boil, the learned roast, an egg.

Alexander Pope 1688–1744: *Imitations of Horace* (1738)

15 A woman always has half an onion left over, no matter what the size of the onion, the dish or the woman.

Terry Pratchett 1948– : *Monstrous Regiment* (2003)

16 Her cooking is the missionary position of cooking. That is how everybody starts.
defending Delia Smith

Egon Ronay: in *Independent on Sunday* 1 November 1998

17 The cook was a good cook, as cooks go; and as cooks go, she went.

Saki 1870–1916: *Reginald* (1904)

18 'But why should you want to shield him?' cried Egbert; 'the man is a common murderer.' 'A common murderer, possibly, but a very uncommon cook.'

Saki 1870–1916: *Beasts and Super-Beasts* (1914)

19 You won't be surprised that diseases are innumerable— count the cooks.

Seneca C.4 BC–AD 65: *Epistles*

20 I want to focus on my salad.
when asked about a congressional investigation into her sale of shares

Martha Stewart 1941– : interviewed on *The Early Show* (CBS) 25 June 2002

21 The most remarkable thing about my mother is that for 30 years she served nothing but leftovers. The original meal was never found.

Tracey Ullman 1959– : in *Observer* 23 May 1999 'Sayings of the Week'

22 And now with some pleasure I find that it's seven; and must cook dinner. Haddock and sausage meat. I think it is true that one gains a certain hold on sausage and haddock by writing them down.

Virginia Woolf 1882–1941: diary, 8 March 1941

Countries and Peoples

See also **America, Australia, Canada, France, Places, Russia**

66 *Abroad is unutterably bloody and foreigners are fiends.* 99
Nancy Mitford

1 It's like Bob Benchley's remark on India—'India, what does the name *not* suggest?' To which Benchley himself gives the answer—'a hell of a lot of things.'

Robert Benchley 1889–1945: Stephen Leacock *The Boy I Left Behind Me* (1947); attributed

2 It's where they commit suicide and the king rides a
bicycle, Sweden.

Alan Bennett 1934– : *Enjoy* (1980)

3 Germans are flummoxed by humour, the Swiss have no
concept of fun, the Spanish think there is nothing at all
ridiculous about eating dinner at midnight, and the
Italians should never, ever have been let in on the
invention of the motor car.

Bill Bryson 1951– : *Neither Here Nor There* (1991)

4 The perpetual lamentations after beef and beer, the stupid
bigoted contempt for every thing foreign, and
insurmountable incapacity of acquiring even a few words
of any language, rendered him like all other English
servants, an encumbrance.

Lord Byron 1788–1824: letter, 14 January 1811

5 I like my 'abroad' to be Catholic and sensual.

Chips Channon 1897–1958: diary 18 January 1924

6 I'm a Red Sea pedestrian, and proud of it!
Graham Chapman as 'Brian'

Graham Chapman 1941–89, **John Cleese** 1939– , et al.: *Monty Python's Life of Brian* (1979 film)

7 Belgium has only one real claim to fame. Thanks to all the
wars that have been fought on its soil, there are more dead
people there than anywhere else in the world. So, while
there's no quality of life in Belgium, there is a simply
wonderful quality of death.

Jeremy Clarkson 1960– : in *Sunday Times* 18 July 1999

8 They're Germans. Don't mention the war.

John Cleese 1939– and **Connie Booth**: *Fawlty Towers* (BBC TV programme, 1975)

9 *the French jazz critic Hugues Panassie had given Condon a
generally favourable notice:*
I don't see why we need a Frenchman to come over here
and tell us how to play American music. I wouldn't think
of going to France and telling him how to jump on a
grape.

Eddie Condon 1905–73: Bill Crow *Jazz Anecdotes* (1990)

10 To speak with your mouth full
And swallow with greed
Are national traits
Of the travelling Swede.

Duff Cooper 1890–1954: Philip Ziegler *Diana Cooper* (1981)

11 In a bar on the Piccola Marina
Life called to Mrs Wentworth-Brewster,
Fate beckoned her and introduced her
Into a rather queer
Unfamiliar atmosphere . . .
Just for fun three young sailors from Messina
Bowed low to Mrs Wentworth-Brewster,
Said 'Scusi' and politely goosed her.
Then there was quite a scena.
Her family, in floods of tears, cried,
'Leave these men, Mama.'
She said, 'They're just high-spirited, like all Italians are
And most of them have a great deal more to offer than
    Papa,
In a bar on the Piccola Marina.'

Noël Coward 1899–1973: 'A Bar on the Piccola Marina' (1954)

12 Don't let's be beastly to the Germans
   When our Victory is ultimately won.
   It was just those nasty Nazis who persuaded them to fight
   And their Beethoven and Bach are really far worse than
       their bite,
   Let's be meek to them—
   And turn the other cheek to them
   And try to bring out their latent sense of fun.

Noël Coward 1899–1973: 'Don't Let's
Be Beastly to the Germans' (1943)

13 Some people . . . may be Rooshans, and others may be
   Prooshans; they are born so, and will please themselves.
   Them which is of other naturs thinks different.

Charles Dickens 1812–70: *Martin
Chuzzlewit* (1844)

14 When you enter a house you take your shoes off
   It's better with your shoes off! . . .
   Get yourself a Geisha. The flower of Asia,
   She's one with whom to take up.
   At night your bed she'll make up,
   And she'll be there when you wake up.

Howard Dietz 1896–1983: 'Get
Yourself a Geisha' (1935)

15 The Arabs are only Jews upon horseback.

Benjamin Disraeli 1804–81: *Tancred*
(1847)

16 *to a Boer who had told her that he could never quite forgive the
British for having conquered his country:*
   I understand that perfectly. We feel very much the same in
   Scotland.

Queen Elizabeth, the Queen Mother
1900–2002: Elizabeth Longford (ed.)
The Oxford Book of Royal Anecdotes
(1989)

17 I'm not Jewish. I only look intelligent.
       German cabaret artist to Nazis in his audience, 1931

Werner Finck 1902– : Humphrey
Carpenter *That Was Satire That Was*
(2000)

18 We sing you the Song of the Rhineland—
   Europe's beauty spot . . .
   That wonderful pretzel-and-stein land
   Can never be forgot!

Ira Gershwin 1896–1983: 'Song of
the Rhineland' (1945)

19 What cleanliness everywhere! You dare not throw your
   cigarette into the lake. No graffiti in the urinals.
   Switzerland is proud of this; but I believe this is just what
   she lacks: manure.

André Gide 1869–1951: diary,
Lucerne, 10 August 1917

20 For he might have been a Roosian,
   A French, or Turk, or Proosian,
   Or perhaps Ital-ian!
   But in spite of all temptations
   To belong to other nations,
   He remains an Englishman!

W. S. Gilbert 1836–1911: *HMS
Pinafore* (1878)

21 Holland . . . lies so low they're only saved by being
   dammed.

Thomas Hood 1799–1845: *Up the
Rhine* (1840) 'Letter from Martha
Penny to Rebecca Page'

22 And we will all go together when we go—
   Every Hottentot and every Eskimo.

Tom Lehrer 1928– : 'We Will All Go
Together When We Go' (1953)

23 ELIZA: The Rain in Spain stays mainly in the plain.
   HIGGINS: By George, she's got it!

Alan Jay Lerner 1918–86: 'The Rain
in Spain' (1956)

24 I'd love to get you
   On a slow boat to China,
   All to myself, alone.

Frank Loesser 1910–69: 'On a Slow
Boat to China' (1948)

25 'We went in [to the European Community],' he said, 'to screw the French by splitting them off from the Germans. The French went in to protect their inefficient farmers from commercial competition. The Germans went in to cleanse themselves of genocide and apply for readmission to the human race.'

Jonathan Lynn 1943– and **Antony Jay** 1930– : *Yes, Minister* vol. 2 (1982)

26 In fact, I'm not really a *Jew*. Just Jew-*ish*. Not the whole hog, you know.

Jonathan Miller 1934– : *Beyond the Fringe* (1960 review) 'Real Class'

27 Frogs . . . are slightly better than Huns or Wops, but abroad is unutterably bloody and foreigners are fiends.

Nancy Mitford 1904–73: *The Pursuit of Love* (1945)

28 The Dutch in old Amsterdam do it,
Not to mention the Finns,
Folks in Siam do it,
Think of Siamese twins.
Some Argentines, without means, do it,
People say, in Boston, even beans do it
Let's do it, let's fall in love.

Cole Porter 1891–1964: 'Let's Do It, Let's Fall in Love' (1928)

29 If you come on a camel, you can park it,
So come to the supermarket
And see
Pe-
king.

Cole Porter 1891–1964: 'Come to the Supermarket in Old Peking' (1958)

30 The people of Crete unfortunately make more history than they can consume locally.

Saki 1870–1916: *Chronicles of Clovis* (1911)

31 All my wife has ever taken from the Mediterranean—from that whole vast intuitive culture—are four bottles of Chianti to make into lamps.

Peter Shaffer 1926– : *Equus* (1973)

32 That's the main trouble with the two nations: bad Brits are snobs, bad Americans are slobs.

Peter Shaffer 1926– : *Whom Do I Have the Honour of Addressing?* (1990)

33 I think he bought his doublet in Italy, his round hose in France, his bonnet in Germany, and his behaviour everywhere.

William Shakespeare 1564–1616: *The Merchant of Venice* (1596–8)

34 England and America are two countries divided by a common language.

George Bernard Shaw 1856–1950: attributed in this and other forms, but not found in Shaw's published writings

35 I look upon Switzerland as an inferior sort of Scotland.

Sydney Smith 1771–1845: letter to Lord Holland, 1815

36 Yesterday, the President met with a group he calls the coalition of the willing. Or, as the rest of the world calls them, Britain and Spain.

Jon Stewart 1962– : *The Daily Show* March 2003

37 *a travelling companion on the Alps:*
They say if the Swiss had designed these mountains, um, they'd be rather flatter.

Paul Theroux 1941– : 'Misery on the Orient Express' in *Atlantic Monthly* July 1975

38 Lump the whole thing! say that the Creator made Italy from designs by Michael Angelo!

Mark Twain 1835–1910: *The Innocents Abroad* (1869)

39 I don't like Norwegians at all. The sun never sets, the bar never opens, and the whole country smells of kippers.

Evelyn Waugh 1903–66: letter to Lady Diana Cooper, 13 July 1934

40 In Italy for thirty years under the Borgias they had warfare, terror, murder, bloodshed—they produced Michelangelo, Leonardo da Vinci and the Renaissance. In Switzerland they had brotherly love, five hundred years of democracy and peace and what did that produce . . . ? The cuckoo clock.

Orson Welles 1915–85: *The Third Man* (1949 film); words added by Welles to Graham Greene's script

41 *of art and the Swiss:*
The sons of patriots are left with the clock that turns the mill, and the sudden cuckoo, with difficulty restrained in its box!
　　For this was Tell a hero! For this did Gessler die!

James McNeill Whistler 1834–1903: lecture in London, 20 February 1885; in *Mr Whistler's 'Ten O'Clock'* (1888)

42 I don't like Switzerland: it has produced nothing but theologians and waiters.

Oscar Wilde 1854–1900: letter from Switzerland, 20 March 1899

The Country

❝ Anybody can be good in the country. ❞
Oscar Wilde

1 I'm proud of George. He's learned a lot about ranching since that first year when he tried to milk the horse. What's worse, it was a male horse.

Laura Bush 1946– : White House Correspondents' Association dinner, 30 April 2005

2 He likes the country, but in truth must own,
Most likes it, when he studies it in town.

William Cowper 1731–1800: 'Retirement' (1782)

3 God made the country, and man made the town.

William Cowper 1731–1800: *The Task* (1785)

4 'You are a pretty urban sort of person though, wouldn't you say?'
'Only nor'nor'east,' I said. 'I know a fox from a fax-machine.'

Stephen Fry 1957– : *The Hippopotamus* (1994)

5 A weekend in the country—
Trees in the orchard call.
When you've examined one tree,
Then you've examined them all.

Ira Gershwin 1896–1983: 'A Weekend in the Country' (*The Barkleys of Broadway*, 1949 film)

6 June is bustin' out all over
The sheep aren't sleepin' any more!
All the rams that chase the ewe sheep
Are determined there'll be new sheep
And the ewe sheep aren't even keepin' score!

Oscar Hammerstein II 1895–1960: 'June is Bustin' Out All Over' (1945)

7 In a mountain greenery
Where God paints the scenery—.

Lorenz Hart 1895–1943: 'Mountain Greenery' (1926)

8 There is nothing good to be had in the country, or if there is, they will not let you have it.

William Hazlitt 1778–1830: *The Round Table* (1817)

9 The Farmer will never be happy again;
He carries his heart in his boots;
For either the rain is destroying his grain
Or the drought is destroying his roots.

A. P. Herbert 1890–1971: 'The Farmer' (1922)

10 Hey, buds below, up is where to grow,
Up with which below can't compare with.
Hurry! It's lovely up here! *Hurry!*

Alan Jay Lerner 1918–86: 'It's Lovely Up Here' (1965)

11 So *that's* what hay looks like.
said at Badminton House, where she was evacuated during the Second World War

Queen Mary 1867–1953: James Pope-Hennessy *Life of Queen Mary* (1959)

12 It is no good putting up notices saying 'Beware of the bull' because very rude things are sometimes written on them. I have found that one of the most effective notices is 'Beware of the Agapanthus'.

Lord Massereene and Ferrard 1914–93: speech on the Wildlife and Countryside Bill, House of Lords 16 December 1980

13 Very few people have settled entirely in the country but have grown at length weary of one another. The lady's conversation generally falls into a thousand impertinent effects of idleness, and the gentleman falls in love with his dogs and horses, and out of love with every thing else.

Lady Mary Wortley Montagu 1689–1762: letter to Edward Wortley Montagu, 12 August 1712

14 Whose woods are whose everybody knows exactly, and everybody knows who got them rezoned for a shopping mall and who couldn't get the financing to begin construction and why it was he couldn't get it.
on a traditional New England community, with reference to Robert Frost's 'Whose woods these are I think I know'

P. J. O'Rourke 1947– : *Parliament of Whores* (1991)

15 A farm is an irregular patch of nettles bounded by short-term notes, containing a fool and his wife who didn't know enough to stay in the city.

S. J. Perelman 1904–79: *The Most of S. J. Perelman* (1959) 'Acres and Pains'

16 Farming, that's the fashion,
Farming, that's the passion
Of our great celebrities of today.
Kit Cornell is shellin' peas,
Lady Mendl's climbin' trees,
Dear Mae West is at her best in the hay . . .
The natives think it's utterly utter
When Margie Hart starts churning her butter . . .
Miss Elsa Maxwell, so the folks tattle,
Got well-goosed while dehorning her cattle . . .
Liz Whitney has, on her bin of manure, a
Clip designed by the Duke of Verdura,
Farming is so charming, they all say.

Cole Porter 1891–1964: 'Farming' (1941)

17 Sylvia . . . was accustomed to nothing much more sylvan than 'leafy Kensington'. She looked on the country as something excellent and wholesome in its way, which was apt to become troublesome if you encouraged it overmuch.

Saki 1870–1916: *The Chronicles of Clovis* (1911)

18 I have no relish for the country; it is a kind of healthy grave.

Sydney Smith 1771–1845: letter to Miss G. Harcourt, 1838

19 Anybody can be good in the country.

Oscar Wilde 1854–1900: *The Picture of Dorian Gray* (1891)

20 What do we see at once but a little robin! There is no need to burst into tears fotherington-tomas swete tho he be. Nor to buzz a brick at it, molesworth 2.
a nature walk at St Custards

Geoffrey Willans 1911–58 and **Ronald Searle** 1920– : *Down with Skool!* (1953)

Cricket

See also **Sports and Games**

❝ *Never read print, it spoils one's eye for the ball.* **❞**

W. G. Grace

---

1 Hey, Jardine, you leave our flies alone.
   called by a spectator to the English captain Douglas Jardine as he brushed the flies away, during the 1932–3 MCC tour of Australia, when England's controversial technique of 'bodyline' bowling resulted in injuries to several of the home batsmen

Anonymous: Jack Fingleton *Cricket Crisis: bodyline and other lines* (1946)

2 *when playing in a Lancashire league game, Dennis Lillee's ball hit the batsman on the leg. Although given out, the batsman remained at the crease, and Lillee insisted forcefully that he must go:*
   I'd love to go Dennis but I daren't move. I think you've broken my bloody leg.

Anonymous: Michael Parkinson *Sporting Lives* (1993)

3 *in Australian cricket, traditional line of wicket-keeper to new batsman:*
   How's the wife and my kids?

Anonymous: Simon Hughes *Yakking Around the World* (2000)

4 *the umpire to the bowler, after 'not out' was called when W. G. Grace was unexpectedly bowled first ball:*
   They have paid to see Dr Grace bat, not to see you bowl.

Anonymous: Harry Furniss *A Century of Grace* (1985); perhaps apocryphal

5 *after South Africa's 'Tufty' Mann had baffled George Mann of Middlesex with three successive deliveries in 1947:*
   It is a clear case of Mann's inhumanity to Mann.

John Arlott 1914–91: *Another Word from Arlott* (1985)

6 *on being approached for a contribution to W. G. Grace's testimonial:*
   It's not in support of cricket but as an earnest protest against golf.

Max Beerbohm 1872–1956: attributed

7 *reflecting on the cricketer Billy Barnes who had made a century at Lord's while tipsy:*
   The modern professional cricketer does not get drunk at Lord's or often get a century there, or anywhere else, before lunch.

Neville Cardus 1889–1975: *Autobiography* (1947)

8 The last positive thing England did for cricket was to invent it.

Ian Chappell 1943– : in *Mail on Sunday* 6 January 2002

9 I couldn't bat for the length of time required to score 500. I'd get bored and fall over.

Denis Compton 1918– : to Brian Lara; in *Daily Telegraph* 27 June 1994

10 That's the trouble with these West Country teams. They bowl and field beautifully for an hour, and then—They begin to think of apples.

C. B. Fry 1872–1956: Iain Wilton *C. B. Fry* (1999)

11 Never read print, it spoils one's eye for the ball.
   habitual advice to his players

W. G. Grace 1848–1915: Harry Furniss *A Century of Grace* (1985)

12 Cricket—a game which the English, not being a spiritual people, have invented in order to give themselves some conception of eternity.

Lord Mancroft 1914– : *Bees in Some Bonnets* (1979)

13 *having watched a match at Lord's for several hours:*
MICHAEL DAVIE: Are you enjoying it?
GROUCHO MARX: It's great. When does it start?

Groucho Marx 1890–1977: in *Daily Telegraph* 13 December 2005

14 He is also too daring for the majority of the black-beards, the brown-beards and the no-beards, and the all-beards, who sit in judgement on batsmen; in short, too daring for those who have never known what it is to dare in cricket. Only for those who have not yet grown to the tyranny of the razor is Gimblett possibly not daring enough.
on Harold Gimblett, sometimes accused of being 'too daring for the greybeards'

R. C. Robertson-Glasgow 1901–65: *Cricket Prints* (1943)

15 He loved to walk sideways towards them, like a grimly playful crab.
of George Gunn's approach to faster bowlers

R. C. Robertson-Glasgow 1901–65: *Cricket Prints* (1943)

16 Personally, I have always looked upon cricket as organized loafing.
view of a future archbishop of Canterbury in 1925

William Temple 1881–1944: Michael Parkinson *Sporting Lives* (1993)

17 I need nine wickets from this match, and you buggers had better start drawing straws to see who I don't get.
to an opposing team

Freddie Trueman 1931–2006: in *Ned Sherrin in his Anecdotage* (1993)

18 *asked if he thought anyone would surpass his achievement in taking 300 Test wickets:*
If anyone beats it, they'll be bloody tired.

Freddie Trueman 1931–2006: in 1964; quoted in obituary, *BBC Sport* (online edition) 1 July 2006

19 Fred, t'definitive volume on t'best fast bowler that ever drew breath.
suggested title for his biography; often quoted as 't'finest bloody fast bowler . . .'

Freddie Trueman 1931–2006: Michael Parkinson *Sporting Profiles* (1995)

20 It's a well-known fact that, when I'm on 99, I'm the best judge of a run in all the bloody world.
to Cyril Washbrook

Alan Wharton 1923–93: Freddie Trueman *You Nearly Had Me That Time* (1978)

21 Cricket is basically baseball on valium.

Robin Williams 1952– : attributed

Crime
See also **The Law, Judges, Punishment**

66 *One restaurant, you're in business, four restaurants it's the Mafia.* 99
Neil Simon

1 *Mafia hitman, on trial in Sicily for a double murder:*
It was not me who killed those two men because that night I was shooting two other men.

Anonymous: in *Mail on Sunday* 4 January 2004 'Quotes of the Year'

2 Sammy, you've already lost one eye. D'you wanna go for two?
gangster threatening Sammy Davis Jr

Anonymous: Donald Zec *Put the Knife in Gently* (2003)

3 When their lordships asked Bacon
How many bribes he had taken
He had at least the grace
To get very red in the face.

Edmund Clerihew Bentley 1875–1956: 'Bacon' (1939)

4 Since it is probable that any book flying a bullet in its title is going to produce a corpse sooner or later—here it is.

Caryl Brahms 1901–82 and **S. J. Simon** 1904–48: *A Bullet in the Ballet* (1937)

5 What is robbing a bank compared with founding a bank?

Bertolt Brecht 1898–1956: *Die Dreigroschenoper* (1928)

6 Thieves respect property. They merely wish the property to become their property that they may more perfectly respect it.

G. K. Chesterton 1874–1936: *The Man who was Thursday* (1908)

7 Thou shalt not steal; an empty feat,
When it's so lucrative to cheat.

Arthur Hugh Clough 1819–61: 'The Latest Decalogue' (1862)

8 Here in our city
We're all of us pretty
Well sure that vice
Will in a trice
Be bundled out of sight,
Old men in lobbies
With dubious hobbies
Can still get the deuce of a fright
In London at night.

Noël Coward 1899–1973: 'London at Night' (1953)

9 Three juvenile delinquents,
Juvenile delinquents,
Happy as can be—we
Waste no time
On the wherefores and whys of it;
We like crime
And that's about the size of it.

Noël Coward 1899–1973: 'Three Juvenile Delinquents' (1949)

10 *of a burglar:*
He found it inconvenient to be poor.

William Cowper 1731–1800: 'Charity' (1782)

11 *a prisoner before Mr Justice Darling objected to being called 'a professional crook':*
PRISONER: I've only done two jobs, and each time I've been nabbed.
LORD DARLING: It has never been suggested that you are successful in your profession.

Lord Darling 1849–1936: Edward Maltby *Secrets of a Solicitor* (1929)

12 It is quite a three-pipe problem, and I beg that you won't speak to me for fifty minutes.

Arthur Conan Doyle 1859–1930: *The Adventures of Sherlock Holmes* (1892) 'The Red-Headed League'

13 'Excellent,' I cried. 'Elementary,' said he.

Arthur Conan Doyle 1859–1930: *The Memoirs of Sherlock Holmes* (1894) 'The Crooked Man'. 'Elementary, my dear Watson' is not found in any book by Conan Doyle

14 Major Strasser has been shot. Round up the usual suspects.

Julius J. Epstein 1909–2001 et al.: *Casablanca* (1942 film)

15 It was beautiful and simple as all truly great swindles are.

O. Henry 1862–1910: *Gentle Grafter* (1908) 'Octopus Marooned'

16 Though he might be more humble, there is no police like Holmes.

Ernest Hornung 1866–1921: Arthur Conan Doyle *Memories and Adventures* (1924)

17 The Warden threw a party at the county jail,
The prison band was there an' they began to wail.
The brass band was jumpin' an' the joint began to swing
You should have heard those knocked out jail birds sing.

Jerry Leiber 1933– and **Mike Stoller** 1933– : 'Jailhouse Rock' (1957)

18 Let it appear in a criminal trial that the accused is a Sunday-school superintendent, and the jury says guilty almost automatically.

H. L. Mencken 1880–1956: *Minority Report* (1956)

19 If I ever hear you accuse the police of using violence on a prisoner in custody again, I'll take you down to the station and beat the eyes out of your head.

Joe Orton 1933–67: *Loot* (1966)

20 The most peaceable way for you, if you do take a thief, is, to let him show himself what he is and steal out of your company.

William Shakespeare 1564–1616: *Much Ado About Nothing* (1598–9)

21 She starts to tell me how she's . . . married to an Italian with four restaurants on Long Island and right away I dig he's in with the mob. I mean one restaurant, you're in business, four restaurants it's the Mafia.

Neil Simon 1927– : *The Gingerbread Lady* (1970)

Critics

❝ A man who knows the way but can't drive the car. **❞**
Kenneth Tynan

1 A bad review may spoil your breakfast but you shouldn't allow it to spoil your lunch.

Kingsley Amis 1922–95: Giles Gordon *Aren't We Due a Royalty Statement?* (1993); attributed

2 Full many a gallant man lies slain
On Waterloo's ensanguined plain,
But none by bullet or by shot
Fell half so flat as Walter Scott.
comment on Scott's poem 'The Field of Waterloo' (1815), sometimes attributed to Thomas Erskine

Anonymous: Una Pope-Hennessy *The Laird of Abbotsford* (1932)

3 This fictional account of the day-by-day life of an English gamekeeper is still of considerable interest to outdoor-minded readers, as it contains many passages on pheasant raising, the apprehending of poachers, ways to control vermin, and other chores and duties of the professional gamekeeper. Unfortunately one is obliged to wade through many pages of extraneous material in order to discover and savour these sidelights on the management of a Midlands shooting estate, and in this reviewer's opinion this book cannot take the place of J. R. Miller's *Practical Gamekeeping*.

Anonymous: review of D. H. Lawrence *Lady Chatterley's Lover*; attributed to *Field and Stream*, c.1928

4 I have always thought it was a sound impulse by which he [Kipling] was driven to put his 'Recessional' into the waste-paper basket, and a great pity that Mrs Kipling fished it out and made him send it to *The Times*.

Max Beerbohm 1872–1956: letter 30 October 1913

5 *apparent reassurance to a leading lady after a particularly bad first night:*
My dear, good is not the word.

Max Beerbohm 1872–1956: attributed; Nigel Rees *Cassell Dictionary of Humorous Quotations* (1999)

6 Critics are like eunuchs in a harem; they know how it's done, they've seen it done every day, but they're unable to do it themselves.

Brendan Behan 1923–64: Jonathon Green (ed.) *A Dictionary of Contemporary Quotations* (1982)

7 Hebrews 13.8. [Jesus Christ, the same yesterday, and today, and forever.]
summing up the long-running 1920s Broadway hit Abie's Irish Rose

Robert Benchley 1889–1945: Peter Hay *Theatrical Anecdotes* (1987)

8 Listen, dear, you couldn't write 'fuck' in the dust on a Venetian blind.
to a Hollywood writer who had criticized Alan Bennett's 'An Englishman Abroad'

Coral Browne 1913–91: attributed

9 Send me no more reviews of any kind.—I will read no more of evil or good in that line.—Walter Scott has not read a review of *himself* for *thirteen years*.

Lord Byron 1788–1824: letter to his publisher John Murray, 3 November 1821

10 You know who the critics are? The men who have failed in literature and art.

Benjamin Disraeli 1804–81: *Lothair* (1870)

11 One of the most characteristic sounds of the English Sunday is the sound of Harold Hobson barking up the wrong tree.

Penelope Gilliatt 1933–93: in *Encore* November–December 1959

12 Asking a working writer what he thinks about critics is like asking a lamp-post how it feels about dogs.

Christopher Hampton 1946– : in *Sunday Times Magazine* 16 October 1977

13 When I read something saying I've not done anything as good as *Catch-22* I'm tempted to reply, Who has?'

Joseph Heller 1923–99: in *Times* 9 June 1993

14 There is a sort of savage nobility about his firm reliance on his own bad taste.
of Richard Bentley's edition of Paradise Lost

A. E. Housman 1859–1936: 'Introductory Lecture' (1892)

15 Criticism is a study by which men grow important and formidable at very small expense.

Samuel Johnson 1709–84: *The Idler* 9 June 1759

16 The quickest way to start a punch-up between two British literary critics is to ask them what they think of the poems of Sir John Betjeman

Philip Larkin 1922–85: introduction to *Collected Poems* (1971)

17 He took the praise as a greedy boy takes apple pie, and the criticism as a good dutiful boy takes senna-tea.
of Bulwer Lytton, whose novels he had criticized

Lord Macaulay 1800–59: letter, 5 August 1831

18 He takes the long review of things;
He asks and gives no quarter.
And you can sail with him on wings
Or read the book. It's shorter.

David McCord 1897–1997: 'To A Certain Most Certainly Certain Critic' (1945)

19 Reviewing here [in Baltimore] is a hazardous occupation. Once I spoke harshly of an eminent American novelist, and he retaliated by telling a very charming woman that I was non compos penis. In time she came to laugh at him as a liar.

H. L. Mencken 1880–1956: letter to Hugh Walpole, 1922

20 And it is that word 'hummy', my darlings, that marks the first place in 'The House at Pooh Corner' at which Tonstant Weader fwowed up.

Dorothy Parker 1893–1967: review in *New Yorker* 20 October 1928

21 For 18 years he *started the day* by reading a French novel (in preparation for his history of them) an act so unnatural to man as to amount almost to genius.

Stephen Potter 1900–69: of the critic G. E. B. Saintsbury; *The Muse in Chains* (1937)

22 Let my people go!
at a viewing of Exodus

Mort Sahl 1926– : attributed, 1961; Nigel Rees *Cassell Dictionary of Humorous Quotations* (1999)

23 Last year I gave several lectures on 'Intelligence and the Appreciation of Music Among Animals'. Today I am going to speak to you about 'Intelligence and the Appreciation of Music Among Critics'. The subject is very similar.

Erik Satie 1866–1925: Nat Shapiro (ed.) *An Encyclopedia of Quotations about Music* (1978)

24 Criticism is not only medicinally salutary: it has positive popular attractions in its cruelty, its gladiatorship, and the gratification given to envy by its attacks on the great, and to enthusiasm by its praises.

George Bernard Shaw 1856–1950: preface to *Plays Unpleasant* (1898)

25 Never pay any attention to what critics say . . . A statue has never been set up in honour of a critic!

Jean Sibelius 1865–1957: Bengt de Törne *Sibelius: A Close-Up* (1937)

26 I never read a book before reviewing it; it prejudices a man so.

Sydney Smith 1771–1845: H. Pearson *The Smith of Smiths* (1934)

27 As learned commentators view
In Homer more than Homer knew.

Jonathan Swift 1667–1745: 'On Poetry' (1733)

28 *John Churton Collins, a rival of Edmund Gosse, launched a bitter critical attack on him. When Gosse took tea with Tennyson he found an ally who defined Collins as:*
A louse in the locks of literature.

Alfred, Lord Tennyson 1809–92: Evan Charteris *Life and Letters of Sir Edmund Gosse* (1931)

29 My dear Sir: I have read your play. Oh, my dear Sir! Yours faithfully.
rejecting a play

Herbert Beerbohm Tree 1852–1917: Peter Hay *Theatrical Anecdotes* (1987)

30 A critic is a man who knows the way but can't drive the car.

Kenneth Tynan 1927–80: in *New York Times Magazine* 9 January 1966

31 The original Greek is of great use in elucidating Browning's translation of the *Agamemnon.*

Robert Yelverton Tyrrell 1844–1914: habitual remark to students; Ulick O'Connor *Oliver St John Gogarty* (1964)

32 Critics search for ages for the wrong word which, to give them credit, they eventually find.

Peter Ustinov 1921–2004: Ned Sherrin *Cutting Edge* (1984)

33 *Norman Mailer, annoyed at Vidal's literary style of criticism, hit him over the head with a glass tumbler:*
Ah, Mailer is, as usual, lost for words.

Gore Vidal 1925– : attributed; in *Guardian* 27 February 1999

34 Said a critic initialled E. N.
'Why does my wife like young men?'
A friend said: 'You fool,
Don't you know that the tool
Is mightier far than the pen?'
in course of a feud with the music critic Ernest Newman

Peter Warlock 1894–1930: attributed

35 Restaurant critics—even great critics are like very bad lovers. They only come once a year, they don't care if you're not ready, they leave without saying a word and then they tell everyone what you did was wrong.

Trevor White 1972– : *Kitchen Con* (2006)

36 WILDE: I shall always regard you as the best critic of my
   plays.
   TREE: But I have never criticized your plays.
   WILDE: That's why.

Oscar Wilde 1854–1900:
conversation with Beerbohm Tree
after the first-night success of *A
Woman of No Importance*; Hesketh
Pearson *Beerbohm Tree* (1956)

37 One must have a heart of stone to read the death of Little
Nell without laughing.

Oscar Wilde 1854–1900: Ada
Leverson *Letters to the Sphinx* (1930)

Dance

❝ *I wish I could shimmy like my sister
Kate.* ❞
Armand J. Piron

1 Do you still play a lot of balls?
   *unnamed headmaster's wife to Humphrey Lyttleton, having
   seen him perform at an Oxford May Ball*

Anonymous: Humphrey Lyttleton *It
Just Occurred to Me . . . : the
reminiscences and thoughts of
Chairman Humph* (2006)

2 I made the little buggers hop.
   on conducting the Diaghilev Ballet

Thomas Beecham 1879–1961:
attributed

3 We are told that her supporting company are all relations,
and I dare say they do better than yours or mine would
under the circumstances.
   *of Carmen Armaya's Spanish Gypsy Dancers at the Prince's
   Theatre*

Caryl Brahms 1901–82: in *Evening
Standard* 1948

4 *the ballet designer Benois:*
   Benois . . . If 'e come.

Caryl Brahms 1901–82 and **S. J.
Simon** 1904–48: *A Bullet in the Ballet*
(1937)

5 Will you, won't you, will you, won't you, will you join the
dance?

Lewis Carroll 1832–98: *Alice's
Adventures in Wonderland* (1865)

6 Though no one ever could be keener
Than little Nina
On quite a number
Of very eligible men who did the Rhumba
When they proposed to her she simply left them flat.
She said that love should be impulsive
But not compulsive
And syncopation
Has a discouraging effect on procreation
And that she'd rather read a book—and that was that!

Noël Coward 1899–1973: 'Nina'
(1945)

7 Stately as a galleon, I sail across the floor,
Doing the Military Two-step, as in the days of yore . . .
So gay the band,
So giddy the sight,
Full evening dress is a must,
But the zest goes out of a beautiful waltz
When you dance it bust to bust.

Joyce Grenfell 1910–79: 'Stately as a
Galleon' (1978)

8 No. You see there are portions of the human anatomy
which would keep swinging after the music had finished.
   *reply to question on whether the fashion for nudity would
   extend to dance*

Robert Helpmann 1909–86:
Elizabeth Salter *Helpmann* (1978)

9 GROUCHO MARX: I could dance with you till the cows come home. On second thoughts, I'd rather dance with the cows till you came home.

Bert Kalmar 1884–1947 et al.: *Duck Soup* (1933 film)

10 Cheek to Cheek
Toes to Toes
Here's a dance you can do on a dime
Knees to Knees
Nose to Nose
Slowly move, and you're doin' 'The Slime'.

Jerry Leiber 1933– : 'The Slime' (1942)

11 He waltzes like a Protestant curate.

Kate O'Brien 1897–1974: *The Last of Summer* (1943)

12 Everyone else at the table had got up to dance, except him and me. There I was, trapped. Trapped like a trap in a trap.

Dorothy Parker 1893–1967: *After Such Pleasures* (1933)

13 I wish I could shimmy like my sister Kate,
She shivers like the jelly on a plate.

Armand J. Piron: 'Shimmy like Kate' (1919)

14 If the Louvre custodian can,
If the Guard Republican can,
If Van Gogh and Matisse and Cézanne can,
Baby, you can can-can too . . .
Lovely Duse in Milan can,
Lucien Guitry and Réjane can,
Sarah Bernhardt upon a divan can,
Baby, you can can-can too.

Cole Porter 1891–1964: 'Can-Can' (1953)

15 [Dancing is] a perpendicular expression of a horizontal desire.

George Bernard Shaw 1856–1950: in *New Statesman* 23 March 1962

16 On the church gate a hand-painted notice with two spelling mistakes announced that owing to the welcome presence of the Redemptorist Fathers in the town there would be no dance on Sunday.

Honor Tracy 1915–89: *Mind You, I've Said Nothing* (1953)

17 'Can you dance?' said the girl. Lancelot gave a short, amused laugh. He was a man who never let his left hip know what his right hip was doing.

P. G. Wodehouse 1881–1975: *Meet Mr Mulliner* (1927)

Death

See also **Epitaphs, Funerals, Last Words, Murder**

❝ *Either he's dead, or my watch has stopped.* ❞
Groucho Marx

1 It's not that I'm afraid to die. I just don't want to be there when it happens.

Woody Allen 1935– : *Death* (1975)

2 *of suicide:*
There have been times when I've thought about it—but with my luck it would probably turn out to be only a temporary solution.

Woody Allen 1935– : attributed; Milton Shulman *It Takes All Sorts* (2003)

3 I don't want to achieve immortality through my work . . . I want to achieve it through not dying.

Woody Allen 1935– : Eric Lax *Woody Allen and his Comedy* (1975)

4 Death has got something to be said for it:
There's no need to get out of bed for it;
Wherever you may be,
They bring it to you, free.

Kingsley Amis 1922–95: 'Delivery
Guaranteed' (1979)

5 Regret to inform you Hand that rocked the cradle kicked
the bucket.

Anonymous: reported telegram; in
Ned Sherrin in his Anecdotage (1993)

6 [Death is] nature's way of telling you to slow down.

Anonymous: American life insurance
proverb, in *Newsweek* 25 April 1960

7 We met . . . Dr Hall in such very deep mourning that
either his mother, his wife, or himself must be dead.

Jane Austen 1775–1817: letter to
Cassandra Austen, 17 May 1799

8 Even death is unreliable: instead of zero it may be some
ghastly hallucination, such as the square root of minus
one.

Samuel Beckett 1906–89: attributed

9 When I came back to Dublin, I was courtmartialled in my
absence and sentenced to death in my absence, so I said
they could shoot me in my absence.

Brendan Behan 1923–64: *Hostage*
(1958)

10 Lord Finchley tried to mend the Electric Light
Himself. It struck him dead: And serve him right!
It is the business of the wealthy man
To give employment to the artisan.

Hilaire Belloc 1870–1953: 'Lord
Finchley' (1911)

11 When I am dead, I hope it may be said:
'His sins were scarlet, but his books were read.'

Hilaire Belloc 1870–1953: 'On His
Books' (1923)

12 What I like about Clive
Is that he is no longer alive.
There is a great deal to be said
For being dead.

Edmund Clerihew Bentley
1875–1956: 'Clive' (1905)

13 I believe in reincarnation, so I've left all my money to
myself.

Tony Blackburn 1943– : in *The Oldie*
May 2003

14 Thou shalt not kill; but need'st not strive
Officiously to keep alive.

Arthur Hugh Clough 1819–61: 'The
Latest Decalogue' (1862)

15 Swans sing before they die: 'twere no bad thing
Should certain persons die before they sing.

Samuel Taylor Coleridge
1772–1834: 'On a Volunteer Singer'
(1834)

16 I'm amazed he was such a good shot.
on being told that his accountant had blown his brains out

Noël Coward 1899–1973: in *Ned
Sherrin's Theatrical Anecdotes* (1991)

17 I read the *Times* and if my name is not in the obits I
proceed to enjoy the day.

Noël Coward 1899–1973: attributed

18 *before his death, Lord Curzon had informed his second wife of
his arrangements for her burial in the family vault at
Kedleston, when he 'placing his hand on one of the niches, said
"This, Gracie dearest, is reserved for you."' In fact he had
already placed in the niche 'a large Foreign Office envelope on
which he had scrawled in blue pencil':*
Reserved for the second Lady Curzon.

Lord Curzon 1859–1925: Harold
Nicolson diary, 13 January 1934

19 He'd make a lovely corpse.

Charles Dickens 1812–70: *Martin
Chuzzlewit* (1844)

20 Can I unmoved see thee dying
On a log,
Expiring frog!

Charles Dickens 1812–70: *Pickwick Papers* (1837)

21 Take away that emblem of mortality.
on being offered an air cushion to sit on, 1881

Benjamin Disraeli 1804–81: Robert Blake *Disraeli* (1966)

22 When I die I want to decompose in a barrel of porter and have it served in all the pubs in Dublin. I wonder would they know it was me?

J. P. Donleavy 1926– : *Ginger Man* (1955)

23 In this world nothing can be said to be certain, except death and taxes.

Benjamin Franklin 1706–90: letter to Jean Baptiste Le Roy, 13 November 1789

24 Bombazine would have shown a deeper sense of her loss.

Elizabeth Gaskell 1810–65: *Cranford* (1853)

25 He makes a very handsome corpse and becomes his coffin prodigiously.

Oliver Goldsmith 1730–74: *The Good-Natured Man* (1768)

26 The babe with a cry brief and dismal,
Fell into the water baptismal;
Ere they gathered its plight,
It had sunk out of sight,
For the depth of the font was abysmal.

Edward Gorey 1925–2000: *The Listing Attic* (1954)

27 'There's been an accident,' they said,
'Your servant's cut in half; he's dead!'
'Indeed!' said Mr Jones, 'and please,
Send me the half that's got my keys.'

Harry Graham 1874–1936: 'Mr Jones' (1899)

28 Billy, in one of his nice new sashes,
Fell in the fire and was burnt to ashes;
Now, although the room grows chilly,
I haven't the heart to poke poor Billy.

Harry Graham 1874–1936: 'Tender-Heartedness' (1899)

29 *Richard Harris, who died of cancer, to diners, while being carried on a stretcher out of the Savoy:*
It was the food. It was the food.

Richard Harris 1930–2002: in *Limerick Leader* (online edition) 7 December 2002

30 Once you're dead, you're made for life.

Jimi Hendrix 1942–70: *c.*1968, attributed; Nigel Rees *Cassell Dictionary of Humorous Quotations* (1999)

31 *during his last illness:*
If Mr Selwyn calls again, show him up: if I am alive I shall be delighted to see him; and if I am dead he would like to see me.

Lord Holland 1705–74: J. H. Jesse *George Selwyn and his Contemporaries* (1844)

32 His death, which happened in his berth,
At forty-odd befell:
They went and told the sexton, and
The sexton tolled the bell.

Thomas Hood 1799–1845: 'Faithless Sally Brown' (1826)

33 I still go up my 44 stairs two at a time, but that is in hopes of dropping dead at the top.

A. E. Housman 1859–1936: letter to Laurence Housman, 9 June 1935

34 At his funeral in Omaha he filled the church to capacity. He was a draw right to the finish.
after the death of the boxer Vince Foster in 1949

Jack Hurley: Jonathon Green and Don Atyeo (eds.) *The Book of Sports Quotes* (1979)

35 I had an interest in death from an early age. It fascinated me. When I heard 'Humpty Dumpty sat on a wall,' I thought, 'Did he fall or was he pushed?'

P. D. James 1920– : in *Paris Review* 1995

36 But there, everything has its drawbacks, as the man said when his mother-in-law died, and they came down upon him for the funeral expenses.

Jerome K. Jerome 1859–1927: *Three Men in a Boat* (1889)

37 Depend upon it, Sir, when a man knows he is to be hanged in a fortnight, it concentrates his mind wonderfully.

Samuel Johnson 1709–84: James Boswell *Life of Samuel Johnson* (1791) 19 September 1777

38 *ex-President Eisenhower's death prevented her photograph appearing on the cover of* Newsweek:
Fourteen heart attacks and he had to die in my week. In MY week.

Janis Joplin 1943–70: in *New Musical Express* 12 April 1969

39 *on how he would kill himself:*
With kindness.

George S. Kaufman 1889–1961: Howard Teichmann *George S. Kaufman* (1973)

40 I detest life-insurance agents; they always argue that I shall some day die, which is not so.

Stephen Leacock 1869–1944: *Literary Lapses* (1910)

41 Death is the most convenient time to tax rich people.

David Lloyd George 1863–1945: in *Lord Riddell's Intimate Diary of the Peace Conference and After, 1918–23* (1933)

42 Alas! Lord and Lady Dalhousie are dead, and buried at last,
Which causes many people to feel a little downcast.

William McGonagall c.1825–1902: 'The Death of Lord and Lady Dalhousie'

43 Beautiful Railway Bridge of the Silv'ry Tay!
Alas, I am very sorry to say
That ninety lives have been taken away
On the last Sabbath day of 1879,
Which will be remembered for a very long time.

William McGonagall c.1825–1902: 'The Tay Bridge Disaster'

44 There is nothing like a morning funeral for sharpening the appetite for lunch.

Arthur Marshall 1910–89: *Life's Rich Pageant* (1984)

45 Either he's dead, or my watch has stopped.

Groucho Marx 1890–1977: in *A Day at the Races* (1937 film; script by Robert Pirosh, George Seaton, and George Oppenheimer)

46 BLUEBOTTLE: You rotten swines. I told you I'd be deaded.

Spike Milligan 1918–2002: *The Hastings Flyer* in *The Goon Show* (BBC radio series) 3 January 1956

47 Death and taxes and childbirth! There's never any convenient time for any of them.

Margaret Mitchell 1900–49: *Gone with the Wind* (1936)

48 Jimmy Hoffa's most valuable contribution to the American labour movement came at the moment he stopped breathing—on July 30th, 1975.

Don E. Moldea: *The Hoffa Wars* (1978)

49 One dies only once, and it's for such a long time!

Molière 1622–73: *Le Dépit amoureux* (performed 1656, published 1662)

50 *on his deathbed, asked by an acquaintance how he was:*
Hovering between wife and death.

James Montgomery: Ulick O'Connor *Oliver St John Gogarty* (1964)

51 *during the Boxer rising it was erroneously reported that those besieged in the Legation quarter of Peking, including the* Times *correspondent Dr Morrison, had been massacred. Morrison cabled the paper:*
Have just read obituary in the Times. Kindly adjust pay to suit.

George Ernest Morrison 1862–1920: Claud Cockburn *In Time of Trouble* (1956); attributed

52 Drink and dance and laugh and lie
Love, the reeling midnight through
For tomorrow we shall die!
(But, alas, we never do.)

Dorothy Parker 1893–1967: 'The Flaw in Paganism' (1937)

53 *on being told by Robert Benchley that Calvin Coolidge had died:*
DOROTHY PARKER: How can they tell?
ROBERT BENCHLEY: He had an erection.

Dorothy Parker 1893–1967: Ned Sherrin in *The Listener* 8 January 1987; Benchley's final remark vouched for by his grandson Peter on the authority of Benchley's widow.

54 Guns aren't lawful;
Nooses give;
Gas smells awful;
You might as well live.

Dorothy Parker 1893–1967: 'Résumé' (1937)

55 Here am I, dying of a hundred good symptoms.

Alexander Pope 1688–1744: to George, Lord Lyttelton, 15 May 1744

56 Not louder shrieks to pitying heav'n are cast,
When husbands or when lapdogs breathe their last.

Alexander Pope 1688–1744: *The Rape of the Lock* (1714)

57 But thousands die, without or this or that,
Die, and endow a college, or a cat.

Alexander Pope 1688–1744: *Epistles to Several Persons* 'To Lord Bathurst' (1733)

58 Luca Brasi sleeps with the fishes.

Mario Puzo 1920–99: *The Godfather* (1972 film); spoken by Richard S. Castellano as Peter Clemenza

59 [Memorial services are the] cocktail parties of the geriatric set.

Ralph Richardson 1902–83: Ruth Dudley Edwards *Harold Macmillan* (1983)

60 The cemetery is a sort of Mayfair of the dead, the most expensive real estate in Buenos Aires.
of the Recoleta Cemetery in Buenos Aires

Robert Robinson 1927– : in *Times* 22 July 1978

61 *the aged President of Magdalen was told of a Fellow's suicide by two colleagues anxious that the news would distress him:*
Don't tell me. Let me guess.

Martin Routh 1755–1854: Dacre Balsdon *Oxford Life* (1957)

62 Waldo is one of those people who would be enormously improved by death.

Saki 1870–1916: *Beasts and Super-Beasts* (1914)

63 Ain't it grand to be blooming well dead?

Leslie Sarony 1897–1985: title of song (1932)

64 The thought of death has now become a part of my life. I read the obituaries every day just for the satisfaction of not seeing my name there.

Neil Simon 1927– : *Last of the Red Hot Lovers* (1970)

65 Well, it only proves what they always say—give the public something they want to see, and they'll come out for it.
on the crowds attending the funeral of the movie tycoon Harry Cohn, 2 March 1958

Red Skelton 1913–97: attributed

66 Death is always a great pity of course but it's not as though the alternative were immortality.

Tom Stoppard 1937– : *Jumpers* (rev. ed. 1986)

67 Early to rise and early to bed makes a male healthy and wealthy and dead.

James Thurber 1894–1961: 'The Shrike and the Chipmunks'; in *New Yorker* 18 February 1939

68 He was just teaching me my death duties.
on her deathbed, having been visited by her solicitor to put her affairs in order

Lady Tree 1863–1937: in *Ned Sherrin in his Anecdotage* (1993)

69 The report of my death was an exaggeration.
usually quoted as, 'Reports of my death have been greatly exaggerated'

Mark Twain 1835–1910: in *New York Journal* 2 June 1897

70 I refused to attend his funeral, but I wrote a very nice letter explaining that I approved of it.
on hearing of the death of a corrupt politician

Mark Twain 1835–1910: James Munson (ed.) *The Sayings of Mark Twain* (1992)

71 *of Truman Capote's death:*
Good career move.

Gore Vidal 1925– : attributed

72 You're here to stay until the rustle in your dying throat relieves you!

H. M. Walker: addressed to Laurel and Hardy in *Beau Hunks* (1931 film; re-named *Beau Chumps* for British audiences)

73 Just think who we'd have been seen dead with!
on discovery that her name, with Noël Coward's, had been on the Nazi blacklist for arrest and probable execution

Rebecca West 1892–1983: postcard to Noël Coward, 1945

74 *at the mention of a huge fee for a surgical operation:*
Ah, well, then, I suppose that I shall have to die beyond my means.

Oscar Wilde 1854–1900: R. H. Sherard *Life of Oscar Wilde* (1906)

75 *of the wallpaper in the room where he was dying:*
One of us must go.

Oscar Wilde 1854–1900: attributed, probably apocryphal

Debt

See also **Money, Poverty**

❝ *If I hadn't my debts I shouldn't have anything to think about.* ❞
Oscar Wilde

1 Cohen owes me ninety-seven dollars.

Irving Berlin 1888–1989: song-title (1913)

2 *on Allied war debts:*
They hired the money, didn't they?

Calvin Coolidge 1872–1933: John H. McKee *Coolidge: Wit and Wisdom* (1933)

3 Any further letters and I shall remove my overdraft.
telegram, c.1959, to his bankers, who had become alarmed at his expensive undergraduate lifestyle

Bobby Corbett 1940–99: in his obituary, *Daily Telegraph* 13 March 1999

4 My feet want to dance in the sun.
My head wants to rest in the shade.
The Lord says, 'Go out and have fun'.
But the Landlord says,
'Your rent ain't paid.'

E. Y. Harburg 1898–1981: 'Necessity' (1947)

5 [My father] taught me two things about bills; always query them and never pay till you have no alternative.

Miles Kington 1941–2008: *Welcome to Kington* (1989)

6 If the spoken word is repeated often enough, it is eventually written and thus made permanent . . . Many a decent man who has written a bad cheque knows the truth of that.

Flann O'Brien 1911–66: *Myles Away from Dublin* (1990)

7 I feel these days like a very large flamingo. No matter what way I turn, there is always a very large bill.

Joseph O'Connor 1963– : *The Secret World of the Irish Male* (1994)

8 The National Debt is a very Good Thing and it would be dangerous to pay it off, for fear of Political Economy.

W. C. Sellar 1898–1951 and **R. J. Yeatman** 1898–1968: *1066 and All That* (1930)

9 One must have some sort of occupation nowadays. If I hadn't my debts I shouldn't have anything to think about.

Oscar Wilde 1854–1900: *A Woman of No Importance* (1893)

Democracy

See also **Government, Politics**

❝ *I never vote for anybody. I always vote against.* ❞
W. C. Fields

1 Elections are won by men and women chiefly because most people vote against somebody rather than for somebody.

Franklin P. Adams 1881–1960: *Nods and Becks* (1944)

2 If the Archangel Gabriel had stood with the name of Winston Churchill, Ken would still have won.
of Ken Livingstone's candidacy as Mayor of London

Jeffrey Archer 1940– : in *Independent on Sunday* 7 May 2000

3 Democracy means government by discussion, but it is only effective if you can stop people talking.

Clement Attlee 1883–1967: speech at Oxford, 14 June 1957

4 A majority is always the best repartee.

Benjamin Disraeli 1804–81: *Tancred* (1847)

5 Hell, I never vote *for* anybody. I always vote *against*.

W. C. Fields 1880–1946: Robert Lewis Taylor *W. C. Fields* (1950)

6 Democracy is the name we give the people whenever we need them.

Robert, Marquis de Flers 1872–1927 and **Armand de Caillavet** 1869–1915: *L'habit vert* (1913)

7 *the personal assistant to the West German Chancellor, on thrills:*
Never mind football! Try parliamentary democracy!

Michael Frayn 1933– : *Democracy* (2003)

8 I always voted at my party's call,
And I never thought of thinking for myself at all.

W. S. Gilbert 1836–1911: *HMS Pinafore* (1878)

9 *on John F. Kennedy's electoral victory in Wisconsin:*
A triumph for democracy. It proves that a millionaire has just as good a chance as anybody else.

Bob Hope 1903–2003: TV programme (1960); William Robert Faith *Bob Hope* (1983)

10 Democracy is the theory that the common people know what they want, and deserve to get it good and hard.

H. L. Mencken 1880–1956: *A Little Book in C major* (1916)

11 Under democracy one party always devotes its energies to trying to prove that the other party is unfit to rule—and both commonly succeed and are right.

H. L. Mencken 1880–1956: *Minority Report* (1956)

12 Every government is a parliament of whores. The trouble is, in a democracy the whores are us.

P. J. O'Rourke 1947– : *Parliament of Whores* (1991)

13 All animals are equal but some animals are more equal than others.

George Orwell 1903–50: *Animal Farm* (1945)

14 *on the death of a supporter of Proportional Representation:*
He has joined what even he would admit to be the majority.

John Sparrow 1906–92: J. A. Gere and John Sparrow (eds.) *Geoffrey Madan's Notebooks* (1981)

15 It's not the voting that's democracy, it's the counting.

Tom Stoppard 1937– : *Jumpers* (1972)

16 Democracy is the recurrent suspicion that more than half of the people are right more than half of the time.

E. B. White 1899–1985: in *New Yorker* 3 July 1944

17 Democracy means simply the bludgeoning of the people by the people for the people.

Oscar Wilde 1854–1900: *Sebastian Melmoth* (1891)

18 *a voter canvassed by Wilkes had declared that he would sooner vote for the devil:*
And if your friend is not standing?

John Wilkes 1727–97: Raymond Postgate 'That Devil Wilkes' (1956 rev. ed.)

Description

66 *Looking like a brown condom full of walnuts.* 99

Clive James

1 Though I yield to no one in my admiration for Mr Coolidge, I do wish he did not look as if he had been weaned on a pickle.

Anonymous: remark recorded in Alice Roosevelt Longworth *Crowded Hours* (1933)

2 Diana Manners has no heart but her brains are in the right place.

Cyril Asquith 1890–1954: J. A. Gere and John Sparrow (eds.) *Geoffrey Madan's Notebooks* (1981)

3 *after a party given by Dorothy Parker:*
The less I behave like Whistler's Mother the night before, the more I look like her the morning after.

Tallulah Bankhead 1903–68: R. E. Drennan *Wit's End* (1973)

4 About as cuddly as a cornered ferret.
of Anne Robinson

Lynn Barber 1944– : in *Times* 27 October 2001

5 His smile bathed us like warm custard.

Basil Boothroyd 1910–88: *Let's Move House* (1977)

6 A high altar on the move.
of Edith Sitwell

Elizabeth Bowen 1899–1973: V. Glendinning *Edith Sitwell* (1981)

7 Damn description, it is always disgusting.

Lord Byron 1788–1824: letter 6 August 1809

8 What can you do with a man who looks like a female llama surprised when bathing?
of Charles de Gaulle

Winston Churchill 1874–1965: in conversation, c.1944; David Fraser *Alanbrooke* (1982)

9 The effect is of a Womble taking Cerberus for a walk.
of Roy Hattersley and his dog Buster

Will Cohn: interview in *Daily Telegraph* 19 September 1998

10 Two bursts in a sofa.
of a lady spectator at Wimbledon with pronouncedly hirsute armpits

Bobby Corbett 1940–99: in his obituary, *Daily Telegraph* 13 March 1999

11 The Henry Fondas lay on the evening like a damp mackintosh.

Noël Coward 1899–1973: diary, 8 May 1960

12 Like the silver plate on a coffin.
describing Robert Peel's smile

John Philpot Curran 1750–1817: quoted by Daniel O'Connell, House of Commons 26 February 1835

13 A day away from Tallulah is like a month in the country.

Howard Dietz 1896–1983: *Dancing in the Dark* (1974)

14 The ministers [on the Treasury Bench] reminded me of one of those marine landscapes not very uncommon on the coast of South America. You behold a range of exhausted volcanoes. Not a flame flickers on a single pallid crest.

Benjamin Disraeli 1804–81: speech at Manchester, 3 April 1872

15 Monsignor was forty-four then, and bustling—a trifle too stout for symmetry, with hair the colour of spun gold, and a brilliant, enveloping personality. When he came into a room clad in his full purple regalia from thatch to toe, he resembled a Turner sunset.

F. Scott Fitzgerald 1896–1940: *This Side of Paradise* (1921)

16 You are so graceful, have you wings?
You have a faceful of nice things
You have no speaking voice, dear . . .
With every word it sings.

Lorenz Hart 1895–1943: 'Thou Swell' (1927)

17 *of Arnold Schwarzenegger:*
I once described him as looking like a brown condom full of walnuts.

Clive James 1939– : in *Daily Mail* 20 August 2003

18 A man who so much resembled a Baked Alaska—sweet, warm and gungy on the outside, hard and cold within.
of C. P. Snow

Francis King 1923– : *Yesterday Came Suddenly* (1993)

19 His appearance with his large features and rich mane of hair suggested the attempt of some archaic sculptor only acquainted with sheep to achieve a lion by hearsay.

Osbert Lancaster 1908–86: *All Done From Memory* (1953)

20 The newspapers say that long streamy flakes of music fall from his string, interspersed with luminous points of sound which ascend the air and appear like stars. This eloquence is quite beyond me.
of Paganini

Lord Macaulay 1800–59: letter, 1831

21 [He looks like] an explosion in a pubic hair factory.
of Paul Johnson

Jonathan Miller 1934– : Alan Watkins *Brief Lives* (1982)

22 Her face showed the kind of ferocious disbelief with which Goneril must have taken the news that her difficult old father King Lear had decided to retire and move in with her.

Frank Muir 1920–98: *The Walpole Orange* (1993)

23 Rudyard Kipling's eyebrows are very odd indeed! They curl up black and furious like the moustache of a Neapolitan tenor.

Harold Nicolson 1886–1968: diary 8 January 1930

24 The beach was almost deserted. The tide was out. Turnstones were turning stones. Oystercatchers were catching oysters. In the marshalling yards, shunting engines were shunting and marshalling.

David Nobbs 1935– : *Going Gently* (2000)

25 The place smelt of apple-scented air freshener, not like apples, but like a committee's idea of what apples smell like.

Joseph O'Connor 1963– : *Cowboys and Indians* (1992)

26 Buckingham Palace looked a vast doll's house that some bullying skinhead big brother had kicked down the Mall.

Joseph O'Connor 1963– : *Cowboys and Indians* (1992)

27 The butler who answered the door—and he took his time about it—looked like a Road Company Robert Morley at the Paper Mill Playhouse.

S. J. Perelman 1904–79: 'Call Me Monty and Grovel Freely'

28 A rose-red sissy half as old as time.

William Plomer 1903–73: 'Playboy of the Demi-World: 1938' (1945)

29 The Cavaliers (Wrong but Wromantic) and the Roundheads (Right but Repulsive).

W. C. Sellar 1898–1951 and **R. J. Yeatman** 1898–1968: *1066 and All That* (1930)

30 Hotter than Uncle Bud's pants on lesbian mud-wrestling night.

Mark Steyn: in *Spectator* 2 October 1999

31 I don't think I have ever seen a Silver Band so nonplussed. It was as though a bevy of expectant wolves had overtaken a sleigh and found no Russian peasant on board.

P. G. Wodehouse 1881–1975: *Uncle Dynamite* (1948)

32 I turned to Aunt Agatha, whose demeanour was now rather like that of one who, picking daisies on the railway, has just caught the down express in the small of the back.

P. G. Wodehouse 1881–1975: *The Inimitable Jeeves* (1923)

33 She fitted into my biggest armchair as if it had been built round her by someone who knew they were wearing armchairs tight about the hips that season.

P. G. Wodehouse 1881–1975: *My Man Jeeves* (1919)

34 Roderick Spode? Big chap with a small moustache and the sort of eye that can open an oyster at sixty paces?

P. G. Wodehouse 1881–1975: *The Code of the Woosters* (1938)

Despair See **Hope and Despair**

Diaries

❝ *Something sensational to read in the train.* ❞
Oscar Wilde

1 A page of my Journal is like a cake of portable soup. A little may be diffused into a considerable portion.

James Boswell 1740–95: *Journal of a Tour to the Hebrides* (1785)

2 What is more dull than a discreet diary? One might just as well have a discreet soul.

Chips Channon 1897–1958: diary, 26 July 1935

3 It is a fair proposition, I think, that the diaries of men who enjoy their own nudity ought not to be published unless they are as interesting as Pepys. Otherwise it is really too distressing for the observer.

Harold Laski 1893–1950: letter to Oliver Wendell Holmes, 23 October 1927

4 To write a diary every day is like returning to one's own vomit.

Enoch Powell 1912–98: interview in *Sunday Times* 6 November 1977

5 I have decided to keep a full journal, in the hope that my life will perhaps seem more interesting when it is written down.

Sue Townsend 1946– : *Adrian Mole: The Wilderness Years* (1993)

6 I always say, keep a diary and some day it'll keep you.

Mae West 1892–1980: *Every Day's a Holiday* (1937 film)

7 I never travel without my diary. One should always have something sensational to read in the train.

Oscar Wilde 1854–1900: *The Importance of Being Earnest* (1895)

Dictionaries

66 *Defining what is unknown in terms of something equally unknown.* 99
Flann O'Brien

1 You can file Madonna's quote in the dictionary of clichés under 'pot and kettle'.
response to her reported comment that he and Jennifer Lopez had courted media attention

Ben Affleck 1972– : in *Sunday Times* 20 June 2004 'Talking Heads'

2 Big dictionaries are nothing but storerooms with infrequently visited and dusty corners.

Richard W. Bailey 1939– : *Images of English* (1991)

3 They are strange beings, these lexicographers.

John Brown 1810–82: *Horae Subsecivae* (rev. ed. 1884)

4 Like Webster's Dictionary, we're Morocco bound.

Johnny Burke 1908–64: *The Road to Morocco* (1942 film), title song

5 The greatest masterpiece in literature is only a dictionary out of order.

Jean Cocteau 1889–1963: attributed

6 The Dictionary has not attempted to rival some of its predecessors in deliberate humour . . . Such rare occasions for a smile as may be found in it are unintentional.

W. A. Craigie 1867–1967: of the *New English Dictionary*; in *The Periodical* 15 February 1928

7 Short dictionaries should be improved because they are intended for people who actually need help.

William Empson 1906–84: attributed

8 *Lexicographer.* A writer of dictionaries, a harmless drudge.

Samuel Johnson 1709–84: *A Dictionary of the English Language* (1755)

9 *of his coinage of the phrase 'life's rich pageant':*
As far as I know, I didn't borrow the words from anywhere else and no less a body than the compilers of *The Oxford Dictionary of Quotations* have since taken an interest in the matter. They have finally decided that the phrase, such as it is, was my own invention and it is to be credited to me. Let me assure you that this small feather in my cap has not gone, so to speak, to my head.

Arthur Marshall 1910–89: *Life's Rich Pageant* (1984)

10 A bad business, opening dictionaries; a thing I very rarely do. I try to make it a rule never to open my mouth, dictionaries, or hucksters' shops.

Flann O'Brien 1911–66: *The Best of Myles* (1968)

11 I suppose that so long as there are people in the world, they will publish dictionaries defining what is unknown in terms of something equally unknown.

Flann O'Brien 1911–66: *Myles Away from Dublin* (1990)

12 *Henry Liddell (1811–98) and Robert Scott (1811–87) were co-authors of the* Greek Lexicon *(1843), Liddell being in the habit of ascribing to his co-author usages which he criticized in his pupils, and which they said that they had culled from the* Lexicon:

Edward Waterfield: L. E. Tanner *Westminster School: A History* (1934)

Two men wrote a lexicon, Liddell and Scott;
Some parts were clever, but some parts were not.
Hear, all ye learned, and read me this riddle,
How the wrong part wrote Scott, and the right part wrote
    Liddell.

13 I've been in *Who's Who*, and I know what's what, but it'll be the first time I ever made the dictionary.
    on having an inflatable life jacket named after her

Mae West 1892–1980: letter to the RAF, early 1940s

Diets

66 *You die of a heart attack but so what? You die thin.* 99

Bob Geldof

1 In Lent she ate onion soup and gave up drink; but otherwise she must have drunk the maximum compatible with survival and sanity.
    of the television cook, Jennifer Paterson

Anonymous: obituary of Jennifer Paterson, in *Daily Telegraph* 11 August 1999

2 I'm afraid I'm addicted to fat and love British beef. BSE holds no terror for me because . . . I am as likely to get it as win the National Lottery.
    on her main difficulty in following a healthy diet

Joan Bakewell 1933– : in *Independent* 30 August 1997 'Quote Unquote'

3 You die of a heart attack but so what? You die thin.
    on the Atkins diet

Bob Geldof 1954– : in *Independent* 23 August 2003

4 I'm of the pie-eaters' liberation front. I'm fat and proud to be fat.

Boris Johnson 1964– : at the Conservative party conference; in *Independent* 5 October 2006

5 I feel about airplanes the way I feel about diets. It seems to me that they are wonderful things for other people to go on.

Jean Kerr 1923–2003: *The Snake Has All the Lines* (1958)

6 Life, if you're fat, is a minefield—you have to pick your way, otherwise you blow up.

Miriam Margolyes 1941– : in *Observer* 9 June 1991

7 Is Elizabeth Taylor fat? Her favourite food is seconds.

Joan Rivers 1933– : attributed

8 Free your mind, and your bottom will follow.

Sarah, Duchess of York 1959– : slimming advice, 2001

Diplomacy

See also **Politics**

66 *Forever poised between a cliché and an indiscretion.* 99

Harold Macmillan

1 The Prime Minister rather enjoyed being led up the garden path by the Taoiseach, but she didn't much like the garden when she got there.
    on negotiations between Margaret Thatcher and Charles Haughey

Anonymous: unnamed civil servant, in *Daily Telegraph* 14 August 1993

2 *on the Council of Europe:*
If you open that Pandora's Box, you never know what Trojan 'orses will jump out.

> **Ernest Bevin** 1881–1951: Roderick Barclay *Ernest Bevin and the Foreign Office* (1975)

3 We exchanged many frank words in our respective languages.

> **Peter Cook** 1937–95: *Beyond the Fringe* (1961 revue)

4 American *diplomacy*. It's like watching somebody trying to do joinery with a chainsaw.

> **James Hamilton-Paterson** 1941– : *Griefwork* (1993)

5 Kissinger brought peace to Vietnam the same way Napoleon brought peace to Europe: by losing.

> **Joseph Heller** 1923–99: *Good as Gold* (1979)

6 Diplomacy—lying in state.

> **Oliver Herford** 1863–1935: Laurence J. Peter (ed.) *Quotations for Our Time* (1977)

7 There cannot be a crisis next week. My schedule is already full.

> **Henry Kissinger** 1923– : in *New York Times Magazine* 1 June 1969

8 *on the life of a Foreign Secretary:*
Forever poised between a cliché and an indiscretion.

> **Harold Macmillan** 1894–1986: in *Newsweek* 30 April 1956

9 I liken the French/British relationship to a very old married couple who often think of killing each other but would never dream of divorce.
> *on the revelation that in 1956 the French Prime Minister Guy Mollet suggested to Anthony Eden a union between the United Kingdom and France*

> **Denis MacShane** 1948– : in *Times* (online edition) 15 January 2007

10 *on the Hoare-Laval pact:*
Sam Hoare was certified by his doctors as unfit for public business, and on his way to the sanatorium he stops off in Paris and allows Laval to do him down.

> **Harold Nicolson** 1886–1968: diary 12 December 1935

11 The French are masters of 'the dog ate my homework' school of diplomatic relations.

> **P. J. O'Rourke** 1947– : *Holidays in Hell* (1988)

12 Wherever there is suffering, injustice and oppression, the Americans will show up, six months late, and bomb the country next to where it's happening.

> **P. J. O'Rourke** 1947– : *Peace Kills* (2004)

13 Lord Palmerston, with characteristic levity had once said that only three men in Europe had ever understood [the Schleswig-Holstein question], and of these the Prince Consort was dead, a Danish statesman (unnamed) was in an asylum, and he himself had forgotten it.

> **Lord Palmerston** 1784–1865: R. W. Seton-Watson *Britain in Europe 1789–1914* (1937)

14 I was wisely seen as unsuitable.
> *admitting he was once rejected by the Diplomatic Corps*

> **Jeremy Paxman** 1950– : in *Observer* 2 May 1999 'Sayings of the Week'

15 The chief distinction of a diplomat is that he can say no in such a way that it sounds like yes.

> **Lester Bowles Pearson** 1897–1972: a Canadian Prime Minister's view; Geoffrey Pearson *Seize the Day* (1993)

16 In return for a handsomely bound facsimile of Palestrina's music, the Vicar of God was rewarded with a signed photograph of the Grocer and a gramophone record of himself conducting an orchestra.
> *of a meeting between the Pope and Edward Heath*

> **Nicholas Shakespeare** 1957– : in *The Spectator* 19/26 December 1992

17 There is a story that when Mrs Thatcher first met Gorbachev he gave her a ball-point and she offered him Labour-voting Scotland.

Nicholas Shakespeare 1957– : in *The Spectator* 19/26 December 1992

18 A diplomat these days is nothing but a head-waiter who's allowed to sit down occasionally.

Peter Ustinov 1921–2004: *Romanoff and Juliet* (1956)

19 An ambassador is an honest man sent to lie abroad for the good of his country.

Henry Wotton 1568–1639: written in the album of Christopher Fleckmore in 1604

Discontent See **Satisfaction and Discontent**

Dogs

❝ A door is what a dog is perpetually on the wrong side of. **❞**
Ogden Nash

1 I look like a young wolf—cuddly in a frightening sort of way.
   Buster's view of himself

Roy Hattersley 1932– : *Buster's Diaries* (1998)

2 Dogs who earn their living by appearing in television commercials in which they constantly and aggressively demand meat should remember that in at least one Far Eastern country they *are* meat.

Fran Lebowitz 1946– : *Social Studies* (1981)

3 A door is what a dog is perpetually on the wrong side of.

Ogden Nash 1902–71: 'A Dog's Best Friend is his Illiteracy' (1953)

4 I am his Highness' dog at Kew;
Pray, tell me sir, whose dog are you?

Alexander Pope 1688–1744: 'Epigram Engraved on the Collar of a Dog which I gave to his Royal Highness' (1738)

5 That indefatigable and unsavoury engine of pollution, the dog.

John Sparrow 1906–92: letter to *Times* 30 September 1975

6 The more one gets to know of men, the more one values dogs.

A. Toussenel 1803–85: *L'Esprit des bêtes* (1847); attributed to Mme Roland in the form 'The more I see of men, the more I like dogs'

7 They say a reasonable amount o' fleas is good fer a dog— keeps him from broodin' over bein' a dog, mebbe.

Edward Noyes Westcott 1846–98: *David Harum* (1898)

8 The Aberdeen terrier gave me an unpleasant look and said something under its breath in Gaelic.

P. G. Wodehouse 1881–1975: *The Code of the Woosters* (1938)

Doubt See **Certainty and Doubt**

Dreams See **Sleep and Dreams**

Dress

❝ *High heels that would have broken the heart of John Calvin.* ❞

Stephen Leacock

1 I had spent the whole of my savings . . . on a suit for the wedding—a remarkable piece of apparel with lapels that had been modelled on the tail fins of a 1957 Coupe de Ville and trousers so copiously flared that when I walked you didn't see my legs move.

Bill Bryson 1951– : *Neither Here Nor There* (1991)

2 You've got so much ice on your hands I could skate on them.
   to Liberace

John Curry 1949–94: Ned Sherrin *Cutting Edge* (1984)

3 *to Sir Frederick Ponsonby, who had proposed accompanying him in a tail-coat:*
I thought everyone must know that a *short* jacket is always worn with a silk hat at a private view in the morning.

Edward VII 1841–1910: Philip Magnus *Edward VII* (1964)

4 *when Lord Harris appeared at Ascot in a brown bowler:*
Goin' rattin', 'Arris?

Edward VII 1841–1910: Michael Hill *Right Royal Remarks* (2003)

5 When he buys his ties he has to ask if gin will make them run.

F. Scott Fitzgerald 1896–1940: *Notebooks* (1978)

6 *Lord Charles Russell had appeared incorrectly dressed at a Court Ball:*
Good evening, sir, I suppose you are the regimental doctor.

George IV 1762–1830: Michael Hill (ed.) *Right Royal Remarks* (2003)

7 *Dame Edna to Judy Steel:*
Tell me the history of that frock, Judy. It's obviously an old favourite. You were wise to remove the curtain rings.

Barry Humphries 1934– : *Another Audience with Dame Edna* (TV, 1984); Nigel Rees (ed.) *Cassell Dictionary of Humorous Quotations* (1999)

8 You should never have your best trousers on when you go out to fight for freedom and truth.

Henrik Ibsen 1828–1906: *An Enemy of the People* (1882)

9 A silk dress in four sections, and shoes with high heels that would have broken the heart of John Calvin.

Stephen Leacock 1869–1944: *Arcadian Adventures with the Idle Rich* (1914)

10 I am not . . . totally unreceptive to colour providing it makes its appearance quietly, deferentially, and without undue fanfare.

Fran Lebowitz 1946– : *Metropolitan Life* (1978)

11 My little rebellion was to have my tie loose, with the top button of my shirt undone, but Paul'd always come up to me and put it straight.

John Lennon 1940–80: *John Lennon: in His Own Words* (1980)

12 *of 'Fred Fernackerpan, a Mystery Goblin', who walked about the town with his trousers deployed à la Grand Old Duke of York:*
And when they were up they were up
And when they were down they were down
And when they were only half way up
He was arrested.

Spike Milligan 1918–2002: Alexander Games *The Essential Spike Milligan* (2002)

13 *on being asked what she wore in bed:*
Chanel No. 5.

Marilyn Monroe 1926–62: Pete Martin *Marilyn Monroe* (1956)

14 The officers of this branch of the Force [the Obscene Publications Squad at Scotland Yard] have a discouraging club tie, on which a book is depicted being cut in half by a larger pair of scissors.

John Mortimer 1923–2009: *Clinging to the Wreckage* (1982)

15 The only really firm rule of taste about cross dressing is that neither sex should ever wear anything they haven't yet figured out how to go to the bathroom in.

P. J. O'Rourke 1947– : *Modern Manners* (1984)

16 Fur is a subject that makes sensitive toes curl in their leather shoes.
  introducing a discussion on fur coats

Jeremy Paxman 1950– : in *Mail on Sunday* 13 February 2000 'Quotes of the Week'

17 My wife liked the costume. She asked me to bring it home.
  on his costume as Achilles in the film Troy

Brad Pitt 1963– : in CBS News (online ed.) 14 May 2004

18 We know Jesus can't have been English. He is always wearing sandals, but never with socks.

Linda Smith 1958–2006: in *Independent* 25 August 1994

19 She wears her clothes, as if they were thrown on her with a pitchfork.

Jonathan Swift 1667–1745: *Polite Conversation* (1738)

20 She wore far too much rouge last night, and not quite enough clothes. That is always a sign of despair in a woman.

Oscar Wilde 1854–1900: *An Ideal Husband* (1895)

Drink

66 *Some weasel took the cork out of my lunch.* 99
W. C. Fields

1 R-E-M-O-R-S-E!
Those dry Martinis did the work for me;
Last night at twelve I felt immense,
Today I feel like thirty cents.
My eyes are bleared, my coppers hot,
I'll try to eat, but I cannot.
It is no time for mirth and laughter,
The cold, grey dawn of the morning after.

George Ade 1866–1944: *The Sultan of Sulu* (1903)

2 Let's get out of these wet clothes and into a dry Martini.

Anonymous: line coined in the 1920s by Robert Benchley's press agent and adopted by Mae West in *Every Day's a Holiday* (1937 film)

3 Somewhere in the limbo which divides perfect sobriety from mild intoxication.

Cyril Asquith 1890–1954: J. A. Gere and John Sparrow (eds.) *Geoffrey Madan's Notebooks* (1981)

4 At Dirty Dick's and Sloppy Joe's
We drank our liquor straight,
Some went upstairs with Margery,
And some, alas, with Kate.

W. H. Auden 1907–73: 'The Sea and the Mirror' (1944)

5 I saw a notice which said 'Drink Canada Dry' and I've just started.

Brendan Behan 1923–64: attributed (probably not original); Nigel Rees *Cassell Dictionary of Humorous Quotations* (1999)

6 *asked to devise an advertising slogan for Guinness:*
Guinness makes you drunk.

Brendan Behan 1923–64: attributed, perhaps apocryphal

7 *on being told that the particular drink he was consuming was slow poison:*
So who's in a hurry?

Robert Benchley 1889–1945: Nathaniel Benchley *Robert Benchley* (1955)

8 Often Daddy sat up very late working on a case of Scotch.

Robert Benchley 1889–1945: *Pluck and Luck* (1925)

9 An admirable man, who puts down half a bottle of whisky a day and has two convictions for drunken driving, but otherwise a pillar of society.

Alan Bennett 1934– : *Getting On* (1972)

10 One evening in October, when I was one-third sober,
An' taking home a 'load' with manly pride;
My poor feet began to stutter, so I lay down in the gutter,
And a pig came up an' lay down by my side;
Then we sang 'It's all fair weather when good fellows get together,'
Till a lady passing by was heard to say:
'You can tell a man who "boozes" by the company he chooses'
And the pig got up and slowly walked away.

Benjamin Hapgood Burt 1880–1950: 'The Pig Got Up and Slowly Walked Away' (1933)

11 'Take some more tea,' the March Hare said to Alice, very earnestly. 'I've had nothing yet,' Alice replied in an offended tone, 'so I can't take more.' 'You mean you can't take *less*,' said the Hatter: 'it's very easy to take *more* than nothing.'

Lewis Carroll 1832–98: *Alice's Adventures in Wonderland* (1865)

12 Tea, although an Oriental,
Is a gentleman at least.
Cocoa is a cad and coward
Cocoa is a vulgar beast.

G. K. Chesterton 1874–1936: 'A Song of Right and Wrong' (1914)

13 I have taken more out of alcohol than alcohol has taken out of me.

Winston Churchill 1874–1965: Quentin Reynolds *By Quentin Reynolds* (1964)

14 *on being invited by a friend to dine at a Middle Eastern restaurant:*
The aftertaste of foreign food spoils the clean, pure flavour of gin for hours.

Eddie Condon 1905–73: Bill Crow *Jazz Anecdotes* (1990)

15 *when seriously ill and given a blood transfusion:*
This must be Fats Waller's blood. I'm getting high.

Eddie Condon 1905–73: Bill Crow *Jazz Anecdotes* (1990)

16 Take the juice of two quarts of whisky.
recommended hangover cure

Eddie Condon 1905–73: in *New York Sunday News* 10 June 1951

17 Sure I eat what I advertise. Sure I eat Wheaties for breakfast. A good bowl of Wheaties with Bourbon can't be beat.
a baseball star's comment

Dizzy Dean: in *Guardian* 23 December 1978 'Sports Quotes of the Year'

18 Therefore I *do* require it, which I makes confession, to be brought reg'lar and draw'd mild.

Charles Dickens 1812–70: *Martin Chuzzlewit* (1844)

19 'Mrs Harris,' I says, 'leave the bottle on the chimley-piece, and don't ask me to take none, but let me put my lips to it when I am so dispoged.'

Charles Dickens 1812–70: *Martin Chuzzlewit* (1844)

20 There is wan thing, an' on'y wan thing, to be said in favour iv dhrink, an' that is that it has caused manny a lady to be loved that otherwise might've died single.

Finley Peter Dunne 1867–1936: *Mr. Dooley Says* (1910)

21 A man shouldn't fool with booze until he's fifty; then he's a damn fool if he doesn't.

William Faulkner 1897–1962: James M. Webb and A. Wigfall Green *William Faulkner of Oxford* (1965)

22 Some weasel took the cork out of my lunch.

W. C. Fields 1880–1946: *You Can't Cheat an Honest Man* (1939 film)

23 I always keep a supply of stimulant handy in case I see a snake—which I also keep handy.

W. C. Fields 1880–1946: Corey Ford *Time of Laughter* (1970); attributed

24 A woman drove me to drink and I never even had the courtesy to thank her.

W. C. Fields 1880–1946: attributed

25 Best while you have it use your breath,
There is no drinking after death.

John Fletcher 1579–1625: *The Bloody Brother, or Rollo Duke of Normandy* (with Ben Jonson and others, performed c.1616)

26 And he that will go to bed sober,
Falls with the leaf still in October.

John Fletcher 1579–1625: *The Bloody Brother, or Rollo Duke of Normandy* (with Ben Jonson and others, performed c.1616)

27 There is no such thing as a small whisky.

Oliver St John Gogarty 1878–1957: attributed

28 From the bathing machine came a din
As of jollification within;
It was heard far and wide,
And the incoming tide
Had a definite flavour of gin.

Edward Gorey 1925–2000: *The Listing Attic* (1954)

29 The House of Lords is sitting in its judicial capacity this afternoon, and while I may be drunk as a lord I must be sober as a judge.
refusing another drink from the political journalist Robin Oakley

Lord Hailsham 1907–2001: anecdote; in *Spectator* 5 April 2003

30 Licker talks mighty loud w'en it git loose fum de jug.

Joel Chandler Harris 1848–1908: *Uncle Remus: His Songs and His Sayings* (1880) 'Plantation Proverbs'

31 I felt that the assortment of tablets that I had been given may have been mis-prescribed, since they seemed to interfere with the pleasant effects of alcohol. In the interests of my health, therefore, I stopped taking them.

Barry Humphries 1934– : *More Please* (1992)

32 We drink one another's healths, and spoil our own.

Jerome K. Jerome 1859–1927: *Idle Thoughts of an Idle Fellow* (1886)

33 Claret is the liquor for boys; port, for men; but he who aspires to be a hero (smiling) must drink brandy.

Samuel Johnson 1709–84: James Boswell *Life of Samuel Johnson* (1791) 7 April 1779

34 When I makes tea I makes tea, as old mother Grogan said. And when I makes water I makes water . . . *Begob, ma'am,* says Mrs Cahill, *God send you don't make them in the one pot.*

James Joyce 1882–1941: *Ulysses* (1922)

35 The Lord above made liquor for temptation
To see if man could turn away from sin.
The Lord above made liquor for temptation—but
With a little bit of luck,
With a little bit of luck,
When temptation comes you'll give right in!

Alan Jay Lerner 1918–86: 'With a Little Bit of Luck' (1956)

36 I don't drink liquor. I don't like it. It makes me feel good.

Oscar Levant 1906–72: in *Time* 5 May 1958

37 Heineken refreshes the parts other beers cannot reach.

Terry Lovelock: slogan for Heineken lager, 1975 onwards

38 Love makes the world go round? Not at all. Whisky makes it go round twice as fast.

Compton Mackenzie 1883–1972: *Whisky Galore* (1947)

39 Prohibition makes you want to cry into your beer and denies you the beer to cry into.

Don Marquis 1878–1937: *Sun Dial Time* (1936)

40 You're not drunk if you can lie on the floor without holding on.

Dean Martin 1917– : Paul Dickson *Official Rules* (1978)

41 I'm ombibulous. I drink every known alcoholic drink, and enjoy them all.

H. L. Mencken 1880–1956: attributed

42 If one glass of stout on a Sunday night is not enough, his spiritual home is the bodega.

J. B. Morton 1893–1975: M. Frayn *The Best of Beachcomber* (1963)

43 Candy
Is dandy
But liquor
Is quicker.

Ogden Nash 1902–71: 'Reflections on Ice-breaking' (1931)

44 *on the water content of a glass of whiskey:*
True, it is nearly impossible to avoid absorbing water in one form or another. But are you quite sane to be paying four shillings for a modest glasheen of it?

Flann O'Brien 1911–66: *Myles Away from Dublin* (1990)

45 Sometimes I have a sherry before dinner.
a notable understatement

Charlie Parker 1920–55: Bill Crow *Jazz Anecdotes* (1990)

46 You can always tell that the crash is coming when I start getting tender about Our Dumb Friends. Three highballs and I think I'm St Francis of Assisi.

Dorothy Parker 1893–1967: *Here Lies* (1939)

47 One more drink and I'd have been under the host.

Dorothy Parker 1893–1967: Howard Teichmann *George S. Kaufman* (1973)

48 So make it another old-fashioned, please.
Leave out the cherry,
Leave out the orange,
Leave out the bitters,
Just make it a straight rye!

Cole Porter 1891–1964: 'Make it Another Old-Fashioned, Please' (1940)

49 Look here, Steward, if this is coffee, I want tea; but if this is tea, then I wish for coffee.

Punch 1841–1992: vol. 123 (1902)

50 And the sooner the tea's out of the way, the sooner we can get out the gin, eh?

Henry Reed 1914–86: *Private Life of Hilda Tablet* (1954 radio play)

51 We want the finest wines available to humanity. And we want them here, and we want them now!

Bruce Robinson 1946– : *Withnail and I* (1987 film), spoken by Richard E. Grant as Withnail

52 Doth it not show vilely in me to desire small beer?

William Shakespeare 1564–1616: *Henry IV, Part 2* (1597)

53 PORTER: Drink, sir, is a great provoker of three things.
MACDUFF: What three things does drink especially
provoke?
PORTER: Marry, sir, nose-painting, sleep, and urine.
Lechery, sir, it provokes, and unprovokes; it provokes
the desire, but it takes away the performance.

William Shakespeare 1564–1616:
Macbeth (1606)

54 Alcohol . . . enables Parliament to do things at eleven at
night that no sane person would do at eleven in the
morning.

George Bernard Shaw 1856–1950:
Major Barbara (1907)

55 Gin was mother's milk to her.

George Bernard Shaw 1856–1950:
Pygmalion (1916)

56 A bumper of good liquor
Will end a contest quicker
Than justice, judge, or vicar.

Richard Brinsley Sheridan
1751–1816: *The Duenna* (1775)

57 But I'm not so think as you drunk I am.

J. C. Squire 1884–1958: 'Ballade of
Soporific Absorption' (1931)

58 There are two things that will be believed of any man
whatsoever, and one of them is that he has taken to drink.

Booth Tarkington 1869–1946:
Penrod (1914)

59 [An alcoholic:] A man you don't like who drinks as much
as you do.

Dylan Thomas 1914–53: Constantine
Fitzgibbon *Life of Dylan Thomas*
(1965)

60 *of Edvard Grieg:*
Checking into the Betty Fjord Clinic.

Dick Vosburgh 1929–2007 and **Denis
King**: *Beauty and the Beards* (2001)

61 What have you been doing in my absinthe?

Dick Vosburgh 1929–2007: *A Saint
She Ain't* (1999)

62 I have a rare intolerance to herbs which means I can only
drink fermented liquids, such as gin.

Julie Walters 1950– : in *Observer* 14
March 1999 'Sayings of the Week'

63 It was my Uncle George who discovered that alcohol was a
food well in advance of medical thought.

P. G. Wodehouse 1881–1975: *The
Inimitable Jeeves* (1923)

64 At the present moment, the whole Fleet's lit up. When I
say 'lit up', I mean lit up by fairy lamps.
*engaged to make a live outside broadcast of the Spithead
Review, Woodrooffe was so overcome by his reunion with
many old Naval colleagues that the celebrations sabotaged
his ability to commentate*

Thomas Woodrooffe 1899–1978:
reporting on the Spithead Review, 20
May 1937

Drugs

❝ I used to be a laboratory myself once. ❞
Keith Richards

1 LSD? Nothing much happened, but I did get the distinct
impression that some birds were trying to communicate
with me.

W. H. Auden 1907–73: George
Plimpton (ed.) *The Writer's Chapbook*
(1989)

2 Cocaine habit-forming? Of course not. I ought to know.
I've been using it for years.

Tallulah Bankhead 1903–68: *Tallulah*
(1952)

3 I'll die young, but it's like kissing God.
on his drug addiction

Lenny Bruce 1925–66: attributed

4 I experimented with marijuana a time or two. And I didn't like it, and I didn't inhale.

Bill Clinton 1946– : in *Washington Post* 30 March 1992

5 *warning his young son John to avoid opium on account of its 'terrible binding effect'*
Have you ever seen the pictures of the wretched poet Coleridge? He smoked opium. Take a look at Coleridge, he was green about the gills and a stranger to the lavatory.

Clifford Mortimer: John Mortimer *Clinging to the Wreckage* (1982)

6 Drugs have taught an entire generation of English kids the metric system.

P. J. O'Rourke 1947– : *Modern Manners* (1984, UK ed.)

7 Sure thing, man. I used to be a laboratory myself once.
on being asked to autograph a fan's school chemistry book

Keith Richards 1943– : in *Independent on Sunday* 7 August 1994

8 Reality is a crutch for people who can't cope with drugs.

Lily Tomlin 1939– : attributed; Phil Hammond and Michael Mosley *Trust Me (I'm a Doctor)* 1999

9 A drug is neither moral or immoral—it's a chemical compound. The compound itself is not a menace to society until a human being treats it as if consumption bestowed a temporary licence to act like an asshole.

Frank Zappa 1940–93: *The Real Frank Zappa Book* (1989)

Economics

See also **Money**

❝ *Balancing the budget is like going to heaven.* **❞**
Phil Gramm

1 No real English gentleman, in his secret soul, was ever sorry for the death of a political economist.

Walter Bagehot 1826–77: *Estimates of some Englishmen and Scotchmen* (1858) 'The First Edinburgh Reviewers'

2 A man explained inflation to his wife thus: 'When we married you measured 36-24-36. Now you're 42-42-42. There's more of you, but you're not worth as much.'

Joel Barnett 1923– : attributed; in *Mail on Sunday* 5 October 2003

3 John Stuart Mill,
By a mighty effort of will,
Overcame his natural *bonhomie*
And wrote 'Principles of Political Economy'.

Edmund Clerihew Bentley 1875–1956: 'John Stuart Mill' (1905)

4 It's the economy, stupid.
slogan on a sign put up at the Clinton presidential campaign headquarters

James Carville 1944– : campaign slogan, 1992

5 I never could make out what those damned dots meant.
as Chancellor, on decimal points

Lord Randolph Churchill 1849–94: W. S. Churchill *Lord Randolph Churchill* (1906)

6 Trickle-down theory—the less than elegant metaphor that if one feeds the horse enough oats, some will pass through to the road for the sparrows.

J. K. Galbraith 1908–2006: *The Culture of Contentment* (1992)

7 I could seek to ease his pain, but only by giving him an aspirin.

the Governor of the Bank of England on economic problems of the small businessman

Eddie George 1938– : interview on *The Money Programme* BBC2 TV, 28 February 1999

8 Balancing the budget is like going to heaven. Everybody wants to do it, but nobody wants to do what you have to do to get there.

Phil Gramm 1942– : in a television interview, 16 September 1990

9 In '29 when the banks went bust,
Our coins still read 'In God We Trust'.

E. Y. Harburg 1898–1981: 'Federal Reserve' (1965)

10 The safest way to double your money is to fold it over and put it in your pocket.

Frank McKinney Hubbard 1868–1930: attributed

11 *claiming to have been the first person to explain monetarism to Margaret Thatcher:*
It makes one feel like the geography teacher who showed a map of the world to Genghis Khan.

Peter Jay 1937– : in *Tory !Tory! Tory!* (BBC Four television documentary) 8 March 2006

12 If economists could manage to get themselves thought of as humble, competent people, on a level with dentists, that would be splendid!

John Maynard Keynes 1883–1946: 'Economic Possibilities for our Grandchildren'; David Howell *Blind Victory* (1986)

13 Expenditure rises to meet income.

C. Northcote Parkinson 1909–93: *The Law and the Profits* (1960)

14 Nothink for nothink 'ere, and precious little for sixpence.

Punch 1841–1992: vol. 57 (1869)

15 Greed—for lack of a better word—is good. Greed is right. Greed works.

Stanley Weiser and **Oliver Stone** 1946– : *Wall Street* (1987 film)

Education

See also **Examinations**

❝ I won't say ours was a tough school, but we had our own coroner. ❞
Lenny Bruce

1 He shows great originality which must be curbed at all costs.

an early school report on Peter Ustinov

Anonymous: Catherine Hurley *Could Do Better* (2003)

2 I read Shakespeare and the Bible and I can shoot dice. That's what I call a liberal education.

Tallulah Bankhead 1903–68: attributed

3 I was not unpopular [at school] . . . It is Oxford that has made me insufferable.

Max Beerbohm 1872–1956: *More* (1899) 'Going Back to School'

4 Someone once said, Rumbold, that education is what is left when you have forgotten all you have ever learned. You appear to be trying to circumvent the process by learning as little as possible.

Alan Bennett 1934– : *Forty Years On* (1969)

5 Education with socialists, it's like sex, all right so long as you don't have to pay for it.

Alan Bennett 1934– : *Getting On* (1972)

6 I went to public school, of course. But looking back on it, I think it may have been Borstal.

Alan Bennett 1934– : *Getting On* (1972)

7 Gentlemen: I have not had your advantages. What poor education I have received has been gained in the University of Life.

Horatio Bottomley 1860–1933: speech at the Oxford Union, 2 December 1920

8 I won't say ours was a tough school, but we had our own coroner. We used to write essays like: What I'm going to be if I grow up.

Lenny Bruce 1925–66: attributed

9 In my day, the principal concerns of university students were sex, smoking dope, rioting and learning. Learning was something you did only when the first three weren't available.

Bill Bryson 1951– : *The Lost Continent* (1989)

10 *of Cambridge University:*
This place is the Devil, or at least his principal residence, they call it the University, but any other appellation would have suited it much better, for study is the last pursuit of the society; the Master eats, drinks, and sleeps, the Fellows drink, dispute and pun, the employments of the undergraduates you will probably conjecture without my description.

Lord Byron 1788–1824: letter, 23 November 1805

11 No academic person is ever voted into the chair until he has reached an age at which he has forgotten the meaning of the word 'irrelevant'.

Francis M. Cornford 1874–1943: *Microcosmographia Academica* (1908)

12 C-l-e-a-n, clean, verb active, to make bright, to scour. W-i-n, win, d-e-r, der, winder, a casement. When the boy knows this out of the book, he goes and does it.

Charles Dickens 1812–70: *Nicholas Nickleby* (1839)

13 EDUCATION.—At Mr Wackford Squeers's Academy, Dotheboys Hall, at the delightful village of Dotheboys, near Greta Bridge in Yorkshire, Youth are boarded, clothed, booked, furnished with pocket-money, provided with all necessaries, instructed in all languages living and dead, mathematics, orthography, geometry, astronomy, trigonometry, the use of the globes, algebra, single stick (if required), writing, arithmetic, fortification, and every other branch of classical literature. Terms, twenty guineas per annum. No extras, no vacations, and diet unparalleled.

Charles Dickens 1812–70: *Nicholas Nickleby* (1839)

14 Ev'ry pedagogue
Goes to bed agog at night—
Doing Collegiana . . . .

Dorothy Fields 1905–74: 'Collegiana' (1924)

15 The clever men at Oxford
Know all that there is to be knowed.
But they none of them know one half as much
As intelligent Mr Toad!

Kenneth Grahame 1859–1932: *The Wind in the Willows* (1908)

16 Common to all staff was a conviction that they could have done better outside education. The teachers believed in a mysterious world outside the school called 'business' where money was handed out freely.

Michael Green 1927– : *The Boy Who Shot Down an Airship* (1988)

17 Education in those elementary subjects which are ordinarily taught to our defenceless children, as reading, writing, and arithmetic.

A. P. Herbert 1890–1971: *Misleading Cases* (1935)

18 Beauty school report
No graduation day for you
Beauty school dropout
Mixed your mid-terms and flunked shampoo.

Jim Jacobs and **Warren Casey**: 'Beauty School Dropout' (1972)

19 Life isn't like coursework, baby. It's one damn essay crisis after another.

Boris Johnson 1964– : in *Observer* 15 May 2005

20 [JOHNSON:] I had no notion that I was wrong or irreverent to my tutor.
[BOSWELL:] That, Sir, was great fortitude of mind.
[JOHNSON:] No, Sir; stark insensibility.

Samuel Johnson 1709–84: James Boswell *Life of Samuel Johnson* (1791) 31 October 1728

21 That state of resentful coma that . . . dons dignify by the name of research.

Harold Laski 1893–1950: letter to Oliver Wendell Holmes, 10 October 1922

22 Most people tire of a lecture in ten minutes; clever people can do it in five. Sensible people never go to lectures at all.

Stephen Leacock 1869–1944: *My Discovery of England* (1922)

23 If you are truly serious about preparing your child for the future, don't teach him to subtract—teach him to deduct.

Fran Lebowitz 1946– : *Social Studies* (1981)

24 Stand firm in your refusal to remain conscious during algebra. In real life, I assure you, there is no such thing as algebra.

Fran Lebowitz 1946– : *Social Studies* (1981)

25 Who walks in the classroom cool and slow?
Who calls his English teacher Daddy-O?

Jerry Leiber 1933– and **Mike Stoller** 1933– : 'Charlie Brown' (1959)

26 University seems to have turned them into Conan the Grammarians, who fret over perfect sentence construction.
of writer friends with degrees in English

Kathy Lette 1958– : in *Daily Telegraph* 30 November 2002

27 At school I never minded the lessons. I just resented having to work terribly hard at playing.

John Mortimer 1923–2009: *A Voyage Round My Father* (1971)

28 The Socratic method is a game at which only one (the professor) can play.

Ralph Nader 1934– : Joel Seligman *The High Citadel* (1978)

29 Liberals have invented whole college majors—psychology, sociology, women's studies— to prove that nothing is anybody's fault.

P. J. O'Rourke 1947– : *Give War a Chance* (1992)

30 The schoolteacher is certainly underpaid as a childminder, but ludicrously overpaid as an educator.

John Osborne 1929–94: in *Observer* 21 July 1985 'Sayings of the Week'

31 I don't think one 'comes down' from Jimmy's university. According to him, it's not even red brick, but white tile.

John Osborne 1929–94: *Look Back in Anger* (1956)

32 GROUCHO MARX: With a little study you'll go a long way, and I wish you'd start now.

S. J. Perelman 1904–79 et al.: *Monkey Business* (1931 film)

33 Good gracious, you've got to educate him first. You can't expect a boy to be vicious till he's been to a good school.

Saki 1870–1916: *Reginald in Russia* (1910)

34 For every person who wants to teach there are approximately thirty who don't want to learn—much.

W. C. Sellar 1898–1951 and **R. J. Yeatman** 1898–1968: *And Now All This* (1932) introduction

35 Me havin' no education, I had to use my brains.

Bill Shankly 1913–81: Hugh McIlvanney *McIlvanney on Football* (1994)

36 Very nice sort of place, Oxford, I should think, for people that like that sort of place. They teach you to be a gentleman there. In the Polytechnic they teach you to be an engineer or such like.

George Bernard Shaw 1856–1950: *Man and Superman* (1903)

37 He who can, does. He who cannot, teaches.

George Bernard Shaw 1856–1950: *Man and Superman* (1903) 'Maxims: Education'

38 *Educ*: during the holidays from Eton.

Osbert Sitwell 1892–1969: entry in *Who's Who* (1929)

39 *replying to Woodrow Wilson's 'And what in your opinion is the trend of the modern English undergraduate?':* Steadily towards drink and women, Mr President.

F. E. Smith 1872–1930: attributed

40 To me education is a leading out of what is already there in the pupil's soul. To Miss Mackay it is a putting in of something that is not there, and that is not what I call education, I call it intrusion.

Muriel Spark 1918–2006: *The Prime of Miss Jean Brodie* (1961)

41 I am putting old heads on your young shoulders . . . all my pupils are the crème de la crème.

Muriel Spark 1918–2006: *The Prime of Miss Jean Brodie* (1961)

42 Soap and education are not as sudden as a massacre, but they are more deadly in the long run.

Mark Twain 1835–1910: *A Curious Dream* (1872) 'Facts concerning the Recent Resignation'

43 'We class schools, you see, into four grades: Leading School, First-rate School, Good School, and School. Frankly,' said Mr Levy, 'School is pretty bad.'

Evelyn Waugh 1903–66: *Decline and Fall* (1928)

44 Any one who has been to an English public school will always feel comparatively at home in prison. It is the people brought up in the gay intimacy of the slums, Paul learned, who find prison so soul-destroying.

Evelyn Waugh 1903–66: *Decline and Fall* (1928)

45 Assistant masters came and went . . . Some liked little boys too little and some too much.

Evelyn Waugh 1903–66: *A Little Learning* (1964)

46 In England, at any rate, education produces no effect whatsoever. If it did, it would prove a serious danger to the upper classes, and probably lead to acts of violence in Grosvenor Square.

Oscar Wilde 1854–1900: *The Importance of Being Earnest* (1895)

47 'Didn't Frankenstein get married?'
'Did he?' said Eggy. 'I don't know. I never met him. Harrow man, I expect.'

P. G. Wodehouse 1881–1975: *Laughing Gas* (1936)

48 A pretty example he sets to this Infants' Bible Class of which he speaks! A few years of sitting at the feet of Harold Pinker and imbibing his extraordinary views on morality and ethics, and every bally child on the list will be serving a long stretch at Wormwood Scrubs for blackmail.

P. G. Wodehouse 1881–1975: *The Code of the Woosters* (1938)

Enemies

❝ *I detest him more than cold boiled veal.* ❞
Lord Macaulay

1 I wouldn't piss in his ear if his brain was on fire.
indicating your level of dislike for someone

Anonymous: quoted as a traditional expression of the Southern US; Bill Clinton *My Life* (2004)

2 I do not love thee, Dr Fell.
The reason why I cannot tell;
But this I know, and know full well,
I do not love thee, Dr Fell.

Thomas Brown 1663–1704: written while an undergraduate at Christ Church, Oxford, of which Dr Fell was Dean

3 Rejoice, rejoice, rejoice.
telephone call to his office on hearing of Margaret Thatcher's fall from power in 1990

Edward Heath 1916–2005: attributed; in *Daily Telegraph* 24 September 1998 (online edition)

4 I detest him more than cold boiled veal.
of the Tory essayist and politician John Wilson Croker

Lord Macaulay 1800–59: letter 5 August 1831

5 People wish their enemies dead—but I do not; I say give them the gout, give them the stone!

Lady Mary Wortley Montagu 1689–1762: W. S. Lewis et al. (eds.) *Horace Walpole's Correspondence* (1973)

6 *a Spanish general, asked on his deathbed if he forgave his enemies:*
I have none. I had them all shot.

Ramón María Narváez 1800–68: Antony Beevor *The Battle For Spain* (2006)

7 Any kiddie in school can love like a fool,
But hating, my boy, is an art.

Ogden Nash 1902–71: 'Plea for Less Malice Toward None' (1933)

8 I find that forgiving one's enemies is a most curious morbid pleasure; perhaps I should check it.

Oscar Wilde 1854–1900: letter ?20 April 1894

9 A man cannot be too careful in the choice of his enemies.

Oscar Wilde 1854–1900: *The Picture of Dorian Gray* (1891)

England
See also **Countries and Peoples, Places**

❝ If an Englishman gets run down by a truck he apologizes to the truck. ❞
Jackie Mason

1 Boasting about modesty is typical of the English.

Anonymous: unattributed; in *Mail on Sunday* 21 February 1999 'Quotes of the Week'

2 An Englishman considers himself a self-made man, and thereby relieves the Almighty of a dreadful responsibility.

Anonymous: unattributed; in *Times* 23 February 1999

3 The English may not like music, but they absolutely love the noise it makes.

Thomas Beecham 1879–1961: in *New York Herald Tribune* 9 March 1961

4 He was born an Englishman and remained one for years.

Brendan Behan 1923–64: *Hostage* (1958)

5 Think of what our Nation stands for,
Books from Boots' and country lanes,
Free speech, free passes, class distinction,
Democracy and proper drains.
Lord, put beneath Thy special care
One-eighty-nine Cadogan Square.

John Betjeman 1906–84: 'In Westminster Abbey' (1940)

6 For 'tis a low, newspaper, humdrum, lawsuit Country.

Lord Byron 1788–1824: *Don Juan* (1819–24)

7 Mad dogs and Englishmen
Go out in the midday sun.
The Japanese don't care to,
The Chinese wouldn't dare to,
The Hindus and Argentines sleep firmly from twelve to
one,
But Englishmen detest a siesta.
In the Philippines, there are lovely screens
To protect you from the glare;
In the Malay states, they have hats like plates
Which the Britishers won't wear.
At twelve noon, the natives swoon,
And no further work is done;
But mad dogs and Englishmen go out in the midday sun.

Noël Coward 1899–1973: 'Mad Dogs and Englishmen' (1931)

8 The English can be explained by their Anglo-Saxon
heritage and the influence of the Methodists. But I prefer to
explain them in terms of tea, roast beef and rain. A people
is first what it eats, drinks and gets pelted with.

Pierre Daninos: *Major Thompson and I* (1957)

9 There is in the Englishman a combination of qualities, a
modesty, an independence, a responsibility, a repose,
combined with an absence of everything calculated to call
a blush into the cheek of a young person, which one
would seek in vain among the Nations of the Earth.

Charles Dickens 1812–70: *Our Mutual Friend* (1865)

10 But 'tis the talent of our English nation,
Still to be plotting some new reformation.

John Dryden 1631–1700: 'The Prologue at Oxford, 1680'

11 Stiff upper lip! Stout fella!
Carry on, old fluff!
Chin up! Keep muddling through!
Stiff upper lip! Stout fella!
When the going's rough—
Pip-pip to Old Man Trouble—and a toodle-oo, too!

Ira Gershwin 1896–1983: 'Stiff Upper Lip' (1937)

12 He is an Englishman!
For he himself has said it,
And it's greatly to his credit,
That he is an Englishman!

W. S. Gilbert 1836–1911: *HMS Pinafore* (1878)

13 Contrary to popular belief, English women do not wear
tweed nightgowns.

Hermione Gingold 1897–1987: in *Saturday Review* 16 April 1955

14 The truth is that every Englishman's house is his hospital,
particularly the bathroom. Patent medicine is the English
patent.

Oliver St John Gogarty 1878–1957: *As I Was Going Down Sackville Street* (1937)

15 Even crushed against his brother in the Tube, the average
Englishman pretends desperately that he is alone.

Germaine Greer 1939– : *The Female Eunuch* (1970)

16 My parents were English. We were too poor to be British.
on his British origins

Bob Hope 1903–2003: in *Times* 29 July 2003

17 Not to be English was for my family so terrible a handicap
as almost to place the sufferer in the permanent invalid
class.

Osbert Lancaster 1908–86: *All Done From Memory* (1953)

18 The old English belief that if a thing is unpleasant it is
automatically good for you.

Osbert Lancaster 1908–86: *Homes Sweet Homes* (1939)

19 In England it is very dangerous to have a sense of humour.

E. V. Lucas 1868–1938: *365 Days and One More* (1926)

20 If an Englishman gets run down by a truck he apologizes to the truck.

Jackie Mason 1931– : in *Independent* 20 September 1990

21 An Englishman, even if he is alone, forms an orderly queue of one.

George Mikes 1912–87: *How to be an Alien* (1946)

22 The English are busy; they don't have time to be polite.

Montesquieu 1689–1755: *Pensées et fragments inédits . . .* (1901)

23 Let us pause to consider the English,
Who when they pause to consider themselves they get all
   reticently thrilled and tinglish,
Because every Englishman is convinced of one thing, viz.:
That to be an Englishman is to belong to the most
   exclusive club there is.

Ogden Nash 1902–71: 'England Expects' (1938)

24 But we, brave Britons, foreign laws despised,
And kept unconquered, and uncivilized.

Alexander Pope 1688–1744: *An Essay on Criticism* (1711)

25 Good evening, England. This is Gillie Potter speaking to you in English.

Gillie Potter 1887–1975: *Heard at Hogsnorton* (opening words of broadcasts, 6 June 1946 and 11 November 1947)

26 It is hard to tell where the MCC ends and the Church of England begins.

J. B. Priestley 1894–1984: in *New Statesman* 20 July 1962

27 She comes from the North, where they live in the fear of Heaven and the Earl of Durham.

Saki 1870–1916: *Reginald* (1904) 'Reginald on Christmas Presents'

28 The Roman Conquest was, however, a *Good Thing*, since the Britons were only natives at the time.

W. C. Sellar 1898–1951 and **R. J. Yeatman** 1898–1968: *1066 and All That* (1930)

29 We really *like* dowdiness in England. It's absolutely incurable in us, I believe.

Peter Shaffer 1926– : *Whom Do I Have the Honour of Addressing?* (1990)

30 An Englishman thinks he is moral when he is only uncomfortable.

George Bernard Shaw 1856–1950: *Man and Superman* (1903)

31 Englishmen never will be slaves: they are free to do whatever the Government and public opinion allow them to do.

George Bernard Shaw 1856–1950: *Man and Superman* (1903)

32 This Englishwoman is so refined
She has no bosom and no behind.

Stevie Smith 1902–71: 'This Englishwoman' (1937)

33 What two ideas are more inseparable than Beer and Britannia?

Sydney Smith 1771–1845: Hesketh Pearson *The Smith of Smiths* (1934)

34 What a pity it is that we have no amusements in England but vice and religion!

Sydney Smith 1771–1845: Hesketh Pearson *The Smith of Smiths* (1934)

35 I think for my part one half of the nation is mad—and the other not very sound.

Tobias Smollett 1721–71: *The Adventures of Sir Launcelot Greaves* (1762)

36 As an Englishman does not travel to see Englishmen, I retired to my room.

Laurence Sterne 1713–68: *A Sentimental Journey* (1768)

37 Now hang it! quoth I, as I looked towards the French coast—a man should know something of his own country too, before he goes abroad.

Laurence Sterne 1713–68: *Tristram Shandy* (1759–67)

38 *on the suggestion that, in his books, washing has some symbolic significance:*
I've noticed that the British are not given to it.

Gore Vidal 1925– : attributed; in *Guardian* 27 February 1999

39 Any who have heard that sound will shrink at the recollection of it; it is the sound of English county families baying for broken glass.

Evelyn Waugh 1903–66: *Decline and Fall* (1928)

40 Other nations use 'force'; we Britons alone use 'Might'.

Evelyn Waugh 1903–66: *Scoop* (1938)

41 He is a typical Englishman, always dull and usually violent.

Oscar Wilde 1854–1900: *An Ideal Husband* (1895)

42 You should study the Peerage, Gerald . . . It is the best thing in fiction the English have ever done.

Oscar Wilde 1854–1900: *A Woman of No Importance* (1893)

43 I like a man to be a clean, strong, upstanding Englishman who can look his gnu in the face and put an ounce of lead in it.

P. G. Wodehouse 1881–1975: *Mr. Mulliner Speaking* (1929)

Environment See **Nature and the Environment**

Epitaphs
See also **Death**

❝ *Keep off the grass.* ❞
Peter Ustinov

1 *invited to write his own epitaph:*
He finally met his deadline.

Douglas Adams 1952–2001: on BBC Radio 4 *Quote Unquote*

2 Whoever treadeth on this stone
I pray you tread most neatly
For underneath this stone do lie
Your honest friend
WILL WHEATLEY.

Anonymous: gravestone at Stepney, London, 10 November 1683; Fritz Spiegl (ed.) *A Small Book of Grave Humour* (1971)

3 In bloom of life
She's snatched from hence
She had not room
To make defence;
For Tiger fierce
Took life away,
And here she lies
In a bed of clay
Until the Resurrection Day.
 of Hannah Twynnoy, who had been attacked by an escaped tiger from a travelling circus in 1703

Anonymous: gravestone in Malmesbury churchyard

4 Here lies a poor woman who always was tired,
For she lived in a place where help wasn't hired.
Her last words on earth were, Dear friends I am going
Where washing ain't done nor sweeping nor sewing,
And everything there is exact to my wishes,
For there they don't eat and there's no washing of dishes
 . . .

Anonymous: epitaph in Bushey churchyard, before 1860; destroyed by 1916

Don't mourn for me now, don't mourn for me never,
For I'm going to do nothing for ever and ever.

5 Here lies Fred,
Who was alive and is dead:
Had it been his father,
I had much rather;
Had it been his brother,
Still better than another;
Had it been his sister,
No one would have missed her;
Had it been the whole generation,
Still better for the nation:
But since 'tis only Fred,
Who was alive and is dead,—
There's no more to be said.
　　epitaph for Frederick, Prince of Wales, killed by a cricket ball
　　in 1751

Anonymous: Horace Walpole
Memoirs of George II (1847)

6 I should like my epitaph to say, 'He helped people see God
in the ordinary things of life, and he made children laugh.'

Revd W. Awdry 1911–97: in
Independent 22 March 1997

7 *suggested epitaph for an unnamed movie queen whose love-life*
had been notorious:
She sleeps alone at last.

Robert Benchley 1889–1945:
attributed

8 John Adams lies here, of the parish of Southwell,
A carrier who carried his can to his mouth well;
He carried so much, and he carried so fast,
He could carry no more—so was carried at last;
For the liquor he drank, being too much for one,
He could not carry off—so he's now carri-on.

Lord Byron 1788–1824: 'Epitaph on
John Adams of Southwell, a Carrier
who Died of Drunkenness' (1807)

9 Alan died suddenly at Saltwood on Sunday 5th September.
He said he would like it to be stated that he regarded
himself as having gone to join Tom and the other dogs.

Alan Clark 1928–99: announcement
in *Times* 8 September 1999

10 *on the death of US President Warren G. Harding:*
The only man, woman or child who wrote a simple
declarative sentence with seven grammatical errors is
dead.

e. e. cummings 1894–1962:
attributed

11 Believing that his hate for queers
Proclaimed his love for God,
He now (of all queer things, my dears)
Lies under his first sod.
　　on John Gordon (1890–1974), editor of the Sunday
　　Express

Paul Dehn 1912–76: Nigel Rees
*Cassell Dictionary of Humorous
Quotations* (1999)

12 Under this stone, Reader, survey
Dead Sir John Vanbrugh's house of clay.
Lie heavy on him, Earth! for he
Laid many heavy loads on thee!

Abel Evans 1679–1737: 'Epitaph on
Sir John Vanbrugh, Architect of
Blenheim Palace'

13 Here lies W. C. Fields. I would rather be living in
Philadelphia.

W. C. Fields 1880–1946: suggested
epitaph for himself; in *Vanity Fair* June
1925

14 Here Skugg
Lies snug
As a bug
In a rug.

Benjamin Franklin 1706–90: letter to
Georgiana Shipley on the death of her
squirrel, 26 September 1772

15 Here lies Nolly Goldsmith, for shortness called Noll,
Who wrote like an angel, but talked like poor Poll.

David Garrick 1717–79: 'Impromptu Epitaph' (written 1773/4)

16 John Le Mesurier wishes it to be known that he conked out on November 15th. He sadly misses family and friends.

John Le Mesurier 1912–83: obituary notice in *Times* 16 November 1983

17 Malcolm Lowry
Late of the Bowery
His prose was flowery
And often glowery
He lived, nightly, and drank, daily,
And died playing the ukelele.
　epitaph he had prepared, which his wife refused to use on his tombstone

Malcolm Lowry 1909–57: Javier Marias *Written Lives* (2000)

18 Poor G.K.C., his day is past—
Now God will know the truth at last.

E. V. Lucas 1868–1938: mock epitaph for G. K. Chesterton; Dudley Barker *G. K. Chesterton* (1973)

19 Here lie I, Martin Elginbrodde:
Hae mercy o' my soul, Lord God;
As I wad do, were I Lord God,
And ye were Martin Elginbrodde.

George MacDonald 1824–1905: *David Elginbrod* (1863)

20 *epitaph for a waiter:*
By and by
God caught his eye.

David McCord 1897–1997: 'Remainders' (1935)

21 Here lies Spike Milligan. I told you I was ill.
his chosen epitaph

Spike Milligan 1918–2002: in *Daily Telegraph* 28 February 2002

22 Beneath this slab
John Brown is stowed.
He watched the ads,
And not the road.

Ogden Nash 1902–71: 'Lather as You Go' (1942)

23 Excuse My Dust.

Dorothy Parker 1893–1967: suggested epitaph for herself; Alexander Woollcott *While Rome Burns* (1934) 'Our Mrs Parker'

24 *epitaph for Maurice Bowra:*
Without you, Heaven would be too dull to bear,
And Hell would not be Hell if you are there.

John Sparrow 1906–92: in *Times Literary Supplement* 30 May 1975

25 Poor Pope will grieve a month, and Gay
A week, and Arbuthnot a day.
St John himself will scarce forbear
To bite his pen, and drop a tear.
The rest will give a shrug, and cry,
'I'm sorry—but we all must die!'

Jonathan Swift 1667–1745: 'Verses on the Death of Dr Swift' (1731)

26 There was a poor poet named Clough,
Whom his friends all united to puff,
But the public, though dull,
Had not such a skull
As belonged to believers in Clough.

Algernon Charles Swinburne 1837–1909: *Essays and Studies* (1875)

27 *when asked what he would like to see on his tombstone:*
Keep off the grass.

Peter Ustinov 1921–2004: attributed; in *Mail on Sunday* 4 April 2004

28 I always thought I'd like my tombstone to be blank. No epitaph, and no name. Well, actually I'd like it to say 'figment'.

Andy Warhol 1927–87: *America* (1985)

29 His friends he loved. His direst earthly foes—
Cats—I believe he did but feign to hate.
My hand will miss the insinuated nose,
Mine eyes the tail that wagged contempt at Fate.

William Watson 1858–1936: 'An Epitaph'

30 Here lies Mr Chesterton,
who to heaven might have gone,
but didn't, when he heard the news
that the place was run by Jews.

Humbert Wolfe 1886–1940: 'G. K. Chesterton' (1925)

Examinations

❝ *I evidently knew more about economics than my examiners.* ❞
John Maynard Keynes

1 Truth is no more at issue in an examination than thirst at a wine-tasting or fashion at a striptease.

Alan Bennett 1934– : *The History Boys* (2004)

2 I wrote my name at the top of the page. I wrote down the number of the question '1'. After much reflection I put a bracket round it thus '(1)'. But thereafter I could not think of anything connected with it that was either relevant or true. . . . It was from these slender indications of scholarship that Mr Welldon drew the conclusion that I was worthy to pass into Harrow. It is very much to his credit.

Winston Churchill 1874–1965: *My Early Life* (1930)

3 He had ambitions, at one time, to become a sex maniac, but he failed his practical.

Les Dawson 1934–93: attributed; Fred Metcalf (ed.) *Penguin Dictionary of Modern Humorous Quotations* (1987)

4 *explaining why he performed badly in the Civil Service examinations:*
I evidently knew more about economics than my examiners.

John Maynard Keynes 1883–1946: Roy Harrod *Life of John Maynard Keynes* (1951)

5 In examinations those who do not wish to know ask questions of those who cannot tell.

Walter Raleigh 1861–1922: *Laughter from a Cloud* (1923) 'Some Thoughts on Examinations'

6 Do not on any account attempt to write on both sides of the paper at once.

W. C. Sellar 1898–1951 and **R. J. Yeatman** 1898–1968: *1066 and All That* (1930) 'Test Paper 5'

7 *Whistler had been found 'deficient in chemistry' in a West Point examination:*
Had silicon been a gas, I would have been a major-general by now.

James McNeill Whistler 1834–1903: E. R. and J. Pennell *The Life of James McNeill Whistler* (1908)

8 *in his viva at Oxford Wilde was required to translate a passage from the Greek version of the New Testament. Having acquitted himself well, he was stopped:*
Oh, do let me go on, I want to see how it ends.

Oscar Wilde 1854–1900: James Sutherland (ed.) *The Oxford Book of Literary Anecdotes* (1975)

Exploration See Travel and Exploration

Faces

> ❝I tried to shave off my eyebrows once and my trousers fell down.❞
>
> **Denis Healey**

1 Frazier is so ugly that he should donate his face to the US Bureau of Wild Life.

Muhammad Ali 1942– : in *Guardian* 23 December 1972 'Sports Quotes of the Year'

2 My job is
Keeping faces clean
And nobody knows
De stubble
I've seen
Burma-Shave.

Anonymous: Burma-Shave advertisement, 1950

3 My face looks like a wedding cake left out in the rain.

W. H. Auden 1907–73: Humphrey Carpenter *W. H. Auden* (1981)

4 In appearance Dior is like a bland country curate made out of pink marzipan.
of Christian Dior

Cecil Beaton 1904–80: *The Glass of Fashion* (1954)

5 He had the sort of face that makes you realise God does have a sense of humour.

Bill Bryson 1951– : *Neither Here Nor There* (1991)

6 *of W. H. Auden's heavily wrinkled face:*
Were a fly to attempt to cross it, it would break its leg.

Lord David Cecil 1902–86: A. L. Rowse diary, 30 May 1960

7 I tried to shave off my eyebrows once and my trousers fell down.

Denis Healey 1917– : in *Observer* 21 August 2005

8 I kept thinking, if his face was that wrinkled, what did his balls look like?
after drawing W. H. Auden

David Hockney 1937– : attributed

9 Americans wear their teeth the way Aussie diggers wear their medals on Anzac day.

Janette Turner Hospital 1942– : *North of Nowhere, South of Loss* (2005)

10 My general appearance, and especially my face, have always been a source of depression to me.

William Orpen 1878–1931: *Stories of Old Ireland and Myself* (1924)

Failure

❝ You tried your best, and you failed miserably. The lesson is, never try. ❞
Matt Groening

1 *during a rehearsal at the Royal Court, Beckett encouraged an actor who had lamented, 'I'm failing':*
Go on failing. Go on. Only next time, try to fail better.

Samuel Beckett 1906–89: Tony Richardson *Long Distance Runner* (1993)

2 In the end we are all sacked and it's always awful.

Alan Clark 1928–99: diary 21 June 1983

3 If at first you don't succeed, failure may be your style.

Quentin Crisp 1908–99: in *Sunday Telegraph* 28 September 1999

4 I don't think we have failed, we have just found another way that doesn't work.
on the ending of an attempted round-the-world balloon flight

Andy Elson: comment, Hamamatsu, Japan, 7 March 1999

5 If at first you don't succeed, try, try again. Then quit. No use being a damn fool about it.

W. C. Fields 1880–1946: attributed

6 Kids, you tried your best, and you failed miserably. The lesson is, never try.
Homer Simpson

Matt Groening 1954– : *The Simpsons* 'Burns' Heir' (1994) written by Jack Richdale

7 Come forth, Lazarus! And he came fifth and lost the job.

James Joyce 1882–1941: *Ulysses* (1922)

8 Anybody seen in a bus over the age of 30 has been a failure in life.

Loelia, Duchess of Westminster 1902–93: in *Times* 4 November 1993; habitual remark

Fame

❝ Stardom isn't a profession; it's an accident. ❞
Lauren Bacall

1 A celebrity is a person who works hard all his life to become well known, and then wears dark glasses to avoid being recognized.

Fred Allen 1894–1956: Laurence J. Peter (ed.) *Quotations for our Time* (1977)

2 To live in *Who's Who*
And to die in *The Times*,
To be one of the few
To live in *Who's Who*,
What would I not do?—
I'd commit frightful crimes
To live in *Who's Who*
And to die in *The Times*.

Anonymous: unattributed; in *Times* 3 January 2004

3 I go in and out of fashion like a double-breasted suit.

Alan Ayckbourn 1939– : in *Observer* 13 August 2000 'They said what . . . ?'

4 Stardom isn't a profession; it's an accident.

Lauren Bacall 1924– : in *Observer* 19 March 1995 'Sayings of the Week'

5 *asked at a press conference what it was like to act with a 'screen legend' like Nicole Kidman:*
She's not a legend, she's a beginner. You can't be a legend at whatever age she is.

6 Being a legend is a hazardous thing if you're *only* a legend. If you can keep updating yourself, then being a legend is just an added bonus.

7 Oh, the self-importance of fading stars. Never mind, they will be black holes one day.

8 Oblivion . . . fame's eternal dumping ground.

9 They were so far down the bill I thought they were the printers.
on Morecambe and Wise in early posters and playbills

10 A legend in his own lunchtime.
of Dennis Main Wilson

11 They usually ask you, 'Are you you?' . . . In fact, I've even been thinking of printing up some cards that just say, 'Yes, I am,' so I can get one out before they even say anything.
on signing autographs

12 *refusing to allow his biographer Sheridan Morley to out him as a homosexual, despite the example of the theatre critic T. C. Worsley:*
You forget that the great British public would not care if Cuthbert Worsley had slept with mice.

13 Fancy being remembered around the world for the invention of a mouse!

14 It's the first time I've opened a pier. Nothing can really prepare you, though last night I opened a tin of tomatoes and declared my bathroom open.
at the official reopening of Cromer's Pier Pavilion, 27 June 2004

15 ARTHUR: I think I'll take a bath.
HOBSON: I'll alert the media.

16 The best fame is a writer's fame: it's enough to get a table at a good restaurant, but not enough that you get interrupted when you eat.

17 *on being asked what it was like to be famous:*
It's like having a string of pearls given you. It's nice, but after a while, if you think of it at all, it's only to wonder if they're real or cultured.

18 You can't shame or humiliate modern celebrities. What used to be called shame and humiliation is now called publicity.

Lauren Bacall 1924– : in *Sunday Telegraph* 12 September 2004

Joan Baez 1941– : in *Independent* 19 January 2004

Jeffrey Bernard 1932–97: in *The Spectator* 18 July 1992

Ambrose Bierce 1842–c.1914: *The Enlarged Devil's Dictionary* (1967)

Eddie Braben 1930– : William Cook (ed.) *Eric Morecambe Unseen* (2005)

David Climie: Ned Sherrin *Theatrical Anecdotes* (1991); also attributed to Christopher Wordsworth of Clifford Makins

Jarvis Cocker 1963– : interview in *Q Magazine* November 1995

Noël Coward 1899–1973: in *Independent on Sunday Magazine* 12 November 1995

Walt Disney 1901–66: during his last illness; Leonard Mosley *Disney's World* (1985)

Stephen Fry 1957– : in *Sunday Times* 4 July 2004 'Talking Heads'

Steve Gordon: *Arthur* (1981 film); Dudley Moore as Arthur Bach, and John Gielgud as his valet Hobson

Fran Lebowitz 1946– : in *Observer* 30 May 1993 'Sayings of the Week'

W. Somerset Maugham 1874–1965: *A Writer's Notebook* (1949) written in 1941

P. J. O'Rourke 1947– : *Give War a Chance* (1992)

19 *autographing a book for a dissatisfied customer:*
CUSTOMER: But usen't you to be J. B. Priestley?
PRIESTLAND: That was a long time ago.

Gerald Priestland 1927–91:
Something Understood (1986)

20 The people, they need to adore me,
So Christian Dior me.

Tim Rice 1944– : *Evita* (1979)

21 Well, not exactly a big star . . . But I once had a sandwich named after me at the Stage Delicatessen.

Neil Simon 1927– : *The Gingerbread Lady* (1970)

22 *to Labour MP Chris Bryant, whose photograph in his Y-fronts had appeared on a gay website:*
Ah, Bryant, there you are. Nearly didn't recognise you with your clothes on.

Nicholas Soames 1948– : attributed; in *Mail on Sunday* 4 January 2004

23 Fame is like V.D. Everybody wants to fuck you until they see what they get.

Sylvester Stallone 1946– : quoted by Sharon Stone, *Graham Norton Show* (Channel 4 TV) 18 December 2003

24 Celebrity is good for kick-starting ideas, but often celebrity is a lead weight around your neck. It's like you pointing at the moon, but people are looking at your finger.
on campaigning

Sting 1951– : in *Mojo* February 1995

25 One day you are a signature, next day you're an autograph.

Billy Wilder 1906–2002: Charlotte Chandler *Nobody's Perfect* (2002)

The Family

See also **Children, Parents**

❝ We have become a grandmother. ❞
Margaret Thatcher

1 What is wrong with a little incest? It is both handy and cheap.

James Agate 1877–1947: on *The Barretts of Wimpole Street*; attributed, perhaps apocryphal

2 And my parents finally realize that I'm kidnapped and they snap into action immediately: They rent out my room.

Woody Allen 1935– : Eric Lax *Woody Allen and his Comedy* (1975)

3 Could you possibly whistle your father and put him back on his lead, please.

Alan Ayckbourn 1939– : *Sisterly Feelings* (1981)

4 Daughters are best. They don't migrate.

Alan Bennett 1934– : *Talking Heads* (1988)

5 My mother-in-law broke up my marriage. My wife came home from work one day and found us in bed together.

Lenny Bruce 1925–66: attributed; Fred Metcalf (ed.) *The Penguin Dictionary of Modern Humorous Quotations*

6 Happiness is having a large, loving, caring, close-knit family in another city.

George Burns 1896–1996: attributed

7 I should, many a good day, have blown my brains out, but for the recollection that it would have given pleasure to my mother-in-law; and, even *then*, if I could have been certain to haunt her . . .

Lord Byron 1788–1824: letter, 28 January 1817

8 I did bring my 11-year-old son Bilak here with his wife who is a similar age. They have recently given born to a baby which we are hoping to sell to singing transvestite Madonna.
as Borat, arriving for the premiere of the film Cultural Learnings of America for Make Benefit Glorious Nation of Kazakhstan

Sacha Baron Cohen 1970– : BBC news, 25 October 2006

9 We must all be very kind to Auntie Jessie,
For she's never been a Mother or a Wife,
You mustn't throw your toys at her
Or make a vulgar noise at her,
She hasn't led a very happy life.

Noël Coward 1899–1973: 'We Must All be Very Kind to Auntie Jessie' (c.1924)

10 If you must go flopping yourself down, flop in favour of your husband and child, and not in opposition to 'em.

Charles Dickens 1812–70: *A Tale of Two Cities* (1859)

11 Your sister is given to government.

Charles Dickens 1812–70: *Great Expectations* (1861)

12 Accidents will occur in the best-regulated families.

Charles Dickens 1812–70: *David Copperfield* (1850)

13 We do everything alike
We look alike, we dress alike,
We walk alike, we talk alike,
and what is more we hate each other very much.

Howard Dietz 1896–1983: 'Triplets' (1937)

14 John Donne, Anne Donne, Un-done.
in a letter to his wife, on being dismissed from the service of his father-in-law, Sir George More

John Donne 1572–1631: Izaak Walton *The Life of Dr Donne* (first printed in *LXXX Sermons*, 1640)

15 You know what they say, if at first you don't succeed, you're not the eldest son.

Stephen Fry 1957– : *Paperweight* (1992)

16 A man . . . is *so* in the way in the house!

Elizabeth Gaskell 1810–65: *Cranford* (1853)

17 He will be six foot two,
My son-in-law;
His haircut will be crew,
My son-in-law.

Ira Gershwin 1896–1983: 'My Son-in-Law' (1946)

18 And so do his sisters, and his cousins and his aunts!
His sisters and his cousins,
Whom he reckons up by dozens,
And his aunts!

W. S. Gilbert 1836–1911: *HMS Pinafore* (1878)

19 T'Morra, t'morra,
Lookin' for t'morra,
My aunt became a spinster that way.

E. Y. Harburg 1898–1981: 'T'Morra' (1944)

20 I'm also told that the latest popular game in America is called Incest—all the family can join in!

Rupert Hart-Davis 1907–99: letter to George Lyttelton, 14 November 1959

21 If Gloria hadn't divorced me she might never have become her own daughter-in-law.
of his ex-wife, Gloria Grahame, who had married her former stepson

Cy Howard 1915–93: in *Ned Sherrin in his Anecdotage* (1993)

22 'It wouldn't hurt us to be nice, would it?'
'That depends on your threshold of pain.'
on being told his aunt was coming to visit

George S. Kaufman 1889–1961: Howard Teichmann *George S. Kaufman* (1973)

23 *of his appointment of his brother Robert:*
I see nothing wrong with giving Robert some legal
experience as Attorney General before he goes out to
practice law.

John F. Kennedy 1917–63: Bill Adler
The Complete Kennedy Wit (1967)

24 BARBARA WALTERS: What would be your first act on
becoming President?
JOHN F. KENNEDY JNR: Call Uncle Teddy and gloat.

John F. Kennedy Jnr. 1960–99: in
Sunday Telegraph 25 July 1999;
recalled by Ted Kennedy at his
nephew's memorial service on 23 July
1999

25 My grandfather had displayed that Jovelike side to his
character of which his family were always nervously
aware.

Osbert Lancaster 1908–86: *All Done
From Memory* (1953)

26 I've been out where the Blues begin,
Stopping at home with my kith and kin,
Where the handclasp's firm, and the smile is humorous,
And Family Friends are a bit too numerous.

Phyllis McGinley 1905–78: 'Ordeal
by Family' (1960)

27 Few misfortunes can befall a boy which bring worse
consequences than to have a really affectionate mother.

W. Somerset Maugham 1874–1965:
A Writer's Notebook (1949), written
in 1896

28 The English take breeding of horses and dogs more
seriously than children. God forbid the wrong drop of
blood should get into their Labrador. But their children
marry everywhere.

Princess Michael of Kent 1945– : in
Observer 20 February 2005

29 One would be in less danger
From the wiles of the stranger
If one's own kin and kith
Were more fun to be with.

Ogden Nash 1902–71: 'Family Court'
(1931)

30 Uncle Carl Laemmle,
Has a very large faemmle.
of a Hollywood mogul much given to nepotism

Ogden Nash 1902–71: Philip French
The Movie Moguls (1969)

31 Bury her naked? My own mum? It's a Freudian
nightmare.

Joe Orton 1933–67: *Loot* (1967)

32 We kept Mommy on a pedestal—it was the only way we
could keep Daddy off her.
of family life as one of twelve children

Dolly Parton 1946– : review of her
show at the Hammersmith Apollo,
London; in *Observer* 24 November
2002

33 I want to spend more time with my family, but I'm not
sure they want to spend more time with me.

Esther Rantzen 1940– : in
Independent 29 April 2000

34 To your tents, O Israel!
to his wife's Rothschild relations one evening at Mentmore

Lord Rosebery 1847–1929: Robert
Rhodes James *Rosebery* (1963);
perhaps apocryphal

35 I find it difficult to take much interest in a man whose
father was a dragon.
*apologizing for his inability to appreciate William Morris's
epic poem* Sigurd the Volsung *(1876)*

Dante Gabriel Rossetti 1828–82:
Osbert Sitwell *Noble Essences* (1950)

36 *Chutzpa* is that quality enshrined in a man who, having
killed his mother and father, throws himself on the mercy
of the court as an orphan.

Leo Rosten 1908–97: *The Joys of
Yiddish* (1968)

37 *questionnaire for would-be Kings in the Wars of the Roses:*
What have you done with your mother? (If *Nun*, write
None.)

W. C. Sellar 1898–1951 and R. J.
Yeatman 1898–1968: *1066 and All
That* (1930)

38 It is a wise father that knows his own child.

William Shakespeare 1564–1616: *The Merchant of Venice* (1596–8)

39 Parentage is a very important profession, but no test of fitness for it is ever imposed in the interest of the children.

George Bernard Shaw 1856–1950: *Everybody's Political What's What?* (1944)

40 My father is a bastard
My Ma's an S.O.B.
My Grandpa's always plastered
My Grandma pushes tea
My sister wears a moustache
My brother wears a dress
Goodness gracious, that's why I'm a mess.

Stephen Sondheim 1930– : 'Gee, Officer Krupke' (1957)

41 'Never was born!' persisted Topsy . . . 'never had no father, nor mother, nor nothin'. I was raised by a speculator, with lots of others.'

Harriet Beecher Stowe 1811–96: *Uncle Tom's Cabin* (1852)

42 The young ladies entered the drawing-room in the full fervour of sisterly animosity.

R. S. Surtees 1805–64: *Mr Sponge's Sporting Tour* (1853)

43 I am Septimus, the most morbid of the Tennysons.
introducing himself to Dante Gabriel Rossetti

Septimus Tennyson 1815–66: Peter Levi *Tennyson* (1993)

44 If a man's character is to be abused, say what you will, there's nobody like a relation to do the business.

William Makepeace Thackeray 1811–63: *Vanity Fair* (1847–8)

45 We have become a grandmother.

Margaret Thatcher 1925– : in *Times* 4 March 1989

46 I'm off to see if X Mansions is really razed to the ground, as I have an uncle who lives there and I know I'm in his will!

Ernest Thesiger 1879–1961: during the war; in *Ned Sherrin in his Anecdotage* (1993)

47 I'm Charley's aunt from Brazil—where the nuts come from.

Brandon Thomas 1856–1914: *Charley's Aunt* (1892)

48 I suppose that the high-water mark of my youth in Columbus, Ohio, was the night the bed fell on my father.

James Thurber 1894–1961: *My Life and Hard Times* (1933)

49 All happy families resemble one another, but each unhappy family is unhappy in its own way.

Leo Tolstoy 1828–1910: *Anna Karenina* (1875–7)

50 Familiarity breeds contempt—and children.

Mark Twain 1835–1910: *Notebooks* (1935)

51 To lose one parent, Mr Worthing, may be regarded as a misfortune; to lose both looks like carelessness.

Oscar Wilde 1854–1900: *The Importance of Being Earnest* (1895)

52 To be born, or at any rate bred, in a hand-bag, whether it had handles or not, seems to me to display a contempt for the ordinary decencies of family life that reminds one of the worst excesses of the French Revolution.

Oscar Wilde 1854–1900: *The Importance of Being Earnest* (1895)

53 It is no use telling me that there are bad aunts and good aunts. At the core, they are all alike. Sooner or later, out pops the cloven hoof.

P. G. Wodehouse 1881–1975: *The Code of the Woosters* (1938)

54 To my daughter Leonora without whose never-failing sympathy and encouragement this book would have been finished in half the time.

P. G. Wodehouse 1881–1975: dedication to *The Heart of a Goof* (1926)

55 As a rule, you see, I'm not lugged into Family Rows. On the occasions when Aunt is calling to Aunt like mastodons bellowing across primeval swamps and Uncle James's letter about Cousin Mabel's peculiar behaviour is being shot round the family circle . . . the clan has a tendency to ignore me.

P. G. Wodehouse 1881–1975: *The Inimitable Jeeves* (1923)

56 It was that strange, almost unearthly light which comes into the eyes of wronged uncles when they see a chance of getting a bit of their own back from erring nephews.

P. G. Wodehouse 1881–1975: *Uncle Dynamite* (1948)

Fashion
See also **Dress**

66 *His socks compelled one's attention without losing one's respect.* 99
Saki

1 It is totally impossible to be well dressed in cheap shoes.

Hardy Amies 1909–2003: *The Englishman's Suit* (1994)

2 *of Asquith's first wife:*
She lived in Hampstead and had no clothes.

Margot Asquith 1864–1945: Chips Channon diary, 31 October 1937

3 I never cared for fashion much. Amusing little seams and witty little pleats. It was the girls I liked.

David Bailey 1938– : in *Independent* 5 November 1990

4 *of Dior's New Look:*
Clothes by a man who doesn't know women, never had one, and dreams of being one!

Coco Chanel 1883–1971: in *Vanity Fair* June 1994

5 He thinks he is a flower to be looked at
And when he pulls his frilly nylon pants right up tight
He feels a dedicated follower of fashion.

Ray Davies 1944– : 'A Dedicated Follower of Fashion' (1966)

6 I guess I'll have to change my plan
I should have realized there'd be another man
Why did I buy those blue pyjamas
Before the big affair began?
I guess I'll have to change my plan.

Howard Dietz 1896–1983: 'I Guess I'll Have to Change My Plan' (1929)

7 Uncool people never hurt anybody—all they do is collect stamps, read science-fiction books and stand on the end of railway platforms staring at trains.

Ben Elton 1959– : in *Radio Times* 18/24 April 1998

8 There are easier things in this life than being a drag queen. But, I ain't got no choice. Try as I may, I just can't walk in flats.

Harvey Fierstein 1954– : *Torch Song Trilogy* (1979)

9 My only complaint about having a father in fashion is that every time I'm about to go to bed with a guy I have to look at my dad's name all over his underwear.

Marci Klein: in *Newsweek* 17 October 1994

10 *when a waiter at Buckingham Palace spilled soup on her dress:*
Never darken my Dior again!

Beatrice Lillie 1894–1989: *Every Other Inch a Lady* (1973)

11 A woman's dress should be like a barbed wire fence: serving its purpose without obstructing the view.

Sophia Loren 1934– : in *Mail on Sunday* 30 March 2003

12 *on reports that 'style guru' Carole Caplin had dressed President Putin's wife for the Russian state visit:*
She made her look like a lampshade in a curry house.

Andrew Marr 1959– : in *Daily Telegraph* 2 July 2003 (online edition)

13 Elizabeth Taylor is wearing Orson Welles designer jeans.

Joan Rivers 1933– : attributed; Ned Sherrin *Cutting Edge* (1984)

14 PIRATE: I'm gonna teach you the meaning of pain.
ELIZABETH: You like pain? Try wearing a corset.

Terry Rossio and **Ted Elliott**: *Pirates of the Caribbean* (2003)

15 I wish I had invented blue jeans.
on his only regret

Yves Saint Laurent 1936–2008: in *Ritz* no. 85 (1984)

16 His socks compelled one's attention without losing one's respect.

Saki 1870–1916: *Chronicles of Clovis* (1911)

17 Her frocks are built in Paris, but she wears them with a strong English accent.

Saki 1870–1916: *Reginald* (1904)

18 If Botticelli were alive today he'd be working for *Vogue*.

Peter Ustinov 1921–2004: in *Observer* 21 October 1962 'Sayings of the Week'

19 I like to dress egos. If you haven't got an ego today, you can forget it.

Gianni Versace 1949–97: in *Guardian* 16 July 1997; obituary

20 It is charming to totter into vogue.

Horace Walpole 1717–97: letter to George Selwyn, 2 December 1765

21 *to Ada Leverson, who with her husband visited Wilde on the morning he left Pentonville:*
How marvellous of you to know exactly the right hat to wear at seven o'clock in the morning to meet a friend who has been away.

Oscar Wilde 1854–1900: Rupert Hart-Davis (ed.) *Selected Letters of Oscar Wilde* (1979)

Film

See also **The Cinema, Film Producers, Film Stars**

> 66 *It's more than magnificent, it's mediocre.* 99
> **Sam Goldwyn**

1 Several tons of dynamite are set off in this picture [*Tycoon*]; none of it under the right people.

James Agee 1909–55: in *The Nation* 14 February 1948

2 Beware geeks bearing scripts.
headline to Nick Lowe's review of Troy

Anonymous: in *Times Literary Supplement* 4 June 2004

3 *Adolph Zukor had protested at the escalating costs of* The Ten Commandments:
What do you want me to do? Stop shooting now and release it as *The Five Commandments*?

Cecil B. De Mille 1881–1959: M. LeRoy *Take One* (1974)

4 A movie so good they named a country after it.
on his film Brazil

Terry Gilliam 1940– : in *Mail on Sunday* 22 August 1999, attributed

5 Let's bring it up to date with some snappy 19th-century dialogue.

Sam Goldwyn 1882–1974: King Vidor *A Tree is a Tree* (1953)

6 *of one of his own films:*
It's more than magnificent, it's mediocre.

Sam Goldwyn 1882–1974: attributed, perhaps apocryphal

7 GOLDWYN: I hope you didn't think it was too blood and thirsty.
THURBER: Not only did I think so but I was horror and struck.
of The Secret Life of Walter Mitty, *Goldwyn's 1947 film of Thurber's story*

Sam Goldwyn 1882–1974: Michael Freedland *The Goldwyn Touch* (1986)

8 It would have been cheaper to lower the Atlantic!
of the disaster movie Raise the Titanic

Lew Grade 1906–98: *Still Dancing: My Story* (1987)

9 *of the film* Lock, Stock and Two Smoking Barrels *starring* Vinnie Jones:
Think of it as a carefully constructed entertainment for the benefit of people who really, really like beer commercials.

Anthony Lane: in *New Yorker* 8 March 1999

10 Do you have any idea how bad the picture is? I'll tell you. Stay away from the neighbourhood where it's playing— don't even go near that street! It might rain—you could get caught in the downpour, and to keep dry you'd have to go inside the theatre.

Herman J. Mankiewicz 1897–1953: attributed

11 I'm not [biting my fingernails]. I'm biting my knuckles. I finished the fingernails months ago.

Joseph L. Mankiewicz 1909–93: while directing *Cleopatra* (1963); Dick Sheppard *Elizabeth* (1975)

12 The slaves . . . are so cordial and upbeat about having their lives and property gentrified in 1776 that you fear for the entire future of the blues.
of The Patriot

Wesley Morris: in *San Francisco Examiner* 28 June 2000

13 It was a cute picture. They used the basic story of *Wuthering Heights* and worked in surfriders.

Neil Simon 1927– : *Last of the Red Hot Lovers* (1970)

14 Anything but Beethoven. Nobody wants to see a movie about a blind composer.

Jack Warner 1892–1978: J. Lawrence *Actor* (1975)

15 I didn't have to act in 'Tarzan, the Ape Man'—just said, 'Me Tarzan, you Jane.'

Johnny Weissmuller 1904–84: in *Photoplay Magazine* June 1932 (the words 'Me Tarzan, you Jane' do not occur in the 1932 film)

16 *asking Graham Greene to give a final polish to a rewrite of the last part of the screenplay for* Ben Hur:
You see, we find a kind of anticlimax after the Crucifixion.

Sam Zimbalist 1904–58: Graham Greene *Ways of Escape* (1980)

Film Producers and Directors
See also **The Cinema, Film**

❝A pig in a silk suit who sends flowers.❞
Katharine Hepburn

1 Cecil B. de Mille
Rather against his will,
Was persuaded to leave Moses
Out of 'The Wars of the Roses'.

Anonymous: J. W. Carter (ed.) *Clerihews* (1938); attributed to Nicolas Bentley

2 What's going on? I have big meetings with important gentiles.
greeting an interviewer

Mel Brooks 1926– : *I Thought I Was Taller: A Short History of Mel Brooks* BBC2 TV 2 October 1981

3 Ah don't believe Ah know which pictures are yours. Do you make the Mickey Mouse brand?
to Irving Thalberg

William Faulkner 1897–1962: Max Wilk *The Wit and Wisdom of Hollywood* (1972)

4 *resigning from the Motion Picture Producers and Distributors of America in 1933:*
Gentlemen, include me out.

Sam Goldwyn 1882–1974: Michael Freedland *The Goldwyn Touch* (1986)

5 PRODUCTION ASSISTANT: But Mr Goldwyn, you said you wanted a spectacle.
GOLDWYN: Yes, but goddam it, I wanted an intimate spectacle!

Sam Goldwyn 1882–1974: attributed, perhaps apocryphal

6 That's the way with these directors, they're always biting the hand that lays the golden egg.

Sam Goldwyn 1882–1974: Alva Johnston *The Great Goldwyn* (1937)

7 Hitchcock was more careful about how the birds were treated than he was about me. I was just there to be pecked.
on the filming of The Birds

Tippi Hedren 1930– : Charlotte Chandler *It's Only A Movie: Alfred Hitchcock* (2005)

8 A pig in a silk suit who sends flowers.
of Sam Spiegel

Katharine Hepburn 1907–2003: Natasha Fraser-Cavassoni *Sam Spiegel* (2003)

9 If I made Cinderella, the audience would immediately be looking for a body in the coach.

Alfred Hitchcock 1899–1980: in *Newsweek* 11 June 1956

10 I can't tell you [the perfect ending to a script] . . . I thought of the answer after 5.30.
to Jack Warner, who imposed a strict nine-to-five-thirty schedule on his scriptwriters

Norman Krasna 1909–84: M. Freedland *Warner Brothers* (1983)

11 Jack Warner has oilcloth pockets so he can steal soup.

Wilson Mizner 1876–1933: Max Wilk *The Wit and Wisdom of Hollywood* (1972)

12 He decided to make it [*Daisy Miller*] exactly as it stood; he crammed James's words into Cybill's mouth like fish into a letterbox.
on Peter Bogdanovich

Frederic Raphael 1931– : *Cuts and Bruises: Personal Terms 3* (2006)

13 Tsar of all the rushes.
of Louis B. Mayer

B. P. Schulberg d. 1957: Norman Zierold *The Hollywood Tycoons* (1969)

14 Once a month the sky falls on my head, I come to, and I see another movie I want to make.

Steven Spielberg 1947– : in *Time* 8 June 1998

15 To Raoul Walsh a tender love scene is burning down a whorehouse.

Jack Warner 1892–1978: P. F. Boller and R. L. Davis *Hollywood Anecdotes* (1988)

16 I like the old masters, by which I mean John Ford, John Ford, and John Ford.

Orson Welles 1915–85: P. F. Boller and R. L. Davis *Hollywood Anecdotes* (1988)

17 Johnny, it's the usual slashed-wrist shot . . . Keep it out of focus. I want to win the foreign picture award.

Billy Wilder 1906–2002: to his lighting cameraman, John Seitz, when filming *Sunset Boulevard* (1950); P. F. Boller and R. L. Davis *Hollywood Anecdotes* (1988)

18 A modern-day Robin Hood, who steals from the rich and steals from the poor.
of Sam Spiegel

Billy Wilder 1906–2002: Natasha Fraser-Cavassoni *Sam Spiegel* (2003)

19 ANONYMOUS: What is an associate producer?
BILLY WILDER: Anybody who's prepared to associate with a
producer.

Billy Wilder 1906–2002: attributed

20 He could do more with a closed door than other directors
could do with an open fly.
of Ernst Lubitsch

Billy Wilder 1906–2002: attributed

21 The first nine commandments for a director are 'Thou
shalt not bore.' The tenth is 'Thou shalt have the right of
final cut.'

Billy Wilder 1906–2002: attributed,
perhaps apocryphal

Film Stars

See also **The Cinema, Film**

**❝ It's not what I do, but the way I do it. It's
not what I say, but the way I say it. ❞**
Mae West

1 Can't act. Slightly bald. Also dances.
studio official's comment on Fred Astaire

Anonymous: Bob Thomas *Astaire*
(1985)

2 They used to shoot her through gauze. You should shoot
me through linoleum.
on Shirley Temple

Tallulah Bankhead 1903–68:
attributed

3 JOE GILLIS: You used to be in pictures. You used to be big.
NORMA DESMOND: I am big. It's the pictures that got small.

Charles Brackett 1892–1969 and
Billy Wilder 1906–2002: *Sunset
Boulevard* (1950 film)

4 When he meets Garbo in a suit of corduroy,
He gives a little frown
And knocks her down.
Oh dear, oh dear, I'm mad about the boy.

Noël Coward 1899–1973: 'Mad
About the Boy' (1932)

5 Like watching an affair between a mad rocking-horse and
a rawhide suitcase.
*of Jeanette MacDonald and Nelson Eddy in the film of his
Bitter Sweet*

Noël Coward 1899–1973: diary 1 July
1946

6 *asked what it was like to kiss Marilyn Monroe:*
It's like kissing Hitler.

Tony Curtis 1925– : A. Hunter *Tony
Curtis* (1985)

7 Nowadays Mitchum doesn't so much act as point his suit
at people.

Russell Davies 1946– : in *Sunday
Times* 18 September 1983

8 *during the making of* Lifeboat *in 1944, Mary Anderson asked
Hitchcock what he thought her 'best side' for photography was:*
My dear, you're sitting on it.

Alfred Hitchcock 1899–1980: D.
Spoto *Life of Alfred Hitchcock* (1983)

9 That man's ears make him look like a taxi-cab with both
doors open.
of Clark Gable

Howard Hughes Jr. 1905–76: Charles
Higham and Joel Greenberg *Celluloid
Muse* (1969)

10 She is a phenomenon of nature, like Niagara Falls or the
Grand Canyon. You can't talk to it. It can't talk to you. All
you can do is stand back and be awed by it.
of Marilyn Monroe

Nunnally Johnson 1897–1977: Peter
Harry Brown and Patte B. Barham
Marilyn, the Last Take (1990)

11 To work as hard as I've worked to accomplish anything and then have some yo-yo come up and say 'Take off those dark glasses and let's have a look at those blue eyes' is really discouraging.

Paul Newman 1925–2008: in *Observer* 5 October 1986 'Sayings of the Week'

12 Elizabeth [Taylor] is a wonderful movie actress: she has a deal with the film lab—she gets better in the bath overnight.

Mike Nichols 1931– : in *Vanity Fair* June 1994

13 Wet, she was a star—dry she ain't.
of the swimmer Esther Williams and her 1940s film career

Joe Pasternak 1901–91: attributed

14 All Americans born between 1890 and 1945 wanted to be movie stars.

Gore Vidal 1925– : *Pink Triangle and Yellow Star* (1982)

15 *on hearing that Ronald Reagan was seeking nomination as Governor of California:*
No, no. Jimmy Stewart for governor—Reagan for his best friend.

Jack Warner 1892–1978: Max Wilk *The Wit and Wisdom of Hollywood* (1972)

16 It's not what I do, but the way I do it. It's not what I say, but the way I say it.

Mae West 1892–1980: G. Eells and S. Musgrove *Mae West* (1989)

17 *on Marilyn Monroe's unpunctuality:*
My Aunt Minnie would always be punctual and never hold up production, but who would pay to see my Aunt Minnie?

Billy Wilder 1906–2002: P. F. Boller and R. L. Davis *Hollywood Anecdotes* (1988)

18 The question is whether Marilyn [Monroe] is a person at all or one of the greatest Dupont products ever invented. She has breasts like granite and a brain like Swiss cheese, full of holes.

Billy Wilder 1906–2002: E. Goodman *The Fifty-Year Decline and Fall of Hollywood* (1961)

Fishing

❝Transcendental meditation with a punch-line.**❞**
Billy Connolly

1 If fishing is a religion, fly fishing is high church.

Tom Brokaw 1940– : in *International Herald Tribune* 10 September 1991

2 I love fishing. It's like transcendental meditation with a punch-line.

Billy Connolly 1942– : *Gullible's Travels* (1982)

3 Fishing is unquestionably a form of madness but, happily, for the once-bitten there is no cure.

Lord Home 1903–95: *The Way the Wind Blows* (1976)

4 Fly fishing may be a very pleasant amusement; but angling or float fishing I can only compare to a stick and a string, with a worm at one end and a fool at the other.

Samuel Johnson 1709–84: attributed; Hawker *Instructions to Young Sportsmen* (1859); also attributed to Jonathan Swift

5 It is to be observed that 'angling' is the name given to fishing by people who can't fish.

Stephen Leacock 1869–1944: attributed

Flattery See **Praise and Flattery**

Food

See also **Cookery, Diets**

> ❝ *Cauliflower is nothing but cabbage with a college education.* ❞
>
> **Mark Twain**

1 The French, they say, live to eat. The English, on the other hand, eat to die.

Martin Amis 1949– : *Money* (1984)

2 I've eaten shepherd's pie at The Ivy and the Savoy, but I've never seen anything like Belmarsh's version.

Jeffrey Archer 1940– : prison diaries, in *Independent* 28 December 2002

3 Shake and shake
The catsup bottle,
None will come,
And then a lot'll.

Richard Armour: Laurence J. Peter (ed.) *Quotations for our Time* (1977)

4 I believe that if ever I had to practise cannibalism, I might manage if there were enough tarragon around.

James Beard 1903–85: in *New York Times* 24 January 1985

5 A gourmet can tell from the flavour whether a woodcock's leg is the one on which the bird is accustomed to roost.

Lucius Beebe 1902–66: Laurence J. Peter (ed.) *Quotations for our Time* (1977)

6 WAITER WITH FISH ORDER: Are you smelt, sir?
JOHN BETJEMAN: Only by the discerning.

John Betjeman 1906–84: Bevis Hillier *Betjeman: the Bonus of Laughter* (2004)

7 Good to eat, and wholesome to digest, as a worm to a toad, a toad to a snake, a snake to a pig, a pig to a man, and a man to a worm.
   on the cycle of digestion

Ambrose Bierce 1842–c.1914: *The Enlarged Devil's Dictionary* (1967)

8 One of the sauces which serve the French in place of a state religion.
   on mayonnaise

Ambrose Bierce 1842–c.1914: *The Enlarged Devil's Dictionary* (1967)

9 Sir Walter Raleigh gripped his seat under the table. He had sailed halfway round the world to find this root, he had faced great perils to bring it back, he had withstood the blandishments of the most expert cajolers at Court, and had not even hinted at the secret of its flavour, he had changed his chef six times, and now Elizabeth of England was tasting it.
He looked at her.
Elizabeth of England spat.
'Not enough salt,' she said.

Caryl Brahms 1901–82 and **S. J. Simon** 1904–48: *No Bed for Bacon* (1941)

10 Some of the waiters discuss the menu with you as if they were sharing wisdom picked up in the Himalayas.

Seymour Britchky: *The Restaurants of New York* (1981 ed.)

11 *Leo Bloom on life in Rio with Swedish Ulla:*
Breakfast on our terrace—many different kinds of herring.

Mel Brooks 1926– and **Thomas Meehan**: *The Producers* (musical, 2001)

12 *asked if he liked vegetables:*
I don't know. I have never eaten them . . . No, that is not quite true. I once ate a pea.

Beau Brummell 1778–1840: Lewis Melville *Beau Brummell* (1924)

13 I'm President of the United States, and I'm not going to eat any more broccoli!

George Bush 1924– : in *New York Times* 23 March 1990

14 The healthy stomach is nothing if not conservative. Few radicals have good digestions.

Samuel Butler 1835–1902: *Notebooks* (1912)

15 Day will break and you'll awake and start to bake a sugar cake for all the boys to see.

Irving Caesar 1895–1996: 'Tea for Two' (1925)

16 'There's nothing like eating hay when you're faint' . . . 'I didn't say there was nothing *better*,' the King replied, 'I said there was nothing *like* it.'

Lewis Carroll 1832–98: *Through the Looking-Glass* (1872)

17 Poets have been mysteriously silent on the subject of cheese.

G. K. Chesterton 1874–1936: *Alarms and Discursions* (1910)

18 Take away that pudding—it has no theme.

Winston Churchill 1874–1965: Lord Home *The Way the Wind Blows* (1976)

19 Open up the caviare
And say Thank God.

Noël Coward 1899–1973: 'Alice is At It Again' (1954)

20 I never see an egg brought on my table but I feel penetrated with the wonderful change it would have undergone but for my gluttony; it might have been a gentle useful hen, leading her chickens with a care and vigilance which speaks shame to many women.

St John de Crévecoeur 1735–1813: *Letters from an American Farmer* (1782)

21 'It's very easy to talk,' said Mrs Mantalini. 'Not so easy when one is eating a demnition egg,' replied Mr Mantalini; 'for the yolk runs down the waistcoat, and yolk of egg does not match any waistcoat but a yellow waistcoat, demmit.'

Charles Dickens 1812–70: *Nicholas Nickleby* (1839)

22 It's a wery remarkable circumstance . . . that poverty and oysters always seem to go together.

Charles Dickens 1812–70: *Pickwick Papers* (1837)

23 Please, sir, I want some more.

Charles Dickens 1812–70: *Oliver Twist* (1838)

24 [Cheese is] milk's leap toward immortality.

Clifton Fadiman 1904–99: *Any Number Can Play* (1957)

25 Roast Beef, Medium, is not only a food. It is a philosophy.

Edna Ferber 1887–1968: foreword to *Roast Beef, Medium* (1911)

26 Ask for heron's eggs whipped with wine into an amber foam.
when asked by a friend what to order in a Lyons teashop

Ronald Firbank 1886–1926: Mervyn Horder *Ronald Firbank: Memoirs and Critiques* (1977)

27 Last night we went to a Chinese dinner at six and a French dinner at nine, and I can feel the sharks' fins navigating unhappily in the Burgundy.

Peter Fleming 1907–71: letter from Yunnanfu, 20 March 1938

28 Of soup and love, the first is the best.

Thomas Fuller 1654–1734: *Gnomologia* (1732)

29 You like potato and I like po-tah-to,
You like tomato and I like to-mah-to;
Potato, po-tah-to, tomato, to-mah-to—
Let's call the whole thing off!

Ira Gershwin 1896–1983: 'Let's Call the Whole Thing Off' (1937)

30 Donuts. Is there anything they *can't* do?
Homer Simpson

Matt Groening 1954– : *The Simpsons* 'Marge vs the Monorail' (2002), written by Conan O'Brien

31 The best number for a dinner party is two—myself and a dam' good head waiter.

Nubar Gulbenkian 1896–1972: in *Daily Telegraph* 14 January 1965

32 'For what we are about to receive,
Oh Lord, 'tis Thee we thank,'
Said the cannibal as he cut a slice
Of the missionary's shank.

E. Y. Harburg 1898–1981: 'The Realist' (1965)

33 I ate his liver with some fava beans and a nice chianti.

Thomas Harris 1940– and **Ted Tally** 1952– : *The Silence of the Lambs* (1991 film)

34 Never eat more than you can lift.
Miss Piggy's advice

Jim Henson 1936– : attributed

35 Oh, I was down by Manly Pier
Drinking tubes of ice-cold beer
With a bucket full of prawns upon me knee.
But when I'd swallowed the last prawn
I had a technicolour yawn
And I chundered in the old Pacific sea.

Barry Humphries 1934– : 'Chunder Down Under' (1964)

36 What proper man would plump for bints
Ahead of After-Eight thin mints?
True pleasure for a man of parts
Is tarts in him, not him in tarts.

Clive James 1939– : Ned Sherrin *Cutting Edge* (1984)

37 Mr Leopold Bloom ate with relish the inner organs of beasts and fowls. He liked thick giblet soup, nutty gizzards, a stuffed roast heart, liverslices fried with crustcrumbs, fried hencod's roes. Most of all he liked grilled mutton kidneys which gave to his palate a fine tang of faintly scented urine.

James Joyce 1882–1941: *Ulysses* (1922)

38 Garlic bread—it's the future, I've tasted it.
Brian Potter envisages a reborn Phoenix Club

Peter Kay 1973– : *Phoenix Nights* 'Brian Gets Everyone Back Together' (Series 2, 2002)

39 Lunch Hollywood-style—a hot dog and vintage wine.

Harry Kurnitz 1907–68: Max Wilk *The Wit and Wisdom of Hollywood* (1971)

40 It has nothing to do with frogs' legs. No amphibian is harmed in the making of this dish.
explaining toad-in-the-hole to an American audience

Nigella Lawson 1960– : in *Sunday Times* 6 October 2002

41 Cannibalism went right out as soon as the American canned food came in.

Stephen Leacock 1869–1944: *The Boy I Left Behind Me* (1947)

42 Large, naked, raw carrots are acceptable as food only to those who live in hutches eagerly awaiting Easter.

Fran Lebowitz 1946– : *Metropolitan Life* (1978)

43 *her anti-aging secrets:*
A love of life, spaghetti and the odd bath in virgin olive oil. Everything I have I owe to spaghetti.

Sophia Loren 1934– : in *Sunday Times* 28 August 2005

44 The piece of cod passeth all understanding.

Edwin Lutyens 1869–1944: Robert Lutyens *Sir Edwin Lutyens* (1942)

45 You are offered a piece of bread and butter that feels like a damp handkerchief and sometimes, when cucumber is added to it, like a wet one.

Compton Mackenzie 1883–1972: *Vestal Fire* (1927)

46 Sushi, crab claws, caviar, little heaps of pink glop . . . A taste of dank rock pools fills my mouth.

Liz McManus 1947– : 'Dwelling Below the Skies' (1997)

47 It's all right, the white wine came up with the fish.
at a formal dinner at the home of the producer Arthur Hornblow Jr., having left the dinner table to be sick

Herman J. Mankiewicz 1897–1953: Max Wilk *The Wit and Wisdom of Hollywood* (1972); also claimed by Howard Dietz

48 'Can I have a table near the floor?'
'Certainly, I'll have the waiter saw the legs off.'

Groucho Marx 1890–1977: attributed

49 [England] is the only country in the world where the food is more dangerous than sex. I mean, a hard cheese will kill you, but a soft cheese will kill you in *seconds*.

Jackie Mason 1931– : in *Independent* 17 February 1989

50 People often feed the hungry so that nothing may disturb their own enjoyment of a good meal.

W. Somerset Maugham 1874–1965: *A Writer's Notebook* (1949) written in 1896

51 *to a friend who had said that he hated English food:*
All you have to do is eat breakfast three times a day.

W. Somerset Maugham 1874–1965: Ted Morgan *Somerset Maugham* (1980)

52 *explaining her dislike of soup:*
I do not believe in building a meal on a lake.

Elsie Mendl 1865–1950: Elsie de Wolfe *After All* (1935)

53 Sue wants a barbecue, Sam wants to boil a ham,
Grace votes for bouillabaisse stew,
Jake wants a weeny-bake, steak and a layer cake,
He'll get a tummy ache too.

Johnny Mercer 1909–76: 'In the Cool, Cool, Cool of the Evening' (1951)

54 Long as there is chicken and gravy on your rice
Ev'rything is nice.

Johnny Mercer 1909–76: 'Lazybones' (1932)

55 No man is lonely eating spaghetti; it requires so much attention.

Christopher Morley 1890–1957: attributed

56 Parsley
Is gharsley.

Ogden Nash 1902–71: 'Further Reflections on Parsley' (1942)

57 *of the wartime food at his prep school:*
There was greasy toad in an equally greasy hole, and a bacon and egg pie so dry and powdery that it was like eating a crumbling 17th-century wattle and daub cottage.

David Nobbs 1935– : *I Didn't Get Where I Am Today* (2003)

58 Never serve oysters in a month that has no paycheck in it.

P. J. O'Rourke 1947– : *The Bachelor Home Companion* (1987)

59 I'll take a lemonade! . . . In a dirty glass!

Norman Panama 1914– and **Melvin Frank** 1913–88: in *Road to Utopia* (1946 film; words spoken by Bob Hope)

60 I had never had a piece of toast
Particularly long and wide,
But fell upon the sanded floor,
And always on the buttered side.

James Payn 1830–98: in *Chambers's Journal* 2 February 1884

61 The mountain sheep are sweeter,
But the valley sheep are fatter;
We therefore deemed it meeter
To carry off the latter.

Thomas Love Peacock 1785–1866: 'The War-Song of Dinas Vawr' (1823)

62 The divine took his seat at the breakfast-table, and began to compose his spirits by the gentle sedative of a large cup of tea, the demulcent of a well-buttered muffin, and the tonic of a small lobster.

Thomas Love Peacock 1785–1866: *Crotchet Castle* (1831)

63 There is no danger of my getting scurvy [while in England], as I have to consume at least two gin-and-limes every evening to keep the cold out.

S. J. Perelman 1904–79: letter, 13 December 1953

64 I've had a taste of society
And society has had a taste of me.
the oyster ending up back in the sea after a day of social climbing

Cole Porter 1891–1964: 'The Tale of the Oyster' (1929)

65 It just proves that fifty million Frenchmen can't be wrong. They eat horses instead of ride them.
having been crippled in a riding accident in 1937

Cole Porter 1891–1964: G. Eells *The Life that Late He Led* (1967)

66 Dinner at the Huntercombes' possessed 'only two dramatic features—the wine was a farce and the food a tragedy'.

Anthony Powell 1905–2000: *The Acceptance World* (1955)

67 Botticelli isn't a wine, you Juggins! Botticelli's a *cheese*!

Punch 1841–1992: vol. 106 (1894)

68 BISHOP: I'm afraid you've got a bad egg, Mr Jones.
CURATE: Oh no, my Lord, I assure you! Parts of it are excellent!

Punch 1841–1992: vol. 109 (1895)

69 Cheese it is a peevish elf
It digests all things but itself.

John Ray 1627–1705: *English Proverbs* (1670)

70 Does the spearmint lose its flavour on the bedpost overnight?

Billy Rose 1899–1966 and **Marty Bloom**: title of song (1924); revived in 1959 by Lonnie Donegan with the title 'Does your chewing-gum lose its flavour on the bedpost overnight?'

71 Like a purée of white kid gloves.
of a dish of lobster Newburg

Philip Sassoon 1888–1939: Chips Channon, diary, 3 June 1939

72 A plague o' these pickle herring!

William Shakespeare 1564–1616: *Twelfth Night* (1601)

73 Then my stomach must digest its waistcoat.
when told that drinking would ruin the coat of his stomach

Richard Brinsley Sheridan 1751–1816: in *Sheridaniana* (1826)

74 OSCAR: I got brown sandwiches and green sandwiches . . . Well, what do you say?
MURRAY: What's the green?
OSCAR: It's either very new cheese or very old meat.

Neil Simon 1927– : *The Odd Couple* (1966)

75 Serenely full, the epicure would say,
Fate cannot harm me, I have dined to-day.

Sydney Smith 1771–1845: Lady Holland *Memoir* (1855) 'Receipt for a Salad'

76 If there is a pure and elevated pleasure in this world it is a roast pheasant with bread sauce. Barn door fowls for dissenters but for the real Churchman, the thirty-nine times articled clerk—the pheasant, the pheasant.

Sydney Smith 1771–1845: letter to R. H. Barham, 15 November 1841

77 Shepherd's pie peppered with actual shepherd on top.
one of Mrs Lovett's variations on Sweeney Todd's human meat pies

Stephen Sondheim 1930– : 'A Little Priest' (1979)

78 Have an egg roll, Mr Goldstone,
Have a napkin, have a chopstick, have a chair!
Have a sparerib, Mr Goldstone—
Any sparerib that I can spare, I'd be glad to share!

Stephen Sondheim 1930– : 'Mr Goldstone, I Love You' (1959)

79 Someone at the table, whose order had not yet arrived, said, 'I think "waiter" is such a funny word. It is we who wait.'

Muriel Spark 1918–2006: *The Finishing School* (2004)

80 For the edible and the readable we give thanks to God, the Author of Life.

Mervyn Stockwood 1913–95: grace for a literary lunch, in Ned Sherrin *Cutting Edge* (1984)

81 I'll fill hup the chinks wi' cheese.

R. S. Surtees 1805–64: *Handley Cross* (1843)

82 MARGARET THATCHER: This food is absolutely delicious.
DENIS THATCHER: So it should be. They're charging like the Light Brigade.
eating in Harry's Bar

Denis Thatcher 1915–2003: attributed; in *Spectator* 20 March 2004

83 *dining with her Cabinet:*
MRS THATCHER: Steak.
WAITER: And the vegetables?
MRS THATCHER: Oh, they'll have steak too.

Margaret Thatcher 1925– : attributed, probably apocryphal

84 *offered jugged hare by his hostess Margaret Taylor, he finally agreed:*
[To] eat the hare of the bitch that dogs me.

Dylan Thomas 1914–53: attributed; Andrew Lycett 'Thomas Untutored' in *Oxford Today* Hilary 2004 (online edition)

85 Cauliflower is nothing but cabbage with a college education.

Mark Twain 1835–1910: *Pudd'nhead Wilson* (1894)

86 'Turbot, Sir,' said the waiter, placing before me two fishbones, two eyeballs, and a bit of black mackintosh.

Thomas Earle Welby 1881–1933: *The Dinner Knell* (1932) 'Birmingham or Crewe?'

87 Beulah, peel me a grape.

Mae West 1892–1980: in *I'm No Angel* (1933 film)

88 MOTHER: It's broccoli, dear.
CHILD: I say it's spinach, and I say the hell with it.

E. B. White 1899–1985: cartoon caption in *New Yorker* 8 December 1928

89 An egg is always an adventure.

Oscar Wilde 1854–1900: Laurence Housman *Echo de Paris: A Study from Life* (1923)

90 When I ask for a watercress sandwich, I do not mean a loaf with a field in the middle of it.

Oscar Wilde 1854–1900: Max Beerbohm letter to Reggie Turner, 15 April 1893

91 I was so darned sorry for poor old Corky that I hadn't the heart to touch my breakfast. I told Jeeves to drink it himself.

P. G. Wodehouse 1881–1975: *My Man Jeeves* (1919)

92 The lunches of fifty-seven years had caused his chest to slip down into the mezzanine floor.

P. G. Wodehouse 1881–1975: *The Heart of a Goof* (1926)

93 What with excellent browsing and sluicing and cheery conversation and what-not, the afternoon passed quite happily.

P. G. Wodehouse 1881–1975: *My Man Jeeves* (1919)

94 JACKIE: Pity there's no such thing as Sugar Replacement Therapy.
VICTORIA: There is. It's called chocolate.

Victoria Wood 1953– : *Mens Sana in Thingummy Doodah* (1990)

95 We ordered our food. David and I ate Dover sole. Ms Fortier ate Mr Blunkett.
dining with David Blunkett and Kimberley Quinn, formerly Fortier

Petronella Wyatt 1969– : in *Sunday Telegraph* 19 December 2004

96 If you dine out of tins, you should have the labels served up with the grub.

Jack B. Yeats 1871–1957: *The Charmed Life* (1938)

97 One doughnut doesn't do a thing. You've got to eat 20 a day for five weeks before you get results.
preparing to play Bridget Jones

Renee Zellweger 1969– : in *Mail on Sunday* 15 June 2003

Foolishness
See also **Ignorance, Stupidity**

❝ *As any fule kno.* **❞**
Geoffrey Willans and Ronald Searle

---

1 *New Year Resolutions*
  1. To refrain from saying witty, unkind things, unless they are really witty and irreparably damaging.
  2. To tolerate fools more gladly, provided this does not encourage them to take up more of my time.

James Agate 1877–1947: diary 2 January 1942

2 Fools have this happiness—to be easy with themselves, and let other people blush for 'em.

Anonymous: in *The Female Tatler* July–August 1709

3 I sometimes wonder if the manufacturers of foolproof items keep a fool or two on their payroll to test things.

Alan Coren 1938–2007: *Seems Like Old Times* (1989)

4 How much a dunce that has been sent to roam
Excels a dunce that has been kept at home?

William Cowper 1731–1800: 'The Progress of Error' (1782)

5 The idiot who praises, with enthusiastic tone,
All centuries but this, and every country but his own.

W. S. Gilbert 1836–1911: *The Mikado* (1885)

6 Oh, innocent victims of Cupid,
Remember this terse little verse;
To let a fool kiss you is stupid,
To let a kiss fool you is worse.

E. Y. Harburg 1898–1981: 'Inscriptions on a Lipstick' (1965)

7 The Lord made Adam,
The Lord made Eve,
He made 'em both a little naïve.

E. Y. Harburg 1898–1981: 'The Begat' (1947)

8 You've heard of people living in a fool's paradise? Well, Leonora has a duplex there.
of Leonora Corbett

George S. Kaufman 1889–1961: Howard Teichmann *George S. Kaufman* (1973)

9 I could name eight people—half of those eight are barmy. How many apples short of a picnic?
on Tory critics

John Major 1943– : comment, 19 September 1993

10 A man may be a fool and not know it, but not if he is married.

H. L. Mencken 1880–1956: Laurence J. Peter (ed.) *Quotations for our Time* (1977)

11 What a waste it is to lose one's mind, or not to have a mind. How true that is.

Dan Quayle 1947– : speech to the United Negro College Fund, whose slogan is 'a mind is a terrible thing to waste'; in *Times* 26 May 1989

12 He does it with a better grace, but I do it more natural.

William Shakespeare 1564–1616: *Twelfth Night* (1601)

13 *Sheridan's son Tom announced that when he became an MP he would proclaim his independence of party by writing 'To Let' on his forehead:*
And, under that, Tom, write 'unfurnished'.

Richard Brinsley Sheridan 1751–1816: Walter Jerrold *Bon-Mots* (1893)

14 'A soldier,' cried my Uncle Toby, interrupting the corporal, 'is no more exempt from saying a foolish thing, Trim, than a man of letters.'—'But not so often, an' please your honour,' replied the corporal.

Laurence Sterne 1713–68: *Tristram Shandy* (1759–67)

15 Major Yammerton was rather a peculiar man, inasmuch as he was an ass, without being a fool.

R. S. Surtees 1805–64: *Ask Mamma* (1858)

16 How haughtily he lifts his nose,
To tell what every schoolboy knows.

Jonathan Swift 1667–1745: 'The Journal' (1727)

17 Hain't we got all the fools in town on our side? and ain't that a big enough majority in any town?

Mark Twain 1835–1910: *The Adventures of Huckleberry Finn* (1884)

18 Man is without any doubt the most interesting fool there is. Also the most eccentric. He hasn't a single written law, in his Bible or out of it, which has any but one purpose and intention—to *limit or defeat a law of God.*

Mark Twain 1835–1910: *Letters from the Earth* (1905–09)

19 As any fule kno.

Geoffrey Willans 1911–58 and **Ronald Searle** 1920– : *Down with Skool!* (1953)

Football
See also **Sports and Games**

❝ I got into moisturiser when I played football. ❞
Vinnie Jones

1 You've got DiCanio, we've
nicked your stereo!
football chant sung by Liverpool fans to West Ham fans to the tune of La donna e mobile

Anonymous: in *Sunday Times* 30 November 2003

2 Why is there only one ball for 22 players? If you gave a ball to each of them, they'd stop fighting for it.
comment of a football widow, posted on an anti-World Cup website

Anonymous: in *Daily Telegraph* 28 December 1998 'Sporting Quotes of the Year'

3 If I had the wings of a sparrow
If I had the arse of a crow
I'd fly over Tottenham tomorrow
And shit on the bastards below.

Anonymous: frequently sung on the Chelsea terraces; Ned Sherrin *Cutting Edge* (1984)

4 He's blond, he's quick,
his name's a porno flick
Emmanuel, Emmanuel.
He's quick, he's blond, he's
won the Coupe du Monde
football chant sung by Arsenal fans when Emmanuel Petit played at Highbury

Anonymous: in *Sunday Times* 30 November 2003

5 *George Best was often told by Matt Busby not to bother to turn up for Busby's team talks to Manchester United:*
It wasn't worth his coming. It was a very simple team talk. All I used to say was: 'Whenever possible, give the ball to George.'

Matt Busby 1909–94: Michael Parkinson *Sporting Lives* (1993)

6 *on meetings with players:*
We talk about it for 20 minutes and then we decide I was right.

7 Football's football; if that weren't the case, it wouldn't be the game it is.

8 United will no longer be a football club, it will be a giant Old Trafford fruit machine.

9 *of Stan Bowles:*
If only he could pass a betting shop like he does a football.

10 One is not amused at that.
reported comment when the disallowing of a goal put England out of the World Cup

11 Football, wherein is nothing but beastly fury, and extreme violence, whereof proceedeth hurt, and consequently rancour and malice do remain with them that be wounded.

12 The only thing that Norwich didn't get was the goal that they finally got.

13 What makes a sane and rational person subject himself to such humiliation? Why on earth does anyone want to become a football referee?

14 The natural state of the football fan is bitter disappointment, no matter what the score.

15 I got into moisturiser when I played football. If you're out in all weathers you have to take care of your face.

16 I don't think some of the people who come to Old Trafford can spell football, never mind understand it.

17 The nice aspect about football is that, if things go wrong, it's the manager who gets the blame.
before his first match as captain of England

18 Football is a simple game; 22 men chase a ball for 90 minutes and at the end, the Germans win.

19 Oh, he's football crazy, he's football mad
And the football it has robbed him o' the wee bit sense he had.
And it would take a dozen skivvies, his clothes to wash and scrub,
Since our Jock became a member of that terrible football club.

20 What's a geriatric? A German footballer scoring three goals.

21 Nobody cares if Le Saux is gay or not. It is the fact that he openly admits to reading *The Guardian* that makes him the most reviled man in football.

Brian Clough 1935–2004: attributed; in *Channel 4 News* 20 September 2004 (online edition)

Garth Crooks 1958– : Barry Fantoni (ed.) *Private Eye's Colemanballs 2* (1984)

Tommy Docherty 1928– : in *Mail on Sunday* 13 September 1998 'Quotes of the Week'

Reg Drury 1928–2003: in *Times* 28 June 2003 (obituary)

Elizabeth II 1926– : in *Daily Telegraph* 28 December 1998 'Sporting Quotes of the Year'

Thomas Elyot 1499–1546: *Book of the Governor* (1531)

Jimmy Greaves 1940– : Barry Fantoni (ed.) *Private Eye's Colemanballs 2* (1984)

Roy Hattersley 1932– : in *Sunday Times* 7 April 2002 'Talking Heads'

Nick Hornby 1957– : *Fever Pitch* (1992)

Vinnie Jones 1965– : in *Independent* 28 December 2002

Roy Keane 1971– : in *Belfast Telegraph* 9 November 2000

Gary Lineker 1960– : in *Independent* 12 September 1990

Gary Lineker 1960– : attributed

Jimmy McGregor: 'Football Crazy' (1960)

Bob Monkhouse 1928–2003: attributed; in *BBC News* (UK edition, online) 29 December 2003

Piers Morgan 1965– : letter to *Guardian*, 5 March 1999

22 To say that these men paid their shillings to watch twenty-two hirelings kick a ball is merely to say that a violin is wood and catgut, that *Hamlet* is so much paper and ink. For a shilling the Bruddersford United AFC offered you Conflict and Art.

J. B. Priestley 1894–1984: *Good Companions* (1929)

23 We didn't underestimate them. They were a lot better than we thought.
on Cameroon's football team

Bobby Robson 1933– : in *Guardian* 24 December 1990 'Sports Quotes of the Year'

24 Some people think football is a matter of life and death . . . I can assure them it is much more serious than that.

Bill Shankly 1913–81: in *Guardian* 24 December 1973 'Sports Quotes of the Year'

25 [Gary Lineker is] the Queen Mother of football.

Arthur Smith 1954– and **Chris England**: *An Evening with Gary Lineker* (1990)

26 The English football team—brilliant on paper, shit on grass.

Arthur Smith 1954– and **Chris England**: *An Evening with Gary Lineker* (1990)

27 Football and cookery are the two most important subjects in the country.
having been appointed a director of Norwich City football club

Delia Smith 1941– : in *Observer* 23 February 1997 'Said and Done'

28 We're having a philosophical discussion about the yob ethics of professional footballers.

Tom Stoppard 1937– : *Professional Foul* (1978)

29 Me and the wife are breeding our own team. When I get home tonight it'll be 'c'mon hen, we need a centre-back.'
comment by the manager of Coventry, whose son is a Sky Blues youth-team player

Gordon Strachan 1957– : in *Daily Telegraph* 28 December 1998 'Sporting Quotes of the Year'

30 REPORTER: So, Gordon, in what areas do you think Middlesbrough were better than you today?
GORDON STRACHAN: What areas? Mainly that big green one out there . . .

Gordon Strachan 1957– : attributed

31 I tell you what son, playing football is a lot easier than directing a funeral.
comparing his two careers

Ray Wilson 1934– : Simon Hattenstone *The Best of Times: What became of the heroes of '66?* (2006)

France

❝ How can you govern a country which has 246 varieties of cheese? ❞
Charles de Gaulle

1 France is the only place where you can make love in the afternoon without people hammering on your door.

Barbara Cartland 1901–2000: in *Guardian* 24 December 1984

2 Every wise and thoroughly worldly wench
Knows there's always something fishy about the French!

Noël Coward 1899–1973: 'There's Always Something Fishy about the French' (1933)

3 How can you govern a country which has 246 varieties of cheese?

Charles de Gaulle 1890–1970: Ernest Mignon *Les Mots du Général* (1962)

4 I hate the French, I hate them all,
From Toulouse Lafucking Trec to Charles de Gaulle.

Paul Scott Goodman: 'I Hate the French' (*Bright Lights, Big City*, 1988 musical, from the book by Jay McInerney)

5 Bonjourr, you cheese-eating surrender monkeys.
Groundskeeper Willie as French teacher

Matt Groening 1954– : *The Simpsons* (1995) 'Round Springfield'

6 The French are always too wordy and need cutting by half before they start.

Miles Kington 1941–2008: in *Spectator* 16 December 2006

7 No matter how politely or distinctly you ask a Parisian a question he will persist in answering you in French.

Fran Lebowitz 1946– : *Metropolitan Life* (1978)

8 Yet, who can help loving the land that has taught us Six hundred and eighty-five ways to dress eggs?

Thomas Moore 1779–1852: *The Fudge Family in Paris* (1818)

9 They order, said I, this matter better in France.

Laurence Sterne 1713–68: opening words of *A Sentimental Journey* (1768)

10 Paris last year. Wonderful town but the French are awful, the waiters and so on, they're tip mad.

Tom Stoppard 1937– : *Neutral Ground* (1983)

11 France is a country where the money falls apart in your hands and you can't tear the toilet paper.

Billy Wilder 1906–2002: Leslie Halliwell *The Filmgoer's Book of Quotes* (1973)

Friends

See also **Enemies**

❝ *He hasn't an enemy in the world, and none of his friends like him.* **❞**
Oscar Wilde

1 I may be wrong, but I have never found deserting friends conciliates enemies.

Margot Asquith 1864–1945: *Lay Sermons* (1927)

2 Champagne for my real friends, and real pain for my sham friends.
his favourite toast

Francis Bacon 1909–92: Michael Peppiatt *Francis Bacon* (1996)

3 It may be more difficult to make new friends as you get older but it is some consolation to know how easy it is to lose them when you are young.

Jeffrey Bernard 1932–97: in *The Spectator* 17 August 1985

4 A person whom we know well enough to borrow from, but not well enough to lend to. A degree of friendship called slight when its object is poor or obscure, and intimate when he is rich or famous.

Ambrose Bierce 1842–c.1914: definition of an acquaintance; *The Cynic's Word Book* (1906)

5 *of a rival:*
Such a clever actress. Pity she does her hair with Bovril.

Mrs Patrick Campbell 1865–1940: in *Ned Sherrin in his Anecdotage* (1993); attributed

6 *during an audience with the Pope:*
I expect you know my friend Evelyn Waugh, who, like your holiness, is a Roman Catholic.

Randolph Churchill 1911–68: attributed; in *Penguin Dictionary of Modern Quotations* (1971)

7 To find a friend one must close one eye. To keep him— two.

Norman Douglas 1868–1952: *South Wind* (1917)

8 [Friends are] God's apology for relations.

Hugh Kingsmill 1889–1949: Michael Holroyd *The Best of Hugh Kingsmill* (1970)

9 Money couldn't buy friends but you got a better class of enemy.

Spike Milligan 1918–2002: *Puckoon* (1963)

10 Scratch a lover, and find a foe.

Dorothy Parker 1893–1967: 'Ballade of a Great Weariness' (1937)

11 If it is abuse,—why one is always sure to hear of it from one damned goodnatured friend or another!

Richard Brinsley Sheridan 1751–1816: *The Critic* (1779)

12 We were in some little time fixed in our seats, and sat with that dislike which people not too good-natured usually conceive of each other at first sight.

Richard Steele 1672–1729: *The Spectator* 1 August 1711

13 You had only two friends in the world, and having killed one you can't afford to irritate the other.

Tom Stoppard 1937– : *Artist Descending a Staircase* (1973)

14 *on Harold Macmillan's sacking seven of his Cabinet on 13 July 1962:*
Greater love hath no man than this, that he lay down his friends for his life.

Jeremy Thorpe 1929– : D. E. Butler and Anthony King *The General Election of 1964* (1965)

15 It takes your enemy and your friend, working together, to hurt you to the heart: the one to slander you and the other to get the news to you.

Mark Twain 1835–1910: *Following the Equator* (1897)

16 Unfortunately we have little in common except a mutual knowledge of a story by Charlotte Yonge in which the hero is an albino curate with eyes like rubies. This is cordial, but not enough.

Sylvia Townsend Warner 1893–1978: letter, 31 October 1967

17 He [Bernard Shaw] hasn't an enemy in the world, and none of his friends like him.

Oscar Wilde 1854–1900: George Bernard Shaw *Sixteen Self Sketches* (1949)

18 *I* go to the OP club [a theatrical society where he would have faced a hostile audience]? I should be like a poor lion in a den of Daniels.

Oscar Wilde 1854–1900: Ford Madox Ford *Return to Yesterday* (1931)

Funerals

> **❝** *I have nothing against undertakers personally.* **❞**
> **Jessica Mitford**

1 You can't get buried quickly at Bexhill on Sea—it's like getting a table at the Caprice.

David Hare 1947– : Richard Eyre *National Service: Diary of a Decade* (2003)

2 *fax sent to Harry Secombe:*
I hope you go before me because I don't want you singing at my funeral.

Spike Milligan 1918–2002: attributed; in *Daily Telegraph* 28 February 2002

3 I have nothing against undertakers personally. It's just that I wouldn't want one to bury my sister.

Jessica Mitford 1917–96: in *Saturday Review* 1 February 1964

4 *on Teddy Kennedy arriving for Aristotle Onassis's funeral:*
Looking like a priestly hustler peddling indulgences.

Christina Onassis 1950–88: Peter Evans *Nemesis: the True Story of Aristotle* (2004)

The Future

See also **Past and Present**

> *❝Cheer up! the worst is yet to come!❞*
>
> **Philander Chase Johnson**

1 Fascism is not in itself a new order of society. It is the future refusing to be born.

Aneurin Bevan 1897–1960: Leon Harris *The Fine Art of Political Wit* (1965)

2 That period of time in which our affairs prosper, our friends are true, and our happiness is assured.

Ambrose Bierce 1842–c.1914: *The Cynic's Word Book* (1906)

3 Predictions can be very difficult—especially about the future.

Niels Bohr 1885–1962: attributed

4 Posterity is as likely to be wrong as anybody else.

Heywood Broun 1888–1939: *Sitting on the World* (1924)

5 You're so lucky! You'll be around to see what happened to Charlotte Church!

Willie Donaldson 1935–2005: Terence Blacker *You Cannot Live as I Have Lived and Not End Up Like This* (2007)

6 I never think of the future. It comes soon enough.

Albert Einstein 1879–1955: interview given on the *Belgenland*, December 1930

7 Why should I write for posterity?
What, if I may be free
To ask a ridiculous question,
Has posterity done for me?

E. Y. Harburg 1898–1981: 'Posterity is Right Around the Corner' (1976)

8 This very remarkable man
Commends a most practical plan:
You can do what you want
If you don't think you can't,
So don't think you can't think you can.

Charles Inge 1868–1957: 'On Monsieur Coué' (1928)

9 You can only predict things after they have happened.

Eugène Ionesco 1912–94: *Le Rhinocéros* (1959)

10 Cheer up! the worst is yet to come!

Philander Chase Johnson 1866–1939: in *Everybody's Magazine* May 1920

11 The bridge to the future is the phallus.

D. H. Lawrence 1885–1930: *Sex, Literature and Censorship* (1955)

12 Soon we'll be sliding down the razor-blade of life.

Tom Lehrer 1928– : 'Bright College Days' (c.1960)

13 *supposed opening words of a letter of dismissal to the* Sun's *astrologer:*
As you will no doubt have foreseen . . .

Kelvin Mackenzie 1946– : attributed, probably apocryphal

Gambling

66 *All life is 6 to 5 against.* 99
Damon Runyon

1 I have a notion that gamblers are as happy as most people—being always excited.

2 Rowe's Rule: the odds are five to six that the light at the end of the tunnel is the headlight of an oncoming train.

3 Never give a sucker an even break.

4 GAMBLER: Say, is this a game of chance?
CUTHBERT J. TWILLIE: Not the way I play it.

5 Two-up is Australia's very own way of parting a fool and his money.

6 *asked how his bridge-partner should have played a hand:* Under an assumed name.

7 I long ago come to the conclusion that all life is 6 to 5 against.

Lord Byron 1788–1824: 'Detached Thoughts' 15 October 1821

Paul Dickson 1939– : in *Washingtonian* November 1978

W. C. Fields 1880–1946: title of a W. C. Fields film (1941); the catch-phrase (Fields's own) is said to have originated in the musical comedy *Poppy* (1923)

W. C. Fields 1880–1946: *My Little Chickadee* (1940 film), spoken by W. C. Fields

Germaine Greer 1939– : in *Observer* 1 August 1982

George S. Kaufman 1889–1961: Scott Meredith *George S. Kaufman and the Algonquin Round Table* (1974)

Damon Runyon 1884–1946: in *Collier's* 8 September 1934, 'A Nice Price'

Games See **Sports and Games**

Gardens

66 *Biennials are the ones that die this year instead of next.* 99
Katharine Whitehorn

1 I'm not a dirt gardener. I sit with my walking stick and point things out that need to be done. After many years, the garden is now totally obedient.

2 Everyone with a garden, however small, should have a few acres of woodland.

3 One thimbleful of water every blue moon does not constitute expertise. Otherwise we should all be fellows of the Royal Horticultural Society.

4 Laid to lawn? This is laid to adventure playground.

Hardy Amies 1909–2003: in *Sunday Times* 11 July 1999

Anonymous: saying, sometimes attributed to Lord Rothschild or to an unidentified Director of the Royal Horticultural Society

Alan Bennett 1934– : *Getting On* (1972)

Basil Boothroyd 1910–88: *Let's Move House* (1977)

5 A delectable sward, shaved as close as a bridegroom and looking just as green.

Basil Boothroyd 1910–88: *Let's Move House* (1977)

6 I will keep returning to the virtues of sharp and swift drainage, whether a plant prefers to be wet or dry . . . I would have called this book Better Drains, but you would never have bought it or borrowed it for bedtime.

Robin Lane Fox 1946– : *Better Gardening* (1982)

7 Eleven months' hard work and one month's acute disappointment.
on gardening

John Heathcoat Amory: attributed; in *Guardian* 3 February 2006

8 I was dosing the greenfly . . . with that frightfully good aerosol defoliant that Picarda got the recipe for from some boffin on the run from Porton Down.

Richard Ingrams 1937– and **John Wells** 1936– : *The Other Half* (1981); 'Dear Bill' letters

9 Mad fools of gardeners go out in the pouring rain
To prove they're Anglo-Saxon
They rarely put their macks on;
Each puts on rubber boots and squelches through moist terrain,
Then leaves the mud and silt on
The Wilton.

Alan Melville 1910–83: *Gnomes and Gardens* (1983)

10 'I distinguish the picturesque and the beautiful, and I add to them, in the laying out of the grounds, a third and distinct character, which I call *unexpectedness*.'
'Pray, Sir,' said Mr Milestone, 'by what name do you distinguish this character, when a person walks round the grounds for a second time?'

Thomas Love Peacock 1785–1866: *Headlong Hall* (1816)

11 'All really grim gardeners possess a keen sense of humus.' Capt. W. D. Pontoon.

W. C. Sellar 1898–1951 and **R. J. Yeatman** 1898–1968: *Garden Rubbish* (1930); chapter heading

12 'I want to be a lawn.' Greta Garbo.

W. C. Sellar 1898–1951 and **R. J. Yeatman** 1898–1968: *Garden Rubbish* (1930); chapter heading

13 Perennials are the ones that grow like weeds, biennials are the ones that die this year instead of next and hardy annuals are the ones that never come up at all.

Katharine Whitehorn 1928– : *Observations* (1970)

The Generation Gap
See also **Children, Parents**

❝ Time to make way for an Older Man. ❞
Maurice Bowra

1 Time is the one thing you have got. If there's one thing I envy you for, it's not your cool and your easy birds . . . it's time.

Alan Bennett 1934– : *Getting On* (1972)

2 They're both on drugs, they both detest you, and neither of them has a job.
on the similarities between teenagers and their grandparents

Jasper Carrott 1945– : in *Observer* 11 January 2004

3 What's the point in growing old if you can't hound and persecute the young?

Kenneth Clarke 1940– : in *Observer* 27 May 2007 'Quotes of the Week'

4 It is the one war in which everyone changes sides.

Cyril Connolly 1903–74: Tom Driberg, speech in House of Commons, 30 October 1959

5 Grown-ups never understand anything for themselves, and it is tiresome for children to be always and forever explaining things to them.

Antoine de Saint-Exupéry 1900–44: *Le Petit Prince* (1943)

6 When I was young, the old regarded me as an outrageous young fellow, and now that I'm old the young regard me as an outrageous old fellow.

Fred Hoyle 1915–2001: in *Scientific American* March 1995

7 What is a teenager in San Francisco to rebel against, for pity's sake? Their parents are all so busy trying to be non-judgemental, it's no wonder they take to dyeing their hair green.

Molly Ivins 1944–2007: in *Dallas Times Herald* 3 February 1987

8 I . . . remember how I regarded adults when I was small. They seemed a grey crew to me, too fond of sitting down, too keen on small talk, too accustomed to having nothing to look forward to.

Ian McEwan 1948– : *Enduring Love* (1998)

9 Remember the battle between the generations twenty-some years ago . . . Well, our parents won. They're out there living the American dream on some damned golf course, and we're stuck with the jobs and haircuts.

P. J. O'Rourke 1947– : *Parliament of Whores* (1991)

10 The young have aspirations that never come to pass, the old have reminiscences of what never happened.

Saki 1870–1916: *Reginald* (1904)

11 The denunciation of the young is a necessary part of the hygiene of older people, and greatly assists the circulation of their blood.

Logan Pearsall Smith 1865–1946: *Afterthoughts* (1931) 'Age and Death'

12 There is more felicity on the far side of baldness than young men can possibly imagine.

Logan Pearsall Smith 1865–1946: *Afterthoughts* (1931) 'Age and Death'

13 When I was a boy of 14, my father was so ignorant I could hardly stand to have the old man around. But when I got to be 21, I was astonished at how much the old man had learned in seven years.

Mark Twain 1835–1910: attributed in *Reader's Digest* September 1939, but not traced in his works

14 Two things my parents did for me as a child stand head and shoulders above what parents usually do for their children. They had me in Egypt and they set me a vivid example of everything I didn't want to be when I grew up.

Jill Tweedie 1936–93: *Eating Children* (1993)

15 When I was your age . . . I had been an inconsolable widower for three months, and was already paying my addresses to your admirable mother.

Oscar Wilde 1854–1900: *An Ideal Husband* (1895)

God
See also **Religion**

❝ I'm sorry, we don't do God. ❞
Alastair Campbell

1 If it turns out that there is a God, I don't think that he's evil. But the worst that you can say about him is that basically he's an underachiever.

Woody Allen 1935– : *Love and Death* (1975 film)

2 If only God would give me some clear sign! Like making a large deposit in my name at a Swiss bank.

Woody Allen 1935– : 'Selections from the Allen Notebooks' in *New Yorker* 5 November 1973

3 God is silent, now if only we can get Man to shut up.

Woody Allen 1935– : 'Remembering Needleman' (1976)

4 God is not dead but alive and working on a much less ambitious project.

Anonymous: graffito quoted in *Guardian* 26 November 1975

5 Dear Sir,
Your astonishment's odd:
I am always about in the Quad.
And that's why the tree
Will continue to be,
Since observed by
Yours faithfully,
God.

Anonymous: reply to verse by Ronald Knox (see **God** 31); Langford Reed *Complete Limerick Book* (1924)

6 Not odd
Of God:
Goyim
Annoy 'im.

Anonymous: in *Leo Rosten's Book of Laughter* (1986); see **God** 13, **God** 23

7 If I were Her what would really piss me off the worst is that they cannot even get My gender right for Christsakes.

Roseanne Arnold 1953– : *Roseanne* (1990)

8 CLAIRE: How do you know you're . . . God?
EARL OF GURNEY: Simple. When I pray to Him I find I'm talking to myself.

Peter Barnes 1931– : *The Ruling Class* (1969)

9 Let us pray to God . . . the bastard! He doesn't exist!

Samuel Beckett 1906–89: *Endgame* (1958)

10 *replying to the Master of Trinity College Cambridge, H. M. Butler, who in proposing the health of the College had said that 'it was well to remember that, at this moment, both the Sovereign and the Prime Minister are Trinity men':*
The Master should have added that he can go further, for it is obvious that the affairs of the world are built upon the momentous fact that God also is a Trinity man.

Augustine Birrell 1850–1933: Harold Laski, letter to Oliver Wendell Holmes, 4 December 1926

11 *Birrell once saw a man treat George Eliot rudely:*
I sat down in a corner and prayed to God to blast him. God did nothing, and ever since I have been an agnostic.

Augustine Birrell 1850–1933: Harold Laski, letter to Oliver Wendell Holmes, 21 January 1928

12 *Boswell's daughter had concluded that God did not exist:*
I looked into Cambrai's *Education of a Daughter*, hoping to have found some simple argument for the being of God. But it is taken for granted.

James Boswell 1740–95: diary, 20 December 1779

13 But not so odd
As those who choose
A Jewish God,
But spurn the Jews.

Cecil Browne 1932– : reply to verse by William Norman Ewer; see **God** 6, **God** 23

14 An apology for the Devil: It must be remembered that we have only heard one side of the case. God has written all the books.

Samuel Butler 1835–1902: *Notebooks* (1912)

15 God will not always be a Tory.

Lord Byron 1788–1824: letter, 2 February 1821

16 I'm sorry, we don't do God.
when Tony Blair was asked about his Christian faith in an interview for Vanity Fair *magazine*

Alastair Campbell 1957– : in *Daily Telegraph* 5 May 2003

17 He's not the Messiah! He's a very naughty boy!
Brian's mother to his would-be followers

Graham Chapman 1941–89, **John Cleese** 1939– , et al.: *Monty Python's Life of Brian* (1979 film)

18 Isn't God a shit?
while reading the Bible straight through for a bet

Randolph Churchill 1911–68: Evelyn Waugh, diary 11 November 1944

19 Thou shalt have one God only; who
Would be at the expense of two?

Arthur Hugh Clough 1819–61: 'The Latest Decalogue' (1862)

20 Do I believe in God? Let's say we have a working relationship.

Noël Coward 1899–1973: Sheridan Morley *The Quotable Noël Coward* (1999)

21 I don't believe in God because I don't believe in Mother Goose.

Clarence Darrow 1857–1938: speech in Toronto in 1930

22 Our only hope rests on the off-chance that God does exist.

Alice Thomas Ellis 1932–2005: *Unexplained Laughter* (1985)

23 How odd
Of God
To choose
The Jews.

William Norman Ewer 1885–1976: *Week-End Book* (1924); see **God** 6, **God** 13

24 Forgive, O Lord, my little jokes on Thee
And I'll forgive Thy great big one on me.

Robert Frost 1874–1963: 'Cluster of Faith' (1962)

25 Did God who gave us flowers and trees,
Also provide the allergies?

E. Y. Harburg 1898–1981: 'A Nose is a Nose is a Nose' (1965)

26 God will pardon me, it is His trade.

Heinrich Heine 1797–1856: on his deathbed, in Alfred Meissner *Heinrich Heine. Erinnerungen* (1856); see **Royalty**

27 The great act of faith is when a man decides he is not God.

Oliver Wendell Holmes Jr. 1841–1935: letter to William James, 24 March 1907

28 *to an undergraduate trying to excuse himself from attendance at early morning chapel on the plea of loss of faith:*
You will find God by tomorrow morning, or leave this college.

Benjamin Jowett 1817–93: Kenneth Rose *Superior Person* (1969)

29 Zeus, 'the God of wine and whoopee'.

Garrison Keillor 1942– : *The Book of Guys* (1994)

30 The peculiar, even unsatisfactory system whereby God never communicated direct with his chosen people but preferred to give the Israelite leaders an off-the-record briefing.

Miles Kington 1941–2008: *Welcome to Kington* (1989)

31 There once was a man who said, 'God
Must think it exceedingly odd
If he finds that this tree
Continues to be
When there's no one about in the Quad.'

Ronald Knox 1888–1957: Langford Reed *Complete Limerick Book* (1924); see **God** 5

32 I don't know why it is that the religious never ascribe common sense to God.

W. Somerset Maugham 1874–1965: *A Writer's Notebook* (1949) written in 1941

33 The chief contribution of Protestantism to human thought is its massive proof that God is a bore.

H. L. Mencken 1880–1956: *Minority Report* (1956)

34 It is impossible to imagine the universe run by a wise, just and omnipotent God, but it is quite easy to imagine it run by a board of gods. If such a board actually exists it operates precisely like the board of a corporation that is losing money.

H. L. Mencken 1880–1956: *Minority Report* (1956)

35 God, to whom, if he existed, I felt I should have nothing very polite to say.

John Mortimer 1923–2009: *Clinging to the Wreckage* (1982)

36 Satan probably wouldn't have talked so big if God had been his wife.

P. J. O'Rourke 1947– : *Modern Manners* (1984)

37 God, whom you doubtless remember as that quaint old subordinate of General Douglas MacArthur.

S. J. Perelman 1904–79: letter to Mel Elliott, 24 April 1951

38 God can stand being told by Professor Ayer and Marghanita Laski that He doesn't exist.

J. B. Priestley 1894–1984: in *Listener* 1 July 1965

39 I've made a lot of mistakes, but, boy, you've made a lot more.
   on what he plans to say to God when they meet

Burt Reynolds 1936– : in *Sunday Times* 17 February 2002

40 Those who set out to serve both God and Mammon soon discover that there is no God.

Logan Pearsall Smith 1865–1946: *Afterthoughts* (1931) 'Other People'

41 For ten years of my life, three times a day, I thanked the Lord for what I was about to receive and thanked him again for what I had just received, and then we lost touch—and I suddenly thought, *where is He now?*

Tom Stoppard 1937– : *Where Are They Now?* (1973)

42 Only one thing, is impossible for God: to find any sense in any copyright law on the planet.

Mark Twain 1835–1910: Notebook 23 May 1903

43 God was left out of the Constitution but was furnished a front seat on the coins of the country.

Mark Twain 1835–1910: *Mark Twain in Eruption* (1940)

44 Even God has become female. God is no longer the bearded patriarch in the sky. He has had a sex change and turned into Mother Nature.

Fay Weldon 1931– : in *Times* 29 August 1998

Golf
See also **Sports and Games**

❝ The uglier a man's legs are, the better he plays golf. ❞
H. G. Wells

1 His drive has gone to pieces, largely through having more hinges in it than a sardine tin. But he could always play his iron shots, and his never-ending chatter must be worth at least two holes to his side.

James Agate 1877–1947: diary, 7 August 1938

2 *on the golf course, on being asked by Nancy Cunard, 'What is your handicap?'*
   Drink and debauchery.

Lord Castlerosse 1891–1943: Philip Ziegler *Diana Cooper* (1981)

3 QUESTION: What is your handicap?
   ANSWER: I'm a colored, one-eyed Jew—do I need anything else?

Sammy Davis Jnr. 1925–90: *Yes I Can* (1965)

4 One who has to shout 'Fore' when he putts.
definition of a Coarse Golfer

Michael Green 1927– : *The Art of Coarse Golf* (1967)

5 Men who would face torture without a word become blasphemous at the short fourteenth. It is clear that the game of golf may well be included in that category of intolerable provocations which may legally excuse or mitigate behaviour not otherwise excusable.

A. P. Herbert 1890–1971: *Misleading Cases* (1935)

6 If you watch a game, it's fun. If you play it, it's recreation. If you work at it, it's golf.

Bob Hope 1903–2003: in *Reader's Digest* October 1958

7 I consider it unsportsmanlike to hit a sitting ball.
on why he disliked golf

Ernest Hornung 1866–1921: attributed; Julian Barnes *Arthur and George* (2005)

8 While tearing off
A game of golf
I may make a play for the caddy.
But when I do
I don't follow through
'Cause my heart belongs to Daddy.

Cole Porter 1891–1964: 'My Heart belongs to Daddy' (1938)

9 I'm playing like Tarzan and scoring like Jane.

Chi Chi Rodrigues 1935– : attributed, 1982

10 Golf is a good walk spoiled.

Mark Twain 1835–1910: Alex Ayres *Greatly Exaggerated: the Wit and Wisdom of Mark Twain* (1988); attributed

11 The uglier a man's legs are, the better he plays golf—it's almost a law.

H. G. Wells 1866–1946: *Bealby* (1915)

12 The least thing upset him on the links. He missed short putts because of the uproar of the butterflies in the adjoining meadows.

P. G. Wodehouse 1881–1975: *The Clicking of Cuthbert* (1922)

13 Golf . . . is the infallible test. The man who can go into a patch of rough alone, with the knowledge that only God is watching him, and play his ball where it lies, is the man who will serve you faithfully and well.

P. G. Wodehouse 1881–1975: *The Clicking of Cuthbert* (1922)

Gossip

66 *Hopefully, there's one good scandal left in me yet.* 99
Diana Rigg

1 I know that's a secret, for it's whispered every where.

William Congreve 1670–1729: *Love for Love* (1695)

2 They come together like the Coroner's Inquest, to sit upon the murdered reputations of the week.

William Congreve 1670–1729: *The Way of the World* (1700)

3 A secret in the Oxford sense: you may tell it to only one person at a time.

Oliver Franks 1905–92: in *Sunday Telegraph* 30 January 1977

4 It's the gossip columnist's business to write about what is none of his business.

Louis Kronenberger 1904–80: *The Cart and the Horse* (1964)

5 I hate to spread rumours, but what else can one do with them?

Amanda Lear: in an interview in 1978; Jonathon Green (ed.) *A Dictionary of Contemporary Quotations* (1978)

6 If you haven't got anything good to say about anyone come and sit by me.

Alice Roosevelt Longworth 1884–1980: maxim embroidered on a cushion; Michael Teague *Mrs L: Conversations with Alice Roosevelt Longworth* (1981)

7 She proceeds to dip her little fountain-pen filler into pots of oily venom and to squirt this mixture at all her friends.
  of the society hostess Mrs Ronnie Greville

Harold Nicolson 1886–1968: diary, 20 July 1937

8 You have dished me up, like a savoury omelette, to gratify the appetite of the reading rabble for gossip.

Thomas Love Peacock 1785–1866: *Crotchet Castle* (1831)

9 I hope there's a tinge of disgrace about me. Hopefully, there's one good scandal left in me yet.

Diana Rigg 1938– : in *Times* 3 May 1999

10 I'm called away by particular business—but I leave my character behind me.

Richard Brinsley Sheridan 1751–1816: *The School for Scandal* (1777)

11 Here is the whole set! a character dead at every word.

Richard Brinsley Sheridan 1751–1816: *The School for Scandal* (1777)

12 It is perfectly monstrous the way people go about, nowadays, saying things against one behind one's back that are absolutely and entirely true.

Oscar Wilde 1854–1900: *A Woman of No Importance* (1893)

13 There is only one thing in the world worse than being talked about, and that is not being talked about.

Oscar Wilde 1854–1900: *The Picture of Dorian Gray* (1891)

Government
See also **Democracy, Politics**

❝ We all know that Prime Ministers are wedded to the truth, but like other married couples they sometimes live apart. ❞
Saki

1 The first requirement of a statesman is that he be dull.

Dean Acheson 1893–1971: in *Observer* 21 June 1970

2 There is, in fact, no law or government at all [in Italy]; and it is wonderful how well things go on without them.

Lord Byron 1788–1824: letter, 2 January 1821

3 Democracy means government by the uneducated, while aristocracy means government by the badly educated.

G. K. Chesterton 1874–1936: in *New York Times* 1 February 1931

4 Like most Chief Whips he [Michael Jopling] knew who the shits were.

Alan Clark 1928–99: diary, 17 June 1987

5 A wartime Minister of Information is compelled, in the national interest, to such continuous acts of duplicity that even his natural hair must grow to resemble a wig.
of Brendan Bracken

Claud Cockburn 1904–81: *Crossing the Line* (1958)

6 MRS THATCHER: I do not create peers to have them vote against me in the House of Lords.
LORD DENHAM: Prime Minister, even you should know better than to expect me to find you a majority during Gold Cup week.
exchange between the Prime Minister and the Leader of the House of Lords

Lord Denham 1927– : Peter Hennessy *The Prime Minister* (2000)

7 Distrust of authority should be the first civic duty.

Norman Douglas 1868–1952: *An Almanac* October (1941)

8 A woolsack without a Lord Chancellor resplendent in his wig will be like Ascot without the hats and morning coats.

Lord Falkland 1935– : in *Independent* 5 July 2003 'Quotes of the Week'

9 Ambassadors cropped up like hay,
Prime Ministers and such as they
Grew like asparagus in May,
And dukes were three a penny.

W. S. Gilbert 1836–1911: *The Gondoliers* (1889)

10 But the privilege and pleasure
That we treasure beyond measure
Is to run on little errands for the Ministers of State.

W. S. Gilbert 1836–1911: *The Gondoliers* (1889)

11 The House of Peers, throughout the war,
Did nothing in particular,
And did it very well.

W. S. Gilbert 1836–1911: *Iolanthe* (1882)

12 'Do you pray for the senators, Dr Hale?' 'No, I look at the senators and I pray for the country.'

Edward Everett Hale 1822–1909: Van Wyck Brooks *New England Indian Summer* (1940)

13 This we learn from Watergate
That almost any creep'll
Be glad to help the Government
Overthrow the people.

E. Y. Harburg 1898–1981: 'History Lesson' (1976)

14 This high official, all allow,
Is grossly overpaid;
There wasn't any Board, and now
There isn't any Trade.

A. P. Herbert 1890–1971: 'The President of the Board of Trade' (1922)

15 People must not do things for fun. We are not here for fun. There is no reference to fun in any Act of Parliament.

A. P. Herbert 1890–1971: *Uncommon Law* (1935) 'Is it a Free Country?'

16 *Alan Clark, then a Parliamentary Under-Secretary at the Department of Employment, asked Douglas Hogg, then a junior Whip, how he was 'keeping all the new boys in order':*
By offering them your job.

Douglas Hogg 1945– : Alan Clark, diary, 28 July 1983

17 Office hours are from 12 to 1 with an hour off for lunch.
of the US Senate

George S. Kaufman 1889–1961: Howard Teichmann *George S. Kaufman* (1973)

18 We are a government of laws. Any laws some government hack can find to louse up a man who's down.

Murray Kempton 1917–97: in *New York Post* 21 December 1955

19 I work for a Government I despise for ends I think criminal.

John Maynard Keynes 1883–1946: letter to Duncan Grant, 15 December 1917

20 How is the world ruled and how do wars start? Diplomats tell lies to journalists and then believe what they read.

Karl Kraus 1874–1936: *Aphorisms and More Aphorisms* (1909)

21 *on suggestions that the US should draft a Constitution for Iraq:* We might as well give them ours. We aren't using it.

Jay Leno 1950– : attributed; in *Mail on Sunday* 7 September 2003

22 One of these days the people of Louisiana are going to get good government—and they aren't going to like it.

Huey Long 1893–1935: attributed

23 *describing the traditional method of running the economy:* [Like] looking up trains in last year's Bradshaw.

Harold Macmillan 1894–1986: as Chancellor of the Exchequer, 1956; in Alistair Horne *Macmillan* (1988)

24 He [Calvin Coolidge] slept more than any other President, whether by day or by night. Nero fiddled, but Coolidge only snored.

H. L. Mencken 1880–1956: in *American Mercury* April 1933

25 The worst government is often the most moral. One composed of cynics is often very tolerant and humane. But when fanatics are on top there is no limit to oppression.

H. L. Mencken 1880–1956: *Minority Report* (1956)

26 There are two reasons for making an appointment. Either there was nobody else; or there *was* somebody else.

Lord Normanbrook 1902–67: Anthony Sampson *The Changing Anatomy of Britain* (1982)

27 I don't want to abolish government. I simply want to reduce it to the size where I can drag it into the bathroom and drown it in the bathtub.

Grover Norquist 1956– : interview on National Public Radio, Morning Edition, 25 May 2001

28 *criticism of an opposition motion to declare general warrants illegal, 17 February 1764:* If I was a Judge, I should pay no more regard to this resolution than to that of a drunken porter.

Fletcher Norton 1716–89: Horace Walpole *Memoirs of the Reign of George III* (1845)

29 Are you labouring under the impression that I read these memoranda of yours? I can't even lift them.
to Leon Henderson

Franklin D. Roosevelt 1882–1945: J. K. Galbraith *Ambassador's Journal* (1969)

30 We all know that Prime Ministers are wedded to the truth, but like other married couples they sometimes live apart.

Saki 1870–1916: *The Unbearable Bassington* (1912)

31 Members [of civil service orders] rise from CMG (known sometimes in Whitehall as 'Call Me God') to the KCMG ('Kindly Call Me God') to—for a select few governors and super-ambassadors—the GCMG ('God Calls Me God').

Anthony Sampson 1926–2004: *Anatomy of Britain* (1962)

32 The art of government is the organization of idolatry.

George Bernard Shaw 1856–1950: *Man and Superman* (1903) 'Maxims: Idolatry'

33 A government which robs Peter to pay Paul can always depend on the support of Paul.

George Bernard Shaw 1856–1950: *Everybody's Political What's What?* (1944)

34 Back in the East you can't do much without the right papers, but *with* the right papers you can do *anything*. They *believe* in papers. Papers are power.

Tom Stoppard 1937– : *Neutral Ground* (1983)

35 The House of Lords, an illusion to which I have never been able to subscribe—responsibility without power, the prerogative of the eunuch throughout the ages.

Tom Stoppard 1937– : *Lord Malquist and Mr Moon* (1966)

36 I don't mind how much my Ministers talk, so long as they do what I say.

Margaret Thatcher 1925– : in *Observer* 27 January 1980

37 *of his first Cabinet meeting as Prime Minister:*
An extraordinary affair. I gave them their orders and they wanted to stay and discuss them.

Duke of Wellington 1769–1852: Peter Hennessy *Whitehall* (1990)

38 I accept that anomalies exist but I would not wish to remove them by taking something from people who already have it.
   on the television licence fee

William Whitelaw 1918–99: in House of Commons, 1 December 1981

39 Now that the House of Commons is trying to become useful, it does a great deal of harm.

Oscar Wilde 1854–1900: *An Ideal Husband* (1895)

40 *the White House in the time of President Eisenhower:*
The Tomb of the Well-Known Soldier.

Emlyn Williams 1905–87: James Harding *Emlyn Williams* (1987)

Grammar

❝ *I was born to be a punctuation vigilante.* **❞**
Lynne Truss

1 Sentence structure is innate but whining is acquired.

Woody Allen 1935– : 'Remembering Needleman' (1976)

2 Would you convey my compliments to the purist who reads your proofs and tell him or her that I write in a sort of broken-down patois which is something like the way a Swiss waiter talks, and that when I split an infinitive, God damn it, I split it so it will stay split.

Raymond Chandler 1888–1959: letter to Edward Weeks, 18 January 1947

3 There was so little English in that answer that President Chirac would have been happy with it.

William Hague 1961– : confronting John Prescott at Prime Minister's questions in the House of Commons, 29 March 2006

4 *on the first-person plural pronoun:*
The only person entitled to use the imperial 'we' in speaking of himself is a king, an editor, and a man with a tapeworm.

Robert G. Ingersoll 1833–99: in *Los Angeles Times* 6 October 1914

5 The subjunctive mood is in its death throes, and the best thing to do is to put it out of its misery as soon as possible.

W. Somerset Maugham 1874–1965: *A Writer's Notebook* (1949) written in 1941

6 Save the gerund and screw the whale.

Tom Stoppard 1937– : *The Real Thing* (1988 rev. ed.)

7 I was born to be a punctuation vigilante.

Lynne Truss 1955– : *Eats, Shoots and Leaves* (2003)

8 Good intentions are invariably ungrammatical.

Oscar Wilde 1854–1900: attributed

Handwriting

❝ The ten commandments in every stroke of the pen, and the moral law all over the page. ❞
Oscar Wilde

1 That exquisite handwriting like a fly which has been trained at the Russian ballet.
   of George Bernard Shaw's handwriting

   James Agate 1877–1947: diary, 22 September 1944

2 I never saw Monty James's writing but doubt whether he can have been more illegible than Lady Colefax: the only hope of deciphering *her* invitations, someone said, was to pin them up on the wall and *run* past them!

   Rupert Hart-Davis 1907–99: letter to George Lyttelton, 13 November 1955

3 The dawn of legibility in his handwriting has revealed his utter inability to spell.

   Ian Hay 1876–1952: attributed; perhaps used in a dramatization of *The Housemaster* (1938)

4 Did you ever get a letter from Monty James? I once had a note from him inviting us to dinner—we guessed that the time was 8 and not 3, as it appeared to be, but all we could tell about the day was that it was not Wednesday.

   George Lyttelton 1883–1962: letter to Rupert Hart-Davis, 9 November 1955

5 *of Foreign Office handwriting:*
   Iron railings leaning out of the perpendicular.

   Lord Palmerston 1784–1865: J. A. Gere and John Sparrow (eds.) *Geoffrey Madan's Notebooks* (1981)

6 No individual word was decipherable, but, with a bold reader, groups could be made to conform to a scheme based on probabilities.

   Edith Œ. Somerville 1858–1949 and **Martin Ross** 1862–1915: *In Mr Knox's Country* (1915)

7 I know that handwriting . . . I remember it perfectly. The ten commandments in every stroke of the pen, and the moral law all over the page.

   Oscar Wilde 1854–1900: *An Ideal Husband* (1895)

8 As regards the mode of copying: of course it is too long for any amanuensis to attempt: and your own handwriting, dear Robbie, in your last letter seems specially designed to remind me that the task is not to be yours.

   Oscar Wilde 1854–1900: letter to Robert Ross from Reading Prison, 1 April 1897

Happiness
See also **Hope and Despair, Satisfaction and Discontent**

❝ Life would be very pleasant if it were not for its enjoyments. ❞
R. S. Surtees

1 No pleasure is worth giving up for the sake of two more years in a geriatric home in Weston-super-Mare.

   Kingsley Amis 1922–95: in *Times* 21 June 1994; attributed

2 Happy as a bastard on Father's Day.
   Australian expression

   Anonymous: Richard Eyre *National Service: Diary of a Decade* (2003)

3 When people say, 'You're breaking my heart,' they do in fact usually mean that you're breaking their genitals.

   Jeffrey Bernard 1932–97: in *Spectator* 31 May 1986

4 Let us have wine and women, mirth and laughter,
Sermons and soda-water the day after.

Lord Byron 1788–1824: *Don Juan* (1819–24)

5 Happiness is . . . finding two olives in your martini when you're hungry.

Johnny Carson 1925–2005: *Happiness is—a Dry Martini* (1966)

6 When constabulary duty's to be done,
A policeman's lot is not a happy one.

W. S. Gilbert 1836–1911: *The Pirates of Penzance* (1879)

7 I can imagine no more comfortable frame of mind for the conduct of life than a humorous resignation.

W. Somerset Maugham 1874–1965: *A Writer's Notebook* (1949) written in 1903

8 The fact that I have no remedy for the sorrows of the world is no reason for my accepting yours. It simply supports the strong probability that yours is a fake.

H. L. Mencken 1880–1956: *Minority Report* (1956)

9 I told him that if somebody liked to dress up in chamois leather and be stung by wasps, I really couldn't see why one should stop him.
recalling a conversation with Lord Longford on pornography

Robert Morley 1908–92: Kenneth Tynan diary, 31 March 1975

10 He's simply got the instinct for being unhappy highly developed.

Saki 1870–1916: *Chronicles of Clovis* (1911)

11 But a lifetime of happiness! No man alive could bear it: it would be hell on earth.

George Bernard Shaw 1856–1950: *Man and Superman* (1903)

12 There are two tragedies in life. One is not to get your heart's desire. The other is to get it.

George Bernard Shaw 1856–1950: *Man and Superman* (1903)

13 MRS BAKER is a woman who has managed to find a little misery in the best of things. Sorrow and trouble are the only things that can make her happy.

Neil Simon 1927– : *Come Blow Your Horn* (1961)

14 Life would be very pleasant if it were not for its enjoyments.

R. S. Surtees 1805–64: *Mr Facey Romford's Hounds* (1865)

15 Have some fun. Buy a big gun.

Richard Thomas and **Stewart Lee**: *Jerry Springer—the Opera* (2003)

16 Let us all be happy, and live within our means, even if we have to borrer the money to do it with.

Artemus Ward 1834–67: *Artemus Ward in London* (1867)

17 A cigarette is the perfect type of a perfect pleasure. It is exquisite, and it leaves one unsatisfied. What more can one want?

Oscar Wilde 1854–1900: *The Picture of Dorian Gray* (1891)

18 All the things I really like to do are either illegal, immoral, or fattening.

Alexander Woollcott 1887–1943: R. E. Drennan *Wit's End* (1973)

Headlines

❝ *Sticks nix hick pix.* ❞
Anonymous

1 Headless Body in Topless Bar.

Anonymous: headline in *New York Post* 15 April 1983

2 HONG KONG POOH-POOHS NICHI NICHI'S DUM-DUMS.
reported headline in Australian newspaper, referring to reports that Hong Kong police denied a claim by the Japanese paper Nichi Nichi Shimbun *that they had used soft-nosed bullets against rioters*

Anonymous: attributed; in *Spectator* 19 December 1998

3 Queen to skip Chuck nups.
  announcing that the Queen would not attend the wedding of Charles, Prince of Wales, and Camilla Parker Bowles

Anonymous: headline in *New York Post* 23 February 2005

4 Sticks nix hick pix.
  on the lack of enthusiasm for farm dramas among rural populations

Anonymous: headline in *Variety* 17 July 1935

5 It's The Sun Wot Won It.
  following the 1992 general election

Anonymous: headline in *Sun* 11 April 1992

6 NUT SCREWS WASHERS AND BOLTS.
  reported headline in a Chinese newspaper above the story of an escapee from an asylum who broke into a laundry and raped several laundresses before escaping

Anonymous: Claud Cockburn *I, Claud* (1967)

7 If Kinnock wins today will the last person to leave Britain please turn out the lights.
  on election day, showing Neil Kinnock's head inside a light bulb

Anonymous: headline in *Sun* 9 April 1992

8 If I rescued a child from drowning, the Press would no doubt headline the story 'Benn grabs child.'

Tony Benn 1925– : in *Observer* 2 March 1975

9 *with which Cockburn claimed to have won a competition at The Times for the dullest headline:*
  Small earthquake in Chile. Not many dead.

Claud Cockburn 1904–81: *In Time of Trouble* (1956)

10 Paralysed Girl Determined to Dance Again.

Michael Frayn 1933– : headline in *The Tin Men* (1966)

11 SIXTY HORSES WEDGED IN CHIMNEY
  The story to fit this sensational headline has not turned up yet.

J. B. Morton 1893–1975: Michael Frayn (ed.) *The Best of Beachcomber* (1963)

12 Marquis's Son Unused to Wine.

Evelyn Waugh 1903–66: headline in *Brideshead Revisited* (1945)

Health
See also **Medicine, Sickness**

❝ It's a question of finding a sickness you like. ❞
Jackie Mason

1 I feel as young as I ever did, apart from the occasional heart attack.

Robert Benchley 1889–1945: attributed

2 In 1969 I gave up women and alcohol. It was the worst 20 minutes of my life.

George Best 1946–2005: attributed

3 The two best exercises in the world are making love and dancing but a simple one is to stand on tiptoe.

Barbara Cartland 1901–2000: in 1972, attributed; in *Guardian* 22 May 2000

4 In the face of such overwhelming statistical possibilities, hypochondria has always seemed to me to be the only rational position to take on life.

John Diamond: *C: Because Cowards Get Cancer Too* (1998)

5 Exercise is the yuppie version of bulimia.

Barbara Ehrenreich 1941– : *The Worst Years of Our Lives* (1991) 'Food Worship'

6 *on Warren Clarke's portrayal of Hill's Superintendent Dalziel:*
REGINALD HILL: For the sake of my art you should be seven stones heavier.
WARREN CLARKE: For the sake of my heart, I shouldn't.

Reginald Hill 1936– : in *Mail on Sunday* 30 July 2000

7 Aromatherapy is like going into the countryside and smelling flowers. It should be available in Parliament. They already have it in some mental hospitals.

Simon Hughes 1951– : in *Independent* 24 January 1998

8 It's no longer a question of staying healthy. It's a question of finding a sickness you like.

Jackie Mason 1931– : attributed

9 My uterine contractions have been bogus for sometime.

Joe Orton 1933–67: *What the Butler Saw* (1969)

10 The only exercise I take is walking behind the coffins of friends who took exercise.

Peter O'Toole 1932– : in *Mail on Sunday* 27 December 1998 'Quotes of the Year'

11 Avoid running at all times.

Leroy ('Satchel') Paige 1906–82: *How To Stay Young* (1953)

12 At 70, I'm in fine fettle for my age, sleep like a babe and feel around 12. The secret? Lots of meat, drink and cigarettes and not giving in to things.

Jennifer Paterson 1928–99: in *Daily Mail* 18 August 1998

13 If God had wanted us to bend over, He would have put diamonds on the floor.

Joan Rivers 1933– : attributed

14 I try to keep fit. I've got these parallel bars at home. I run at them and try to buy a drink from both of them.

Arthur Smith 1954– : attributed

15 When people discussed tonics, pick-me-ups after a severe illness, she kept to herself the prescription of a quick dip in bed with someone you liked but were not in love with. A shock of sexual astonishment which could make you feel astonishingly well and high spirited.

Mary Wesley 1912–2002: *Not That Sort of Girl* (1987)

16 *'Thatchcard' carried in her handbag:*
Under no circumstances whatsoever do I wish to be visited in hospital by Margaret Thatcher.

Mary Wesley 1912–2002: attributed

17 I don't take enough exercise, but what is the longest-lived animal in the world? The giant tortoise is 120 years old and it hardly moves.

Terry Wogan 1938– : in *Times* 23 June 2007

Heaven and Hell

❝*I have friends in both places.***❞**
Mark Twain

1 *of Lord Curzon, who at the age of thirty-nine had been created Viceroy of India:*
For all the rest of his life Curzon was influenced by his sudden journey to heaven at the age of thirty-nine, and then by his return seven years later to earth, for the remainder of his mortal existence.

Lord Beaverbrook 1879–1964: *Men and Power* (1956)

2 All are inclined to believe what they covet, from a lottery-ticket up to a passport to Paradise,—in which, from description, I see nothing very tempting.

Lord Byron 1788–1824: diary 27 November 1813

3 I always say, as you know, that if my fellow citizens want to go to Hell I will help them. It's my job.

Oliver Wendell Holmes Jr. 1841–1935: letter to Harold Laski, 4 March 1920

4 Whose love is given over-well
Shall look on Helen's face in hell
Whilst they whose love is thin and wise
Shall see John Knox in Paradise.

Dorothy Parker 1893–1967: 'Partial Comfort' (1937)

5 The Devil himself had probably re-designed Hell in the light of information he had gained from observing airport layouts.

Anthony Price 1928– : *The Memory Trap* (1989)

6 My idea of heaven is, eating *pâté de foie gras* to the sound of trumpets.

Sydney Smith 1771–1845: view ascribed by Smith to his friend Henry Luttrell; Peter Virgin *Sydney Smith* (1994)

7 I have friends in both places.

Mark Twain 1835–1910: Archibald Henderson *Mark Twain* (1911)

8 If Max [Beaverbrook] gets to Heaven he won't last long. He will be chucked out for trying to pull off a merger between Heaven and Hell . . . after having secured a controlling interest in key subsidiary companies in both places, of course.

H. G. Wells 1866–1946: A. J. P. Taylor *Beaverbrook* (1972)

History

66 *History repeats itself; historians repeat one other.* 99
Rupert Brooke

1 I want to see the hand of history on his collar.
woman queueing to see the Prime Minister at the Hutton Inquiry

Anonymous: in *Mail on Sunday* 31 August 2003

2 History is a commentary on the various and continuing incapabilities of men. What is history? History is women following behind with the buckets.

Alan Bennett 1934– : *The History Boys* (2004)

3 I was still a medieval historian, not a profession, I imagine, with a high sexual strike rate.

Alan Bennett 1934– : *Untold Stories* (2005)

4 An account, mostly false, of events, mostly unimportant, which are brought about by rulers, mostly knaves, and soldiers, mostly fools.
definition of history

Ambrose Bierce 1842–c.1914: *The Cynic's Word Book* (1906)

5 History repeats itself; historians repeat one other.

Rupert Brooke 1887–1915: letter to Geoffrey Keynes, 4 June 1906

6 People who make history know nothing about history. You can see that in the sort of history they make.

G. K. Chesterton 1874–1936: J. A. Gere and John Sparrow (eds.) *Geoffrey Madan's Notebooks* (1981)

7 History teaches us that men and nations behave wisely once they have exhausted all other alternatives.

Abba Eban 1915–2002: speech in London 16 December 1970

8 History is more or less bunk.

Henry Ford 1863–1947: in *Chicago Tribune* 25 May 1916

9 History is not what you thought. *It is what you can remember.*

W. C. Sellar 1898–1951 and **R. J. Yeatman** 1898–1968: *1066 and All That* (1930) 'Compulsory Preface'

10 AMERICA was thus clearly top nation, and History came to a .

W. C. Sellar 1898–1951 and **R. J. Yeatman** 1898–1968: *1066 and All That* (1930)

11 SWINDON: What will history say?
BURGOYNE: History, sir, will tell lies as usual.

George Bernard Shaw 1856–1950: *The Devil's Disciple* (1901)

12 History is about arrogance, vanity and vapidity—who better than me to present it?

David Starkey 1945– : in *Mail on Sunday* 10 October 2004

13 Like most of those who study history, he [Napoleon III] learned from the mistakes of the past how to make new ones.

A. J. P. Taylor 1906–90: in *Listener* 6 June 1963

14 History gets thicker as it approaches recent times.

A. J. P. Taylor 1906–90: *English History 1914–45* (1965), bibliography

15 *on being asked what would have happened in 1963, had Khrushchev and not Kennedy been assassinated:*
With history one can never be certain, but I think I can safely say that Aristotle Onassis would not have married Mrs Khrushchev.

Gore Vidal 1925– : in *Sunday Times* 4 June 1989

16 Thanks to modern technology . . . history now comes equipped with a fast-forward button.

Gore Vidal 1925– : *Screening History* (1992)

17 Human history becomes more and more a race between education and catastrophe.

H. G. Wells 1866–1946: *Outline of History* (1920)

18 The one duty we owe to history is to rewrite it.

Oscar Wilde 1854–1900: *Intentions* (1891) 'The Critic as Artist' pt. 1

19 History started badly and hav been geting steadily worse.

Geoffrey Willans 1911–58 and **Ronald Searle** 1920– : *Down with Skool!* (1953)

Holidays

66 *After you've spent 8 hours reading on the beach you don't feel like turning in early with a good book.* 99
Arthur Smith

1 The sort of place to send your mother-in-law for a month, all expenses paid.
of Pakistan, in a BBC Radio interview, 17 March 1984; in April 1984 he was fined £1000 for making the remark by the Test and County Cricket Board

Ian Botham 1955– : in *Times* 20 March 1984

2 What kind of holiday can you take when you live in almost continual sunshine in an olive grove in the mountains, which is only twenty minutes away from the beaches and the sea?

Patrick Campbell 1913–80: *Gullible Travels* (1969)

3 There's sand in the porridge and sand in the bed, And if this is pleasure we'd rather be dead.

Noël Coward 1899–1973: 'The English Lido' (1928)

4 Cannot avoid contrasting deliriously rapid flight of time when on a holiday with very much slower passage of days, and even hours, in other and more familiar surroundings.

E. M. Delafield 1890–1943: *The Diary of a Provincial Lady* (1930)

5 I don't think we can do better than 'Good old Broadstairs'.

George Grossmith 1847–1912 and **Weedon Grossmith** 1854–1919: *The Diary of a Nobody* (1894)

6 I suppose we all have our recollections of our earlier holidays, all bristling with horror.

Flann O'Brien 1911–66: *Myles Away from Dublin* (1990)

7 I like to have exciting evenings on holiday, because after you've spent 8 hours reading on the beach you don't feel like turning in early with a good book.

Arthur Smith 1954– : *The Live Bed Show* (1995)

8 A weekend in the country
With the panting
And the yawns
With the crickets and the pheasants
And the orchards and the hay,
With the servants and the peasants,
We'll be laying our plans
While we're playing croquet
For a weekend in the country
So inactive one has to lie down.
A weekend in the country
Where we're twice as upset
As in town.

Stephen Sondheim 1930– : 'A Weekend in the Country' (1972)

9 The Victorians had not been anxious to go away for the weekend. The Edwardians, on the contrary, were nomadic.

T. H. White 1906–64: *Farewell Victoria* (1933)

10 I wish I'd given Spain a miss this year—I nearly plumped for a crochet week in Rhyl. I was going to have a stab at a batwing blouson.

Victoria Wood 1953– : *Mens Sana in Thingummy Doodah* (1990)

Hollywood
See also **The Cinema, Film**

❝ *A place where they'll pay you a thousand dollars for a kiss and fifty cents for your soul.* ❞
Marilyn Monroe

1 Hollywood is a place where people from Iowa mistake each other for stars.

Fred Allen 1894–1956: Maurice Zolotow *No People like Show People* (1951)

2 I'm not very keen on Hollywood. I'd rather have a nice cup of cocoa really.

Noël Coward 1899–1973: letter to his mother, 1937; Cole Lesley *The Life of Noel Coward* (1976)

3 Remember all the time . . . that Hollywood is an Oriental city. As long as you do that you might survive.

Olivia De Havilland 1916– : Dirk Bogarde *Snakes and Ladders* (1978)

4 Hollywood is bounded on the north, south, east, and west by agents.

William Fadiman: *Hollywood Now* (1972)

5 Working in Hollywood does give one a certain expertise in the field of prostitution.

Jane Fonda 1937– : J. R. Colombo *Wit and Wisdom of the Moviemakers* (1979)

6 The only place you can wake up in the morning and hear the birds coughing in the trees.

Joe Frisco: attributed

7 Hollywood is strange when you're in trouble. Everyone is afraid it's contagious.

Judy Garland 1922–69: Simon Rose *Classic Film Guide* (1995)

8 There's lots of nice guys walking around Hollywood, but they ain't eating.

Henry Hathaway 1898–1985: in *Times* 22 March 1969

9 Every country gets the circus it deserves. Spain gets bullfights. Italy gets the Catholic Church. America Hollywood.

Erica Jong 1942– : *How to Save Your Own Life* (1977)

10 Behind the phoney tinsel of Hollywood lies the real tinsel.

Oscar Levant 1906–72: Laurence J. Peter (ed.) *Quotations for our Time* (1977)

11 Being a writer in Hollywood is like going into Hitler's Eagle's Nest with a great idea for a bar-mitzvah.

David Mamet 1947– : in *Sunday Times* 1 August 2004

12 Hooray for Hollywood,
Where you're terrific if you're even good!

Johnny Mercer 1909–76: 'Hooray for Hollywood' (*Hollywood Hotel*, 1938 musical)

13 A trip through a sewer in a glass-bottomed boat.

Wilson Mizner 1876–1933: Alva Johnston *The Legendary Mizners* (1953), reworked by Mayor Jimmy Walker into 'A reformer is a guy who rides through a sewer in a glass-bottomed boat'

14 Hollywood is a place where they'll pay you a thousand dollars for a kiss and fifty cents for your soul.

Marilyn Monroe 1926–62: J. R. Colombo *Wit and Wisdom of the Moviemakers* (1979)

15 Hollywood, the Versailles of Los Angeles.

Jan Morris 1926– : *Destinations* (1980)

16 The only 'ism' in Hollywood is plagiarism.

Dorothy Parker 1893–1967: attributed

17 Oh, it's all right. You make a little money and get caught up on your debts. We're up to 1912 now . . .

Dorothy Parker 1893–1967: Max Wilk *The Wit and Wisdom of Hollywood* (1972)

18 Hollywood money isn't money. It's congealed snow, melts in your hand, and there you are.

Dorothy Parker 1893–1967: Malcolm Cowley (ed.) *Writers at Work* 1st Series (1958)

19 Hollywood: They know only one word of more than one syllable here, and that is fillum.

Louis Sherwin: Laurence J. Peter (ed.) *Quotations for our Time* (1977)

20 This is the biggest electric train any boy ever had!

Orson Welles 1915–85: Leo Rosten *Hollywood* (1941)

The Home

See also **Housework**

66 *All I need is room enough to lay a hat and a few friends.* 99
Dorothy Parker

1 The premises are so delightfully extensive, that two people might live together without ever seeing, hearing, or meeting.
   of Newstead Abbey

Lord Byron 1788–1824: letter 30 (31?) August 1811

2 They tell me there is no more toilet paper in the house. How can I be expected to act a romantic part and remember to order TOILET PAPER!

Mrs Patrick Campbell 1865–1940: Margot Peters *Mrs Pat* (1984)

3 My old man said, 'Follow the van,
   Don't dilly-dally on the way!'
   Off went the cart with the home packed in it,
   I walked behind with my old cock linnet.
   But I dillied and dallied, dallied and dillied,
   Lost the van and don't know where to roam.

Charles Collins: 'Don't Dilly-Dally on the Way' (1919, with Fred Leigh); popularized by Marie Lloyd

4 Love and a cottage! Eh, Fanny! Ah, give me indifference and a coach and six!

George Colman, the Elder 1732–94 and **David Garrick** 1717–79: *The Clandestine Marriage* (1766)

5 Tho' the pipes that supply the bathroom burst
   And the lavatory makes you fear the worst,
   It was used by Charles the First
   Quite informally,
   And later by George the Fourth
   On a journey North.

Noël Coward 1899–1973: 'The Stately Homes of England' (1938)

6 Though the fact that they have to be rebuilt
   And frequently mortgaged to the hilt
   Is inclined to take the gilt
   Off the gingerbread,
   And certainly damps the fun
   Of the eldest son.

Noël Coward 1899–1973: 'The Stately Homes of England' (1938)

7 Mrs Crupp had indignantly assured him that there wasn't room to swing a cat there; but, as Mr Dick justly observed to me, sitting down on the foot of the bed, nursing his leg, 'You know, Trotwood, I don't want to swing a cat. I never do swing a cat. Therefore, what does that signify to *me*!'

Charles Dickens 1812–70: *David Copperfield* (1850)

8 *congratulating Margaret Thatcher on* 10 *Downing Street:*
   I never seem to meet a good estate agent.

John Gielgud 1904–2000: Sheridan Morley *Asking for Trouble* (2002)

9 There's no greater bliss in life than when the plumber eventually comes to unblock your drains. No writer can give that sort of pleasure.

Victoria Glendinning 1937– : in *Observer* 3 January 1993

10 What's the good of a home if you are never in it?

George Grossmith 1847–1912 and **Weedon Grossmith** 1854–1919: *The Diary of a Nobody* (1894)

11 I want a house that has got over all its troubles; I don't want to spend the rest of my life bringing up a young and inexperienced house.

Jerome K. Jerome 1859–1927: *They and I* (1909)

12 Although very few people are actually called upon to live in palaces a very large number are unwilling to admit the fact.

Osbert Lancaster 1908–86: *Homes Sweet Homes* (1939)

13 All I need is room enough to lay a hat and a few friends.

Dorothy Parker 1893–1967: R. E. Drennan *Wit's End* (1973)

14 Home life as we understand it is no more natural to us than a cage is natural to a cockatoo.

George Bernard Shaw 1856–1950: *Getting Married* (1911) preface 'Hearth and Home'

15 *on being encountered drinking a glass of wine in the street, while watching his theatre, the Drury Lane, burn down, on 24 February 1809:*
A man may surely be allowed to take a glass of wine by his own fireside.

Richard Brinsley Sheridan 1751–1816: T. Moore *Life of Sheridan* (1825)

16 Is that bottle just going to sit up there or are you going to turn it into a lamp?

Neil Simon 1927– : *Last of the Red Hot Lovers* (1970)

17 It looks different when you're sober. I thought I had twice as much furniture.

Neil Simon 1927– : *The Gingerbread Lady* (1970)

18 I have heard of a man who had a mind to sell his house, and therefore carried a piece of brick in his pocket, which he shewed as a pattern to encourage purchasers.

Jonathan Swift 1667–1745: *The Drapier's Letters* (1724)

19 *asked who wore the trousers at home:*
I do. I wear the trousers. And I wash and iron them, too.

Denis Thatcher 1915–2003: attributed; in *Times* 27 June 2003

20 The national sport of England is obstacle racing. People fill their rooms with useless and cumbersome furniture, and spend the rest of their lives in trying to dodge it.

Herbert Beerbohm Tree 1852–1917: Hesketh Pearson *Beerbohm Tree* (1956)

21 I am returned to my own Lares and Penates—to my dogs and cats.

Horace Walpole 1717–97: letter, 25 October 1775

Honours

See also **Awards**

> ❝*Thieves break in, moths corrupt, but an OBE goes on for ever.*❞
> **Fay Weldon**

---

1 Gongs and medals and ribbons really belong on a Christmas tree.

J. G. Ballard 1930–2009: in *Independent* 14 July 2004

2 You should always accept because of the pain it brings to your enemies.

Maurice Bowra 1898–1971: quoted by Peter Hennessy in evidence to the House of Commons Select Committee on Public Administration, 11 March 2004

3 Had they sent me ¼ lb of good tobacco, the addition to my happiness had probably been suitabler and greater!
on being awarded the Prussian Order of Merit

Thomas Carlyle 1795–1881: letter to his brother John Carlyle, 14 February 1874

4 Now Mr Schlesinger, we must try and get this *straight*.
adjusting the ribbon of a CBE round the sizeable neck of John Schlesinger; he took it as a tactful recognition of his sexual orientation

Elizabeth II 1926– : Alan Bennett diary 2003, in *London Review of Books* 8 January 2004

5 I feel very humble. But I think I have the strength of character to fight it.
on receiving a Congressional Gold Medal from President Kennedy

Bob Hope 1903–2003: attributed; in *Times* 29 July 2003

6 *on his acceptance of an OBE:*
Someone had to accept one, otherwise there would be shelves full of them left.

Roy Hudd 1936– : in *Sunday Times* 4 January 2004

7 I can't see the sense in it really. It makes me a Commander of the British Empire. They might as well make me a Commander of Milton Keynes—at least that exists.
on receiving an honorary CBE in 1992

Spike Milligan 1918–2002: attributed; in *Daily Telegraph* 28 February 2002

8 A very useful institution. It fosters a wholesome taste for bright colours, and gives old men who have good legs an excuse for showing them.
of the Order of the Garter, which had been awarded to both his father and grandfather as well as the early Cecils

Lord Salisbury 1830–1903: in Houghton Papers; Andrew Roberts *Salisbury: Victorian Titan* (1999)

9 In the end I accepted the honour, because during dinner Venables told me, that, if I became Poet Laureate, I should always when I dined out be offered the liver-wing of a fowl.
on being made Poet Laureate in 1850

Alfred, Lord Tennyson 1809–92: in *Alfred Lord Tennyson: A Memoir by his Son* (1897) vol. 1

10 *congratulated on being awarded a baronetcy:*
Thanks—but more importantly than that, I have just been elected a member of Sunningdale Golf Club.

Denis Thatcher 1915–2003: attributed; in *Times* 27 June 2003

11 The cross of the Legion of Honour has been conferred upon me. However, few escape that distinction.

Mark Twain 1835–1910: *A Tramp Abroad* (1880)

12 I had another convulsion of pleasure when Yale made me a Doctor of Literature, because I was not competent to doctor anybody's literature but my own.

Mark Twain 1835–1910: *Autobiography* (1924)

13 People fail you, children disappoint you, thieves break in, moths corrupt, but an OBE goes on for ever.

Fay Weldon 1931– : *Praxis* (1978)

14 An OBE is what you get if you clean the toilets well at King's Cross Station.
explaining why he turned down an OBE in the Queen's 80th birthday honours' list

Michael Winner 1935– : in *Independent* 29 May 2006

Hope and Despair

See also **Happiness, Satisfaction and Discontent**

❝ *Blessed is the man who expects nothing, for he shall never be disappointed.* ❞
Alexander Pope

1 *seeing a commemorative stone engraved 'Laid by the Poet Laureate' (John Masefield):*
Every nice girl's ambition.

John Betjeman 1906–84: Bevis Hillier *Betjeman: the Bonus of Laughter* (2004)

2 A minor form of despair, disguised as a virtue.
definition of patience

Ambrose Bierce 1842–c.1914: *The Devil's Dictionary* (1911)

3 I don't consider myself a pessimist. I think of a pessimist as someone who is waiting for it to rain. And I feel soaked to the skin.

Leonard Cohen 1934– : in *Observer* 2 May 1993

4 There are bad times just around the corner,
There are dark clouds travelling through the sky
And it's no good whining
About a silver lining
For we know from experience that they won't roll by,
With a scowl and a frown
We'll keep our peckers down
And prepare for depression and doom and dread,
We're going to unpack our troubles from our old kitbag
And wait until we drop down dead.

Noël Coward 1899–1973: 'There are Bad Times Just Around the Corner' (1953)

5 I have known him come home to supper with a flood of tears, and a declaration that nothing was now left but a jail; and go to bed making a calculation of the expense of putting bow-windows to the house, 'in case anything turned up,' which was his favourite expression.

Charles Dickens 1812–70: *David Copperfield* (1850)

6 but wotthehell
archy wotthehell
it s cheerio
my deario that
pulls a lady through.

Don Marquis 1878–1937: *archy and mehitabel* (1927) 'cheerio my deario'

7 but wotthehell archy wotthehell
jamais triste archy jamais triste
that is my motto.

Don Marquis 1878–1937: *archy and mehitabel* (1927) 'mehitabel sees paris'

8 When I am sad and weary
When I think all hope has gone
When I walk along High Holborn
I think of you with nothing on.

Adrian Mitchell 1932– : 'Celia, Celia'

9 'Blessed is the man who expects nothing, for he shall never be disappointed' was the ninth beatitude.

Alexander Pope 1688–1744: letter to Fortescue, 23 September 1725

10 Why, even the janitor's wife
Has a perfectly good love life
And here am I
Facing tomorrow
Alone with my sorrow
Down in the depths on the ninetieth floor.

Cole Porter 1891–1964: 'Down in the Depths' (1936)

11 'Do you know what a pessimist is?' 'A man who thinks everybody is as nasty as himself, and hates them for it.'

George Bernard Shaw 1856–1950: *An Unsocial Socialist* (1887)

12 *the wife of a late 19th-century master at Eton College:*
In all disagreeable circumstances remember the three things which I always say to myself:
I am an Englishwoman.
I was born in wedlock.
I am on dry land.

Blanche Warre-Cornish: *Bensoniana & Cornishiana* (1935)

13 If you think nobody cares if you're alive, try missing a couple of car payments.

Earl Wilson 1907–87: attributed

Hospitality

❝ *Some people can stay longer in an hour than others can in a week.* ❞
William Dean Howells

1 *opening a lecture at Strathclyde University, immediately after her husband's trial for perjury; the audience included many journalists:*
Good morning, and a special welcome to those of you who are new to the field of quantum solar energy conversion.

Mary Archer 1944– : in *Sunday Times* 29 July 2001

2 *an assiduous hostess:*
She arranged that motor-cars, golf-caddies and fishing gillies were lurking like wild beasts round the corner, ready to pounce.

E. F. Benson 1867–1940: *The Climber* (1908)

3 *instructions to strangers trying to find their way around Drumlanrig Castle:*
Turn right at the Rembrandt then left at the Leonardo.

Jane, Duchess of Buccleuch and Queensberry: attributed; in *Mail on Sunday* 31 August 2003

4 Hospitality consists in a little fire, a little food, and an immense quiet.

Ralph Waldo Emerson 1803–82: journal, 1865

5 Here you are again, older faces and younger clothes.
 a famous hostess's habitual greeting to guests

Mamie Stuyvesant Fish 1853–1915: attributed

6 A host is like a general: misfortunes often reveal his genius.

Horace 65–8 BC: *Satires*

7 Some people can stay longer in an hour than others can in a week.

William Dean Howells 1837–1920: attributed

8 *when visiting Chequers:*
Come on, young Blair, where's the whisky?

Derry Irvine 1940– : attributed; Anthony Howard in *Times* 10 June 2003

9 I really felt for you in the scene in which you tried to make the party go.
 to Judith Anderson after her Lady Macbeth *in 1937*

Queen Mary 1867–1953: Adrian Woolhouse *Angus Macbean Face-maker* (2006)

Hotels

❝ *There is a French widow in every bedroom.* ❞
Gerard Hoffnung

1 All through the night there's a friendly receptionist
Welcome to Holiday Inn.

Dorothy Fields 1905–74: 'Welcome to Holiday Inn' (1973)

2 The cushions had cushions, the curtains looked like duvets.
 of a typical English country house hotel

A. A. Gill 1954– : *Starcrossed* (1999)

3 The chambermaid is very kind,
She always thinks we're so refined.
Of course, she's deaf and dumb and blind—
No fools we—
In our little den of iniquity.

Lorenz Hart 1895–1943: 'In Our Little Den of Iniquity' (*Pal Joey*, 1940 musical)

4 *supposedly quoting a letter from a Tyrolean landlord:*
Standing among savage scenery, the hotel offers
stupendous revelations. There is a French widow in every
bedroom, affording delightful prospects.

Gerard Hoffnung 1925–59: speech at
the Oxford Union, 4 December 1958

5 We were served the sort of dinner you might get in a
remarkably well-run open prison.

Alexei Sayle 1952– : *Overtaken*
(2003)

6 The great advantage of a hotel is that it's a refuge from
home life.

George Bernard Shaw 1856–1950:
You Never Can Tell (1898)

Housework

66 *After the first four years the dirt doesn't
get any worse.* 99
Quentin Crisp

1 Conran's Law of Housework—it expands to fill the time
available plus half an hour.

Shirley Conran 1932– : *Superwoman
2* (1977)

2 *of Greta Garbo:*
A rather boring old Swede, but luckily she loves doing the
washing-up.

Gladys Cooper 1888–1971: Sheridan
Morley *Asking for Trouble* (2002)

3 There was no need to do any housework at all. After the
first four years the dirt doesn't get any worse.

Quentin Crisp 1908–99: *The Naked
Civil Servant* (1968)

4 I hate housework! You make the beds, you do the dishes—
and six months later you have to start all over again.

Joan Rivers 1933– : attributed, 1984

5 Hatred of domestic work is a natural and admirable result
of civilization.

Rebecca West 1892–1983: in *The
Freewoman* 6 June 1912

6 Everything's getting on top of me. I can't switch off. I've
got a self-cleaning oven—I have to get up in the night to
see if it's doing it.

Victoria Wood 1953– : *Mens Sana in
Thingummy Doodah* (1990)

The Human Race

66 *Man is the Only Animal that Blushes. Or
needs to.* 99
Mark Twain

1 Well, of course, people are only human . . . But it really
does not seem much for them to be.

Ivy Compton-Burnett 1884–1969: *A
Family and a Fortune* (1939)

2 They are usually a mistake.
of other people

Quentin Crisp 1908–99: in *Spectator*
20 November 1999

3 I got disappointed in human nature as well and gave it up
because I found it too much like my own.

J. P. Donleavy 1926– : *A Fairy Tale of
New York* (1973)

4 That habit of treading in ruts and trooping in companies
which men share with sheep.

A. E. Housman 1859–1936: 'The
Editing of Juvenal' (1905)

5 Men have an extraordinarily erroneous opinion of their
position in nature; and the error is ineradicable.

W. Somerset Maugham 1874–1965:
A Writer's Notebook (1949) written in
1896

6 Man is one of the toughest of animated creatures. Only the anthrax bacillus can stand so unfavourable an environment for so long a time.

H. L. Mencken 1880–1956: *Minority Report* (1956)

7 I wish I loved the Human Race;
I wish I loved its silly face;
I wish I liked the way it walks;
I wish I liked the way it talks;
And when I'm introduced to one
I wish I thought *What Jolly Fun!*

Walter Raleigh 1861–1922: 'Wishes of an Elderly Man' (1923)

8 I'm dealing in rock'n'roll. I'm, like, I'm not a bona fide human being.

Phil Spector 1940– : attributed

9 He's an animal lover . . . People he don't like so much.

Tom Stoppard 1937– : *Neutral Ground* (1983)

10 The only man who wasn't spoilt by being lionized was Daniel.

Herbert Beerbohm Tree 1852–1917: Hesketh Pearson *Beerbohm Tree* (1956)

11 Man is the Only Animal that Blushes. Or needs to.

Mark Twain 1835–1910: *Following the Equator* (1897)

12 Reality is something the human race doesn't handle very well.

Gore Vidal 1925– : in *Radio Times* 3 January 1990

13 This world is a comedy to those that think, a tragedy to those that feel.

Horace Walpole 1717–97: letter to Anne, Countess of Upper Ossory, 16 August 1776

14 'Have you ever seen Spode eat asparagus?'
'No.'
'Revolting. It alters one's whole conception of Man as Nature's last word.'

P. G. Wodehouse 1881–1975: *The Code of the Woosters* (1938)

Humility

❝I don't do humble. And I don't do oppressed.❞
Robert Kilroy-Silk

1 I've never had a humble opinion. If you've got an opinion, why be humble about it?

Joan Baez 1941– : in *Observer* 29 February 2004

2 I don't do humble. And I don't do oppressed.

Robert Kilroy-Silk 1942– : in *Sunday Times* 13 June 2004

3 In 1969 I published a small book on Humility. It was a pioneering work which has not, to my knowledge, been superseded.

Lord Longford 1905–2001: in *The Tablet* 22 January 1994

4 *Wayne and Garth meet Alice Cooper:*
We're not worthy! We're not worthy!

Mike Myers 1963– : *Wayne's World* (1992 film)

5 Do you imagine I am going to pronounce the name of my beautiful theatre in a hired cab?
refusing to give directions to His Majesty's theatre to a cab-driver

Herbert Beerbohm Tree 1852–1917: Neville Cardus *Sir Thomas Beecham* (1961)

6 Charity, dear Miss Prism, charity! None of us are perfect. I myself am peculiarly susceptible to draughts.

Oscar Wilde 1854–1900: *The Importance of Being Earnest* (1895)

Humour

See also **Wit and Wordplay**

66 *What do you mean, funny? Funny-peculiar or funny ha-ha?* 99

Ian Hay

1 Among all kinds of writing, there is none in which authors are more apt to miscarry than in works of humour, as there is none in which they are more ambitious to excel.

Joseph Addison 1672–1719: *The Spectator* 10 April 1711

2 The marvellous thing about a joke with a double meaning is that it can only mean one thing.

Ronnie Barker 1929–2005: *Sauce* (1977)

3 In Milwaukee last month a man died laughing over one of his own jokes. That's what makes it so tough for us outsiders. We have to fight home competition.

Robert Benchley 1889–1945: R. E. Drennan *Wit's End* (1973)

4 Mark my words, when a society has to resort to the lavatory for its humour, the writing is on the wall.

Alan Bennett 1934– : *Forty Years On* (1969)

5 The world dwindles daily for the humorist . . . Jokes are fast running out, for a joke must transform real life in some perverse way, and real life has begun to perform the same operation perfectly professionally upon itself.

Craig Brown 1957– : *Craig Brown's Greatest Hits* (1993)

6 When you tell an Iowan a joke, you can see a kind of race going on between his brain and his expression.

Bill Bryson 1951– : *The Lost Continent* (1989)

7 Without humour you cannot run a sweetie-shop, let alone a nation.

John Buchan 1875–1940: *Castle Gay* (1930)

8 Good jests ought to bite like lambs, not dogs: they should cut, not wound.

Charles II 1630–85: attributed; Stephen Leacock 'A Rehabilitation of Charles II' in *Essays and Literary Studies* (1916)

9 A joke's a very serious thing.

Charles Churchill 1731–64: *The Ghost* (1763)

10 Reality goes bounding past the satirist like a cheetah laughing as it lopes ahead of the greyhound.

Claud Cockburn 1904–81: *Crossing the Line* (1958)

11 Freud's theory was that when a joke opens a window and all those bats and bogeymen fly out, you get a marvellous feeling of relief and elation. The trouble with Freud is that he never had to play the old Glasgow Empire on a Saturday night after Rangers and Celtic had both lost.

Ken Dodd 1927– : in *Guardian* 30 April 1991 (quoted in many, usually much contracted, forms since the mid-1960s)

12 A difference of taste in jokes is a great strain on the affections.

George Eliot 1819–80: *Daniel Deronda* (1876)

13 Comedy, like sodomy, is an unnatural act.

Marty Feldman 1933–83: in *Times* 9 June 1969

14 The funniest thing about comedy is that you never know why people laugh. I know *what* makes them laugh but trying to get your hands on the *why* of it is like trying to pick an eel out of a tub of water.

W. C. Fields 1880–1946: Richard J. Anobile *A Flask of Fields* (1972)

15 It is easy to forget that the most important aspect of comedy, after all, its great saving grace, is its ambiguity. You can simultaneously laugh at a situation, *and* take it seriously.

Stephen Fry 1957– : *Paperweight* (1992)

16 There's a weight of intellect behind my comedy.
David Brent's self-analysis

Ricky Gervais 1961– and **Stephen Merchant**: *The Office* (Series 1, Episode 2; 2001)

17 'Tis ever thus with simple folk—an accepted wit has but to say 'Pass the mustard', and they roar their ribs out!

W. S. Gilbert 1836–1911: *The Yeoman of the Guard* (1888)

18 The Irish have wit but little humour. They cannot laugh at the battle while they are involved in the broil of life.

Oliver St John Gogarty 1878–1957: *Tumbling in the Hay* (1939)

19 What do you mean, funny? Funny-peculiar or funny ha-ha?

Ian Hay 1876–1952: *The Housemaster* (1938)

20 A sober God-fearing man whose idea of a good joke was to lie about his age.

Joseph Heller 1923–99: *Catch-22* (1961)

21 My idea of an ideal programme would be a show where I would have all the questions and some other bastard would have to figure out the funny answers.

Groucho Marx 1890–1977: letter, 10 October 1940

22 It's an odd job, making decent people laugh.

Molière 1622–73: *La Critique de l'école des femmes* (1663)

23 They laughed when I said I was going to be a comedian . . . They're not laughing now.

Bob Monkhouse 1928–2003: attributed; *BBC News* 29 December 2003 (online edition)

24 I knew nothing about farce until I read [Feydeau's] *Puce à l'Oreille*, and had no idea what a deadly serious business it is.

John Mortimer 1923–2009: *Clinging to the Wreckage* (1982)

25 Good taste and humour . . . are a contradiction in terms, like a chaste whore.

Malcolm Muggeridge 1903–90: in *Time* 14 September 1953

26 Another day gone and no jokes.

Flann O'Brien 1911–66: *The Best of Myles* (1968)

27 That's the Irish people all over—they treat a joke as a serious thing and a serious thing as a joke.

Sean O'Casey 1880–1964: *The Shadow of a Gunman* (1923)

28 Humour is, by its nature, more truthful than factual.

P. J. O'Rourke 1947– : *Parliament of Whores* (1991)

29 Laughter is pleasant, but the exertion is too much for me.

Thomas Love Peacock 1785–1866: *Nightmare Abbey* (1818)

30 Everything is funny as long as it is happening to Somebody Else.

Will Rogers 1879–1935: *The Illiterate Digest* (1924) 'Warning to Jokers: lay off the prince'

31 All humour is based on hostility—that's why World War Two was funny.

Neil Simon 1927– : *Laughter on the 23rd Floor* (1993)

32 Love, marriage and kids are fine, but I wouldn't give up an hour of comedy for them.

Frank Skinner 1957– : in *Times* 11 August 2007

33 There are three basic rules for great comedy. Unfortunately no-one can remember what they are.

Arthur Smith 1954– : attributed

34 For every ten jokes, thou hast got an hundred enemies.

Laurence Sterne 1713–68: *Tristram Shandy* (1769)

35 It would be a sad reflection on any satirical programme if no one ended up taking offence at some point.

Meera Syal 1963– : in *Independent* 30 November 2002

36 Humour is emotional chaos remembered in tranquillity.

James Thurber 1894–1961: in *New York Post* 29 February 1960

37 That joke was lost on the foreigner—guides cannot master the subtleties of the American joke.

Mark Twain 1835–1910: *The Innocents Abroad* (1869)

38 Laughter would be bereaved if snobbery died.

Peter Ustinov 1921–2004: in *Observer* 13 March 1955

39 Mucky jokes. Obscenity—it's all the go nowadays. By law, you see. You're allowed to do it. You can say bum, you can say po, you can say anything . . . Well, he said it! The thin one! He said bum one night. I heard him! Satire!

Keith Waterhouse 1929– and **Willis Hall**: 'Close Down' in David Frost and Ned Sherrin *That Was The Week That Was* (1963)

40 It's hard to be funny when you have to be clean.

Mae West 1892–1980: Joseph Weintraub *The Wit and Wisdom of Mae West* (1967)

41 Madeleine Bassett laughed the tinkling, silvery laugh that had got her so disliked by the better element.

P. G. Wodehouse 1881–1975: *The Code of the Woosters* (1938)

42 She had a penetrating sort of laugh. Rather like a train going into a tunnel.

P. G. Wodehouse 1881–1975: *The Inimitable Jeeves* (1923)

Hypocrisy

❝*Most people sell their souls, and live with a good conscience on the proceeds.*❞
Logan Pearsall Smith

1 There are moments when we in the British press can show extraordinary sensitivity; these moments usually coincide with the death of a proprietor, or a proprietor's wife.

Craig Brown 1957– : *Craig Brown's Greatest Hits* (1993)

2 In England the only homage which they pay to Virtue—is hypocrisy.

Lord Byron 1788–1824: letter, 11 May 1821

3 We are so very 'umble.
   Uriah Heep

Charles Dickens 1812–70: *David Copperfield* (1850)

4 He combines the manners of a Marquis with the morals of a Methodist.

W. S. Gilbert 1836–1911: *Ruddigore* (1887)

5 Hypocrisy is not generally a social sin, but a virtue.

Judith Martin 1938– : *Miss Manners' Guide to Rearing Perfect Children* (1985)

6 *the hypocritical Quaker, Ephraim Smooth, hears violin music:* I must shut my ears. The man of sin rubbeth the hair of the horse to the bowels of the cat.

John O'Keeffe 1747–1833: *Wild Oats* (1791)

7 Most people sell their souls, and live with a good conscience on the proceeds.

Logan Pearsall Smith 1865–1946: *Afterthoughts* (1931) 'Other People'

8 Of all the cants which are canted in this canting world,— though the cant of hypocrites may be the worst,—the cant of criticism is the most tormenting!

Laurence Sterne 1713–68: *Tristram Shandy* (1759–67)

9 I hope you have not been leading a double life, pretending to be wicked and being really good all the time. That would be hypocrisy.

Oscar Wilde 1854–1900: *The Importance of Being Earnest* (1895)

Ideas

❝ *I had a monumental idea this morning, but I didn't like it.* **❞**

Sam Goldwyn

1 I ran into Isosceles. He has a great idea for a new triangle!

2 An original idea. That can't be too hard. The library must be full of them.

3 I had a monumental idea this morning, but I didn't like it.

4 The chief end of man is to frame general ideas—and . . . no general idea is worth a damn.

5 It is better to entertain an idea than to take it home to live with you for the rest of your life.

6 A household where a total unawareness of the world of ideas not only existed but was regarded as a matter for congratulation.

7 There are some ideas so wrong that only a very intelligent person could believe in them.

8 The English approach to ideas is not to kill them, but to let them die of neglect.

9 I believe what I said yesterday. I don't know what I said, but I know what I think . . . and I assume it's what I said.

Woody Allen 1935– : *If the Impressionists had been Dentists*

Stephen Fry 1957– : *The Liar* (1991)

Sam Goldwyn 1882–1974: N. Zierold *Hollywood Tycoons* (1969)

Oliver Wendell Holmes Jr. 1841–1935: letter to Morris R. Cohen, 12 April 1915

Randall Jarrell 1914–65: *Pictures from an Institution* (1954)

Osbert Lancaster 1908–86: *All Done From Memory* (1953)

George Orwell 1903–50: attributed

Jeremy Paxman 1950– : *The English: a portrait of a people* (1998)

Donald Rumsfeld 1932– : Pentagon press briefing, 21 February 2002

Ignorance

❝ *You know everybody is ignorant, only on different subjects.* **❞**

Will Rogers

1 Mr Kremlin himself was distinguished for ignorance, for he had only one idea,—and that was wrong.

2 *on being asked why he had defined* pastern *as the 'knee' of a horse:*
Ignorance, madam, pure ignorance.

3 *in response to the comment on another lawyer, 'It may be doubted whether any man of our generation has plunged more deeply into the sacred fount of learning':*
Or come up drier.

4 A bishop wrote gravely to the *Times* inviting all nations to destroy 'the formula' of the atomic bomb. There is no simple remedy for ignorance so abysmal.

5 What's it all about . . . ?

Benjamin Disraeli 1804–81: *Sybil* (1845)

Samuel Johnson 1709–84: James Boswell *Life of Samuel Johnson* (1791) 1755

Abraham Lincoln 1809–65: Leon Harris *The Fine Art of Political Wit* (1965)

Peter Medawar 1915–87: *The Hope of Progress* (1972)

Bill Naughton 1910–92: *Alfie* (1966 film); spoken by Michael Caine as Alfie

6 You know everybody is ignorant, only on different subjects.

Will Rogers 1879–1935: in *New York Times* 31 August 1924

7 Reports that say that something hasn't happened are always interesting to me, because as we know, there are known knowns; there are things we know we know. We also know there are known unknowns; that is to say we know there are some things we do not know. But there are also unknown unknowns—the ones we don't know we don't know.

Donald Rumsfeld 1932– : news briefing, February 2002; the statement won the Plain English Campaign's Foot in Mouth award

8 Ignorance is like a delicate exotic fruit; touch it and the bloom is gone.

Oscar Wilde 1854–1900: *The Importance of Being Earnest* (1895)

Indexes
See also **Books**

❝ *I wasn't even in the index.* **❞**
Edwina Currie

1 If you don't find it in the Index, look very carefully through the entire catalogue.

Anonymous: in *Consumer's Guide, Sears, Roebuck and Co.* (1897); Donald E. Knuth *Sorting and Searching* (1973)

2 Whenever I am sent a new book on the lively arts, the first thing I do is look for myself in the index.

Julie Burchill 1960– : *The Spectator* 16 January 1992

3 I wasn't even in the index.
  on John Major's autobiography

Edwina Currie 1946– : in *Times* 28 September 2002

4 *the Editors' acknowledgements:*
  Their thanks are also due to their wife for not preparing the index wrong. There is no index.

W. C. Sellar 1898–1951 and **R. J. Yeatman** 1898–1968: *1066 and All That* (1930)

5 An index is a great leveller.

George Bernard Shaw 1856–1950: G. N. Knight *Indexing* (1979); attributed, perhaps apocryphal

6 Should not the Society of Indexers be known as Indexers, Society of, The?

Keith Waterhouse 1929– : *Bookends* (1990)

Insults and Invective

❝ *Simply a shiver looking for a spine to run up.* **❞**
Paul Keating

1 Lord Birkenhead is very clever but sometimes his brains go to his head.

Margot Asquith 1864–1945: in *Listener* 11 June 1953 'Margot Oxford' by Lady Violet Bonham Carter

2 The *t* is silent, as in *Harlow*.
  to Jean Harlow, who had been mispronouncing her first name

Margot Asquith 1864–1945: T. S. Matthews *Great Tom* (1973)

3 I married beneath me, all women do.

Nancy Astor 1879–1964: in *Dictionary of National Biography 1961–1970* (1981)

4 NANCY ASTOR: If I were your wife I would put poison in your coffee!
WINSTON CHURCHILL: And if I were your husband I would drink it.

Nancy Astor 1879–1964: Consuelo Vanderbilt Balsan *Glitter and Gold* (1952)

5 I didn't know he'd been knighted. I knew he'd been doctored.
on Malcolm Sargent's knighthood

Thomas Beecham 1879–1961: attributed

6 The 'g' is silent—the only thing about her that is.
of Camille Paglia

Julie Burchill 1960– : in *The Spectator* 16 January 1992

7 Lillian Gish may be a charming person, but she is not Ophelia. She comes on stage as if she had been sent for to sew rings on the new curtains.

Mrs Patrick Campbell 1865–1940: Margot Peters *Mrs Pat* (1984)

8 I have derived continued benefit from criticism at all periods of my life and I do not remember any time when I was ever short of it.

Winston Churchill 1874–1965: in House of Commons 27 November 1914

9 [Clement Attlee is] a modest man who has a good deal to be modest about.

Winston Churchill 1874–1965: in *Chicago Sunday Tribune Magazine of Books* 27 June 1954

10 A sheep in sheep's clothing.
of Clement Attlee

Winston Churchill 1874–1965: Lord Home *The Way the Wind Blows* (1976)

11 BESSIE BRADDOCK: Winston, you're drunk.
CHURCHILL: Bessie, you're ugly. But tomorrow I shall be sober.

Winston Churchill 1874–1965: an exchange with the Labour MP Bessie Braddock; J. L. Lane (ed.) *Sayings of Churchill* (1992)

12 *Henry Clay of Virginia unexpectedly moved out of the way of his political rival, John Randolph of Roanoke:*
JOHN RANDOLPH: I never sidestep skunks.
HENRY CLAY: I always do.

Henry Clay 1777–1852: Robert V. Remini *Henry Clay* (1991)

13 A sophistical rhetorician, inebriated with the exuberance of his own verbosity.
of Gladstone

Benjamin Disraeli 1804–81: in *Times* 29 July 1878

14 [*The Sun Also Rises* is about] bullfighting, bullslinging, and bull—.

Zelda Fitzgerald 1900–47: Marion Meade *What Fresh Hell Is This?* (1988)

15 A very weak-minded fellow I am afraid, and, like the feather pillow, bears the marks of the last person who has sat on him!
of Lord Derby

Earl Haig 1861–1928: letter to Lady Haig, 14 January 1918

16 His thoughts are seldom consecutive.
He just can write.
I know a movie executive
Who's twice as bright.

Lorenz Hart 1895–1943: 'Take Him' (*Pal Joey*, 1940 musical)

17 *on being criticized by Geoffrey Howe:*
Like being savaged by a dead sheep.

Denis Healey 1917– : speech, House of Commons 14 June 1978

18 Some men are born mediocre, some men achieve mediocrity, and some men have mediocrity thrust upon them. With Major Major it had been all three.

Joseph Heller 1923–99: *Catch-22* (1961)

19 Such cruel glasses.
of Robin Day

Frankie Howerd 1922–92: in *That Was The Week That Was* (BBC television series, from 1963)

20 So dumb he can't fart and chew gum at the same time.
of Gerald Ford

Lyndon Baines Johnson 1908–73: Richard Reeves *A Ford, not a Lincoln* (1975)

21 Is not a Patron, my Lord, one who looks with unconcern on a man struggling for life in the water, and, when he has reached ground, encumbers him with help? The notice which you have been pleased to take of my labours, had it been early, had been kind; but it has been delayed till I am indifferent, and cannot enjoy it; till I am solitary, and cannot impart it; till I am known, and do not want it.

Samuel Johnson 1709–84: letter to Lord Chesterfield, 7 February 1755; James Boswell *Life of Samuel Johnson* (1791)

22 This man [Lord Chesterfield] I thought had been a Lord among wits; but, I find, he is only a wit among Lords.

Samuel Johnson 1709–84: James Boswell *Life of Samuel Johnson* (1791) (1754)

23 This little flower, this delicate little beauty, this cream puff, is supposed to be beyond personal criticism . . . He is simply a shiver looking for a spine to run up.
of John Hewson, the Australian Liberal leader

Paul Keating 1944– : in *Ned Sherrin in his Anecdotage* (1993)

24 The truckman, the trashman and the policeman on the block may call me Alice but you may not.
to Senator Joseph McCarthy

Alice Roosevelt Longworth 1884–1980: Michael Teague *Mrs. L* (1981)

25 *on hearing that a Hollywood agent had swum safely in shark-infested waters:*
I think that's what they call professional courtesy.

Herman J. Mankiewicz 1897–1953: attributed; Nigel Rees *Cassell Dictionary of Humorous Quotations* (1999)

26 I never forget a face, but in your case I'll be glad to make an exception.

Groucho Marx 1890–1977: Leo Rosten *People I have Loved, Known or Admired* (1970) 'Groucho'

27 The majority of the members of the Irish parliament are professional politicians, in the sense that otherwise they would not be given jobs minding mice at crossroads.

Flann O'Brien 1911–66: *The Hair of the Dogma* (1977)

28 If you say a modern celebrity is an adulterer, a pervert and a drug addict, all it means is that you've read his autobiography.

P. J. O'Rourke 1947– : *Give War a Chance* (1992)

29 *to Clare Boothe Luce, who had stood aside for her saying, 'Age before Beauty':*
Pearls before swine.

Dorothy Parker 1893–1967: R. E. Drennan *Wit's End* (1973)

30 The affair between Margot Asquith and Margot Asquith will live as one of the prettiest love stories in all literature.

Dorothy Parker 1893–1967: review of Margot Asquith's *Lay Sermons*; in *New Yorker* 22 October 1927

31 I'm not offended at all, because I know I'm not a dumb blonde. I also know I'm not blonde.

Dolly Parton 1946– : M. Palmer *Small Talk, Big Names: 40 Years of Rock Quotes* (1993)

32 Let Sporus tremble—'What? that thing of silk,
Sporus, that mere white curd of ass's milk?
Satire or sense, alas! can Sporus feel?
Who breaks a butterfly upon a wheel?'

Alexander Pope 1688–1744: of Lord Hervey; 'An Epistle to Dr Arbuthnot' (1735)

33 A cherub's face, a reptile all the rest.

> **Alexander Pope** 1688–1744: of Lord Hervey; 'An Epistle to Dr Arbuthnot' (1735)

34 A wit with dunces, and a dunce with wits.

> **Alexander Pope** 1688–1744: *The Dunciad* (1742)

35 Don't look at me, Sir, with—ah—in that tone of voice.

> **Punch** 1841–1992: vol. 87 (1884)

36 BEATRICE: I wonder that you will still be talking, Signior Benedick: nobody marks you.
BENEDICK: What! my dear Lady Disdain, are you yet living?

> **William Shakespeare** 1564–1616: *Much Ado About Nothing* (1598–9)

37 Diana Rigg is built like a brick mausoleum with insufficient flying buttresses.
review of Abelard and Heloise *in 1970*

> **John Simon** 1925– : Diana Rigg *No Turn Unstoned* (1982)

38 *on being approached by the secretary of the Athenaeum, which he had been in the habit of using as a convenience on the way to his office:*
Good God, do you mean to say this place is a club?

> **F. E. Smith** 1872–1930: attributed

39 JUDGE: You are extremely offensive, young man.
SMITH: As a matter of fact, we both are, and the only difference between us is that I am trying to be, and you can't help it.

> **F. E. Smith** 1872–1930: Lord Birkenhead *Earl of Birkenhead* (1933)

40 *on a proposal to surround St Paul's with a wooden pavement:*
Let the Dean and Canons lay their heads together and the thing will be done.

> **Sydney Smith** 1771–1845: H. Pearson *The Smith of Smiths* (1934)

41 Science is his forte, and omniscience his foible.
of William Whewell, master of Trinity College, Cambridge

> **Sydney Smith** 1771–1845: Isaac Todhunter *William Whewell* (1876)

42 I regard you with an indifference closely bordering on aversion.

> **Robert Louis Stevenson** 1850–94: *New Arabian Nights* (1882)

43 *when pressed by a gramophone company for a written testimonial:*
Sirs, I have tested your machine. It adds a new terror to life and makes death a long-felt want.

> **Herbert Beerbohm Tree** 1852–1917: Hesketh Pearson *Beerbohm Tree* (1956)

44 *to Richard Adams, who had described Vidal's novel on Lincoln as 'meretricious'*
Really? Well, meretricious and a happy New Year to you too!
earlier uses of the response are attributed to Franklin P. Adams in the 1930s, and the NBC radio show starring the Marx Brothers, Flywheel, Shyster and Flywheel, *in 1933*

> **Gore Vidal** 1925– : on *Start the Week*, BBC radio, 1970s

45 Every other inch a gentleman.

> **Rebecca West** 1892–1983: of Michael Arlen; Victoria Glendinning *Rebecca West* (1987)

46 CECILY: When I see a spade I call it a spade.
GWENDOLEN: I am glad to say that I have never seen a spade.

> **Oscar Wilde** 1854–1900: *The Importance of Being Earnest* (1895)

47 [EARL OF SANDWICH:] 'Pon my soul, Wilkes, I don't know whether you'll die upon the gallows or of the pox.
[WILKES:] That depends, my Lord, whether I first embrace your Lordship's principles, or your Lordship's mistresses.

> **John Wilkes** 1727–97: Charles Petrie *The Four Georges* (1935); probably apocryphal

Intelligence and Intellectuals

See also **The Mind**

❝ *Genius is one per cent inspiration, ninety-nine per cent perspiration.* **❞**

Thomas Alva Edison

1 To the man-in-the-street, who, I'm sorry to say,
Is a keen observer of life,
The word 'Intellectual' suggests straight away
A man who's untrue to his wife.

W. H. Auden 1907–73: *New Year Letter* (1941)

2 I am sure some people think I have not got the brains to be that clever, but I do have the brains.
on how he intentionally picked up a yellow card in England's World Cup match against Wales

David Beckham 1975– : in *Mail on Sunday* 17 October 2004

3 Men of genius are so few that they ought to atone for their fewness by being at any rate ubiquitous.

Max Beerbohm 1872–1956: letter to W. B. Yeats, 11 July 1911

4 But—Oh! ye lords of ladies intellectual,
Inform us truly, have they not hen-pecked you all?

Lord Byron 1788–1824: *Don Juan* (1819–24)

5 MAN OF CULTURE: I like my painting muddy
And all my verse obscure
My music without melody
You see I'm most mature.

Ronald Duncan 1914–82: *This Way to the Tomb* (1946)

6 Genius is one per cent inspiration, ninety-nine per cent perspiration.

Thomas Alva Edison 1847–1931: said c.1903; in *Harper's Monthly Magazine* September 1932

7 With the thoughts I'd be thinkin'
I could be another Lincoln,
If I only had a brain.

E. Y. Harburg 1898–1981: 'If I Only Had a Brain' (1939)

8 Zip! Walter Lippman wasn't brilliant today,
Zip! Will Saroyan ever write a great play?
Zip! I was reading Schopenhauer last night.
Zip! And I think that Schopenhauer was right!
satirizing the intellectual pretensions of Gypsy Rose Lee

Lorenz Hart 1895–1943: 'Zip' (1940)

9 Probably the greatest concentration of talent and genius in this house except for perhaps those times when Thomas Jefferson ate alone.
of a dinner for Nobel Prizewinners at the White House

John F. Kennedy 1917–63: in *New York Times* 30 April 1962

10 *I think, therefore I am* is the statement of an intellectual who underrates toothaches.

Milan Kundera 1929– : *Immortality* (1991)

11 No one in this world, so far as I know—and I have searched the records for years, and employed agents to help me—has ever lost money by underestimating the intelligence of the great masses of the plain people.

H. L. Mencken 1880–1956: in *Chicago Tribune* 19 September 1926

12 My wish was that my husband should be distinguished for intellect, and my children too. I have had my wish,—and I now wish that there were a little less intellect in the family so as to allow for a little more common sense.

Frances Rossetti 1800–86: William Rossetti (ed.) *Dante Gabriel Rossetti: His Family Letters with a Memoir* (1895)

13 You can persuade a man to believe almost anything provided he is clever enough, but it is much more difficult to persuade someone less clever.

Tom Stoppard 1937– : *Professional Foul* (1978)

14 What is a highbrow? He is a man who has found something more interesting than women.

Edgar Wallace 1875–1932: in *New York Times* 24 January 1932

15 I have nothing to declare except my genius.

Oscar Wilde 1854–1900: at the New York Custom House; Frank Harris *Oscar Wilde* (1918)

16 'Jeeves is a wonder.'
'A marvel.'
'What a brain.'
'Size nine-and-a-quarter, I should say.'
'He eats a lot of fish.'

P. G. Wodehouse 1881–1975: *Thank You, Jeeves* (1934)

17 'Well, I think you're a pig.'
'A pig, maybe, but a shrewd, levelheaded pig. I wouldn't touch the project with a bargepole.'

P. G. Wodehouse 1881–1975: *The Code of the Woosters* (1938)

18 I know I've got a degree. Why does that mean I have to spend my life with intellectuals? I've got a life-saving certificate but I don't spend my evenings diving for a rubber brick with my pyjamas on.

Victoria Wood 1953– : *Mens Sana in Thingummy Doodah* (1990)

Invective See **Insults and Invective**

Ireland and the Irish
See also **Countries and Peoples, Places**

❝ *I'm Irish. We think sideways.* **❞**
Spike Milligan

1 PAT: He was an Anglo-Irishman.
MEG: In the blessed name of God what's that?
PAT: A Protestant with a horse.

Brendan Behan 1923–64: *Hostage* (1958)

2 We've never been cool, we're hot. Irish people are Italians who can't dress, Jamaicans who can't dance.

Bono 1960– : interview, 25 February 2001; in *Independent* 26 February 2001

3 Where would the Irish be without someone to be Irish at?

Elizabeth Bowen 1899–1973: *The House in Paris* (1935)

4 We rose to bring about Eutopia,
But all we got was Dev's myopia.

Oliver St John Gogarty 1878–1957: letter to James Montgomery; Ulick O'Connor *Oliver St John Gogarty* (1964)

5 Ireland is a small but insuppressible island half an hour nearer the sunset than Great Britain.

Thomas Kettle 1880–1916: 'On Crossing the Irish Sea'

6 The Irish, he says, don't care for clean government; they want Irish government.

Stephen Leacock 1869–1944: *Arcadian Adventures with the Idle Rich* (1914)

7 I'm Irish. We think sideways.

Spike Milligan 1918–2002: in *Independent on Sunday* 20 June 1999

8 Our ancestors believed in magic, prayers, trickery, browbeating and bullying: I think it would be fair to sum that list up as 'Irish politics'.

Flann O'Brien 1911–66: *The Hair of the Dogma* (1977)

9 He'd . . . settled into a life of Guinness, sarcasm and late late nights, the kind of life that American academics think real Dubliners lead.

Joseph O'Connor 1963– : *Cowboys and Indians* (1991)

10 Gladstone . . . spent his declining years trying to guess the answer to the Irish Question; unfortunately whenever he was getting warm, the Irish secretly changed the Question.

W. C. Sellar 1898–1951 and **R. J. Yeatman** 1898–1968: *1066 and All That* (1930)

11 An Irishman's heart is nothing but his imagination.

George Bernard Shaw 1856–1950: *John Bull's Other Island* (1907)

12 *denying that he was Irish:*
Because a man is born in a stable, that does not make him a horse.

Duke of Wellington 1769–1852: Paul Johnson (ed.) *The Oxford Book of Political Anecdotes* (1986)

Journalism

See also **Newspapers**

“ *Saying 'Lord Jones Dead' to people who never knew that Lord Jones was alive.* ”
G. K. Chesterton

1 At certain times each year, we journalists do almost nothing except apply for the Pulitzers and several dozen other major prizes. During these times you could walk right into most newsrooms and commit a multiple axe murder naked, and it wouldn't get reported in the paper because the reporters and editors would all be too busy filling out prize applications.

Dave Barry 1948– : in *Miami Herald* 29 March 1987

2 *to Nicholas Phipps, who had announced that he was an efficient hack rather than a creative writer:*
Creative writers are two a penny. Efficient hacks are very rare.

Lord Beaverbrook 1879–1964: in *Daily Telegraph* 17 July 2004 (obituary of Nicholas Phipps)

3 When a dog bites a man, that is not news, because it happens so often. But if a man bites a dog, that is news.

John B. Bogart 1848–1921: F. M. O'Brien *The Story of the* [New York] *Sun* (1918); often attributed to Charles A. Dana

4 *on being asked whether George Mair had been a fastidious journalist:*
He once telephoned a semicolon from Moscow.

James Bone: James Agate diary, 31 October 1935

5 Journalism could be described as turning one's enemies into money.

Craig Brown 1957– : in *Daily Telegraph* 28 September 1990

6 A would-be satirist, a hired buffoon,
A monthly scribbler of some low lampoon,
Condemned to drudge, the meanest of the mean,
And furbish falsehoods for a magazine.
  of journalists

Lord Byron 1788–1824: 'English Bards and Scotch Reviewers' (1809)

7 Let's face it, sports writers, we're not hanging around with brain surgeons.

Jimmy Cannon 1910–73: attributed

8 *explaining the craft of sports writers:*
We work in the toy department.

9 When seagulls follow a trawler, it is because they think sardines will be thrown into the sea.

10 Journalism largely consists in saying 'Lord Jones Dead' to people who never knew that Lord Jones was alive.

11 You are misunderstood, maligned, viewed by the press as a Pulitzer Prize ready to be won.
on the problems of investigative journalism for politicians

12 The first law of journalism—to confirm existing prejudice rather than contradict it.

13 Thou god of our idolatry, the press . . .
Thou fountain, at which drink the good and wise;
Thou ever-bubbling spring of endless lies;
Like Eden's dread probationary tree,
Knowledge of good and evil is from thee.

14 If you lose your temper at a newspaper columnist, he'll be rich, or famous, or both.

15 Power without responsibility: the prerogative of the harlot throughout the ages.
summing up the view of Lord Beaverbrook, who had said to Kipling: 'What I want is power. Kiss 'em one day and kick 'em the next'; Stanley Baldwin, Kipling's cousin, subsequently obtained permission to use the phrase in a speech in London on 18 March 1931

16 I think it well to remember that, when writing for the newspapers, we are writing for an elderly lady in Hastings who has two cats of which she is passionately fond. Unless our stuff can successfully compete for her interest with those cats, it is no good.

17 I like to do my principal research in bars, where people are more likely to tell the truth or, at least, lie less convincingly than they do in briefings and books.

18 No government in history has been as obsessed with public relations as this one . . . Speaking for myself, if there is a message I want to be off it.

19 More like a gentleman than a journalist.

20 My belief is that 'recluse' is a codeword generated by journalists . . . meaning 'doesn't like to talk to reporters'.

21 Comment is free but facts are on expenses.

22 Up to a point, Lord Copper.

Jimmy Cannon 1910–73: Michael Parkinson *Sporting Lives* (1993)

Eric Cantona 1966– : at the end of a press conference, 31 March 1995

G. K. Chesterton 1874–1936: *Wisdom of Father Brown* (1914)

Lawton Chiles 1930– : in *St Petersburg (Florida) Times* 6 March 1991

Alexander Cockburn 1941– : in 1974; Jonathon Green *Says Who?* (1988)

William Cowper 1731–1800: 'The Progress of Error' (1782)

James Hagerty 1936– : the view of President Eisenhower's press secretary; Jonathon Green *Says Who?* (1988)

Rudyard Kipling 1865–1936: in *Kipling Journal* December 1971

Willmott Lewis 1877–1950: Claud Cockburn *In Time of Trouble* (1957)

P. J. O'Rourke 1947– : *Holidays in Hell* (1988)

Jeremy Paxman 1950– : in *Daily Telegraph* 3 July 1998

J. B. Priestley 1894–1984: of Bruce Richmond, editor of *The Times Literary Supplement*; letter to Edward Davison, 23 June 1924

Thomas Pynchon 1937– : in a telephone conversation with CNN, 1997; in *Guardian* 5 May 2003

Tom Stoppard 1937– : *Night and Day* (1978)

Evelyn Waugh 1903–66: *Scoop* (1938)

23 They had loitered together of old on many a doorstep and forced an entry into many a stricken home.

Evelyn Waugh 1903–66: *Scoop* (1938)

24 A journalist is somebody who possesses himself of a fantasy and lures the truth towards it.

Arnold Wesker 1932– : *Journey into Journalism* (1977)

25 There is a journalistic curse of Eve. The woman who writes is always given anti-feminist books to review.

Rebecca West 1892–1983: in *The Clarion* 21 November 1913

26 *the difference between journalism and literature:*
Journalism is unreadable, and literature is not read.

Oscar Wilde 1854–1900: 'The Critic as Artist' (1891)

27 You cannot hope
to bribe or twist,
thank God! the
British journalist.
But, seeing what
the man will do
unbribed, there's
no occasion to.

Humbert Wolfe 1886–1940: 'Over the Fire' (1930)

28 Rock journalism is people who can't write interviewing people who can't talk for people who can't read.

Frank Zappa 1940–93: Linda Botts *Loose Talk* (1980)

Judges

See also **Crime and Punishment, The Law**

> **❝** *I could have been a judge but I never had the Latin.* **❞**
> **Peter Cook**

1 Reform! Reform! Aren't things bad enough already?

Mr Justice Astbury 1860–1939: attributed

2 *affecting not to recognize Lord Campbell, the newly appointed Lord Chancellor, whom he encountered enveloped in a huge fur coat:*
I beg your pardon, My Lord. I mistook you for the Great Seal.

Richard Bethell 1800–73: J. B. Atlay *Victorian Chancellors* (1908)

3 CONVICTED CRIMINAL: As God is my judge—I am innocent.
LORD BIRKETT: He isn't; I am, and you're not!

Lord Birkett 1883–1962: attributed; Matthew Parris *Scorn* (1994)

4 I always approach Judge [Lemuel] Shaw as a savage approaches his fetish, knowing that he is ugly but feeling that he is great.

Rufus Choate 1799–1859: Van Wyck Brooks *The Flowering of New England* (1936)

5 I don't want to know what the law is, I want to know who the judge is.

Roy M. Cohn 1927–86: in *New York Times Book Review* 3 April 1988

6 Did you mail that cheque to the Judge?

Roy M. Cohn 1927–86: spoken to an aide, at breakfast with Ned Sherrin, 1978

7 Yes, I could have been a judge but I never had the Latin, never had the Latin for the judging, I just never had sufficient of it to get through the rigorous judging exams. They're noted for their rigour. People come staggering out saying, 'My God, what a rigorous exam'—and so I became a miner instead.

Peter Cook 1937–95: *Beyond the Fringe* (1961 revue)

8 *the judge Sir James Mansfield had suggested that the Court might sit on Good Friday:*
If your Lordship pleases. But your Lordship will be the first judge who has done so since Pontius Pilate.
   the Court did not sit

William Davy d. 1780: Edward Parry *The Seven Lamps of Advocacy* (1923)

9 *of Judges Learned and Augustus Hand:*
Quote Learned, and follow 'Gus'.

Robert H. Jackson 1892–1954: Hershel Shanks *The Art and Craft of Judging* (1968)

10 I always feel that there should be some comfort derived from any question from the bench. It is clear proof that the inquiring Justice is not asleep.

Robert H. Jackson 1892–1954: 'Advocacy before the Supreme Court: Suggestions for Effective Presentation' (1951)

11 Mr Justice Cocklecarrot began the hearing of a very curious case yesterday. A Mrs Tasker is accused of continually ringing the doorbell of a Mrs Renton, and then, when the door is opened, pushing a dozen red-bearded dwarfs into the hall and leaving them there.

J. B. Morton 1893–1975: *Diet of Thistles* (1938)

12 Poor fellow, I suppose he fancied he was on the bench.
   on hearing that a judge had slept through his play Pizarro

Richard Brinsley Sheridan 1751–1816: Walter Jerrold *Bon-Mots* (1893)

13 JUDGE: I have read your case, Mr Smith, and I am no wiser now than I was when I started.
SMITH: Possibly not, My Lord, but far better informed.

F. E. Smith 1872–1930: Lord Birkenhead *F. E.* (1959)

14 JUDGE WILLIS: Mr Smith, have you ever heard of a saying by Bacon—the great Bacon—that youth and discretion are ill-wed companions?
SMITH: Indeed I have, your Honour; and has your Honour ever heard of a saying by Bacon—the great Bacon—that a much talking Judge is like an ill-tuned cymbal?

F. E. Smith 1872–1930: Lord Birkenhead *F. E.* (1959)

Language
See also **Grammar, Languages, Words**

❝ *The sort of English up with which I will not put.* ❞
Winston Churchill

1 Don't swear, boy. It shows a lack of vocabulary.

Alan Bennett 1934– : *Forty Years On* (1969)

2 This is the sort of English up with which I will not put.

Winston Churchill 1874–1965: Ernest Gowers *Plain Words* (1948) 'Troubles with Prepositions'

3 Stars, Charlie had noticed before, always spoke slowly. Listening to Warren Beatty being interviewed was like waiting for speech to finish being invented.

Ray Connolly: *Shadows on a Wall* (1994)

4 Where in this small-talking world can I find
A longitude with no platitude?

Christopher Fry 1907–2005: *The Lady's not for Burning* (1949)

5 Backward ran sentences until reeled the mind.
satirizing the style of Time *magazine*

Wolcott Gibbs 1902–58: in *New Yorker* 28 November 1936 'Time . . . Fortune . . . Life . . . Luce'

6 When you're lying awake with a dismal headache, and
repose is taboo'd by anxiety,
I conceive you may use any language you choose to
indulge in, without impropriety.

W. S. Gilbert 1836–1911: *Iolanthe* (1882)

7 Though 'Bother it' I may
Occasionally say,
I never use a big, big D—

W. S. Gilbert 1836–1911: *HMS Pinafore* (1878)

8 The minute a phrase becomes current it becomes an
apology for not thinking accurately to the end of the
sentence.

Oliver Wendell Holmes Jr. 1841–1935: letter to Harold Laski, 2 July 1917

9 My spelling is Wobbly. It's good spelling but it Wobbles,
and the letters get in the wrong places.

A. A. Milne 1882–1956: *Winnie-the-Pooh* (1926)

10 'Feather-footed through the plashy fen passes the questing
vole' . . . 'Yes,' said the Managing Editor. 'That must be
good style.'

Evelyn Waugh 1903–66: *Scoop* (1938)

Languages

See also **Language, Words**

66 *The interpreter is the hardest to be understood of the two!* 99
Richard Brinsley Sheridan

1 The Norwegian language has been described as German
spoken underwater.

Anonymous: Nigel Rees *Cassell Dictionary of Humorous Quotations* (1999)

2 If you understand English, press 1. If you do not
understand English, press 2.
recorded message on Australian tax helpline

Anonymous: in *Mail on Sunday* 30 July 2000 'Quotes of the Week'

3 The letter is written in the tongue of the Think Tanks, a
language more difficult to master than Basque or Navaho
and spoken only where strategic thinkers clump together
in Institutes.

Russell Baker 1925– : in *New York Times* 8 April 1981

4 Albanian . . . a language that sounded comic with all its
pffts, pees, wees, pings and fitts.

Cecil Beaton 1904–80: diary, August 1940

5 Is there no Latin word for Tea? Upon my soul, if I had
known that I would have let the vulgar stuff alone.

Hilaire Belloc 1870–1953: 'On Tea' (1908)

6 You know the trouble with the French, they don't even
have a word for entrepreneur.

George W. Bush 1946– : attributed, probably apocryphal

7 JOSEPHINE BAKER: Donnez-moi une tasse de café, s'il vous
plait.
MARY CAMPBELL: Honey, talk out of the mouth you was
born with.
*exchange between Josephine Baker, who had moved to
France from America, and who was staying with Lorenz
Hart's parents, and Mary Campbell, who was the Harts'
cook*

Mary Campbell: Samuel Marx and Jan Clayton *Rodgers and Hart* (1975)

8 Speak in French when you can't think of the English for a thing.

Lewis Carroll 1832–98: *Through the Looking-Glass* (1872)

9 *on speaking French fluently rather than correctly:*
It's nerve and brass, *audace* and disrespect, and leaping-before-you-look and what-the-hellism, that must be developed.

Diana Cooper 1892–1986: Philip Ziegler *Diana Cooper* (1981)

10 If the King's English was good enough for Jesus Christ, it's good enough for Texas.
view of the first woman Governor of Texas, 1924

Miriam A. 'Ma' Ferguson 1875–1961: Christopher Meyer *D.C. Confidential* (2005)

11 Anglish is what we don' know
Spanglish is langlish we know.

Dorothy Fields 1905–74: 'Spanglish' (1973)

12 I hear it's the Hebrew in Heaven, sir. Spanish is seldom spoken.

Ronald Firbank 1886–1926: *Concerning the Eccentricities of Cardinal Pirelli* (1926)

13 Weep not for little Léonie
Abducted by a French Marquis!
Though loss of honour was a wrench
Just think how it's improved her French.

Harry Graham 1874–1936: 'Compensation' (1930)

14 All pro athletes are bilingual. They speak English and profanity.

Gordie Howe 1928– : in *Toronto Star* 27 May 1975

15 There even are places where English completely disappears.
In America, they haven't used it for years!
Why can't the English teach their children how to speak?

Alan Jay Lerner 1918–86: 'Why Can't the English?' (1956)

16 *when Khrushchev began banging his shoe on the desk:*
Perhaps we could have a translation, I could not quite follow.

Harold Macmillan 1894–1986: during his speech to the United Nations, 29 September 1960

17 Listen, someone's screaming in agony—fortunately I speak it fluently.

Spike Milligan 1918–2002: *The Goon Show* 'The Scarlet Capsule' (BBC Radio, 1959)

18 I can speak Esperanto like a native.

Spike Milligan 1918–2002: attributed; in *Daily Telegraph* 28 February 2002

19 Waiting for the German verb is surely the ultimate thrill.

Flann O'Brien 1911–66: *The Hair of the Dogma* (1977)

20 *on being told there was no English word equivalent to sensibilité:*
Yes we have. Humbug.

Lord Palmerston 1784–1865: attributed

21 Don't you guys know you're in Hollywood? Speak German.
when a number of people began speaking in Hungarian at a Hollywood party

Otto Preminger 1906–86: Anthony Heilbut *Exiled in Paradise* (1983)

22 KENNETH: If you're so hot, you'd better tell me how to say she has ideas above her station.
BRIAN: Oh, yes, I forgot. It's fairly easy, old boy. *Elle a des idées au-dessus de sa gare.*
KENNETH: You can't do it like that. You can't say *au-dessus de sa gare*. It isn't that sort of station.

Terence Rattigan 1911–77: *French without Tears* (1937)

23 Remember that you are a human being with a soul and the divine gift of articulate speech: that your native language is the language of Shakespeare and Milton and The Bible; and don't sit there crooning like a bilious pigeon.

George Bernard Shaw 1856–1950: *Pygmalion* (1916)

24 Egad I think the interpreter is the hardest to be understood of the two!

Richard Brinsley Sheridan 1751–1816: *The Critic* (1779)

25 They spell it Vinci and pronounce it Vinchy; foreigners always spell better than they pronounce.

Mark Twain 1835–1910: *The Innocents Abroad* (1869)

26 I once heard a Californian student in Heidelberg say, in one of his calmest moods, that he would rather decline two drinks than one German adjective.

Mark Twain 1835–1910: *A Tramp Abroad* (1880)

27 An unalterable and unquestioned law of the musical world required that the German text of French operas sung by Swedish artists should be translated into Italian for the clearer understanding of English-speaking audiences.

Edith Wharton 1862–1937: *The Age of Innocence* (1920)

28 There had crept a look of furtive shame, the shifty, hangdog look which announces that an Englishman is about to talk French.

P. G. Wodehouse 1881–1975: *The Luck of the Bodkins* (1935)

29 '*Faute de* what?'
'*Mieux*, m'lord. A French expression. We should say "For want of anything better."'
'What asses these Frenchmen are. Why can't they talk English?'
'They are possibly more to be pitied than censured, m'lord. Early upbringing no doubt has a lot to do with it.'

P. G. Wodehouse 1881–1975: *Ring for Jeeves* (1953)

Last Words
See also **Death**

66 *Die, my dear Doctor, that's the last thing I shall do!* 99
Lord Palmerston

1 I will not go down to posterity talking bad grammar.

Benjamin Disraeli 1804–81: while correcting proofs of his last Parliamentary speech, 31 March 1881; Robert Blake *Disraeli* (1966)

2 No it is better not. She would only ask me to take a message to Albert.
near death, declining a proposed visit from Queen Victoria

Benjamin Disraeli 1804–81: Robert Blake *Disraeli* (1966)

3 Channel 5 is all shit, isn't it?

Adam Faith 1940–2002: attributed; in *Guardian* 13 May 2003

4 *on his deathbed in 1936, when someone remarked 'Cheer up, your Majesty, you will soon be at Bognor again':*
Bugger Bognor.

George V 1865–1936: Kenneth Rose *King George V* (1983); attributed

5 'Hallelujah!', Was the only observation
That escaped Lieutenant-Colonel Mary Jane
When she tumbled off the platform in the
station,
And was cut in little pieces by the train.

Mary Jane, the train is through yer:
Hallelujah, Hallelujah!
We will gather up the fragments that remain.

A. E. Housman 1859–1936:
'Hallelujah!'

6 *Lady Eldon had suggested that she should read to him from his
own New Testament:*
No . . . Awfully jolly of you to suggest it, though.

Ronald Knox 1888–1957: Evelyn
Waugh *Life of Ronald Knox*

7 I'm always angry when I'm dying.
John Mortimer's father's last words

Clifford Mortimer: John Mortimer *A
Voyage Round My Father* (1971)

8 Die, my dear Doctor, that's the last thing I shall do!

Lord Palmerston 1784–1865: E.
Latham *Famous Sayings and their
Authors* (1904)

9 Put that bloody cigarette out!
before being shot by a sniper in World War One

Saki 1870–1916: attributed, perhaps
apocryphal

10 They couldn't hit an elephant at this distance.
*immediately prior to being killed by enemy fire at the battle
of Spotsylvania in the American Civil War, May 1864*

John Sedgwick d. 64: Robert E.
Denney *The Civil War Years* (1992)

11 If this is dying, then I don't think much of it.

Lytton Strachey 1880–1932: Michael
Holroyd *Lytton Strachey* (1967)

12 I find, then, I am but a bad anatomist.
*cutting his throat in prison, he severed his windpipe instead
of his jugular, and lingered for several days*

Wolfe Tone 1763–98: Oliver Knox
Rebels and Informers (1998)

13 This is no time for making new enemies.
on being asked to renounce the Devil, on his deathbed

Voltaire 1694–1778: attributed

The Law
See also **Crime and Punishment, Judges**

❝ *If this is justice, I am a banana.* ❞
Ian Hislop

1 *an Irish judge dismissing a prisoner in the 19th century:*
You have been acquitted by a Limerick jury, and you may
now leave the dock without any other stain upon your
character.

Richard Adams: Maurice Healy *The
Old Munster Circuit* (1939)

2 I have knowingly defended a number of guilty men. But
the guilty never escape unscathed. My fees are sufficient
punishment for anyone.

F. Lee Bailey 1933– : in *Los Angeles
Times* 9 January 1972

3 Equity does not demand that its suitors shall have led
blameless lives.

Louis Brandeis 1856–1941: in
Loughran v. Loughran 1934

4 Lawyers charge a fortune to handle a bond offering. You
know what it takes to handle a bond offering? The mental
capacities of a filing cabinet.

Jimmy Breslin 1929– : in *Legal Times*
17 January 1983

5 As a moth is drawn to the light, so is a litigant drawn to
the United States. If he can only get his case into their
courts, he stands to win a fortune.

Lord Denning 1899–1999: *Smith
Kline & French Laboratories Ltd. v.
Bloch* 1983

6 'Little to do, and plenty to get, I suppose?' said Sergeant
Buzfuz, with jocularity. 'Oh, quite enough to get, sir, as
the soldier said ven they ordered him three hundred and
fifty lashes,' replied Sam. 'You must not tell us what the
soldier, or any other man, said, sir,' interposed the judge;
'it's not evidence.'

Charles Dickens 1812–70: *Pickwick
Papers* (1837)

7 'If the law supposes that,' said Mr Bumble . . . 'the law is a
ass—a idiot.'

Charles Dickens 1812–70: *Oliver
Twist* (1838)

8 The one great principle of the English law is, to make
business for itself.

Charles Dickens 1812–70: *Bleak
House* (1853)

9 This contract is so one-sided that I am surprised to find it
written on both sides of the paper.

Lord Evershed 1899–1966: Lord
Denning *Closing Chapter* (1983)

10 I was sued by a woman who claimed that she became
pregnant because she watched me on the television and I
bent her contraceptive coil.

Uri Geller 1946– : in *Sunday Times*
17 December 2000

11 When I was a lad I served a term
As office boy to an Attorney's firm.
I cleaned the windows and I swept the floor,
And I polished up the handle of the big front door.
I polished up that handle so carefullee
That now I am the Ruler of the Queen's Navee!

W. S. Gilbert 1836–1911: *HMS
Pinafore* (1878)

12 The Law is the true embodiment
Of everything that's excellent.
It has no kind of fault or flaw,
And I, my Lords, embody the Law.

W. S. Gilbert 1836–1911: *Iolanthe*
(1882)

13 Let's find out what everyone is doing,
And then stop everyone from doing it.

A. P. Herbert 1890–1971: 'Let's Stop
Somebody from Doing Something'
(1930)

14 *an attempt is made to write a cheque on a cow:*
'Was the cow crossed?'
'No, your worship, it was an open cow.'

A. P. Herbert 1890–1971:
Uncommon Law (1935) 'The
Negotiable Cow'

15 *on the award of £600,000 libel damages to Sonia Sutcliffe
against Private Eye:*
If this is justice, I am a banana.

Ian Hislop 1960– : in *Guardian* 25
May 1989

16 Legal writing is one of those rare creatures, like the rat
and the cockroach, that would attract little sympathy even
as an endangered species.

Richard Hyland 1949– : 'A Defense
of Legal Writing' (1986)

17 Johnson observed, that 'he did not care to speak ill of any
man behind his back, but he believed the gentleman was
an *attorney*.'

Samuel Johnson 1709–84: James
Boswell *Life of Samuel Johnson*
(1791) 1770

18 Sergeant, arrest most of these people.
often quoted as 'arrest most of those vicars'

Philip King c.1905–79 and **Falkland
Carey**: *See How They Run* (1947)

19 *when Knox was Attorney General Theodore Roosevelt
requested a legal justification for his acquisition of the Panama
Canal:*
Oh, Mr President, do not let so great an achievement suffer
from any taint of legality.

Philander C. Knox 1853–1921: Tyler
Dennett *John Hay: From Poetry to
Politics*

20 If you want to get ahead in this world get a lawyer—not a
book.
on self-help books

Fran Lebowitz 1946– : *Social Studies*
(1981)

21 Whatever fees we [Judge Logan and I] earn at a distance, if not paid *before*, we notice we never hear of after the work is done. We therefore, are growing a little sensitive on the point.

Abraham Lincoln 1809–65: letter 2 November 1842

22 Sue me, sue me
Shoot bullets through me
I love you.

Frank Loesser 1910–69: 'Sue Me' (1950)

23 However harmless a thing is, if the law forbids it most people will think it wrong.

W. Somerset Maugham 1874–1965: *A Writer's Notebook* (1949) written in 1896

24 Injustice is relatively easy to bear; what stings is justice.

H. L. Mencken 1880–1956: *Prejudices, Third Series* (1922)

25 Here [in Paris] they hang a man first, and try him afterwards.

Molière 1622–73: *Monsieur de Pourceaugnac* (1670)

26 I don't know as I want a lawyer to tell me what I cannot do. I hire him to tell me how to do what I want to do.

J. P. Morgan 1837–1913: Ida M. Tarbell *The Life of Elbert H. Gary* (1925)

27 No brilliance is needed in the law. Nothing but common sense, and relatively clean finger nails.

John Mortimer 1923–2009: *A Voyage Round My Father* (1971)

28 As it was once put to me, always remember that [as a barrister] you are in the position of a cabman on the rank, bound to answer the first hail.

Ralph Neville: in *Times* 16 June 1913

29 The Polis as Polis, in this city, is Null an' Void!

Sean O'Casey 1880–1964: *Juno and the Paycock* (1925)

30 Policemen, like red squirrels, must be protected.

Joe Orton 1933–67: *Loot* (1967)

31 Going to court is just an expensive habit.

Keith Richards 1943– : Barbara Charone *Keith Richards* (1979)

32 Went down and spoke at some lawyers' meeting last night. They didn't think much of my little squib yesterday about driving the shysters out of their profession. They seemed to kinder doubt just who would have to leave.

Will Rogers 1879–1935: 'Mr. Rogers is Hob Nobbing With Leaders of the Bar'

33 The first thing we do, let's kill all the lawyers.

William Shakespeare 1564–1616: *Henry VI, Part 2* (1592)

34 The sound of tireless voices is the price we pay for the right to hear the music of our own opinions.

Adlai Stevenson 1900–65: *The Guide to American Law* (1984)

35 Some circumstantial evidence is very strong, as when you find a trout in the milk.

Henry David Thoreau 1817–62: diary, 11 November 1850

36 What chance has the ignorant, uncultivated liar against the educated expert? What chance have I . . . against a lawyer?

Mark Twain 1835–1910: 'On the Decay of the Art of Lying' (1882)

37 Whenever a copyright law is to be made or altered, then the idiots assemble.

Mark Twain 1835–1910: *Notebook* 23 May 1903

38 Naturally a detective doesn't want to look like a detective, and give the whole thing away right at the start.

P. G. Wodehouse 1881–1975: *The Man with Two Left Feet* (1917)

39 Asking the ignorant to use the incomprehensible to decide the unknowable.

Hiller B. Zobel 1932– : 'The Jury on Trial' in *American Heritage* July–August 1995; see **Sports and Games** 41

Leisure See **Work and Leisure**

Letters

❝ *Dear 338171 (May I call you 338?).* **❞**
Noël Coward

1 *formula with which to return unsolicited manuscripts:*
Mr James Agate regrets that he has no time to bother about the enclosed in which he has been greatly interested.

James Agate 1877–1947: diary, 3 January 1936

2 It would have been less heterodox
If he had put the letter in the letter-o-box.
the Babes-in-the-Wood discovering a letter pinned to a tree by Robin Hood, in an Oxford pantomime in 1953

Brian Brindley: Ned Sherrin *Cutting Edge* (1984)

3 I am not a cautious letter-writer and generally say what comes uppermost at the moment.

Lord Byron 1788–1824: letter to Mary Shelley, 9 October 1822

4 WITWOUD: Madam, do you pin up your hair with all your letters?
MILLAMANT: Only with those in verse, Mr Witwoud. I never pin up my hair with prose.

William Congreve 1670–1729: *The Way of the World* (1700)

5 Regarding yours, dear Mrs Worthington, of Wednesday the 23rd.

Noël Coward 1899–1973: 'Mrs Worthington' (1935)

6 Dear 338171 (May I call you 338?).

Noël Coward 1899–1973: letter to T. E. Lawrence, 25 August 1930

7 Sir, My pa requests me to write to you, the doctors considering it doubtful whether he will ever recuvver the use of his legs which prevents his holding a pen.

Charles Dickens 1812–70: *Nicholas Nickleby* (1839)

8 It is wonderful how much news there is when people write every other day; if they wait for a month, there is nothing that seems worth telling.

O. Douglas 1877–1948: *Penny Plain* (1920)

9 [Charles Lamb's] sayings are generally like women's letters; all the pith is in the postscript.

William Hazlitt 1778–1830: *Conversations of James Northcote* (1826–7)

10 A man seldom puts his authentic self into a letter. He writes it to amuse a friend or to get rid of a social or business obligation, which is to say, a nuisance.

H. L. Mencken 1880–1956: *Minority Report* (1956)

11 I have made this [letter] longer than usual, only because I have not had the time to make it shorter.

Blaise Pascal 1623–62: *Lettres Provinciales* (1657)

12 Laura's repeated assurances to me that she had both replied to your letter and that she was about to do so are, I think, characteristic of a mind at bay.

S. J. Perelman 1904–79: letter 17 October 1948

13 *responding to a savage review by Rudolph Louis in* Münchener
Neueste Nachrich *7 February 1906:*
I am sitting in the smallest room of my house. I have your
review before me. In a moment it will be behind me.

Max Reger 1873–1916: Nicolas
Slonimsky *Lexicon of Musical Invective*
(1953)

14 *circular sent out to forestall unwanted visitors:*
Mr J. Ruskin is about to begin a work of great importance
and therefore begs that in reference to calls and
correspondence you will consider him dead for the next
two months.

John Ruskin 1819–1900: attributed

15 *Wilde had sent a letter on 'Fashion in Dress' to the* Daily
Telegraph, *but explained in a covering letter to the proprietor:*
I don't wish to sign my name, though I am afraid
everybody will know who the writer is: one's style is one's
signature always.

Oscar Wilde 1854–1900: letter, 2
February 1891

16 I have no need of your God-damned sympathy. I only wish
to be entertained by some of your grosser reminiscences.

Alexander Woollcott 1887–1943:
letter to Rex O'Malley, 1942

Libraries

See also **Books**

> ❝ *I thought it might sober me up to sit in a
> library.* ❞
> **F. Scott Fitzgerald**

1 RUTH: They'll sack you.
NORMAN: They daren't. I reorganized the Main Index.
When I die, the secret dies with me.

Alan Ayckbourn 1939– : *Round and
Round the Garden* (1975)

2 If you file your waste-paper basket for 50 years, you have
a public library.

Tony Benn 1925– : in *Daily Telegraph*
5 March 1994

3 What a sad want I am in of libraries, of books to gather
facts from! Why is there not a Majesty's library in every
county town? There is a Majesty's jail and gallows in
every one.

Thomas Carlyle 1795–1881: diary, 18
May 1832

4 There is nowhere in the world where sleep is so deep as in
the libraries of the House of Commons.

Chips Channon 1897–1958: diary, 16
December 1937

5 Th' first thing to have in a libry is a shelf. Fr'm time to
time this can be decorated with lithrachure. But th' shelf is
th' main thing.

Finley Peter Dunne 1867–1936: *Mr
Dooley Says* (1910)

6 I've been drunk for about a week now, and I thought it
might sober me up to sit in a library.

F. Scott Fitzgerald 1896–1940: *The
Great Gatsby* (1925)

7 Mr Cobb took me into his library and showed me his
books, of which he had a complete set.

Ring Lardner 1885–1933: R. E.
Drennan *Wit's End* (1973)

8 'Our library,' said the president, 'two hundred thousand
volumes!' 'Aye,' said the minister, 'a powerful heap of
rubbish, I'll be bound!'

Stephen Leacock 1869–1944:
*Arcadian Adventures with the Idle
Rich* (1914)

9 E. W. B. Nicholson [Bodley's Librarian] spending three
days at the London Docks, watching outgoing ships, after
losing a book from Bodley, which was afterwards
discovered slightly out of place on the shelf.

Falconer Madan 1851–1935: J. A.
Gere and John Sparrow (eds.)
Geoffrey Madan's Notebooks (1981)

10 Those dreadful detective stories. Another corpse in the library this evening. Really, you know, too much of a good thing. Fourth this week. No doubt trouble is shortage of libraries.

Flann O'Brien 1911–66: *The Best of Myles* (1968)

11 The Librarian was, of course, very much in favour of reading in general, but readers in particular got on his nerves . . . He liked people who loved and respected books, and the best way to do that, in the Librarian's opinion, was to leave them on the shelves where Nature intended them to be.

Terry Pratchett 1948– : *Men at Arms* (1993)

Lies
See also **Truth**

66 *Only his attempt to put an herbaceous border on stark reality.* 99
Oliver St John Gogarty

1 It reminds me of the small boy who jumbled his biblical quotations and said: 'A lie is an abomination unto the Lord, and a very present help in trouble.'

Anonymous: recalled by Adlai Stevenson; Bill Adler *The Stevenson Wit* (1966)

2 She [Lady Desborough] tells enough white lies to ice a wedding cake.

Margot Asquith 1864–1945: Lady Violet Bonham Carter 'Margot Oxford' in *Listener* 11 June 1953

3 Matilda told such Dreadful Lies,
It made one Gasp and Stretch one's Eyes;
Her Aunt, who, from her Earliest Youth,
Had kept a Strict Regard for Truth,
Attempted to Believe Matilda:
The effort very nearly killed her.

Hilaire Belloc 1870–1953: 'Matilda' (1907)

4 For every time She shouted 'Fire!'
They only answered 'Little Liar!'
And therefore when her Aunt returned,
Matilda, and the House, were Burned.

Hilaire Belloc 1870–1953: 'Matilda' (1907)

5 That branch of the art of lying which consists in very nearly deceiving your friends without quite deceiving your enemies.
   of propaganda

Francis M. Cornford 1874–1943: *Microcosmographia Academica* (1922 ed.)

6 There are three kinds of lies: lies, damned lies and statistics.

Benjamin Disraeli 1804–81: attributed to Disraeli in Mark Twain *Autobiography* (1924)

7 What you take for lying in an Irishman is only his attempt to put an herbaceous border on stark reality.

Oliver St John Gogarty 1878–1957: *Going Native* (1940)

8 By the time you say you're his,
Shivering and sighing
And he vows his passion is
Infinite, undying—
Lady, make a note of this:
One of you is lying.

Dorothy Parker 1893–1967: 'Unfortunate Coincidence' (1937)

9 *on being told that Lord Astor claimed that her allegations, concerning himself and his house parties at Cliveden, were untrue:*
He would, wouldn't he?

Mandy Rice-Davies 1944– : in *Guardian* 1 July 1963

10 A little inaccuracy sometimes saves tons of explanation.

Saki 1870–1916: *The Square Egg* (1924)

11 In exceptional circumstances it is necessary to say something that is untrue in the House of Commons.

William Waldegrave 1946– : in *Guardian* 9 March 1994

12 Untruthful! My nephew Algernon? Impossible! He is an Oxonian.

Oscar Wilde 1854–1900: *The Importance of Being Earnest* (1895)

Life and Living

See also **Lifestyle**

❝ *Life is something to do when you can't get to sleep.* ❞
Fran Lebowitz

1 I feel that life is—is divided up into the horrible and the miserable.

Woody Allen 1935– : *Annie Hall* (1977 film, with Marshall Brickman)

2 Alun's life was coming to consist more and more exclusively of being told at dictation speed what he knew.

Kingsley Amis 1922–95: *The Old Devils* (1986)

3 Life is a sexually transmitted disease.

Anonymous: graffito found on the London Underground

4 The only thing I regret about my life is the length of it. If I had to live my life again I'd make all the same mistakes—only sooner.

Tallulah Bankhead 1903–68: Laurence J. Peter (ed.) *Quotations for our Time* (1977)

5 Brought up in the provinces in the forties and fifties one learned early the valuable lesson that life is generally something that happens elsewhere.

Alan Bennett 1934– : introduction to *Talking Heads* (1988)

6 It's as large as life, and twice as natural!

Lewis Carroll 1832–98: *Through the Looking-Glass* (1872)

7 It's a funny old world—a man's lucky if he gets out of it alive.

Walter de Leon and **Paul M. Jones**: *You're Telling Me* (1934 film); spoken by W. C. Fields

8 *Auntie Mame's view:*
Life is a banquet, and some poor suckers are starving to death.

Patrick Dennis et al.: *Auntie Mame* (1956)

9 Life is a Cabaret, old chum
Come to the Cabaret.

Fred Ebb: 'Cabaret' (1965)

10 Life is just one damned thing after another.

Elbert Hubbard 1859–1915: in *Philistine* December 1909, (often attributed to Frank Ward O'Malley)

11 Life is something to do when you can't get to sleep.

Fran Lebowitz 1946– : *Metropolitan Life* (1978)

12 Laugh it off, laugh it off; it's all part of life's rich pageant.

Arthur Marshall 1910–89: *The Games Mistress* (recorded monologue, 1937)

13 Moderation in all things. Not too much of life. It often lasts too long.

H. L. Mencken 1880–1956: *Minority Report* (1956)

14 Life is a shit sandwich and every day you take another bite.
a pro football player's view

Joe Schmidt: Jonathon Green and Don Atyeo (eds.) *The Book of Sports Quotes* (1979)

15 I *love* living. I have some problems with my *life*, but living is the best thing they've come up with so far.

Neil Simon 1927– : *Last of the Red Hot Lovers* (1970)

16 Life is a gamble at terrible odds—if it was a bet, you wouldn't take it.

Tom Stoppard 1937– : *Rosencrantz and Guildenstern are Dead* (1967)

17 The world is rather tiresome, I must say—everything at sixes and at sevens—ladies in love with buggers, and buggers in love with womanisers, and the price of coal going up too. Where will it all end?
in the midst of Ralph Partridge's pursuit of Dora Carrington

Lytton Strachey 1880–1932: letter to Dora Carrington, 11 July 1919

18 Above all, gentlemen, not the slightest zeal.

Charles-Maurice de Talleyrand 1754–1838: P. Chasles *Voyages d'un critique à travers la vie et les livres* (1868)

19 Oh, isn't life a terrible thing, thank God?

Dylan Thomas 1914–53: *Under Milk Wood* (1954)

20 What a queer thing Life is! So unlike anything else, don't you know, if you see what I mean.

P. G. Wodehouse 1881–1975: *My Man Jeeves* (1919)

Lifestyle

66 *Never try to keep up with the Joneses. Drag them down to your level.* 99
Quentin Crisp

1 Have fun. And go home when you're tired.

George Abbott 1887–1995: in obituary, *New York Times* 2 February 1995

2 What is the secret of my long life? I really don't know—cigarettes, whisky and wild, wild women!
the oldest British survivor of the First World War

Henry Allingham 1896– : in *Daily Telegraph* 10 November 2005 (online edition)

3 Never try to keep up with the Joneses. Drag them down to your level. It's cheaper that way.

Quentin Crisp 1908–99: in *Times* 22 November 1999

4 If *A* is a success in life, then *A* equals *x* plus *y* plus *z*. Work is *x*; *y* is play; and *z* is keeping your mouth shut.

Albert Einstein 1879–1955: in *Observer* 15 January 1950

5 There's nothing in the middle of the road but yellow stripes and dead armadillos.

Jim Hightower 1943– : attributed, 1984

6 Puberty is a phase . . . Fifteen years of rejection is a lifestyle.

Susan Kolinsky: *Sex and the City* 'The Turtle and the Hare'(1998), spoken by Stanford (Willie Garson)

7 You only live once, and the way I live, once is enough.

Frank Sinatra 1915–98: attributed, in *Times* 16 May 1998

8 Why is he living among those men
Who talk like Barbie and look like Ken?
on the last straight man in gay Chelsea

Glenn Slater: *The New Yorkers* (2000)

9 As life goes on, don't you find that all you need is about two real friends, a regular supply of books, and a Peke?

P. G. Wodehouse 1881–1975: letter 28 October 1930

10 The others had their drugs and booze. I had my women. I thought that was safer: you can't overdose on women.

Bill Wyman 1936– : in *Independent* 26 October 2002

Literature

See also **Books, Poetry and Poets, Writers and Writing**

66 *When I want to read a novel, I write one.* 99

Benjamin Disraeli

1 A swear-word in a rustic slum
A simple swear-word is to some,
To Masefield something more.

Max Beerbohm 1872–1956: *Fifty Caricatures* (1912)

2 The literary gift is a mere accident—is as often bestowed on idiots who have nothing to say worth hearing as it is denied to strenuous sages.

Max Beerbohm 1872–1956: letter to George Bernard Shaw, 21 September 1903

3 Remote and ineffectual Don
That dared attack my Chesterton.

Hilaire Belloc 1870–1953: 'Lines to a Don' (1910)

4 We were put to Dickens as children but it never quite took. That unremitting humanity soon had me cheesed off.

Alan Bennett 1934– : *The Old Country* (1978)

5 Literature's always a good card to play for Honours. It makes people think that Cabinet ministers are educated.

Arnold Bennett 1867–1931: *The Title* (1918)

6 Dr Weiss, at forty, knew that her life had been ruined by literature.

Anita Brookner 1928– : *A Start in Life* (1981)

7 'The whole of this unfortunate business,' said Dr Lyster, 'has been the result of PRIDE AND PREJUDICE.'

Fanny Burney 1752–1840: *Cecilia* (1782)

8 We learn from Horace, Homer sometimes sleeps;
We feel without him: Wordsworth sometimes wakes.

Lord Byron 1788–1824: *Don Juan* (1819–24)

9 You praise the firm restraint with which they write—
I'm with you there, of course:
They use the snaffle and the curb all right,
But where's the bloody horse?

Roy Campbell 1901–57: 'On Some South African Novelists' (1930)

10 'What is the use of a book', thought Alice, 'without pictures or conversations?'

Lewis Carroll 1832–98: *Alice's Adventures in Wonderland* (1865)

11 If my books had been any worse, I should not have been invited to Hollywood, and if they had been any better, I should not have come.

Raymond Chandler 1888–1959: letter to Charles W. Morton, 12 December 1945

12 A literary man—*with* a wooden leg.

Charles Dickens 1812–70: *Our Mutual Friend* (1865)

13 When I want to read a novel, I write one.

Benjamin Disraeli 1804–81: W. Monypenny and G. Buckle *Life of Benjamin Disraeli* (1920)

14 *listening to readings from Tolkien's* Lord of the Rings:
Oh fuck, not another elf!

Hugh Dyson 1896–1975: A. N. Wilson *C. S. Lewis* (1990)

15 The mama of dada.
of Gertrude Stein

Clifton Fadiman 1904–99: *Party of One* (1955)

16 How rare, how precious is frivolity! How few writers can prostitute all their powers! They are always implying, 'I am capable of higher things.'

E. M. Forster 1879–1970: *Abinger Harvest* (1936)

17 What greater service could I have performed for German literature than that I didn't bother with it?

Frederick the Great 1712–86: K. Biedermann *Friedrich der Grosse* (1859)

18 The work of Henry James has always seemed divisible by a simple dynastic arrangement into three reigns: James I, James II, and the Old Pretender.

Philip Guedalla 1889–1944: *Supers and Supermen* (1920) 'Some Critics'

19 The cheerful clatter of Sir James Barrie's cans as he went round with the milk of human kindness.

Philip Guedalla 1889–1944: *Supers and Supermen* (1920) 'Some Critics'

20 He knew everything about literature except how to enjoy it.

Joseph Heller 1923–99: *Catch-22* (1961)

21 It takes a great deal of history to produce a little literature.

Henry James 1843–1916: *Hawthorne* (1879)

22 A beginning, a muddle, and an end.
on the 'classic formula' for a novel

Philip Larkin 1922–85: in *New Fiction* January 1978

23 From the moment I picked up your book until I laid it down, I was convulsed with laughter. Some day I intend reading it.

Groucho Marx 1890–1977: a blurb written for S. J. Perelman's 1928 book *Dawn Ginsberg's Revenge*

24 *explaining to Queen Victoria why he did not wish to read* Oliver Twist*:*
It's all among workhouses and Coffin Makers and Pickpockets . . . I wish to avoid them.

Lord Melbourne 1779–1848: A. N. Wilson *The Victorians* (2002)

25 I have only ever read one book in my life, and that is *White Fang*. It's so frightfully good I've never bothered to read another.
Uncle Matthew's view of literature

Nancy Mitford 1904–73: *Love in a Cold Climate* (1949)

26 And I'll stay off Verlaine too; he was always chasing Rimbauds.

Dorothy Parker 1893–1967: 'The Little Hours' (1939)

27 If, with the literate, I am
Impelled to try an epigram,
I never seek to take the credit;
We all assume that Oscar said it.

Dorothy Parker 1893–1967: 'A Pig's-Eye View of Literature' (1937)

28 Nearly all our best men are dead! Carlyle, Tennyson, Browning, George Eliot!—I'm not feeling very well myself.

Punch 1841–1992: vol. 104 (1893)

29 I have known her pass the whole evening without mentioning a single book, or *in fact anything unpleasant*, at all.

Henry Reed 1914–86: *A Very Great Man Indeed* (1953)

30 In view of her penchant
For something romantic,
De Sade is too trenchant
And Dickens too frantic,
And Stendhal would ruin
The plan of attack
As there isn't much blue in
The Red and the Black.

Stephen Sondheim 1930– : 'Now' (1972)

31 You're familiar with the tragedies of antiquity, are you? The great homicidal classics?

Tom Stoppard 1937– : *Rosencrantz and Guildenstern are Dead* (1967)

32 Like playing Beethoven on the kazoo.
on his translation of Shakespeare into text messages

John Sutherland 1938– : in *Mail on Sunday* 20 November 2005

33 Any writer worth his salt knows that only a small proportion of literature does more than partly compensate people for the damage they have suffered in learning to read.

Rebecca West 1892–1983: Peter Vansittart *Path from a White Horse* (1985), author's note

34 Meredith's a prose Browning, and so is Browning.

Oscar Wilde 1854–1900: *Intentions* (1891) 'The Critic as Artist'

Living See **Life and Living**

Love
See also **Marriage, Sex**

❝ Love is the delusion that one woman differs from another. ❞
H. L. Mencken

1 We men have got love well weighed up; our stuff
Can get by without it.
Women don't seem to think that's good enough;
They write about it.

Kingsley Amis 1922–95: 'A Bookshop Idyll' (1956)

2 Even logical positivists are capable of love.

A. J. Ayer 1910–89: Kenneth Tynan *Profiles* (1989)

3 Women who love the same man have a kind of bitter freemasonry.

Max Beerbohm 1872–1956: *Zuleika Dobson* (1911)

4 Make love to every woman you meet. If you get five percent on your outlays it's a good investment.

Arnold Bennett 1867–1931: Laurence J. Peter (ed.) *Quotations for our Time* (1977)

5 Miss Joan Hunter Dunn, Miss Joan Hunter Dunn,
How mad I am, sad I am, glad that you won.
The warm-handled racket is back in its press,
But my shock-headed victor, she loves me no less.

John Betjeman 1906–84: 'A Subaltern's Love-Song' (1945)

6 The ability to make love frivolously is the chief characteristic which distinguishes human beings from beasts.

Heywood Broun 1888–1939: Howard Teichmann *George S. Kaufman* (1973)

7 Would I were free from this restraint,
Or else had hopes to win her;
Would she could make of me a saint,
Or I of her a sinner.

William Congreve 1670–1729: 'Pious Selinda Goes to Prayers' (song)

8 What do you get when you kiss a guy?
You get enough germs to catch pneumonia.
After you do, he'll never phone you.

Hal David 1921– : 'I'll Never Fall In Love Again' (1968)

9 They made love as though they were an endangered species.

Peter de Vries 1910–93: Laurence J. Peter (ed.) *Quotations for our Time* (1977)

10 Did you ever hear of Captain Wattle?
He was all for love, and a little for the bottle.

Charles Dibdin 1745–1814: 'Captain Wattle and Miss Roe' (1797)

11 Barkis is willin'.

Charles Dickens 1812–70: *David Copperfield* (1850)

12 Oh, Mrs Corney, what a prospect this opens! What a opportunity for a jining of hearts and house-keepings!

Charles Dickens 1812–70: *Oliver Twist* (1838)

13 The magic of first love is our ignorance that it can ever end.

Benjamin Disraeli 1804–81: *Henrietta Temple* (1837)

14 What is commonly called love, namely the desire of satisfying a voracious appetite with a certain quantity of delicate white human flesh.

Henry Fielding 1707–54: *Tom Jones* (1749)

15 I'm afraid I was very much the traditionalist. I went down on one knee and dictated a proposal which my secretary faxed over straight away.

Stephen Fry 1957– and **Hugh Laurie**: *A Bit More Fry and Laurie* (1991)

16 How happy could I be with either,
Were t'other dear charmer away!

John Gay 1685–1732: *The Beggar's Opera* (1728)

17 Holding hands at midnight
'Neath a starry sky . . .
Nice work if you can get it,
And you can get it if you try.

Ira Gershwin 1896–1983: 'Nice Work If You Can Get It' (1937)

18 With love to lead the way,
I've found more clouds of grey
Than any Russian play
Could guarantee . . .
. . . When ev'ry happy plot
Ends with the marriage knot—
And there's no knot for me.

Ira Gershwin 1896–1983: 'But Not For Me' (1930)

19 Love is sweeping the country;
Waves are hugging the shore;
All the sexes
From Maine to Texas
Have never known such love before.

Ira Gershwin 1896–1983: 'Love is Sweeping the Country' (1931)

20 So I fell in love with a rich attorney's
Elderly ugly daughter.

W. S. Gilbert 1836–1911: *Trial by Jury* (1875)

21 I never meant to marry my second wife. I only meant to rob her.

Rich Hall 1954– : *Otis Lee Crenshaw: I Blame Society*

22 In the spring a young man's fancy lightly turns to thoughts of love;
And in summer,
and in autumn,
and in winter—
See above.

E. Y. Harburg 1898–1981: 'Tennyson Anyone?' (1965)

23 When I'm not near the girl I love,
I love the girl I'm near.
. . . When I can't fondle the hand I'm fond of
I fondle the hand at hand.

E. Y. Harburg 1898–1981: 'When I'm Not Near the Girl I Love' (1947)

24 The broken dates,
The endless waits,
The lovely loving and the hateful hates,
The conversation and the flying plates—
I wish I were in love again.

Lorenz Hart 1895–1943: 'I Wish I Were in Love Again' (1937)

25 When love congeals
It soon reveals
The faint aroma of performing seals,
The double crossing of a pair of heels.
I wish I were in love again!

Lorenz Hart 1895–1943: 'I Wish I
Were in Love Again' (1937)

26 Love's like the measles—all the worse when it comes late
in life.

Douglas Jerrold 1803–57: *The Wit
and Opinions of Douglas Jerrold*
(1859) 'Love'

27 Another bride, another June,
Another sunny honeymoon,
Another season, another reason,
For makin' whoopee!

Gus Kahn 1886–1941: 'Makin'
Whoopee' (1928)

28 Snug as two baboons—in a bamboo tree
I'll bamboozle you
And you'll bamboozle me
By a goona goona goona,
by a goona goona goona lagoon.

John Latouche 1917–56: 'The Goona
Goona Goona Lagoon' (*The Golden
Apple*, 1954 musical)

29 You ain't nothin' but a hound dog,
Quit snoopin' round my door
You can wag your tail but I ain't gonna feed you no more.

Jerry Leiber 1933– and Mike
Stoller 1933– : 'Hound Dog' (1956)

30 Tell me, George, if you had to do it all over would you fall
in love with yourself again.
    to George Gershwin

Oscar Levant 1906–72: David Ewen
The Story of George Gershwin (1943)

31 Love's a disease. But curable.

Rose Macaulay 1881–1958: *Crewe
Train* (1926)

32 Bed. No woman is worth more than a fiver unless you're
in love with her. Then she's worth all she costs you.

W. Somerset Maugham 1874–1965:
A Writer's Notebook (1949) written in
1903

33 Love is the delusion that one woman differs from another.

H. L. Mencken 1880–1956:
Chrestomathy (1949)

34 You want to get three feet up a bull's ass, just listen to the
whisperings of sweethearts.

Anthony Minghella 1954–2008: *Cold
Mountain* (2003 film); spoken by
Ruby Thewes (Renee Zellweger)

35 Oh, life is a glorious cycle of song,
A medley of extemporanea;
And love is a thing that can never go wrong;
And I am Marie of Roumania.

Dorothy Parker 1893–1967:
'Comment' (1937)

36 Four be the things I'd been better without:
Love, curiosity, freckles, and doubt.

Dorothy Parker 1893–1967:
'Inventory' (1937)

37 Most gentlemen don't like love,
They just like to kick it around.

Cole Porter 1891–1964: 'Most
Gentlemen don't like Love' (1938)

38 I get no kick from champagne,
Mere alcohol doesn't thrill me at all,
So tell me why should it be true
That I get a kick out of you?

Cole Porter 1891–1964: 'I Get a Kick
Out of You' (1934)

39 There are various ways of mending a broken heart, but
perhaps going to a learned conference is one of the more
unusual.

Barbara Pym 1913–80: *No Fond
Return of Love* (1961)

40 ELAINE: *Romantic?* In your mother's clean apartment with
two glasses from Bloomingdale's and your rubbers
dripping on the newspaper?
BARNEY: It was my belief that romance is inspired by the
participants and not the accoutrements.

Neil Simon 1927– : *Last of the Red Hot Lovers* (1970)

41 Loving you
Is not a choice
And not much reason
To rejoice.

Stephen Sondheim 1930– : *Passion* (1994) 'Loving You'

42 Out upon it, I have loved
Three whole days together;
And am like to love three more,
If it prove fair weather.

Time shall moult away his wings,
Ere he shall discover
In the whole wide world again
Such a constant lover.

John Suckling 1609–42: 'A Poem with the Answer' (1659)

43 Love is the fart
Of every heart:
It pains a man when 'tis kept close,
And others doth offend, when 'tis let loose.

John Suckling 1609–42: 'Love's Offence' (1646)

44 If love is the answer, could you rephrase the question?

Lily Tomlin 1939– : attributed; David Housham and John Frank-Keyes *Funny Business* (1992)

45 Love conquers all things—except poverty and toothache.

Mae West 1892–1980: attributed

46 To love oneself is the beginning of a lifelong romance.

Oscar Wilde 1854–1900: *An Ideal Husband* (1895)

47 For the first time since sudden love had thrown them into
each other's arms, she had found herself beginning to
wonder if her Blair was quite the godlike superman she
had supposed. There even flashed through her mind a
sinister speculation as to whether, when you came right
down to it, he wasn't something of a pill.

P. G. Wodehouse 1881–1975: *Hot Water* (1932)

48 Ernest Plinlimmon was not one of your butterflies who flit
from flower to flower. He was an average adjuster, and
average adjusters are like chartered accountants. When
they love, they give their hearts for ever.

P. G. Wodehouse 1881–1975: *Lord Emsworth and Others* (1937)

49 LILL: He loves me. He's just waiting till the children are
settled.
VICTORIA: What in—sheltered housing?

Victoria Wood 1953– : *Mens Sana in Thingummy Doodah* (1990)

Management

See also **Bureaucracy**

> 66 *Only the paranoid survive.* 99
> **Andrew Grove**

1 Assistant heads must roll!
traditional solution to management problems in broadcasting

Anonymous: in *Guardian* 30 June 2004

2 We trained hard . . . but it seemed that every time we were beginning to form up into teams we would be reorganized. I was to learn later in life that we tend to meet any new situation by reorganizing; and a wonderful method it can be for creating the illusion of progress while producing confusion, inefficiency, and demoralization.

Anonymous: modern saying, frequently (and wrongly) attributed to Petronius Arbiter

3 It was not unlike watching the Prague Spring in reverse.
on the arrival of John Birt as Director General of the BBC

David Benedictus 1938– : *Dropping Names* (2005)

4 Meetings are a great trap. However, they are indispensable when you don't want to do anything.

J. K. Galbraith 1908–2006: diary, 22 April 1961

5 When people say. 'Oh, would you rather be thought of as a funny man or a great boss?' My answer's always the same: to me they're not mutually exclusive.
David Brent as manager

Ricky Gervais 1961– and **Stephen Merchant**: *The Office* (Series 1, Episode 2; 2001)

6 Only the paranoid survive.
dictum on which he has long run his company, the Intel Corporation

Andrew Grove 1936– : in *New York Times* 18 December 1994

7 The man who is denied the opportunity of taking decisions of importance begins to regard as important the decisions he is allowed to take.

C. Northcote Parkinson 1909–93: *Parkinson's Law* (1958)

8 It is difficult to get a man to understand something when his salary depends on his not understanding it.

Upton Sinclair 1878–1968: *I, Candidate for Governor* (1935)

9 Lunch is for wimps.

Stanley Weiser and **Oliver Stone** 1946– : *Wall Street* (1987 film)

10 Don't say yes until I finish talking!
characteristic instruction

Darryl F. Zanuck 1902–79: Mel Gussow *Don't Say Yes Until I Finish Talking* (1971)

Marriage

See also **Love, Sex**

66 *Advice to persons about to marry.—'Don't.'* **99**

Punch

1 It was partially my fault that we got divorced . . . I tended to place my wife under a pedestal.

Woody Allen 1935– : 'I Had a Rough Marriage' (monologue, 1964)

2 My wife was an immature woman . . . I would be home in the bathroom, taking a bath, and my wife would walk in whenever she felt like it and sink my boats.

Woody Allen 1935– : 'I Had a Rough Marriage' (monologue, 1964)

3 Your experience will be a lesson to all us men to be careful not to marry ladies in very high positions.
to Lord Snowdon on the break-up of his marriage to Princess Margaret

Idi Amin 1925–2003: attributed; Nigel Rees *Cassell Dictionary of Humorous Quotations* (1999)

4 After a while, marriage is a sibling relationship—marked by occasional, and rather regrettable, episodes of incest.

Martin Amis 1949– : *Yellow Dog* (2003)

5 [Marriage is] the only war where one sleeps with the enemy.

Anonymous: Mexican saying; Ned Sherrin *Cutting Edge* (1984)

6 Bigamy is having one husband too many. Monogamy is the same.

Anonymous: Erica Jong *Fear of Flying* (1973)

7 They start with all that sucking and blowing and in the end you lose your house.
comparing marriage to the Florida hurricanes

Anonymous: in *New Statesman* 20 November 2000

8 I think we explored the further reaches of 'for better or for worse'.
on her marriage during the 1980s

Mary Archer 1944– : at Jeffrey Archer's trial for perjury, London, 29 June 2001

9 It is a truth universally acknowledged, that a single man in possession of a good fortune, must be in want of a wife.

Jane Austen 1775–1817: *Pride and Prejudice* (1813)

10 A fate worse than marriage. A sort of eternal engagement.

Alan Ayckbourn 1939– : *Living Together* (1975)

11 Marriage is very difficult if you're a woman and a writer. No wonder Virginia Woolf committed suicide.

Beryl Bainbridge 1933– : attributed

12 A man cannot marry before he has studied anatomy and has dissected at the least one woman.

Honoré de Balzac 1799–1850: *Physiology of Marriage* (1904)

13 Opposites, opposites,
Where Momma won't sit Poppa sits.

Lionel Bart 1930– : *Blitz!* (1962)

14 I've known for years our marriage has been a mockery. My body lying there night after night in the wasted moonlight. I know now how the Taj Mahal must feel.

Alan Bennett 1934– : *Habeas Corpus* (1973)

15 Being a husband is a whole-time job. That is why so many husbands fail. They cannot give their entire attention to it.

Arnold Bennett 1867–1931: *The Title* (1918)

16 Never marry a man who hates his mother, because he'll end up hating you.

Jill Bennett 1931–90: in *Observer* 12 September 1982 'Sayings of the Week'

17 My wife's gone to the country
Hooray! Hooray!
She thought it best, I need a rest,
That's why she's gone away.

Irving Berlin 1888–1989 and **George Whiting**: 'My Wife's Gone To The Country' (1910)

18 Love matches are formed by people who pay for a month of honey with a life of vinegar.

Countess of Blessington 1789–1849: *Desultory Thoughts and Reflections* (1839)

19 Even quarrels with one's husband are preferable to the ennui of a solitary existence.
view of the estranged American wife of Napoleon Bonaparte's brother Jerome

Elizabeth Patterson Bonaparte 1785–1879: Eugene L. Didier *The Life and Letters of Madame Bonaparte* (1879)

20 'Vladimir,' said Natasha, 'do you love me?' 'Toujours,' said Stroganoff, with wariness. An unusual emotion for a honeymooning husband when this particular question crops up. But Stroganoff was lying in the upper berth of a railway compartment and Natasha was in the lower berth so the question could not be an overture to a delightful interlude but merely the prelude to some less delightful demand.

Caryl Brahms 1901–82 and **S. J. Simon** 1904–48: *Six Curtains for Stroganova* (1945)

21 *to his butler, who had resigned because of Lady Braxfield's constant scolding:*
Lord! ye've little to complain o': ye may be thankfu' ye're no married to her.

Lord Braxfield 1722–99: Henry Cockburn *Memorials of his Time* (1856)

22 It was very good of God to let Carlyle and Mrs Carlyle marry one another and so make only two people miserable instead of four.

Samuel Butler 1835–1902: letter, 21 November 1884

23 Think you, if Laura had been Petrarch's wife, He would have written sonnets all his life?

Lord Byron 1788–1824: *Don Juan* (1819–24)

24 I have great hopes that we shall love each other all our lives as much as if we had never married at all.

Lord Byron 1788–1824: letter to Annabella Milbanke, 5 December 1814

25 Love and marriage, love and marriage, Go together like a horse and carriage.

Sammy Cahn 1913– : 'Love and Marriage' (1955)

26 The deep, deep peace of the double-bed after the hurly-burly of the chaise-longue.

Mrs Patrick Campbell 1865–1940: Alexander Woollcott *While Rome Burns* (1934) 'The First Mrs Tanqueray'

27 Translations (like wives) are seldom strictly faithful if they are in the least attractive.

Roy Campbell 1901–57: in *Poetry Review* June–July 1949

28 I am not at all the sort of person you and I took me for.

Jane Carlyle 1801–66: letter to Thomas Carlyle, 7 May 1822

29 Yblessed be god that I have wedded fyve! Welcome the sixte, whan that evere he shal.

Geoffrey Chaucer c.1343–1400: *The Canterbury Tales* 'The Wife of Bath's Prologue'

30 If you are afraid of loneliness, don't get married.

Anton Chekhov 1860–1904: attributed

31 *of her future son-in-law John Betjeman:* We invite people like that to our houses, but we don't marry them.

Lady Chetwode d. 1946: Maurice Bowra *Memories 1898–1939* (1966)

32 Every woman should marry an archaeologist because she grows increasingly attractive to him as she grows increasingly to resemble a ruin.

Agatha Christie 1890–1976: Russell H. Fitzgibbon *The Agatha Christie Companion* (1980); attributed, perhaps apocryphal

33 The most happy marriage I can picture or imagine to myself would be the union of a deaf man to a blind woman.

Samuel Taylor Coleridge 1772–1834: Thomas Allsop *Letters, Conversations, and Recollections of S. T. Coleridge* (1836)

34 I've never yet met a man who could look after me. I don't need a husband. What I need is a wife.

Joan Collins 1933– : in *Sunday Times* 27 December 1987

35 Marriage is a feast where the grace is sometimes better than the dinner.

Charles Caleb Colton 1780–1832: *Lacon* (1822)

36 Courtship to marriage, as a very witty prologue to a very dull play.

William Congreve 1670–1729: *The Old Bachelor* (1693)

37 Nay, for my part I always despised Mr Tattle of all things; nothing but his being my husband could have made me like him less.

William Congreve 1670–1729: *Love for Love* (1695)

38 Tho' marriage makes man and wife one flesh, it leaves 'em still two fools.

William Congreve 1670–1729: *The Double Dealer* (1694)

39 SHARPER: Thus grief still treads upon the heels of pleasure: Married in haste, we may repent at leisure.
SETTER: Some by experience find those words mis-placed: At leisure married, they repent in haste.

William Congreve 1670–1729: *The Old Bachelor* (1693)

40 Marriage is a wonderful invention; but, then again, so is a bicycle repair kit.

Billy Connolly 1942– : Duncan Campbell *Billy Connolly* (1976)

41 There is no more sombre enemy of good art than the pram in the hall.

Cyril Connolly 1903–74: *Enemies of Promise* (1938)

42 The figure is unbelievable—just because she cooked a few meals now and again and wrote a few books.
   on the £10 million divorce settlement awarded to Caroline Conran

Terence Conran 1931– : in *Mail on Sunday* 6 July 1997 'Quotes of the Week'

43 One of those looks which only a quarter-century of wedlock can adequately marinate.

Alan Coren 1938–2007: *Seems Like Old Times* (1989)

44 'What are your views on marriage?'
   'Rather garbled.'

Noël Coward 1899–1973: in *Ned Sherrin's Theatrical Anecdotes* (1991); attributed

45 She very soon married this short young man
   Who talked about soldiers all day
   But who wasn't above
   Making passionate love
   In a coarse, rather Corsican way.

Noël Coward 1899–1973: 'Josephine' (1946)

46 So basically you're saying marriage is just a way of getting out of an embarrassing pause in conversation.

Richard Curtis 1956– : *Four Weddings and a Funeral* (1994 film)

47 It's my old girl that advises. She has the head. But I never own to it before her. Discipline must be maintained.

Charles Dickens 1812–70: *Bleak House* (1853)

48 I revere the memory of Mr F. as an estimable man and most indulgent husband, only necessary to mention Asparagus and it appeared or to hint at any little delicate thing to drink and it came like magic in a pint bottle it was not ecstasy but it was comfort.

Charles Dickens 1812–70: *Little Dorrit* (1857)

49 I have always thought that every woman should marry, and no man.

Benjamin Disraeli 1804–81: *Lothair* (1870)

50 No man is regular in his attendance at the House of Commons until he is married.

Benjamin Disraeli 1804–81: Hesketh Pearson *Dizzy* (1951)

51 Here lies my wife; here let her lie!
   Now she's at peace and so am I.

John Dryden 1631–1700: epitaph; attributed but not traced in his works

52 I don't think matrimony consistent with the liberty of the subject.

George Farquhar 1678–1707: *The Twin Rivals* (1703)

53 His designs were strictly honourable, as the phrase is; that is, to rob a lady of her fortune by way of marriage.

Henry Fielding 1707–54: *Tom Jones* (1749)

54 Keep your eyes wide open before marriage, half shut afterwards.

Benjamin Franklin 1706–90: *Poor Richard's Almanack* (1738)

55 The awe and dread with which the untutored savage contemplates his mother-in-law are amongst the most familiar facts of anthropology.

James George Frazer 1854–1941: *The Golden Bough* (2nd ed., 1900)

56 I support gay marriage because I believe they have a right to be just as miserable as the rest of us.

Kinky Friedman 1944– : quoted on CBS News, 21 August 2005

57 He taught me housekeeping; when I divorce I keep the house.

Zsa Zsa Gabor 1919– : of her fifth husband; Ned Sherrin *Cutting Edge* (1984)

58 A man in love is incomplete until he has married. Then he's finished.

Zsa Zsa Gabor 1919– : in *Newsweek* 28 March 1960

59 *when asked how many husbands she had had:*
You mean apart from my own?

    Zsa Zsa Gabor 1919– : K. Edwards *I Wish I'd Said That* (1976)

60 *on Sinatra's marriage to the young, severely cropped Mia Farrow:*
Frank always did want a fag with a pussy.

    Ava Gardner 1922–90: Lee Server *Ava Gardner* (2006)

61 The comfortable estate of widowhood, is the only hope that keeps up a wife's spirits.

    John Gay 1685–1732: *The Beggar's Opera* (1728)

62 Do you think your mother and I should have lived comfortably so long together, if ever we had been married?

    John Gay 1685–1732: *The Beggar's Opera* (1728)

63 POLLY: Then all my sorrows are at an end.
MRS PEACHUM: A mighty likely speech, in troth, for a wench who is just married!

    John Gay 1685–1732: *The Beggar's Opera* (1728)

64 Imagine signing a lease together;
And hanging a Matisse together;
Being alone and baking bread together.
Reading the *New Yorker* in bed together!
Starting a family tree together!
Voting for the GOP together!

    Ira Gershwin 1896–1983: 'There's Nothing Like Marriage for People' (1946)

65 By god, D. H. Lawrence was right when he had said there must be a dumb, dark, dull, bitter belly-tension between a man and a woman, and how else could this be achieved save in the long monotony of marriage?

    Stella Gibbons 1902–89: *Cold Comfort Farm* (1932)

66 When you marry your mistress you create a job vacancy.
marrying Lady Annabel Birley in 1978

    James Goldsmith 1933–97: G. Wansell *Tycoon* (1987)

67 I . . . chose my wife, as she did her wedding gown, not for a fine glossy surface, but such qualities as would wear well.

    Oliver Goldsmith 1730–74: *The Vicar of Wakefield* (1766)

68 I don't think I'll get married again. I'll just find a woman I don't like and give her a house.

    Lewis Grizzard 1946–94: attributed

69 My mother said it was simple to keep a man, you must be a maid in the living room, a cook in the kitchen and a whore in the bedroom. I said I'd hire the other two and take care of the bedroom bit.

    Jerry Hall 1956– : in *Observer* 6 October 1985 'Sayings of the Week'

70 I married many men,
A ton of them,
And yet I was untrue to none of them
Because I bumped off ev'ry one of them
To keep my love alive.
Sir Paul was frail,
He looked a wreck to me.
At night he was a horse's neck to me.
So I performed an appendectomy
To keep my love alive.

    Lorenz Hart 1895–1943: 'To Keep My Love Alive' (1943)

71 It was not totally inconceivable that she could have joined me as my wife at No. 10.
on the TV starlet Jayne Mansfield

    Edward Heath 1916–2005: in *Sunday Times* 6 February 2000

72 The critical period in matrimony is breakfast-time.

    A. P. Herbert 1890–1971: *Uncommon Law* (1935) 'Is Marriage Lawful?'

73 Holy deadlock.

    A. P. Herbert 1890–1971: title of novel (1934)

74 A TV host asked my wife, 'Have you ever considered divorce?' She replied: 'Divorce never, murder often.'

Charlton Heston 1924–2008: in *Independent* 21 July 1999

75 Hogamus, higamous
Man is polygamous
Higamus, hogamous
Woman monogamous.

William James 1842–1910: in *Oxford Book of Marriage* (1990)

76 *of a man who remarried immediately after the death of a wife with whom he had been unhappy:*
The triumph of hope over experience.

Samuel Johnson 1709–84: James Boswell *Life of Samuel Johnson* (1791) 1770

77 I want you to assist me in forcing her on board the lugger; once there, I'll frighten her into marriage.

John Benn Johnstone 1803–91: *The Gipsy Farmer* (performed 1845); since quoted as 'Once aboard the lugger and the maid is mine'

78 The best thing about being married is having someone who puts out the rubbish.

Ulrika Jonsson 1967– : in *Mail on Sunday* 30 October 2005 'Quotes of the Week'

79 I've been married six months. She looks like a million dollars, but she only knows a hundred and twenty words and she's only got two ideas in her head.

Eric Linklater 1899–1974: *Juan in America* (1931)

80 Did you ever look through a microscope at a drop of pond water? You see plenty of love there. All the amoebae getting married. I presume they think it very exciting and important. We don't.

Rose Macaulay 1881–1958: *Crewe Train* (1926)

81 Don't worry if you never marry. It will save you a lot of vexation.
   last words of advice to Petronella Wyatt

Princess Margaret 1930–2002: in *Sunday Times* 17 February 2002

82 *to her husband, who had asked the age of a flirtatious starlet with noticeably thick legs:*
For God's sake, Walter, why don't you chop off her legs and read the rings?

Carol Matthau 1925–2003: Truman Capote *Answered Prayers* (1986)

83 No matter how happily a woman may be married, it always pleases her to discover that there is a nice man who wishes she were not.

H. L. Mencken 1880–1956: *Chrestomathy* (1949)

84 Kissing don't last: cookery do!

George Meredith 1828–1909: *The Ordeal of Richard Feverel* (1859)

85 There once was an old man of Lyme
Who married three wives at a time,
When asked 'Why a third?'
He replied, 'One's absurd!
And bigamy, Sir, is a crime!'

William Cosmo Monkhouse 1840–1901: *Nonsense Rhymes* (1902)

86 One doesn't have to get anywhere in a marriage. It's not a public conveyance.

Iris Murdoch 1919–99: *A Severed Head* (1961)

87 I'm Henery the Eighth, I am!
Henery the Eighth, I am, I am!
I got married to the widow next door,
She's been married seven times before.
Every one was a Henery,
She wouldn't have a Willie or a Sam.
I'm her eighth old man named Henery
I'm Henery the Eighth, I am!

Fred Murray: 'I'm Henery the Eighth, I Am!' (1911)

88 To keep your marriage brimming
With love in the loving cup,
Whenever you're wrong, admit it,
Whenever you're right, shut up.

Ogden Nash 1902–71: 'A Word to Husbands' (1957)

89 To Wanda, the only item of essential equipment—apart from a Rolex watch (boiled in a stew by Afghans to test its waterproof qualities)—not lost, stolen or simply worn out in the course of some thirty years of travel together.

Eric Newby 1919– : *On the Shores of the Mediterranean* (1984); dedication to his wife

90 *to his wife Vita Sackville-West:*
A crushed life is what I lead, similar to that of the hen you ran over the other day.

Harold Nicolson 1886–1968: diary, 8 October 1958

91 'It was she as set her bonnet at him!' cried Mrs Williams, who had never yet let her husband finish a sentence since his 'I will' at Trinity Church, Plymouth Dock, in 1782 [eighteen years before].

Patrick O'Brian 1914–2000: *Master and Commander* (1970)

92 Marriage may often be a stormy lake, but celibacy is almost always a muddy horsepond.

Thomas Love Peacock 1785–1866: *Melincourt* (1817)

93 Strange to say what delight we married people have to see these poor fools decoyed into our condition.

Samuel Pepys 1633–1703: diary, 25 December 1665

94 Tolerance is the one essential ingredient . . . You can take it from me that the Queen has the quality of tolerance in abundance.
his recipe for a successful marriage, 19 November 1997, marking their golden wedding anniversary

Prince Philip, Duke of Edinburgh 1921– : in *Times* 20 November 1997

95 They dream in courtship, but in wedlock wake.

Alexander Pope 1688–1744: *Translations from Chaucer* (1714)

96 HE: Have you heard Professor Munch
Ate his wife and divorced his lunch?
SHE: Well, did you evah!
What a swell party this is.

Cole Porter 1891–1964: 'Well, Did You Evah!' (1939)

97 I'm a maid who would marry
And will take with no qualm
Any Tom, Dick or Harry,
Any Harry, Dick or Tom.

Cole Porter 1891–1964: 'Tom, Dick or Harry' (1948)

98 WIFE OF TWO YEARS' STANDING: Oh yes! I'm sure he's not so fond of me as at first. He's away so much, neglects me dreadfully, and he's so cross when he comes home. What *shall* I do?
WIDOW: Feed the brute!

Punch 1841–1992: vol. 89 (1885)

99 Advice to persons about to marry.—'Don't.'

Punch 1841–1992: vol. 8 (1845)

100 BISHOP: Who is it that sees and hears all we do, and before whom even I am but as a crushed worm?
PAGE: The Missus, my Lord.

Punch 1841–1992: vol. 79 (1880)

101 A husband is what is left of a lover, after the nerve has been extracted.

Helen Rowland 1875–1950: *A Guide to Men* (1922)

102 *the Lord Chief Justice was once asked by a lady what was the maximum punishment for bigamy:*
Two mothers-in-law.

Lord Russell of Killowen 1832–1900: Edward Abinger *Forty Years at the Bar* (1930)

103 I think that gay marriage is something that should be between a man and a woman.

Arnold Schwarzenegger 1947– : in *CCN.com* (online edition) 28 August 2003

104 But for marriage 'tis good for nothing, but to make friends fall out.

Thomas Shadwell c.1642–92: *The Sullen Lovers* (1668)

105 A young man married is a man that's marred.

William Shakespeare 1564–1616: *All's Well that Ends Well* (1603–4)

106 Many a good hanging prevents a bad marriage.

William Shakespeare 1564–1616: *Twelfth Night* (1601)

107 It is a woman's business to get married as soon as possible, and a man's to keep unmarried as long as he can.

George Bernard Shaw 1856–1950: *Man and Superman* (1903)

108 Marriage is popular because it combines the maximum of temptation with the maximum of opportunity.

George Bernard Shaw 1856–1950: *Man and Superman* (1903) 'Maxims: Marriage'

109 'Tis safest in matrimony to begin with a little aversion.

Richard Brinsley Sheridan 1751–1816: *The Rivals* (1775)

110 Take care of him. And make him feel important. And if you can do that, you'll have a happy and wonderful marriage. Like two out of every ten couples.

Neil Simon 1927– : *Barefoot in the Park* (1964)

111 PAUL: You want me to be rich and famous, don't you?
CORRIE: During the day. At night I want you to be here and sexy.

Neil Simon 1927– : *Barefoot in the Park* (1964)

112 My definition of marriage . . . it resembles a pair of shears, so joined that they cannot be separated; often moving in opposite directions, yet always punishing anyone who comes between them.

Sydney Smith 1771–1845: Lady Holland *Memoir* (1855)

113 The concerts you enjoy together
Neighbours you annoy together
Children you destroy together,
That keep marriage intact.

Stephen Sondheim 1930– : 'The Little Things You Do Together' (1970)

114 My brother Toby, quoth she, is going to be married to Mrs Wadman. Then he will never, quoth my father, lie *diagonally* in his bed again as long as he lives.

Laurence Sterne 1713–68: *Tristram Shandy* (1759–67)

115 Even if we take matrimony at its lowest, even if we regard it as no more than a sort of friendship recognised by the police.

Robert Louis Stevenson 1850–94: *Virginibus Puerisque* (1881)

116 *on how she survived her divorces:*
The first one's the hardest, then you know the routine.

Elizabeth Taylor 1932– : in *Observer* 25 July 2004 'They said what?'

117 A husband should not insult his wife publicly, at parties. He should insult her in the privacy of the home.

James Thurber 1894–1961: *Thurber Country* (1953)

118 That's my first wife up there and this is the *present* Mrs Harris.

James Thurber 1894–1961: cartoon caption in *New Yorker* 16 March 1933

119 Don't get mad, get everything.
advice to wronged wives

Ivana Trump 1949– : spoken in *The First Wives Club* (film, 1996)

120 LADY BRUTE: 'Tis a hard fate I should not be believed.
SIR JOHN: 'Tis a damned atheistical age, wife.

John Vanbrugh 1664–1726: *The Provoked Wife* (1697)

121 Marriage isn't a word . . . it's a *sentence*!

King Vidor 1895–1982: in *The Crowd* (1928 film)

122 He is dreadfully married. He's the most married man I ever saw in my life.

Artemus Ward 1834–67: *Artemus Ward's Lecture* (1869) 'Brigham Young's Palace'

123 Marriage is a great institution, but I'm not ready for an institution yet.

Mae West 1892–1980: Laurence J. Peter (ed.) *Quotations for our Time* (1977); attributed

124 An engagement should come on a young girl as a surprise, pleasant or unpleasant, as the case may be.

Oscar Wilde 1854–1900: *The Importance of Being Earnest* (1895)

125 Twenty years of romance make a woman look like a ruin; but twenty years of marriage make her something like a public building.

Oscar Wilde 1854–1900: *A Woman of No Importance* (1893)

126 GERRY: We can't get married at all . . . I'm a man.
OSGOOD: Well, nobody's perfect.

Billy Wilder 1906–2002 and **I. A. L. Diamond** 1915–88: *Some Like It Hot* (1959 film; closing words)

127 *when courting his future wife (whom he married in 1949):*
I would worship the ground you walk on, Audrey, if you only lived in a better neighbourhood.

Billy Wilder 1906–2002: M. Zolotow *Billy Wilder in Hollywood* (1977)

128 Marriage is a bribe to make a housekeeper think she's a householder.

Thornton Wilder 1897–1975: *The Merchant of Yonkers* (1939)

129 Chumps always make the best husbands. When you marry, Sally, grab a chump. Tap his forehead first, and if it rings solid, don't hesitate. All the unhappy marriages come from the husbands having brains.

P. G. Wodehouse 1881–1975: *The Adventures of Sally* (1920)

130 There are men who fear repartee in a wife more keenly than a sword.

P. G. Wodehouse 1881–1975: *Jill the Reckless* (1922)

131 'Tis my maxim, he's a fool that marries, but he's a greater that does not marry a fool.

William Wycherley c.1640–1716: *The Country Wife* (1675)

Medicine
See also **Sickness and Health**

❝Being hugged by Diana Rigg is worth three sessions of chemotherapy.❞
Robert Runcie

1 I am dying with the help of too many physicians.

Alexander the Great 356–323 BC: attributed

2 *doctor's advice to Bond star Roger Moore after he had been fitted with a heart pacemaker:*
Keep paying the electricity bill.

Anonymous: in *Mail on Sunday* 4 January 2004 'Quotes of the Year'

3 She has her high days and low days, a bit like the church. It depends what miracle drug the doctor's currently got her on.

Alan Ayckbourn 1939– : *Joking Apart* (1979)

4 Medicinal discovery,
It moves in mighty leaps,
It leapt straight past the common cold
And gave it us for keeps.

Pam Ayres 1947– : 'Oh no, I got a cold' (1976)

5 Hark! the herald angels sing!
Beecham's Pills are just the thing,
Two for a woman, one for a child . . .
Peace on earth and mercy mild!

Thomas Beecham 1879–1961:
advertising jingle devised for his
father, but not used; Neville Cardus
Sir Thomas Beecham (1961)

6 Physicians of the Utmost Fame
Were called at once; but when they came
They answered, as they took their Fees,
'There is no Cure for this Disease.'

Hilaire Belloc 1870–1953: 'Henry
King' (1907)

7 Dr Sillitoes's got him on tablets for depression. It's not
mental, in fact it's quite widespread. A lot of better-class
people get it apparently.

Alan Bennett 1934– : *Enjoy* (1980)

8 I was in for ten hours and had 40 pints, beating my
previous record by 20 minutes.
*comparing transfusions with drinking, during the BBC's
Sports Personality of the Year Awards*

George Best 1946–2005: in *Mail on
Sunday* 15 December 2002

9 One on whom we set our hopes when ill, and our dogs
when well.
definition of a physician

Ambrose Bierce 1842–c.1914: *The
Devil's Dictionary* (1911)

10 I don't believe in vitamin pills. I swear by men, darling—
and as many as possible.

Joan Collins 1933– : in *Independent*
10 June 2000 'Quotes of the Week'

11 And, on the label of the stuff,
He wrote this verse;
Which one would think was clear enough,
And terse:—
When taken,
To be well shaken.

George Colman the Younger
1762–1836: 'The Newcastle
Apothecary' (1797)

12 Meaty jelly, too, especially when a little salt, which is the
case when there's ham, is mellering to the organ.

Charles Dickens 1812–70: *Our
Mutual Friend* (1865)

13 *epigram on Dr John Lettsom, who would sign his prescriptions
'I. Lettsom':*
Whenever patients come to I,
I physics, bleeds, and sweats 'em;
If after that they choose to die,
What's that to me!—*I letts 'em.*

Thomas Erskine 1750–1823: *Poetical
Works* (1823)

14 A cousin of mine who was a casualty surgeon in
Manhattan tells me that he and his colleagues had a one-
word nickname for bikers: Donors. Rather chilling.

Stephen Fry 1957– : *Paperweight*
(1992)

15 I came in here in all good faith to help my country. I don't
mind giving a reasonable amount [of blood], but a pint . . .
why that's very nearly an armful. I'm sorry. I'm not
walking around with an empty arm for anybody.

Ray Galton 1930– and **Alan
Simpson** 1929– : *The Blood Donor*
(1961 television programme, words
spoken by Tony Hancock)

16 Any man who goes to a psychiatrist should have his head
examined.

Sam Goldwyn 1882–1974: Norman
Zierold *Moguls* (1969)

17 What's the bleeding time?

Richard Gordon 1921– et al.: *Doctor
in the House* (1954 film), spoken by
James Robertson Justice

18 If you have a stomach ache, in France you get a
suppository, in Germany a health spa, in the United States
they cut your stomach open and in Britain they put you
on a waiting list.

Phil Hammond 1955– and **Michael
Mosley** : *Trust Me (I'm a Doctor)*
(1999)

19 When our organs have been transplanted
And the new ones made happy to lodge in us,
Let us pray one wish be granted—
We retain our zones erogenous.

E. Y. Harburg 1898–1981: 'Seated One Day at the Organ' (1965)

20 Hungry Joe collected lists of fatal diseases and arranged them in alphabetical order so that he could put his finger without delay on any one he wanted to worry about.

Joseph Heller 1923–99: *Catch-22* (1961)

21 The kind of doctor I want is one who, when he's not examining me, is home studying medicine.

George S. Kaufman 1889–1961: Howard Teichmann *George S. Kaufman* (1973)

22 In disease Medical Men guess: if they cannot ascertain a disease, they call it nervous.

John Keats 1795–1821: J. A. Gere and John Sparrow (eds.) *Geoffrey Madan's Notebooks* (1981); attributed

23 The medics can now stretch your life out an additional dozen years but they don't tell you that most of these years are going to be spent flat on your back while some ghoul with thick glasses and a matted skull peers at you through a machine that's hot out of 'Space Patrol'.

Groucho Marx 1890–1977: letter 23 December 1954

24 All the errors that lead to burst appendixes are made by family doctors. The patient usually is sick enough to call for help, but by the time he gets to the specialist he is too far gone for it.

H. L. Mencken 1880–1956: *Minority Report* (1956)

25 GÉRONTE: It seems to me you are locating them wrongly: the heart is on the left and the liver is on the right.
SGANARELLE: Yes, in the old days that was so, but we have changed all that, and we now practise medicine by a completely new method.

Molière 1622–73: *Le Médecin malgré lui* (1667)

26 I only take Viagra when I'm with more than one woman.

Jack Nicholson 1937– : in *Mail on Sunday* 8 February 2004

27 I fear that being a patient in any hospital in Ireland calls for two things—holy resignation and an iron constitution.

Flann O'Brien 1911–66: *Myles Away from Dublin* (1990)

28 The desire to take medicine is perhaps the greatest feature which distinguishes man from animals.

William Osler 1849–1919: H. Cushing *Life of Sir William Osler* (1925)

29 As for consulting a dentist regularly, my punctuality practically amounted to a fetish. Every twelve years I would drop whatever I was doing and allow wild Caucasian ponies to drag me to a reputable orthodontist.

S. J. Perelman 1904–79: *The Most of S. J. Perelman* (1959) 'Dental or Mental, I Say It's Spinach'

30 He said my bronchial tubes were entrancing,
My epiglottis filled him with glee,
He simply loved my larynx
And went wild about my pharynx,
But he never said he loved me.

Cole Porter 1891–1964: 'The Physician' (1933)

31 Cured yesterday of my disease,
I died last night of my physician.

Matthew Prior 1664–1721: 'The Remedy Worse than the Disease' (1727)

32 Being hugged by Diana Rigg is worth three sessions of chemotherapy.
after his appearance on Loose Ends *with Diana Rigg, 15 April 2000*

Robert Runcie 1921–2000: letter to the Editor, April 2000

33 There would never be any public agreement among doctors if they did not agree to agree on the main point of the doctor being always in the right.

George Bernard Shaw 1856–1950: preface to *The Doctor's Dilemma* (1911)

34 There is at bottom only one genuinely scientific treatment for all diseases, and that is to stimulate the phagocytes.

George Bernard Shaw 1856–1950: *The Doctor's Dilemma* (1911)

35 I can't stand whispering. Every time a doctor whispers in the hospital, next day there's a funeral.

Neil Simon 1927– : *The Gingerbread Lady* (1970)

36 A psychiatrist is a man who goes to the Folies-Bergère and looks at the audience.

Mervyn Stockwood 1913–95: in *Observer* 15 October 1961

37 Randolph Churchill went into hospital . . . to have a lung removed. It was announced that the trouble was not 'malignant' . . . it was a typical triumph of modern science to find the only part of Randolph that was not malignant and remove it.

Evelyn Waugh 1903–66: 'Irregular Notes 1960–65'; diary March 1964

38 Sir Roderick Glossop . . . is always called a nerve specialist, because it sounds better, but everybody knows that he's really a sort of janitor to the looney-bin.

P. G. Wodehouse 1881–1975: *The Inimitable Jeeves* (1923)

39 *on being given aspirin from a small tin box by Jeeves:*
Thank you, Jeeves. Don't slam the lid.

P. G. Wodehouse 1881–1975: *Ring for Jeeves* (1953)

Men
See also **Men and Women**

❝ *Men are animals and as such are entitled to humane treatment.* **❞**
Germaine Greer

1 Women were brought up to believe that men were the answer. They weren't. They weren't even one of the questions.

Julian Barnes 1946– : *Staring at the Sun* (1986)

2 My mother wanted me to be a nice boy. I didn't let her down. I don't smoke, drink or mess around with women.

Julian Clary 1959– : in *Independent* 2 March 1996 'Quote Unquote'

3 Faded boys, jaded boys, come what may,
Art is our inspiration,
And as we are the reason for the 'Nineties' being gay,
We all wear a green carnation.

Noël Coward 1899–1973: 'Green Carnation' (1929)

4 We are lads. We have burgled houses and nicked car stereos, and we like girls and swear and go to the football and take the piss.

Noel Gallagher 1967– : interview in *Melody Maker* 30 March 1996

5 *asked by John Ford what she saw in a 120lb runt like Frank Sinatra:*
Well, John, Frank's 10lb of runt, and 110lb of cock.

Ava Gardner 1922–90: Lee Server *Ava Gardner* (2006)

6 Francesca di Rimini, miminy, piminy,
Je-ne-sais-quoi young man!

W. S. Gilbert 1836–1911: *Patience* (1881)

7 A greenery-yallery, Grosvenor Gallery,
Foot-in-the-grave young man!

W. S. Gilbert 1836–1911: *Patience* (1881)

8 Men are animals and as such are entitled to humane treatment and should not be trapped or shot or bred for food or fur.

Germaine Greer 1939– : in *Mail on Sunday* 7 March 1999 'Quotes of the Week'

9 *asked about his hard-man image:*
Neanderthal. A glowering thug, the Terminator in shorts. And that's just my wife's opinion.

Martin Johnson 1970– : Martin Johnson *Autobiography* (2003)

10 Years ago, manhood was an opportunity for achievement, and now it is a problem to be overcome.

Garrison Keillor 1942– : *The Book of Guys* (1994)

11 There is nothing about which men lie so much as about their sexual powers. In this at least every man is, what in his heart he would like to be, a Casanova.

W. Somerset Maugham 1874–1965: *A Writer's Notebook* (1949) written in 1941

12 He's an oul' butty o' mine—oh, he's a darlin' man, a daarlin' man.

Sean O'Casey 1880–1964: *Juno and the Paycock* (1925)

13 The follies which a man regrets most, in his life, are those which he didn't commit when he had the opportunity.

Helen Rowland 1875–1950: *A Guide to Men* (1922)

14 God made him, and therefore let him pass for a man.

William Shakespeare 1564–1616: *The Merchant of Venice* (1596–8)

15 You men are unaccountable things; mad till you have your mistresses, and then stark mad till you are rid of 'em again.

John Vanbrugh 1664–1726: *The Provoked Wife* (1697)

16 A hard man is good to find.

Mae West 1892–1980: attributed

17 Many a fellow who looks like the dominant male and has himself photographed smoking a pipe curls up like carbon paper when confronted by an aunt.

P. G. Wodehouse 1881–1975: *The Mating Season* (1949)

Men and Women
See also **Men, Women and Woman's Role**

❝ *When women go wrong, men go right after them.* ❞
Mae West

1 *'Mrs Merton' to Debbie McGee:*
But what first, Debbie, attracted you to millionaire Paul Daniels?

Caroline Aherne 1963– : *The Mrs Merton Show* (BBC TV)

2 *announcing the break-up of Ken and Barbie's 43-year romance:*
Like other Hollywood couples, their celebrity romance has come to an end.

Russell Arons: in *CNN.com* (online edition) 12 February 2004

3 All women dress like their mothers, that is their tragedy. No man ever does. That is his.

Alan Bennett 1934– : *Forty Years On* (1969)

4 We sat in the car park till twenty to one
And now I'm engaged to Miss Joan Hunter Dunn.

John Betjeman 1906–84: 'A Subaltern's Love-Song' (1945)

5 Too many rings around Rosie
Never got Rosie a ring.

Irving Caesar 1895–1996: 'Too Many Rings around Rosie' (1925)

6 AMANDA: I've been brought up to believe that it's beyond the pale, for a man to strike a woman.
ELYOT: A very poor tradition. Certain women should be struck regularly, like gongs.

Noël Coward 1899–1973: *Private Lives* (1930)

7 Last year my wife ran off with the fellow next door and I must admit, I still miss him.

Les Dawson 1934–93: attributed

8 ''Cos a coachman's a privileged indiwidual,' replied Mr Weller, looking fixedly at his son. ''Cos a coachman may do vithout suspicion wot other men may not; 'cos a coachman may be on the wery amicablest terms with eighty mile o' females, and yet nobody think that he ever means to marry any vun among them.'

Charles Dickens 1812–70: *Pickwick Papers* (1837)

9 The feminist movement seems to have beaten the manners out of men, but I didn't see them put up a lot of resistance.

Clarissa Dickson Wright: in *Mail on Sunday* 24 September 2000 'Quotes of the Week'

10 *a fellow Congressman attacked a piece of women's rights legislation with the words, 'I've always thought of women as kissable, cuddly, and smelling good'*:
That's what I feel about men. I only hope you haven't been disappointed as often as I have.

Millicent Fenwick 1910–92: in *Ned Sherrin in his Anecdotage* (1993)

11 I will not . . . sulk about having no boyfriend, but develop inner poise and authority and sense of self as woman of substance, complete *without* boyfriend, as best way to obtain boyfriend.

Helen Fielding 1958– : *Bridget Jones's Diary* (1996)

12 The minute you walked in the joint,
I could see you were a man of distinction,
A real big spender.
Good looking, so refined,
Say, wouldn't you like to know what's going on in my mind?
So let me get right to the point.
I don't pop my cork for every guy I see.
Hey! big spender, spend a little time with me.

Dorothy Fields 1905–74: 'Big Spender' (1966)

13 A fine romance with no kisses.
A fine romance, my friend, this is.
We should be like a couple of hot tomatoes,
But you're as cold as yesterday's mashed potatoes.

Dorothy Fields 1905–74: 'A Fine Romance' (1936)

14 *estranged husband of Liza Minnelli*:
I'd give up all my Shirley Temple dolls to get Liza back.

David Gest: attributed; in *Sunday Times* 14 December 2003 'Talking Heads'

15 If they ever invent a vibrator that can open pickle jars, we've had it.
on the bleak future facing men

Jeff Green: in *Mail on Sunday* 21 March 1999 'Quotes of the Week'

16 If a man asks you to have plastic surgery, he doesn't want you, he wants a trophy.

Jerry Hall 1956– : in *Observer* 12 September 2004

17 Our days will be so ecstatic
Our nights will be so exotic
For I'm a neurotic erratic
And you're an erratic erotic.

E. Y. Harburg 1898–1981: 'Courtship in Greenwich Village' (1965)

18 I'm wild again,
Beguiled again,
A simpering, whimpering child again—
Bewitched, bothered and bewildered am I.
Couldn't sleep
And wouldn't sleep

Lorenz Hart 1895–1943: 'Bewitched, Bothered and Bewildered' (1940)

Until I could sleep where I shouldn't sleep—
Bewitched, bothered and bewildered am I.

19 Take him, I won't put a price on him
Take him, he's yours
Take him, pyjamas look nice on him
But how he snores!

Lorenz Hart 1895–1943: 'Take Him' (1940)

20 KATHARINE HEPBURN: I fear I may be too tall for you, Mr. Tracy.
SPENCER TRACY: Don't worry, I'll cut you down to my size. *apocryphal account of their first meeting in 1942; it was the film director Joe Mankiewicz who said to Hepburn, 'He'll cut you down to size'*

Katharine Hepburn 1907–2003: Bill Davidson *Spencer Tracy* (1987)

21 A woman's mind is cleaner than a man's; she changes it more often.

Oliver Herford 1863–1935: attributed; Evan Esar and Nicolas Bentley (eds.) *Treasury of Humorous Quotations* (1951)

22 Brought up in an epoch when ladies apparently rolled along on wheels, Mr Quarles was peculiarly susceptible to calves.

Aldous Huxley 1894–1963: *Point Counter Point* (1928)

23 If men could get pregnant, abortion would be a sacrament.

Florynce Kennedy 1916–2001: 'The Verbal Karate of Florynce R. Kennedy' (1973)

24 Being kissed by a man who *didn't* wax his moustache was—like eating an egg without salt.

Rudyard Kipling 1865–1936: *The Story of the Gadsbys* (1889) 'Poor Dear Mamma'

25 The female sex has no greater fan than I, and I have the bills to prove it.

Alan Jay Lerner 1918–86: *The Street Where I Live* (1978)

26 Yes, why can't a woman be more like a man?
Men are so honest, so thoroughly square;
Eternally noble, historically fair;
Who when you win will always give your back a pat—
Why can't a woman be like that?

Alan Jay Lerner 1918–86: 'A Hymn to Him' (1956)

27 But let a woman in your life
And your serenity is through!
She'll redecorate your home
From the cellar to the dome;
Then get on to the enthralling
Fun of overhauling
You.

Alan Jay Lerner 1918–86: 'I'm an Ordinary Man' (1956)

28 *comment made by the estranged wife of Selwyn Lloyd:*
How could any woman love a man who wears a cardigan over his pyjamas?

Elizabeth Lloyd 1928– : attributed; Alan Watkins in *Spectator* 14 June 2003

29 Brother, do you know a nicer occupation,
Matter of fact, neither do I,
Than standing on the corner
Watching all the girls go by?

Frank Loesser 1910–69: 'Standing on the Corner' (1956)

30 Oh! to be loved by a man I respect,
To bask in the glow of his perfectly understandable neglect.

Frank Loesser 1910–69: 'Happy to Keep his Dinner Warm' (1961)

31 When you meet a gent paying all sorts of rent
For a flat that would flatten the Taj Mahal,
Call it sad, call it funny
But it's better than even money
That the guy's only doing it for some doll.

Frank Loesser 1910–69: 'Guys and Dolls' (1950)

32 So then he said that he used to be a member of the choir
himself, so who was he to cast the first rock at a girl like I.

Anita Loos 1893–1981: *Gentlemen Prefer Blondes* (1925)

33 *approaching an unwelcoming Greta Garbo and peering up*
under the brim of her floppy hat:
Pardon me, Ma'am . . . I thought you were a guy I knew
in Pittsburgh.

Groucho Marx 1890–1977: David Niven *Bring on the Empty Horses* (1975)

34 I suppose true sexual equality will come when a general
called Anthea is found having an unwise lunch with a
young, unreliable male model from Spain.

John Mortimer 1923–2009: in *The Spectator* 26 March 1994

35 He tells you when you've got on too much lipstick,
And helps you with your girdle when your hips stick.

Ogden Nash 1902–71: 'The Perfect Husband' (1949)

36 A little incompatibility is the spice of life, particularly if he
has income and she is pattable.

Ogden Nash 1902–71: *Versus* (1949)

37 Twenty years ago when we had no respect for women
they just used to say, 'You're chucked.' And now we do
respect them we have to lie to them sensitively.

Simon Nye 1958– : *Men Behaving Badly* (ITV, series 1, 1992) 'Intruders'

38 I killin' meself workin', an' he sthruttin' about from
mornin' till night like a paycock!

Sean O'Casey 1880–1964: *Juno and the Paycock* (1925)

39 Men seldom make passes
At girls who wear glasses.

Dorothy Parker 1893–1967: 'News Item' (1937)

40 Woman lives but in her lord;
Count to ten, and man is bored.
With this the gist and sum of it,
What earthly good can come of it?

Dorothy Parker 1893–1967: 'General Review of the Sex Situation' (1937)

41 Some get a kick from cocaine.
I'm sure that if I took even one sniff
That would bore me terrific'ly too,
Yet I get a kick out of you.

Cole Porter 1891–1964: 'I Get a Kick out of You' (1934)

42 Of course, I'm awfly glad that Mother had to marry
Father,
But I hate men.

Cole Porter 1891–1964: 'I Hate Men' (1948)

43 The breeze is chasing the zephyr,
The moon is chasing the sea,
The bull is chasing the heifer,
But nobody's chasing me.

Cole Porter 1891–1964: 'Nobody's Chasing Me' (1950)

44 You're the Nile,
You're the Tow'r of Pisa,
You're the smile
On the Mona Lisa.
I'm a worthless check, a total wreck, a flop,
But if, baby, I'm the bottom
You're the top!

Cole Porter 1891–1964: 'You're the Top' (1934)

45 All my life I've loved a womanly woman and admired a
manly man, but I never could stand a boily boy.

Lord Rosebery 1847–1929: George Cornwallis-West *Edwardian Heydays* (1930)

46 The material for this book was collected directly from nature at great personal risk by the author.
  in capitals, on the flyleaf of her book

Helen Rowland 1875–1950: *A Guide to Men* (1922)

47 Only the male intellect, clouded by sexual impulse, could call the undersized, narrow-shouldered, broad-hipped, and short-legged sex the fair sex.

Arthur Schopenhauer 1788–1860: 'On Women' (1851), tr. E. Belfort Bax

48 Say that she rail; why then I'll tell her plain
  She sings as sweetly as a nightingale:
  Say that she frown; I'll say she looks as clear
  As morning roses newly washed with dew:
  Say she be mute and will not speak a word;
  Then I'll commend her volubility,
  And say she uttereth piercing eloquence.

William Shakespeare 1564–1616: *The Taming of the Shrew* (1592)

49 *an unknown woman wrote to Shaw suggesting that as he had the greatest brain in the world, and she the most beautiful body, they ought to produce the most perfect child:*
  What if the child inherits my body and your brains?

George Bernard Shaw 1856–1950: Hesketh Pearson *Bernard Shaw* (1942)

50 You think that you are Ann's suitor; that you are the pursuer and she the pursued . . . Fool: it is you who are the pursued, the marked down quarry, the destined prey.

George Bernard Shaw 1856–1950: *Man and Superman* (1903)

51 Won't you come into the garden? I would like my roses to see you.

Richard Brinsley Sheridan 1751–1816: to a young lady; attributed

52 You've got to understand, in a way a thirty-three-year-old guy is a lot younger than a twenty-four-year-old girl. That is, he may not be ready for marriage yet.

Neil Simon 1927– : *Come Blow Your Horn* (1961)

53 From my experience of life I believe my personal motto should be 'Beware of men bearing flowers.'

Muriel Spark 1918–2006: *Curriculum Vitae* (1992)

54 A lady, if surprised by melancholy, might go to bed with a chap, once; or a thousand times if consumed by passion. But twice . . . *twice* . . . A lady might think she'd been taken for a tart.

Tom Stoppard 1937– : *Night and Day* (1978)

55 Yes, I am a fatal man, Madame Fribsbi. To inspire hopeless passion is my destiny.

William Makepeace Thackeray 1811–63: *Pendennis* (1848–50)

56 Werther had a love for Charlotte
  Such as words could never utter;
  Would you know how first he met her?
  She was cutting bread and butter.

William Makepeace Thackeray 1811–63: 'Sorrows of Werther' (1855)

57 In Europe, when a rich woman has an affair with a conductor, they have a baby. In America, she endows an orchestra for him.

Edgar Varèse 1885–1965: Herman G. Weinberg *Saint Cinema* (1970)

58 I don't want anyone to notice that I've been chucked, well, not even chucked, to be chucked you have to have been going out with someone, I've been . . . sort of sampled.

Arabella Weir: *Does My Bum Look Big in This?* (1997)

59 A man has one hundred dollars and you leave him with two dollars, that's subtraction.

Mae West 1892–1980: Joseph Weintraub *Peel Me a Grape* (1975)

60 Is that a gun in your pocket, or are you just glad to see me?

Mae West 1892–1980: Joseph Weintraub *Peel Me a Grape* (1975), usually quoted as 'Is that a pistol in your pocket . . . '

61 When women go wrong, men go right after them.

Mae West 1892–1980: in *She Done Him Wrong* (1933 film)

62 *asked by the gossip columnist Hedda Hopper how she knew so much about men:*
Baby, I went to night school.

Mae West 1892–1980: Max Wilk *The Wit and Wisdom of Hollywood* (1972)

63 Whatever women do they must do twice as well as men to be thought half as good. Luckily, this is not difficult.

Charlotte Whitton 1896–1975: in *Canada Month* June 1963

64 All women become like their mothers. That is their tragedy. No man does. That's his.

Oscar Wilde 1854–1900: *The Importance of Being Earnest* (1895); the same words occur in dialogue form in *A Woman of No Importance* (1893)

65 Girls are just friends who give you erections.
reporting his teenage son's words

Nigel Williams 1948– : *Fortysomething* (1999)

66 When I was a young boy
My mama said to me
There's only one girl in the world for you
And she probably lives in Tahiti.

Wreckless Eric 1954– : 'Whole Wide World' (song)

67 A mistress should be like a little country retreat near the town, not to dwell in constantly, but only for a night and away.

William Wycherley c.1640–1716: *The Country Wife* (1675)

Middle Age
See also **Old Age, Youth**

❝ *20 to 40 is the fillet steak of life. After that it's all short cuts.* **❞**
Philip Larkin

1 Years ago we discovered the exact point, the dead centre of middle age. It occurs when you are too young to take up golf and too old to rush up to the net.

Franklin P. Adams 1881–1960: *Nods and Becks* (1944)

2 I recently turned 60. Practically a third of my life is over.

Woody Allen 1935– : in *Observer* 'Sayings of the Week' 10 March 1996

3 You are thirty-two. You are rapidly approaching the age when your body, whether it embarrasses you or not, begins to embarrass other people.

Alan Bennett 1934– : *Getting On* (1972)

4 Whenever the talk turns to age, I say I am 49 plus VAT.

Lionel Blair 1936– : in *Mail on Sunday* 6 June 1999

5 After forty a woman has to choose between losing her figure or her face. My advice is to keep your face, and stay sitting down.

Barbara Cartland 1901–2000: Libby Purves 'Luncheon à la Cartland'; in *Times* 6 October 1993

6 Middle age is when your broad mind and narrow waist begin to change places.

E. Joseph Crossman: attributed

7 Nobody loves a fairy when she's forty.

Arthur W. D. Henley: title of song (1934)

8 20 to 40 is the fillet steak of life. After that it's all short cuts.

Philip Larkin 1922–85: comment, in *Philip Larkin Documentary* (Channel 4 TV) 6 July 2003

9 *of Zsa Zsa Gabor:*
She's discovered the secret of perpetual middle age.

Oscar Levant 1906–72: attributed

10 I have a bone to pick with Fate.
Come here and tell me, girlie,
Do you think my mind is maturing late,
Or simply rotted early?

Ogden Nash 1902–71: 'Lines on Facing Forty' (1942)

11 As invariably happens after one passes 40, the paper sagged open to the obituary page.

S. J. Perelman 1904–79: 'Swindle Sheet with Blueblood Engrailed Arrant Fibs Rampant'

12 When I was cuter,
Each night meant another suitor,
I sleep easier now.

Cole Porter 1891–1964: 'I Sleep Easier Now' (1950)

13 It is one of the consolations of middle-aged reformers that the good they inculcate must live after them if it is to live at all.

Saki 1870–1916: *Beasts and Super-Beasts* (1914)

14 Maturity is a high price to pay for growing up.

Tom Stoppard 1937– : *Where Are They Now?* (1973)

15 From birth to 18 a girl needs good parents. From 18 to 35, she needs good looks. From 35 to 55, good personality. From 55 on, she needs good cash.

Sophie Tucker 1884–1966: Michael Freedland *Sophie* (1978)

16 Thirty-five is a very attractive age. London society is full of women of the very highest birth who have, of their own free choice, remained thirty-five for years.

Oscar Wilde 1854–1900: *The Importance of Being Earnest* (1895)

The Mind

See also **Intelligence and Intellectuals**

❝ *Insanity is hereditary. You can get it from your children.* ❞
Sam Levenson

1 If I am out of my mind, it's all right with me, thought Moses Herzog.

Saul Bellow 1915–2005: *Herzog* (1961) opening sentence

2 The asylums of this country are full of the sound of mind disinherited by the out of pocket.

Alan Bennett 1934– : *The Madness of George III* (performed 1991)

3 An apparatus with which we think that we think.
definition of the brain

Ambrose Bierce 1842–c.1914: *Cynic's Word Book* (1906)

4 *Charles Condomine declining psychoanalysis:*
I refuse to endure months of expensive humiliation only to be told at the end of it that at the age of four I was in love with my rocking-horse.

Noël Coward 1899–1973: *Blithe Spirit* (1941)

5 'I am inclined to think—' said I [Dr Watson]. 'I should do so,' Sherlock Holmes remarked, impatiently.

Arthur Conan Doyle 1859–1930: *The Valley of Fear* (1915)

6 There was only one catch and that was Catch-22, which specified that a concern for one's own safety in the face of dangers that were real and immediate was the process of a rational mind . . . Orr would be crazy to fly more missions and sane if he didn't, but if he was sane he had to fly

Joseph Heller 1923–99: *Catch-22* (1961)

them. If he flew them he was crazy and didn't have to; but if he didn't want to he was sane and had to.

7 Psychiatry is a waste of good couches. Why should I make a psychiatrist laugh, and then pay him?

Kathy Lette 1958– : in *Times* 27 October 2001

8 Insanity is hereditary. You can get it from your children.

Sam Levenson 1911–80: *You Can Say That Again, Sam!* (1975)

9 If the nineteenth century was the age of the editorial chair, ours is the century of the psychiatrist's couch.

Marshall McLuhan 1911–80: *Understanding Media* (1964)

10 'Do you know if there was any insanity in her family?' 'Insanity? No, I never heard of any. Her father lives in West Kensington, but I believe he's sane on all other subjects.'

Saki 1870–1916: *Beasts and Super-Beasts* (1914)

11 O Lord, Sir—when a heroine goes mad she always goes into white satin.

Richard Brinsley Sheridan 1751–1816: *The Critic* (1779)

12 Noble deeds and hot baths are the best cures for depression.

Dodie Smith 1896–1990: *I Capture the Castle* (1949)

13 Not body enough to cover his mind decently with; his intellect is improperly exposed.

Sydney Smith 1771–1845: Lady Holland *Memoir* (1855)

14 I must have a prodigious quantity of mind; it takes me as much as a week, sometimes, to make it up.

Mark Twain 1835–1910: *The Innocents Abroad* (1869)

15 A neurosis is a secret you don't know you're keeping.

Kenneth Tynan 1927–80: Kathleen Tynan *Life of Kenneth Tynan* (1987)

16 Dr Tayler's thoughts are very white and pure, recalling in their disorder a draper's shop on the last day of a great white sale.

Rebecca West 1892–1983: in *The Clarion* 7 March 1913

Mistakes and Misfortunes

❝ *We don't just have egg on our face. We have omelette all over our suits.* ❞
Tom Brokaw

1 Instead of being arrested, as we stated, for kicking his wife down a flight of stairs and hurling a lighted kerosene lamp after her, the Revd James P. Wellman died unmarried four years ago.

Anonymous: from an American newspaper, quoted by Burne-Jones in a letter to Lady Horner; J. A. Gere and John Sparrow (eds.) *Geoffrey Madan's Notebooks* (1981)

2 *waiter delivering champagne to George Best's hotel room:* Tell me, Mr Best, where did it all go wrong? *£20,000 in cash was scattered on the bed, which also contained Miss World*

Anonymous: attributed

3 I'm not going to make the same mistake once. *on marriage*

Warren Beatty 1937– : attributed; Bob Chieger *Was It Good For You Too?* (1983)

4 My only solution for the problem of habitual accidents . . . is to stay in bed all day. Even then, there is always the chance that you will fall out.

Robert Benchley 1889–1945: *Chips off the old Benchley* (1949) 'Safety Second'

5 George the Third
Ought never to have occurred.
One can only wonder
At so grotesque a blunder.

Edmund Clerihew Bentley
1875–1956: 'George the Third'
(1929)

6 The younger Van Eyck
Was christened Jan, and not Mike,
The thought of this curious mistake
Often kept him awake.

Edmund Clerihew Bentley
1875–1956: 'Van Eyck' (1905)

7 My misdeeds are accidental happenings and merely the
result of having been in the wrong bar or bed at the wrong
time, say most days between midday and midnight.

Jeffrey Bernard 1932–97: in *The
Spectator* 18 July 1992

8 Calamities are of two kinds: misfortune to ourselves, and
good fortune to others.

Ambrose Bierce 1842–c.1914: *The
Cynic's Word Book* (1906)

9 *on premature calls of a win in Florida in the presidential
election of 2000:*
We don't just have egg on our face. We have omelette all
over our suits.

Tom Brokaw 1940– : in *Atlanta
Constitution-Journal* 9 November
2000 (online edition)

10 Of all the horrid, hideous notes of woe,
Sadder than owl-songs or the midnight blast,
Is that portentous phrase, 'I told you so.'

Lord Byron 1788–1824: *Don Juan*
(1819–24)

11 *Edith Evans repeatedly inserted the word* 'very' *into a line of*
Hay Fever:
No, no, Edith. The line is, 'You can see as far as Marlow
on a clear day.' On a *very* clear day you can see Marlow
and Beaumont and Fletcher.

Noël Coward 1899–1973: Cole Lesley
The Life of Noël Coward (1976)

12 It was a moment of madness for which I have
subsequently paid a very, very heavy price.
*of the episode on Clapham Common leading to his
resignation as Welsh Secretary*

Ron Davies 1946– : interview with
BBC Wales and HTV, 30 October 1998

13 If Gladstone fell into the Thames, that would be
misfortune; and if anybody pulled him out, that, I
suppose, would be a calamity.

Benjamin Disraeli 1804–81: Leon
Harris *The Fine Art of Political Wit*
(1965)

14 Something nasty in the woodshed.

Stella Gibbons 1902–89: *Cold
Comfort Farm* (1932)

15 I left the room with silent dignity, but caught my foot in
the mat.

George Grossmith 1847–1912 and
Weedon Grossmith 1854–1919: *The
Diary of a Nobody* (1894)

16 I was mistaken for a prostitute once in the last war. When
a GI asked me what I charged, I said, 'Well, dear, what do
your mother and sisters normally ask for?'

Thora Hird 1911–2003: in
Independent 27 February 1999

17 Higgledy—Piggledy
Andrea Doria
Lines in the name of this
Glorious boat.
As I sit writing these
Non-navigational
Verses a—CRASH! BANG! BLURP!
GLUB . . . (end of quote).

John Hollander 1929– : 'Last Words'
(1966)

18 Well, I'm still here.

after erroneous reports of his death, marked by tributes paid to him in Congress

Bob Hope 1903–2003: in *Mail on Sunday* 7 June 1998 'Quotes of the Week'

19 The Achilles heel which has bitten us in the backside all year has stood out like a sore thumb.

Andy King 1956– : in *Observer* 18 December 2005

20 When I make a mistake, it's a beaut.

Fiorello H. La Guardia 1882–1947: on his appointment of Herbert O'Brien as a judge; William Manners *Patience and Fortitude* (1976)

21 I've no sympathy with people to whom things happen. It may be that their luck was bad, but is that to count in their favour?

Cormac McCarthy 1933– : *All the Pretty Horses* (1993)

22 now and then
there is a person born
who is so unlucky
that he runs into accidents
which started to happen
to somebody else.

Don Marquis 1878–1937: *archys life of mehitabel* (1933) 'archy says'

23 Erratum. In my article on the price of milk, 'horses' should have read 'cows' throughout.

J. B. Morton 1893–1975: *Sideways Through Borneo* (1937)

24 I actually slipped on a hamburger in Hamburg once, and almost fell off stage.

Keith Richards 1943– : *Keith Richards: in His Own Words* (1994)

25 *a postcard of the Venus de Milo sent to his niece:*
See what'll happen to you if you don't stop biting your finger-nails.

Will Rogers 1879–1935: Bennett Cerf *Shake Well Before Using* (1948)

26 *For* Pheasant *read* Peasant, throughout.

W. C. Sellar 1898–1951 and **R. J. Yeatman** 1898–1968: *1066 and All That* (1930); errata

27 *when the news that Sheridan's Drury Lane theatre was on fire reached the House of Commons, a motion was made to adjourn the debate on the campaign in Spain:*
Whatever might be the extent of the individual calamity, I do not consider it of a nature worthy to interrupt the proceedings on so great a national question.

Richard Brinsley Sheridan 1751–1816: speech, House of Commons, 24 February 1809

28 Well, if I called the wrong number, why did you answer the phone?

James Thurber 1894–1961: cartoon caption in *New Yorker* 5 June 1937

29 Wardrobe malfunction.

explanation for the exposure of Janet Jackson's right breast on prime time American television during the Super Bowl

Justin Timberlake 1981– : in *Daily Telegraph* 3 February 2004 (online edition)

30 If we had had more time for discussion we should probably have made a great many more mistakes.

Leon Trotsky 1879–1940: *My Life* (1930)

31 *to his troop sergeant after sustaining serious wounds trying to unblock a jammed machine gun:*
Kiss me, Chudleigh

Auberon Waugh 1939–2001: anecdote; in *Daily Telegraph* 18 January 2001

32 Unseen, in the background, Fate was quietly slipping the lead into the boxing gloves.

P. G. Wodehouse 1881–1975: *Very Good, Jeeves* (1930)

33 He felt like a man who, chasing rainbows, has had one of them suddenly turn and bite him in the leg.

P. G. Wodehouse 1881–1975: *Eggs, Beans, and Crumpets* (1940)

Money

See also **Debt, Poverty, Wealth**

❝ *There's only one thing to do with loose change of course. Tighten it.* **❞**
Flann O'Brien

1 Money is better than poverty, if only for financial reasons.

Woody Allen 1935– : *Without Feathers* (1976) 'Early Essays'

2 Money, it turned out, was exactly like sex, you thought of nothing else if you didn't have it and thought of other things if you did.

James Baldwin 1924–87: in *Esquire* May 1961 'Black Boy looks at the White Boy'

3 We live by the Golden Rule. Those who have the gold make the rules.

Buzzie Bavasi 1914–2008: attributed; A. J. Maikovich and M. D. Brown (eds.) *Sports Quotations* (2000)

4 I'm tired of Love: I'm still more tired of Rhyme.
But Money gives me pleasure all the time.

Hilaire Belloc 1870–1953: 'Fatigued' (1923)

5 HOLDUP MAN: Quit stalling—I said your money or your life.
JACK BENNY: I'm thinking it over!

Jack Benny 1894–1974: one of Jack Benny's most successful gags; Irving Fein *Jack Benny* (1976)

6 'First you schange me schmall scheque?' 'No.'

Caryl Brahms 1901–82 and **S. J. Simon** 1904–48: *A Bullet in the Ballet* (1937)

7 I never loved a dear gazelle—
Nor anything that cost me much:
High prices profit those who sell,
But why should I be fond of such?

Lewis Carroll 1832–98: 'Tema con Variazioni'

8 Saving is a very fine thing. Especially when your parents have done it for you.

Winston Churchill 1874–1965: J. A. Sutcliffe (ed.) *The Sayings of Winston Churchill* (1992)

9 Annual income twenty pounds, annual expenditure nineteen nineteen six, result happiness. Annual income twenty pounds, annual expenditure twenty pounds ought and six, result misery.

Charles Dickens 1812–70: *David Copperfield* (1850)

10 When you don't have any money, the problem is food. When you have money, it's sex. When you have both it's health.

J. P. Donleavy 1926– : *The Ginger Man* (1955)

11 We don't wake up for less than $10,000 a day.
of herself and supermodel Christy Turlington; often quoted as, 'I don't get out of bed for less than $10,000 a day'

Linda Evangelista 1965– : in *Vogue* October 1990

12 I like Chopin and Bizet, and the voice of Doris Day,
Gershwin songs and old forgotten carols.
But the music that excels is the sound of oil wells
As they slurp, slurp, slurp into the barrels.

My little home will be quaint as an old parasol,
Instead of fitted carpets I'll have money wall to wall.
I want an old-fashioned house

Marve Fisher: 'An Old-Fashioned Girl' (1954)

With an old-fashioned fence
And an old-fashioned millionaire.

13 A bank is a place where they lend you an umbrella in fair
weather and ask for it back when it begins to rain.

Robert Frost 1874–1963: in
Muscatine Journal 22 August 1961

14 Economy was always 'elegant', and money-spending
always 'vulgar' and ostentatious— a sort of sour-
grapeism, which made us very peaceful and satisfied.

Elizabeth Gaskell 1810–65: *Cranford*
(1853)

15 Money, wife, is the true fuller's earth for reputations, there
is not a spot or a stain but what it can take out.

John Gay 1685–1732: *The Beggar's
Opera* (1728)

16 The shares are a penny, and ever so many are taken by
Rothschild and Baring,
And just as a few are allotted to you, you awake with a
shudder despairing.

W. S. Gilbert 1836–1911: *Iolanthe*
(1882)

17 Good news rarely comes in a brown envelope.

Henry D'Avigdor Goldsmid 1909–76:
John Betjeman, letter to Tom Driberg,
21 July 1976

18 *on being told that money doesn't buy happiness:*
But it upgrades despair so beautifully.

Richard Greenberg: *Hurrah at Last*
(1999)

19 Money is what you'd get on beautifully without if only
other people weren't so crazy about it.

Margaret Case Harriman: Laurence J.
Peter (ed.) *Quotations for our Time*
(1977)

20 A bank is a place that will lend you money if you can
prove that you don't need it.

Bob Hope 1903–2003: Alan
Harrington *Life in the Crystal Palace*
(1959)

21 When a feller says, 'It hain't the money, but th' principle
o' th' thing,', it's the money.

Frank McKinney Hubbard
1868–1930: *Hoss Sense and
Nonsense* (1926)

22 *to Joynson-Hicks, who had acquired his double-barrelled
surname through marriage with an heiress:*
On the spur of the moment I can think of no better
example of unearned increment than the hyphen in the
right honourable gentleman's name.

David Lloyd George 1863–1945:
Leon Harris *The Fine Art of Political
Wit* (1965)

23 There's only one thing to do with loose change of course.
Tighten it.

Flann O'Brien 1911–66: *The Best of
Myles* (1968)

24 'My boy,' he says, 'always try to rub up against money,
for if you rub up against money long enough, some of it
may rub off on you.'

Damon Runyon 1884–1946: in
Cosmopolitan August 1929, 'A Very
Honourable Guy'

25 *on being asked what* Rosencrantz and Guildenstern are Dead
was about:
It's about to make me very rich.

Tom Stoppard 1937– : attributed; in
Daily Telegraph 27 February 1999

26 The elegant simplicity of the three per cents.

Lord Stowell 1745–1836: Lord
Campbell *Lives of the Lord
Chancellors* (1857)

27 Money won't buy happiness, but it will pay the salaries of
a large research staff to study the problem.

Bill Vaughan: Laurence J. Peter (ed.)
Quotations for Our Time (1977)

Morality

See also **Virtue and Vice**

> **❝ My will is strong, but my won't is weak. ❞**
> **Cole Porter**

1 *asking Robbie Ross to keep away from the scandal-touched Reggie Turner:*
He is very weak and you, if I remember rightly, are wicked.

Max Beerbohm 1872–1956: letter, spring 1895

2 I am all for morality now—and shall confine myself henceforward to the strictest adultery—which you will please recollect is all that that virtuous wife of mine has left me.

Lord Byron 1788–1824: letter 29 October 1819

3 Throwing acid is wrong—in some people's eyes.

Jimmy Carr 1972– : in *Guardian* 19 August 2002

4 To be absolutely honest, what I feel really bad about is that I don't feel worse. That's the ineffectual liberal's problem in a nutshell.

Michael Frayn 1933– : in *Observer* 8 August 1965

5 If people want a sense of purpose, they should get it from their archbishops. They should not hope to receive it from their politicians.

Harold Macmillan 1894–1986: in conversation 1963; Henry Fairlie *The Life of Politics* (1968)

6 I think fidelity is a very good idea—now that I can't walk.

John Mortimer 1923–2009: in *Mail on Sunday* 4 January 2004 'Quotes of the Year'

7 I'm very mild, I'm very meek,
My will is strong, but my won't is weak;
So don't look at me that way!

Cole Porter 1891–1964: 'Don't Look at Me That Way' (*Paris*, 1928 musical)

8 People will do things from a sense of duty which they would never attempt as a pleasure.

Saki 1870–1916: *The Chronicles of Clovis* (1911)

9 There is such a thing as letting one's aesthetic sense override one's moral sense . . . I believe you would have condoned the South Sea Bubble and the persecution of the Albigenses if they had been carried out in effective colour schemes.

Saki 1870–1916: *The Toys of Peace* (1919)

10 Dost thou think, because thou art virtuous, there shall be no more cakes and ale?

William Shakespeare 1564–1616: *Twelfth Night* (1601)

11 When a stupid man is doing something he is ashamed of, he always declares that it is his duty.

George Bernard Shaw 1856–1950: *Caesar and Cleopatra* (1901)

12 PICKERING: Have you no morals, man?
DOOLITTLE: Can't afford them, Governor.

George Bernard Shaw 1856–1950: *Pygmalion* (1916)

13 If your morals make you dreary, depend upon it they are wrong.

Robert Louis Stevenson 1850–94: *Across the Plains* (1892)

14 BELINDA: Ay, but you know we must return good for evil.
LADY BRUTE: That may be a mistake in the translation.

John Vanbrugh 1664–1726: *The Provoked Wife* (1697)

15 Moral indignation is jealousy with a halo.

H. G. Wells 1866–1946: *The Wife of Sir Isaac Harman* (1914)

16 On an occasion of this kind it becomes more than a moral duty to speak one's mind. It becomes a pleasure.

Oscar Wilde 1854–1900: *The Importance of Being Earnest* (1895)

Murder

❝ You can't chop your poppa up in Massachusetts. ❞

Michael Brown

1 Lizzie Borden took an axe
And gave her mother forty whacks;
When she saw what she had done
She gave her father forty-one!

Anonymous: popular rhyme in circulation after the acquittal of Lizzie Borden, in June 1893, from the charge of murdering her father and stepmother at Fall River, Massachusetts on 4 August 1892

2 I feel we are so busy compromising at every turn that we can't say 'murder is wrong' in case it upsets some murderers.

Alan Ayckbourn 1939– : in *Guardian* 4 September 2002

3 You can't chop your poppa up in Massachusetts,
Not even if it's planned as a surprise
No you can't chop your poppa up in Massachusetts
You know how neighbours love to criticize.

Michael Brown: 'Lizzie Borden' (1952)

4 The Stately Homes of England,
Tho' rather in the lurch,
Provide a lot of chances
For Psychical Research —
There's the ghost of a crazy younger son
Who murdered, in thirteen fifty-one,
An extremely rowdy Nun
Who resented it,
And people who come to call
Meet her in the hall.

Noël Coward 1899–1973: *The Stately Homes of England* (1938)

5 *on being asked whether he thought that Dr John Bodkin Adams, acquitted of murdering an elderly female patient, had actually been guilty:*
He must have had quite a lot of explaining to do to the recording angel.

Lord Hailsham 1907–2001: in an interview; John Mortimer *Character Parts* (1986)

6 Television has brought back murder into the home—where it belongs.

Alfred Hitchcock 1899–1980: in *Observer* 19 December 1965

7 English law does not permit good persons, as such, to strangle bad persons, as such.

T. H. Huxley 1825–95: letter in *Pall Mall Gazette*, 31 October 1866

8 It was not until several weeks after he had decided to murder his wife that Dr Bickleigh took any active steps in the matter. Murder is a serious business.

Francis Iles 1893–1970: *Malice Aforethought* (1931)

9 The National Rifle Association says guns don't kill people, people do. But I think the gun helps. Just standing there, going 'Bang!'—that's not going to kill too many people.

Eddie Izzard 1962– : *Dress to Kill* (stageshow, San Francisco, 1998)

10 We'll murder them all amid laughter and merriment,
Except for a few we'll take home to experiment.
My pulse will be quickenin' with each drop of strychnine
we feed to a pigeon.
(It just takes a smidgin!)
To poison a pigeon in the park.

Tom Lehrer 1928– : 'Poisoning Pigeons in the Park' (1953)

11 You can always count on a murderer for a fancy prose style.

Vladimir Nabokov 1899–1977: *Lolita* (1955)

12 *Julius Caesar of his assassins:*
Infamy, infamy, they've all got it in for me!

Talbot Rothwell 1916–74: *Carry on, Cleo* (1964); according to Frank Muir's letter to the *Guardian*, 22 July 1995, the line had actually been written by him and Denis Norden for a radio sketch for 'Take It From Here', and was later used by Rothwell with their permission

13 I met Murder on the way—
He had a mask like Castlereagh.

Percy Bysshe Shelley 1792–1822: 'The Mask of Anarchy' (1819)

14 By the argument of counsel it was shown that at half-past ten in the morning on the day of the murder . . . [the defendant] became insane, and remained so for eleven and a half hours exactly.

Mark Twain 1835–1910: 'A New Crime' (1875)

15 *justification for poisoning his sister-in-law*
She had very thick ankles.

Thomas Griffiths Wainewright 1794–1852: in *Dictionary of National Biography* (1917–)

Music
See also **Musicians, Songs and Singing**

❝ *Wagner has lovely moments but awful quarters of an hour.* ❞
Gioacchino Rossini

1 I can't listen to too much Wagner, ya know? I start to get the urge to conquer Poland.

Woody Allen 1935– : *Manhattan Murder Mystery* (1998 film)

2 All music is folk music, I ain't never heard no horse sing a song.

Louis Armstrong 1901–71: in *New York Times* 7 July 1971

3 *when asked what jazz is:*
If you still have to ask . . . shame on you.

Louis Armstrong 1901–71: Max Jones et al. *Salute to Satchmo* (1970) (sometimes quoted 'Man, if you gotta ask you'll never know')

4 I love Wagner, but the music I prefer is that of a cat hung up by its tail outside a window and trying to stick to the panes of glass with its claws.

Charles Baudelaire 1821–67: Nat Shapiro (ed.) *An Encyclopedia of Quotations about Music* (1978)

5 What can you do with it? It's like a lot of yaks jumping about.
on the third movement of Beethoven's Seventh Symphony

Thomas Beecham 1879–1961: Harold Atkins and Archie Newman *Beecham Stories* (1978)

6 Why do we have to have all these third-rate foreign conductors around—when we have so many second-rate ones of our own?

Thomas Beecham 1879–1961: L. Ayre *Wit of Music* (1966)

7 The musical equivalent of the Towers of St Pancras Station.

Thomas Beecham 1879–1961: describing Elgar's 1st Symphony; Neville Cardus *Sir Thomas Beecham* (1961)

8 There are two golden rules for an orchestra: start together and finish together. The public doesn't give a damn what goes on in between.

Thomas Beecham 1879–1961: Harold Atkins and Archie Newman *Beecham Stories* (1978)

9 [The piano is] a parlour utensil for subduing the impenitent visitor. It is operated by depressing the keys of the machine and the spirits of the audience.

Ambrose Bierce 1842–c.1914: *The Enlarged Devil's Dictionary* (1967)

10 A variable resource centre whose viability depends upon the business plan of the Controller of Radio 3.
describing the BBC's symphony orchestras

John Birt 1944– : attributed, in *Spectator* 2 September 2000

11 Extraordinary how potent cheap music is.

Noël Coward 1899–1973: *Private Lives* (1930); see **Music** 60

12 The tuba is certainly the most intestinal of instruments—the very lower bowel of music.

Peter de Vries 1910–93: *The Glory of the Hummingbird* (1974)

13 I don't like composers who think. It gets in the way of their plagiarism.

Howard Dietz 1896–1983: *Dancing in the Dark* (1974)

14 *a trumpet player had been suggested with the endorsement 'he's a nice guy':*
Nice guys are a dime a dozen! Get me a prick that can play!

Tommy Dorsey 1905–56: Bill Crow *Jazz Anecdotes* (1990)

15 I hate music, especially when it's played.

Jimmy Durante 1893–1980: Nat Shapiro (ed.) *An Encyclopedia of Quotations about Music* (1978)

16 Playing 'Bop' is like scrabble with all the vowels missing.

Duke Ellington 1899–1974: in *Look* 10 August 1954

17 'Tis wonderful how soon a piano gets into a log hut on the frontier.

Ralph Waldo Emerson 1803–82: 'Civilization' (1870)

18 *message sent after the Grenadier Guards had played an arrangement of Richard Strauss' Elektra:*
His Majesty does not know what the Band has just played, but it is *never* to be played again.

George V 1865–1936: Osbert Sitwell *Left Hand, Right Hand* (1945)

19 Slap that bass—
Use it like a tonic.
Slap that bass
Keep your Philharmonic.
Zoom, zoom, zoom—
And the milk and honey'll flow!

Ira Gershwin 1896–1983: 'Slap that Bass' (1937)

20 Then they began to sing
That extremely lovely thing,
'*Scherzando! ma non troppo ppp.*'

W. S. Gilbert 1836–1911: 'Story of Prince Agib' (1869)

21 I only know two tunes. One of them is 'Yankee Doodle' and the other isn't.

Ulysses S. Grant 1822–85: Nat Shapiro (ed.) *An Encyclopedia of Quotations about Music* (1978)

22 Music helps not the toothache.

George Herbert 1593–1633: *Outlandish Proverbs* (1640)

23 Classic music is th'kind that we keep thinkin'll turn into a tune.

Frank McKinney Hubbard 1868–1930: *Comments of Abe Martin and His Neighbors* (1923)

24 A pianoforte is a harp in a box.

Leigh Hunt 1784–1859: *The Seer* (1840)

25 *on the performance of a celebrated violinist:*
Difficult do you call it, Sir? I wish it were impossible.

Samuel Johnson 1709–84: William Seward *Supplement to the Anecdotes of Distinguished Persons* (1797)

26 If you play that score one more time before we open, people are going to think we're doing a revival.
to George Gershwin

George S. Kaufman 1889–1961: Howard Teichmann *George S. Kaufman* (1973)

27 HAMMERSTEIN: Here is a story laid in China about an Italian told by an Irishman. What kind of music are you going to write?
KERN: It'll be good Jewish music.
in the 1930s, discussing with Oscar Hammerstein II a musical to be based on Donn Byrne's novel Messer Marco Polo

Jerome Kern 1885–1945: Gerald Bordman *Jerome Kern* (1980)

28 I don't like jazz. When I hear jazz, it's as if I had gas on the stomach. I used to think it was static when I heard it on the radio.

Nikita Khrushchev 1894–1971: in *Encounter* April 1963

29 A carpenter's hammer, in a warm summer noon, will fret me into more than midsummer madness. But those unconnected, unset sounds are nothing to the measured malice of music.

Charles Lamb 1775–1834: *Elia* (1823)

30 A squeak's heard in the orchestra
The leader draws across
The intestines of the agile cat
The tail of the noble hoss.

G. T. Lanigan 1845–86: *The Amateur Orlando* (1875)

31 Mine was the kind of piece in which nobody knew what was going on, including the composer, the conductor, and the critics. Consequently I got pretty good notices.

Oscar Levant 1906–72: *A Smattering of Ignorance* (1940)

32 If I play Tchaikovsky I play his melodies and skip his spiritual struggles . . . If there's any time left over I fill in with a lot of runs up and down the keyboard.

Liberace 1919–87: Stuart Hall and Paddy Whannel (eds.) *The Popular Arts* (1964)

33 I don't like my music, but what is my opinion against that of millions of others.

Frederick Loewe 1904–88: Nat Shapiro (ed.) *An Encyclopedia of Quotations about Music* (1978)

34 On seeing Niagara Falls, Mahler exclaimed: 'Fortissimo at last!'

Gustav Mahler 1860–1911: K. Blaukopf *Gustav Mahler* (1973)

35 If you're in jazz and more than ten people like you, you're labelled commercial.

Herbie Mann 1930– : Henry Pleasants *Serious Music and all that Jazz!* (1969)

36 *lead singer of Coldplay:*
I know you think we just sit and count money, but sometimes we do other things, like teach the drummer to play piano.

Chris Martin 1977– : in *Sunday Times* 12 June 2005

37 If I had the power, I would insist on all oratorios being sung in the costume of the period—with a possible exception in the case of *The Creation.*

Ernest Newman 1868–1959: in *New York Post* 1924; Nat Shapiro (ed.) *An Encyclopedia of Quotations about Music* (1978)

38 I have been told that Wagner's music is better than it sounds.

Bill Nye 1850–96: Mark Twain *Autobiography* (1924)

39 What a terrible revenge by the culture of the Negroes on that of the whites!
of jazz

Ignacy Jan Paderewski 1860–1941: Nat Shapiro (ed.) *An Encyclopedia of Quotations about Music* (1978)

40 If anyone has conducted a Beethoven performance, and then doesn't have to go to an osteopath, then there's something wrong.

Simon Rattle 1955– : in *Guardian* 31 May 1990

41 Of course we've all *dreamed* of reviving the *castrati*; but it's needed Hilda to take the first practical steps towards making them a reality . . . She's drawn up a list of well-known singers who she thinks would benefit . . . It's only a question of getting them to agree.

Henry Reed 1914–86: *Private Life of Hilda Tablet* (1954)

42 To the social-minded, a definition for Concert is: that which surrounds an intermission.

Ned Rorem 1923– : *The Final Diary* (1974)

43 It is a music one must hear several times. I am not going again.
of Tannhäuser

Gioacchino Rossini 1792–1868: L. de Hegermann-Lindencrone *In the Courts of Memory* (1912)

44 Wagner has lovely moments but awful quarters of an hour.

Gioacchino Rossini 1792–1868: to Emile Naumann, April 1867

45 Applause is a receipt, not a note of demand.

Artur Schnabel 1882–1951: in *Saturday Review of Literature* 29 September 1951

46 I know two kinds of audiences only—one coughing, and one not coughing.

Artur Schnabel 1882–1951: *My Life and Music* (1961)

47 You are there and I am here; but where is Beethoven?
to his conductor during a Beethoven rehearsal

Artur Schnabel 1882–1951: Nat Shapiro (ed.) *An Encyclopedia of Quotations about Music* (1978)

48 I am delighted to add another unplayable work to the repertoire. I want the Concerto to be difficult and I want the little finger to become longer. I can wait.
of his Violin Concerto

Arnold Schoenberg 1874–1951: Joseph Machlis *Introduction to Contemporary Music* (1963)

49 I have a reasonable good ear in music: let us have the tongs and the bones.

William Shakespeare 1564–1616: *A Midsummer Night's Dream* (1595–6)

50 Hell is full of musical amateurs: music is the brandy of the damned.

George Bernard Shaw 1856–1950: *Man and Superman* (1903)

51 I absolutely forbid such outrage. If *Pygmalion* is not good enough for your friends with its own verbal music . . . let them try Mozart's *Cosi Fan Tutti*, or at least Offenbach's *Grand Duchess*.

George Bernard Shaw 1856–1950: refusing to allow a musical based on *Pygmalion*; Caryl Brahms and Ned Sherrin *Song by Song* (1984)

52 If one will only take the precaution to go in long enough after it commences and to come out long before it is over you will not find it wearisome.
of Gounod's La Rédemption

George Bernard Shaw 1856–1950: in *The World* 22 February 1893

53 I play all my country and western music backwards. Your lover returns, your dog comes back to life and you cease to be an alcoholic.

Linda Smith 1958–2006: in *Daily Telegraph* (obituary), 1 March 2006

54 Nothing can be more disgusting than an oratorio. How absurd to see 500 people fiddling like madmen about Israelites in the Red Sea!

Sydney Smith 1771–1845: Hesketh Pearson *The Smith of Smiths* (1934)

55 Jazz will endure, just as long as people hear it through their feet instead of their brains.

John Philip Sousa 1854–1932: Nat Shapiro (ed.) *An Encyclopedia of Quotations about Music* (1978)

56 Satisfied great success.
reply to telegram from Billy Rose, suggesting that reorchestration by Robert Russell Bennett might make a ballet which was 'a great success' even more successful

Igor Stravinsky 1882–1971: in *Ned Sherrin in his Anecdotage* (1993)

57 I would like to thank Beethoven, Brahms, Wagner, Strauss, Rimsky-Korsakov.

Dmitri Tiomkin 1899–1979: Oscar acceptance speech for the score of *The High and the Mighty* in 1955; Nat Shapiro (ed.) *An Encyclopedia of Quotations about Music* (1978)

58 I assure you that the typewriting machine, when played with expression, is not more annoying than the piano when played by a sister or near relation.

Oscar Wilde 1854–1900: letter to Robert Ross from Reading Prison, 1 April 1897

59 Musical people are so absurdly unreasonable. They always want one to be perfectly dumb at the very moment when one is longing to be absolutely deaf.

Oscar Wilde 1854–1900: *An Ideal Husband* (1895)

60 He reminds us how cheap potent music can be.
of the popular pianist Richard Clayderman

Richard Williams: Ned Sherrin *Cutting Edge* (1984); see **Music** 11

Musicians
See also **Music**

> ❝ Please do not shoot the pianist. He is doing his best. ❞
> **Anonymous**

1 The music teacher came twice each week to bridge the awful gap between Dorothy and Chopin.

George Ade 1866–1944: Nat Shapiro (ed.) *An Encyclopedia of Quotations about Music* (1978)

2 There's no need for Peter Pears
To give himself airs.
He has them written
By Benjamin Britten.

Anonymous: a verse from *Punch*; in *Ned Sherrin in his Anecdotage* (1993)

3 I prefer to face the wrath of the police than the wrath of Sir John Barbirolli.
a member of the Hallé orchestra on a speeding charge

Anonymous: Ned Sherrin *Cutting Edge* (1984)

4 *printed notice in an American dancing saloon:*
Please do not shoot the pianist. He is doing his best.

Anonymous: Oscar Wilde *Impressions of America* 'Leadville' (c. 1882–3)

5 A musicologist is a man who can read music but can't hear it.

Thomas Beecham 1879–1961: H. Proctor-Gregg *Beecham Remembered* (1976)

6 No wonder Bob Geldof is such an expert on famine. He's been feeding off 'I Don't Like Mondays' for 30 years.

Russell Brand 1975– : at the Edinburgh Festival, 2006, in *Independent* 26 August 2006

7 Tchaikovsky thought of committing suicide for fear of being discovered as a homosexual, but today, if you are a composer and *not* homosexual, you might as well put a bullet through your head.

Sergei Diaghilev 1872–1929: Vernon Duke *Listen Here!* (1963)

8 Everybody told me you can't get far
On thirty-seven dollars and a Jap guitar.

Steve Earle 1954– : 'Guitar Town'
(1986 song)

9 QUESTION: Mr. Sullivan's music . . . reminds me so much of
dear Baytch [Bach]. Do tell me: what is Baytch doing
just now? Is he still composing?
ANSWER: Just now, as a matter of fact, dear Baytch is by
way of decomposing.

W. S. Gilbert 1836–1911: Hesketh
Pearson *Gilbert and Sullivan* (1947)

10 *after Yehudi Menuhin's violin solo at Anthony Asquith's
memorial service, 1968:*
Never could abide a fiddler.

Rex Harrison 1908–90: remark to
Dirk Bogarde; Dirk Bogarde *A
Particular Friendship* (1989)

11 QUESTION: Do you play the guitar with your teeth?
HENDRIX: No, with my ears.

Jimi Hendrix 1942–70: in
International Times 2–15 February
1968

12 There is no doubt that the first requirement for a composer
is to be dead.

Arthur Honegger 1892–1955: *Je suis
compositeur* (1951)

13 Some cry up Haydn, some Mozart,
Just as the whim bites; for my part
I care not a farthing candle
For either of them, or for Handel.

Charles Lamb 1775–1834: 'Free
Thoughts on Several Eminent
Composers' (1830)

14 I continue to listen gamely to Archie Shepp (who is
wearing a beard now) in the hope that it will one day all
cease to sound like 'Flight of the Bumble Bee' scored for
bagpipes and concrete mixer.

Philip Larkin 1922–85: *All What Jazz*
(1985)

15 ANONYMOUS: Is Ringo the best drummer in the world?
JOHN LENNON: He's not even the best drummer in the band.

John Lennon 1940–80: attributed

16 Leonard Bernstein has been disclosing musical secrets that
have been known for over four hundred years.

Oscar Levant 1906–72: *Memoirs of
an Amnesiac* (1965)

17 In the 1960s, the record companies seemed to sign
anything with long hair; if it was a sheepdog, so what.

Nick Mason 1944– : N. Shaffner *A
Saucerful of Secrets: the Pink Floyd
Odyssey* (1991)

18 I'm told that Saint-Saëns has informed a delighted public
that since the war began he has composed music for the
stage, melodies, an elegy and a piece for the trombone. If
he'd been making shell-cases instead it might have been
all the better for music.

Maurice Ravel 1875–1937: letter to
Jean Marnold, 7 October 1916

19 Suddenly he was a big pop star. He could do whatever he
wanted. Hence vodka, beer, anything . . . He took it all too
far, and boy, he couldn't play guitar. Dave Bowie
reference.
on Sid Vicious

Johnny Rotten 1956– : John Lydon,
with Keith and Kent Zimmerman
Rotten: no Irish, no Blacks, no Dogs
(1994)

20 Ravel refuses the Legion of Honour, but all his music
accepts it.

Erik Satie 1866–1925: Jean Cocteau
Le Discours d'Oxford (1956)

21 *asked how he could play so well when he was loaded:*
I practise when I'm loaded.

Zoot Sims 1925–85: Bill Crow *Jazz
Anecdotes* (1990)

22 I don't have time to sit down and write. When I think of a
melody, I call my answering machine and sing it.

Britney Spears 1981– : in *Observer* 9
January 2005

23 'What do you think of Beethoven?'
'I love him, especially his poems.'

Ringo Starr 1940– : at a press
conference during the Beatles' first
American tour in 1964; Hunter Davies
The Beatles (1985)

24 On matters of intonation and technicalities I am more than a martinet—I am a martinetissimo!

Leopold Stokowski 1882–1977: Nat Shapiro (ed.) *An Encyclopedia of Quotations about Music* (1978)

25 After I die, I shall return to earth as the doorkeeper of a bordello and I won't let one of you in.
to his orchestra during a difficult rehearsal

Arturo Toscanini 1867–1957: Nat Shapiro (ed.) *An Encyclopedia of Quotations about Music* (1978)

26 Comrade Zhdanov is no professional musician. But oh, how well he knows folk song! When he recently visited our Piatnitzky Choir, we asked him: 'Is it true, Comrade Zhdanov, that you know 600 folk songs?' 'No,' he said, 'not 600, but I suppose I do know about 300.' How much better our composers would write if they knew folk songs as Andrei Alexandrovich does!
on the musical expertise of A. A. Zhdanov, Stalin's 'cultural commissar'

Vladimir Zakharov: Alexander Werth *Musical Uproar in Moscow* (1949)

Names

❝I remember your name perfectly; but I just can't think of your face.❞
William Archibald Spooner

1 Can I speak to Mr S. P. Eagle—this is Mr C. O. Hen.
friend's joke on Sam Spiegel's change of name

Anonymous: Natasha Fraser-Cavassoni *Sam Spiegel* (2003)

2 The reason Michael Jackson entitled his album *Bad* was because he couldn't spell *Indescribable*.

Anonymous: in 1987; Nigel Rees (ed.) *Cassell Dictionary of Humorous Quotations* (1999)

3 I never really needed a nickname at school. Although it was bad for me it was much worse for my sister Ophelia.

Ed Balls 1967– : in *Independent* 24 September 2007

4 *of Arianna Stassinopoulos:*
So boring you fall asleep halfway through her name.

Alan Bennett 1934– : attributed; in *Observer* 18 September 1983

5 'You mustn't mention the Shah out loud.' . . . 'We had better call him Marjoribanks, if we want to remember who we mean.'

Robert Byron 1905–41: *The Road to Oxiana* (1937)

6 *fashionable children's names of which Camden disapproved:*
The new names, Free-gift, Reformation, Earth, Dust, Ashes . . . which have lately been given by some to their children.

William Camden 1551–1623: *Remains* (1605)

7 They *will* call me Mrs Pat. I can't stand it. The 'Pat' is the last straw that breaks the Campbell's back.

Mrs Patrick Campbell 1865–1940: attributed

8 *of Alfred Bossom:*
Who is this man whose name is neither one thing nor the other?

Winston Churchill 1874–1965: attributed

9 *nickname for Cecil Beaton:*
Malice in Wonderland.

Jean Cocteau 1889–1963: attributed; Hugo Young in *Guardian* 24 January 2004

10 Rip-Van-With-It.
nickname for Cecil Beaton

Cyril Connolly 1903–74: Hugo Vickers (ed.) *The Unexpurgated Beaton* (2002)

11 One theory is that I was named after the opera and the other that my mum was sitting in her boudoir wondering what to call me and glanced at her Carmen rollers. I prefer the Bizet theory.

Carmen Ejogo: in *Observer* 26 March 2000 'They said what . . . ?'

12 *on J. P. Horrocks-Taylor's slipping Mick English's rugby tackle to score:*
Horrocks went one way, Taylor went the other, and I was left holding his bloody hyphen.

Mick English: in *Sunday Times* 2 September 1990

13 Colin is the sort of name you give your goldfish for a joke.

Colin Firth 1960– : in *Observer* 1 September 2002

14 Every Tom, Dick and Harry is called Arthur.

Sam Goldwyn 1882–1974: to Arthur Hornblow, who was planning to name his son Arthur; Michael Freedland *The Goldwyn Touch* (1986)

15 *Yossarian*—the very sight of the name made him shudder. There were so many esses in it. It just had to be subversive.

Joseph Heller 1923–99: *Catch-22* (1961)

16 It was an odious, alien, distasteful name, that just did not inspire confidence. It was not at all like such clean, crisp, honest, American names as Cathcart, Peckem and Dreedle.

Joseph Heller 1923–99: *Catch-22* (1961)

17 The batsman's Holding, the bowler's Willey.

Brian Johnston 1912–94: attributed; comment at a Test Match as Michael Holding faced Peter Willey

18 In the last Parliament, the House of Commons had more MPs called John than all the women MPs put together.

Tessa Jowell 1947– : in *Independent on Sunday* 14 March 1999 'Quotes'

19 If you should have a boy do not christen him John . . . 'Tis a bad name and goes against a man. If my name had been Edmund I should have been more fortunate.

John Keats 1795–1821: letter to his sister-in-law, 13 January 1820

20 Many people ask what are Beatles? Why Beatles? Ugh, Beatles, how did the name arrive? So we will tell you. It came in a vision—a man appeared on a flaming pie and said unto them 'From this day on you are Beatles with an A'.

John Lennon 1940–80: in *Mersey Beat* 6–20 July 1961

21 One day I'll be famous! I'll be proper and prim;
Go to St James so often I will call it St Jim!

Alan Jay Lerner 1918–86: 'Just You Wait' (*My Fair Lady*, 1956 musical)

22 *pointing out that if she had kept her first husband's name she would still be 'Mrs Wisdom':*
That would have been asking for trouble.

Doris Lessing 1919– : in *Times* 15 July 2000

23 Obadiah Bind-their-kings-in-chains-and-their-nobles-with-links-of-iron.

Lord Macaulay 1800–59: 'The Battle of Naseby' (1824), fictitious author's name

24 No, I'm breaking it in for a friend.
when asked if Groucho were his real name

Groucho Marx 1890–1977: attributed

25 *on why she had named her canary 'Onan':*
Because he spills his seed on the ground.

Dorothy Parker 1893–1967: John Keats *You Might as Well Live*

26 Why should people I have never met, who read me in bed and in the bathtub, think of me as 'Sam'.
insisting that his first name be represented by the initial 'S.' on the title-pages of his books

Samuel ('Sam') Schoenbaum 1927–96: in *Times* 25 April 1996; obituary

27 *of Jeffrey Archer's title:*
Lord Archer of Weston-Super-Mare—the only seaside pier on which Danny La Rue has not performed.

Neil Shand: *Loose Ends* monologue, 1999

28 *wondering why, since he was Irish, he was not O'Sheridan:*
For in truth we owe everybody.

Richard Brinsley Sheridan 1751–1816: Walter Jerrold *Bon-Mots* (1893)

29 I remember your name perfectly; but I just can't think of your face.

William Archibald Spooner 1844–1930: attributed; in *Penguin Dictionary of Quotations* (1960)

30 Bingo Bolger-Baggins a bad name. Let Bingo = Frodo.
on the first draft of The Lord of the Rings

J. R. R. Tolkien 1892–1973: note, c.1938; Humphrey Carpenter *J. R. R. Tolkien* (1977)

31 We do have these extraordinary names . . . When you see the sign 'African Primates Meeting' you expect someone to produce bananas.
address at his retirement service, Cape Town, 23 June 1996

Desmond Tutu 1931– : in *Daily Telegraph* 24 June 1996

32 *on being asked by William Carlos Williams how he had chosen the name 'West':*
Horace Greeley said, 'Go West, young man.' So I did.

Nathanael West 1903–40: Jay Martin *Nathanael West* (1970)

Nature and the Environment

❝ *When the sukebind hangs heavy from the wains.* **❞**
Stella Gibbons

1 I can remember when the air was clean and sex was dirty.

George Burns 1896–1996: attributed, perhaps apocryphal

2 I find it hard to understand why one should look for sermons in stones when the inability to preach is so attractive a feature of stones.

Northrop Frye 1912–91: *The Bush Garden* (1971)

3 Every year, in the fulness o' summer, when the sukebind hangs heavy from the wains . . . 'tes the same. And when the spring comes her hour is upon her again. 'Tes the hand of Nature and we women cannot escape it.

Stella Gibbons 1902–89: *Cold Comfort Farm* (1932)

4 What do we chop, when we chop a tree?
A thousand things that you daily see.
A baby's crib, the poet's chair,
The soap box down in Union Square.
A pipe for Dad, a bat for brother,
An extra broom for dear old mother.

E. Y. Harburg 1898–1981: 'Song of the Woodman' (1936)

5 Man he eat the barracuda,
Barracuda eat the bass
Bass he eat the little flounder,
'Cause the flounder lower class.
Little flounder eat the sardine
That's nature's plan.
Sardine eat the little worm,
Little worm eat man.

E. Y. Harburg 1898–1981: 'For Every Fish' (1957)

6 I find it hard to accept, difficult to swallow, the new term 'ecology' which has come to us . . . It sounds a little too much like being sick.

Stephen Leacock 1869–1944: *The Boy I Left Behind Me* (1947)

7 Worship of nature may be ancient, but seeing nature as cuddlesome, hug-a-bear and too cute for words is strictly a modern fashion.

P. J. O'Rourke 1947– : *Parliament of Whores* (1991)

8 The green belt was a Labour idea and we are determined to build on it.

John Prescott 1938– : attributed by Paddy Ashdown, in *Independent* 22 September 1999; perhaps apocryphal

9 [Richard Nixon is] the kind of politician who would cut down a redwood tree, and then mount the stump and make a speech on conservation.

Adlai Stevenson 1900–65: Fawn M. Brodie *Richard Nixon* (1983)

10 *on the Falklands campaign, 1982:*
It is exciting to have a real crisis on your hands, when you have spent half your political life dealing with humdrum issues like the environment.

Margaret Thatcher 1925– : speech to Scottish Conservative Party conference, 14 May 1982

11 BRICK: Well, they say nature hates a vacuum, Big Daddy.
BIG DADDY: That's what they say, but sometimes I think that a vacuum is a hell of a lot better than some of the stuff that nature replaces it with.

Tennessee Williams 1911–83: *Cat on a Hot Tin Roof* (1955)

Newspapers
See also **Journalism, Headlines**

❝ *I once put 'exclusive' on the weather by mistake.* **❞**
Piers Morgan

1 I read the newspapers avidly. It is my one form of continuous fiction.

Aneurin Bevan 1897–1960: in *Times* 29 March 1960

2 More than one newspaper has been ruined by the brilliant writer in the editor's chair.

Lord Camrose 1879–1954: Leonard Russell et al. *The Pearl of Days: An Intimate Memoir of the Sunday Times* (1972)

3 'I believe that nothing in the newspapers is ever true,' said Madame Phoebus. 'And that is why they are so popular,' added Euphrosyne, 'the taste of the age being decidedly for fiction.'

Benjamin Disraeli 1804–81: *Lothair* (1870)

4 Where it will all end, knows God!
satirizing the style of Time *magazine*

Wolcott Gibbs 1902–58: in *New Yorker* 28 November 1936

5 The witness replied that his leading articles [in *The Observer*] were half-way between a cold bath and a religious exercise, and that this was the place which they occupied, very fitly, in the life of the nation.

A. P. Herbert 1890–1971: *Misleading Cases* (1935)

6 Editor: a person employed by a newspaper, whose business it is to separate the wheat from the chaff, and to see that the chaff is printed.

Elbert Hubbard 1859–1915: *The Roycroft Dictionary* (1914)

7 A newspaper which weighs as much as the *Oxford Dictionary of Quotations* and a very large haddock.
of the Sunday edition of the New York Times

Bernard Levin 1928–2004: *In These Times* (1986)

8 The British Press is always looking for stuff to fill the space between their cartoons.

Bernadette Devlin McAliskey 1947– : comment, 1970

9 You should always believe all you read in the newspapers, as this makes them more interesting.

Rose Macaulay 1881–1958: *A Casual Commentary* (1926)

10 People don't actually read newspapers. They get into them every morning, like a hot bath.

Marshall McLuhan 1911–80: in 1965; Jonathon Green (ed.) *A Dictionary of Contemporary Quotations* (1982)

11 The art of newspaper paragraphing is to stroke a platitude until it purrs like an epigram.

Don Marquis 1878–1937: E. Anthony *O Rare Don Marquis* (1962)

12 When newspapers became solvent they lost a good deal of their old venality, but at the same time they became increasingly cautious, for capital is always timid.

H. L. Mencken 1880–1956: *Minority Report* (1956)

13 Whenever I see a newspaper I think of the poor trees. As trees they provide beauty, shade and shelter. But as paper all they provide is rubbish.

Yehudi Menuhin 1916–99: Jonathon Green (ed.) *Contemporary Quotations* (1982)

14 Exclusives aren't what they used to be. We tend to put 'exclusive' on everything just to annoy other papers. I once put 'exclusive' on the weather by mistake.

Piers Morgan 1965– : in *Independent on Sunday* 14 March 1999 'Quotes'

15 *asked why he had allowed Page 3 to develop:*
I don't know. The editor did it when I was away.

Rupert Murdoch 1931– : in *Guardian* 25 February 1994

16 *on being telephoned by the* Sunday Express *to ask what was his main wish for 1956:*
Not to be telephoned by the *Sunday Express* when I am busy.

Harold Nicolson 1886–1968: diary, 29 December 1955

17 If a newspaper prints a sex crime, it is smut: but when the *New York Times* prints it it is a sociological study.

Adolph S. Ochs 1858–1935: Laurence J. Peter (ed.) *Quotations for our Time* (1977)

18 No self-respecting fish would be wrapped in a Murdoch newspaper.

Mike Royko 1932– : before resigning from the Chicago *Sun-Times* when the paper was sold to Rupert Murdoch in 1984; Karl E. Meyer (ed.) *Pundits, Poets, and Wits* (1990)

19 *of the* Daily Mail*:*
By office boys for office boys.

Lord Salisbury 1830–1903: H. Hamilton Fyfe *Northcliffe, an Intimate Biography* (1930)

20 Ever noticed that no matter what happens in one day, it exactly fits in the newspaper?

Jerry Seinfeld 1954– : in *Mail on Sunday* 11 February 2007

21 The newspapers! Sir, they are the most villainous—licentious—abominable—infernal—Not that I ever read them—No—I make it a rule never to look into a newspaper.

Richard Brinsley Sheridan 1751–1816: *The Critic* (1779)

22 Accuracy to a newspaper is what virtue is to a lady; but a newspaper can always print a retraction.

Adlai Stevenson 1900–65: *The Wit and Wisdom of Adlai Stevenson* (1965)

23 I'm with you on the free press. It's the newspapers I can't stand.

Tom Stoppard 1937– : *Night and Day* (1978)

24 Freedom of the press in Britain means freedom to print such of the proprietor's prejudices as the advertisers don't object to.

Hannen Swaffer 1879–1962: Tom Driberg *Swaff* (1974)

25 It is part of the social mission of every great newspaper to provide a refuge and a home for the largest possible number of salaried eccentrics.

Lord Thomson of Fleet 1894–1976: in *Observer* 22 November 1959 'Sayings of the Week'

26 There are laws to protect the freedom of the press's speech, but none that are worth anything to protect the people from the press.

Mark Twain 1835–1910: 'License of the Press' (1873)

27 *The Beast* stands for strong mutually antagonistic governments everywhere . . . Self-sufficiency at home, self-assertion abroad.

Evelyn Waugh 1903–66: *Scoop* (1938)

28 Newspapers, even, have degenerated. They may now be absolutely relied upon.

Oscar Wilde 1854–1900: *The Decay of Lying* (1891)

New York

66 *A helluva town.* **99**
Betty Comden and Adolph Green

1 New York makes one think of the collapse of civilization, about Sodom and Gomorrah, the end of the world. The end wouldn't come as a surprise here. Many people already bank on it.

Saul Bellow 1915–2005: *Mr Sammler's Planet* (1970)

2 New York, New York,—a helluva town,
The Bronx is up but the Battery's down,
And people ride in a hole in the ground:
New York, New York,—It's a helluva town.

Betty Comden 1917–2006 and **Adolph Green** 1915–2002: 'New York, New York' (1945)

3 Nearly all th' most foolish people in th' counthry an' manny iv th' wisest goes to Noo York. Th' wise people ar-re there because th' foolish wint first. That's th' way th' wise men make a livin'.

Finley Peter Dunne 1867–1936: *Mr. Dooley's Opinions* (1902)

4 Broadway's turning into Coney,
Champagne Charlie's drinking gin.
Old New York is new and phoney—
Give it back to the Indians.

Lorenz Hart 1895–1943: 'Give it back to the Indians' (1940)

5 New York, New York, so good they named it twice.

Gerard Kenny 1947– : 'New York, New York' (1978 song)

6 There are no available men in their thirties in New York. Giuliani had them removed along with the homeless.

Michael Patrick King: *Sex and the City* 'Valley of the Twenty-Something Guys' (1998); spoken by Miranda

7 When people start writing about New York, they tend to go get a thesaurus and find all the synonyms for dysfunctional.

James J. Lack: in *Times* 22 October 2002

8 *sitting in a New York bar in the 1940s:*
Oh, to be back in Hollywood, wishing I was back in New York.

Herman J. Mankiewicz 1897–1953: James Sanders *Celluloid Skyline: New York and the Movies* (2001)

Old Age

See also **Middle Age, Youth**

❝ *To what do I attribute my longevity? Bad luck.* ❞

Quentin Crisp

---

1 If you want to be adored by your peers and have standing ovations wherever you go—live to be over ninety.

George Abbott 1887–1995: in *Times* 2 February 1995; obituary

2 Mr Salteena was an elderly man of 42.

Daisy Ashford 1881–1972: *The Young Visiters* (1919)

3 To me old age is always fifteen years older than I am.

Bernard Baruch 1870–1965: in *Newsweek* 29 August 1955

4 In England, you see, age wipes the slate clean . . . If you live to be ninety in England and can still eat a boiled egg they think you deserve the Nobel Prize.

Alan Bennett 1934– : *An Englishman Abroad* (1989)

5 Here I sit, alone and sixty,
Bald, and fat, and full of sin,
Cold the seat and loud the cistern,
As I read the Harpic tin.

Alan Bennett 1934– : 'Place Names of China' (parody of John Betjeman)

6 *on reaching the age of 100:*
If I'd known I was gonna live this long, I'd have taken better care of myself.

Eubie Blake 1883–1983: in *Observer* 13 February 1983 'Sayings of the Week'; also claimed by Adolph Zukor on reaching 100

7 'You are old, Father William,' the young man said,
'And your hair has become very white;
And yet you incessantly stand on your head—
Do you think, at your age, it is right?'

Lewis Carroll 1832–98: *Alice's Adventures in Wonderland* (1865)

8 I'll tell thee everything I can:
There's little to relate.
I saw an aged, aged man,
A-sitting on a gate.

Lewis Carroll 1832–98: *Through the Looking-Glass* (1872)

9 Old age is the outpatients' department of Purgatory.

Lord Hugh Cecil 1869–1956: John Betjeman, letter to Tom Driberg, 21 July 1976

10 *in his old age Churchill overheard one of two new MPs whisper to the other, 'They say the old man's getting a bit past it':*
And they say the old man's getting deaf as well.

Winston Churchill 1874–1965: K. Halle *The Irrepressible Churchill* (1985)

11 *it was pointed out to the aged Winston Churchill that his fly-button was undone:*
No matter. The dead bird does not leave the nest.

Winston Churchill 1874–1965: Rupert Hart-Davis letter to George Lyttelton, 5 January 1957

12 How foolish to think that one can ever slam the door in the face of age. Much wiser to be polite and gracious and ask him to lunch in advance.

Noël Coward 1899–1973: diary, 3 June 1956

13 To what do I attribute my longevity? Bad luck.

Quentin Crisp 1908–99: in *Spectator* 20 November 1999

14 *approaching his 80th birthday:*
While there's snow on the roof, it doesn't mean the fire
has gone out in the furnace.

John G. Diefenbaker 1895–1979:
attributed, 1991

15 Before I go to meet my Maker,
I want to use the salt left in my shaker.
I want to find out if it's true
The Blue Danube is really blue,
Before I kiss the world goodbye.

Howard Dietz 1896–1983: 'Before I
Kiss the World Goodbye' (1963)

16 Although I am 92, my brain is 30 years old.

Alfred Eisenstaedt 1898–1995: to a
reporter in 1991, in *Life* 24 August
1995

17 As Groucho Marx once said, 'Anyone can get old—all you
have to do is to live long enough.'

Elizabeth II 1926– : speech at her
official 80th birthday lunch, 15 June
2006, in *Independent on Sunday* 18
June 2006

18 Being an old maid is like death by drowning, a really
delightful sensation after you cease to struggle.

Edna Ferber 1887–1968: R. E.
Drennan *Wit's End* (1973)

19 After the age of 80, you seem to be having breakfast every
five minutes.

Christopher Fry 1907–2005:
attributed; in *Spectator* 7 December
2002

20 Methus'lah live nine hundred years,
Methus'lah live nine hundred years
But who calls dat livin'
When no gal'll give in
To no man what's nine hundred years?

Ira Gershwin 1896–1983: 'It Ain't
Necessarily So' (1935)

21 I've got to take under my wing,
Tra la,
A most unattractive old thing,
Tra la,
With a caricature of a face.

W. S. Gilbert 1836–1911: *The
Mikado* (1885)

22 At forty I lost my illusions,
At fifty I lost my hair,
At sixty my hope and teeth were gone,
And my feet were beyond repair.
At eighty life has clipped my claws,
I'm bent and bowed and cracked;
But I can't give up the ghost because
My follies are intact.

E. Y. Harburg 1898–1981:
'Gerontology or Springtime for
Senility' (1965)

23 W'en folks git ole en strucken wid de palsy, dey mus speck
ter be laff'd at.

Joel Chandler Harris 1848–1908:
Nights with Uncle Remus (1883)

24 To my deafness I'm accustomed,
To my dentures I'm resigned,
I can manage my bifocals,
But Oh, how I miss my mind.

Lord Home 1903–95: John G. Murray
*A Gentleman Publisher's
Commonplace Book* (1996)

25 Nobody in Beverly Hills grows old. It's a violation of a city
ordinance.

Bob Hope 1903–2003: attributed; in
Times 24 September 2003

26 I still go up my 44 stairs two at a time, but that is in hopes
of dropping dead at the top.

A. E. Housman 1859–1936: letter to
Laurence Housman, 9 June 1935

27 When I am an old woman I shall wear purple
With a red hat which doesn't go, and doesn't suit me.
And I shall spend my pension on brandy and summer
    gloves
And satin sandals, and say we've got no money for butter.

Jenny Joseph 1932– : 'Warning' (1974)

28 H: We met at nine
   G: We met at eight
   H: I was on time
   G: No, you were late
   H: Ah yes! I remember it well.

Alan Jay Lerner 1918–86: 'I Remember It Well' (1957)

29 The fountain of youth is dull as paint.
Methuselah is my favourite saint.
I've never been so comfortable before.
Oh I'm so glad I'm not young any more.

Alan Jay Lerner 1918–86: 'I'm Glad I'm Not Young Any More' (1957)

30 The thing about getting old is the number of things you
think that you can't say aloud because it would be too
shocking.

Doris Lessing 1919– : in *Times* 15 July 2000

31 In one old people's home they changed the words of the
song to 'When I'm 84' as they considered 64 to be young.
I might do that.

Paul McCartney 1942– : in *Times* 14 October 2006

32 *of an elderly guest:*
Talk about over 70. She can do 8 times more than I can
and reduces me to a pudding of exhaustion.

Nancy Mitford 1904–73: letter 15 October 1953

33 Senescence begins
And middle age ends
The day your descendants
Outnumber your friends.

Ogden Nash 1902–71: 'Crossing the Border' (1964)

34 There's one more terrifying fact about old people: I'm
going to be one soon.

P. J. O'Rourke 1947– : *Parliament of Whores* (1991)

35 When men grow virtuous in their old age, they only make
a sacrifice to God of the devil's leavings.

Alexander Pope 1688–1744: *Miscellanies* (1727) 'Thoughts on Various Subjects'

36 Growing old is like being increasingly penalized for a crime
you haven't committed.

Anthony Powell 1905–2000: *Temporary Kings* (1973)

37 *when his age was contrasted with that of his opponent Walter
Mondale (born 1928):*
I am not going to make age an issue in this campaign. I
am not going to exploit for political purposes my
opponent's youth and inexperience.

Ronald Reagan 1911–2004: television debate, 21 October 1984

38 As I grow older and older,
And totter towards the tomb,
I find that I care less and less
Who goes to bed with whom.

Dorothy L. Sayers 1893–1957: 'That's Why I Never Read Modern Novels'; Janet Hitchman *Such a Strange Lady* (1975)

39 *a final letter to a young correspondent, a year before his death:*
Dear Elise,
Seek younger friends; I am extinct.

George Bernard Shaw 1856–1950: letter, 1949

40 The House of Lords is a perfect eventide home.

Baroness Stocks 1891–1975: *My Commonplace Book* (1970)

41 *to a young diplomat who boasted of his ignorance of whist:*
What a sad old age you are preparing for yourself.

Charles-Maurice de Talleyrand
1754–1838: J. Amédée Pichot
Souvenirs Intimes sur M. de Talleyrand
(1870)

42 *on how he knows he's getting old:*
My children are doing me in history now.

David Trimble 1944– : in *Mail on Sunday* 27 May 2007

43 *on growing old:*
I feel I can talk with more authority, especially when I say, 'I don't know'.
  at the age of 78

Peter Ustinov 1921–2004: interview in *Independent* 28 July 1999

44 One should never make one's début with a scandal. One should reserve that to give an interest to one's old age.

Oscar Wilde 1854–1900: *The Picture of Dorian Gray* (1891)

45 Though well stricken in years the old blister becomes on these occasions as young as he feels, which seems to be about twenty-two.

P. G. Wodehouse 1881–1975: *Uncle Dynamite* (1948)

Opera

❝ *Italian chefs screaming risotto recipes at each other.* ❞
Aristotle Onassis

1 I do not mind what language an opera is sung in so long as it is a language I don't understand.

Edward Appleton 1892–1965: in *Observer* 28 August 1955

2 The opera ain't over 'til the fat lady sings.

Dan Cook: in *Washington Post* 3 June 1978

3 People are wrong when they say that the opera isn't what it used to be. It is what it used to be—that's what's wrong with it.

Noël Coward 1899–1973: *Design for Living* (1933)

4 Opera is when a guy gets stabbed in the back and, instead of bleeding, he sings.

Ed Gardner 1901–63: *Duffy's Tavern* (US radio programme, 1940s)

5 Opera in English is, in the main, just about as sensible as baseball in Italian.

H. L. Mencken 1880–1956: Laurence J. Peter (ed.) *Quotations for our Time* (1977)

6 *view of opera before he met Maria Callas:*
Italian chefs screaming risotto recipes at each other.

Aristotle Onassis 1906–75: Peter Evans *Nemesis: the True Story of Aristotle* (2004)

7 *Parsifal* is the kind of opera that starts at six o'clock. After it has been going three hours, you look at your watch and it says 6.20.

David Randolph 1914– : Nat Shapiro (ed.) *An Encyclopedia of Quotations about Music* (1978)

8 [Gutrune] is the only woman that Siegfried has ever come across who hasn't been his aunt . . . I'm not making this up, you know!

Anna Russell 1911–2006: 'The Ring of the Nibelung'

9 The first act of the three occupied two hours. I enjoyed that in spite of the singing.

Mark Twain 1835–1910: *What is Man?* (1906)

Parents

See also **Children, The Family**

❝ A Jewish man with parents alive is a fifteen-year-old boy. ❞
Philip Roth

1 Money—the one thing that keeps us in touch with our children.

Gyles Brandreth 1948– : in *Times 2* February 2002

2 The authoritarian, didactic, primitive Irish parent is world famous—as is his frequently neurotic, deceitful and anxious child.

Noel Browne 1915–97: in 1973, attributed

3 *to his daughter's date:*
Anything happens to my daughter, I got a .45 and a shovel. I doubt anybody would miss you.

Amy Heckering: *Clueless* (1995 film); spoken by Mel Horowitz (Dan Hedeya)

4 Mom and Pop were just a couple of kids when they got married. He was eighteen, she was sixteen, and I was three.

Billie Holiday 1915–59: *Lady Sings the Blues* (1958) opening words

5 *on hearing a report that his son Charles James Fox was to be married:*
He will be obliged to go to bed at least one night of his life.

Lord Holland 1705–74: Christopher Hobhouse *Fox* (1934)

6 If I'm more of an influence to your son as a rapper than you are as a father . . . you got to look at yourself as a parent.

Ice Cube 1970– : to Mike Sager in *Rolling Stone* 4 October 1990

7 In case it is one of mine.
  patting children in Chelsea on the head as he passed by

Augustus John 1878–1961: Michael Holroyd *Augustus John* (1975)

8 *to Nina Hamnett:*
We have become, Nina, the sort of people our parents warned us about.

Augustus John 1878–1961: attributed; Nigel Rees *Cassell Dictionary of Humorous Quotations* (1999)

9 Fathers don't curse, they disinherit. Mothers curse.

Irma Kurtz: *Malespeak* (1986)

10 *explaining her mother's insistence on taking her own bidet with her when she travelled:*
My poor, dear mother suffers from a bidet-fixe.

Karen Lancaster d. 1964: Osbert Lancaster *With an Eye to the Future* (1967)

11 They fuck you up, your mum and dad.
They may not mean to, but they do.
They fill you with the faults they had
And add some extra, just for you.

Philip Larkin 1922–85: 'This Be The Verse' (1974)

12 Parents should conduct their arguments in quiet, respectful tones, but in a foreign language. You'd be surprised what an inducement that is to the education of children.

Judith Martin 1938– : 'Advice from Miss Manners', column in *Washington Post* 1979–82

13 A Jewish man with parents alive is a fifteen-year-old boy, and will remain a fifteen-year-old boy until *they die*!

Philip Roth 1933– : *Portnoy's Complaint* (1967)

14 I did not throw myself into the struggle for life: I threw my mother into it. I was not a staff to my father's old age: I hung on to his coat tails.

George Bernard Shaw 1856–1950: preface to *The Irrational Knot* (1905)

15 If you must hold yourself up to your children as an object lesson (which is not at all necessary), hold yourself up as a warning and not as an example.

George Bernard Shaw 1856–1950: *Parents and Children* (1914)

16 I wish either my father or my mother, or indeed both of them, as they were in duty both equally bound to it, had minded what they were about when they begot me.

Laurence Sterne 1713–68: *Tristram Shandy* (1759–67)

17 And her mother came too!

Dion Titheradge: title of song (1921)

18 I have four sons and three stepsons. I have learnt what it is like to step on Lego with bare feet.

Fay Weldon 1931– : in *Independent* 6 July 2002

19 In our society . . . mothers go on getting blamed until they're eighty, but shouldn't take it personally.

Katharine Whitehorn 1928– : *Observations* (1970)

Parties

See also **Society and Social Life**

❝ You need an orgy, once in a while. ❞
Ogden Nash

---

1 I've been to a marvellous party,
We didn't start dinner till ten
And young Bobbie Carr
Did a stunt at the bar
With a lot of extraordinary men.

Noël Coward 1899–1973: 'I've been to a Marvellous Party' (1938)

2 You know I hate parties. My idea of hell is a very large party in a cold room, where everybody has to play hockey properly.

Stella Gibbons 1902–89: *Cold Comfort Farm* (1932)

3 At every party there are two kinds of people—those who want to go home and those who don't. The trouble is, they are usually married to each other.

Ann Landers 1918–2002: in *International Herald Tribune* 19 June 1991

4 Home is heaven and orgies are vile,
But you *need* an orgy, once in a while.

Ogden Nash 1902–71: 'Home, 99⁴⁴⁄₁₀₀% Sweet Home' (1935)

5 Unless your life is going well you don't dream of giving a party. Unless you can look in the mirror and see a benign and generous and healthy human being, you shrink from acts of hospitality.

Carol Shields 1935–2003: *Larry's Party* (1997)

6 Gee, what a terrific party. Later on we'll get some fluid and embalm each other.

Neil Simon 1927– : *The Gingerbread Lady* (1970)

7 I made a terrible social gaffe. I went to a Ken and Barbie party dressed as Klaus Barbie.

Arthur Smith 1954– and **Chris England**: *An Evening with Gary Lineker* (1990)

8 An office party is not, as is sometimes supposed, the Managing Director's chance to kiss the tea-girl. It is the tea-girl's chance to kiss the Managing Director.

Katharine Whitehorn 1928– : *Roundabout* (1962) 'The Office Party'

9 Of course I don't want to go to a cocktail party . . . If I wanted to stand around with a load of people I don't know eating bits of cold toast I can get caught shoplifting and go to Holloway.

Victoria Wood 1953– : *Mens Sana in Thingummy Doodah* (1990)

Past and Present

See also **The Future**

❝ We mustn't prejudge the past. ❞

William Whitelaw

1 'The first ten million years were the worst,' said Marvin, 'and the second ten million years, they were the worst too. The third ten million I didn't enjoy at all. After that I went into a bit of a decline.'

Douglas Adams 1952–2001: *Restaurant at the End of the Universe* (1980)

2 Nostalgia isn't what it used to be.

Anonymous: graffito (taken as title of book by Simone Signoret, 1978)

3 The world has turned upside down. The best golfer in the world is black; the best rapper in the world is white; and now there is a war and, guess what, Germany doesn't want to be in it.

Alan Bennett 1934– : diary 2003, in *London Review of Books* 8 January 2004

4 It's not perfect, but to me on balance Right Now is a lot better than the Good Old Days.

Maeve Binchy 1940– : in *Irish Times* 15 November 1997

5 The rule is, jam to-morrow and jam yesterday—but never jam today.

Lewis Carroll 1832–98: *Through the Looking-Glass* (1872)

6 What a Royal Academy,
Too Alma-Tademy,
Practical, mystical,
Over-artistical,
Highly pictorial,
Albert Memorial
Century this has been.

Noël Coward 1899–1973: 'What a Century' (1953)

7 I do not know which makes a man more conservative—to know nothing but the present, or nothing but the past.

John Maynard Keynes 1883–1946: *The End of Laissez-Faire* (1926)

8 Industrial archaeology . . . believes that a thing that doesn't work any more is far more interesting than a thing that still works.

Miles Kington 1941–2008: *Nature Made Ridiculously Simple* (1983)

9 Weren't the eighties grand? Cash grew on trees or, anyway, coca bushes. The rich roamed the land in vast herds hunted by proud, free tribes of investment brokers who lived a simple life in tune with money.

P. J. O'Rourke 1947– : introduction to the second edition of *The Bachelor Home Companion* (1993)

10 They spend their time mostly looking forward to the past.

John Osborne 1929–94: *Look Back in Anger* (1956)

11 There's a million more important things going on in the world today. New countries are being born. They're getting ready to send men to the moon. I just can't get excited about making wax fruit.

Neil Simon 1927– : *Come Blow Your Horn* (1961)

12 It used to be a good hotel, but that proves nothing—I used to be a good boy.

Mark Twain 1835–1910: *The Innocents Abroad* (1869)

13 It is the spirit of the age to believe that any fact, no matter how suspect, is superior to any imaginative exercise, no matter how true.

Gore Vidal 1925– : in *Encounter* December 1967

14 We mustn't prejudge the past.

William Whitelaw 1918–99: in *Times* 2 July 1999; attributed

15 Hindsight is always twenty-twenty.

Billy Wilder 1906–2002: J. R. Columbo *Wit and Wisdom of the Moviemakers* (1979)

People and Personalities

66 *That's the trouble with Anthony—half mad baronet, half beautiful woman.* 99
R. A. Butler

---

1 By appointment: teddy bear to the nation.
heading to profile of John Betjeman

Anonymous: Alan Bell 'Times Profile: Sir John Betjeman' in *Times* 20 September 1982

2 Sorry, girls—he's married.
John Lennon's TV subtitle during the Beatles' appearance on the Ed Sullivan Show, 9 February 1964

Anonymous: Philip Norman *Shout!: the true story of the Beatles* (1981)

3 *of Gordon Brown:*
A man who can lighten a room by leaving it.

Anonymous: Tom Bower *Gordon Brown* (2004)

4 My name is George Nathaniel Curzon,
I am a most superior person.
My face is pink, my hair is sleek,
I dine at Blenheim once a week.
of Lord Curzon

Anonymous: *The Masque of Balliol* (c.1870), in W. G. Hiscock *The Balliol Rhymes* (1939, the last two lines are a later addition); see **People** 31

5 My God, there are two of them!
cry from the gallery of the Glasgow Empire as Mike Winters followed Bernie Winters on to the stage

Anonymous: unattributed

6 *on Vita Sackville-West's appearance in a* tableau vivant:
Dear old Vita, all aqua, no vita, was as heavy as frost.

Margot Asquith 1864–1945: Philip Ziegler *Diana Cooper* (1981)

7 He came to see me this morning—positively reeking of Horlicks.
of Adrian Boult

Thomas Beecham 1879–1961: Ned Sherrin *Cutting Edge* (1984)

8 Byron!—he would be all forgotten today if he had lived to be a florid old gentleman with iron-grey whiskers, writing very long, very able letters to *The Times* about the Repeal of the Corn Laws.

Max Beerbohm 1872–1956: *Zuleika Dobson* (1911)

9 He's always backing into the limelight.
of T. E. Lawrence

Lord Berners 1883–1950: oral tradition

10 The meringue-utan.
of Rosamond Lehmann

Maurice Bowra 1898–1971: in *Spectator* 17 July 1999; attributed

11 *jumping from a second storey window:*
I'm Superjew!

Lenny Bruce 1925–66: in *Observer* 21 August 1966

12 I kind of like ducking questions.

George W. Bush 1946– : in April 2004; Graydon Carter *What We've Lost* (2004)

13 That's the trouble with Anthony—half mad baronet, half beautiful woman.
of Anthony Eden

R. A. Butler 1902–82: attributed

14 He is a person of very *epic* appearance—and has a fine head as far as the outside goes—and wants nothing but taste to make the inside equally attractive.
of Robert Southey

Lord Byron 1788–1824: letter, 30 September 1813

15 *of the vegetarian George Bernard Shaw:*
If you give him meat no woman in London will be safe.

Mrs Patrick Campbell 1865–1940: Frank Harris *Contemporary Portraits* (1919)

16 *after meeting Irving Berlin and supposing him to be Isaiah Berlin:*
Berlin's just like most bureaucrats. Wonderful on paper but disappointing when you meet them face to face.

Winston Churchill 1874–1965: Laurence Bergreen *As Thousands Cheer* (1990)

17 I had to pull him out, otherwise nobody would have believed I didn't push him in.
on rescuing David Frost from drowning

Peter Cook 1937–95: Nigel Rees (ed.) *A Year of Stings and Squelches* (1985)

18 I view this able and energetic man with some detachment. He is loyal to his own career but only incidentally to anything or anyone else.
of Richard Crossman

Hugh Dalton 1887–1962: diary 17 September 1941

19 The laugh in mourning.
of Eamonn de Valera

Oliver St John Gogarty 1878–1957: Ulick O'Connor *Oliver St John Gogarty* (1964)

20 Peter Mandelson is someone who can skulk in broad daylight.

Simon Hoggart 1946– : in *Guardian* 10 July 1998

21 I'd rather be Frank Capra than God. If there is a Frank Capra.

Garson Kanin 1912–99: in *Times* 16 March 1999; attributed

22 It was like watching someone organize her own immortality. Every phrase and gesture was studied. Now and again, when she said something a little out of the ordinary, she wrote it down herself in a notebook.
of Virginia Woolf

Harold Laski 1893–1950: letter to Oliver Wendell Holmes, 30 November 1930

23 He was the chilli to Paul's jam, the knuckle to his duster, the pole to his lap-dancer, the 'sod off' to his 'nice-to-meet-you', the hallucinogenic icing to Paul's birthday cake.
on John Lennon

Roger McGough 1937– : *Said and Done* (2005)

24 Many people see Eva Peron as either a saint or the incarnation of Satan. That means I can definitely identify with her.

Madonna 1958– : in *Newsweek* 5 February 1996

25 There were three things that Chico was always on—a phone, a horse or a broad.

Groucho Marx 1890–1977: Ned Sherrin *Cutting Edge* (1984)

26 Nothing ever made me more doubtful of T. E. Lawrence's genuineness than that he so heartily trusted two persons whom I knew to be bogus.

W. Somerset Maugham 1874–1965: *A Writer's Notebook* (1949) written in 1941

27 *asked if she really had nothing on in the* [calendar] *photograph:*
I had the radio on.

Marilyn Monroe 1926–62: in *Time* 11 August 1952

28 The triumph of sugar over diabetes.
of J. M. Barrie

George Jean Nathan 1882–1958: Robin May *The Wit of the Theatre* (1969)

29 Oh, that Bernadette Shaw! What a chatterbox! Nags away from arsehole to breakfast-time but never sees what's staring her in the face.

Peter Nichols 1927– : *Privates on Parade* (1977)

30 A big cat detained briefly in a poodle parlour, sharpening her claws on the velvet.
of Lady Thatcher in the House of Lords

Matthew Parris 1949– : *Look Behind You!* (1993)

31 My name is Mandy: Peter B.
I'm back in charge—don't mess with me.
My cheeks are drawn, my face is bony,
The line I take comes straight from Tony.

Matthew Parris 1949– : in *Times* 21 October 1999; see **People** 4

32 An elderly fallen angel travelling incognito.
of André Gide

Peter Quennell 1905– : *The Sign of the Fish* (1960)

33 Any man who hates dogs and babies can't be all bad.
of W. C. Fields, and often attributed to him

Leo Rosten 1908–97: speech at Masquers' Club dinner, 16 February 1939

34 Through it all, I have remained consistently and nauseatingly adorable. In fact, I have been known to cause diabetes.

Meg Ryan 1961– : at Women in Hollywood luncheon, 1999

35 He [Macaulay] is like a book in breeches.

Sydney Smith 1771–1845: Lady Holland *Memoir* (1855)

36 Daniel Webster struck me much like a steam-engine in trousers.

Sydney Smith 1771–1845: Lady Holland *Memoir* (1855)

37 That great Cham of literature, Samuel Johnson.

Tobias Smollett 1721–71: letter to John Wilkes, 16 March 1759

38 I can't say whether I see myself as a comedian, a singer or an entertainer. I think I'm a plumber.

Vivian Stanshall 1943–95: L. Randall and C. Welch *Ginger Geezer: the life of Vivian Stanshall* (2002)

39 Her conception of God was certainly not orthodox. She felt towards Him as she might have felt towards a glorified sanitary engineer; and in some of her speculations she seems hardly to distinguish between the Deity and the Drains.
of Florence Nightingale

Lytton Strachey 1880–1932: *Eminent Victorians* (1918)

40 [Charles Laughton] walks top-heavily, like a salmon standing on its tail.

Kenneth Tynan 1927–80: *Profiles* (ed. Kathleen Tynan, 1989)

41 Forty years ago he was Slightly in *Peter Pan,* and you might say that he has been wholly in *Peter Pan* ever since.
of Noël Coward

Kenneth Tynan 1927–80: *Curtains* (1961)

42 A triumph of the embalmer's art.
of Ronald Reagan

Gore Vidal 1925– : in *Observer* 26 April 1981

43 Of course, I believe in the Devil. How otherwise would I account for the existence of Lord Beaverbrook?

Evelyn Waugh 1903–66: L. Gourlay *The Beaverbrook I Knew* (1984)

44 *to a gentleman who had accosted him in the street saying, 'Mr Jones, I believe?':*
If you believe that, you'll believe anything.
George Jones RA (1786–1869), painter of military subjects, bore a striking resemblance to Wellington

Duke of Wellington 1769–1852: Elizabeth Longford *Pillar of State* (1972)

45 The only Greek Tragedy I know.
of Spyros Skouras, Head of Fox Studios

Billy Wilder 1906–2002: attributed, perhaps apocryphal

46 She is so odd a blend of Little Nell and Lady Macbeth. It is not so much the familiar phenomenon of a hand of steel in a velvet glove as a lacy sleeve with a bottle of vitriol concealed in its folds.
of Dorothy Parker

Alexander Woollcott 1887–1943: *While Rome Burns* (1934)

Peoples See **Countries and Peoples**

Personalities See **People and Personalities**

Philosophy

66 *Apart from the known and the unknown, what else is there?* 99
Harold Pinter

1 *intervening at a New York party between Mike Tyson and Naomi Campbell:*
TYSON: Do you know who the f— I am? I'm the heavyweight champion of the world.
AYER: And I am the former Wykeham Professor of Logic. We are both pre-eminent in our field. I suggest we talk about this like rational men.

A. J. Ayer 1910–89: Ben Rogers *A. J. Ayer: a Life* (1999)

2 I have tried too in my time to be a philosopher; but, I don't know how, cheerfulness was always breaking in.

Oliver Edwards 1711–91: James Boswell *Life of Samuel Johnson* (1934 ed.) 17 April 1778

3 The philosopher is like a mountaineer who has with difficulty climbed a mountain for the sake of the sunrise, and arriving at the top finds only fog . . . He must be an honest man if he doesn't tell you that the spectacle was stupendous.

W. Somerset Maugham 1874–1965: *A Writer's Notebook* (1949) written in 1896

4 Philosophy consists very largely of one philosopher arguing that all others are jackasses. He usually proves it, and I should add that he usually proves that he is one himself.

H. L. Mencken 1880–1956: *Minority Report* (1956)

5 I like your playing very much.
to Jean-Paul Sartre

Charlie Parker 1920–55: John Szwed *So What: the life of Miles Davis* (2002)

6 Apart from the known and the unknown, what else is there?

Harold Pinter 1930–2008: *The Homecoming* (1965)

7 Sometimes I sits and thinks, and then again I just sits.

Punch 1841–1992: vol. 131 (1906)

8 My German engineer, I think is a fool. He thinks nothing empirical is Knowable—I asked him to admit that there was not a rhinoceros in the room, but he wouldn't.
of Wittgenstein

Bertrand Russell 1872–1970: letter to Lady Ottoline Morrell, November 1911

9 *on the speaker's choice of subject at university:*
Almost everyone who didn't know what to do, did philosophy. Well, that's logical.

Tom Stoppard 1937– : *Albert's Bridge* (1969)

10 The safest general characterization of the European philosophical tradition is that it consists of a series of footnotes to Plato.

Alfred North Whitehead 1861–1947: *Process and Reality* (1929)

11 What is your aim in philosophy?—To show the fly the way out of the fly-bottle.

Ludwig Wittgenstein 1889–1951: *Philosophische Untersuchungen* (1953)

12 You would not like Nietzsche, sir. He is fundamentally unsound.

P. G. Wodehouse 1881–1975: *My Man Jeeves* (1919)

Places

See also **America, Countries, England, Ireland, Scotland, Wales**

66 *Addresses are given to us to conceal our whereabouts.* 99
Saki

1 He was glued to Soho, a fairly common but chronic attachment some of us formed. There is no known cure for it except the road to Golders Green.

Jeffrey Bernard 1932–97: in *The Spectator* 8 March 1986

2 For Cambridge people rarely smile,
Being urban, squat, and packed with guile.

Rupert Brooke 1887–1915: 'The Old Vicarage, Grantchester' (1915)

3 I had forgotten just how flat and empty it [middle America] is. Stand on two phone books almost anywhere in Iowa and you get a view.

Bill Bryson 1951– : *The Lost Continent* (1989)

4 *of Herat:*
Here at last is Asia without an inferiority complex.

Robert Byron 1905–41: *The Road to Oxiana* (1937)

5 BASIL: May I ask what you were hoping to see out of a Torquay bedroom window? Sydney Opera House, perhaps? The Hanging Gardens of Babylon? Herds of wildebeeste sweeping majestically . . .

John Cleese 1939– and **Connie Booth**: *Fawlty Towers* (1979) 'Communication Problems'

6 Very flat, Norfolk.

Noël Coward 1899–1973: *Private Lives* (1930)

7 In Manhattan, every flat surface is a potential stage and every inattentive waiter an unemployed, possibly unemployable, actor.

Quentin Crisp 1908–99: 'Love Lies Bleeding' (Channel 4 TV), 6 August 1991; Nigel Rees (ed.) *Cassell Dictionary of Humorous Quotations* (1999)

8 Kent, sir—everybody knows Kent—apples, cherries, hops, and women.

Charles Dickens 1812–70: *Pickwick Papers* (1837)

9 They used to say that Cambridge was the first stopping place for the wind that swept down from the Urals: in the thirties that was as true of the politics as the weather.

Stephen Fry 1957– : *The Liar* (1991)

10 The Pacific Ocean was a body of water surrounded on all sides by elephantiasis and other dread diseases.

Joseph Heller 1923–99: *Catch-22* (1961)

11 Broadbosomed, bold, becalm'd, benign
Lies Balham foursquare on the Northern Line.
Matched by no marvel save in Eastern scene,
A rose-red city half as gold as green.

Frank Muir 1920–98 and **Denis Norden** 1922– : 'Balham—Gateway to the South' *Third Division* (BBC Third Programme, 1948); Nigel Rees (ed.) *Cassell Dictionary of Humorous Quotations* (1999)

12 The lush pastrami beds of the West Forties knew him not.

S. J. Perelman 1904–79: 'The Swirling Cape and the Low Bow'

13 Addresses are given to us to conceal our whereabouts.

Saki 1870–1916: *Reginald in Russia* (1910)

14 Wensleydale lies between Tuesleydale and Thursleydale.

Arthur Smith 1954– : attributed

Poetry
See also **Literature, Poets, Writers and Writing**

❝ *I'd as soon write free verse as play tennis with the net down.* ❞
Robert Frost

1 There was a young man called MacNabbiter
Who had an organ of prodigious diameter.
But it was not the size
That gave girls the surprise,
'Twas his rhythm—Iambic Pentameter.

Anonymous: in *Ned Sherrin in his Anecdotage* (1993)

2 There was a young man from Peru
Whose limericks stopped at line two.

Anonymous: Harry Mathews and Alastair Brotchie (eds) *Oulipo Compendium* (1998)

3 Poetry is the only art people haven't yet learnt to consume like soup.

W. H. Auden 1907–73: in *New York Times* 1960

4 I have but with some difficulty *not* added any more to this snake of a poem [*The Giaour*]—which has been lengthening its rattles every month.

Lord Byron 1788–1824: letter 26 August 1813

5 'I can repeat poetry as well as other folk if it comes to that—' 'Oh, it needn't come to that!' Alice hastily said.

Lewis Carroll 1832–98: *Through the Looking-Glass* (1872)

6 'By God,' quod he, 'for pleynly, at a word,
Thy drasty rymyng is nat worth a toord!'

Geoffrey Chaucer c.1343–1400: *The Canterbury Tales* 'Sir Thopas'

7 Sometimes poetry is emotion recollected in a highly emotional state.

Wendy Cope 1945– : 'An Argument with Wordsworth' (1992)

8 *Laman Blanchard, a young poet, had submitted some verses entitled 'Orient Pearls at Random Strung' to* Household Words:
Dear Blanchard, too much string—Yours. C.D.

Charles Dickens 1812–70: Frederick Locker-Lampson *My Confidences* (1896)

9 So poetry, which is in Oxford made
An art, in London only is a trade.

John Dryden 1631–1700: 'Prologue to the University of Oxon . . . at the Acting of *The Silent Woman*' (1673)

10 Immature poets imitate; mature poets steal.

T. S. Eliot 1888–1965: *The Sacred Wood* (1920) 'Philip Massinger'

11 I'd as soon write free verse as play tennis with the net down.

Robert Frost 1874–1963: Edward Lathem *Interviews with Robert Frost* (1966)

12 There are the women whose husbands I meet on aeroplanes
Who close their briefcases and ask, 'What are *you* in?'
I look in their eyes, I tell them I am in poetry . . . .

Donald Hall 1928– : 'To a Waterfowl' (1971)

13 I did not begin to write poetry in earnest until the really emotional part of my life was over; and my poetry, so far as I could make out, sprang chiefly from physical conditions, such as a relaxed sore throat during my most prolific period.

A. E. Housman 1859–1936: letter, 5 February 1933

14 Mr Stone's hexameters are verses of no sort, but prose in ribands.

A. E. Housman 1859–1936: in *Classical Review* 1899

15 The notion of expressing sentiments in short lines having similar sounds at their ends seems as remote as mangoes on the moon.

Philip Larkin 1922–85: letter to Barbara Pym, 22 January 1975

16 Writing a book of poetry is like dropping a rose petal down the Grand Canyon and waiting for the echo.

Don Marquis 1878–1937: E. Anthony *O Rare Don Marquis* (1962)

17 My favourite poem is the one that starts 'Thirty days hath September' because it actually tells you something.

Groucho Marx 1890–1977: Ned Sherrin *Cutting Edge* (1984); attributed

18 All that is not prose is verse; and all that is not verse is prose.

Molière 1622–73: *Le Bourgeois Gentilhomme* (1671)

19 M. JOURDAIN: What? when I say: 'Nicole, bring me my slippers, and give me my night-cap,' is that prose?
PHILOSOPHY TEACHER: Yes, Sir.
M. JOURDAIN: Good heavens! For more than forty years I have been speaking prose without knowing it.

Molière 1622–73: *Le Bourgeois Gentilhomme* (1671)

20 And he, whose fustian's so sublimely bad,
It is not poetry, but prose run mad.

Alexander Pope 1688–1744: 'An Epistle to Dr Arbuthnot' (1735)

21 Of all the literary scenes
Saddest this sight to me:
The graves of little magazines
Who died to make verse free.

Keith Preston 1884–1927: 'The Liberators'

22 I picture him as short and tan.
We'd meet, perhaps, in Hindustan.
I'd say, with admirable *élan*,
'Ah, Anantanarayanan—'.

John Updike 1932–2009: 'I Missed His Book, But I Read His Name' (1964)

23 All bad poetry springs from genuine feeling.

Oscar Wilde 1854–1900: 'The Critic as Artist' (1891)

24 Peotry is sissy stuff that rhymes. Weedy people sa la and fie and swoon when they see a bunch of daffodils.

Geoffrey Willans 1911–58 and **Ronald Searle** 1920– : *Down with Skool!* (1953)

Poets

See also **Poetry**

❝ *They're mostly wicked as a ginless tonic*
And wild as pension plans. ❞
Wendy Cope

1 How thankful we ought to be that Wordsworth was only a poet and not a musician. Fancy a symphony by Wordsworth! Fancy having to sit it out! And fancy what it would have been if he had written fugues!

Samuel Butler 1835–1902: *Notebooks* (1912)

2 The Edinburgh praises Jack Keats or Ketch or whatever his names are;—why his is the Onanism of poetry.

Lord Byron 1788–1824: letter to his publisher John Murray, 4 November 1820

3 Even the greatest poets need something to cling to. Keats had Beauty; Milton had God. T. S. Eliot's standby was Worry.

John Carey 1934– : in *Sunday Times* 25 September 1988

4 It is hard to be a poet maudit when you have a good tan.

Leonard Cohen 1934– : Ira B. Nadel *Various Positions: a life of Leonard Cohen* (1996)

5 I used to think all poets were Byronic —
Mad, bad and dangerous to know.
And then I met a few. Yes it's ironic —
I used to think all poets were Byronic.
They're mostly wicked as a ginless tonic
And wild as pension plans.

Wendy Cope 1945– : 'Triolet' (1986)

6 *the young Stephen Spender had told Eliot of his wish to become a poet:*
I can understand your wanting to write poems, but I don't quite know what you mean by 'being a poet' . . .

T. S. Eliot 1888–1965: Stephen Spender *World within World* (1951)

7 Osbert was wonderful, as you would expect, and Edith, of course, but then we had this rather lugubrious man in a suit, and he read a poem . . . I think it was called The Desert. And first the girls got the giggles and then I did and then even the King.
   of an evening at Windsor during the war, arranged by Osbert Sitwell, at which T. S. Eliot read from 'The Waste Land' to the King and Queen and the Princesses

Queen Elizabeth, the Queen Mother 1900–2002: private conversation, reported in *Spectator* 30 June 1990

8 What is a modern poet's fate?
To write his thoughts upon a slate;
The critic spits on what is done,
Gives it a wipe—and all is gone.

Thomas Hood 1799–1845: 'A Joke', in Hallam Tennyson *Alfred Lord Tennyson* (1897); not found in Hood's *Complete Works*

9 *a nineteenth-century headmaster of Eton:*
I wish Shelley had been at Harrow.

James John Hornby 1826–1909: Henry S. Salt *Percy Bysshe Shelley* (1896)

10 In barrenness, at any rate, I hold a high place among English poets, excelling even Gray.

A. E. Housman 1859–1936: letter 28 February 1910

11 Dr Donne's verses are like the peace of God; they pass all understanding.

James I 1566–1625: remark recorded by Archdeacon Plume (1630–1704)

12 *on the relative merits of two minor poets:*
Sir, there is no settling the point of precedency between a
louse and a flea.

Samuel Johnson 1709–84: James
Boswell *Life of Samuel Johnson*
(1791) 1783

13 We had the old crow over at Hull recently, looking like a
Christmas present from Easter Island.
of Ted Hughes

Philip Larkin 1922–85: letter, 1975

14 *on being asked by Stephen Spender in the 1930s how best a
poet could serve the Communist cause:*
Go to Spain and get killed. The movement needs a Byron.

Harry Pollitt 1890–1960: Frank
Johnson *Out of Order* (1982);
attributed, perhaps apocryphal

15 While pensive poets painful vigils keep,
Sleepless themselves, to give their readers sleep.

Alexander Pope 1688–1744: *The
Dunciad* (1742)

16 Sir, I admit your gen'ral rule
That every poet is a fool:
But you yourself may serve to show it,
That every fool is not a poet.

Alexander Pope 1688–1744:
'Epigram from the French' (1732)

17 For years a secret shame destroyed my peace—
I'd not read Eliot, Auden or MacNeice.
But then I had a thought that brought me hope—
Neither had Chaucer, Shakespeare, Milton, Pope.

Justin Richardson: 'Take Heart,
Illiterates' (1966)

18 I made my then famous declaration (among 100 people) 'I
am a Socialist, an Atheist and a Vegetarian' (ergo, a true
Shelleyan), whereupon two ladies who had been
palpitating with enthusiasm for Shelley under the
impression that he was a devout Anglican, resigned on the
spot.

George Bernard Shaw 1856–1950:
letter 1 March 1908

19 Life's a curse, love's a blight, God's a blaggard, cherry
blossom is quite nice.
on A. E. Housman

Tom Stoppard 1937– : *The Invention
of Love* (1997)

20 I may as well tell you, here and now, that if you are going
about the place thinking things pretty, you will never
make a modern poet. Be poignant, man, be poignant!

P. G. Wodehouse 1881–1975: *The
Small Bachelor* (1927)

Political Parties

**❝The Labour Party is going around stirring
up apathy.❞**
William Whitelaw

1 I realize I am about as welcome in the Tory party as
Banquo's ghost.

Jonathan Aitken 1942– : in *Sunday
Times* 15 February 2004

2 CHILD: Mamma, are Tories born wicked, or do they grow
   wicked afterwards?
MOTHER: They are born wicked, and grow worse.

Anonymous: G. W. E. Russell
Collections and Recollections (1898)

3 Don't be stupid, be a smarty,
Come and join the Nazi Party.

Mel Brooks 1926– : 'Springtime for
Hitler', lyric from *The Producers* (2001
musical)

4 A liberal is a man who leaves the room before the fight
begins.

Heywood Broun 1888–1939: R. E.
Drennan *Wit's End* (1973)

5 'A sound Conservative government,' said Taper, musingly. 'I understand: Tory men and Whig measures.'

Benjamin Disraeli 1804–81: *Coningsby* (1844)

6 The right hon. Gentleman caught the Whigs bathing, and walked away with their clothes.
on Sir Robert Peel's abandoning protection in favour of free trade, traditionally the policy of the [Whig] *Opposition*

Benjamin Disraeli 1804–81: speech, House of Commons 28 February 1845

7 I never dared be radical when young
For fear it would make me conservative when old.

Robert Frost 1874–1963: 'Precaution' (1936)

8 I often think it's comical
How Nature always does contrive
That every boy and every gal,
That's born into the world alive,
Is either a little Liberal,
Or else a little Conservative!

W. S. Gilbert 1836–1911: *Iolanthe* (1882)

9 Conservatives do not believe that the political struggle is the most important thing in life . . . The simplest of them prefer fox-hunting—the wisest religion.

Lord Hailsham 1907–2001: *The Case for Conservatism* (1947)

10 *at a photocall when Lady Thatcher said to him 'You should be on my right':*
That would be difficult.

Edward Heath 1916–2005: in *Times* 24 April 1999 'Quotes of the Week'

11 Testators would do well to provide some indication of the particular Liberal Party which they have in mind, such as a telephone number or a Christian name.

A. P. Herbert 1890–1971: *Misleading Cases* (1935)

12 The Tory Party only panics in a crisis.

Iain Macleod 1913–70: attributed

13 *on privatization:*
First of all the Georgian silver goes, and then all that nice furniture that used to be in the saloon. Then the Canalettos go.

Harold Macmillan 1894–1986: speech to the Tory Reform Group, 8 November 1985

14 Labour is led by an upper-class public school man, the Tories by a self-made grammar school lass who worships her creator, though she is democratic enough to talk down to anyone.

Austin Mitchell 1934– : *Westminster Man* (1982)

15 I have only one firm belief about the American political system, and that is this: God is a Republican and Santa Claus is a Democrat.

P. J. O'Rourke 1947– : *Parliament of Whores* (1991)

16 Having committed political suicide, the Conservative Party is now living to regret it.

Chris Patten 1944– : attributed, 2003; the remark was subsequently considered for a Plain English Foot in Mouth Award

17 Tory and Whig in turns shall be my host,
I taste no politics in boiled and roast.

Sydney Smith 1771–1845: letter to John Murray, November 1834

18 I like a lot of Republicans . . . Indeed, there are some I would trust with anything—anything, that is, except public office.

Adlai Stevenson 1900–65: in *New York Times* 15 August 1952

19 The Labour Party is going around stirring up apathy.

William Whitelaw 1918–99: recalled by Alan Watkins as a characteristic 'Willieism', in *Observer* 1 May 1983

20 The average footslogger in the New South Wales Right . . . generally speaking carries a dagger in one hand and a Bible in the other and doesn't put either to really elegant use.

Neville Wran 1926– : in 1973; Michael Gordon *A Question of Leadership* (1993)

Politicians

See also **People and Personalities, Politics, Presidents, Prime Ministers**

66 *I never saw so many shocking bad hats in my life.* 99
Duke of Wellington

1 Dalton McGuinty: He's an evil reptilian kitten-eater from another planet.
   Canadian Conservative press release attacking the Liberal leader (now premier) during September 2003 Ontario election campaign

Anonymous: in *London Free Press News* 13 September 2003

2 Here lieth Robin Crookback, unjustly reckoned
A Richard the Third, he was Judas the Second.

Anonymous: contemporary verse on Robert Cecil's death; P. M. Handover *The Second Cecil* (1959)

3 In good King Charles's golden days,
When loyalty no harm meant;
A furious High-Churchman I was,
And so I gained preferment.
Unto my flock I daily preached,
Kings are by God appointed,
And damned are those who dare resist,
Or touch the Lord's Anointed.
And this is law, I will maintain,
Unto my dying day, Sir,
That whatsoever King shall reign,
I will be the Vicar of Bray, sir!

Anonymous: *British Musical Miscellany* (1734) 'The Vicar of Bray'

4 They [parliament] are a lot of hard-faced men who look as if they had done very well out of the war.

Stanley Baldwin 1867–1947: J. M. Keynes *Economic Consequences of the Peace* (1919)

5 Beaverbrook is so pleased to be in the Government that he is like the town tart who has finally married the Mayor!

Beverley Baxter 1891–1964: Chips Channon diary 12 June 1940

6 I am the very master of the multipurpose metaphor,
I put them into speeches which I always feel the better for.
The speed of my delivery is totally vehicular,
I'm burning with a passion about nothing in particular.
I'm well acquainted too with matters technological,
I'm able to explain myself in phrases tautological.
My language is poetical and full of hidden promises . . .
It's like the raging torrent of a thousand Dylan Thomases.

Alistair Beaton: 'I am the very Model . . . ', sung by Pooh-Bach (*Minister for everything else. Formerly Neil Kinnock*) in Ned Sherrin and Alistair Beaton *The Metropolitan Mikado* (1985)

7 Always threatening resignation, he never signed off.
   of Lord Derby

Lord Beaverbrook 1879–1964: *Men and Power* (1956)

8 Sir! you have disappointed us!
We had intended you to be
The next Prime Minister but three:
The stocks were sold; the Press was squared;
The Middle Class was quite prepared.
But as it is! . . . My language fails!
Go out and govern New South Wales!

Hilaire Belloc 1870–1953: 'Lord Lundy' (1907)

9 I am not going to spend any time whatsoever in attacking the Foreign Secretary . . . If we complain about the tune, there is no reason to attack the monkey when the organ grinder is present.

Aneurin Bevan 1897–1960: during a debate on the Suez crisis, House of Commons 16 May 1957

10 The right kind of leader for the Labour Party . . . a desiccated calculating machine.
generally taken as referring to Hugh Gaitskell, although Bevan specifically denied it in an interview with Robin Day on 28 April 1959

Aneurin Bevan 1897–1960: Michael Foot *Aneurin Bevan* (1973) vol. 2

11 *Attlee is said to have remarked that Herbert Morrison was his own worst enemy:*
Not while I'm alive he ain't.

Ernest Bevin 1881–1951: Paul Johnson (ed.) *The Oxford Book of Political Anecdotes* (1986), introduction; also attributed to Bevin of Aneurin Bevan

12 *of David Cameron as Conservative Leader:*
Cameron's actually a serious threat to me. He does Tony Blair much better than I do.

Rory Bremner 1961– : attributed

13 *of the popularity of Margaret Thatcher:*
The further you got from Britain, the more admired you found she was.

James Callaghan 1912–2005: in *Spectator* 1 December 1990

14 QUESTION: What are the desirable qualifications for any young man who wishes to become a politician?
MR CHURCHILL: It is the ability to foretell what is going to happen tomorrow, next week, next month, and next year. And to have the ability afterwards to explain why it didn't happen.

Winston Churchill 1874–1965: B. Adler *Churchill Wit* (1965)

15 There but for the grace of God, goes God.
of Stafford Cripps

Winston Churchill 1874–1965: P. Brendon *Churchill* (1984)

16 a politician is an arse upon
which everyone has sat except a man.

e. e. cummings 1894–1962: *1 x 1* (1944)

17 It is not necessary that every time he rises he should give his famous imitation of a semi-house-trained polecat.
of Norman Tebbit

Michael Foot 1913– : speech in the House of Commons 2 March 1978

18 *on being asked immediately after the Munich crisis if he were not worn out by the late nights:*
No, not exactly. But it spoils one's eye for the high birds.

Lord Halifax 1881–1959: Paul Johnson (ed.) *The Oxford Book of Political Anecdotes* (1986)

19 That's Lazarus with a triple bypass.
asked if he thought he could regain leadership of his party

John Howard 1939– : at a press conference, 9 May 1989; David Barnett *John Howard: Prime Minister* (1997)

20 A stable or a zoo is better, at least there you have a donkey that carries a load and a cow that provides milk.
view of her fellow members of the Afghan parliament

Malalai Joya 1978– : in *Independent* 22 May 2007

21 *having been dissuaded from writing a story which would have been soundly based:*
I decided that for Peter Mandelson the truth was like a second home: he didn't live there all the time.

Trevor Kavanagh 1943– : in *Times* 7 May 2003

22 *on the calibre of MPs:*
In Victorian and Edwardian times, the cleverest people went into politics. Now they go to Goldman Sachs.

Kelvin Mackenzie 1946– : in *Observer* 16 January 2005

23 did you ever
notice that when
a politician
does get an idea
he usually
gets it all wrong.

Don Marquis 1878–1937: *archys life of mehitabel* (1933) 'archygrams'

24 He had the geniality of the politician who for years has gone out of his way to be cordial with everyone he meets.

W. Somerset Maugham 1874–1965: *A Writer's Notebook* (1949) written in 1938

25 If I saw Mr Haughey buried at midnight at a crossroads, with a stake driven through his heart—politically speaking—I should continue to wear a clove of garlic round my neck, just in case.

Conor Cruise O'Brien 1917–2008: in *Observer* 10 October 1982

26 DEMOSTHENES: The Athenians will kill thee, Phocion, should they go crazy.
PHOCION: But they will kill thee, should they come to their senses.

Phocion c.402–317 BC: Plutarch *Life of Phocion and Cato the Younger* (Loeb ed., 1919)

27 Gordon Brown is from Mars, David Cameron is from Venus.

Andrew Rawnsley 1962– : in *Observer* 19 November 2006

28 He may be a son of a bitch, but he's our son of a bitch.
on President Somoza of Nicaragua, 1938

Franklin D. Roosevelt 1882–1945: Jonathon Green *The Book of Political Quotes* (1982)

29 *on deciding to run for Governor of California:*
The most difficult decision I've ever made in my entire life, except for the one in 1978 when I decided to get a bikini wax.

Arnold Schwarzenegger 1947– : on the NBC TV *Tonight Show* 6 August 2003

30 He didn't inhale, he didn't insert. He won't invade.
on Bill Clinton and Kosovo

Neil Shand: *Loose Ends* monologue, 1999

31 *explaining to his fellow columnist Simon Hoggart why he avoided meeting MPs:*
If I knew them, it might spoil the purity of my hatred.

Norman Shrapnel 1912–2004: in *Guardian* 3 February 2004

32 A politician is a man who understands government, and it takes a politician to run a government. A statesman is a politician who's been dead 10 or 15 years.

Harry S. Truman 1884–1972: in *New York World Telegram and Sun* 12 April 1958

33 I never saw so many shocking bad hats in my life.
on seeing the first Reformed Parliament

Duke of Wellington 1769–1852: W. Fraser *Words on Wellington* (1889)

34 If the country doesn't go to the dogs or the Radicals, we shall have you Prime Minister, some day.

Oscar Wilde 1854–1900: *An Ideal Husband* (1895)

Politics

See also **Democracy, Diplomacy, Government, Presidents, Prime Ministers**

66 *If voting changed anything they'd abolish it.* **99**

Ken Livingstone

1 Being an MP is the sort of job all working-class parents want for their children—clean, indoors and no heavy lifting.

2 When the political columnists say 'Every thinking man' they mean themselves, and when candidates appeal to 'Every intelligent voter' they mean everybody who is going to vote for them.

3 Practical politics consists in ignoring facts.

4 *annotation to a ministerial brief, said to have been read out inadvertently in the House of Lords:*
This is a rotten argument, but it should be good enough for their lordships on a hot summer afternoon.

5 *Je suis Marxiste—tendance Groucho.*
I am a Marxist—of the Groucho tendency.

6 [The War Office kept three sets of figures:] one to mislead the public, another to mislead the Cabinet, and the third to mislead itself.

7 From politics, it was an easy step to silence.

8 There are three classes which need sanctuary more than others—birds, wild flowers, and Prime Ministers.

9 Vote for the man who promises least; he'll be the least disappointing.

10 Damn it all, you can't have the crown of thorns *and* the thirty pieces of silver.
on his position in the Labour Party, c.1956

11 There are two ways of getting into the Cabinet—you can crawl in or kick your way in.

12 A strife of interests masquerading as a contest of principles. The conduct of public affairs for private advantage.

13 My God! They've shot our fox!
on hearing of the resignation of Hugh Dalton, Chancellor of the Exchequer in the Labour Government, after a leakage of Budget secrets

14 Have you ever seen a candidate talking to a rich person on television?

Diane Abbott 1953– : in *Observer* 30 January 1994 'Sayings of the Week'

Franklin P. Adams 1881–1960: *Nods and Becks* (1944)

Henry Brooks Adams 1838–1918: *The Education of Henry Adams* (1907)

Anonymous: Lord Home *The Way the Wind Blows* (1976)

Anonymous: slogan found at Nanterre in Paris, 1968

Herbert Asquith 1852–1928: Alistair Horne *Price of Glory* (1962)

Jane Austen 1775–1817: *Northanger Abbey* (1818)

Stanley Baldwin 1867–1947: in *Observer* 24 May 1925

Bernard Baruch 1870–1965: Meyer Berger *New York* (1960)

Aneurin Bevan 1897–1960: Michael Foot *Aneurin Bevan* (1973) vol. 2

Aneurin Bevan 1897–1960: attributed

Ambrose Bierce 1842–c.1914: *The Enlarged Devil's Dictionary* (1967)

Nigel Birch 1906–81: on 13 November 1947

Art Buchwald 1925– : Laurence J. Peter (ed.) *Quotations for our Time* (1977)

15 The US presidency is a Tudor monarchy plus telephones.

Anthony Burgess 1917–93: George Plimpton (ed.) *Writers at Work* 4th Series (1977)

16 In politics you must always keep running with the pack. The moment that you falter and they sense that you are injured, the rest will turn on you like wolves.

R. A. Butler 1902–82: Dennis Walters *Not Always with the Pack* (1989)

17 *to Franklin Roosevelt on the likely duration of the Yalta conference with Stalin:*
I do not see any other way of realizing our hopes about World Organization in five or six days. Even the Almighty took seven.

Winston Churchill 1874–1965: *The Second World War* (1954) vol. 6

18 Politics are almost as exciting as war and quite as dangerous. In war you can only be killed once, but in politics—many times.

Winston Churchill 1874–1965: attributed

19 There are no true friends in politics. We are all sharks circling, and waiting, for traces of blood to appear in the water.

Alan Clark 1928–99: diary, 30 November 1990

20 There's nothing so improves the mood of the Party as the imminent execution of a senior colleague.

Alan Clark 1928–99: diary, 13 July 1990

21 Safe is spelled D-U-L-L. Politics has got to be a fun activity. *on being selected as parliamentary candidate for Kensington and Chelsea, 24 January 1997*

Alan Clark 1928–99: in *Daily Telegraph* 25 January 1997

22 M is for Marx
And Movement of Masses
And Massing of Arses.
And Clashing of Classes.

Cyril Connolly 1903–74: 'Where Engels Fears to Tread'

23 The only safe pleasure for a parliamentarian is a bag of boiled sweets.

Julian Critchley 1930–2000: in *Listener* 10 June 1982

24 The duty of an Opposition [is] very simple . . . to oppose everything, and propose nothing.

Lord Derby 1799–1869: quoting 'Mr Tierney, a great Whig authority'; House of Lords 4 June 1841

25 'It's always best on these occasions to do what the mob do.' 'But suppose there are two mobs?' suggested Mr Snodgrass. 'Shout with the largest,' replied Mr Pickwick.

Charles Dickens 1812–70: *Pickwick Papers* (1837)

26 Men destined to the highest places should beware of badinage . . . An insular country subject to fogs, and with a powerful middle class, requires grave statesmen.

Benjamin Disraeli 1804–81: *Endymion* (1880)

27 Think of it! A second Chamber selected by the Whips. A seraglio of eunuchs.

Michael Foot 1913– : speech in the House of Commons 3 February 1969

28 The prospect of a lot
Of dull MPs in close proximity,
All thinking for themselves is what
No man can face with equanimity.

W. S. Gilbert 1836–1911: *Iolanthe* (1882)

29 When in that House MPs divide,
If they've a brain and cerebellum too,
They have to leave that brain outside,
And vote just as their leaders tell 'em to.

W. S. Gilbert 1836–1911: *Iolanthe* (1882)

30 Once the toothpaste is out of the tube, it is awfully hard to get it back in.

H. R. Haldeman 1929–93: to John Dean; *Hearings Before the Select Committee on Presidential Campaign Activities of US Senate: Watergate and Related Activities* (1973)

31 DEALER: How about Dave Zimmerman?
BEN: Davie's too bright.
2: What about Walt Gustafson?
BEN: Walt died last night.
3:How about Frank Monohan?
4: What about George Gale?
BEN: Frank ain't a citizen
And George is in jail.
5: We could run Al Wallenstein.
BEN: He's only twenty three.
DEALER: How about Ed Peterson?
2: You idiot, that's me!
ALL: Politics and Poker . . .

Sheldon Harnick 1924– : 'Politics and Poker' (1959)

32 I cannot and will not cut my conscience to fit this year's fashions.

Lillian Hellman 1905–84: letter to John S. Wood, 19 May 1952, in *US Congress Committee Hearing on Un-American Activities* (1952)

33 *of Labour's 'prawn cocktail offensive' prior to the 1992 election campaign:*
Never before have so many crustaceans died in vain.

Michael Heseltine 1933– : speech, 1992

34 Oliver Cromwell aimed to bring about the kingdom of God on earth and founded the British Empire.

Christopher Hill 1912–2003: *A Turbulent, Seditious, and Factious People: John Bunyan and his Church, 1628-1688* (1988)

35 A little rebellion now and then is a good thing.

Thomas Jefferson 1743–1826: letter to James Madison, 30 January 1787

36 BOSWELL: So, Sir, you laugh at schemes of political improvement.
JOHNSON: Why, Sir, most schemes of political improvement are very laughable things.

Samuel Johnson 1709–84: James Boswell *Life of Samuel Johnson* (1791) 26 October 1769

37 Gratitude is not a normal feature of political life.

Lord Kilmuir 1900–67: *Political Adventure* (1964)

38 Since when was fastidiousness a quality useful for political advancement?

Bernard Levin 1928–2004: *If You Want My Opinion* (1992)

39 If voting changed anything they'd abolish it.

Ken Livingstone 1945– : in *Independent* 12 April 1996

40 If you want to succeed in politics, you must keep your conscience well under control.

David Lloyd George 1863–1945: Lord Riddell diary 23 April 1919

41 As usual the Liberals offer a mixture of sound and original ideas. Unfortunately none of the sound ideas is original and none of the original ideas is sound.

Harold Macmillan 1894–1986: speech to London Conservatives, 7 March 1961

42 *statement at London airport on leaving for a Commonwealth tour, 7 January 1958, following the resignation of the Chancellor of the Exchequer and others:*
I thought the best thing to do was to settle up these little local difficulties, and then turn to the wider vision of the Commonwealth.

Harold Macmillan 1894–1986: in *Times* 8 January 1958

43 It has always seemed to me more artistic, when the curtain falls on the last performance, to accept the inevitable *E finita la commedia*. It is tempting, perhaps, but unrewarding to hang about the greenroom after final retirement from the stage.

Harold Macmillan 1894–1986: *At the End of the Day* (1973)

44 There are three bodies no sensible man directly challenges: the Roman Catholic Church, the Brigade of Guards and the National Union of Mineworkers.

Harold Macmillan 1894–1986: in *Observer* 22 February 1981

45 I have never found in a long experience of politics that criticism is ever inhibited by ignorance.

Harold Macmillan 1894–1986: Leon Harris *The Fine Art of Politcal Wit* (1965)

46 *when Rab Butler produced a pile of papers:*
MACMILLAN: What are those?
BUTLER: Policies.
MACMILLAN: Oh, I beg you, not policies. They come back to haunt you. Give them broad sunlit uplands, dear boy.

Harold Macmillan 1894–1986: at a meeting in the family home, Birch grove in Sussex, recalled by Macmillan's grandson, the Earl of Stockton; attributed, in *Times* 16 July 2006

47 A political culture that has no time for lunch is no culture at all.

Andrew Marr 1959– : in *Independent* 11 January 2003

48 I thought you were the original professor of rotational medicine.
to Bernard Ingham, who was appearing before the Commons public administration select committee

Rhodri Morgan 1939– : in *Mail on Sunday* 7 June 1998 'Quotes of the Week'

49 I'm not going to rearrange the furniture on the deck of the Titanic.
having lost five of the last six primaries as President Ford's campaign manager

Rogers Morton 1914–79: in *Washington Post* 16 May 1976

50 Politics is the diversion of trivial men who, when they succeed at it, become important in the eyes of more trivial men.

George Jean Nathan 1882–1958: attributed

51 *Nigel Nicolson, who in 1956 abstained from voting with the Government on the Suez Crisis and subsequently lost his seat, reflecting on the Maastricht vote:*
One final tip to rebels: always have a second profession in reserve.

Nigel Nicolson 1917–2004: in *The Spectator* 7 November 1992

52 I will be sad if I either look up or down after my death and don't see my son fast asleep on the same benches on which I have slept.

Lord Onslow 1938– : in *Times* 31 October 1998 'Quotes of the Week'

53 Politics are, like God's infinite mercy, a last resort.

P. J. O'Rourke 1947– : *Parliament of Whores* (1991)

54 Men enter local politics solely as a result of being unhappily married.

C. Northcote Parkinson 1909–93: *Parkinson's Law* (1958)

55 Being an MP feeds your vanity and starves your self-respect.

Matthew Parris 1949– : in *Times* 9 February 1994

56 Politics is supposed to be the second oldest profession. I have come to realize that it bears a very close resemblance to the first.

Ronald Reagan 1911–2004: at a conference in Los Angeles, 2 March 1977

57 The more you read and observe about this Politics thing, you got to admit that each party is worse than the other.

Will Rogers 1879–1935: *The Illiterate Digest* (1924)

58 It's not cricket to picket.

Harold Rome 1908–93: song-title (1937)

59 Sing us a song
Of social significance.
All other tunes are taboo
It must be packed with social fact
Or we won't love you!

Harold Rome 1908–93: 'Sing a Song of Social Significance' (1937)

60 He knows nothing; and he thinks he knows everything. That points clearly to a political career.

George Bernard Shaw 1856–1950: *Major Barbara* (1907)

61 Anarchism is a game at which the police can beat you.

George Bernard Shaw 1856–1950: *Misalliance* (1914)

62 Nature has no cure for this sort of madness [Bolshevism], though I have known a legacy from a rich relative work wonders.

F. E. Smith 1872–1930: *Law, Life and Letters* (1927)

63 Minorities . . . are almost always in the right.

Sydney Smith 1771–1845: H. Pearson *The Smith of Smiths* (1934)

64 *on the quality of debate in the House of Lords:*
It is, I think, good evidence of life after death.

Donald Soper 1903–98: in *Listener* 17 August 1978

65 An independent is a guy who wants to take the politics out of politics.

Adlai Stevenson 1900–65: Bill Adler *The Stevenson Wit* (1966)

66 I will make a bargain with the Republicans. If they will stop telling lies about Democrats, we will stop telling the truth about them.

Adlai Stevenson 1900–65: speech during 1952 Presidential campaign; Leon Harris *The Fine Art of Political Wit* (1965)

67 *on why he did not become a politician:*
I could not stand the strain of having to be right all the time.

Peter Ustinov 1921–2004: in *Saga Magazine* August 1999

68 If you want to rise in politics in the United States there is one subject you must stay away from, and that is politics.

Gore Vidal 1925– : in *Observer* 28 June 1987 'Sayings of the Week'

69 The public say they are getting cynical about politicians; they should hear how politicians talk about them.

George Walden 1939– : *Lucky George* (1999)

70 *on Marxism, from an expert on ants:*
Wonderful theory, wrong species.

Edward O. Wilson 1929– : in *Los Angeles Times* 21 October 1994

Poverty
See also **Debt, Money**

❝ *It's no disgrace t'be poor, but it might as well be.* ❞
Frank McKinney Hubbard

1 She was poor but she was honest
Victim of a rich man's game.
First he loved her, then he left her,
And she lost her maiden name . . .
It's the same the whole world over,
It's the poor wot gets the blame,
It's the rich wot gets the gravy.
Ain't it all a bleedin' shame?

Anonymous: 'She was Poor but she was Honest'; sung by British soldiers in the First World War

2 Anyone who has ever struggled with poverty knows how extremely expensive it is to be poor.

James Baldwin 1924–87: *Nobody Knows My Name* (1961) 'Fifth Avenue, Uptown: a letter from Harlem'

3 The murmuring poor, who will not fast in peace.

George Crabbe 1754–1832: 'The Newspaper' (1785)

4 There is a wealth of poverty in Northern Ireland which must be overcome.

Lord Enniskillen 1918–89: speech in the House of Lords, 3 December 1968

5 Gee, I'd like to see you looking swell, Baby,
Diamond bracelets Woolworth doesn't sell, Baby,
Till that lucky day, you know darned well, Baby
I can't give you anything but love.

Dorothy Fields 1905–74: 'I Can't Give You Anything But Love' (1928)

6 My problem lies in reconciling my gross habits with my net income.

Errol Flynn 1909–59: Jane Mercer *Great Lovers of the Movies* (1975)

7 What throws a monkey wrench in
A fella's good intention?
That nasty old invention—
Necessity!

E. Y. Harburg 1898–1981: 'Necessity' (1947)

8 It's so bad being homeless in the winter. They should go somewhere hot like the Caribbean where they can eat free fish all day.
  at a Cosmopolitan party

Lady Victoria Hervey 1976– : attributed; in *Sunday Telegraph* 28 December 2003

9 It's no disgrace t'be poor, but it might as well be.

Frank McKinney Hubbard 1868–1930: *Short Furrows* (1911)

10 Everyone was poor and proud. My parents didn't know anything to be proud of, so they just carried on.

Patrick Kavanagh 1904–67: *The Green Fool* (1938)

11 Up and down the City Road,
In and out the Eagle,
That's the way the money goes—
Pop goes the weasel!

W. R. Mandale: 'Pop Goes the Weasel' (1853); also attributed to Charles Twiggs

12 If only Bapu [Gandhi] knew the cost of setting him up in poverty!

Sarojini Naidu 1879–1949: A. Campbell-Johnson *Mission with Mountbatten* (1951)

13 Look at me. Worked myself up from nothing to a state of extreme poverty.

S. J. Perelman 1904–79, **Will B. Johnstone**, and **Arthur Sheekman**: *Monkey Business* (1931 film)

14 LABRAX: One letter more than a medical man, that's what I am.
GRIPUS: Then you're a mendicant?
LABRAX: You've hit the point.

Plautus c.250–184 BC: *Rudens*

15 How can I ever start
To tell what's in my heart
At the sight of a dime
Of a shiny new dime.

Harold Rome 1908–93: 'The Face on the Dime' (1946)

16 The greatest of evils and the worst of crimes is poverty . . . our first duty—a duty to which every other consideration should be sacrificed—is not to be poor.

George Bernard Shaw 1856–1950: *Major Barbara* (1907) preface

17 You may tempt the upper classes
With your villainous demi-tasses,
But: Heaven will protect a working-girl!

Edgar Smith 1857–1938: 'Heaven Will Protect the Working-Girl' (1909)

18 Poverty is no disgrace to a man, but it is confoundedly inconvenient.

Sydney Smith 1771–1845: J. Potter Briscoe *Sydney Smith: His Wit and Wisdom* (1900)

19 I am pent up in frowzy lodgings, where there is not room enough to swing a cat.

Tobias Smollett 1721–71: *Humphry Clinker* (1771)

20 He was a gentleman who was generally spoken of as having nothing a-year, paid quarterly.

R. S. Surtees 1805–64: *Mr Sponge's Sporting Tour* (1853)

21 How to live well on nothing a year.

William Makepeace Thackeray 1811–63: *Vanity Fair* (1847–8)

22 I wonder what the poor people are doin' tonight. I'd love to be doin' it with 'em.

Fats Waller 1904–43: catchphrase, in Joel Vance *Fats Waller: his life and times* (1979)

23 As for the virtuous poor, one can pity them, of course, but one cannot possibly admire them.

Oscar Wilde 1854–1900: *Sebastian Melmoth* (1891)

24 Like dear St Francis of Assisi I am wedded to Poverty: but in my case the marriage is not a success.

Oscar Wilde 1854–1900: letter June 1899

Power

❝ The Pope! How many divisions has he got? ❞
Joseph Stalin

1 Whatever happens we have got
The Maxim Gun, and they have not.

Hilaire Belloc 1870–1953: *The Modern Traveller* (1898)

2 Anybody that wants the presidency so much that he'll spend two years organizing and campaigning for it is not to be trusted with the office.

David Broder 1929– : in *Washington Post* 18 July 1973

3 She cannot see an institution without hitting it with her handbag.
of Margaret Thatcher

Julian Critchley 1930–2000: in *Times* 21 June 1982

4 So long as men worship the Caesars and Napoleons, Caesars and Napoleons will duly arise and make them miserable.

Aldous Huxley 1894–1963: *Ends and Means* (1937)

5 I don't want loyalty. I want *loyalty*. I want him to kiss my ass in Macy's window at high noon and tell me it smells like roses. I want his pecker in my pocket.

Lyndon Baines Johnson 1908–73: David Halberstam *The Best and the Brightest* (1972)

6 Better to have him inside the tent pissing out, than outside pissing in.
of J. Edgar Hoover

Lyndon Baines Johnson 1908–73: David Halberstam *The Best and the Brightest* (1972)

7 Castro couldn't even go to the bathroom unless the Soviet Union put the nickel in the toilet.

Richard Milhous Nixon 1913–94: interview, September 1980

8 I'll make him an offer he can't refuse.

Mario Puzo 1920–99: *The Godfather* (1969)

9 Seven months ago I could give a single command and 541,000 people would immediately obey it. Today I can't get a plumber to come to my house.

H. Norman Schwarzkopf III 1934– : in *Newsweek* 11 November 1991; see **Presidents** 24

10 The Pope! How many divisions has *he* got?
   on being asked to encourage Catholicism in Russia by way of
   conciliating the Pope

Joseph Stalin 1879–1953: on 13 May 1935

11 He seemed much greater than a private citizen while he
   still was a private citizen, and by everyone's consent
   capable of reigning if only he had not reigned.
   of the Emperor Galba

Tacitus AD 56–after 117: *Histories*

12 Children and zip fasteners do not respond to force . . .
   Except occasionally.

Katharine Whitehorn 1928– :
Observations (1970)

Praise and Flattery

66 *Flattery hurts no one, that is, if he doesn't*
inhale. 99
Adlai Stevenson

1 We authors, Ma'am.
   to Queen Victoria after the publication of Leaves from the
   Journal of our Life in the Highlands *in 1868*

Benjamin Disraeli 1804–81: Elizabeth
Longford *Victoria R.I.* (1964);
attributed

2 Your Majesty is the head of the literary profession.
   to Queen Victoria after the publication of Leaves from the
   Journal of our Life in the Highlands *in 1868*

Benjamin Disraeli 1804–81: Hesketh
Pearson *Dizzy* (1951); attributed

3 Please don't be too effusive.
   adjuration to the Prime Minister, at their weekly meeting on
   the speech he was to make to celebrate her golden wedding;
   see **Prime Ministers** 6

Elizabeth II 1926– : in *Daily
Telegraph* 21 November 1997

4 I live for your agglomerated lucubrations.
   to H. G. Wells

Henry James 1843–1916: letter, 18
November 1902

5 Consider with yourself what your flattery is worth before
   you bestow it so freely.
   to Hannah More

Samuel Johnson 1709–84: James
Boswell *Life of Johnson* (1791)

6 You're the top! You're the Coliseum,
   You're the top! You're the Louvre Museum,
   You're a melody
   From a symphony by Strauss,
   You're a Bendel bonnet,
   A Shakespeare sonnet,
   You're Mickey Mouse!

Cole Porter 1891–1964: 'You're the
Top' (1934)

7 I used your soap two years ago; since then I have used no
   other.

Punch 1841–1992: vol. 86 (1884)

8 What really flatters a man is that you think him worth
   flattering.

George Bernard Shaw 1856–1950:
John Bull's Other Island (1907)

9 Among the smaller duties of life, I hardly know one more
   important than that of not praising where praise is not
   due.

Sydney Smith 1771–1845: Saba
Holland *Memoir* (1855)

10 I suppose flattery hurts no one, that is, if he doesn't inhale.

Adlai Stevenson 1900–65: television
broadcast, 30 March 1952

Prejudice and Tolerance

66 *Tolerance is only another name for indifference.* 99
W. Somerset Maugham

1 You take the girl, and I'll keep the car, okay? That's the problem, right?
to a policeman, on being stopped in Philadelphia while driving his Ferrari with a white woman passenger

Miles Davis 1926–91: John Szwed *So What: the life of Miles Davis* (2002)

2 Being a star has made it possible for me to get insulted in places where the average Negro could never *hope* to go and get insulted.

Sammy Davis Jnr. 1925–90: *Yes I Can* (1965)

3 I always suspected she had Scotch blood in her veins, anything else I could have looked over in her from a regard to the family.

Maria Edgeworth 1767–1849: *Castle Rackrent* (1800)

4 CONGRESSMAN STARNES: You are quoting from this Marlowe. Is he a Communist?
HALLIE FLANAGAN: I am very sorry. I was quoting from Christopher Marlowe.

Hallie Flanagan 1890–1969: in hearing on the Federal Theatre Project by the House Un-American Activities Committee, 6 December 1938

5 CONGRESSMAN STARNES: I believe Mr Euripides was guilty of teaching class consciousness also, wasn't he?
HALLIE FLANAGAN: I believe that was alleged against all the Greek dramatists.

Hallie Flanagan 1890–1969: in hearing on the Federal Theatre Project by the House Un-American Activities Committee, 6 December 1938

6 Wouldn't it be a hell of a thing if all this was burnt cork and you people were being tolerant for nothing?

Dick Gregory 1932– : *Nigger* (1965)

7 You gotta say this for the white race—its self-confidence knows no bounds. Who else could go to a small island in the South Pacific where there's no poverty, no crime, no unemployment, no war and no worry—and call it a 'primitive society'?

Dick Gregory 1932– : *From the Back of the Bus* (1962)

8 Without the aid of prejudice and custom, I should not be able to find my way across the room.

William Hazlitt 1778–1830: 'On Prejudice' (1830)

9 'It's powerful,' he said.
'What?'
'That one drop of Negro blood—because just *one* drop of black blood makes a man coloured. *One* drop—you are a Negro!'

Langston Hughes 1902–67: *Simple Takes a Wife* (1953)

10 If there were any of Australia's original inhabitants living in Melbourne they were kept well out of the way of nice people; unless, of course, they could sing.

Barry Humphries 1934– : *More Please* (1992)

11 When they call you articulate, that's another way of saying 'He talks good for a black guy'.

Ice-T 1958– : in *Independent* 30 December 1995 'Interviews of the Year'

12 *refused admittance to a smart Californian beach club:*
Since my daughter is only half-Jewish, could she go in the water up to her knees?

Groucho Marx 1890–1977: in *Observer* 21 August 1977

13 Tolerance is only another name for indifference.

W. Somerset Maugham 1874–1965: *A Writer's Notebook* (1949) written in 1896

14 The South African police would leave no stone unturned to see that nothing disturbed the even terror of their lives.

Tom Sharpe 1928– : *Indecent Exposure* (1973)

15 You must always look for the *Ulsterior motive*.
of C. S. Lewis as an Ulsterman

J. R. R. Tolkien 1892–1973: A. N. Wilson *Life of C. S. Lewis* (1986)

16 I have a distinct impression that the anthropologists' version of that famous quote from Alexander Pope's essay runs: 'The proper study of mankind is *black* man, or if not actually black, at least poor and a long way off.'

Jill Tweedie 1936–93: *It's Only Me* (1980)

17 I have never derived any pleasure from spanking black girls: it conflicts with my belief in civil liberties.

Kenneth Tynan 1927–80: diary, 28 December 1976

Present see **Past and Present**

Presidents

See also **Politicians, Politics**

66 *The vice-presidency isn't worth a pitcher of warm piss.* 99
John Nance Garner

1 Richard Nixon impeached himself. He gave us Gerald Ford as his revenge.

Bella Abzug 1920– : in *Rolling Stone*; Linda Botts *Loose Talk* (1980)

2 *of Woodrow Wilson:*
When the President proposed to the second Mrs Wilson, she was so surprised that she fell out of bed.

Anonymous: anecdote, probably apocryphal; recalled by Anthony Howard in *Times* 1 April 2003

3 I said to him the other day, 'George, if you really want to end tyranny in this world, you're going to have to stay up later' . . . Nine o'clock and Mr Excitement here is in bed, and I am watching *Desperate Housewives*.
on life with George W. Bush

Laura Bush 1946– : White House Correspondents' Association dinner, 30 April 2005

4 God Almighty was satisfied with Ten Commandments. Mr Wilson requires Fourteen Points.

Georges Clemenceau 1841–1929: during the Peace Conference negotiations in 1919; Leon Harris *The Fine Art of Political Wit* (1965)

5 A hard dog to keep on the porch.
on her husband, Bill Clinton

Hillary Rodham Clinton 1947– : in *Guardian* 2 August 1999

6 Mr Speaker, the Honourable Gentleman has conceived three times and brought forth nothing.
when Lincoln, making his first speech in the Illinois legislature, had three times begun 'Mr Speaker, I conceive'

Stephen A. Douglas 1813–61: Leon Harris *The Fine Art of Political Wit* (1965)

7 *on his office:*
The vice-presidency isn't worth a pitcher of warm piss.

John Nance Garner 1868–1967: O. C. Fisher *Cactus Jack* (1978) ch. 11

8 I was elected to lead, not to read.
President Arnold Schwarzenegger

Matt Groening 1954– et al.: *The Simpsons Movie* (2007)

9 Higgledy-Piggledy
Benjamin Harrison
Twenty-third President,
Was, and, as such,
Served between Clevelands, and
Save for this trivial
Idiosyncrasy
Didn't do much.

John Hollander 1929– : 'Historical Reflections' (1966)

10 I performed for twelve presidents and entertained six.

Bob Hope 1903–2003: in *Times* 29 July 2003

11 I was happy when I first heard Ronald Reagan was running for the presidency. I've always thought, once you're in show business you should stay in it.

Bob Hope 1903–2003: attributed

12 Ronald Reagan, the President who never told bad news to the American people.

Garrison Keillor 1942– : *We Are Still Married* (1989), introduction

13 The pay is good and I can walk to work.

John F. Kennedy 1917–63: attributed; James B. Simpson (ed.) *Simpson's Contemporary Quotations* (1988)

14 Hillary Clinton said she hopes America is ready for a woman in the Oval Office. That was the great thing about her husband, Bill: he was always ready for a woman in the Oval Office.

Jay Leno 1950– : in *Mail on Sunday* 5 November 2006 Quotes of the week'

15 If there had been any formidable body of cannibals in the country he would have promised to provide them with free missionaries fattened at the taxpayer's expense.
of Harry Truman's success in the 1948 presidential campaign

H. L. Mencken 1880–1956: in *Baltimore Sun* 7 November 1948

16 The battle for the mind of Ronald Reagan was like the trench warfare of World War I. Never have so many fought so hard for such barren terrain.

Peggy Noonan 1950– : *What I Saw at the Revolution* (1990)

17 I trust Bush with my daughter, but I trust Clinton with my job.

Craig Paterson: in *Independent* 1 February 2003

18 Poor George, he can't help it—he was born with a silver foot in his mouth.
of George Bush Snr

Ann Richards 1933–2006: keynote speech at the Democratic convention, in *Independent* 20 July 1988

19 McKinley has no more backbone than a chocolate éclair!

Theodore Roosevelt 1858–1919: Harry Thurston Peck *Twenty Years of the Republic* (1906)

20 *on being a father as well as President*
I can do one of two things. I can be president of the United States or I can control Alice. I cannot possibly do both.

Theodore Roosevelt 1858–1919: John Lewis-Stempel *Fatherhood: An Anthology* (2001)

21 If I talk over people's heads, Ike must talk under their feet.

Adlai Stevenson 1900–65: during the Presidential campaign of 1952; Bill Adler *The Stevenson Wit* (1966)

22 *of Eisenhower's presidential campaign in 1956:*
The General has dedicated himself so many times he must feel like the cornerstone of a public building.

Adlai Stevenson 1900–65: Leon Harris *The Fine Art of Political Wit* (1965)

23 We elected a President, not a Pope.
to journalists at the White House, 5 February 1998

Barbra Streisand 1942– : reported by James Naughtie, BBC Radio 4, Today programme, 6 February 1998

24 He'll sit right here and he'll say do this, do that! And nothing will happen. Poor Ike—it won't be a bit like the Army.

Harry S. Truman 1884–1972: *Harry S. Truman* (1973); see **Power** 9

Pride

See also **Humility**

> 66 *I had to choose between honest arrogance and hypocritical humility.* 99
> **Frank Lloyd Wright**

1 His opinion of himself, having once risen, remained at 'set fair'.

Arnold Bennett 1867–1931: *The Card* (1911)

2 *on stepping from his bath in the presence of a startled President Roosevelt:*
The Prime Minister has nothing to hide from the President of the United States.

Winston Churchill 1874–1965: as recalled by Roosevelt's son in *Churchill* (BBC television series presented by Martin Gilbert, 1992)

3 Every day when he looked into the glass, and gave the last touch to his consummate toilette, he offered his grateful thanks to Providence that his family was not unworthy of him.

Benjamin Disraeli 1804–81: *Lothair* (1870)

4 Modest? My word, no . . . He was an all-the-lights-on man.

Henry Reed 1914–86: *A Very Great Man Indeed* (1953 radio play) in *Hilda Tablet and Others*

5 But be not afraid of greatness: some men are born great, some achieve greatness, and some have greatness thrust upon them.

William Shakespeare 1564–1616: *Twelfth Night* (1601)

6 I have often wished I had time to cultivate modesty . . . But I am too busy thinking about myself.

Edith Sitwell 1887–1964: in *Observer* 30 April 1950

7 I am the Dean of Christ Church, Sir:
There's my wife; look well at her.
She's the Broad and I'm the High;
We are the University.
  the first couplet was unofficially altered to: 'I am the Dean, and this is Mrs Liddell; | She the first, and I the second fiddle.'

Cecil Spring-Rice 1859–1918: *The Masque of Balliol* (composed by and current among members of Balliol College, Oxford, in the 1870s)

8 Of all my verse, like not a single line;
But like my title, for it is not mine.
That title from a better man I stole;
Ah, how much better, had I stol'n the whole!

Robert Louis Stevenson 1850–94: *Underwoods* (1887) foreword

9 When I pass my name in such large letters I blush, but at the same time instinctively raise my hat.

Herbert Beerbohm Tree 1852–1917: Hesketh Pearson *Beerbohm Tree* (1956)

10 *on being asked to name the best living author writing in English:*
No one working in the English language now comes close to my exuberance, my passion, my fidelity to words.

Jeanette Winterson 1959– : in *Sunday Times* 13 March 1994

11 Early in life I had to choose between honest arrogance and hypocritical humility. I chose honest arrogance and have seen no occasion to change.

Frank Lloyd Wright 1867–1959: Herbert Jacobs *Frank Lloyd Wright* (1965)

Prime Ministers
See also **Politicians, Politics**

❝ *Every Prime Minister needs a Willie.* **❞**
Margaret Thatcher

1 It is fitting that we should have buried the Unknown Prime Minister [Bonar Law] by the side of the Unknown Soldier.

Herbert Asquith 1852–1928: Robert Blake *The Unknown Prime Minister* (1955)

2 He [Lloyd George] can't see a belt without hitting below it.

Margot Asquith 1864–1945: in *Listener* 11 June 1953 'Margot Oxford' by Lady Violet Bonham Carter

3 Few thought he was even a starter
There were many who thought themselves smarter
But he ended PM
CH and OM
An earl and a knight of the garter.

Clement Attlee 1883–1967: describing himself; letter to Tom Attlee, 8 April 1956

4 [Lloyd George] did not seem to care which way he travelled providing he was in the driver's seat.

Lord Beaverbrook 1879–1964: *The Decline and Fall of Lloyd George* (1963)

5 Listening to a speech by Chamberlain is like paying a visit to Woolworth's: everything in its place and nothing above sixpence.

Aneurin Bevan 1897–1960: Michael Foot *Aneurin Bevan* (1962) vol.1

6 I am from the Disraeli school of Prime Ministers in their relations with the Monarch.
at the Queen's golden wedding celebration; see **Praise** 3

Tony Blair 1953– : speech, 20 November 1997

7 If he ever went to school without any boots it was because he was too big for them.
referring to Harold Wilson in a speech at the Conservative Party Conference

Ivor Bulmer-Thomas 1905–93: in *Manchester Guardian* 13 October 1949

8 *on the younger Pitt's maiden speech:*
Not merely a chip of the old 'block', but the old block itself.

Edmund Burke 1729–97: N. W. Wraxall *Historical Memoirs of My Own Time* (1904 ed.)

9 Pitt is to Addington
As London is to Paddington.

George Canning 1770–1827: 'The Oracle' (c.1803)

10 For the purposes of recreation he [Gladstone] has selected the felling of trees, and we may usefully remark that his amusements, like his politics, are essentially destructive . . . The forest laments in order that Mr Gladstone may perspire.

Lord Randolph Churchill 1849–94: speech on Financial Reform, delivered in Blackpool, 24 January 1884

11 I remember, when I was a child, being taken to the celebrated Barnum's circus, which contained an exhibition of freaks and monstrosities, but the exhibit on the programme which I most desired to see was the one described as 'The Boneless Wonder'. My parents judged that that spectacle would be too revolting and demoralizing for my youthful eyes, and I have waited 50 years to see the boneless wonder sitting on the Treasury Bench.
of Ramsay Macdonald

Winston Churchill 1874–1965: speech in the House of Commons 28 January 1931

12 In the depths of that dusty soul is nothing but abject surrender.
of Neville Chamberlain

Winston Churchill 1874–1965: Leon Harris *The Fine Art of Political Wit* (1965)

13 Tony Blair has now had 10 years as a leader of the party and been Prime Minister since 1997. That's enough for the Archangel Gabriel. And Mr Blair is not the Archangel Gabriel.

Tam Dalyell 1932– : in *Guardian* 5 March 2004 (online edition)

14 Palmerston is now seventy. If he could prove evidence of his potency in his electoral address he'd sweep the country.
to the suggestion that capital could be made from one of Palmerston's affairs

Benjamin Disraeli 1804–81: Hesketh Pearson *Dizzy* (1951); attributed, probably apocryphal

15 *Disraeli was asked on what, offering himself for Marylebone, he intended to stand:*
On my head.

Benjamin Disraeli 1804–81: *Lord Beaconsfield's Correspondence with his Sister 1832–1852* (1886)

16 INTERVIEWER: What three skills should every great Prime Minister have? Did you have them?
HEATH: Patience, stamina and good luck. Two out of three isn't bad!

Edward Heath 1916–2005: in *Independent* 25 November 1998

17 JOHN MAJOR: Tell me, do you mind dreadfully not having been Prime Minister?
ROY JENKINS: No not at all—but tell me, do *you* mind dreadfully actually having been Prime Minister?

Roy Jenkins 1920–2003: anecdote recalled by Anthony Howard, in *Times* 1 April 2003

18 *of Tony Blair:*
He believes in magic. That if you say a thing, it is true. He's not very bright.

Doris Lessing 1919– : in *Sunday Times* 28 March 2004

19 *on being asked what place Arthur Balfour would have in history:*
He will be just like the scent on a pocket handkerchief.

David Lloyd George 1863–1945: Thomas Jones diary, 9 June 1922

20 [Churchill] would make a drum out of the skin of his mother in order to sound his own praises.

David Lloyd George 1863–1945: Paul Johnson (ed.) *The Oxford Book of Political Anecdotes* (1986)

21 He might make an adequate Lord Mayor of Birmingham in a lean year.
of Neville Chamberlain

David Lloyd George 1863–1945: Leon Harris *The Fine Art of Political Wit* (1965)

22 Well, it was the best I could do, seated as I was between Jesus Christ and Napoleon Bonaparte.
on the outcome of the Peace Conference negotiations in 1919 between himself, Woodrow Wilson, and Georges Clemenceau

David Lloyd George 1863–1945: Leon Harris *The Fine Art of Political Wit* (1965)

23 *after forming the National Government, 25 August 1931:*
Tomorrow every Duchess in London will be wanting to kiss me!

Ramsay MacDonald 1866–1937: Viscount Snowden *An Autobiography* (1934)

24 Every Prime Minister needs a Willie.
at the farewell dinner for William Whitelaw

Margaret Thatcher 1925– : in *Guardian* 7 August 1991

25 I think sometimes the Prime Minister should be intimidating. There's not much point being a weak, floppy thing in the chair, is there?

Margaret Thatcher 1925– : on 'The Thatcher Years' (BBC 1), 21 October 1993

Prizes See **Awards and Prizes**

Progress

See also **Science, Technology**

❝Vorwärts! Avanti! Onwards! Full speed ahead! **❞**
George Santayana

1 Everywhere one looks, decadence. I saw a bishop with a moustache the other day.

Alan Bennett 1934– : *Forty Years On* (1969)

2 All progress is based upon a universal innate desire on the part of every organism to live beyond its income.

Samuel Butler 1835–1902: *Notebooks* (1912)

3 Now, *here*, you see, it takes all the running *you* can do, to keep in the same place. If you want to get somewhere else, you must run at least twice as fast as that!

Lewis Carroll 1832–98: *Through the Looking-Glass* (1872)

4 To you, Baldrick, the Renaissance was just something that happened to other people, wasn't it?

Richard Curtis 1956– and **Ben Elton** 1959– : *Blackadder II* (1987) television series

5 Mechanics, not microbes, are the menace to civilization.

Norman Douglas 1868–1952: introduction to *The Norman Douglas Limerick Book* (1967)

6 Think what we would have missed if we had never . . . used a mobile phone or surfed the Net—or, to be honest, listened to other people talking about surfing the Net.
  reflecting on developments in the past 50 years

Elizabeth II 1926– : in *Daily Telegraph* 21 November 1997

7 The civilized man has built a coach, but has lost the use of his feet.

Ralph Waldo Emerson 1803–82: 'Self-Reliance' (1841)

8 *on being asked what he thought of modern civilization:*
  That would be a good idea.
    while visiting England in 1930

Mahatma Gandhi 1869–1948: E. F. Schumacher *Good Work* (1979)

9 They all laughed at Christopher Columbus
  When he said the world was round
  They all laughed when Edison recorded sound
  They all laughed at Wilbur and his brother
  When they said that man could fly;
  They told Marconi
  Wireless was a phony—
  It's the same old cry!

Ira Gershwin 1896–1983: 'They All Laughed' (1937)

10 Don't get smart alecksy,
  With the galaxy
  Leave the atom alone.

E. Y. Harburg 1898–1981: 'Leave the Atom Alone' (1957)

11 Push de button!
  Up de elevator!
  Push de button!
  Out de orange juice!
  Push de button!
  From refrigerator
  Come banana short-cake and frozen goose!

E. Y. Harburg 1898–1981: 'Push de Button' (1957)

12 You can't say civilization don't advance, however, for in every war they kill you in a new way.

Will Rogers 1879–1935: in *New York Times* 23 December 1929

13 The cry was for vacant freedom and indeterminate progress: *Vorwärts! Avanti! Onwards! Full speed ahead!*, without asking whether directly before you was not a bottomless pit.

George Santayana 1863–1952: *My Host the World* (1953)

14 You started something which you can't stop. You want a self-limiting revolution but it's like trying to limit influenza.

Tom Stoppard 1937– : *Squaring the Circle* (1984)

15 A swell house with . . . all the modern inconveniences.

Mark Twain 1835–1910: *Life on the Mississippi* (1883)

Publishing

> **❝** *I suppose publishers are untrustworthy. They certainly always look it.* **❞**
> **Oscar Wilde**

1 *telegram from an impatient author who had sent her play to a theatrical management:*
AUTHOR: Please give immediate decision; have other irons in the fire.
MANAGEMENT: Suggest removing irons and inserting manuscript.

Anonymous: Christine Campbell Thomson *I am a Literary Agent* (1951)

2 If I had been someone not very clever, I would have done an easier job like publishing. That's the easiest job I can think of.

A. J. Ayer 1910–89: attributed

3 Times have changed since a certain author was executed for murdering his publisher. They say that when the author was on the scaffold he said goodbye to the minister and to the reporters, and then he saw some publishers sitting in the front row below, and to them he did not say goodbye. He said instead, 'I'll see you later.'

J. M. Barrie 1860–1937: speech at Aldine Club, New York, 5 November 1896

4 In a profession where simple accountancy is preferable to a degree in English, illiteracy is not considered to be a great drawback.

Dominic Behan 1928– : *The Public World of Parable Jones* (1989)

5 The ever-increasing dullness and oddity of Oxford books is an old favourite among humorists, who are always trying to think up new and hilariously tedious 'The Oxford Book of . . . ' titles.

Craig Brown 1957– : *Craig Brown's Greatest Hits* (1993)

6 I have seen enough of my publishers to know that they have no ideas of their own about literature save what they can clutch at as believing it to be a straight tip from a business point of view.

Samuel Butler 1835–1902: *Notebooks* (1912)

7 The poem will please if it is lively—if it is stupid it will fail—but I will have none of your damned cutting and slashing.

Lord Byron 1788–1824: letter to his publisher John Murray, 6 April 1819

8 *at a literary dinner during the Napoleonic Wars, Thomas Campbell proposed a toast to Napoleon:*
Gentlemen, you must not mistake me. I admit that the French Emperor is a tyrant. I admit he is a monster. I admit that he is the sworn foe of our nation, and, if you will, of the whole human race. But, gentlemen, we must be just to our great enemy. We must not forget that he once shot a bookseller.

Thomas Campbell 1777–1844: G. O. Trevelyan *The Life of Lord Macaulay* (1876)

9 Now Barabbas was a publisher.

Thomas Campbell 1777–1844: attributed, in Samuel Smiles *A Publisher and his Friends: Memoir and Correspondence of the late John Murray* (also attributed, wrongly, to Byron); see **Publishing** 12

10 Aren't we due a royalty statement?
  to his literary agent

Charles, Prince of Wales 1948– : Giles Gordon *Aren't We Due a Royalty Statement?* (1993)

11 *on being sent the manuscript of* Travels with my Aunt, *Greene's American publishers had cabled, 'Terrific book, but we'll need to change the title':*
No need to change title. Easier to change publishers.

Graham Greene 1904–91: telegram to his American publishers in 1968; Giles Gordon *Aren't We Due a Royalty Statement?* (1993)

12 I always thought Barabbas was a much misunderstood man . . .
  a publisher's view

Peter Grose: letter, 25 May 1983; see **Publishing** 9

13 You cannot or at least you should not try to argue with authors. Too many are like children whose tears can suddenly be changed to smiles if they are handled in the right way.
  a publisher's view

Michael Joseph 1897–1958: *The Adventure of Publishing* (1949)

14 The relationship of an agent to a publisher is that of a knife to a throat.
  an American agent's view

Marvin Josephson: Ned Sherrin *Cutting Edge* (1984)

15 A publisher who writes is like a cow in a milk bar.

Arthur Koestler 1905–83: Jonathon Green (ed.) *A Dictionary of Contemporary Quotations* (1982)

16 There is some kind of notion abroad that because a book is humorous the publisher has to be funnier and madder than hell in marketing it.

S. J. Perelman 1904–79: letter to Bennett Cerf, 23 July 1937

17 I suppose publishers are untrustworthy. They certainly always look it.

Oscar Wilde 1854–1900: letter February 1898

18 All a publisher has to do is write cheques at intervals, while a lot of deserving and industrious chappies rally round and do the real work.

P. G. Wodehouse 1881–1975: *My Man Jeeves* (1919)

19 The literary agent was a grim, hard-bitten person, to whom, when he called at their offices to arrange terms, editors kept their faces turned so that they might at least retain their back collar studs.

P. G. Wodehouse 1881–1975: *Meet Mr Mulliner* (1927)

20 Being published by the Oxford University Press is rather like being married to a duchess: the honour is almost greater than the pleasure.

G. M. Young 1882–1959: Rupert Hart-Davis letter to George Lyttelton, 29 April 1956

Punishment

See also **Crime, The Law**

❝ Death to anyone who drops chewing gum. **❞**
Steven Norris

1 *to a prison visitor who asked if he were sewing:*
No, reaping.

Horatio Bottomley 1860–1933: S. T. Felstead *Horatio Bottomley* (1936)

2 It's over, and can't be helped, and that's one consolation, as they always says in Turkey, ven they cuts the wrong man's head off.

Charles Dickens 1812–70: *Pickwick Papers* (1837)

3 Thwackum was for doing justice, and leaving mercy to heaven.

Henry Fielding 1707–54: *Tom Jones* (1749)

4 Hanging is too good for him. He must be posted to the infantry.
on being asked to endorse the execution of a cavalryman who sodomized his horse

Frederick the Great 1712–86: Giles MacDonogh *Frederick the Great: a Life in Deed and Letters* (1999)

5 Awaiting the sensation of a short, sharp shock,
From a cheap and chippy chopper on a big black block.

W. S. Gilbert 1836–1911: *The Mikado* (1885)

6 As some day it may happen that a victim must be found,
I've got a little list—I've got a little list
Of society offenders who might well be under ground
And who never would be missed—who never would be missed!

W. S. Gilbert 1836–1911: *The Mikado* (1885)

7 Something lingering, with boiling oil in it, I fancy.

W. S. Gilbert 1836–1911: *The Mikado* (1885)

8 *on the campaign trail for Mayor of London:*
Death to anyone who drops chewing gum.

Steven Norris 1945– : in *Sunday Times* 13 June 2004

9 In sentencing a man for one crime, we may well be putting him beyond the reach of the law in respect of those crimes which he has not yet had an opportunity to commit. The law, however, is not to be cheated in this way. I shall therefore discharge you.

N. F. Simpson 1919– : *One Way Pendulum* (1960)

10 *Alf Garnett's view:*
Better to hang somebody than not to hang anybody at all.

Johnny Speight 1921–98: *In Sickness and in Health* (1985–92); spoken by Warren Mitchell

Quotations

❝ I always have a quotation for everything—it saves original thinking. **❞**
Dorothy L. Sayers

1 To-day I am a lamppost against which no anthologist lifts his leg.

James Agate 1877–1947: diary, 21 August 1941

2 Ah, yes! I wrote the 'Purple Cow'—
I'm sorry, now, I wrote it!
But I can tell you anyhow,
I'll kill you if you quote it!

Gelett Burgess 1866–1951: *The Burgess Nonsense Book* (1914) 'Confessional'

3 It would be nice if sometimes the kind things I say were considered worthy of quotation. It isn't difficult, you know, to be witty or amusing when one has something to say that is destructive, but damned hard to be clever and quotable when you are singing someone's praises.

Noël Coward 1899–1973: William Marchant *The Pleasure of His Company* (1981)

4 I know heaps of quotations, so I can always make quite a fair show of knowledge.

O. Douglas 1877–1948: *The Setons* (1917)

5 Next to the originator of a good sentence is the first quoter of it.

Ralph Waldo Emerson 1803–82: *Letters and Social Aims* (1876)

6 *advice for House of Commons quotations:*
No Greek; as much Latin as you like: never French in any circumstance: no English poet unless he has completed his century.

Charles James Fox 1749–1806: J. A. Gere and John Sparrow (eds.) *Geoffrey Madan's Notebooks* (1981)

7 A cannibal, but one with better table manners.
of the editor of the Oxford Dictionary of Twentieth Century Quotations

Bevis Hillier 1940– : in *Spectator* 19 December 1998

8 But I have long thought that if you knew a column of advertisements by heart, you could achieve unexpected felicities with them. You can get a happy quotation anywhere if you have the eye.

Oliver Wendell Holmes Jr. 1841–1935: letter to Harold Laski, 31 May 1923

9 You must not treat my immortal works as quarries to be used at will by the various hacks whom you may employ to compile anthologies.

A. E. Housman 1859–1936: letter to his publisher Grant Richards, 29 June 1907

10 He wrapped himself in quotations—as a beggar would enfold himself in the purple of emperors.

Rudyard Kipling 1865–1936: *Many Inventions* (1893)

11 My favourite quotation is eight pounds ten for a second-hand suit.

Spike Milligan 1918–2002: on *Quote . . . Unquote* (BBC Radio) 1 January 1979; Nigel Rees (ed.) *Cassell Dictionary of Humorous Quotations* (1999)

12 He liked those literary cooks
Who skim the cream of others' books;
And ruin half an author's graces
By plucking bon-mots from their places.

Hannah More 1745–1833: *Florio* (1786)

13 His works contain nothing worth quoting; and a book that furnishes no quotations is, *me judice*, no book—it's a plaything.

Thomas Love Peacock 1785–1866: *Crotchet Castle* (1831)

14 Misquotation is, in fact, the pride and privilege of the learned. A widely-read man never quotes accurately, for the rather obvious reason that he has read too widely.

Hesketh Pearson 1887–1964: *Common Misquotations* (1934) introduction

15 An anthology is like all the plums and orange peel picked out of a cake.

Walter Raleigh 1861–1922: letter to Mrs Robert Bridges, 15 January 1915

16 I always have a quotation for everything—it saves original thinking.

Dorothy L. Sayers 1893–1957: *Have His Carcase* (1932)

17 It seems pointless to be quoted if one isn't going to be quotable . . . It's better to be quotable than honest.

Tom Stoppard 1937– : in *Guardian* 21 March 1973

18 What a good thing Adam had. When he said a good thing he knew nobody had said it before.

Mark Twain 1835–1910: *Notebooks* (1935)

Reading

66 *I read part of it all the way through.* 99
Sam Goldwyn

1 The world may be full of fourth-rate writers but it's also full of fourth-rate readers.

Stan Barstow 1928– : in *Daily Mail* 15 August 1989

2 *on hearing that* Watership Down *was a novel about rabbits written by a civil servant:*
I would rather read a novel about civil servants written by a rabbit.

Craig Brown 1957– : attributed; probably apocryphal

3 The ideal reader of my novels is a lapsed Catholic and a failed musician, short-sighted, colour-blind, auditorily biased, who has read the books that I have read. He should also be about my age.

Anthony Burgess 1917–93: George Plimpton (ed.) *Writers at Work* 4th Series (1977)

4 You couldn't even read the Gettysburg Address. So who cares anyway where Gettysburg lived?

Betty Comden 1917–2006 and **Adolph Green** 1915–2002: *Singin' in the Rain* (1952)

5 Arrival of Book of the Month choice, and am disappointed. History of a place I am not interested in, by an author I do not like.

E. M. Delafield 1890–1943: *The Diary of a Provincial Lady* (1930)

6 *to an author who had presented him with an unwelcome book:*
Many thanks. I shall lose no time in reading it.

Benjamin Disraeli 1804–81: Wilfrid Meynell *The Man Disraeli* (1903)

7 *on the difficulties of reading the novels of Sir Walter Scott:*
He shouldn't have written in such small print.

O. Douglas 1877–1948: *The Setons* (1917)

8 I read part of it all the way through.

Sam Goldwyn 1882–1974: N. Zierold *Hollywood Tycoons* (1969)

9 Henry Kissinger may be a great writer, but anyone who finishes his book is definitely a great reader.

Walter Isaacson 1952– : in *The Week* 20 March 1999 'Wit and Wisdom'

10 [ELPHINSTON:] What, have you not read it through?
[JOHNSON:] No, Sir, do *you* read books *through*?

Samuel Johnson 1709–84: James Boswell *Life of Samuel Johnson* (1791) 19 April 1773

11 [*The Compleat Angler*] is acknowledged to be one of the world's books. Only the trouble is that the world doesn't read its books, it borrows a detective story instead.

Stephen Leacock 1869–1944: *The Boy I Left Behind Me* (1947)

12 Don't read much but love books about homos.
to Gore Vidal, on her taste in reading

Ethel Merman 1909–84: Fred Kaplan *Gore Vidal* (1999)

13 Reading isn't an occupation we encourage among police officers. We try to keep the paper work down to a minimum.

Joe Orton 1933–67: *Loot* (1967)

14 What really knocks me out is a book that, when you're all done reading it, you wish the author that wrote it was a terrific friend of yours and you could call him up on the phone whenever you felt like it.

J. D. Salinger 1919– : *Catcher in the Rye* (1951)

15 People say that life is the thing, but I prefer reading.

Logan Pearsall Smith 1865–1946: *Afterthoughts* (1931) 'Myself'

16 '*Classic.*' A book which people praise and don't read.

Mark Twain 1835–1910: *Following the Equator* (1897)

Religion
See also **The Clergy, God**

❝ *No praying, it spoils business.* **❞**
Thomas Otway

1 We have in England a particular bashfulness in every thing that regards religion.

Joseph Addison 1672–1719: *The Spectator* 15 August 1712

2 As Sir Roger is landlord to the whole congregation, he keeps them in very good order, and will suffer nobody to sleep in it [the church] besides himself; for if by chance he has been surprised into a short nap at sermon, upon recovering out of it, he stands up, and looks about him; and if he sees anybody else nodding, either wakes them himself, or sends his servant to them.

Joseph Addison 1672–1719: *The Spectator* 9 July 1711

3 *a rhyming marriage licence, said to have been composed for an al fresco ceremony outside Lichfield:*
Under an oak in stormy weather
I joined this rogue and whore together;
And none but he who rules the thunder
Can put this rogue and whore asunder.

Anonymous: has been attributed to Swift, but of doubtful authenticity; C. H. Wilson *Swiftiana* (1804)

4 Bernard always had a few prayers in the hall and some whiskey afterwards as he was rarther pious but Mr Salteena was not very addicted to prayers so he marched up to bed.

Daisy Ashford 1881–1972: *The Young Visiters* (1919)

5 I've a definite sense of spirituality. I want Brooklyn to be christened, but don't know into what religion yet.

David Beckham 1975– : in *Daily Mail* 5 September 2002

6 Gentlemen, I am a Catholic . . . If you reject me on account of my religion, I shall thank God that He has spared me the indignity of being your representative.

Hilaire Belloc 1870–1953: speech to voters of South Salford, 1906

7 FOSTER: I'm still a bit hazy about the Trinity, sir.
SCHOOLMASTER: Three in one, one in three, perfectly straightforward. Any doubts about that see your maths master.

Alan Bennett 1934– : *Forty Years On* (1969)

8 Broad of Church and 'broad of Mind',
Broad before and broad behind,
A keen ecclesiologist,
A rather dirty Wykehamist.

John Betjeman 1906–84: 'The Wykehamist' (1931)

9 So, Lord, reserve for me a crown,
And do not let my shares go down.

John Betjeman 1906–84: 'In Westminster Abbey' (1940)

10 The Church's Restoration
In eighteen-eighty-three
Has left for contemplation
Not what there used to be.

John Betjeman 1906–84: 'Hymn' (1931)

11 *of Bede Griffiths's visiting India with the intention of reconciling the Roman Catholic and Hindu faiths:*
I suppose he's trying to combine Mumbo with Jumbo in roughly equal proportions.

John Betjeman 1906–84: Bevis Hillier *Betjeman: the Bonus of Laughter* (2004)

12 If Jesus had been killed 20 years ago, Catholic school children would be wearing little electric chairs around their necks instead of crosses.

Lenny Bruce 1925–66: attributed

13 An atheist is a man who has no invisible means of support.

John Buchan 1875–1940: H. E. Fosdick *On Being a Real Person* (1943)

14 Thanks to God, I am still an atheist.

Luis Buñuel 1900–83: *Le Monde* 16 December 1959

15 Christians have burnt each other, quite persuaded That all the Apostles would have done as they did.

Lord Byron 1788–1824: *Don Juan* (1819–24)

16 I am always most religious upon a sunshiny day.

Lord Byron 1788–1824: 'Detached Thoughts' 15 October 1821

17 The two dangers which beset the Church of England are good music and bad preaching.

Lord Hugh Cecil 1869–1956: K. Rose *The Later Cecils* (1975)

18 Blessed are the cheesemakers.
a misheard beatitude

Graham Chapman 1941–89, **John Cleese** 1939– , et al.: *Monty Python's Life of Brian* (1979 film)

19 Is man an ape or an angel? Now I am on the side of the angels.

Benjamin Disraeli 1804–81: speech at Oxford, 25 November 1864

20 A Protestant, if he wants aid or advice on any matter, can only go to his solicitor.

Benjamin Disraeli 1804–81: *Lothair* (1870)

21 Said Waldershare, 'Sensible men are all of the same religion.' 'And pray what is that?' . . . 'Sensible men never tell.'

Benjamin Disraeli 1804–81: *Endymion* (1880)

22 A lady, if undressed at Church, looks silly, One cannot be devout in dishabilly.

George Farquhar 1678–1707: *The Stage Coach* (1704)

23 *Lady Carina Fitzalan-Howard was asked if her future husband David Frost were religious:*
Yes, he thinks he's God Almighty.

Carina Frost 1952– : in *Sunday Times* 28 July 1985

24   What after all
Is a halo? It's only one more thing to keep clean.

Christopher Fry 1907–2005: *The Lady's not for Burning* (1949)

25 A Consumer's Guide to Religion—The Best Buy—Church of England. It's a jolly friendly faith. If you are one, there's no onus to make everyone else join. In fact no one need ever know.

Robert Gillespie and **Charles Lewson**: *That Was The Week That Was* BBC television 1962

26 *at Oxford, to an angry crowd who thought she was Charles II's French Catholic mistress the Duchess of Portsmouth:*
Pray, good people, be civil. I am the Protestant whore.

Nell Gwyn 1650–87: B. Bevan *Nell Gwyn* (1969)

27 No matter how I probe and prod
I cannot quite believe in God.
But oh! I hope to God that he
Unswervingly believes in me.

E. Y. Harburg 1898–1981: 'The Agnostic' (1965)

28 For a halo up in heaven
I have never been too keen.
Who needs another gadget
That a fellow has to clean?

E. Y. Harburg 1898–1981: 'The Man who has Everything' (1965)

29 When Messiah comes,
He will say to us
'I apologise that I took so long,
But I had a little trouble finding you.
Over here a few and over there a few—
You were hard to reunite,
But everything is going to be all right.
Up in heaven there
How I wrang my hands
When they exiled you from the Promised Land.
In Babylon you went like castaways
On the first of many, many moving days.
What a day and what a blow,
How terrible I felt you'll never know!'

Sheldon Harnick 1924– : 'When Messiah Comes' (1964)

30 The Revised Prayer Book: a sort of attempt to suppress burglary by legalizing petty larceny.

Dean Inge 1860–1954: J. A. Gere and John Sparrow (eds.) *Geoffrey Madan's Notebooks* (1981)

31 *imagining how a Church of England Inquisition might have worked*
'Cake or death?' 'Cake, please.'

Eddie Izzard 1962– : *Dress to Kill* (stage show, San Francisco, 1998)

32 All moanday, tearsday, wailsday, thumpsday, frightday, shatterday till the fear of the Law.

James Joyce 1882–1941: *Finnegans Wake* (1939)

33 When suave politeness, tempering bigot zeal,
Corrected *I believe* to *One does feel*.

Ronald Knox 1888–1957: 'Absolute and Abitofhell' (1913)

34 'Oh, a cheque, I think,' said the rector; 'one can do so much more with it, after all.' 'Precisely,' said his father; he was well aware of many things that can be done with a cheque that cannot possibly be done with a font.

Stephen Leacock 1869–1944: *Arcadian Adventures with the Idle Rich* (1914)

35 It's nice to have a nun around. Gives the place a bit of glamour.

Graham Linehan and **Arthur Mathews**: 'Grant Unto Him Eternal Rest' (1995), episode from *Father Ted* (Channel 4 TV, 1995–8)

36 That the Almighty would send down His wisdom on the Queen's Ministers, who sorely need it.
prayer delivered in Crathie church, to Queen Victoria's amusement

Dr Macgregor: Arthur Ponsonby *Henry Ponsonby* (1942)

37 *Mahaffy had been asked 'Are you saved?' by 'a zealot who cornered him in a railway carriage':*
To tell you the truth, my good fellow, I am; but it was such a narrow squeak it does not bear talking about.

John Pentland Mahaffy 1839–1919: Oliver St John Gogarty *It Isn't This Time of Year at All* (1954)

38 You can't run the Church on Hail Marys.
view of a Vatican banker

Archbishop Paul Marcinkus 1922–2006: in *Independent* 23 February 2006

39 The spirituality of man is most apparent when he is eating a hearty dinner.

W. Somerset Maugham 1874–1965: *A Writer's Notebook* (1949) written in 1897

40 Things have come to a pretty pass when religion is allowed to invade the sphere of private life.
on hearing an evangelical sermon

Lord Melbourne 1779–1848: G. W. E. Russell *Collections and Recollections* (1898)

41 Puritanism. The haunting fear that someone, somewhere, may be happy.

H. L. Mencken 1880–1956: *Christomathy* (1949)

42 It is now quite lawful for a Catholic woman to avoid pregnancy by a resort to mathematics, though she is still forbidden to resort to physics and chemistry.

H. L. Mencken 1880–1956: *Notebooks* (1956) 'Minority Report'

43 The orgasm has replaced the Cross as the focus of longing and the image of fulfilment.

Malcolm Muggeridge 1903–90: *Tread Softly* (1966)

44 King David and King Solomon
Led merry, merry lives,
With many, many lady friends,
And many, many wives;
But when old age crept over them—
With many, many qualms!—
King Solomon wrote the Proverbs
And King David wrote the Psalms.

James Ball Naylor 1860–1945: 'King David and King Solomon' (1935)

45 God is a man, so it must be all rot.
   just before her marriage to Robert Graves in 1917

Nancy Nicholson d. 1977: R. Graves *Goodbye to All That* (1929)

46 You are not an agnostic . . . You are just a fat slob who is too lazy to go to Mass.

Conor Cruise O'Brien 1917–2008: attributed

47 There's no reason to bring religion into it. I think we ought to have as great a regard for religion as we can, so as to keep it out of as many things as possible.

Sean O'Casey 1880–1964: *The Plough and the Stars* (1926)

48 Good manners can replace religious beliefs. In the Anglican Church they already have. Etiquette (and quiet, well-cut clothes) are devoutly worshipped by Anglicans.

P. J. O'Rourke 1947– : *Modern Manners* (1984)

49 He was an embittered atheist (the sort of atheist who does not so much disbelieve in God as personally dislike Him), and took a sort of pleasure in thinking that human affairs would never improve.

George Orwell 1903–50: *Down and Out in Paris and London* (1933)

50 No praying, it spoils business.

Thomas Otway 1652–85: *Venice Preserved* (1682)

51 God and the doctor we alike adore
But only when in danger, not before;
The danger o'er, both are alike requited,
God is forgotten, and the Doctor slighted.

John Owen c. 1563–1622: *Epigrams*

52 I've been a sinner, I've been a scamp,
But now I'm willin' to trim my lamp,
So blow, Gabriel, blow!

Cole Porter 1891–1964: 'Blow, Gabriel, Blow' (1934)

53 How can you expect to convert England if you use a cope like that?

Augustus Welby Pugin 1812–52: to an unidentified Catholic priest; Bernard Ward *The Sequel to Catholic Emancipation* (1915)

54 I have wondered at times about what the Ten Commandments would have looked like if Moses had run them through the US Congress.

Ronald Reagan 1911–2004: attributed

55 Prove to me that you're no fool
Walk across my swimming pool.

Tim Rice 1944– : 'Herod's Song' (1970)

56 I always claim the mission workers came out too early to catch any sinners on this part of Broadway. At such an hour the sinners are still in bed resting up from their sinning of the night before, so they will be in good shape for more sinning a little later on.

Damon Runyon 1884–1946: in *Collier's* 28 January 1933, 'The Idyll of Miss Sarah Brown'

57 I was told that the Chinese said they would bury me by the Western Lake and build a shrine to my memory. I have some slight regret that this did not happen as I might have become a god, which would have been very *chic* for an atheist.

Bertrand Russell 1872–1970: *Autobiography* (1968)

58 People may say what they like about the decay of Christianity; the religious system that produced green Chartreuse can never really die.

Saki 1870–1916: *Reginald* (1904)

59 Every reformation must have its victims. You can't expect the fatted calf to share the enthusiasm of the angels over the prodigal's return.

Saki 1870–1916: *Reginald* (1904)

60 Didn't some cynical critic say the Church of England is the only barrier between England and Christianity?

Saki 1870–1916: *Mrs Elmsley* (1911, published as by Hector Munro)

61 The conversion of England was thus effected by the landing of St Augustine in Thanet and other places, which resulted in the country being overrun by a Wave of Saints. Among these were St Ive, St Pancra, the great St Bernard (originator of the clerical collar), St Bee, St Ebb, St Neot (who invented whisky), St Kit and St Kin, and the Venomous Bead (author of *The Rosary*).

W. C. Sellar 1898–1951 and **R. J. Yeatman** 1898–1968: *1066 and All That* (1930)

62 Christianity never got any grip of the world until it virtually reduced its claims on the ordinary citizen's attention to a couple of hours every seventh day, and let him alone on week-days.

George Bernard Shaw 1856–1950: preface to *Getting Married* (1911)

63 How can what an Englishman believes be heresy? It is a contradiction in terms.

George Bernard Shaw 1856–1950: *Saint Joan* (1924)

64 I have not the smallest influence over Lord Byron, in this particular, and if I had, I certainly should employ it to eradicate from his great mind the delusions of Christianity, which, in spite of his reason, seem perpetually to recur.

Percy Bysshe Shelley 1792–1822: letter 11 April 1822

65 Baptists are only funny underwater.

Neil Simon 1927– : *Laughter on the 23rd Floor* (1994)

66 I'm a dyslexic Satanist; I worship the drivel.

Linda Smith 1958–2006: in *Daily Telegraph* (obituary), 1 March 2006

67 Deserves to be preached to death by wild curates.

Sydney Smith 1771–1845: Lady Holland *Memoir* (1855)

68 His followers threw a Rosary and a Bible at me, which I felt was at least an ecumenical gesture, and there was a near riot.
of Ian Paisley

Donald Soper 1903–98: speech in the House of Lords, 3 December 1968

69 Protestant women may take the pill. Roman Catholic women must keep taking The Tablet.

Irene Thomas 1919–2001: in *Guardian* 28 December 1990

70 Dr Gwynne himself, though a religious man, was also a thoroughly practical man of the world, and he regarded with no favourable eye the tenets of anyone who looked on the two things as incompatible.

Anthony Trollope 1815–82: *Barchester Towers* (1857)

71 When the missionaries came to Africa, they had the Bible and we had the land. They said: 'Let us pray'. We closed our eyes. When we opened them we had the Bible and they had the land.

Desmond Tutu 1931– : attributed; in *Mail on Sunday* 14 March 2004

72 Why did the Catholics invent the confessional? What is that but a phone box?

Peter Ustinov 1921–2004: *Monsieur René* (1999)

73 Why do born-again people so often make you wish they'd never been born the first time?

Katharine Whitehorn 1928– : attributed

74 THE ARCHDEACON: Her deafness is a great privation to her. She can't even hear my sermons now.

Oscar Wilde 1854–1900: *A Woman of No Importance* (1893)

Retirement

66 *The transition from Who's Who to Who's He.* 99

Eddie George

1 I go to Bournemouth in lieu of Paradise.
on retiring from Eton

Lord Hugh Cecil 1869–1956: in *Dictionary of National Biography* (1917–)

2 If anything could have pulled me out of retirement, it would have been an Indiana Jones film. But in the end, retirement is just too damned much fun.

Sean Connery 1930– : in *Observer* 10 June 2007

3 The transition from Who's Who to Who's He.
view of the former Governor of the Bank of England

Eddie George 1938– : in *Independent* 29 December 2003

4 I contemplate retirement every evening, and then I forget about it in the morning.

Peter Ustinov 1921–2004: in *Times* 30 March 2004

Royalty

66 *I left England when I was four because I found out I could never be King.* 99

Bob Hope

1 She is only 5ft 4in, and to make someone that height look regal is difficult. Fortunately she holds herself very well.
of Queen Elizabeth II

Hardy Amies 1909–2003: interview in *Sunday Telegraph* 9 February 1997

2 When I appear in public people expect me to neigh, grind my teeth, paw the ground and swish my tail—none of which is easy.

Anne, Princess Royal 1950– : in *Observer* 22 May 1977

3 *notice affixed to the gates of St James's Palace during one of George II's absences in Hanover:*
Lost or strayed out of this house a man who has left a wife and six children on the parish . . . [A reward of four shillings and sixpence is offered] Nobody judging him to deserve a crown.

Anonymous: Duke of Windsor 'My Hanoverian Ancestors' (unpublished reminiscences); Elizabeth Longford (ed.) *The Oxford Book of Royal Anecdotes* (1989)

4 King's Moll Reno'd in Wolsey's Home Town.

Anonymous: US newspaper headline on Wallis Simpson's divorce proceedings in Ipswich

5 *it was said that during a cruise Caroline of Brunswick would sleep in a tent on deck with her majordomo, and take a bath in her cabin either with him or in his presence:*
The Grand Master of St Caroline has found promotion's path;

Anonymous: Roger Fulford *The Trial of Queen Caroline* (1967)

He is made both Knight Companion and Commander of the Bath.

6 *Caroline of Brunswick, estranged wife of George IV, while attending the debate in the House of Lords on the Bills of Pains and Penalties whereby George IV was attempting to divorce her, habitually fell asleep:*
Her conduct at present no censure affords,
She sins not with courtiers but sleeps with the Lords.

Anonymous: Roger Fulford *The Trial of Queen Caroline* (1967)

7 Most Gracious Queen, we thee implore
To go away and sin no more,
But if that effort be too great,
To go away at any rate.

Anonymous: epigram on Queen Caroline, quoted in a letter from Francis Burton to Lord Colchester, 15 November 1820

8 As Jordan's high and mighty squire
Her playhouse profits deigns to skim,
Some folks audaciously enquire:
If *he* keeps *her,* or *she* keeps *him?*
  of the Duke of Clarence (later William IV) and his mistress, the actress Mrs Jordan

Anonymous: Philip Ziegler *King William IV* (1971)

9 Lousy but loyal.

Anonymous: London East End slogan at George V's Jubilee, 1935

10 How different, how very different from the home life of our own dear Queen!

Anonymous: comment overheard at a performance of Cleopatra by Sarah Bernhardt (probably apocryphal)

11 Which King did you say?

Anonymous: BBC receptionist to King Haakon of Norway; in *Ned Sherrin in his Anecdotage* (1993)

12 *comment made to Cecil Beaton by a lady-in-waiting to the exiled Queen Geraldine of Albania:*
Of course, we'll go back there one day. Meanwhile, we have to make a new life for ourselves at the Ritz.

Anonymous: Cecil Beaton diary 1940

13 One of Edward's Mistresses was Jane Shore, who has had a play written about her, but it is a tragedy and therefore not worth reading.

Jane Austen 1775–1817: *The History of England* (written 1791)

14 Fate wrote her a most tremendous tragedy, and she played it in tights.
  of Caroline of Brunswick, wife of George IV

Max Beerbohm 1872–1956: *The Yellow Book* (1894)

15 Green with lust and sick with shyness
Let me lick your lacquered toes,
Gosh, oh gosh, your Royal Highness,
Put your finger up my nose.
  parodic poem on John Betjeman's being presented with the Duff Cooper Memorial Prize by Princess Margaret

Maurice Bowra 1898–1971: attributed; in *Daily Telegraph* 10 February 2002 (online edition)

16 *William IV, on his way to dissolve Parliament, with uproar growing in both Houses over the Reform Bill and a cannon heralding his approach, asked his Lord Chancellor what the noise could be:*
If you please, Your Majesty, it is the Lords debating.

Lord Brougham 1778–1868: *Works of Henry Lord Brougham* (1872)

17 'Where shall I begin, please your Majesty?' he asked.
'Begin at the beginning,' the King said, gravely, 'and go on till you come to the end: then stop.'

Lewis Carroll 1832–98: *Alice's Adventures in Wonderland* (1865)

18 I shall be an autocrat: that's my trade. And the good Lord will forgive me: that's his.

Catherine the Great 1729–96: attributed

19 We saw Queen Mary looking like the Jungfrau, white and sparkling in the sun.

Chips Channon 1897–1958: diary, 22 June 1937

20 He had been, he said, an unconscionable time dying; but he hoped that they would excuse it.

Charles II 1630–85: Lord Macaulay *History of England* (1849)

21 I've tried him drunk and I've tried him sober but there's nothing in him.
   of his niece Anne's husband George of Denmark

Charles II 1630–85: Gila Curtis *The Life and Times of Queen Anne* (1972)

22 This is very true: for my words are my own, and my actions are my ministers'.

Charles II 1630–85: reply to 'The King's Epitaph'; *Thomas Hearne: Remarks and Collections* (1885–1921) 17 November 1706; see **Royalty** 56

23 *on being asked the identity of the small man sharing an open carriage with the large Queen Salote of Tonga in the British Coronation procession:*
   Her lunch.

Noël Coward 1899–1973: attributed, but denied by Coward as offensive to Queen Salote; Dick Richards *The Wit and Wisdom of Noël Coward* (1968)

24 Everyone likes flattery; and when you come to Royalty you should lay it on with a trowel.

Benjamin Disraeli 1804–81: G. W. E. Russell *Collections and Recollections* (1898)

25 I never deny; I never contradict; I sometimes forget.
   of his dealings as Prime Minister with Queen Victoria

Benjamin Disraeli 1804–81: Elizabeth Longford *Victoria R. I.* (1964)

26 I had three concubines, who in three diverse properties diversely excelled. One, the merriest; another the wiliest; the third, the holiest harlot in my realm, as one whom no man could get out of the church lightly to any place but it were to his bed.

Edward IV 1442–83: Thomas More *The History of Richard III*, composed about 1513

27 *to the Archbishop of Canterbury after the service of celebration at St Paul's for Queen Victoria's Diamond Jubilee in 1897:*
   I have no objection whatsoever to the notion of the Eternal Father, but every objection to the concept of an eternal mother.

Edward VII 1841–1910: attributed, perhaps apocryphal

28 *on being asked if Queen Victoria would be happy in heaven:*
   She will have to walk behind the angels—and she won't like that.

Edward VII 1841–1910: attributed, perhaps apocryphal

29 I think everybody really will concede that on this, of all days, I should begin my speech with the words 'My husband and I'.

Elizabeth II 1926– : speech at Guildhall, London, on her 25th wedding anniversary

30 *on being asked, just after George VI's accession, if she had seen Chips Channon's new gold dinner service in his Belgravia home:*
   Oh no, we're not nearly grand enough to be asked there.

Queen Elizabeth, the Queen Mother 1900–2002: attributed, perhaps apocryphal

31 I hate all Boets and Bainters.

George I 1660–1727: John Campbell *Lives of the Chief Justices* (1849) 'Lord Mansfield'

32 *when Queen Caroline, on her deathbed, urged him to marry again:*
   No, I shall have mistresses.
   the Queen replied, 'Oh, my God! That won't make any difference'

George II 1683–1760: John Hervey *Memoirs of the Reign of George II* (1848)

33 *the Duke of Clarence had told his father that he made his mistress Mrs Jordan an allowance of £1000 per year:*
A thousand, a thousand; too much; too much! Five hundred quite enough! Quite enough!

George III 1738–1820: Brian Fothergill *Dorothy Jordan* (1965)

34 *on first seeing Caroline of Brunswick, his future wife:*
Harris, I am not well; pray get me a glass of brandy.

George IV 1762–1830: Earl of Malmesbury *Diaries and Correspondence* (1844), 5 April 1795

35 *in conversation with Anthony Eden, 23 December 1935, following Samuel Hoare's resignation as Foreign Secretary:*
I said to your predecessor: 'You know what they're all saying, no more coals to Newcastle, no more Hoares to Paris.' The fellow didn't even laugh.

George V 1865–1936: Earl of Avon *Facing the Dictators* (1962)

36 *on H. G. Wells's comment on 'an alien and uninspiring court':*
I may be uninspiring, but I'll be damned if I'm an alien!

George V 1865–1936: Sarah Bradford *George VI* (1989); attributed

37 *to Brigadier Hinde, who had replied to the question, 'Have we met before?' with 'I don't think so':*
You should bl-bloody well know.

George VI 1895–1952: Lord Carver *Out of Step* (1989)

38 Ah'm sorry your Queen has to pay taxes. She's not a wealthy woman.

John Paul Getty 1892–1976: in *Ned Sherrin in his Anecdotage* (1993); attributed

39 *of the Emperor Gordian:*
Twenty-two acknowledged concubines, and a library of sixty-two thousand volumes, attested the variety of his inclinations, and from the productions which he left behind him, it appears that the former as well as the latter were designed for use rather than ostentation. [Footnote] By each of his concubines the younger Gordian left three or four children. His literary productions were by no means contemptible.

Edward Gibbon 1737–94: *The Decline and Fall of the Roman Empire* (1776–88)

40 Another damned, thick, square book! Always scribble, scribble, scribble! Eh! Mr Gibbon?

Duke of Gloucester 1743–1805: Henry Best *Personal and Literary Memorials* (1829); also attributed to the Duke of Cumberland and King George III

41 I left England when I was four because I found out I could never be King.

Bob Hope 1903–2003: from the Bob Hope Joke Files stored in two vaults of his Toluca Lake estate office; William Robert Faith *Bob Hope* (1983)

42 *notice on a playbill sent to her former lover, the Duke of Clarence, refusing repayment of her allowance:*
Positively no money refunded after the curtain has risen.

Mrs Jordan 1762–1816: Duke of Windsor 'My Hanoverian Ancestors' (unpublished reminiscences); Elizabeth Longford (ed.) *The Oxford Book of Royal Anecdotes* (1989)

43 Not a fatter fish than he
Flounders round the polar sea.
See his blubber—at his gills
What a world of drink he swills . . .
By his bulk and by his size
By his oily qualities
This (or else my eyesight fails)
This should be the Prince of Wales.

Charles Lamb 1775–1834: anonymously written in 1812; Elizabeth Longford (ed.) *Oxford Book of Royal Anecdotes* (1989)

44 What do the simple folk do?
... I have been informed
By those who know them well,
They find relief in quite a clever way.
When they're sorely pressed
They whistle for a spell:
And whistling seems to brighten up their day.
And that's what simple folk do;
So they say.

Alan Jay Lerner 1918–86: 'What Do the Simple Folk Do?' (1960)

45 *England had declared war on France two weeks after the accession of Queen Anne:*
It means I'm growing old when ladies declare war on me.

Louis XIV 1638–1715: Gila Curtis *The Life and Times of Queen Anne* (1972)

46 My children are not royal, they just happen to have the Queen as their aunt.

Princess Margaret 1930–2002: Elizabeth Longford (ed.) *The Oxford Book of Royal Anecdotes* (1989)

47 *on being told that one of the Royal paintings was a Mercier, not by Nollekens:*
We prefer the picture to remain as by Nollekens.

Queen Mary 1867–1953: Michael Hill (ed.) *Right Royal Remarks* (2003)

48 *on the abdication:*
Really, this might be Rumania.

Queen Mary 1867–1953: Michael Hill (ed.) *Right Royal Remarks* (2003)

49 For 50 years and more, Elizabeth Windsor has maintained her dignity, her sense of duty, and her hairstyle.
accepting an Oscar for Best actress for her part in The Queen

Helen Mirren 1945– : in *Independent on Sunday* 4 March 2007

50 Superior to her waiting nymphs,
As lobster to attendant shrimps.
of Queen Caroline of Ansbach when dressed in pink

Lady Mary Wortley Montagu 1689–1762: 'Epistle to Lord Hervey on the King's Birthday'

51 She's head of a dysfunctional family—if she lived on a council estate in Sheffield, she'd probably be in council care.
on the Queen

Michael Parkinson 1935– : in *Mail on Sunday* 17 January 1999 'Quotes of the Week'

52 *after the death in childbirth of the Prince Regent's daughter Charlotte, four of the Regent's brothers married in an attempt to provide an heir to the throne:*
Yoics! the Royal sport's begun!
I'faith but it is glorious fun,
For hot and hard each Royal pair
Are at it hunting for an heir.

Peter Pindar 1738–1819: Elizabeth Longford (ed.) *The Oxford Book of Royal Anecdotes* (1989)

53 Here thou, great Anna! whom three realms obey,
Dost sometimes counsel take—and sometimes tea.

Alexander Pope 1688–1744: *The Rape of the Lock* (1714)

54 The Right Divine of Kings to govern wrong.

Alexander Pope 1688–1744: *The Dunciad* (1742)

55 She made the butler
She made the groom
She made the maid who made the room.
on Catherine the Great of Russia

Cole Porter 1891–1964: 'Kate the Great' (1934)

56 Here lies a great and mighty king
Whose promise none relies on;
He never said a foolish thing,
Nor ever did a wise one.

Lord Rochester 1647–80: 'The King's Epitaph' (an alternative first line reads: 'Here lies our sovereign lord the King'); see **Royalty** 22

57 *at the funeral of Edward VII the Kaiser asked Roosevelt to call on him the next day 'at two o'clock sharp—for I can give you only 45 minutes':*
I will be there at two, but unfortunately I have just 20 minutes to give you.

Theodore Roosevelt 1858–1919: attributed, perhaps apocryphal

58 The *éminence cerise*, the bolster behind the throne.
of Queen Elizabeth the Queen Mother

Will Self 1961– : in *Independent on Sunday* 8 August 1999

59 *questionnaire for would-be Kings in the Wars of the Roses:*
Are you Edmund Mortimer? If not, have you got him?

W. C. Sellar 1898–1951 and **R. J. Yeatman** 1898–1968: *1066 and All That* (1930)

60 The cruel Queen died and a post-mortem examination revealed the word 'CALLOUS' engraved on her heart.
of Mary Tudor

W. C. Sellar 1898–1951 and **R. J. Yeatman** 1898–1968: *1066 and All That* (1930)

61 Charles II was always very merry and was therefore not so much a king as a Monarch.

W. C. Sellar 1898–1951 and **R. J. Yeatman** 1898–1968: *1066 and All That* (1930)

62 *when preaching before Charles II and his court:*
My lord, you snore so loud you will wake the king.

Dr South 1634–1716: to Lord Lauderdale; Arthur Bryant *King Charles II* (rev. ed. 1964)

63 Sire, your majesty seems to have won the race.
after the Battle of the Boyne to James II, who had complained that Lady Tyrconnel's countrymen had run away

Lady Tyrconnel d. 1731: Elizabeth Longford (ed.) *The Oxford Book of Royal Anecdotes* (1989)

64 He speaks to Me as if I was a public meeting.
of Gladstone

Queen Victoria 1819–1901: G. W. E. Russell *Collections and Recollections* (1898)

65 *when forced by a mob to cheer George IV's wife Caroline of Brunswick:*
God Save the Queen, and may all your wives be like her!

Duke of Wellington 1769–1852: Elizabeth Longford *Wellington: Pillar of State* (1972); also attributed to Lord Anglesey and others

66 *having been wakened with the news of his accession, William IV returned to bed:*
To enjoy the novelty of sleeping with a queen.

William IV 1765–1837: Duke of Windsor 'My Hanoverian Ancestors' (unpublished reminiscences); Elizabeth Longford (ed.) *The Oxford Book of Royal Anecdotes* (1989)

67 I'm doing pretty well considering. In the past, when anyone left the Royal family they had you beheaded.

Sarah, Duchess of York 1959– : in *Independent* 8 July 2000 'Quotes of the Week'

Russia

> 66 *Miles of cornfields, and ballet in the evening.* 99
> **Alan Hackney**

1 I gather it has now been decided not to embrace the Russian bear, but to hold out a hand and accept its paw gingerly. No more. The worst of both worlds.

Chips Channon 1897–1958: diary, 16 May 1939

2 Miles of cornfields, and ballet in the evening.

Alan Hackney: *Private Life* (1958) (later filmed as *I'm All Right Jack*, 1959)

3 *on being asked in the 1960s what it was like touring with the Benny Goodman band in Communist Russia:*
When you're with Benny Goodman, every day is like touring in Russia.

Zoot Sims 1925–85: Humphrey Lyttleton *It Just Occurred to Me . . . : the reminiscences and thoughts of Chairman Humph* (2006)

4 I was born under a squandering Tsar.

Dick Vosburgh 1929–2007 and **Denis King**: *Beauty and the Beards* (2001)

5 I cannot see much future for Russian humorists. They have a long way to go before they can play the Palladium.

P. G. Wodehouse 1881–1975: *Plum Pie* (1966)

Satisfaction and Discontent
See also **Happiness, Hope and Despair**

❝ *If not actually disgruntled, he was far from being gruntled.* ❞
P. G. Wodehouse

1 *Mr Bennet dissuading his daughter Mary from continuing to sing:*
You have delighted us long enough.

Jane Austen 1775–1817: *Pride and Prejudice* (1813)

2 *when asked what was the best day of her life:*
It was a night.

Brigitte Bardot 1934– : in *Independent on Sunday* 3 October 2004

3 *asked if he had any regrets:*
Yes, I haven't had enough sex.

John Betjeman 1906–84: on *Time With Betjeman* (BBC TV), February 1983; Nigel Rees (ed.) *Cassell Dictionary of Humorous Quotations* (1999)

4 Does he paint? He would fain write a poem.
Does he write? He would fain paint a picture.

Robert Browning 1812–89: 'One Word More' (1855)

5 I ask very little. Some fragments of Pamphilides, a Choctaw blood-mask, the prose of Scaliger the Elder, a painting by Fuseli, an occasional visit to the all-in wrestling, or to my meretrix; a cook who can produce a passable 'poulet à la Khmer', a Pong vase. Simple tastes, you will agree, and it is my simple habit to indulge them.

Cyril Connolly 1903–74: *The Condemned Playground* 'Told in Gath', a parody of Aldous Huxley

6 If, of all words of tongue and pen,
The saddest are, 'It might have been,'
More sad are these we daily see:
'It is, but hadn't ought to be!'

Bret Harte 1836–1902: 'Mrs Judge Jenkins' (1867)

7 Frankly, my dear, I don't give a damn.

Sidney Howard 1891–1939: *Gone with the Wind* (1939 film, based on the novel by Margaret Mitchell); spoken by Clark Gable as Rhett Butler

8 You were only supposed to blow the bloody doors off!

Troy Kennedy-Martin 1932– : *The Italian Job* (1969 film); spoken by Michael Caine as Charlie Croker

9 I can tolerate without discomfort being waited on hand and foot.

Osbert Lancaster 1908–86: *All Done From Memory* (1953)

10 When fortune empties her chamberpot on your head,
smile—and say 'we are going to have a summer shower'.

John A. Macdonald 1851–91: spoken
c. 1875

11 It's no go the Yogi-Man, it's no go Blavatsky,
All we want is a bank balance and a bit of skirt in a taxi.

Louis MacNeice 1907–63: 'Bagpipe
Music' (1938)

12 I test my bath before I sit,
And I'm always moved to wonderment
That what chills the finger not a bit
Is so frigid upon the fundament.

Ogden Nash 1902–71: 'Samson
Agonistes' (1942)

13 My life was simply hellish
I didn't stand a chance
I thought that I would relish
A tomb like General Grant's
But now I feel so swellish
So Elsa Maxwellish
That I'm giving a dance.

Cole Porter 1891–1964: 'I'm
Throwing a Ball Tonight' (1940)

14 'I must be going,' said Mrs Eggelby, in a tone which had
been thoroughly sterilised of even perfunctory regret.

Saki 1870–1916: *Beasts and Super-
Beasts* (1914)

15 My birthday. No adequate fuss made.

Barbara Skelton 1916–96: diary, 26
June 1952

16 His strongest tastes were negative. He abhorred plastics,
Picasso, sunbathing and jazz—everything in fact that had
happened in his own lifetime.

Evelyn Waugh 1903–66: *The Ordeal
of Gilbert Pinfold* (1957)

17 It's better to be looked over than overlooked.

Mae West 1892–1980: *Belle of the
Nineties* (1934 film)

18 Ice formed on the butler's upper slopes.

P. G. Wodehouse 1881–1975: *Pigs
Have Wings* (1952)

19 He spoke with a certain what-is-it in his voice, and I could
see that, if not actually disgruntled, he was far from being
gruntled.

P. G. Wodehouse 1881–1975: *The
Code of the Woosters* (1938)

Science

See also **Progress, Technology**

❝ *Such wholesale returns of conjecture out of
such a trifling investment of fact.* **❞**
Mark Twain

1 All I know about the becquerel is that, like the Italian lira,
you need an awful lot to amount to very much.

Arnold Allen 1924– : in *Financial
Times* 19 September 1986

2 Multiplication is vexation,
Division is as bad;
The Rule of Three doth puzzle me,
And Practice drives me mad.

Anonymous: in *Lean's Collectanea*
(1904), possibly 16th-century

3 When I find myself in the company of scientists, I feel like
a shabby curate who has strayed by mistake into a
drawing room full of dukes.

W. H. Auden 1907–73: *The Dyer's
Hand* (1963)

4 The Microbe is so very small
You cannot make him out at all.
But many sanguine people hope
To see him through a microscope.

Hilaire Belloc 1870–1953: 'The Microbe' (1897)

5 Sir Humphrey Davy
Abominated gravy.
He lived in the odium
Of having discovered Sodium.

Edmund Clerihew Bentley 1875–1956: 'Sir Humphrey Davy' (1905)

6 Basic research is what I am doing when I don't know what I am doing.

Werner von Braun 1912–77: R. L. Weber *A Random Walk in Science* (1973)

7 Let's be frank, the Italians' technological contribution to humankind stopped with the pizza oven.

Bill Bryson 1951– : *Neither Here Nor There* (1991)

8 There was a young lady named Bright,
Whose speed was far faster than light;
She set out one day
In a relative way
And returned on the previous night.

Arthur Buller 1874–1944: 'Relativity' (1923)

9 If they are worthy of the name, they are indeed about God's path and about his bed and spying out all his ways.
of scientists

Samuel Butler 1835–1902: *Notebooks* (1912)

10 *to an elderly scientist who had bored her by talking interminably about the social organization of ants, which have 'their own police force and their own army'*:
No navy, I suppose?'

Mrs Patrick Campbell 1865–1940: James Agate diary, 11 February 1944

11 If an elderly but distinguished scientist says that something is possible he is almost certainly right, but if he says that it is impossible he is very probably wrong.

Arthur C. Clarke 1917–2008: in *New Yorker* 9 August 1969

12 I have no more faith in men of science being infallible than I have in men of God being infallible, principally on account of them being men.

Noël Coward 1899–1973: diary, 1 July 1946

13 Equations are more important to me, because politics is for the present, but an equation is something for eternity.

Albert Einstein 1879–1955: Stephen Hawking *A Brief History of Time* (1988)

14 If I could remember the names of all these particles I'd be a botanist.

Enrico Fermi 1901–54: R. L. Weber *More Random Walks in Science* (1973)

15 Someone told me that each equation I included in the book would halve the sales.

Stephen Hawking 1942– : *A Brief History of Time* (1988)

16 Cosmologists are often in error, but never in doubt.

Lev Landau 1908–68: attributed in Simon Singh *Big Bang* (2004)

17 It was Einstein who made the real trouble. He announced in 1905 that there was no such thing as absolute rest. After that there never was.

Stephen Leacock 1869–1944: *The Boy I Left Behind Me* (1947)

18 When Rutherford was done with the atom all the solidity was pretty well knocked out of it.

Stephen Leacock 1869–1944: *The Boy I Left Behind Me* (1947)

19 My theory [is] that modern science was largely conceived of as an answer to the servant problem and that it is generally practised by those who lack a flair for conversation.

Fran Lebowitz 1946– : *Metropolitan Life* (1978)

20 It is a good morning exercise for a research scientist to discard a pet hypothesis every day before breakfast.

Konrad Lorenz 1903–89: *On Aggression* (1966)

21 The scientist who yields anything to theology, however slight, is yielding to ignorance and false pretences, and as certainly as if he granted that a horse-hair put into a bottle of water will turn into a snake.

H. L. Mencken 1880–1956: *Minority Report* (1956)

22 To mistrust science and deny the validity of the scientific method is to resign your job as a human. You'd better go look for work as a plant or wild animal.

P. J. O'Rourke 1947– : *Parliament of Whores* (1991)

23 Aristotle maintained that women have fewer teeth than men; although he was twice married, it never occurred to him to verify this statement by examining his wives' mouths.

Bertrand Russell 1872–1970: *Impact of Science on Society* (1952)

24 Science becomes dangerous only when it imagines that it has reached its goal.

George Bernard Shaw 1856–1950: preface to *The Doctor's Dilemma* (1911)

25 He had been eight years upon a project for extracting sunbeams out of cucumbers, which were to be put into vials hermetically sealed, and let out to warm the air in raw inclement summers.

Jonathan Swift 1667–1745: *Gulliver's Travels* (1726)

26 Her own mother lived the latter years of her life in the horrible suspicion that electricity was dripping invisibly all over the house.

James Thurber 1894–1961: *My Life and Hard Times* (1933)

27 There is something fascinating about science. One gets such wholesale returns of conjecture out of such a trifling investment of fact.

Mark Twain 1835–1910: *Life on the Mississippi* (1883)

28 It was absolutely marvellous working for Pauli. You could ask him anything. There was no worry that he would think a particular question was stupid, since he thought *all* questions were stupid.

Victor Weisskopf 1908–2002: in *American Journal of Physics* 1977

Scotland

See also **Countries and Peoples, Places**

66 *That state of mind which cartographers seek to define as Scotland.* 99
Claud Cockburn

1 There are few more impressive sights in the world than a Scotsman on the make.

J. M. Barrie 1860–1937: *What Every Woman Knows* (performed 1908)

2 A young Scotsman of your ability let loose upon the world with £300, what could he not do? It's almost appalling to think of; especially if he went among the English.

J. M. Barrie 1860–1937: *What Every Woman Knows* (1918)

3 I had occasion, not for the first time, to thank heaven for that state of mind which cartographers seek to define as Scotland.

Claud Cockburn 1904–81: *Crossing the Line* (1958)

4 They christened their game golf because they were Scottish and revelled in meaningless Celtic noises in the back of the throat.

Stephen Fry 1957– : *Paperweight* (1992)

5 Norway, too, has noble wild prospects; and Lapland is remarkable for prodigious noble wild prospects. But, Sir, let me tell you, the noblest prospect which a Scotchman ever sees, is the high road that leads him to England!

Samuel Johnson 1709–84: James Boswell *Life of Samuel Johnson* (1791) 6 July 1763

6 *Oats.* A grain, which in England is generally given to horses, but in Scotland supports the people.

Samuel Johnson 1709–84: *A Dictionary of the English Language* (1755)

7 Can the United States ever become genuinely civilized? Certainly it is possible. Even Scotland has made enormous progress since the Eighteenth Century, when, according to Macaulay, most of it was on the cultural level of Albania.

H. L. Mencken 1880–1956: *Minority Report* (1956)

8 No McTavish
Was ever lavish.

Ogden Nash 1902–71: 'Genealogical Reflection' (1931)

9 Scotland has too many ninety-minute patriots whose nationalist outpourings are expressed only at major sporting events.

Jim Sillars 1937– : television interview following the 1992 general election; in *The Herald* 24 April 1992

10 That knuckle-end of England—that land of Calvin, oat-cakes, and sulphur.

Sydney Smith 1771–1845: Lady Holland *Memoir* (1855)

11 It requires a surgical operation to get a joke well into a Scotch understanding. Their only idea of wit . . . is laughing immoderately at stated intervals.

Sydney Smith 1771–1845: Lady Holland *Memoir* (1855)

12 It is never difficult to distinguish between a Scotsman with a grievance and a ray of sunshine.

P. G. Wodehouse 1881–1975: *Blandings Castle and Elsewhere* (1935)

Secrecy
See also **Security**

❝ Being an enigma at 30 shows a lack of imagination. ❞
John Peel

1 *of the 19th-century diarist Charles Greville:*
For fifty years he listened at the door
He heard some secrets and invented more.

Charles M. Andrews 1863–1943: 'These Forty Years', annual address of the President of the American Historical Association, 27 December 1924

2 A Company for carrying on an undertaking of Great Advantage, but no one to know what it is.

Anonymous: Company Prospectus at the time of the South Sea Bubble (1711)

3 See all your best work go unnoticed.

Anonymous: advertisement for staff for MI5, 2005

4 Everyone has a skeleton in their closet. The difference between Bill Clinton and myself is that he has a walk-in closet.

Pat Buchanan 1938– : in *Sunday Times* 21 November 1999

5 Secrets with girls, like loaded guns with boys,
Are never valued till they make a noise.

George Crabbe 1754–1832: *Tales of the Hall* (1819) 'The Maid's Story'

6 When I was nine I remember one of my most secret vices was to wait till everybody had gone out and listen to the last scene of Siegfried again. I was so worried about this I didn't want anyone to know.

Colin Davis 1927– : Anthony Clare *In the Psychiatrist's Chair III* (1998)

7 We never knows wot's hidden in each other's hearts; and if we had glass winders there, we'd need keep the shutters up, some on us, I do assure you!

Charles Dickens 1812–70: *Martin Chuzzlewit* (1844)

8 Anonymous, unseen—
You're dealing with the all-time king or queen
Of undercover loves.
The author of this valentine wore gloves.

Sophie Hannah 1971– : 'Poem for a Valentine Card' (1995)

9 That's another of those irregular verbs, isn't it? I give confidential briefings; you leak; he has been charged under Section 2a of the Official Secrets Act.

Jonathan Lynn 1943– and **Antony Jay** 1930– : *Yes Prime Minister* (1987) vol. 2 'Man Overboard'

10 *of Bob Dylan:*
Being an enigma at 20 is fun, being an enigma at 30 shows a lack of imagination, and being an enigma at Dylan's age is just plain daft.

John Peel 1939–2004: in *Observer* 18 October 1987

Security

66 *The best leaks always take place in the urinal.* 99
John Cole

1 I came to the conclusion that a man who could give such pleasure with his pen couldn't be much of a secret agent. I may well be wrong.
view of the IRA army council's head of civilian intelligence on John Betjeman's role as a press attaché in wartime Dublin

Diarmuid Brennan: report, c.1941; in *Guardian* 22 April 2000

2 Is that man crazy? He thinks there's a bug behind all the pictures.
as Director of the CIA, having visited Harold Wilson during Wilson's last premiership

George Bush 1924– : Peter Hennessy *The Prime Minister: the Office and its Holders since 1945* (2000)

3 The best leaks always take place in the urinal.

John Cole 1927– : in *Independent* 3 June 1996

4 The spy who came in for a cardie.
on 85-year-old Melita Nelson, exposed in 1999 as having spied for Russia in the Cold War

Mike Coleman 1946– : on *Loose Ends* (BBC Radio 4) 18 September 1999

5 If a man cannot keep a measly affair secret, what is he doing in charge of the Intelligence Service?
on the break-up of the marriage of Foreign Secretary Robin Cook

Frederick Forsyth 1938– : in *Guardian* 14 January 1998

6 Truth is suppressed, not to protect the country from enemy agents but to protect the Government of the day against the people.

Roy Hattersley 1932– : in *Independent* 18 February 1995

7 It's been a huge advantage during my professional career that I've always looked like a cheerful, fat missionary. It wouldn't be any use if you went around looking sinister, would it?
view of one of MI6's most senior controllers

Daphne Park 1921– : in *Daily Telegraph* 24 April 2003

8 BLAIR: Everybody knows their safe house. Red Square we call it.
HOGBIN: We call it Dunkremlin.

Tom Stoppard 1937– : *The Dog It Was That Died* (1983)

Self-Knowledge and Self-Deception

See also **Character**

❝ I wouldn't say I was the best manager, but I was in the top one. ❞
Brian Clough

1 Lady Kill-Chairman, who is one of the greatest gossips in the kingdom, and knows everybody but herself.

Anonymous: in *The Female Tatler* December 1709

2 A person of low taste, more interested in himself than in me.
definition of an egotist

Ambrose Bierce 1842–c.1914: *Cynic's Word Book* (1906)

3 Our polite recognition of another's resemblance to ourselves.
definition of admiration

Ambrose Bierce 1842–c.1914: *Cynic's Word Book* (1906)

4 I think that most people who have dealt with me think that I am a pretty straight sort of guy.
on the handling of the decision to exempt Formula One motor racing from a proposed ban on tobacco advertising

Tony Blair 1953– : 'On the Record' interview with John Humphrys, 16 November 1997

5 They misunderestimated me.

George W. Bush 1946– : speech in Bentonville, Arkansas, November 2000

6 It exactly resembles a superannuated Jesuit . . . though my mind misgives me that it is hideously like. If it is—I can not be long for this world—for it overlooks seventy.
of a bust of himself by Bartolini

Lord Byron 1788–1824: letter 23 September 1822

7 The Crown Prince Umberto is charm itself, but has no great intelligence. He reminds me of myself.

Chips Channon 1897–1958: diary (undated entry); introduction to *Chips: the Diaries of Sir Henry Channon* (1993)

8 I wouldn't say I was the best manager, but I was in the top one.

Brian Clough 1935–2004: attributed; in *Scotsman* 21 September 2004 (online edition)

9 Long experience has taught me that to be criticized is not always to be wrong.

Anthony Eden 1897–1977: speech at Lord Mayor's Guildhall banquet during the Suez crisis; in *Daily Herald* 10 November 1956

10 *to a footman who had accidentally spilt cream over him:*
My good man, I'm not a strawberry!

Edward VII 1841–1910: William Lanceley *From Hall-Boy to House-Steward* (1925)

11   I tell you,
Miss, I knows an undesirable character
When I see one; I've been one myself for years.

Christopher Fry 1907–2005: *Venus Observed* (1950)

12 Bono wants to change the world by embracing it. I get angry and want to punch its light out. We are the Laurel and Hardy of international politics.

Bob Geldof 1954– : in *Observer* 6 March 2005

13 All my shows are great. Some of them are bad. But they are all great.

Lew Grade 1906–98: in *Observer* 14 September 1975

14 The photograph is not quite true to my own notion of my gentleness and sweetness of nature, but neither perhaps is my external appearance.

A. E. Housman 1859–1936: letter, 12 June 1922

15 Without exactly *telling* them that I felt like a man swimming towards a raft in a sea of circling fins, I constructed a cry for help masterfully disguised as a manifesto.

Clive James 1939– : *The Dreaming Swimmer* (1992)

16 For self-revelation, whether it be a Tudor villa on the by-pass or a bomb-proof chalet at Berchtesgaden, there's no place like home.

Osbert Lancaster 1908–86: *Homes Sweet Homes* (1939)

17 I am not the type who wants to go back to the land; I am the type who wants to go back to the hotel.

Fran Lebowitz 1946– : *Social Studies* (1981)

18 Underneath this flabby exterior is an enormous lack of character.

Oscar Levant 1906–72: *Memoirs of an Amnesiac* (1965)

19 I believe that Sir Isaiah Berlin is the only man in Britain who talks more rapidly than I do, and even that is a close-run thing.

Bernard Levin 1928–2004: *In These Times* (1986)

20 I have low self-esteem, but I express it the healthy way . . . by eating a box of Double-Stuf Oreos.

Terri Minsky: *Sex and the City* 'The Baby Shower (1998), spoken by Miranda (Cynthia Nixon)

21 [I am] a doormat in a world of boots.

Jean Rhys c.1890–1979: in *Guardian* 6 December 1990

22 You're so vain
You probably think this song is about you.

Carly Simon 1945– : 'You're So Vain' (1972 song)

23 I can put two and two together, you know. Do not think you are dealing with a man who has lost his grapes.

Tom Stoppard 1937– : *Another Moon Called Earth* (1983)

24 The kind of person who embarks on an endless leap-frog down to the great moral issues. I put a position, rebut it, refute it, refute the rebuttal and rebut the refutation. Endlessly.
    on himself

Tom Stoppard 1937– : Mel Gussow *Conversations with Stoppard* (1995)

25 Satire is a sort of glass, wherein beholders do generally discover everybody's face but their own.

Jonathan Swift 1667–1745: *The Battle of the Books* (1704) preface

26 'He has a profound contempt for human nature.'
'Of course, he is much given to introspection.'
    of Fouché

Charles-Maurice de Talleyrand 1754–1838: Leon Harris *The Fine Art of Political Wit* (1965)

27 I am extraordinarily patient, provided I get my own way in the end.

Margaret Thatcher 1925– : in *Observer* 4 April 1989

28 Pavarotti is not vain, but conscious of being unique.

Peter Ustinov 1921–2004: in *Independent on Sunday* 12 September 1993

29 I'm the girl who lost her reputation and never missed it.

Mae West 1892–1980: P. F. Boller and R. L. Davis *Hollywood Anecdotes* (1988)

30 I don't at all like knowing what people say of me behind my back. It makes me far too conceited.

Oscar Wilde 1854–1900: *An Ideal Husband* (1895)

Sex

See also **Love, Marriage**

> **❝** *I've been around so long, I knew Doris Day before she was a virgin.* **❞**
> **Groucho Marx**

1 Don't knock masturbation. It's sex with someone I love.

Woody Allen 1935– : *Annie Hall* (1977 film, with Marshall Brickman)

2 That [sex] was the most fun I ever had without laughing.

Woody Allen 1935– : *Annie Hall* (1977 film, with Marshall Brickman)

3 My love life is terrible. The last time I was inside a woman was when I visited the Statue of Liberty.

Woody Allen 1935– : *Crimes and Misdemeanors* (1989 film)

4 Is sex dirty? Only if it's done right.

Woody Allen 1935– : *Everything You Always Wanted to Know about Sex* (1972 film)

5 I think people should mate for life. Like pigeons, or Catholics.

Woody Allen 1935– and **Marshall Brickman** 1941– : *Manhattan* (1979 film), spoken by Woody Allen

6 A fast word about oral contraception. I asked a girl to go to bed with me and she said 'no'.

Woody Allen 1935– : at a night-club in Washington, April 1965

7 On bisexuality: It immediately doubles your chances for a date on Saturday night.

Woody Allen 1935– : in *New York Times* 1 December 1975

8 *a former girlfriend's description of being made love to by Nicholas Soames:*
Like having a large wardrobe fall on top of you with the key still in the lock.

Anonymous: Gyles Brandreth *Breaking the Code* (1999)

9 You should make a point of trying every experience once, excepting incest and folk-dancing.

Anonymous: Arnold Bax *Farewell My Youth* (1943), quoting 'a sympathetic Scot'

10 Would you like to sin
With Elinor Glyn
On a tigerskin?
Or would you prefer
To err
With her
On some other fur?

Anonymous: verse alluding to Elinor Glyn's romantic novel *Three Weeks* (1907); A. Glyn *Elinor Glyn* (1955)

11 You're the burning heat of a bridal suite in use.
You're the breasts of Venus,
You're King Kong's penis,
You're self abuse.
You're an arch

Anonymous: parody version of Cole Porter's 'You're the Top' (1934), possibly by Porter

In the Rome collection
You're the starch
In a groom's erection.

12 'My mother made me a homosexual.'
'If I send her the wool will she make me one?'

Anonymous: New York graffito of the 1970s

13 Let us honour if we can
The vertical man
Though we value none
But the horizontal one.

W. H. Auden 1907–73: 'To Christopher Isherwood' (1930)

14 Give me chastity and continency—but not yet!

St Augustine of Hippo AD 354–430: *Confessions* (AD 397–8)

15 Norman doesn't bother with secret signals. It was just wham, thump and there we both were on the rug.

Alan Ayckbourn 1939– : *Table Manners* (1975)

16 My mother used to say, Delia, if S-E-X ever rears its ugly head, close your eyes before you see the rest of it.

Alan Ayckbourn 1939– : *Bedroom Farce* (1978)

17 I'll come and make love to you at five o'clock. If I'm late start without me.

Tallulah Bankhead 1903–68: Ted Morgan *Somerset Maugham* (1980)

18 Bendor says that Beauchamp is a bugler.
when Bendor, Duke of Westminster, tried to explain his brother-in-law's homosexuality to his sister

Lady Beauchamp 1876–1936: in *Daily Telegraph* 16 November 2005

19 I've no feeling in this arm and I can hardly see. Which knocks out at least three erogenous zones for a kick-off.

Alan Bennett 1934– : *Enjoy* (1980)

20 *on being told by her son that lesbians are women who sleep together:*
MRS HOPKINS: Well, that's nothing. I slept with your Auntie Phyllis all during the air raids.

Alan Bennett 1934– : *Me! I'm Afraid of Virginia Woolf* (1978)

21 I'm a trisexual. I'll try anything once.

Jenny Bicks: *Sex and the City* 'Boy, Girl, Boy, Girl . . . ' (2000), spoken by Samantha (Kim Cattrall)

22 *at the age of ninety-seven, Blake was asked at what age the sex drive goes:*
You'll have to ask somebody older than me.

Eubie Blake 1883–1983: in *Ned Sherrin in his Anecdotage* (1993)

23 *on being told he should not marry anyone as plain as his fiancée:*
My dear fellow, buggers can't be choosers.

Maurice Bowra 1898–1971: Hugh Lloyd-Jones *Maurice Bowra: a Celebration* (1974)

24 Genitals are a great distraction to scholarship.

Malcolm Bradbury 1932– : *Cuts* (1987)

25 If homosexuality were the normal way, God would have made Adam and Bruce.

Anita Bryant 1940– : in *New York Times* 5 June 1977

26 I'm afraid, you know, there isn't as much of this about as you seem to think.
on Julian Barnes's suggestion, c.1970, that 'blow-job' should be included in the Supplement to the Oxford English Dictionary

Robert Burchfield 1923–2004: quoted by Julian Barnes in *Imagine* (BBC2, 18 December 2003)

27 It was the afternoon of my eighty-first birthday, and I was in bed with my catamite when Ali announced that the archbishop had come to see me.

Anthony Burgess 1917–93: *Earthly Powers* (1980); opening sentence

28 He said it was artificial respiration, but now I find I am to have his child.

Anthony Burgess 1917–93: *Inside Mr Enderby* (1963)

29 What men call gallantry, and gods adultery,
Is much more common where the climate's sultry.

Lord Byron 1788–1824: *Don Juan* (1819–24)

30 A little still she strove, and much repented,
And whispering 'I will ne'er consent'—consented.

Lord Byron 1788–1824: *Don Juan* (1819–24)

31 *on homosexuality:*
It doesn't matter what you do in the bedroom as long as you don't do it in the street and frighten the horses.

Mrs Patrick Campbell 1865–1940: Daphne Fielding *The Duchess of Jermyn Street* (1964)

32 Do not adultery commit;
Advantage rarely comes of it.

Arthur Hugh Clough 1819–61: 'The Latest Decalogue' (1862)

33 The House of Commons en bloc do it,
Civil Servants by the clock do it.

Noël Coward 1899–1973: 'Let's Do It' (with acknowledgements to Cole Porter) (1940s)

34 I became one of the stately homos of England.

Quentin Crisp 1908–99: *The Naked Civil Servant* (1968)

35 For flavour, Instant Sex will never supersede the stuff you had to peel and cook.

Quentin Crisp 1908–99: in *Sunday Telegraph* 28 September 1999

36 *in 1951 the homosexual Labour politician Tom Driberg married a widow; he later complained:*
She broke her marriage vows; she tried to sleep with me.

Tom Driberg 1905–76: in Ned Sherrin in his *Anecdotage* (1993)

37 Seduction is often difficult to distinguish from rape. In seduction, the rapist bothers to buy a bottle of wine.

Andrea Dworkin 1946–2005: *Letters from a War Zone* (1988)

38 He in a few minutes ravished this fair creature, or at least would have ravished her, if she had not, by a timely compliance, prevented him.

Henry Fielding 1707–54: *Jonathan Wild* (1743)

39 My dad told me, 'Anything worth having is worth waiting for.' I waited until I was fifteen.

Zsa Zsa Gabor 1919– : attributed; Bob Chieger *Was It Good For You?* (1983)

40 Sex was a competitive event in those days and the only thing you could take as a certainty was that everyone else was lying, just as you were.

Bob Geldof 1954– : *Is That It?* (1986)

41 Only the Lion and the Cock;
As Galen says, withstand Love's shock.
So, dearest, do not think me rude
If I yield now to lassitude,
But sympathize with me. I know
You would not have me roar or crow.

Oliver St John Gogarty 1878–1957: 'After Galen' (1957)

42 'Ye'es, ye'es,' he finally observed with a certain dry relish, 'ye'es, I think I see some adulterers down there.'
in the Press Gallery of the House of Commons during the Profumo scandal

Maurice Green 1906–87: recorded by Colin Welch; Ned Sherrin *Cutting Edge* (1984)

43 Masturbation is the thinking man's television.

Christopher Hampton 1946– : *The Philanthropist* (1970)

44 The trouble with a virgin is
She's always on the verge.
A virgin is the worst
Her method is reversed
She'll lead a horse to water
And then let him die of thirst.

E. Y. Harburg 1898–1981: 'Never Trust a Virgin' (1961)

45 It's not a good idea to fall asleep while you're actually having sexual intercourse.

Hugh Hefner 1926– : in *Mail on Sunday* 22 August 2004

46 I regret to say that we of the FBI are powerless to act in cases of oral-genital intimacy, unless it has in some way obstructed interstate commerce.

J. Edgar Hoover 1895–1972: Irving Wallace et al. *Intimate Sex Lives of Famous People* (1981)

47 My father told me all about the birds and the bees, the liar—I went steady with a woodpecker until I was 21.

Bob Hope 1903–2003: attributed; in *Times* 29 July 2003

48 I am trisexual. The Army, the Navy, and the Household Cavalry.

Brian Desmond Hurst 1895–1986: Christopher Robbins *The Empress of Ireland* (2004)

49 I can't get no satisfaction
I can't get no girl reaction.

Mick Jagger 1943– and **Keith Richards** 1943– : '(I Can't Get No) Satisfaction' (1965)

50 There is no unhappier creature on earth than a fetishist who yearns to embrace a woman's shoe and has to embrace the whole woman.

Karl Kraus 1874–1936: *Aphorisms and More Aphorisms* (1909)

51 Sexual intercourse began
In nineteen sixty-three
(Which was rather late for me)—
Between the end of the *Chatterley* ban
And the Beatles' first L.P.

Philip Larkin 1922–85: 'Annus Mirabilis' (1974)

52 Surely the sex business isn't worth all this damned fuss? I've met only a handful of people who cared a biscuit for it.
on reading Lady Chatterley's Lover

T. E. Lawrence 1888–1935: Christopher Hassall *Edward Marsh* (1959)

53 He was into animal husbandry—until they caught him at it.

Tom Lehrer 1928– : in *An Evening Wasted with Tom Lehrer* (record album, 1953); Nigel Rees (ed.) *Cassell Dictionary of Humorous Quotations* (1999)

54 *on lesbianism:*
I can understand two men. There is something to get hold of. But how do two insides make love?

Lydia Lopokova 1892–1981: A. J. P. Taylor letter 5 November 1973

55 Is sex dirty? Only when you don't take a bath.

Madonna 1958– : *Madonna: in Her Own Words* (1990)

56 Many years ago I chased a woman for almost two years, only to discover that her tastes were exactly like mine: we both were crazy about girls.

Groucho Marx 1895–1977: letter 28 March 1955

57 I've been around so long, I knew Doris Day before she was a virgin.

Groucho Marx 1890–1977: Max Wilk *The Wit and Wisdom of Hollywood* (1972)

58 I always thought music was more important than sex—then I thought if I don't hear a concert for a year-and-a-half it doesn't bother me.

Jackie Mason 1931– : in *Guardian* 17 February 1989

59 Continental people have sex life; the English have hot-water bottles.

George Mikes 1912–87: *How to be an Alien* (1946)

60 Men who blow themselves up are promised 72 virgins in paradise. That's a high price to pay for a shag.

Shazia Mirza 1976– : at the Edinburgh Festival, 2006, in *Independent* 26 August 2006

61 *on tantric sex:*
I prefer the plumber position. You stay in all day and nobody comes.

John Mortimer 1923–2009: in *Times* 24 February 2003

62 An orgy looks particularly alluring seen through the mists of righteous indignation.

Malcolm Muggeridge 1903–90: *The Most of Malcolm Muggeridge* (1966) 'Dolce Vita in a Cold Climate'

63 Not tonight, Josephine.

Napoleon I 1769–1821: attributed, but probably apocryphal; R. H. Horne *The History of Napoleon* (1841) describes the circumstances in which the affront might have occurred

64 I toiled on a farm tilling soybeans,
In a struggle to chasten my brain,
But the girl beans got in with the boy beans,
And I never struggled again.

Ogden Nash 1902–71: in *One Touch of Venus* (1943 musical film)

65 She was as happy as the dey was long.
   of the relationship between Caroline of Brunswick, estranged wife of George IV, and the dey (or governor) of Algiers

Lord Norbury 1745–1831: attributed; Nigel Rees *Cassell Dictionary of Humorous Quotations* (1998)

66 GARY: She put me right on a few technical details, yes.
DERMOT: She said it was like sleeping with a badly-informed labrador.

Simon Nye 1958– : *Men Behaving Badly* (ITV, series 1, 1992) 'Intruders'

67 You were born with your legs apart. They'll send you to the grave in a Y-shaped coffin.

Joe Orton 1933–67: *What the Butler Saw* (1969)

68 MIKE: There's no word in the Irish language for what you were doing.
WILSON: In Lapland they have no word for snow.

Joe Orton 1933–67: *The Ruffian on the Stair* (rev. ed. 1967)

69 His second question was, 'How queer are you?' If I myself had small talent to amuse, I could at least make an effort to please. 'Oh, about twenty per cent.' 'Really! Are you? I'm ninety-five.'

John Osborne 1929–94: recollection of a conversation with Noël Coward in 1966; *Almost a Gentleman* (1991)

70 Thank God we're normal,
Yes, this is our finest shower!

John Osborne 1929–94: *The Entertainer* (1957)

71 *on her abortion:*
It serves me right for putting all my eggs in one bastard.

Dorothy Parker 1893–1967: John Keats *You Might as well Live* (1970)

72 On a sofa upholstered in panther skin
Mona did researches in original sin.

William Plomer 1903–73: 'Mews Flat Mona' (1960)

73 Birds do it, bees do it,
Even educated fleas do it.
Let's do it, let's fall in love.

Cole Porter 1891–1964: 'Let's Do It' (1954; words added to the 1928 original)

74 Mister Harris, Plutocrat,
Wants to give my cheek a pat.
If a Harris pat
Means a Paris hat,
Bébé!

Cole Porter 1891–1964: 'Always True to You in my Fashion' (*Kiss Me Kate* 1949 musical)

75 No, no; for my virginity,
When I lose that, says Rose, I'll die:
Behind the elms last night, cried Dick,
Rose, were you not extremely sick?

Matthew Prior 1664–1721: 'A True Maid' (1718)

76 Your idea of fidelity is not having more than one man in bed at the same time.

Frederic Raphael 1931– : *Darling* (1965)

77 I mean to have you, even if it must be burglary.

Bruce Robinson 1946– : *Withnail and I* (1987 film), spoken by Richard Griffiths as Monty to Paul McGann as Marwood

78 Sex is something I really don't understand too hot. You never know *where* the hell you are. I keep making up these sex rules for myself, and then I break them right away.

J. D. Salinger 1919– : *The Catcher in the Rye* (1951)

79 *the practice in a New York bath house was for someone wanting a partner to leave the cubicle door open. A young man, entering John Schlesinger's cubicle, recoiled on seeing 'this mound of flesh':*
ANONYMOUS: Oh, please. I couldn't. You've got to be kidding.
JOHN SCHLESINGER: A simple *No* will suffice.

John Schlesinger 1926–2003: Alan Bennett diary 2003, in *London Review of Books* 8 January 2004; a similar story was quoted to the Editor in the 1960s by the American writer Burt Shevelove as happening to him

80 Is it not strange that desire should so many years outlive performance?

William Shakespeare 1564–1616: *Henry IV, Part 2* (1597)

81 *of Marina, a beautiful virgin:*
She would serve after a long voyage at sea.

William Shakespeare 1564–1616: *Pericles* (1606–8)

82 How long do you want to wait until you start enjoying life? When you're sixty-five you get social security, not girls.

Neil Simon 1927– : *Come Blow Your Horn* (1961)

83 Where is she at the moment? Alone with probably the most attractive man she's ever met. Don't tell me *that* doesn't beat hell out of hair curlers and the *Late Late Show.*

Neil Simon 1927– : *Barefoot in the Park* (1964)

84 Fancy meeting someone and forgetting you've slept with them. It's not good, is it?

Arthur Smith 1954– : *The Live Bed Show* (1995)

85 How can a bishop marry? How can he flirt? The most he can say is, 'I will see you in the vestry after service.'

Sydney Smith 1771–1845: Lady Holland *Memoir* (1855)

86 BONES: A consummate artist, sir. I felt it deeply when she retired.
GEORGE: Unfortunately she retired from consummation about the same time as she retired from artistry.

Tom Stoppard 1937– : *Jumpers* (rev. ed. 1986)

87 [CHAIRMAN OF MILITARY TRIBUNAL:] What would you do if you saw a German soldier trying to violate your sister?
[STRACHEY:] I would try to get between them.

Lytton Strachey 1880–1932: in Robert Graves *Good-bye to All That* (1929); otherwise rendered as, 'I should interpose my body'

88 Masturbation: the primary sexual activity of mankind. In the nineteenth century, it was a disease; in the twentieth, it's a cure.

Thomas Szasz 1920– : *The Second Sin* (1973)

89 Gomer Owen who kissed her once by the pig-sty when she wasn't looking and never kissed her again although she was looking all the time.

Dylan Thomas 1914–53: *Under Milk Wood* (1954)

90 Chasing the naughty couples down the grassgreen gooseberried double bed of the wood.

Dylan Thomas 1914–53: *Under Milk Wood* (1954)

91 Dip me in chocolate and throw me to the lesbians.

Richard Thomas and **Stewart Lee**: *Jerry Springer—the Opera* (2003)

92 Enjoy your supper, Mr Percy, the port is on the chim-a-ney piece, and it's *still* adultery!
on finding her husband Herbert Beerbohm Tree dining à deux with the young and handsome actor Esmé Percy

Lady Tree 1863–1937: attributed, perhaps apocryphal

93 Enter the strumpet voluntary.

Kenneth Tynan 1927–80: of a guest at an Oxford party; attributed

94 I'm all for bringing back the birch, but only between consenting adults.

Gore Vidal 1925– : in *Sunday Times Magazine* 16 September 1973

95 All this fuss about sleeping together. For physical pleasure I'd sooner go to my dentist any day.

Evelyn Waugh 1903–66: *Vile Bodies* (1930)

96 In my day, I would only have sex with a man if I found him extremely attractive. These days, girls seem to choose them in much the same way as they might choose to suck on a boiled sweet.

Mary Wesley 1912–2002: in *Independent* 18 October 1997 'Quote Unquote'

97 Why don't you come up sometime, and see me?
usually quoted as, 'Why don't you come up and see me sometime?'

Mae West 1892–1980: in *She Done Him Wrong* (1933 film)

98 It's not the men in my life that counts—it's the life in my men.

Mae West 1892–1980: in *I'm No Angel* (1933 film)

Shopping

❝ If it's shiny, I buy it. ❞
Graham Norton

1 We used to build civilizations. Now we build shopping malls.

Bill Bryson 1951– : *Neither Here Nor There* (1991)

2 Always buy a good pair of shoes and a good bed—if you're not in one you're in the other.
advice from her mother

Gloria Hunniford 1941– : in *Mail on Sunday* 16 June 2002

3 If it's shiny, I buy it.
on buying clothes

Graham Norton 1963– : in *Observer* 13 June 2004

4 When in doubt buy shoes.

Marcelle D'Argy Smith: attributed; in *Independent* 20 August 1997

Sickness

See also **Health, Medicine**

❝ I wish I had the voice of Homer To sing of rectal carcinoma. ❞
J. B. S. Haldane

1 *Christopher Isherwood, apologising for his bad cold, had said that he should probably have cancelled his dinner invitation to Axelrod and Frederic Raphael:*
My dear Christopher, any cold of yours is a cold of mine.

George Axelrod 1922– : quoted by Frederic Raphael in *Times Literary Supplement* 4 February 2000

2 He was a very fine doctor. Very little he couldn't put right when he set his mind to it. Rita's knee got the better of him, though.

Alan Ayckbourn 1939– : *Sisterly Feelings* (1981)

3 What's happened to the galloping consumption you had last Thursday? Slowed down to a trot I suppose.

Alan Bennett 1934– : *Habeas Corpus* (1973)

4 I'm not unwell. I'm fucking dying.

Jeffrey Bernard 1932–97: in conversation with Dominic Lawson; in *The Spectator* 19 February 1994

5 A cough so robust that I tapped into two new seams of phlegm.

Bill Bryson 1951– : *Neither Here Nor There* (1991)

6 What fun—dear little Sidney
Produced a spectacular stone in his kidney,
He's had eleven
So God's in His heaven
And that is the end of the news.

Noël Coward 1899–1973: 'That is the End of the News' (1945)

7 The nurse sleeps sweetly, hired to watch the sick,
Whom, snoring, she disturbs.

William Cowper 1731–1800: *The Task* (1785)

8 This cough I've got is hacking,
The pain in my head is wracking,
I hardly need to mention my flu.
The Board of Health has seen me
They want to quarantine me,
I might as well be miserable with you.

Howard Dietz 1896–1983: 'Miserable with You' (1931)

9 I wish I had the voice of Homer
To sing of rectal carcinoma,
Which kills a lot more chaps, in fact,
Than were bumped off when Troy was sacked.

J. B. S. Haldane 1892–1964: 'Cancer's a Funny Thing'; Ronald Clark *J. B. S.* (1968)

10 My final word, before I'm done,
Is 'Cancer can be rather fun'.
Thanks to the nurses and Nye Bevan
The NHS is quite like heaven
Provided one confronts the tumour
With a sufficient sense of humour.

J. B. S. Haldane 1892–1964: 'Cancer's a Funny Thing'; Ronald Clark *J. B. S.* (1968)

11 *on reticent British acting:*
I am well, except for a slight cold caught watching Sir Gerald du Maurier making love.

George S. Kaufman 1889–1961: Ilka Chase *Past Imperfect* (1942)

12 You can feed her all day with the vitamin A and the Bromo fizz,
But the medicine never gets anywhere near where the trouble is,
If she's getting a kind of a name for herself, and the name ain't his—
A person . . . can develop a cough.

Frank Loesser 1910–69: 'Adelaide's Lament', reprise (1950)

13 In other words just from waiting around
For that plain little band of gold
A person . . . can develop a cold.
You can spray her wherever you figure the streptococci lurk.
You can give her a shot for whatever she's got but it just won't work.
If she's tired of getting the fish-eye from the hotel clerk,
A person . . . can develop a cold.

Frank Loesser 1910–69: 'Adelaide's Lament' (1950)

14 Besides death, constipation is the big fear in hospitals.

Robert McCrum 1953– : *My Year Off* (1998)

15 *on hearing of the illness of Traill, who in 1904 had beaten him for the Provostship of Trinity Dublin:*
Nothing trivial, I hope.

John Pentland Mahaffy 1839–1919: Ulick O'Connor *Oliver St John Gogarty* (1964)

16 To talk of diseases is a sort of *Arabian Nights* entertainment.

William Osler 1849–1919: Oliver Sacks *The Man Who Mistook his Wife for a Hat* (1985)

17 Hypochondria is the one disease I haven't got.

David Renwick 1951– and **Andrew Marshall**: *The Burkiss Way* (BBC Radio, 1978); Nigel Rees *Cassell Dictionary of Humorous Quotations* (1999)

18 In rural cottage life not to have rheumatism is as glaring an omission as not to have been presented at Court would be in more ambitious circumstances.

Saki 1870–1916: *The Toys of Peace* (1919)

19 When men die of disease they are said to die from natural causes. When they recover (and they mostly do) the doctor gets the credit of curing them.

George Bernard Shaw 1856–1950: preface to *The Doctor's Dilemma* (1911)

20 My aunt died of influenza: so they said. But it's my belief they done the old woman in.

George Bernard Shaw 1856–1950: *Pygmalion* (1916)

21 BUDDY: . . . Do you feel any better?
MOTHER: How do I know? I feel too sick to tell.

Neil Simon 1927– : *Come Blow Your Horn* (1961)

22 *on hearing that Peter Sellers had suffered a heart attack:*
What do you mean, heart attack? You've got to have a heart before you can have an attack.

Billy Wilder 1906–2002: Roger Lewis *The Life and Death of Peter Sellers* (1994)

Singing see **Songs and Singing**

Sleep and Dreams

66 There ain't no way to find out why a snorer can't hear himself snore. 99
Mark Twain

1 'It would make anyone go to sleep, that bedstead would, whether they wanted to or not.' 'I should think,' said Sam . . . 'poppies was nothing to it.'

Charles Dickens 1812–70: *Pickwick Papers* (1837)

2 Try thinking of love, or something.
Amor vincit insomnia.

Christopher Fry 1907–2005: *A Sleep of Prisoners* (1951)

3 Sleep is when all the unsorted stuff comes flying out as from a dustbin upset in a high wind.

William Golding 1911–93: *Pincher Martin* (1956)

4 I want something that will keep me awake thinking it was the food I ate and not the show I saw.
after a disastrous preview

George S. Kaufman 1889–1961: Howard Teichmann *George S. Kaufman* (1973)

5 I love sleep because it is both pleasant and safe to use.

Fran Lebowitz 1946– : *Metropolitan Life* (1978)

6 And so to bed.

Samuel Pepys 1633–1703: diary 20 April 1660

7 Men who are unhappy, like men who sleep badly, are always proud of the fact.

Bertrand Russell 1872–1970: *The Conquest of Happiness* (1930)

8 Many's the long night I've dreamed of cheese—toasted, mostly.

Robert Louis Stevenson 1850–94: *Treasure Island* (1883)

9 There ain't no way to find out why a snorer can't hear himself snore.

Mark Twain 1835–1910: *Tom Sawyer Abroad* (1894)

10 I haven't been to sleep for over a year. That's why I go to bed early. One needs more rest if one doesn't sleep.

Evelyn Waugh 1903–66: *Decline and Fall* (1928)

Smoking

❝A custom . . . hateful to the nose.❞
James I

1 I have to smoke more [cigarettes] than most people—because the ones I smoke are very small and full of holes.

Beryl Bainbridge 1933– : in *Daily Telegraph* 28 February 1998

2 It has been said that cigarettes are the only product that, if used according to the manufacturer's instructions, have a very high chance of killing you.

Michael Buerk 1946– : in *Sunday Times* 11 July 1999

3 The pipe with solemn interposing puff,
Makes half a sentence at a time enough;
The dozing sages drop the drowsy strain,
Then pause, and puff—and speak, and pause again.

William Cowper 1731–1800: 'Conversation' (1782)

4 A custom loathsome to the eye, hateful to the nose, harmful to the brain, dangerous to the lungs, and in the black, stinking fume thereof, nearest resembling the horrible Stygian smoke of the pit that is bottomless.

James I 1566–1625: *A Counterblast to Tobacco* (1604)

5 This very night I am going to leave off tobacco! Surely there must be some other world in which this unconquerable purpose shall be realized.

Charles Lamb 1775–1834: letter to Thomas Manning, 26 December 1815

6 I smoked my first cigarette and kissed my first woman on the same day. I have never had time for tobacco since.

Arturo Toscanini 1867–1957: in *Observer* 30 June 1946

Snobbery

See also **Class**

❝The trouble with Michael [Heseltine] is that he had to buy all his furniture.❞
Michael Jopling

1 I am not quite a gentleman but you would hardly notice it but can't be helped anyhow.

Daisy Ashford 1881–1972: *The Young Visiters* (1919)

2 Sir Walter Elliot, of Kellynch-hall, in Somersetshire, was a man who, for his own amusement, never took up any book but the Baronetage; there he found occupation for an idle hour, and consolation in a distressed one.

Jane Austen 1775–1817: *Persuasion* (1818)

3 Vulgarity has its uses. Vulgarity often cuts ice which refinement scrapes at vainly.

Max Beerbohm 1872–1956: letter, 21 May 1921

4 Sapper, Buchan, Dornford Yates, practitioners in that school of Snobbery with Violence that runs like a thread of good-class tweed through twentieth-century literature.

Alan Bennett 1934– : *Forty Years On* (1969)

5 From Poland to polo in one generation.
   of Darryl Zanuck

Arthur Caesar d. 1953: Max Wilk *The Wit and Wisdom of Hollywood* (1972)

6 Just because I have made a point of never losing my accent it doesn't mean I am an eel-and-pie yob.

Michael Caine 1933– : in *Times* 15 April 2000 'Quotes of the Week'

7 Why cannot you go down to Bristol and see some of the third and fourth class people there, and they'll do just as well?
   to Charles Dickens, who had told her of his proposed trip to America

Lady Holland 1770–1845: U. Pope-Hennessy *Charles Dickens* (1947)

8 The trouble with Michael is that he had to buy all his furniture.
   of Michael Heseltine

Michael Jopling 1930– : Alan Clark diary 17 June 1987

9 *as an undergraduate Curzon requested permission to be allowed to attend a ball in London in honour of the Empress Augusta of Germany:*
   I don't think much of Empresses. Good morning.

Benjamin Jowett 1817–93: Kenneth Rose *Superior Person* (1969)

10 These are the same old fogies who doffed their lids and tugged the forelock to the British establishment.

Paul Keating 1944– : of Australian Conservative supporters of Great Britain, House of Representatives, 27 February 1992

11 *the Duchess of Devonshire had called on Queen Mary to apologize for her son's marrying the dancer Adele Astaire:*
   Don't worry. I have a niece called Smith.

Queen Mary 1867–1953: in *Times* 1 June 1994; obituary of Lady May Abel Smith

12 *on being told that Clare Boothe Luce was always kind to her inferiors:*
   And where does she find them?

Dorothy Parker 1893–1967: Marion Meade *What Fresh Hell is This?* (1988)

13 Whenever he met a great man he grovelled before him, and my-lorded him as only a free-born Briton can do.

William Makepeace Thackeray 1811–63: *Vanity Fair* (1847–8)

Society and Social Life
See also **Parties**

66 *You can be in the Horseguards and still be common, dear.* 99
Terence Rattigan

1 CECIL BEATON: What on earth can I become?
   FRIEND: I shouldn't bother too much. Just become a friend of the Sitwells and see what happens.

Anonymous: at the outset of Cecil Beaton's career; Laurence Whistler *The Laughter and the Urn* (1985)

2 Though you would often in the fifteenth century have heard the snobbish Roman say, in a would-be off-hand tone, 'I am dining with the Borgias tonight,' no Roman ever was able to say, 'I dined last night with the Borgias.'

Max Beerbohm 1872–1956: *And Even Now* (1920)

3 Anger and the gravest suspicions about everybody had kept her young and on the boil.

E. F. Benson 1867–1940: *Miss Mapp* (1922)

4 Phone for the fish-knives, Norman
   As Cook is a little unnerved;
   You kiddies have crumpled the serviettes
   And I must have things daintily served.

John Betjeman 1906–84: 'How to get on in Society' (1954)

5 Gaily into Ruislip Gardens
Runs the red electric train,
With a thousand Ta's and Pardon's
Daintily alights Elaine;
Hurries down the concrete station
With a frown of concentration,
Out into the outskirt's edges
Where a few surviving hedges
Keep alive our lost Elysium—rural Middlesex again.

John Betjeman 1906–84: 'Middlesex' (1954)

6 I'm a man more dined against than dining.

Maurice Bowra 1898–1971: John Betjeman *Summoned by Bells* (1960)

7 NINOTCHKA: Why should you carry other people's bags?
PORTER: Well, that's my business, Madame.
NINOTCHKA: That's no business. That's social injustice.
PORTER: That depends on the tip.

Charles Brackett 1892–1969 and **Billy Wilder** 1906–2002: *Ninotchka* (1939 film, with Walter Reisch)

8 Children of the Ritz,
Mentally congealed
Lilies of the Field
We say just how we want our quails done,
And then we go and have our nails done.

Noël Coward 1899–1973: 'Children of the Ritz' (1932)

9 In London, at the Café de Paris, I sang to café society; in Las Vegas, at the Desert Inn, I sang to Nescafé society.

Noël Coward 1899–1973: Sheridan Morley *The Quotable Noël Coward* (1999)

10 I notice she likes lights and commotion, which goes to show she has social instincts.

Ronald Firbank 1886–1926: *Valmouth* (1919)

11 The very pink of perfection.

Oliver Goldsmith 1730–74: *She Stoops to Conquer* (1773)

12 I'm Burlington Bertie
I rise at ten thirty and saunter along like a toff,
I walk down the Strand with my gloves on my hand,
Then I walk down again with them off.

W. F. Hargreaves 1846–1919: 'Burlington Bertie from Bow' (1915)

13 I do wish we could chat longer, but I'm having an old friend for dinner.

Thomas Harris 1940– and **Ted Tally** 1952– : *The Silence of the Lambs* (1991 film)

14 Already at four years of age I had begun to apprehend that refinement was very often an extenuating virtue; one that excused and eclipsed almost every other unappetizing trait.

Barry Humphries 1934– : *More Please* (1992)

15 Hail him like Etonians, without a single word,
Absolutely silent and indefinitely bored.

Ronald Knox 1888–1957: 'Magister Reformator' (1906)

16 PLEASE ACCEPT MY RESIGNATION. I DON'T WANT TO BELONG TO ANY CLUB THAT WILL ACCEPT ME AS A MEMBER.

Groucho Marx 1890–1977: telegram; *Groucho and Me* (1959)

17 You can be in the Horseguards and still be common, dear.

Terence Rattigan 1911–77: *Separate Tables* (1954) 'Table Number Seven'

18 All decent people live beyond their incomes nowadays, and those who aren't respectable live beyond other peoples'.

Saki 1870–1916: *Chronicles of Clovis* (1911)

19 MENDOZA: I am a brigand: I live by robbing the rich.
TANNER: I am a gentleman: I live by robbing the poor.

George Bernard Shaw 1856–1950: *Man and Superman* (1903)

20 MRS CANDOUR: I'll swear her colour is natural—I have seen it come and go—
LADY TEAZLE: I dare swear you have, ma'am; it goes of a night and comes again in the morning.

Richard Brinsley Sheridan 1751–1816: *The School for Scandal* (1777)

21 I must say I take off my hat to you, coming home with Rembrandt place mats for your mother. It's those little touches that lift adultery out of the moral arena and make it a matter of style.

Tom Stoppard 1937– : *The Real Thing* (1988 rev. ed.)

22 GERALD: I suppose society is wonderfully delightful!
LORD ILLINGWORTH: To be in it is merely a bore. But to be out of it simply a tragedy.

Oscar Wilde 1854–1900: *A Woman of No Importance* (1893)

23 Never speak disrespectfully of Society, Algernon. Only people who can't get into it do that.

Oscar Wilde 1854–1900: *The Importance of Being Earnest* (1895)

24 Yes, dear Frank [Harris], we believe you: you have dined in every house in London, *once*.

Oscar Wilde 1854–1900: William Rothenstein *Men and Memories* (1931)

25 Radical Chic . . . is only radical in Style; in its heart it is part of Society and its tradition—Politics, like Rock, Pop, and Camp, has its uses.

Tom Wolfe 1931– : in *New York* 8 June 1970

Songs and Singing

See also **Opera**

❝ *By the Great Wobbly top note of Jeanette Macdonald!* ❞

Dick Vosburgh

1 A town-and-country soprano of the kind often used for augmenting grief at a funeral.

George Ade 1866–1944: Nat Shapiro (ed.) *An Encyclopedia of Quotations about Music* (1978)

2 It is a pity that the composer did not leave directions as to how flat he really did want it sung.

Anonymous: review in *West Wilts Herald* 1893; Ned Sherrin *Cutting Edge* (1984)

3 In saloons and drab hallways
You are what I'll grab, always
Our love will be as grand
As Paul Whiteman's band
And will weigh as much as Paul weighs.
See how I dispense
Rhymes which are immense;
But do they make sense?
Not
Always.

Anonymous: a 1930s parody of Irving Berlin's 'Always' in Lorenz Hart's rhyming style; Ned Sherrin *Cutting Edge* (1984)

4 A gender bender I
A creature of illusion,
Of genital confusion,
A gorgeous butterfly.
My list of hits is long
Through every passion ranging,

Alistair Beaton and **Ned Sherrin** 1931–2007: a parody of Gilbert and Sullivan's 'A Wandering Minstrel I' in *The Metropolitan Mikado* (1985)

To every fashion changing,
I tune my latent song.

5 Today if something is not worth saying, people sing it.

Pierre-Augustin Caron de Beaumarchais 1732–99: *Le Barbier de Séville* (1775)

6 'Mr Nash, I can't hear you. Sing up!'
'How do you expect me to sing my best in this position, Sir Thomas?'
'In that position, my dear fellow, I have given some of my best performances.'
to a tenor in rehearsals for La Bohème *while lying on Mimi's bed*

Thomas Beecham 1879–1961: Ned Sherrin *Cutting Edge* (1984)

7 I was just wondering, is this the place where I'm supposed to be drowned by the waves or by the orchestra?
the tenor in The Wreckers *explaining to Sir Thomas Beecham why he had stopped*

John Coates 1865–1941: ; C. Reid *Sir Thomas Beecham* (1961)

8 In writing songs I've learned as much from Cézanne as I have from Woody Guthrie.

Bob Dylan 1941– : Clinton Heylin *Dylan: Behind the Shades* (1991)

9 DYLAN: I *do* know what my songs are about.
PLAYBOY: And what's that?
DYLAN: Oh, some are about four minutes; some are about five, and some, believe it or not, are about eleven.

Bob Dylan 1941– : interview in *Playboy* March 1966

10 Maybe the most that you can expect from a relationship that goes bad is to come out of it with a few good songs.

Marianne Faithfull 1946– : *Faithfull* (1994)

11 LEW FIELDS: Ladies don't write lyrics.
DOROTHY FIELDS: I'm no lady, I'm your daughter.
to her father

Dorothy Fields 1905–74: Caryl Brahms and Ned Sherrin *Song by Song* (1984)

12 Jerry Kern didn't write 'Ol' Man River', *my* husband did! What Kern wrote was dum-dum-*dee*-dum.

Dorothy Hammerstein: attributed, but probably apocryphal (and specifically denied in conversation with Editor)

13 People never talked about my music. They just counted how many knickers were on the stage.

Tom Jones 1940– : in *Sunday Times* 18 June 2000

14 *refusing to accept further changes to lyrics:*
Call me Miss Birdseye. This show is frozen!

Ethel Merman 1909–84: in *Times* 13 July 1985

15 Clichés make the best songs. I put down every one I can find.

Bob Merrill 1921–98: in *New York Times* 19 February 1998

16 I'm not afraid to say that I think Band Aid was diabolical . . . In the first instance the record itself was absolutely tuneless. One can have great concern for the people of Ethiopia, but it's another thing to inflict daily torture on the people of England.

Morrissey 1959– : in *Time Out* March 1985

17 'Who wrote that song?'
'Rodgers and Hammerstein. If you can imagine it taking *two* men to write one song.'
of 'Some Enchanted Evening' (1949)

Cole Porter 1891–1964: G. Eells *The Life that Late He Led* (1967)

18 I lift up my finger and I say 'tweet tweet'.

Leslie Sarony 1897–1985: title of song (1929)

19 Tenors are usually short, stout men (except when they are Wagnerian tenors, in which case they are large, stout men) made up predominantly of lungs, rope-sized vocal chords, large frontal sinuses, thick necks, thick heads, tantrums and *amour propre* . . . It is certain that they are a race apart, a race that tends to operate reflexively rather than with due process of thought.

Harold Schonberg 1915– : in *Show* December 1961

20 All the grittiness of *The Fantastics*.

Stephen Sondheim 1930– : of one of his own lyrics; in conversation

21 The words, which ageing senators have called 'Drug Orientated', are about a jealous man with exceptionally good eyesight. Honest.
on his song 'I Can See For Miles'

Pete Townshend 1945– : Clinton Heylin (ed.) *The Penguin Book of Rock & Roll Writing* 1992

22 By the Great Wobbly top note of Jeanette Macdonald!

Dick Vosburgh 1929–2007: *A Saint She Ain't* (1999)

23 Leonard, we know you're great, but we don't know if you're any good.
the president of CBS Records to Leonard Cohen in 1984

Walter Yetnikoff: Ira B. Nadel *Various Positions: a life of Leonard Cohen* (1996)

Speeches

“*The most popular speaker is the one who sits down before he stands up.*”
John Pentland Mahaffy

1 I do not object to people looking at their watches when I am speaking. But I strongly object when they start shaking them to make certain they are still going.

Lord Birkett 1883–1962: in *Observer* 30 October 1960

2 Ah yes, the foreign affairs debate. Dear Anthony will make the speech which dear Anthony always makes so well.
on Anthony Eden

R. A. Butler 1902–82: attributed; in *Spectator* 14 June 2003

3 Castroenteritis.
describing Fidel Castro's speaking style

Guillermo Cabrera Infante 1929–2005: *Mea Cuba* (1994)

4 ALEXANDER SMYTH: You, sir, speak for the present generation, but I speak for posterity.
HENRY CLAY: Yes, and you seem resolved to speak until the arrival of *your* audience.

Henry Clay 1777–1852: in the US Senate; Robert V. Remini *Henry Clay* (1991)

5 *opening a Red Cross bazaar at Oxford:*
Desperately accustomed as I am to public speaking.

Noël Coward 1899–1973: Dick Richards *The Wit of Noël Coward* (1968)

6 DR WHO: Lots of planets have a north.
actor Christopher Eccleston, explaining his northern accent

Russell T. Davies 1963– : *Dr Who* BBC1 TV, 26 March 2005

7 Hubert Humphrey talks so fast that listening to him is like trying to read *Playboy* magazine with your wife turning the pages.

Barry Goldwater 1909–98: attributed; Ned Sherrin *Cutting Edge* (1984)

8 Please can we have no more complaints about the pauses in Tony Blair's speeches. They are the best parts.

David Guest: letter to *Daily Telegraph* 17 February 2005

9 Lisp: to call a spade a thpade.

Oliver Herford 1863–1935: attributed; Evan Esar and Nicolas Bentley (eds.) *The Treasury of Humorous Quotations* (1951)

10 a *'close second'* to Robert Benchley's choice of the most disagreeable combination of words in English:
Would you care to say a few words?

Richard Ingrams 1937– : in *Observer* 29 August 2004 (see also **Words** 7)

11 Actors use pauses. Mortals use 'um'.

Simon Jenkins 1943– : in *Independent on Sunday* 28 March 2004

12 I may not know much, but I know chicken shit from a chicken salad.
on a speech by Richard Nixon

Lyndon Baines Johnson 1908–73: Merle Miller *Lyndon* (1980)

13 Did you ever think that making a speech on economics is a lot like pissing down your leg? It seems hot to you, but it never does to anyone else.
to J. K. Galbraith

Lyndon Baines Johnson 1908–73: J. K. Galbraith *A Life in Our Times* (1981)

14 *on Winston Churchill at a dinner at the London School of Economics:*
He searched always to end a sentence with a climax. He looked for antithesis like a monkey looking for fleas.

Harold Laski 1893–1950: letter to Oliver Wendell Holmes, 7 May 1927

15 The most popular speaker is the one who sits down before he stands up.

John Pentland Mahaffy 1839–1919: W. B. Stanford and R. B. McDowell *Mahaffy* (1971)

16 I speak with more passion on a full bladder.
refusing an invitation to use the Gents before a broadcast

Enoch Powell 1912–98: in *Times* 21 January 2004

17 When someone asks a question about sex in Hyde Park you double the crowd and halve the argument.

Donald Soper 1903–98: attributed, in *Times* 23 December 1998

18 I fear I cannot make an amusing speech. I have just been reading a book which says that 'all geniuses are devoid of humour'.

Stephen Spender 1909–95: speech in a debate at the Cambridge Union, January 1938

19 Nixon's farm policy is vague, but he is going a long way towards slowing the corn surplus by his speeches.

Adlai Stevenson 1900–65: Bill Adler *The Stevenson Wit* (1966)

20 Whales only get killed when they spout.
declining a request to be interviewed

Denis Thatcher 1915–2003: in *Times* 8 July 2003

21 Reading a speech with his usual sense of discovery.
of ex-President Eisenhower at the Republican convention of 1964

Gore Vidal 1925– : in *New York Review of Books* 29 September 1983

Sports and Games
See also **Baseball, Boxing, Cricket, Football, Golf, Tennis**

❝ We break bones and we lose teeth. We play rugby. ❞
Martin Johnson

1 Well rowed, Balliol!
shouted by a member of the audience when the film Sanders of the River *was shown in Oxford in the 1930s*

Anonymous: traditional story

2 *on being asked why he did not hunt:*
I do not see why I should break my neck because a dog chooses to run after a nasty smell.

Arthur James Balfour 1848–1930: Ian Malcolm *Lord Balfour: A Memory* (1930)

3 Playing snooker gives you firm hands and helps to build up character. It is the ideal recreation for dedicated nuns.
view of the Pope's emissary, attending a sponsored snooker championship at Tyburn convent

Luigi Barbarito 1922– : in *Daily Telegraph* 15 November 1989

4 If you think squash is a competitive activity, try flower arrangement.

Alan Bennett 1934– : *Talking Heads* (1988)

5 Oh wasn't it naughty of Smudges?
Oh, Mummy, I'm sick with disgust.
She threw me in front of the Judges
And my silly old collarbone's bust.

John Betjeman 1906–84: 'Hunter Trials' (1954)

6 I do not participate in any sport with ambulances at the bottom of the hill.

Erma Bombeck 1927–96: attributed; A. J. Maikovich and M. Brown (eds.) *Sports Quotations* (2000)

7 A man described as a 'sportsman' is generally a bookmaker who takes actresses to night clubs.

Jimmy Cannon 1910–73: in *New York Post* c.1951–54 'Nobody Asked Me, But . . . '

8 The trouble with referees is that they just don't care which side wins.
a US basketball player's view

Tom Canterbury: in *Guardian* 24 December 1980 'Sports Quotes of the Year'

9 His blade struck the water a full second before any other: the lad had started well. Nor did he flag as the race wore on . . . as the boats began to near the winning-post, his oar was dipping into the water nearly *twice* as often as any other.
often quoted as, 'All rowed fast, but none so fast as stroke'

Desmond Coke 1879–1931: *Sandford of Merton* (1903)

10 He just can't believe what isn't happening to him.

David Coleman: in *Guardian* 24 December 1980 'Sports Quotes of the Year'

11 That's the fastest time ever run—but it's not as fast as the world record.

David Coleman: Barry Fantoni (ed.) *Private Eye's Colemanballs 3* (1986)

12 Makes me want to yell from St Paul's steeple
The people I'd like to shoot are the shooting people.

Howard Dietz 1896–1983: 'By Myself' (1937)

13 The thing about sport, any sport, is that swearing is very much part of it.

Jimmy Greaves 1940– : in *Observer* 1 January 1989 'Sayings of the Year'

14 Vladimir, Vladimir, Vladimir Kuts
Nature's attempt at an engine in boots.
on the Russian runner Vladimir Kuts in 1956

A. P. Herbert 1890–1971: Ned Sherrin *Cutting Edge* (1984)

15 What you've got to remember about Michael is that under that cold professional Germanic exterior beats a heart of stone.
of Michael Schumacher

Damon Hill 1960– : in May 2000

16 Get your retaliation in first.

Carwyn James 1929–83: to the British Lions team in 1971; quoted in David Pickering (ed.) *Cassell's Sports Quotations* (2002)

17 The only athletic sport I ever mastered was backgammon.

Douglas Jerrold 1803–57: Walter Jerrold *Douglas Jerrold* (1914)

18 We all get cut and we all get stitched up. We get stud marks down our bodies, we break bones and we lose teeth. We play rugby.

Martin Johnson 1970– : Martin Johnson *Autobiography* (2003)

19 It is very strange, and very melancholy, that the paucity of human pleasures should persuade us ever to call hunting one of them.

Samuel Johnson 1709–84: Hester Lynch Piozzi *Anecdotes of . . . Johnson* (1786)

20 I remain of the opinion that there is no game from bridge to cricket that is not improved by a little light conversation; a view which . . . is shared only by a small and unjustly despised minority.

Osbert Lancaster 1908–86: *All Done From Memory* (1953)

21 Sport is an inarticulate human expression and its practitioners should not be blamed for being, a lot of the time, pretty inarticulate.

Rod Liddle 1960– : in *Times* April 2004

22 Rodeoing is about the only sport you can't fix. You'd have to talk to the bulls and the horses, and they wouldn't understand you.

Bill Linderman 1922–61: in 1961; Jonathon Green and Don Atyeo (eds.) *The Book of Sports Quotes* (1979)

23 If you shout hooray for the Pennsylvania Dutchmen
Every team that they play will be carried away with a
    crutch when
They're out on the field if they're wearing the shield of the
    Dutchmen.

Hugh Martin and **Ralph Blane**: 'Buckle Down Winsocki' (1941)

24 I hate all sports as rabidly as a person who likes sports hates common sense.

H. L. Mencken 1880–1956: Laurence J. Peter (ed.) *Quotations for our Time* (1977)

25 Sport, as I have discovered, fosters international hostility and leads the audience, no doubt from boredom, to assault and do grievous bodily harm while watching it.

John Mortimer 1923–2009: *Clinging to the Wreckage* (1982)

26 There's been a colour clash: both teams are wearing white.

John Motson: in 'Colemanballs' column in *Private Eye*; Ned Sherrin *Cutting Edge* (1984)

27 The sport of ski-ing consists of wearing three thousand dollars' worth of clothes and equipment and driving two hundred miles in the snow in order to stand around at a bar and get drunk.

P. J. O'Rourke 1947– : *Modern Manners* (1984)

28 Most of their discourse was about hunting, in a dialect I understand very little.

Samuel Pepys 1633–1703: diary, 22 November 1663

29 *Goering's excuse for being late was a shooting party:*
Animals, I hope.

Eric Phipps 1875–1945: Ned Sherrin *Cutting Edge* (1984); attributed

30 SHE: Are you fond of riding, dear?
Kindly tell me, if so.
HE: Yes, I'm fond of riding, dear,
But in the morning, no.

Cole Porter 1891–1964: 'But in the Morning, No' (1939)

31 *preparing to play rugby:*
All you need to do to warm up, is sit on the bog, have a crap and read the match programme.

Dean Richards 1963– : Martin Johnson *Autobiography* (2003)

32 A handicapper being a character who can dope out from the form what horses ought to win the races, and as long as his figures turn out all right, a handicapper is spoken of most respectfully by one and all, although of course when he begins missing out for any length of time as

Damon Runyon 1884–1946: *Take it Easy* (1938); 'All Horse Players Die Broke'

handicappers are bound to do, he is no longer spoken of respectfully, or even as a handicapper. He is spoken of as a bum.

33 You do not keep accounts and tell everybody that you think you are all square at the end of the year. You lie and you know it.

S. J. Simon 1904–48: *Why You Lose at Bridge* (1945)

34 I can't see who's in the lead but it's either Oxford or Cambridge.

John Snagge 1904–96: C. Dodd *Oxford and Cambridge Boat Race* (1983)

35 It ar'n't that I loves the fox less, but that I loves the 'ound more.

R. S. Surtees 1805–64: *Handley Cross* (1843)

36 'Unting is all that's worth living for—all time is lost wot is not spent in 'unting—it is like the hair we breathe—if we have it not we die—it's the sport of kings, the image of war without its guilt, and only five-and-twenty per cent of its danger.

R. S. Surtees 1805–64: *Handley Cross* (1843)

37 I am here to propose a toast to the sports writers. It's up to you whether you stand or not.

Freddie Trueman 1931–2006: Michael Parkinson *Sporting Lives* (1993)

38 The atmosphere here is a cross between the Munich Beer Festival and the Coliseum at Rome when the Christians were on the menu.
   at a darts match

Sid Waddell 1940– : in 1980, attributed

39 I have observed in women of her type a tendency to regard all athletics as inferior forms of foxhunting.

Evelyn Waugh 1903–66: *Decline and Fall* (1928)

40 I used to think the only use for it [sport] was to give small boys something else to kick besides me.

Katharine Whitehorn 1928– : *Observations* (1970)

41 The English country gentleman galloping after a fox—the unspeakable in full pursuit of the uneatable.

Oscar Wilde 1854–1900: *A Woman of No Importance* (1893); see **The Law** 39

42 The fascination of shooting as a sport depends almost wholly on whether you are at the right or wrong end of a gun.

P. G. Wodehouse 1881–1975: attributed

43 Jogging is for people who aren't intelligent enough to watch television.

Victoria Wood 1953– : *Mens Sana in Thingummy Doodah* (1990)

Stupidity

66 *Seriousness is stupidity sent to college.* **99**
P. J. O'Rourke

1 *shouting at his whist partner:*
Ye stupid auld bitch—I beg yer pardon, mem. I mistook ye for my wife.

Lord Braxfield 1722–99: attributed; quoted in *Literary Review* November 2003

2 COMMENT: One never hears of Baldwin nowadays — he might as well be dead.
   CHURCHILL: No, not dead. But the candle in that great turnip has gone out.

Winston Churchill 1874–1965: Harold Nicolson's diary, August 1950

3 *to a subordinate:*
You couldn't pour piss out of a boot if the instructions were printed on the heel.

Lyndon Baines Johnson 1908–73: Robert Caro *The Years of Lyndon Johnson: Master of the Senate*

4 Seriousness is stupidity sent to college.

P. J. O'Rourke 1947– : *Give War a Chance* (1992)

5 Better to keep your mouth shut and appear stupid than to open it and remove all doubt.

Mark Twain 1835–1910: James Munson (ed.) *The Sayings of Mark Twain* (1992); attributed, perhaps apocryphal

Success

See also **Failure**

❝ *Be nice to people on your way up because you'll meet 'em on your way down.* ❞
Wilson Mizner

1 Success is the one unpardonable sin against our fellows.

Ambrose Bierce 1842–c.1914: *The Enlarged Devil's Dictionary* (1967)

2 In the end, the golden goose will be cooked.
debate on antisocial behaviour

David Blunkett 1947– : in House of Commons, 19 January 2004

3 Where did we go right?
of an unexpected success

Mel Brooks 1926– : *The Producers* (1967 film), spoken by Zero Mostel

4 Not for Clan Campbell the loser's mentality that participation is as important as winning.

Alastair Campbell 1957– : in *Times* 24 January 2004

5 I am that twentieth-century failure, a happy undersexed celibate.

Denise Coffey: Ned Sherrin *Cutting Edge* (1984)

6 Whom the gods wish to destroy they first call promising.

Cyril Connolly 1903–74: *Enemies of Promise* (1938)

7 I think that's just another word for a washed-up has-been.
on being an 'icon'

Bob Dylan 1941– : in *Mail on Sunday* 18 January 1998 'Quotes of the Week'

8 All the rudiments of success in life can be found in ironing a pair of trousers.

Chris Eubank 1966– : in *Independent* 6 September 2003

9 *of David Steel, Leader of the Liberal Party:*
He's passed from rising hope to elder statesman without any intervening period whatsoever.

Michael Foot 1913– : in the House of Commons, 28 March 1979

10 *formula for success:*
Rise early. Work late. Strike oil.

John Paul Getty 1892–1976: attributed

11 You win some, you lose some, and then there's that little-known third category.
summing up the 2000 presidential election in Florida

Albert Gore Jr. 1948– : speech in Florida, 7 May 2001

12 My son, the world is your lobster.

Leon Griffiths 1928–92: *Minder* (TV series); Nigel Rees (ed.) *Cassell Dictionary of Humorous Quotations* (1999)

13 Well, we knocked the bastard off!
on conquering Mount Everest, 1953

Edmund Hillary 1919–2008: *Nothing Venture, Nothing Win* (1975)

14 It is sobering to consider that when Mozart was my age he had already been dead for a year.

Tom Lehrer 1928– : N. Shapiro (ed.) *An Encyclopedia of Quotations about Music* (1978)

15 How to succeed in business without really trying.

Shepherd Mead 1914– : title of book (1952)

16 The theory seems to be that as long as a man is a failure he is one of God's children, but that as soon as he succeeds he is taken over by the Devil.

H. L. Mencken 1880–1956: *Minority Report* (1956)

17 Be nice to people on your way up because you'll meet 'em on your way down.

Wilson Mizner 1876–1933: Alva Johnston *The Legendary Mizners* (1953)

18 The world is divided into people who do things and people who get the credit. Try, if you can, to belong to the first class. There's far less competition.

Dwight Morrow 1873–1931: letter to his son; Harold Nicolson *Dwight Morrow* (1935)

19 David Frost has risen without trace.

Kitty Muggeridge 1903–94: said c.1965 to Malcolm Muggeridge

20 It is difficult to soar like an eagle when you are surrounded by turkeys.
 words embroidered on a cushion for her husband John Osborne

Helen Osborne 1939–2004: in *Daily Telegraph* 14 January 2004

21 I never climbed any ladder: I have achieved eminence by sheer gravitation.

George Bernard Shaw 1856–1950: preface to *The Irrational Knot* (1905)

22 President George W. Bush overcame an incredible lack of obstacles to achieve his success.

Jon Stewart 1962– : in concert at the Prince Edward Theatre, 11 December 2005

23 People who reach the top of the tree are only those who haven't got the qualifications to detain them at the bottom.

Peter Ustinov 1921–2004: interview with David Frost in 1969

24 Whenever a friend succeeds, a little something in me dies.

Gore Vidal 1925– : in *Sunday Times Magazine* 16 September 1973

25 Moderation is a fatal thing, Lady Hunstanton. Nothing succeeds like excess.

Oscar Wilde 1854–1900: *A Woman of No Importance* (1893)

26 Success is a science; if you have the conditions, you get the result.

Oscar Wilde 1854–1900: letter ?March–April 1883

27 *to the actor Victor Spinetti:*
 Ah, Victor, still struggling to keep your head below water.

Emlyn Williams 1905–87: attributed; Ned Sherrin *Cutting Edge* (1984)

The Supernatural

❝ *I don't believe in astrology; I'm a Sagittarius and we're sceptical.* ❞
Arthur C. Clarke

1 *on spiritualism:*
 I always knew the living talked rot, but it's nothing to the rot the dead talk.

Margot Asquith 1864–1945: Chips Channon diary, 20 December 1937

2 I don't believe in astrology; I'm a Sagittarius and we're sceptical.

Arthur C. Clarke 1917–2008: attributed; Nigel Rees *Cassell Dictionary of Humorous Quotations* (1999)

3 *asked if he was superstitious:*
 Only about thirteen in a bed.

Noël Coward 1899–1973: Anna Massey *Telling Some Tales* (2007)

4 The only contact I ever made with the dead was when I spoke to a journalist from the *Sun*.

Morrissey 1959– : David Bret *Morrissey: Landscapes of the Mind* (1994)

5 Mr Geller may have psychic powers by means of which he can bend spoons; if so, he appears to be doing it the hard way.

James Randi 1928– : *The Supernatural A-Z: the truth and the lies* (1995)

Taxes

❝ *Income Tax has made more Liars out of the American people than Golf.* ❞
Will Rogers

1 Tax collectors who'll never know the invigorating joys of treading water in the deep end without a life belt.

Jeffrey Bernard 1932–97: in *The Spectator* 3 March 1984

2 It was as true . . . as taxes is. And nothing's truer than them.

Charles Dickens 1812–70: *David Copperfield* (1850)

3 The collection of a lunatic and inequitable tax, however few the victims, must tend to breed an un-English dislike of taxation in general.

A. P. Herbert 1890–1971: *Misleading Cases* (1935)

4 *Excise.* A hateful tax levied upon commodities.

Samuel Johnson 1709–84: *A Dictionary of the English Language* (1755)

5 Logic and taxation are not always the best of friends.

James C. McReynolds 1862–1946: concurring in *Sonneborn Bros. v. Cureton* 1923

6 I'm up to my neck in the real world, every day. Just you try doing your VAT return with a head full of goblins.

Terry Pratchett 1948– : in *Sunday Times* 27 February 2000 'Talking Heads'

7 Income Tax has made more Liars out of the American people than Golf.

Will Rogers 1879–1935: *The Illiterate Digest* (1924) 'Helping the Girls with their Income Taxes'

8 What is the difference between a taxidermist and a tax collector? The taxidermist takes only your skin.

Mark Twain 1835–1910: *Notebook* 30 December 1902

Technology
See also **Progress, Science**

❝ *The thing with high-tech is that you always end up using scissors.* ❞
David Hockney

1 When man wanted to make a machine that would walk he created the wheel, which does not resemble a leg.

Guillaume Apollinaire 1880–1918: *Les Mamelles de Tirésias* (1918)

2 Inanimate objects are classified scientifically into three major categories—those that don't work, those that break down, and those that get lost.

Russell Baker 1925– : in *New York Times* 18 June 1968

3 Electric typewriters keep going 'mmmmmmm—what are you waiting for?'

Anthony Burgess 1917–93: Clare Boylan (ed.) *The Agony and the Ego* (1993)

4 The first rule of intelligent tinkering is to save all the parts.

Paul Ralph Ehrlich 1932– : in *Saturday Review* 5 June 1971

5 Why sir, there is every possibility that you will soon be able to tax it!
to Gladstone, when asked about the usefulness of electricity

Michael Faraday 1791–1867: W. E. H. Lecky *Democracy and Liberty* (1899 ed.)

6 Technology . . . the knack of so arranging the world that we need not experience it.

Max Frisch 1911–91: *Homo Faber* (1957)

7 The itemised phone bill ranks up there with suspender belts, Sky Sports Channels and Loaded magazine as inventions women could do without.

Maeve Haran 1932– : in *Mail on Sunday* 25 April 1999

8 The thing with high-tech is that you always end up using scissors.

David Hockney 1937– : in *Observer* 10 July 1994 'Sayings of the Week'

9 Take up car maintenance and find the class is full of other thirty-something women like me, looking for a fella.

Marian Keyes: 'Late Opening at the Last Chance Saloon' (1997)

10 No man can hear his telephone ring without wishing heartily that Alexander Graham Bell had been run over by an ice wagon at the age of four.

H. L. Mencken 1880–1956: Marion Elizabeth Rodgers *Mencken: The American Iconoclast* (2005)

11 When the inventor of the drawing board messed things up, what did he go back to?

Bob Monkhouse 1928–2003: attributed; in *Guardian* 29 December 2003 (online edition)

12 Dr Strabismus (Whom God Preserve) of Utrecht has patented a new invention. It is an illuminated trouser-clip for bicyclists who are using main roads at night.

J. B. Morton 1893–1975: *Morton's Folly* (1933)

13 Father had a secret of making inanimate objects appear to possess malevolent life of their own, and sometimes it was hard to believe that his tools and materials were not really in a conspiracy against him.

Frank O'Connor 1903–66: *An Only Child* (1961)

14 The photographer is like the cod which produces a million eggs in order that one may reach maturity.

George Bernard Shaw 1856–1950: introduction to the catalogue for Alvin Langdon Coburn's exhibition at the Royal Photographic Society, 1906

15 He put this engine [a watch] to our ears, which made an incessant noise like that of a water-mill; and we conjecture it is either some unknown animal, or the god that he worships; but we are more inclined to the latter opinion.

Jonathan Swift 1667–1745: *Gulliver's Travels* (1726)

16 JACKIE: (*very slowly*) Take Tube A and apply to Bracket D.
VICTORIA: Reading it slower does not make it any easier to do.

Victoria Wood 1953– : *Mens Sana in Thingummy Doodah* (1990)

Telegrams

❝ *put corpse on ice till close of play.* **❞**
E. M. Grace

1 Along the electric wire the message came:
He is not better—he is much the same.
parodic poem on the illness of the Prince of Wales, later King Edward VII

Anonymous: F. H. Gribble *Romance of the Cambridge Colleges* (1913); sometimes attributed to Alfred Austin (1835–1913), Poet Laureate

2 *as a young* Times *correspondent in America, Claud Cockburn received a telegram authorizing him to report a murder in Al Capone's Chicago:*
BY ALL MEANS COCKBURN CHICAGOWARDS. WELCOME STORIES EX-CHICAGO NOT UNDULY EMPHASISING CRIME.

Anonymous: Claud Cockburn *In Time of Trouble* (1956)

3 *telegraph message on arriving in Venice:*
STREETS FLOODED. PLEASE ADVISE.

Robert Benchley 1889–1945: R. E. Drennan *Wit's End* (1973)

4 HOW DARE YOU BECOME PRIME MINISTER WHEN I'M AWAY GREAT LOVE CONSTANT THOUGHT VIOLET.
to her father, H. H. Asquith, 7 April 1908

Violet Bonham Carter 1887–1969: Mark Bonham Carter and Mark Pottle (eds.) *Lantern Slides* (1996)

5 *to Irving Thalberg on the birth of his son:*
CONGRATULATIONS ON YOUR LATEST PRODUCTION. AM SURE IT WILL LOOK BETTER AFTER IT'S BEEN CUT.

Eddie Cantor 1892–1964: Max Wilk *The Wit and Wisdom of Hollywood* (1972)

6 *appeal to his wife:*
AM IN MARKET HARBOROUGH. WHERE OUGHT I TO BE?

G. K. Chesterton 1874–1936: *Autobiography* (1936)

7 Dear Mrs A.,
Hooray, hooray,
At last you are deflowered.
On this as every other day
I love you—Noel Coward.

Noël Coward 1899–1973: telegram to Gertrude Lawrence, 5 July 1940 (the day after her wedding)

8 HAVE MOVED HOTEL EXCELSIOR COUGHING MYSELF INTO A FIRENZE.
telegram from Florence

Noël Coward 1899–1973: Angus McGill and Kenneth Thomson *Live Wires* (1982)

9 LEGITIMATE AT LAST WONT MOTHER BE PLEASED.
on Gertrude Lawrence's first straight role

Noël Coward 1899–1973: Sheridan Morley *A Talent to Amuse* (1969)

10 *sent to his partner Jack Wilson in New York in 1938 as the threat of war increased:*
GRAVE POSSIBILITY WAR WITHIN FEW WEEKS OR DAYS MORE IF THIS HAPPENS POSTPONEMENT REVUE INEVITABLE AND ANNIHILATION ALL OF US PROBABLE.

Noël Coward 1899–1973: Sheridan Morley *A Talent to Amuse* (1969)

11 *despite the threat of war, arrangements for the revue* Set to Music *went ahead:*
SUGGEST YOU ENGAGE EIGHT REALLY BEAUTIFUL SHOWGIRLS MORE OR LESS SAME HEIGHT NO REAL TALENT REQUIRED.

Noël Coward 1899–1973: telegram to Jack Wilson; Sheridan Morley *A Talent to Amuse* (1969)

12 *in 1916 Norman Douglas had slipped bail on a charge of an indecent offence with a young man. He returned twenty-five years later, sending this telegram to a friend:*
FEEL LIKE A BOY AGAIN.

Norman Douglas 1868–1952: Angus McGill and Kenneth Thomson *Live Wires* (1982)

13 *sent by a cricket-playing coroner, W. G. Grace's elder brother, to postpone an inquest:*
PUT CORPSE ON ICE TILL CLOSE OF PLAY.

E. M. Grace d. 1911: A. A. Thomson *The Great Cricketer* (1957); perhaps apocryphal

14 *response to a telegraphic enquiry,* HOW OLD CARY GRANT?: OLD CARY GRANT FINE. HOW YOU?

Cary Grant 1904–86: R. Schickel *Cary Grant* (1983)

15 LAST SUPPER AND ORIGINAL CAST COULDN'T DRAW IN THIS HOUSE.
    telegram to his father during a bad week with a stock company

George S. Kaufman 1889–1961: Angus McGill and Kenneth Thomson *Live Wires* (1982)

16 *Carl Laemmle Jr. had sent a telegram to his father,* PLEASE WIRE MORE MONEY AM TALKING TO FRENCH COUNT RE MOVIE: NO MONEY TILL YOU LEARN TO SPELL.

Carl Laemmle 1867–1939: Angus McGill and Kenneth Thomson *Live Wires* (1982)

17 *an estate agent in Bermuda told her that the house she was considering came with a maid, a secretary, and a chauffeur:* AIRMAIL PHOTOGRAPH OF CHAUFFEUR.

Beatrice Lillie 1894–1989: Angus McGill and Kenneth Thomson *Live Wires* (1982)

18 *telegram to Mrs Sherwood on the arrival of her baby:* GOOD WORK, MARY. WE ALL KNEW YOU HAD IT IN YOU.

Dorothy Parker 1893–1967: Alexander Woollcott *While Rome Burns* (1934)

19 *to a couple who had married after living together:* WHAT'S NEW?

Dorothy Parker 1893–1967: S. T. Brownlow (ed.) *The Sayings of Dorothy Parker* (1992)

20 *cables were soon arriving . . . 'Require earliest name life story photograph American nurse upblown Adowa.' We replied:* NURSE UNUPBLOWN.

Evelyn Waugh 1903–66: *Waugh in Abyssinia* (1936)

21 FEAR I MAY NOT BE ABLE TO REACH YOU IN TIME FOR THE CEREMONY. DON'T WAIT.
    telegram of apology for missing Oscar Wilde's wedding

James McNeill Whistler 1834–1903: E. J. and R. Pennell *The Life of James McNeill Whistler* (1908)

22 *his wife had requested him, when in Paris, to buy and send her a bidet:* UNABLE OBTAIN BIDET. SUGGEST HANDSTAND IN SHOWER.

Billy Wilder 1906–2002: Leslie Halliwell *Filmgoer's Book of Quotes* (1973)

23 At this point in the proceedings there was another ring at the front door. Jeeves shimmered out and came back with a telegram.

P. G. Wodehouse 1881–1975: *Carry On, Jeeves!* (1925)

24 I HAVE BEEN LOOKING AROUND FOR AN APPROPRIATE WOODEN GIFT AND AM PLEASED HEREBY TO PRESENT YOU WITH ELSIE FERGUSON'S PERFORMANCE IN HER NEW PLAY.
    congratulatory telegram for George S. Kaufman's fifth wedding anniversary

Alexander Woollcott 1887–1943: Howard Teichmann *George S. Kaufman* (1973)

Television
See also **Broadcasting**

❝ Never miss a chance to have sex or appear on television. ❞
Gore Vidal

1 TV—a clever contraction derived from the words Terrible Vaudeville . . . we call it a medium because nothing's well done.

Goodman Ace 1899–1982: letter to Groucho Marx, c.1953

2 The best that can be said for Norwegian television is that it gives you the sensation of a coma without the worry and inconvenience.

Bill Bryson 1951– : *Neither Here Nor There* (1991)

3 Television is more interesting than people. If it were not, we should have people standing in the corners of our rooms.

Alan Coren 1938–2007: attributed; in *The Penguin Dictionary of Twentieth-Century Quotations* (1993)

4 Television is for appearing on, not looking at.

Noël Coward 1899–1973: Dick Richards *The Wit of Noël Coward* (1968)

5 There was never sex in Ireland before television.

Oliver J. Flanagan 1920–87: c.1965, attributed

6 *returning to a Saturday slot with* Strictly Come Dancing: I've always felt that on Saturday nights there is a kinder audience. That's probably because they're drunk.

Bruce Forsyth 1928– : in *BBC News* (online edition) 21 April 2004

7 Being taken no notice of in 10 million homes.
  of appearing on television

David Hare 1947– : *Amy's View* (1997)

8 It's television, you see. If you are not on the thing every week, the public think you are either dead or deported.

Frankie Howerd 1922–92: attributed

9 Television is simultaneously blamed, often by the same people, for worsening the world and for being powerless to change it.

Clive James 1939– : *Glued to the Box* (1981); introduction

10 *Television?* The word is half Greek, half Latin. No good can come of it.

C. P. Scott 1846–1932: view of the editor of the *Manchester Guardian*; Asa Briggs *The BBC: the First Fifty Years* (1985)

11 I didn't create Alf Garnett. Society did. I just grassed on him.

Johnny Speight 1921–98: in *Mail on Sunday* 27 December 1998 'Quotes of the Year'

12 My show is the stupidest show on TV. If you are watching it, get a life.

Jerry Springer 1944– : in *Independent on Sunday* 7 March 1999

13 It always makes me laugh when people ask why anyone would want to do a sitcom in America. If it runs five years, you never have to work again.

Twiggy 1949– : in *Independent* 4 October 1997 'Quote Unquote'

14 Never miss a chance to have sex or appear on television.

Gore Vidal 1925– : attributed; Bob Chieger *Was It Good For You Too?* (1983)

15 *of television:*
  It used to be that we in films were the lowest form of art. Now we have something to look down on.

Billy Wilder 1906–2002: A. Madsen *Billy Wilder* (1968)

Tennis

❝ You cannot be serious! ❞
John McEnroe

1 In other sports, the lateral euphemism is still in its infancy (at Wimbledon, for example, they have only just realized that 'perfectionist' can be used to represent 'extremely bad-tempered'). In soccer, the form of the encoded adjective is well developed. 'Tenacious', for example, always means 'small'.

Julian Barnes 1946– : in *Observer* 4 July 1982

2 Miss J. Hunter Dunn, Miss J. Hunter Dunn,
 Furnish'd and burnish'd by Aldershot sun,
 What strenuous singles we played after tea,
 We in the tournament—you against me.

 Love-thirty, love-forty, oh! weakness of joy,
 The speed of a swallow, the grace of a boy,
 With carefullest carelessness, gaily you won,
 I am weak from your loveliness, Joan Hunter Dunn.

John Betjeman 1906–84: 'A Subaltern's Love-Song' (1945)

3 No one is more sensitive about his game than a weekend tennis player.

Jimmy Cannon 1910–73: in *New York Post* c.1955 'Nobody Asked Me, But . . . '

4 I call tennis the McDonald's of sport—you go in, they make a quick buck out of you, and you're out.

Pat Cash 1965– : in *Independent on Sunday* 4 July 1999

5 New Yorkers love it when you spill your guts out there. Spill your guts at Wimbledon and they make you stop and clean it up.

Jimmy Connors 1952– : at Flushing Meadow; in *Guardian* 24 December 1984 'Sports Quotes of the Year'

6 Like a Volvo, Borg is rugged, has good after-sales service, and is very dull.

Clive James 1939– : in *Observer* 29 June 1980

7 You cannot be serious!

John McEnroe 1959– : said to tennis umpire at Wimbledon, early 1980s

8 I threw the kitchen sink at him, but he went to the bathroom and got his tub.
 defeated by Roger Federer in the Wimbledon Final, 2004

Andy Roddick 1982– : interview (BBC1), 4 July 2004

9 All gong and no dinner . . . we just wish Anna would finally win something aside from hearts.
 of the Russian tennis star Anna Kournikova at Wimbledon 2000

Tim Sheridan: 'The Word from Wimbledon' (online report) 10 July 2000

The Theatre
See also **Acting, Actors**

66 *The play was a great success, but the audience was a total failure.* 99
Oscar Wilde

1 Welcome to the Theatre,
 To the magic, to the fun!
 Where painted trees and flowers grow,
 And laughter rings fortissimo,
 And treachery's sweetly done.

Lee Adams: 'Welcome to the Theatre' (1970)

2 Shaw's plays are the price we pay for Shaw's prefaces.

James Agate 1877–1947: diary 10 March 1933

3 Why don't actors look out of the window in the morning? Because then they'd have nothing to do in the afternoon.
 old theatre joke

Anonymous: Michael Simkins *What's My Motivation?* (2004)

4 STUDENT: Did Hamlet actually have an affair with Ophelia?
 ACTOR-MANAGER: In our company, always.

Anonymous: Cedric Hardwicke *A Victorian in Orbit* (1961)

5 There is less in this than meets the eye.

Tallulah Bankhead 1903–68: of a revival of Maeterlinck's play 'Aglavaine and Selysette'; Alexander Woollcott *Shouts and Murmurs* (1922)

6 This [*Oh, Calcutta!*] is the kind of show to give pornography a dirty name.

Clive Barnes 1927– : in *New York Times* 18 June 1969

7 God, send me some good actors. Cheap.

Lilian Baylis 1874–1937: Sybil Thorndike *Lilian Baylis* (1938)

8 Enter Michael Angelo. Andrea del Sarto appears for a moment at a window. Pippa passes.

Max Beerbohm 1872–1956: *Seven Men* (1919)

9 *on being asked 'What was the message of your play' after a performance of* The Hostage:
Message? Message? What the hell do you think I am, a bloody postman?

Brendan Behan 1923–64: Dominic Behan *My Brother Brendan* (1965)

10 ANONYMOUS: Why did you go on stage?
MICHAEL BLAKEMORE: To get out of the audience.

Michael Blakemore 1928– : attributed; in *Times* 29 December 2003

11 A play wot I wrote.

Eddie Braben 1930– : spoken by Ernie Wise; Gary Morecambe and Martin Stirling *Behind the Sunshine* (1994)

12 *on hearing the Cockney playwright Henry Arthur Jones reading his play* Michael and his Lost Angel (*1896*):
But it's so *long*, Mr. Jones—even *without* the *h*'s.

Mrs Patrick Campbell 1865–1940: Margot Peters *Mrs Pat* (1984)

13 They eat their young.
on Glasgow music hall audiences

Harry Chapman: attributed; see **Children** 18

14 *of Lionel Bart's musical* Blitz:
Just as long as the real thing and twice as noisy.

Noël Coward 1899–1973: Sheridan Morley *The Quotable Noël Coward* (1999)

15 Stop being gallant
And don't be such a bore,
Pack up your talent,
There's always plenty more
And if you lose hope
Take dope
And lock yourself in the John,
Why must the show go on?

Noël Coward 1899–1973: 'Why Must the Show Go On?' (1955)

16 It's about as long as *Parsifal*, and not as funny.
on Camelot

Noël Coward 1899–1973: Dick Richards *The Wit of Noël Coward* (1968)

17 Shut up, Arnold, or I'll direct this play the way you wrote it!

John Dexter: to the playwright Arnold Wesker; in *Ned Sherrin in his Anecdotage* (1993)

18 The plot can be hot—simply teeming with sex,
A gay divorcee who is after her ex.
It could be Oedipus Rex,
Where a chap kills his father
And causes a lot of bother.
The clerk
Who is thrown out of work

Howard Dietz 1896–1983: 'That's Entertainment' (1953)

By the boss
Who is thrown for a loss
By the skirt
Who is doing him dirt.
The world is a stage
The stage is a world of entertainment.

19 Ridiculous farces worthy of Canadian savages.
   of Shakespeare's plays

Frederick the Great 1712–86: Giles MacDonogh *Frederick the Great* (1999)

20 Prologues precede the piece—in mournful verse;
   As undertakers—walk before the hearse.

David Garrick 1717–79: prologue to Arthur Murphy's *The Apprentice* (1756)

21 Applause, applause!
   Vociferous applause
   From orchestra to gallery
   Could mean a raise in salary.
   Give out, give in!—
   Be noisy, make a din!
   (The manager, he audits our plaudits.)

Ira Gershwin 1896–1983: 'Applause, Applause' (1953)

22 *a Broadway producer after a play about Napoleon had failed:*
   Never, never, will I do another play where a guy writes with a feather.

Max Gordon: attributed by Arthur Miller; in *Ned Sherrin's Theatrical Anecdotes* (1991)

23 I have knocked everything but the knees of the chorus girls, and nature has anticipated me there.

Percy Hammond: Ned Sherrin *Cutting Edge* (1984)

24 If any play has been produced only twice in three hundred years, there must be some good reason for it.

Rupert Hart-Davis 1907–99: letter to George Lyttelton, 7 July 1957

25 I remember it well. That was the tour the Doge of Venice gave Lancelot Gobbo clap.

Ronald Harwood 1934– : *The Dresser* (1980)

26 The difficulty about a theatre job is that it interferes with party-going.

Barry Humphries 1934– : *More Please* (1992)

27 I'll come no more behind your scenes, David; for the silk stockings and white bosoms of your actresses excite my amorous propensities.
   John Wilkes recalls the remark [to Garrick] *in the form:*
   'the silk stockings and white bosoms of your actresses do make my genitals to quiver'

Samuel Johnson 1709–84: James Boswell *Life of Samuel Johnson* (1791) 1750

28 Mixed notices—they were good and rotten.
   after sharing a flop, The Channel Road (*1929*)*, with Alexander Woollcott*

George S. Kaufman 1889–1961: Howard Teichmann *George S. Kaufman* (1973)

29 I thought I heard one of the original lines of the show.
   of the Marx Brothers' ad-libbing

George S. Kaufman 1889–1961: Howard Teichmann *George S. Kaufman* (1973)

30 There was laughter in the back of the theatre, leading to the belief that someone was telling jokes back there.

George S. Kaufman 1889–1961: Howard Teichmann *George S. Kaufman* (1973)

31 Well, Marc, there's only one thing we can do. We've got to call the audience in tomorrow morning for a ten o'clock rehearsal.
   to convince Marc Connelly that a line would not work

George S. Kaufman 1889–1961: Howard Teichmann *George S. Kaufman* (1973)

32 Satire is what closes Saturday night.

George S. Kaufman 1889–1961:
Scott Meredith *George S. Kaufman and his Friends* (1974)

33 Beware of flu. Avoid crowds. See *Someone in the House.*
   advertisement for his unsuccessful revision of the Broadway play, staged during the influenza epidemic of 1918

George S. Kaufman 1889–1961:
Howard Teichmann *George S. Kaufman: an intimate portrait* (1972)

34 Murder was one thing Hamlet sure did enjoy.
   He was, how shall I say, quite a mischievious boy;
   And the moral of this story was very, very plain;
   You'd better get a mussle if you've got a great Dane!

Frank Loesser 1910–69: 'Hamlet' (1949)

35 I didn't like the play, but then I saw it under adverse conditions—the curtain was up.

Groucho Marx 1890–1977: ad-lib, attributed in an interview by Marx to George S. Kaufman; Peter Hay *Broadway Anecdotes* (1989)

36 A play in which nothing happens, twice.
   reviewing Waiting for Godot *in* Irish Times, *1954*

Vivian Mercier 1919–89: *Beckett/Beckett* (1977)

37 Don't clap too hard—it's a very old building.

John Osborne 1929–94: *The Entertainer* (1957)

38 In fact, now that you've got me right down to it, the only thing I didn't like about *The Barretts of Wimpole Street* was the play.

Dorothy Parker 1893–1967: review in *New Yorker* 21 February 1931

39 *House Beautiful* is play lousy.

Dorothy Parker 1893–1967: review in *New Yorker* 1933

40 There still remains, to mortify a wit,
   The many-headed monster of the pit.

Alexander Pope 1688–1744: *Imitations of Horace* (1737)

41 Another pain where the ulcers grow,
   Another op'nin' of another show.

Cole Porter 1891–1964: 'Another Op'nin', Another Show' (1948)

42 We open in Venice,
   We next play Verona,
   Then on to Cremona.
   Lotsa laughs in Cremona.

Cole Porter 1891–1964: 'We Open in Venice' (1948)

43 Brush up your Shakespeare,
   Start quoting him now.
   Brush up your Shakespeare
   And the women you will wow . . .
   If she says your behaviour is heinous
   Kick her right in the 'Coriolanus'.
   Brush up your Shakespeare
   And they'll all kowtow.

Cole Porter 1891–1964: 'Brush Up your Shakespeare' (1948)

44 It is better to have written a damned play, than no play at all—it snatches a man from obscurity.

Frederic Reynolds 1764–1841: *The Dramatist* (1789)

45 You've got to perform in a role hundreds of times. In keeping it fresh one can become a large, madly humming, demented refrigerator.

Ralph Richardson 1902–83: in *Time* 21 August 1978

46 The most lamentable comedy, and most cruel death of Pyramus and Thisby.

William Shakespeare 1564–1616: *A Midsummer Night's Dream* (1595–6)

47 *Exit, pursued by a bear.*

William Shakespeare 1564–1616: stage direction in *The Winter's Tale* (1610–11)

48 You don't expect me to know what to say about a play when I don't know who the author is, do you?

George Bernard Shaw 1856–1950: *Fanny's First Play* (1914)

49 My intention is to do to the play what Hamlet himself longed to do to his mother.

Arthur Smith 1954– : *Arthur Smith's Hamlet*

50 Something appealing,
Something appalling,
Something for everyone:
A comedy tonight!

Stephen Sondheim 1930– : 'Comedy Tonight' (1962)

51 It's pure theatrical Viagra.
   on The Blue Room, starring Nicole Kidman

Charles Spencer 1955– : in *Daily Telegraph* 24 September 1999

52 I can do you blood and love without the rhetoric, and I can do you blood and rhetoric without the love, and I can do you all three concurrent or consecutive, but I can't do you love and rhetoric without the blood. Blood is compulsory—they're all blood, you see.

Tom Stoppard 1937– : *Rosencrantz and Guildenstern are Dead* (1967)

53 To sum up: your father, whom you love, dies, you are his heir, you come back to find that hardly was the corpse cold before his young brother popped onto his throne and into his sheets, thereby offending both legal and natural practice. Now why exactly are you behaving in this extraordinary manner?

Tom Stoppard 1937– : *Rosencrantz and Guildenstern Are Dead* (1967)

54 *Moby Dick* nearly became the tragedy of a man who could not make up his nose.
   on Welles's production of Moby Dick *in 1955, when his false nose fell off on the first night, alluding to the publicity for Olivier's* Hamlet *as 'the tragedy of a man who could not make up his mind'*

Kenneth Tynan 1927–80: *A View of the English Stage* (1975)

55 I've never much enjoyed going to plays . . . The unreality of painted people standing on a platform saying things they've said to each other for months is more than I can overlook.

John Updike 1932–2009: George Plimpton (ed.) *Writers at Work* 4th Series (1977)

56 In the old days, you went from ingénue to old bag with a long stretch of unemployment in between.

Julie Walters 1950– : in *Sunday Times* 26 May 2002

57 When you think about it, what other playwrights are there besides O'Neill, Tennessee and me?

Mae West 1892–1980: G. Eells and S. Musgrove *Mae West* (1989)

58 The play was a great success, but the audience was a total failure.

Oscar Wilde 1854–1900: after the first performance of *Lady Windermere's Fan*; Peter Hay *Theatrical Anecdotes* (1987)

59 *on Irving's revival of* Macbeth *at the Lyceum, with Ellen Terry as Lady Macbeth:*
Judging from the banquet, Lady Macbeth seems an economical housekeeper and evidently patronises local industries for her husband's clothes and the servants' liveries, but she takes care to do all her shopping in Byzantium.

Oscar Wilde 1854–1900: Rupert Hart-Davis (ed.) *The Letters of Oscar Wilde* (1962)

60 *the impresario Binkie Beaumont had been greatly impressed by*
The Wind of Heaven *(1945):*
BEAUMONT: I've read your new play, Emlyn, and I like it
twice as much as your last.
WILLIAMS: Does that mean you're going to pay me twice
my usual royalties?

Emlyn Williams 1905–87: James
Harding *Emlyn Williams* (1987)

61 *on the Company of Four's poorly attended revival of his play*
Spring 1600 *in 1945:*
The Lyric housed the Company of Four and the Audience
of Two.

Emlyn Williams 1905–87: James
Harding *Emlyn Williams* (1987)

62 Musical comedy is the Irish stew of drama. Anything may
be put into it, with the certainty that it will improve the
general effect.

P. G. Wodehouse 1881–1975: *The
Man with Two Left Feet* (1917)

Time

❝ *Life is too short to stuff a mushroom.* ❞
Shirley Conran

1 Time is an illusion. Lunchtime doubly so.

Douglas Adams 1952–2001: *The
Hitch Hiker's Guide to the Galaxy*
(1979)

2 I do love deadlines. I love the whooshing sound they make
as they go past.

Douglas Adams 1952–2001: in
Guardian 14 May 2001

3 *on receiving an invitation for 9 a.m.:*
Oh, are there two nine o'clocks in the day?

Tallulah Bankhead 1903–68:
attributed, perhaps apocryphal

4 *to an effusive greeting 'I haven't seen you for 41 years':*
I thought I told you to wait in the car.

Tallulah Bankhead 1903–68:
attributed; Nigel Rees *Cassell
Dictionary of Humorous Quotations*
(1999)

5 VLADIMIR: That passed the time.
ESTRAGON: It would have passed in any case.
VLADIMIR: Yes, but not so rapidly.

Samuel Beckett 1906–89: *Waiting
for Godot* (1955)

6 I am a sundial, and I make a botch
Of what is done much better by a watch.

Hilaire Belloc 1870–1953: 'On a
Sundial' (1938)

7 *on running the London Marathon:*
I've set myself a target. I'm going for less than eleven-and-
a-half days.

Jo Brand 1957– : in *Observer* 27
February 2005

8 *arriving at Dublin Castle for the handover by British forces on
16 January 1922, and being told that he was seven minutes
late:*
We've been waiting 700 years, you can have the seven
minutes.

Michael Collins 1880–1922: Tim Pat
Coogan *Michael Collins* (1990);
attributed, perhaps apocryphal

9 Life is too short to stuff a mushroom.

Shirley Conran 1932– : *Superwoman*
(1975)

10 There was a pause—just long enough for an angel to pass,
flying slowly.

Ronald Firbank 1886–1926:
Vainglory (1915)

11 I'll be with you in the squeezing of a lemon.

Oliver Goldsmith 1730–74: *She
Stoops to Conquer* (1773)

12 We have passed a lot of water since then.

Sam Goldwyn 1882–1974: E. Goodman *The Fifty-Year Decline of Hollywood* (1961); attributed, possibly apocryphal

13 Time spent on any item of the agenda will be in inverse proportion to the sum involved.

C. Northcote Parkinson 1909–93: *Parkinson's Law* (1958)

14 Wherever I travel I'm too late. The orgy has moved elsewhere.

Mordecai Richler 1931–2001: *Shovelling Trouble* (1972) 'A Sense of the Ridiculous'

15 An artist must organize his life. Here is the exact timetable of my daily activities. Get up: 7.18 am; be inspired: 10.23 to 11.47 am. I take lunch at 12.11 pm and leave the table at 12.14 pm.

Erik Satie 1866–1925: *Memoirs of an Amnesiac* (1914)

16 Eternity's a terrible thought. I mean, where's it all going to end?

Tom Stoppard 1937– : *Rosencrantz and Guildenstern are Dead* (1967)

17 *to a man in the street, carrying a grandfather clock:*
My poor fellow, why not carry a watch?

Herbert Beerbohm Tree 1852–1917: Hesketh Pearson *Beerbohm Tree* (1956)

Titles

❝ *No stronger craving in the world than that of the rich for titles.* **❞**
Hesketh Pearson

1 Your official signature 'Archibald the Arctic' is the most romantic signature in the world and just one point ahead of 'William of Argyll and the Isles'.
  to first Bishop of the Arctic, 1937

John Buchan 1875–1940: Archibald Lang Fleming *Archibald the Arctic* (1957)

2 Hit me with your Rhythm Stick.

Ian Dury 1942–2000: song title (1978)

3 *leading title on the autumn list of 'a new publishing house that would be sure to fail':*
Canada, Our Good Neighbour to the North.

Robert Gottlieb: in *Ned Sherrin in his Anecdotage* (1993)

4 *alleged response to being addressed as 'Mr Kingsley' rather than 'Sir Ben' on the set of his new film:*
It's a small word. It's not long. And it's not difficult to remember.

Ben Kingsley 1943– : attributed; in *Times* 17 June 2003

5 Goodness gracious me.

David Lee 1926– and **Herbert Kretzmer** 1925– : title of song (1960), sung by Peter Sellers and Sophia Loren as characters from their 1960 film *The Millionairess*, which later inspired the BBC radio and television comedy show *Goodness Gracious Me* (1996–2001)

6 Rum, Bum and Concertina.

George Melly 1926–2007: title of autobiography (1977)

7 There is no stronger craving in the world than that of the rich for titles, except perhaps that of the titled for riches.

Hesketh Pearson 1887–1964: *The Pilgrim Daughters* (1961)

8 If you are called Wayne or you say 'serviette' instead of 'napkin', it's unlikely you've got a title.

Meera Syal 1963– : in *Independent* 21 July 2001

9 *bestseller on punctuation named from the story of a panda which obeys a badly punctuated wildlife manual:*
Eats, shoots and leaves.

Lynne Truss 1955– : book title, 2003

10 *title for a language-monitoring organization:*
Association for the Annihilation of the Aberrant Apostrophe.

Keith Waterhouse 1929– : in *Daily Mail* 22 February 1988

Tolerance See **Prejudice and Tolerance**

Towns and Cities

See also **New York**

66 *Toronto is a kind of New York operated by the Swiss.* **99**
Peter Ustinov

1 God made the harbour, and that's all right, but Satan made Sydney.

Anonymous: unnamed Sydney citizen; Mark Twain *More Tramps Abroad* (1897)

2 New York is big but this is Biggar.

Anonymous: slogan for the town of Biggar in Saskatchewan

3 Toronto the Good.
ironic nickname used by 'hilarious drunks'

Anonymous: Robert Thomas Allen *When Toronto was for Kids* (1961)

4 I passed through Glasgow on my way here and couldn't help noticing how different it was from Venice.

Raymond Asquith 1878–1916: letter to Mrs Horner, 28 September 1904

5 One has no great hopes from Birmingham. I always say there is something direful in the sound.

Jane Austen 1775–1817: *Emma* (1816)

6 Tell someone that you live, or have lived, in Leeds and they are quite likely to say, 'Well, it's easy to get out of.'

Alan Bennett 1934– : *Telling Tales* (2000)

7 Come, friendly bombs, and fall on Slough!
It isn't fit for humans now.

John Betjeman 1906–84: 'Slough' (1937)

8 And this is good old Boston,
The home of the bean and the cod,
Where the Lowells talk to the Cabots
And the Cabots talk only to God.

John Collins Bossidy 1860–1928: verse spoken at Holy Cross College alumni dinner in Boston, Massachusetts, 1910

9 A big hard-boiled city with no more personality than a paper cup.

Raymond Chandler 1888–1959: *The Little Sister* (1949)

10 People don't talk in Paris; they just look lovely . . . and eat.

Chips Channon 1897–1958: diary 22 May 1951

11 For some guys
The dream is Paris,
But I found a shrine
Where Hollywood Boulevard crosses Vine.

Ervin Drake: 'My Hometown' (1964)

12 Last week, I went to Philadelphia, but it was closed.

W. C. Fields 1880–1946: Richard J. Anobile *Godfrey Daniels* (1975); attributed

13 The people of Berlin are doing very exciting things with their city at the moment. Basically they had this idea of just knocking it through.

Stephen Fry 1957– and **Hugh Laurie**: *A Bit More Fry and Laurie* (1991)

14 Cities are above
The quarrels that were hapless.
Look who's making love:
St Paul and Minneap'lis!

Ira Gershwin 1896–1983: 'Love is Sweeping the Country' (1931)

15 I met him in Boston
In the native quarter.
He was from Harvard
Just across the border.

Sheldon Harnick 1924– : 'The Boston Beguine' (1952)

16 Liverpool, though not very delightful as a place of residence, is a most convenient and admirable point to get away from.

Nathaniel Hawthorne 1804–64: *Our Old Home* (1863)

17 Try Manchester after midnight and you'll think you've walked into the Book of Revelations.

Howard Jacobson: *The Mighty Waltzer* (1999)

18 When a man is tired of London, he is tired of life; for there is in London all that life can afford.

Samuel Johnson 1709–84: James Boswell *Life of Samuel Johnson* (1791) 20 September 1777

19 Fleet-street has a very animated appearance; but I think the full tide of human existence is at Charing-Cross.

Samuel Johnson 1709–84: James Boswell *Life of Samuel Johnson* (1791) 2 April 1775

20 According to legend, Telford is so dull that the bypass was built before the town.
    on the Midlands new-town

Victor Lewis-Smith: in *Evening Standard* 9 December 1994

21 You're from Big D,
My, oh yes, I mean Big D, little a, double l-a-s
And that spells Dallas, my darlin' darlin' Dallas,
Don't it give you pleasure to confess
That you're from Big D?
My, oh yes!

Frank Loesser 1910–69: 'Big D' (1956)

22 *Ogden Nash had had his car broken into in Boston:*
I'd expect to be robbed in Chicago
But not in the land of the cod,
So I hope that the Cabots and Lowells
Will mention the matter to God.

Ogden Nash 1902–71: David Frost and Michael Shea *The Mid-Atlantic Companion* (1986)

23 Saigon is like all the other great modern cities of the world. It's the mess left over from people getting rich.

P. J. O'Rourke 1947– : *Give War a Chance* (1992)

24 Last Sunday afternoon
I took a trip to Hackensack
But after I gave Hackensack the once-over
I took the next train back.
I happen to like New York.

Cole Porter 1891–1964: 'I Happen to Like New York' (1931)

25 City of perspiring dreams.
    of Cambridge

Frederic Raphael 1931– : *The Glittering Prizes* (1976)

26 He took offence at my description of Edinburgh as the Reykjavik of the South.

Tom Stoppard 1937– : *Jumpers* (1972)

27 Toronto is a kind of New York operated by the Swiss.

Peter Ustinov 1921–2004: in *Globe & Mail* 1 August 1987; attributed

28 Brighton looks like a town that is constantly helping the police with their enquiries.

Keith Waterhouse 1929– : quoted by the author in conversation with the Editor

Transport

❝ *Walk! Not bloody likely. I am going in a taxi.* ❞

George Bernard Shaw

1 *of Annie's parking:*
That's OK, we can walk to the kerb from here.

Woody Allen 1935– : *Annie Hall* (1977 film)

2 Railways and the Church have their critics, but both are the best ways of getting a man to his ultimate destination.

Revd W. Awdry 1911–97: in *Daily Telegraph* 22 March 1997; obituary

3 The freeway is . . . the place where they [Angelenos] spend the two calmest and most rewarding hours of their daily lives.

Reynar Banham 1922–88: *Los Angeles: the Architecture of Four Ecologies* (1971)

4 We're gonna need a bigger boat!

Peter Benchley 1940– : *Jaws* (1975 film); spoken by Roy Schneider as Chief Brody

5 He [Benchley] came out of a night club one evening and, tapping a uniformed figure on the shoulder, said, 'Get me a cab.' The uniformed figure turned around furiously and informed him that he was not a doorman but a rear admiral. 'O.K.,' said Benchley, 'Get me a battleship.'

Robert Benchley 1889–1945: in *New Yorker* 5 January 1946

6 Q: If Mrs Thatcher were run over by a bus . . . ?
LORD CARRINGTON: It wouldn't dare.

Lord Carrington 1919– : during the Falklands War; Russell Lewis *Margaret Thatcher* (1984)

7 The only way of catching a train I ever discovered is to miss the train before.

G. K. Chesterton 1874–1936: attributed; Evan Esar and Nicolas Bentley (eds.) *Treasury of Humorous Quotations* (1951)

8 The ski are the most capricious things upon the earth.

Arthur Conan Doyle 1859–1930: 'Crossing an Alpine Pass' (1894)

9 That monarch of the road,
Observer of the Highway Code,
That big six-wheeler
Scarlet-painted
London Transport
Diesel-engined
Ninety-seven horse power
Omnibus!

Michael Flanders 1922–75 and **Donald Swann** 1923–94: 'A Transport of Delight' (c.1956)

10 Sir, Saturday morning, although recurring at regular and well-foreseen intervals, always seems to take this railway by surprise.

W. S. Gilbert 1836–1911: letter to the station-master at Baker Street, on the Metropolitan line; John Julius Norwich *Christmas Crackers* (1980)

11 For you dream you are crossing the Channel, and tossing about in a steamer from Harwich—
Which is something between a large bathing machine and a very small second class carriage.

W. S. Gilbert 1836–1911: *Iolanthe* (1882)

12 What is this that roareth thus?
Can it be a Motor Bus?
Yes, the smell and hideous hum
Indicat Motorem Bum! . . .
How shall wretches live like us
Cincti Bis Motoribus?
Domine, defende nos
Contra hos Motores Bos!

A. D. Godley 1856–1925: letter to C.
R. L. Fletcher, 10 January 1914

13 Aunt Jane observed, the second time
She tumbled off a bus,
'The step is short from the Sublime
To the Ridiculous.'

Harry Graham 1874–1936:
'Equanimity' (1899)

14 'Glorious, stirring sight!' murmured Toad, never offering
to move. 'The poetry of motion! The *real* way to travel!
The *only* way to travel! Here today—in next week
tomorrow! Villages skipped, towns and cities jumped—
always somebody else's horizon! O bliss! O poop-poop! O
my! O my!'

Kenneth Grahame 1859–1932: *The
Wind in the Willows* (1908)

15 *of Bishop Patrick's fatal error in crossing the street:*
The light of God was with him,
But the traffic light was not.

E. Y. Harburg 1898–1981: 'Lead
Kindly Light' (1965)

16 There once was a man who said, 'Damn!
It is borne in upon me I am
An engine that moves
In predestinate grooves,
I'm not even a bus, I'm a tram.'

Maurice Evan Hare 1886–1967:
'Limerick' (1905)

17 The defendant is clearly one who insufficiently appreciates
the value of the motor car to the human race. But we
must not allow our natural detestation for such an
individual to cloud our judgment.

A. P. Herbert 1890–1971: *Misleading
Cases* (1935)

18 Home James, and don't spare the horses.

Fred Hillebrand 1893– : title of song
(1934)

19 Cyclists see motorists as tyrannical and uncaring.
Motorists believe cyclists are afflicted by a perversion.

Boris Johnson 1964– : in *Observer*
28 December 2003

20 The automobile changed our dress, manners, social
customs, vacation habits, the shape of our cities,
consumer purchasing patterns, common tastes and
positions in intercourse.

John Keats 1920– : *The Insolent
Chariots* (1958)

21 FATHER STACK: While you were out, I got the keys to your
car. And drove it into a big wall. And if you don't like it,
tough. I've had my fun, and that's all that matters.

Graham Linehan and **Arthur
Mathews**: 'New Jack City' (1996),
episode from *Father Ted* (Channel 4
TV, 1995–8)

22 *on a car called by Macmillan 'Mrs Thatcher':*
This car makes a noise if you don't fasten your seat belt,
and a light starts flashing if you don't close the door. It's a
very bossy car.

Harold Macmillan 1894–1986:
Ludovic Kennedy *On My Way to the
Club* (1989)

23 In Milan, traffic lights are instructions. In Rome, they are
suggestions. In Naples, they are Christmas decorations.

Antonio Martino 1942– : in *Sunday
Times* 24 February 2002

24 I've tried walking sideways, and walking to the front,
But people laughed, and said, 'It's a publicity stunt.'

Spike Milligan 1918–2002: 'I'm
Walking Backwards for Christmas'
(1956)

25 *seeing the Morris Minor prototype in 1945:*
It looks like a poached egg—we can't make that.

Lord Nuffield 1877–1963: attributed

26 People who spend most of their natural lives riding iron bicycles over the rocky roadsteads of this parish get their personalities mixed up with the personalities of their bicycles as a result of the interchanging of the atoms of each of them and you would be surprised at the number of people in these parts who nearly are half people and half bicycles.

Flann O'Brien 1911–66: *The Third Policeman* (1967)

27 Why is it no one ever sent me yet
One perfect limousine, do you suppose?
Ah no, it's always just my luck to get
One perfect rose.

Dorothy Parker 1893–1967: 'One Perfect Rose' (1937)

28 Back in the house, I felt someone had put planks in my legs and turned my buttocks into wooden boxes.
his first experience of riding

V. S. Pritchett 1900–97: *Midnight Oil* (1971)

29 Sure, the next train has gone ten minutes ago.

Punch 1841–1992: vol. 60 (1871)

30 What is better than presence of mind in a railway accident? Absence of body.

Punch 1841–1992: vol. 16 (1849)

31 Denis Norden thought that Johann Strauss's car would have been registered as—123 123.

Steve Race 1921– : in *The Bibliophile* September 2000; attributed

32 Take most people, they're crazy about cars. They worry if they get a little scratch on them, and they're always talking about how many miles they get to a gallon . . . I don't even like *old* cars. I mean they don't even interest me. I'd rather have a goddam horse. A horse is at least *human*, for God's sake.

J. D. Salinger 1919– : *The Catcher in the Rye* (1951)

33 Walk! Not bloody likely. I am going in a taxi.

George Bernard Shaw 1856–1950: *Pygmalion* (1916)

34 I wonder if there are enough traffic cones for every student to have one in their bedroom.

Arthur Smith 1954– and **Chris England**: *An Evening with Gary Lineker* (1990)

35 BOATMAN: I 'ad that Christopher Marlowe in the back of my boat.

Tom Stoppard 1937– : *Shakespeare in Love* (1999 film, screenplay by Tom Stoppard and Mark Norman)

36 MAGNUS: How long have you been a pedestrian?
SIMON: Ever since I could walk.

Tom Stoppard 1937– : *The Real Inspector Hound* (1968)

37 *on the construction of the Canadian Pacific Railway across Canada:*
Building that railroad would have made a Canadian out of the German Emperor.

William Cornelius Van Horne 1843–1915: in *Canadian Encyclopedia* (1988) vol. 1

Travel and Exploration

&&*Worth seeing, yes; but not worth going to see.*,,
Samuel Johnson

1 In America there are two classes of travel—first class, and with children.

Robert Benchley 1889–1945: *Pluck and Luck* (1925)

2 I encountered Mr. Hackman, an Englishman, who has been walking the length and breadth of Europe for several years. I enquired of him what were his chief observations. He replied gruffly, 'I never look up', and went on his way.

N. Brooke: in 1796; Duncan Minshull *The Vintage Book of Walking* (2000)

3 But the principal failing occurred in the sailing,
And the Bellman, perplexed and distressed,
Said he *had* hoped, at least, when the wind blew due East,
That the ship would *not* travel due West!

Lewis Carroll 1832–98: *The Hunting of the Snark* (1876) 'Fit the Second: The Bellman's Speech'

4 They say travel broadens the mind; but you must have the mind.

G. K. Chesterton 1874–1936: 'The Shadow of the Shark' (1921)

5 *on travelling to the US:*
I'm often unlucky enough to be picked out for those 'special searches' due to my obvious resemblance to Mr bin Laden.

Joan Collins 1933– : in *Sunday Times* 29 February 2004

6 Why do the wrong people travel, travel, travel,
When the right people stay back home?
What compulsion compels them
And who the hell tells them
To drag their cans to Zanzibar
Instead of staying quietly in Omaha?

Noël Coward 1899–1973: 'Why do the Wrong People Travel?' (1961)

7 *on his arrival in Turkey:*
I am of course known here as English Delight.

Noël Coward 1899–1973: Sheridan Morley *The Quotable Noël Coward* (1999)

8 Luggage left alone unloaded
Will be immediately exploded.

April De Angelis 1955– : Jonathan Dove and April De Angelis *Flight* (1998 opera)

9 A person can be stranded and get by, even though she will be imperilled; two people with a German shepherd and no money are in a mess.

Andrea Dworkin 1946–2005: *Letters from a War Zone* (1988)

10 At my age travel broadens the behind.

Stephen Fry 1957– : *The Liar* (1991)

11 Abroad is bloody.

George VI 1895–1952: W. H. Auden *A Certain World* (1970)

12 So think twice my friends, before you doubt Columbus,
Just imagine what happens to Posterity without
    Columbus.
No New York, and no skyscrapers,
No funnies in the papers,
No automat nickels,
No Heinz and his pickles,
No land of the Brave and the Free.

Ira Gershwin 1896–1983: 'The Nina, the Pinta, the Santa Maria' (1945)

13 And bound on that journey you find your attorney (who
    started that morning from Devon);
He's a bit undersized, and you don't feel surprised when he
    tells you he's only eleven.

W. S. Gilbert 1836–1911: *Iolanthe* (1882)

14 *on the Giant's Causeway:*
Worth seeing, yes; but not worth going to see.

Samuel Johnson 1709–84: James Boswell *Life of Samuel Johnson* (1791) 12 October 1779

15 What good is speed if the brain has oozed out on the way?

Karl Kraus 1874–1936: 'The Discovery of the North Pole'

16 Thanks to the interstate highway system, it is now possible to travel from coast to coast without seeing anything.

Charles Kuralt 1934–97: *On the Road* (1980)

17 I wouldn't mind seeing China if I could come back the same day.

Philip Larkin 1922–85: *Required Writing* (1983), interview with *Observer*, 1979

18 At first, you fear you will die; then, after it has a good hold on you, you fear you won't die.
   on seasickness

Jack London 1876–1916: *The Cruise of the Snark* (1911)

19 A sure cure for seasickness is to sit under a tree.

Spike Milligan 1918–2002: attributed; in *Daily Telegraph* 28 February 2002

20 She said that all the sights in Rome were called after London cinemas.

Nancy Mitford 1904–73: *Pigeon Pie* (1940)

21 *filling in an embarkation form on a channel crossing:*
   HAROLD NICOLSON: What age are you going to put, Osbert?
   OSBERT SITWELL: What sex are you going to put, Harold?

Harold Nicolson 1886–1968: attributed, perhaps apocryphal

22 Everybody in fifteenth-century Spain was wrong about where China was and as a result, Columbus discovered Caribbean vacations.

P. J. O'Rourke 1947– : *Parliament of Whores* (1991)

23 In these days of rapid and convenient travel . . . to come from Leighton Buzzard does not necessarily denote any great strength of character. It might only mean mere restlessness.

Saki 1870–1916: *The Chronicles of Clovis* (1911)

24 If it's Tuesday, this must be Belgium.

David Shaw: film title (1969)

25 *on airline food:*
   The shiny stuff is tomatoes.
   The salad lies in a group.
   The curly stuff is potatoes,
   The stuff that moves is soup.
   Anything that is white is sweet,
   Anything that is brown is meat.
   Anything that is grey—don't eat.

Stephen Sondheim 1930– : 'Do I Hear a Waltz?' (1965)

26 In Turkey it was always 1952, in Malaysia 1937; Afghanistan was 1910 and Bolivia 1949. It is twenty years ago in the Soviet Union, ten in Norway, five in France. It is always last year in Australia and next week in Japan.

Paul Theroux 1941– : *The Kingdom by the Sea* (1983)

27 *asked why he had come to America:*
   In pursuit of my life-long quest for naked women in wet mackintoshes.

Dylan Thomas 1914–53: Constantine Fitzgibbon *Dylan Thomas* (1965); attributed

28 It is not worthwhile to go around the world to count the cats in Zanzibar.

Henry David Thoreau 1817–62: *Walden* (1854) 'Conclusion'

29 Done the elephants, done the poverty.
   after a cricket tour of India

Phil Tufnell 1961– : attributed; in *Times Literary Supplement* 28 July 2000

30 Commuter—one who spends his life
   In riding to and from his wife;
   A man who shaves and takes a train,
   And then rides back to shave again.

E. B. White 1899–1985: 'The Commuter' (1982)

Trust and Treachery

See also **Security**

❝ Once bitten by a snake you feel suspicious even when you see a piece of rope. ❞
Dalai Lama

---

1 Outside Shakespeare the word treason to me means nothing. Only, you pissed in our soup and we drank it.
Coral Browne to Guy Burgess

Alan Bennett 1934– : *An Englishman Abroad* (1989)

2 The only recorded instance in history of a rat swimming *towards* a sinking ship.
of a former Conservative who proposed to stand as a Liberal

Winston Churchill 1874–1965: Leon Harris *The Fine Art of Political Wit* (1965)

3 Frankly speaking it is difficult to trust the Chinese. Once bitten by a snake you feel suspicious even when you see a piece of rope.

Dalai Lama 1935– : attributed, 1981

4 *discussing a friend with Robert Lajeunesse:*
LAJEUNESSE: He deserves to be betrayed.
FEYDEAU: And even so, his wife has to help him.

Georges Feydeau 1862–1921: Caryl Brahms and Ned Sherrin *Ooh! La-La!* (1973)

5 When I was at Cambridge it was, naturally enough I felt, my ambition to be approached in some way by an elderly homosexual don and asked to spy for or against my country.

Stephen Fry 1957– : *Paperweight* (1992)

6 It is rather like sending your opening batsmen to the crease only for them to find the moment that the first balls are bowled that their bats have been broken before the game by the team captain.

Geoffrey Howe 1926– : resignation speech as Deputy Prime Minister, House of Commons 13 November 1990

7 If you paved the way from here to Broken Hill with Bibles, and if that man Hitler swore an oath on every one of them, I wouldn't believe a goddam bloody word he said.

William Morris Hughes 1862–1952: John Thompson *On Lips of Living Men* (1962)

8 *Pension.* Pay given to a state hireling for treason to his country.

Samuel Johnson 1709–84: *A Dictionary of the English Language* (1755)

9 Never trust a man who combs his hair straight from his left armpit.
of the careful distribution of hair on General MacArthur's balding head

Alice Roosevelt Longworth 1884–1980: Michael Teague *Mrs L* (1981)

10 Defectors are like grapes. The first pressings from them are the best. The third and fourth lack body.

Maurice Oldfield 1915–81: Chapman Pincher in *Mail on Sunday* 19 September 1982; attributed

11 Never take a reference from a clergyman. They always want to give someone a second chance.

Lady Selborne 1858–1950: K. Rose *The Later Cecils* (1975)

12 [Treason], Sire, is a question of dates.

Charles-Maurice de Talleyrand 1754–1838: Duff Cooper *Talleyrand* (1932)

13 He trusted neither of them as far as he could spit, and he was a poor spitter, lacking both distance and control.

P. G. Wodehouse 1881–1975: *Money in the Bank* (1946)

Truth

See also **Lies**

66 *There was things which he stretched, but mainly he told the truth.* 99
Mark Twain

1 The pursuit of truth is chimerical . . . What we should pursue is the most convenient arrangement of our ideas.

Samuel Butler 1835–1902: *Notebooks* (1912)

2 'Tis strange—but true; for truth is always strange; Stranger than fiction.

Lord Byron 1788–1824: *Don Juan* (1819–24)

3 He occasionally stumbled over the truth, but hastily picked himself up and hurried on as if nothing had happened. *of Stanley Baldwin*

Winston Churchill 1874–1965: J. L. Lane (ed.) *The Sayings of Winston Churchill* (1992)

4 Our old friend . . . economical with the *actualité*.

Alan Clark 1928–99: under cross-examination at the Old Bailey during the Matrix Churchill case; in *Independent* 10 November 1992

5 Something unpleasant is coming when men are anxious to tell the truth.

Benjamin Disraeli 1804–81: *The Young Duke* (1831)

6 It is always the best policy to speak the truth—unless, of course, you are an exceptionally good liar.

Jerome K. Jerome 1859–1927: in *The Idler* February 1892

7 Never tell a story because it is true: tell it because it is a good story.

John Pentland Mahaffy 1839–1919: W. B. Stanford and R. B. McDowell *Mahaffy* (1971)

8 I never give them [the public] hell. I just tell the truth, and they think it is hell.

Harry S. Truman 1884–1972: in *Look* 3 April 1956

9 'The Adventures of Tom Sawyer' . . . was made by Mr Mark Twain, and he told the truth, mainly. There was things which he stretched, but mainly he told the truth.

Mark Twain 1835–1910: *The Adventures of Huckleberry Finn* (1884)

10 Get your facts first, and then you can distort 'em as much as you please.

Mark Twain 1835–1910: Rudyard Kipling *From Sea to Sea* (1899)

11 The truth is rarely pure, and never simple.

Oscar Wilde 1854–1900: *The Importance of Being Earnest* (1895)

The Universe

66 *Space is almost infinite. As a matter of fact, we think it is infinite.* 99
Dan Quayle

1 Had I been present at the Creation, I would have given some useful hints for the better ordering of the universe.

Alfonso, King of Castile 1221–84: on studying the Ptolemaic system (attributed)

2 'I quite realized,' said Columbus,
'That the Earth was not a rhombus,
But I *am* a little annoyed
To find it an oblate spheroid.'

Edmund Clerihew Bentley 1875–1956: 'Columbus' (1929)

3 *on hearing that Margaret Fuller 'accepted the universe':*
Gad! she'd better!

Thomas Carlyle 1795–1881: William James *Varieties of Religious Experience* (1902)

4 Twinkle, twinkle, little bat!
How I wonder what you're at!
Up above the world you fly!
Like a teatray in the sky.

Lewis Carroll 1832–98: *Alice's Adventures in Wonderland* (1865)

5 The world has treated me very well, but then I haven't treated it so badly either.

Noël Coward 1899–1973: Sheridan Morley *The Quotable Noël Coward* (1999)

6   Listen: there's a hell
Of a good universe next door; let's go.

e. e. cummings 1894–1962: *1 x 1* (1944)

7 The world is disgracefully managed, one hardly knows to whom to complain.

Ronald Firbank 1886–1926: *Vainglory* (1915)

8 Now, my own suspicion is that the universe is not only queerer than we suppose, but queerer than we *can* suppose.

J. B. S. Haldane 1892–1964: *Possible Worlds* (1927)

9 If this planet is a sample,
Or a preview if you will,
Or a model demonstration
Of the great designer's stall,
I say without hesitation,
'Thank you, no reincarnation.'

E. Y. Harburg 1898–1981: 'Letter to my Gaza' (1976)

10 To make the longest story terse,
Be it blessing, be it curse
The Lord designed the Universe
With built in obsolescence . . .

E. Y. Harburg 1898–1981: 'The Odds on Favourite' (1976)

11 The only lyric writer on the Broadway treadmill to get comic with the cosmic.
    of E. Y. Harburg

John Lahr 1941– : Ned Sherrin *Cutting Edge* (1984)

12 I don't think there's intelligent life on other planets. Why should other planets be any different from this one?

Bob Monkhouse 1928–2003: attributed; in *BBC News* 29 December 2003 (online edition)

13 The Greeks said God was always doing geometry, modern physicists say he's playing roulette, everything depends on the observer, the universe is a totality of observations, it's a work of art created by us.

Iris Murdoch 1919–99: *The Good Apprentice* (1985)

14 Space is almost infinite. As a matter of fact, we think it is infinite.

Dan Quayle 1947– : in *Daily Telegraph* 8 March 1989

Virtue and Vice
See also **Morality**

> **❝** *I think I could be a good woman if I had five thousand a year.* **❞**
William Makepeace Thackeray

1 I'm as pure as the driven slush.

Tallulah Bankhead 1903–68: in *Saturday Evening Post* 12 April 1947

2 All things are capable of excess. Absence of morbid moisture is a Whig virtue. But morbid dryness is a Whig vice.

Max Beerbohm 1872–1956: letter July 1928

3 A dead sinner revised and edited.
 definition of a saint

Ambrose Bierce 1842–c.1914: *The Devil's Dictionary* (1911)

4 The rain, it raineth on the just
And also on the unjust fella:
But chiefly on the just, because
The unjust steals the just's umbrella.

Lord Bowen 1835–94: Walter Sichel *Sands of Time* (1923)

5 An original something, fair maid, you would win me
To write—but how shall I begin?
For I fear I have nothing original in me—
Excepting Original Sin.

Thomas Campbell 1777–1844: 'To a Young Lady, Who Asked Me to Write Something Original for Her Album' (1843)

6 The difference between him and Arthur is that Arthur is wicked and moral, Asquith is good and immoral.
 comparing Herbert Asquith with Arthur Balfour

Winston Churchill 1874–1965: E. T. Raymond *Mr Balfour* (1920)

7 In former days, everyone found the assumption of innocence so easy; today we find fatally easy the assumption of guilt.

Amanda Cross 1926–2003: *Poetic Justice* (1970)

8 Lydia was tired of being good. She felt it didn't altogether suit her. It made her feel a little dowdy, as though she had taken up residence in the suburbs of morality.

Alice Thomas Ellis 1932–2005: *Unexplained Laughter* (1985)

9 The louder he talked of his honour, the faster we counted our spoons.

Ralph Waldo Emerson 1803–82: *The Conduct of Life* (1860)

10 But if he does really think that there is no distinction between virtue and vice, why, Sir, when he leaves our houses, let us count our spoons.

Samuel Johnson 1709–84: James Boswell *Life of Samuel Johnson* (1791) 14 July 1763

11 He that but looketh on a plate of ham and eggs to lust after it, hath already committed breakfast with it in his heart.

C. S. Lewis 1898–1963: letter, 10 March 1954

12 honesty is a good
thing but
it is not profitable to
its possessor
unless it is
kept under control.

Don Marquis 1878–1937: *archys life of mehitabel* (1933) 'archygrams'

13 *on being discovered by his wife with a chorus girl:*
I wasn't kissing her, I was just whispering in her mouth.

Chico Marx 1891–1961: Groucho Marx and Richard J. Anobile *Marx Brothers Scrapbook* (1973)

14 If only the good were a little less heavy-footed!

W. Somerset Maugham 1874–1965: *A Writer's Notebook* (1949) written in 1896

15 Decency is Indecency's conspiracy of silence.

George Bernard Shaw 1856–1950: *Man and Superman* (1903) 'Maxims: Decency'

16 Self-denial is not a virtue: it is only the effect of prudence on rascality.

George Bernard Shaw 1856–1950: *Man and Superman* (1903)

17 I think I could be a good woman if I had five thousand a year.

William Makepeace Thackeray 1811–63: *Vanity Fair* (1847–8)

18 Barring that natural expression of villainy which we all have, the man looked honest enough.

Mark Twain 1835–1910: *A Curious Dream* (1872) 'A Mysterious Visit'

19 Her virtue was that she said what she thought, her vice that what she thought didn't amount to much.

Peter Ustinov 1921–2004: attributed; in *Daily Telegraph* 30 March 2004

20 When I'm good, I'm very, very good, but when I'm bad, I'm better.

Mae West 1892–1980: in *I'm No Angel* (1933 film)

21 I used to be Snow White . . . but I drifted.

Mae West 1892–1980: Joseph Weintraub *Peel Me a Grape* (1975)

22 Between two evils, I always pick the one I never tried before.

Mae West 1892–1980: in *Klondike Annie* (1936 film)

23 To err is human—but it feels divine.

Mae West 1892–1980: attributed; Fred Metcalf (ed.) *Penguin Dictionary of Modern Humorous Quotations* (1987)

24 I can resist everything except temptation.

Oscar Wilde 1854–1900: *Lady Windermere's Fan* (1892)

25 A little sincerity is a dangerous thing, and a great deal of it is absolutely fatal.

Oscar Wilde 1854–1900: 'The Critic as Artist' (1891)

Wales

See also **Countries and Peoples, Places**

❝ The land of my fathers. My fathers can have it. ❞
Dylan Thomas

1 *the cover of the Eurostat Yearbook 2004 showed the coastline of the British Isles beginning at the Welsh Border:*
Peter Mandelson has hardly been in Brussels two weeks and already Wales has fallen into the Irish Sea.

Michael Ancram 1945– : in *Independent* 7 October 2004

2 *a Board Member objecting to Richard Burton's candidature for leading a Welsh National Theatre Company, after hearing of Burton's international triumphs:*
Yes, but what has he done for Wales?

Anonymous: in *Ned Sherrin's Theatrical Anecdotes* (1992)

3 It profits a man nothing to give his soul for the whole world . . . But for Wales—!

Robert Bolt 1924–95: *A Man for All Seasons* (1960)

4 Now I perceive the devil understands Welsh.

William Shakespeare 1564–1616: *Henry IV, Part 1* (1597)

5 The land of my fathers. My fathers can have it.

Dylan Thomas 1914–53: *Adam* December 1953

6 There are still parts of Wales where the only concession to gaiety is a striped shroud.

Gwyn Thomas 1913–81: in *Punch* 18 June 1958

7 'I often think,' he continued, 'that we can trace almost all the disasters of English history to the influence of Wales!'

Evelyn Waugh 1903–66: *Decline and Fall* (1928)

8 The Welsh remain the only race whom you can vilify without being called a racist.

A. N. Wilson 1950– : in *Sunday Times* 23 April 2000 'Talking Heads'

War

See also **The Armed Forces**

66 *The quickest way of ending a war is to lose it.* 99

George Orwell

1 *of the retreat from Dunkirk, May 1940:*
The noise, my dear! And the people!

Anonymous: Anthony Rhodes *Sword of Bone* (1942)

2 Kitchener is a great poster.

Margot Asquith 1864–1945: *More Memories* (1933)

3 After each war there is a little less democracy to save.

Brooks Atkinson 1894–1984: *Once Around the Sun* (1951) 7 January

4 Well, if you knows of a better 'ole, go to it.

Bruce Bairnsfather 1888–1959: *Fragments from France* (1915)

5 *on becoming aware of the Nazi threat:*
I shall put warmonger on my passport.

Robert Byron 1905–41: *The Road to Oxiana* (1980 ed.); introduction

6 *of Viscount Montgomery:*
In defeat unbeatable: in victory unbearable.

Winston Churchill 1874–1965: Edward Marsh *Ambrosia and Small Beer* (1964)

7 They found more dangerous chemicals in Coca-Cola's Dasani mineral water than they did in the whole of Iraq.

Robin Cook 1946–2005: in *Observer* 29 August 2004

8 Though Waterloo was won upon the playing fields of Eton, The next war will be photographed, and lost, by Cecil Beaton.

Noël Coward 1899–1973: 'Bright Young People' (1931)

9 *when Park Lane was bombed:*
I was under the table with the telephone and Shakespeare.

Emerald Cunard 1872–1948: Chips Channon diary, 20 March 1945

10 A war hasn't been fought this badly since Olaf the Hairy, High Chief of all the Vikings, ordered 80,000 battle helmets with the horns on the inside.

Richard Curtis 1956– and **Ben Elton** 1959– : *Blackadder Goes Forth* (1989) 'Major Star'

11 I gave my life for freedom—This I know: For those who bade me fight had told me so.

William Norman Ewer 1885–1976: 'Five Souls' (1917)

12 There never was a good war, or a bad peace.

Benjamin Franklin 1706–90: letter to Josiah Quincy, 11 September 1783

13 Fortunately, just when things were blackest, the war broke out.

Joseph Heller 1923–99: *Catch-22* (1961)

14 I'd like to see the government get out of war altogether and leave the whole field to private industry.

Joseph Heller 1923–99: *Catch-22* (1961)

15 All the same, sir, I would put some of the colonies in your wife's name.
the Chief Rabbi to George VI, summer 1940

Joseph Herman Hertz 1872–1946: Chips Channon diary, 3 June 1943

16 *of war in Iraq:*
Vietnam without the mosquitoes.

Carl Hiaasen 1953– : attributed; in *Guardian* 23 October 2004

17 TRENTINO (Louis Calhern): I am willing to do anything to prevent this war.
FIREFLY (Groucho Marx): It's too late. I've already paid a month's rent on the battlefield.

Bert Kalmar 1884–1947 et al.: *Duck Soup* (1933 film)

18 I think from now on they're shooting without a script.
comment on the German invasion of Russia

George S. Kaufman 1889–1961:
Howard Teichmann *George S.
Kaufman* (1973)

19 All castles had one major weakness. The enemy used to
get in through the gift shop.

Peter Kay 1973– : attributed; in *Nuts*
May 2005

20 Gentlemen, you can't fight in here. This is the war room.

Stanley Kubrick 1928–99, **Terry
Southern**, and **Peter George**: *Dr
Strangelove* (1963 film)

21 If we'd had as many soldiers as that, we'd have won the
war!
on seeing the number of Confederate troops in Gone with
the Wind *at the 1939 premiere*

Margaret Mitchell 1900–49: W. G.
Harris *Gable and Lombard* (1976)

22 Like many men of my generation, I had an opportunity to
give war a chance, and I promptly chickened out.

P. J. O'Rourke 1947– : *Give War a
Chance* (1992)

23 The quickest way of ending a war is to lose it.

George Orwell 1903–50: in *Polemic*
May 1946 'Second Thoughts on
James Burnham'

24 Little girl . . . Sometime they'll give a war and nobody will
come.

Carl Sandburg 1878–1967: *The
People, Yes* (1936); 'Suppose They
Gave a War and Nobody Came?' was
the title of a 1970 film

25 'Our armies swore terribly in Flanders,' cried my uncle
Toby,—'but nothing to this.'

Laurence Sterne 1713–68: *Tristram
Shandy* (1759–67)

26 The First World War had begun—imposed on the
statesmen of Europe by railway timetables. It was an
unexpected climax to the railway age.

A. J. P. Taylor 1906–90: *The First
World War* (1963)

27 *Evelyn Waugh, returning from Crete in 1941, was asked his
impression of his first battle:*
Like German opera, too long and too loud.

Evelyn Waugh 1903–66: Christopher
Sykes *Evelyn Waugh* (1975)

28 I am in consultation with my editors on the subject. We
think it a very promising little war. A microcosm you
might say, of world drama.

Evelyn Waugh 1903–66: *Scoop*
(1938)

29 As Lord Chesterfield said of the generals of his day, 'I only
hope that when the enemy reads the list of their names, he
trembles as I do.'
*usually quoted 'I don't know what effect these men will have
upon the enemy, but, by God, they frighten me'*

Duke of Wellington 1769–1852:
letter, 29 August 1810

30 *of an early attempt to write about Waterloo:*
Write the history of a battle? As well write the history of a
ball!

Duke of Wellington 1769–1852:
Richard Holmes *Firing Line* (1986)

31 Good-bye-ee! — Good-bye-ee!
Wipe the tear, baby dear, from your eye-ee.
Tho' it's hard to part, I know,
I'll be tickled to death to go.
Don't cry-ee — don't sigh-ee!
There's a silver lining in the sky-ee!
Bonsoir, old thing! cheerio! chin-chin!
Nahpoo! Toodle-oo! Good-bye-ee!

R. P. Weston 1878–1936 and **Bert
Lee** 1880–1936: 'Good-bye-ee!'
(c.1915)

32 *of Sir Charles Napier's conquest of Sindh:*
Peccavi—I have Sindh.
reworking Latin peccavi *I have sinned*

Catherine Winkworth 1827–78: in
Punch 18 May 1844, supposedly sent
by Napier to Lord Ellenborough

33 'Anything in the papers, Jeeves?' 'Some slight friction threatening in the Balkans, sir.'

P. G. Wodehouse 1881–1975: *The Inimitable Jeeves* (1923)

Wealth

See also **Money, Poverty**

> ❝The meek shall inherit the earth, but not the mineral rights. ❞
> **John Paul Getty**

1 *Ali G interviewing David and Victoria Beckham:*
So they is some people who suddenly get loads of money who become very tasteless. How has you two managed to avoid that?

Ali G (Sacha Baron Cohen) 1970– :
in *Sunday Times* 11 February 2001

2 It was a sumpshous spot all done up in gold with plenty of looking glasses.

Daisy Ashford 1881–1972: *The Young Visiters* (1919)

3 If you would know what the Lord God thinks of money, you have only to look at those to whom he gives it.

Maurice Baring 1874–1945: Malcolm Cowley (ed.) *Writers at Work* (1958) 1st series

4 I can walk. It's just that I'm so rich I don't need to.

Alan Bennett 1934– : *Forty Years On* (1969)

5 People say I wasted my money. I say 90 per cent went on women, fast cars and booze. The rest I wasted.

George Best 1946–2005: in *Daily Telegraph* 29 December 1990

6 A very rich person should leave his kids enough to do anything but not enough to do nothing.

Warren Buffett 1930– : quoted in *Fortune Magazine* (online edition) 25 June 2006

7 Mrs Budge Bulkeley, worth £32,000,000, has arrived here [Isfahan] accompanied by some lesser millionairesses. They are in great misery because the caviare is running out.
on fellow travellers in Persia

Robert Byron 1905–41: *The Road to Oxiana* (1937)

8 When I hear a rich man described as a colourful character I figure he's a bum with money.

Jimmy Cannon 1910–73: in *New York Post* c.1955 'Nobody Asked Me, But . . . '

9 I really love having money, because it lets me be lazy. Work's really overrated.

Charlotte Church 1986– : in *Times* 9 September 2007

10 The Rich aren't like us—they pay less taxes.

Peter de Vries 1910–93: in *Washington Post* 30 July 1989

11 £40,000 a year [is] a moderate income—such a one as a man might jog on with.

Lord Durham 1792–1840: Herbert Maxwell *The Creevey Papers* (1903); letter from Mr Creevey to Miss Elizabeth Ord, 13 September 1821

12 I used to walk in the shade,
With those blues on parade,
But I'm not afraid.
This Rover crossed over.
If I never have a cent
I'll be rich as Rockefeller,

Dorothy Fields 1905–74: 'On the Sunny Side of the Street' (1930)

Gold dust on my feet,
On the sunny side of the street.

13 A rich man is nothing but a poor man with money.

W. C. Fields 1880–1946: attributed

14 The meek shall inherit the earth, but not the mineral rights.

John Paul Getty 1892–1976: Robert Lenzner *The Great Getty*; attributed

15 *aged seven, when his brother asked why he was not interested in learning to read:*
Because when I grow up I'm going to be a millionaire and hire someone to read for me.

James Goldsmith 1933–97: Juan Fallon *Billionaire: the life and times of Sir James Goldsmith* (1991)

16 What a night—the furs, the jewels, the glamour . . . I haven't seen so much expensive jewellery go by since I watched Sammy Davis Jr.'s home sliding down Coldwater Canyon.
   hosting the Oscars, 1978

Bob Hope 1903–2003: attributed; in *Lansing State Journal* 28 July 2003

17 Poor Harold, he can live on his income all right, but he no longer can live on the income from his income.
   of Harold Vanderbilt

George S. Kaufman 1889–1961: Howard Teichmann *George S. Kaufman* (1973)

18 Wealth and power are much more likely to be the result of breeding than they are of reading.
   on self-help books

Fran Lebowitz 1946– : *Social Studies* (1981)

19 When I want a peerage, I shall buy it like an honest man.

Lord Northcliffe 1865–1922: Tom Driberg *Swaff* (1974)

20 The average millionaire is only the average dishwasher dressed in a new suit.

George Orwell 1903–50: *Down and Out in Paris and London* (1933)

21 Where would the Rockefellers be today if sainted old John D. had gone on selling short-weight kerosene (paraffin to you) to widows and orphans instead of wisely deciding to mulct the whole country?

S. J. Perelman 1904–79: letter 25 October 1976

22 I've a shooting box in Scotland,
I've a chateau in Touraine,
I've a silly little chalet
In the Interlaken Valley,
I've a hacienda in Spain,
I've a private fjord in Norway,
I've a villa close to Rome,
And in travelling
It's really quite a comfort to know
That you're never far from home!

Cole Porter 1891–1964: 'I've a Shooting Box in Scotland' (1916)

23 HE: Who wants to be a millionaire?
SHE: I don't.
HE: Have flashy flunkeys ev'rywhere?
SHE: I don't . . .
HE: Who wants a marble swimming pool too?
SHE: I don't.
HE: And I don't,
BOTH: 'Cause all I want is you.

Cole Porter 1891–1964: 'Who Wants to be a Millionaire?' (1956)

24 A kiss on the hand may be quite continental,
But diamonds are a girl's best friend . . .
Men grow cold as girls grow old
And we all lose our charms in the end.
But square cut or pear shape,

Leo Robin 1900–84: 'Diamonds are a Girl's Best Friend' (1949)

These rocks won't lose their shape,
Diamonds are a girl's best friend.

25 Never invest your money in anything that eats or needs repainting.

Billy Rose 1899–1966: in *New York Post* 26 October 1957

26 I am a Millionaire. That is my religion.

George Bernard Shaw 1856–1950: *Major Barbara* (1907)

27 It is the wretchedness of being rich that you have to live with rich people.

Logan Pearsall Smith 1865–1946: *Afterthoughts* (1931)

28 To suppose, as we all suppose, that we could be rich and not behave as the rich behave, is like supposing that we could drink all day and keep absolutely sober.

Logan Pearsall Smith 1865–1946: *Afterthoughts* (1931)

29 It was very prettily said, that we may learn the little value of fortune by the persons on whom heaven is pleased to bestow it.

Richard Steele 1672–1729: *The Tatler* 27 July 1710

30 I've been poor and I've been rich—rich is better.

Sophie Tucker 1884–1966: attributed

31 I sometimes wished he would realize that he was poor instead of being that most nerve-racking of phenomena, a rich man without money.

Peter Ustinov 1921–2004: *Dear Me* (1977)

32 Real diamonds! They must be worth their weight in gold.

Billy Wilder 1906–2002 and **I. A. L. Diamond** 1915–88: *Some Like it Hot* (1959 film); spoken by Marilyn Monroe as Sugar Kane

33 I am grateful for the blessings of wealth, but it hasn't changed who I am. My feet are still on the ground. I'm just wearing better shoes.

Oprah Winfrey 1954– : in *Independent on Sunday* 18 July 2004

The Weather

❝ It was such a lovely day I thought it was a pity to get up. ❞
W. Somerset Maugham

1 When the foal and broodmare hinny,
And in every cut-down spinney
Ladysmocks grow mauve and mauver,
Then the winter days are over.
Sometimes misquoted as, 'Spring is here, winter is over; the cuckoo-flower gets mauver and mauver'

Alfred Austin 1835–1913: *Fortunatus the Pessimist* (1892)

2 *on being asked why he never sunbathed in California instead of sitting under a sun-lamp:*
And get hit by a meteor?

Robert Benchley 1889–1945: R. E. Drennan *Wit's End* (1973)

3 Springtime for Hitler and Germany . . .
Winter for Poland and France.

Mel Brooks 1926– : 'Springtime for Hitler', lyric from Mel Brooks and Thomas Meehan *The Producers* (2001 musical)

4 The English winter—ending in July,
To recommence in August.

Lord Byron 1788–1824: *Don Juan* (1819–24)

5 Summer has set in with its usual severity.

Samuel Taylor Coleridge 1772–1834: letter to Vincent Novello, 9 May 1826

6 It ain't a fit night out for man or beast.

W. C. Fields 1880–1946: adopted by Fields but claimed by him not to be original; letter 8 February 1944

7 A woman rang to say she heard there was a hurricane on the way. Well don't worry, there isn't.
   weather forecast on the night before serious gales in southern England

Michael Fish 1944– : BBC TV, 15 October 1987

8 Some are weather-wise, some are otherwise.

Benjamin Franklin 1706–90: *Poor Richard's Almanac* (1735) February

9 I said, 'It is most extraordinary weather for this time of year.' He replied, 'Ah, it isn't this time of year at all.'

Oliver St John Gogarty 1878–1957: *It Isn't This Time of Year At All* (1954)

10 April in Fairbanks
   There's nothing more appealing
   You feel your blood congealing
   In April in Fairbanks.

Murray Grand 1919–2007: 'April in Fairbanks' (1952)

11 The weather is like the Government, always in the wrong.

Jerome K. Jerome 1859–1927: *Idle Thoughts of an Idle Fellow* (1889)

12 When two Englishmen meet, their first talk is of the weather.

Samuel Johnson 1709–84: *The Idler* 24 June 1758

13 The most serious charge which can be brought against New England is not Puritanism but February.

Joseph Wood Krutch 1893–1970: *The Twelve Seasons* (1949) 'February'

14 SHE: I really can't stay
   HE: But baby it's cold outside.

Frank Loesser 1910–69: 'Baby, It's Cold Outside' (1949)

15 The rain drove us into the church—our refuge, our strength, our only dry place . . . Limerick gained a reputation for piety, but we knew it was only the rain.

Frank McCourt 1930– : *Angela's Ashes* (1996)

16 It was such a lovely day I thought it was a pity to get up.

W. Somerset Maugham 1874–1965: *Our Betters* (1923)

17 Winter is icummen in,
   Lhude sing Goddamm,
   Raineth drop and staineth slop,
   And how the wind doth ramm!
   Sing: Goddamm.

Ezra Pound 1885–1972: 'Ancient Music' (1917)

18 Come December, people always say, 'Isn't it cold?' Well, of course it's cold. It's the middle of winter. You don't wander around at midnight saying, 'Isn't it dark?'

Arthur Smith 1954– : *Arthur Smith's Hamlet*

19 Thank heavens, the sun has gone in, and I don't have to go out and enjoy it.

Logan Pearsall Smith 1865–1946: *Afterthoughts* (1931)

20 Let no man boast himself that he has got through the perils of winter till at least the seventh of May.

Anthony Trollope 1815–82: *Doctor Thorne* (1858)

21 Cold! If the thermometer had been an inch longer we'd all have frozen to death.

Mark Twain 1835–1910: Opie Read *Mark Twain and I* (1940)

22 The way to ensure summer in England is to have it framed and glazed in a comfortable room.

Horace Walpole 1717–97: letter to Revd William Cole, 28 May 1774

23 It was the wrong kind of snow.
explaining disruption on British Rail

Terry Worrall: as quoted in *Evening Standard* 12 February 1991

Weddings

66 *And how's the groom? Why, he's slightly fried.* **99**
Cole Porter

1 If it were not for the presents, an elopement would be preferable.

George Ade 1866–1944: *Forty Modern Fables* (1901)

2 Egghead weds hourglass.
on the marriage of Arthur Miller and Marilyn Monroe

Anonymous: headline in *Variety* 1956; attributed

3 They stood before the altar and supplied
The fire themselves in which their fat was fried.

Ambrose Bierce 1842–c.1914: *The Enlarged Devil's Dictionary* (1967)

4 I am about to be married—and am of course in all the misery of a man in pursuit of happiness.

Lord Byron 1788–1824: letter, 15 October 1814

5 How was the wedding?
Brief, to the point and not unduly musical.

Noël Coward 1899–1973: *Shadow Play*

6 I love to cry at weddings, anybody's weddings anytime!
. . . anybody's weddings just so long as it's not mine!

Dorothy Fields 1905–74: 'I Love to Cry at Weddings' (1966)

7 I'm getting married in the morning!
Ding dong! The bells are gonna chime.
Pull out the stopper!
Let's have a whopper!
But get me to the church on time!

Alan Jay Lerner 1918–86: 'Get Me to the Church on Time' (1956)

8   The trouble
with being best man is, you don't get a chance to prove it.

Les A. Murray 1938– : *The Boys Who Stole the Funeral* (1989)

9 *agreeing with the comment, at her remarriage to Alan Campbell in 1950, that some of those present had not spoken to each other for years:*
Including the bride and groom.

Dorothy Parker 1893–1967: Marion Meade *What Fresh Hell Is This?* (1988)

10 It feels so fine to be a bride,
And how's the groom? Why, he's slightly fried,
It's delightful, it's delicious, it's de-lovely.

Cole Porter 1891–1964: 'It's De-lovely' (1936)

11 *telegram supposedly sent to Tom Driberg on the occasion of Driberg's wedding:*
I pray that the church is not struck by lightning.

Evelyn Waugh 1903–66: attributed; Nigel Rees (ed.) *Cassell Dictionary of Humorous Quotations* (1999)

12 Nothing so surely introduces a sour note into a wedding ceremony as the abrupt disappearance of the groom in a cloud of dust.

P. G. Wodehouse 1881–1975: *A Pelican at Blandings* (1969)

Wine

❝ *I'm only a beer teetotaller, not a champagne teetotaller.* **❞**
George Bernard Shaw

1 The teacher I most wanted to emulate, however, was single, drank wine and had been gassed in World War I. Of his three admirable traits, there was only one I wanted to copy, and sure enough, to this day, I love the sound of a popping cork.

Russell Baker 1925– : column in *New York Times*; Ned Sherrin *Cutting Edge* (1984)

2 *of claret:*
It would be port if it could.

Richard Bentley 1662–1742: R. C. Jebb *Bentley* (1902)

3 And Noah he often said to his wife when he sat down to dine,
'I don't care where the water goes if it doesn't get into the wine.'

G. K. Chesterton 1874–1936: 'Wine and Water' (1914)

4 *when the Queen accepted a second glass of wine at lunch:*
Do you think it's wise, darling? You know you've got to rule this afternoon.

Queen Elizabeth, the Queen Mother 1900–2002: Compton Miller *Who's Really Who* (1983)

5 When at dinner and supper, I drank, I know not how, of my own accord, so much wine, that I was even almost foxed and my head ached all night. So home.

Samuel Pepys 1633–1703: diary 29 September 1661

6 Was I a good year?

Michael Pertwee 1916–91: *A Funny Thing Happened on the Way to the Forum* (film, 1966)

7 A good general rule is to state that the bouquet is better than the taste, and vice versa.
on wine-tasting

Stephen Potter 1900–69: *One-Upmanship* (1952)

8 I'm only a beer teetotaller, not a champagne teetotaller.

George Bernard Shaw 1856–1950: *Candida* (1898)

9 Good God! I've never drunk a vintage that starts with the number two before.

Nicholas Soames 1948– : in *Daily Mail* 5 June 2003

10 BRINDLEY: It does say Burgundy on the bottle.
MARKS: It's the old wine ramp, vicar! Cheapish, reddish and Spanish.

Tom Stoppard 1937– : *Where Are They Now?* (1973)

11 Champagne certainly gives one werry gentlemanly ideas, but for a continuance, I don't know but I should prefer mild hale.

R. S. Surtees 1805–64: *Jorrocks's Jaunts and Jollities* (1838)

12 It's a naïve domestic Burgundy without any breeding, but I think you'll be amused by its presumption.

James Thurber 1894–1961: cartoon caption in *New Yorker* 27 March 1937

Wit and Wordplay

See also **Humour**

66 *I'm on the horns of a Dalai Lama.* 99

Dick Vosburgh

---

1 An ill-favoured thing, but Minoan.
supposedly a comment by the archaeologist Sir Arthur Evans on finding a fragment of Cretan pottery

Anonymous: in 'Quote . . . Unquote' Newsletter, April 1995

2 Wild horses on their bended knees would not get me out there.

Alan Bennett 1934– : *Forty Years On* (1969)

3 There's an element of mockery here I don't like. I don't mind your tongue being in your cheek, but I suspect your heart is there with it.

Alan Bennett 1934– : *Forty Years On* (1969)

4 My problem was that I was always missing. Miss World, Miss England, Miss UK . . .

George Best 1946–2005: Joe Lovejoy *Bestie* (1998)

5 'That's the reason they're called lessons,' the Gryphon remarked: 'because they lessen from day to day.'

Lewis Carroll 1832–98: *Alice's Adventures in Wonderland* (1865)

6 'Curiouser and curiouser!' cried Alice.

Lewis Carroll 1832–98: *Alice's Adventures in Wonderland* (1865)

7 A wit should be no more sincere than a woman constant; one argues a decay of parts, as t'other of beauty.

William Congreve 1670–1729: *The Way of the World* (1700)

8 His wit invites you by his looks to come,
But when you knock it never is at home.

William Cowper 1731–1800: 'Conversation' (1782)

9 Staircase wit.
the witty riposte one thinks of only when one has left the drawing-room and is already on the way downstairs

Denis Diderot 1713–84: in *Paradoxe sur le Comédien* (written 1773–8, published 1830)

10 O lovely O most charming pug
Thy graceful air and heavenly mug . . .
His noses cast is of the roman
He is a very pretty weoman
I could not get a rhyme for roman
And was oblidged to call it weoman.

Marjory Fleming 1803–11: 'Sonnet'

11 You've got to take the bull between your teeth.

Sam Goldwyn 1882–1974: N. Zierold *Hollywood Tycoons* (1969)

12 I can answer you in two words, im-possible.

Sam Goldwyn 1882–1974: Alva Johnston *The Great Goldwyn* (1937); apocryphal

13 Those who cannot miss an opportunity of saying a good thing . . . are not to be trusted with the management of any great question.

William Hazlitt 1778–1830: *Characteristics* (1823)

14 Dentist fills wrong cavity.
report of a dentist convicted of interfering with a patient

Ben Hecht 1894–1964: attributed

15 *on being told that the publisher of* Bentley's Miscellany *had thought of calling it* The Wits' Miscellany:
You need not have gone to the other extremity.

Douglas Jerrold 1803–57: Charles Cowden Clarke *Recollections of Writers* (1878)

16 It's hard not to write satire.

Juvenal c.AD 60–c.130: *Satires*

17 *Ira Gershwin had noticed two aged men entering the theatre:*
GERSHWIN: That must be Gilbert and Sullivan coming to fix the show.
KAUFMAN: Why don't you put jokes like that into your lyrics?

George S. Kaufman 1889–1961: Howard Teichmann *George S. Kaufman* (1973)

18 '*Succès d'estime*' translates as 'a success that ran out of steam'.

George S. Kaufman 1889–1961: Philip Furia *Ira Gershwin* (1996)

19 The greatest thing since they reinvented unsliced bread.

William Keegan 1938– : in *Observer* 13 December 1987

20 [*Shogun* ended with] almost everybody except Richard Chamberlain being killed in the city of Osaka. *Moral—* Never give Osaka an even break.

Herbert Kretzmer 1925– : review of the miniseries *Shogun*; Ned Sherrin *Cutting Edge* (1984)

21 Many of us can still remember the social nuisance of the inveterate punster. This man followed conversation as a shark follows a ship.

Stephen Leacock 1869–1944: *The Boy I Left Behind Me* (1947)

22 Epigram: a wisecrack that played Carnegie Hall.

Oscar Levant 1906–72: in *Coronet* September 1958

23 *for a poem on being Poet Laureate:*
It's hard to get your words' worth from a poet.

Roger McGough 1937– : attributed

24 *on being asked how to make an epigram by a young man in the flying corps:*
You merely loop the loop on a commonplace and come down between the lines.

W. Somerset Maugham 1874–1965: *A Writer's Notebook* (1949) written in 1933

25 Satire is a lesson, parody is a game.

Vladimir Nabokov 1899–1977: *Strong Opinions* (1974)

26 The dusk was performing its customary intransitive operation of 'gathering'.

Flann O'Brien 1911–66: *The Best of Myles* (1968)

27 *to the British actor Herbert Marshall who annoyed her by repeated references to his busy 'shedule':*
I think you're full of skit.

Dorothy Parker 1893–1967: Marion Meade *What Fresh Hell Is This?* (1988)

28 The pellet with the poison's in the vessel with the pestle. The chalice from the palace has the brew that is true.

Norman Panama 1914– and **Melvin Frank** 1913–88: *The Court Jester* (1955 film); spoken by Danny Kaye)

29 You beat your pate, and fancy wit will come:
Knock as you please, there's nobody at home.

Alexander Pope 1688–1744: 'Epigram: You beat your pate' (1732)

30 ADVERTISEMENT: Rice is nice, but ricicles are twicicles as nicicles.
CEDRIC PRICE: But testicles is besticles
in a Cambridge cinema watching the advertisments

Cedric Price 1934–2003: Alan Bennett diary 2003, in *London Review of Books* 8 January 2004

31 I see a voice: now will I to the chink,
To spy an I can hear my Thisby's face.

William Shakespeare 1564–1616: *A Midsummer Night's Dream* (1595–6)

32 Comparisons are odorous.

William Shakespeare 1564–1616: *Much Ado About Nothing* (1598–9)

33 An aspersion upon my parts of speech!

Richard Brinsley Sheridan 1751–1816: *The Rivals* (1775)

34 He is the very pineapple of politeness!

Richard Brinsley Sheridan 1751–1816: *The Rivals* (1775)

35 If I reprehend any thing in this world, it is the use of my oracular tongue, and a nice derangement of epitaphs!

Richard Brinsley Sheridan 1751–1816: *The Rivals* (1775)

36 No caparisons, Miss, if you please!—Caparisons don't become a young woman.

Richard Brinsley Sheridan
1751–1816: *The Rivals* (1775)

37 She's as headstrong as an allegory on the banks of the Nile.

Richard Brinsley Sheridan
1751–1816: *The Rivals* (1775)

38 'I can't see the Speaker,
Pray, Hal, do you?'
'Not see the Speaker, Bill?
Why I see *two*.'
recalling an epigram commemorating the drunkenness of Pitt and Henry Dundas in the House of Commons

Richard Brinsley Sheridan
1751–1816: Walter Jerrold *Bon-Mots* (1893)

39 LADY SNEERWELL: There's no possibility of being witty without a little ill-nature; the malice of a good thing is the barb that makes it stick.

Richard Brinsley Sheridan
1751–1816: *The School for Scandal* (1777)

40 A man might sit down as systematically, and successfully, to the study of wit as he might to the study of mathematics . . . By giving up only six hours a day to being witty, he should come on prodigiously before midsummer.

Sydney Smith 1771–1845: *Sketches of Moral Philosophy* (1849)

41 *on seeing Mrs Grote in a huge rose-coloured turban:*
Now I know the meaning of the word 'grotesque'.

Sydney Smith 1771–1845: Peter Virgin *Sydney Smith* (1994)

42 *a toast:*
To our queer old dean.

William Archibald Spooner
1844–1930: *Oxford University What's What* (1948); attributed, perhaps apocryphal

43 *to an undergraduate:*
You have tasted your worm, you have hissed my mystery lectures, and you must leave by the first town drain.

William Archibald Spooner
1844–1930: *Oxford University What's What* (1948); attributed, perhaps apocryphal

44 My parents bought a lavatory from a travelling circus, under the fond delusion that a Chipperfield commode was a desirable thing to have about the house.
at a British Antique Dealers' Association dinner in the 1970s

Tom Stoppard 1937– : attributed; in *Spectator* 19 December 1998

45 Do you think Diaghilev was the kind of person about whom you could say, 'Hail, Fellatio, well met?'

Peter Ustinov 1921–2004: John Drummond *Tainted by Experience* (2000); attributed

46 I'm aghast! If there ever was one.

Dick Vosburgh 1929–2007: *A Saint She Ain't* (1999)

47 I'm on the horns of a Dalai Lama.

Dick Vosburgh 1929–2007: *A Saint She Ain't* (1999)

48 *the American lexicographer Noah Webster was said to have been found by his wife embracing a chambermaid:*
MRS WEBSTER: Noah, I'm surprised.
NOAH WEBSTER: No, my dear. You are amazed. It is we who are surprised.

Noah Webster 1758–1843: apocryphal; William Safire in *New York Times* 15 October 1973

49 'Sesquippledan,' he would say. 'Sesquippledan verboojuice.'

H. G. Wells 1866–1946: *The History of Mr Polly* (1909)

50 OSCAR WILDE: How I wish I had said that.
WHISTLER: You will, Oscar, you will.

James McNeill Whistler 1834–1903: in R. Ellman *Oscar Wilde* (1987)

51 Oscar . . . picks from our platters the plums for the puddings he peddles in the provinces.

James McNeill Whistler 1834–1903: in *World* November 1886

52 I summed up all systems in a phrase, and all existence in an epigram.

Oscar Wilde 1854–1900: letter, from Reading Prison, to Lord Alfred Douglas, January–March 1897

Women and Woman's Role
See also **Men and Women**

> 66 *A woman's preaching is like a dog's walking on his hinder legs.* 99
> **Samuel Johnson**

1 The trouble with women in an orchestra is that if they are attractive it will upset my players and if they're not it will upset me.

Thomas Beecham 1879–1961: Harold Atkins and Archie Newman *Beecham Stories* (1978)

2 Zuleika, on a desert island, would have spent most of her time in looking for a man's footprint.

Max Beerbohm 1872–1956: *Zuleika Dobson* (1911)

3 The suffragettes were triumphant. Woman's place was in the gaol.

Caryl Brahms 1901–82 and **S. J. Simon** 1904–48: *No Nightingales* (1944)

4 I heard a man say that brigands demand your money *or* your life, whereas women require both.

Samuel Butler 1835–1902: *Further Extracts from Notebooks* (1934)

5 It was a blonde. A blonde to make a bishop kick a hole in a stained glass window.

Raymond Chandler 1888–1959: *Farewell, My Lovely* (1940)

6 I let go of her wrists, closed the door with my elbow and slid past her. It was like the first time. 'You ought to carry insurance on those,' I said.

Raymond Chandler 1888–1959: *The Little Sister* (1949)

7 Ful weel she soong the service dyvyne,
Entuned in hir nose ful semely;
And Frenssh she spak ful faire and fetisly,
After the scole of Stratford atte Bowe,
For Frenssh of Parys was to hire unknowe.

Geoffrey Chaucer c.1343–1400: of the Prioress; *The Canterbury Tales* 'The General Prologue'

8 When a woman isn't beautiful, people always say, 'You have lovely eyes, you have lovely hair.'

Anton Chekhov 1860–1904: *Uncle Vanya* (1897)

9 A woman can become a man's friend only in the following stages—first an acquaintance, next a mistress, and only then a friend.

Anton Chekhov 1860–1904: *Uncle Vanya* (1897)

10 O'erjoy'd was he to find
That, though on pleasure she was bent,
She had a frugal mind.

William Cowper 1731–1800: 'John Gilpin' (1785)

11 I'd have opened a knitting shop in Carlisle and been a part of life.
on his regret at not being born female

Quentin Crisp 1908–99: in *Spectator* 20 November 1999

12 A good uniform must work its way with the women, sooner or later.

Charles Dickens 1812–70: *Pickwick Papers* (1837)

13 She's the sort of woman . . . one would almost feel disposed to bury for nothing: and do it neatly, too!

Charles Dickens 1812–70: *Martin Chuzzlewit* (1844)

14 A woman needs a man like a fish needs a bicycle.

Irina Dunn: graffito written 1970; attributed to Dunn by Gloria Steinem in *Time* 9 October 2000

15 Plain women he regarded as he did the other severe facts of life, to be faced with philosophy and investigated by science.

George Eliot 1819–80: *Middlemarch* (1871–2)

16 No woman can be a beauty without a fortune.

George Farquhar 1678–1707: *The Beaux' Stratagem* (1707)

17 'O! help me, heaven,' she prayed, 'to be decorative and to do right!'

Ronald Firbank 1886–1926: *The Flower Beneath the Foot* (1923)

18 The more underdeveloped the country, the more overdeveloped the women.

J. K. Galbraith 1908–2006: in *Time* 17 October 1969

19 I must have women. There is nothing unbends the mind like them.

John Gay 1685–1732: *The Beggar's Opera* (1728)

20 She may very well pass for forty-three
In the dusk with a light behind her!

W. S. Gilbert 1836–1911: *Trial by Jury* (1875)

21 To everybody's prejudice I know a thing or two;
I can tell a woman's age in half a minute—and I do!

W. S. Gilbert 1836–1911: *Princess Ida* (1884)

22 When lovely woman stoops to folly
And finds too late that men betray,
What charm can soothe her melancholy,
What art can wash her guilt away?

Oliver Goldsmith 1730–74: *The Vicar of Wakefield* (1766)

23 I didn't fight to get women out from behind the vacuum cleaner to get them onto the board of Hoover.

Germaine Greer 1939– : in *Guardian* 27 October 1986

24 She who must be obeyed.

Rider Haggard 1856–1925: *She* (1887)

25 Other girls are coy and hard to catch,
But other girls ain't havin' any fun.
Ev'ry time I lose a wrestlin' match
I have a funny feelin' that I won.

Oscar Hammerstein II 1895–1960: 'I Cain't Say No' (1943)

26 When she's narrow, she's narrow as an arrow
And she's broad, where a broad, should be broad.

Oscar Hammerstein II 1895–1960: 'Honey Bun' (1949)

27 I'm just a fool when lights are low,
I cain't be prissy and quaint.
I ain't the type thet c'n faint,
How c'n I be whut I ain't,
I cain't say no!

Oscar Hammerstein II 1895–1960: 'I Cain't Say No' (1943)

28 When Grandma was a lassie
That tyrant known as man
Thought a woman's place
Was just the space
Around a fryin' pan.

It was good enough for Grandma
But it ain't good enough for us!

E. Y. Harburg 1898–1981: 'It was Good Enough for Grandma' (1944)

29 Starlet is the name for any woman under thirty not actively employed in a brothel.

Ben Hecht 1894–1964: E. Goodman *The Fifty-Year Decline and Fall of Hollywood* (1961)

30 Other people's babies—
That's my life!
Mother to dozens,
And nobody's wife.
 of a nanny

A. P. Herbert 1890–1971: 'Other People's Babies' (1930)

31 A woman's preaching is like a dog's walking on his hinder legs. It is not done well; but you are surprised to find it done at all.

Samuel Johnson 1709–84: James Boswell *Life of Samuel Johnson* (1791) 31 July 1763

32 Remember, you're fighting for this woman's honour . . . which is probably more than she ever did.

Bert Kalmar 1884–1947 et al.: *Duck Soup* (1933 film); spoken by Groucho Marx

33 When you get to a man in the case,
They're like as a row of pins—
For the Colonel's Lady an' Judy O'Grady
Are sisters under their skins!

Rudyard Kipling 1865–1936: 'The Ladies' (1896)

34 I can stretch a greenback dollar from here to Kingdom
Come.
I can play the numbers, pay my bills, an' still end up with
some
I got a twenty dollar piece says
There ain't nothin' I can't do.
I can make a dress out of a feed bag an' I can make a man
out of you.
'Cause I'm a woman
W-O-M-A-N
I'll say it again.

Jerry Leiber 1933– : 'I'm a Woman' (1962)

35 Thank heaven for little girls!
For little girls get bigger every day.

Alan Jay Lerner 1918–86: 'Thank Heaven for Little Girls' (1958)

36 Women do not find it difficult nowadays to behave like men, but they often find it extremely difficult to behave like gentlemen.

Compton Mackenzie 1883–1972: *Literature in My Time* (1933)

37 When women kiss it always reminds one of prize-fighters shaking hands.

H. L. Mencken 1880–1956: *Chrestomathy* (1949)

38 BETTY FRIEDAN: Don't you hate women being treated as a sexual plaything?
JESSICA MITFORD: But Betty, you're not a plaything, you're a war toy!

Jessica Mitford 1917–96: attributed; in *Guardian* 7 February 2006

39 'Always be civil to the girls, you never know who they may marry' is an aphorism which has saved many an English spinster from being treated like an Indian widow.

Nancy Mitford 1904–73: *Love in a Cold Climate* (1949)

40 I have never had any great esteem for the generality of the fair sex, and my only consolation for being of that gender has been the assurance it gave me of never being married to anyone amongst them.

Lady Mary Wortley Montagu 1689–1762: letter to Mrs Calthorpe, 7 December 1723

41 Be plain in dress and sober in your diet;
In short my deary, kiss me, and be quiet.

Lady Mary Wortley Montagu 1689–1762: 'A Summary of Lord Lyttelton's Advice'

42 My only books
Were woman's looks,
And folly's all they've taught me.

Thomas Moore 1779–1852: *Irish Melodies* (1807) 'The time I've lost in wooing'

43 The thinking man's crumpet.
of Joan Bakewell

Frank Muir 1920–98: attributed

44 There was a young belle of old Natchez
Whose garments were always in patchez.
When comment arose
On the state of her clothes,
She drawled, When Ah itchez, Ah scratchez.

Ogden Nash 1902–71: 'Requiem' (1938)

45 Feminism is the result of a few ignorant and literal-minded women letting the cat out of the bag about which is the superior sex.

P. J. O'Rourke 1947– : *Modern Manners* (1984)

46 I'd the upbringing a nun would envy . . . Until I was fifteen I was more familiar with Africa than my own body.

Joe Orton 1933–67: *Entertaining Mr Sloane* (1964)

47 She's like the old line about justice—not only must be done, but must be seen to be done.

John Osborne 1929–94: *Time Present* (1968)

48 That woman speaks eighteen languages, and can't say No in any of them.

Dorothy Parker 1893–1967: Alexander Woollcott *While Rome Burns* (1934)

49 And there was that wholesale libel on a Yale prom. If all the girls attending it were laid end to end, Mrs Parker said, she wouldn't be at all surprised.

Dorothy Parker 1893–1967: Alexander Woollcott *While Rome Burns* (1934)

50 You can lead a horticulture, but you can't make her think.

Dorothy Parker 1893–1967: John Keats *You Might as well Live* (1970)

51 A busted, disgusted cocotte am I,
Undesired on my tired little bottom, I,
While those fat femmes du monde
With the men whom once I owned
Splash around like hell-bound hippopotami.

Cole Porter 1891–1964: 'The Cocotte' (1933)

52 It's not 'cause I wouldn't,
It's not 'cause I shouldn't,
And, Lord knows, it's not 'cause I couldn't,
It's simply because I'm the laziest gal in town.

Cole Porter 1891–1964: 'The Laziest Girl in Town' (1927)

53 I do see her in tough joints more than somewhat.

Damon Runyon 1884–1946: in *Collier's* 22 May 1930 'Social Error'

54 O! when she's angry she is keen and shrewd.
She was a vixen when she went to school:
And though she be but little, she is fierce.

William Shakespeare 1564–1616: *A Midsummer Night's Dream* (1595–6)

55 The lady doth protest too much, methinks.

William Shakespeare 1564–1616: *Hamlet* (1601)

56 The fickleness of the women I love is only equalled by the infernal constancy of the women who love me.

George Bernard Shaw 1856–1950: *The Philanderer* (1898)

57 Here's to the ladies who lunch—
Everybody laugh—
Lounging in their caftans and planning a brunch
On their own behalf . . .
Off to the gym
Then to a fitting
Claiming they're fat,
And looking grim
'Cause they've been sitting
Choosing a hat—
Does anyone still wear a hat?
I'll drink to that . . .

Stephen Sondheim 1930– : 'The Ladies who Lunch' (1970)

... Another long exhausting day,
Another thousand dollars
A Matinée, a Pinter play,
Perhaps a piece of Mahler's—
I'll drink to that.
And one for Mahler ...

... A toast to that invincible bunch
The dinosaurs surviving the crunch
Let's hear it for the ladies who lunch.

58 A woman seldom writes her mind but in her postscript.

Richard Steele 1672–1729: *The Spectator* 31 May 1711

59 We are becoming the men we wanted to marry.

Gloria Steinem 1934– : in *Ms* July/August 1982

60 There are worse occupations in this world than feeling a woman's pulse.

Laurence Sterne 1713–68: *A Sentimental Journey* (1768)

61 I had never seen a naked woman, and the way things were going I was never likely to. My family owned land.

Tom Stoppard 1937– : *Artist Descending a Staircase* (1973)

62 It's the last thing one would have expected of a woman who runs a donkey sanctuary—concubine to an opium addict.

Tom Stoppard 1937– : *The Dog It Was That Died* (1983)

63 I blame the women's movement for 10 years in a boiler suit.

Jill Tweedie 1936–93: attributed

64 When once a woman has given you her heart, you can never get rid of the rest of her body.

John Vanbrugh 1664–1726: *The Relapse* (1696)

65 The Queen is most anxious to enlist every one who can speak or write to join in checking this mad, wicked folly of 'Woman's Rights', with all its attendant horrors, on which her poor feeble sex is bent, forgetting every sense of womanly feeling and propriety.

Queen Victoria 1819–1901: letter to Theodore Martin, 29 May 1870

66 The world is full of care, much like unto a bubble;
Woman and care, and care and women, and women and
    care and trouble.

Nathaniel Ward 1578–1652: epigram, attributed by Ward to a lady at the Court of the Queen of Bohemia; *The Simple Cobbler of Aggawam in America* (1647)

67 I will not stand for being called a woman in my own house.

Evelyn Waugh 1903–66: *Scoop* (1938)

68 I myself have never been able to find out precisely what feminism is: I only know that people call me a feminist whenever I express sentiments that differentiate me from a doormat or a prostitute.

Rebecca West 1892–1983: in 1913; *The Young Rebecca* (1982)

69 Glitter and be gay,
That's the part I play.
Here I am, unhappy chance.
Forced to bend my soul
To a sordid role,
Victimized by bitter, bitter circumstance.

Richard Wilbur 1921– : 'Glitter and be Gay' (1956)

70 One should never trust a woman who tells one her real age. A woman who would tell one that, would tell one anything.

Oscar Wilde 1854–1900: *A Woman of No Importance* (1893)

71 Many a woman has a past, but I am told that she has at least a dozen, and that they all fit.

Oscar Wilde 1854–1900: *Lady Windermere's Fan* (1892)

Wordplay See **Wit and Wordplay**

Words

See also **Language**

❝ *Some word that teems with hidden meaning—like Basingstoke.* ❞

W. S. Gilbert

1 HONEY: I wonder if you could show me where the . . . I want to . . . put some powder on my nose.
GEORGE: Martha, won't you show her where we keep the . . . euphemism?

Edward Albee 1928– : *Who's Afraid of Virginia Woolf* (1964)

2 The most beautiful words in the English language are not 'I love you' but 'It's benign'.

Woody Allen 1935– : *Deconstructing Harry* (1997 film)

3 *after reports that cafeterias in Washington had changed the name of 'french fries' to 'freedom fries' in response to French criticism of American policy in Iraq:*
I don't want to have to refer to my French fry potatoes as freedom fries, and I don't want to have to freedom kiss my wife.

Woody Allen 1935– : in *Independent* 7 June 2003

4 *version of an old joke:*
VICTOR LEWIS SMITH: You clearly don't know the difference between a Joist and a Girder.
IRISH BUILDER: Yes I do. Joist wrote Ulysses and Girder wrote Faust.

Anonymous: in *Evening Standard* 12 September 2003

5 *as a young serviceman Dennis Potter was summoned for help with spelling by an elderly Major:*
How you do spell 'accelerator'? I've been all through the blasted 'Ex's' in this bloody dictionary.

Anonymous: related by Dennis Potter during the launch of his television show *Lipstick on Your Collar*; in *Ned Sherrin in his Anecdotage* (1993)

6 Serendipity means searching for a needle in a haystack and instead finding a farmer's daughter.

Anonymous: in 'Quote . . . Unquote' Newsletter, July 1995, as quoted by Sir Herman Bondi

7 The English language may hold a more disagreeable combination of words than 'The doctor will see you now.' I am willing to concede something to the phrase 'Have you anything to say before the current is turned on'.

Robert Benchley 1889–1945: *Love Conquers All* (1923); (see also **Speeches** 10)

8 You see it's like a portmanteau—there are two meanings packed up into one word.

Lewis Carroll 1832–98: *Through the Looking-Glass* (1872)

9 'There's glory for you!' 'I don't know what you mean by "glory",' Alice said. 'I meant, "there's a nice knock-down argument for you!" ' 'But "glory" doesn't mean "a nice knock-down argument",' Alice objected. 'When *I* use a word,' Humpty Dumpty said in a rather scornful tone, 'it means just what I choose it to mean—neither more nor less.'

Lewis Carroll 1832–98: *Through the Looking-Glass* (1872)

10 It depends on what the meaning of 'is' is.
 videotaped evidence to the grand jury; tapes broadcast 21
 September 1998

Bill Clinton 1946– : in *Guardian* 22 September 1998

11 Euphemisms are unpleasant truths wearing diplomatic cologne.

Quentin Crisp 1908–99: *Manners from Heaven* (1984)

12 'Do you spell it with a "V" or a "W"?' inquired the judge. 'That depends upon the taste and fancy of the speller, my Lord,' replied Sam [Weller].

Charles Dickens 1812–70: *Pickwick Papers* (1837)

13 Two such wonderful phrases—'I understand perfectly' and 'That is a lie'—a précis of life, aren't they?

Brian Friel 1929– : *The Communication Cord* (1983)

14 Excluding two-letter prepositions and 'an', I imagine *me* is the most used two-letter word in Songdom. 'I' (leaving out indefinite article 'a') is doubtless the most used one-letter word (and everywhere else, for that matter). 'You' (if definite article 'the' bows out) is the most frequent three-letter word. 'Love' probably gets the four-letter nod (referring strictly to songs that can be heard in the home). In the five-letter stakes I would wager that 'heart' and 'dream' photo-finish in a dead heat. As for words of more than five letters, you're on your own.

Ira Gershwin 1896–1983: *Lyrics on Several Occasions: A Brief Concordance* (1977)

15 Some word that teems with hidden meaning—like Basingstoke.

W. S. Gilbert 1836–1911: *Ruddigore* (1887)

16 It's exactly where a thought is lacking
 That, just in time, a word shows up instead.

Goethe 1749–1832: *Faust* (1808) pt 1

17 Words are chameleons, which reflect the colour of their environment.

Learned Hand 1872–1961: in *Commissioner v. National Carbide Corp.* (1948)

18 Together they go places . . . Words make you think a thought. Music makes you feel a feeling. A song makes you feel a thought . . . The greatest romance in the life of a lyricist is when the right word meets the right note; often however, a Park Avenue phrase elopes with a Bleeker Street chord resulting in a shotgun wedding and a quickie divorce.

E. Y. Harburg 1898–1981: lecture given at the New York YMCA in 1970

19 Is there, can there be, such a word as *purposive?* There is: it was invented by a surgeon in 1855; and instead of being kept on the top shelf of an anatomical museum it is exhibited in both these volumes.

A. E. Housman 1859–1936: in *Cambridge Review* 1917

20 I understand your new play is full of single entendre.

George S. Kaufman 1889–1961: to Howard Dietz on *Between the Devil*; Howard Teichmann *George S. Kaufman* (1973)

21 I can't do splat . . . It doesn't translate.
 the British Consul when asked to translate a description of
 the effect of a dum-dum bullet on the human skull

John le Carré 1931– : *Single & Single* (1999)

22 In my youth there were words you couldn't say in front of a girl; now you can't say 'girl'.

Tom Lehrer 1928– : in *Sunday Telegraph* 10 March 1996 'Spirits of the Age'

23 Avant-garde? That's the French for bullshit.

John Lennon 1940–80: attributed

24 Hypochondria is Greek for 'men'.

Kathy Lette 1958– : in *Mail on Sunday* 4 April 2004

25 I know
That's she's sweeter 'n sugar—
But oh!
You can't rhyme 'sugar'!

Frank Loesser 1910–69: 'I'm Ridin'
for a Fall' in *Thank Your Lucky Stars*
(1943 musical film)

26 They say the definition of ambivalence is watching your
mother-in-law drive over a cliff in your new Cadillac.

David Mamet 1947– : in *Guardian*
19 February 2000

27 I often think how much easier life would have been for me
and how much time I should have saved if I had known
the alphabet. I can never tell where I and J stand without
saying G, H to myself first.

W. Somerset Maugham 1874–1965:
A Writer's Notebook (1949) written in
1941

28 He respects Owl, because you can't help respecting
anybody who can spell TUESDAY, even if he doesn't spell it
right; but spelling isn't everything. There are days when
spelling Tuesday simply doesn't count.

A. A. Milne 1882–1956: *The House at
Pooh Corner* (1928)

29 Words are like leaves; and where they most abound,
Much fruit of sense beneath is rarely found.

Alexander Pope 1688–1744: *An
Essay on Criticism* (1711)

30 Good authors too, who once knew better words
Now only use four-letter words
Writing prose
Anything goes.

Cole Porter 1891–1964: 'Anything
Goes' (1934)

31 The trouble with words is that you never know whose
mouth they've been in.

Dennis Potter 1935–94: attributed

32 Make me a beautiful word for doing things tomorrow; for
that surely is a great and blessed invention.

George Bernard Shaw 1856–1950:
Back to Methuselah (1921)

33 I asked my teacher what an oxymoron was and he said, 'I
don't know what an "oxy" is, bastard.

Arthur Smith 1954– and **Chris
England**: *An Evening with Gary
Lineker* (1990)

34 *prescription when J. H. Thomas complained of 'an 'ell of an
'eadache':*
A couple of aspirates.

F. E. Smith 1872–1930: in *Ned
Sherrin in his Anecdotage* (1993)

35 Man does not live by words alone, despite the fact that he
sometimes has to eat them.

Adlai Stevenson 1900–65: *The Wit
and Wisdom of Adlai Stevenson*
(1965)

36 REPORTER: Can we have a quick word please?
GORDON STRACHAN: Velocity [walks off].

Gordon Strachan 1957– : Leo
Moynihan *Gordon Strachan* (2004)

37 By hard, honest labour I've dug all the large words out of
my vocabulary . . . I never write metropolis for seven cents
because I can get the same money for city. I never write
policeman, because I can get the same money for *Cop*.

Mark Twain 1835–1910: *Mark
Twain's Speeches* (1923)

38 *defining 'narcissistic':*
An adjective currently used to describe anyone better-
looking than oneself.

Gore Vidal 1925– : attributed; in
Mail on Sunday 2 June 2002

39 It is a pity that Chawcer, who had geneyus, was so
unedicated. He's the wuss speller I know of.

Artemus Ward 1834–67: *Artemus
Ward in London* (1867)

40 A chair is a piece of furniture. I am not a chair because no
one has ever sat on me.
*on Jack Straw's announcement that Parliamentary language
will now be gender-neutral*

Ann Widdecombe 1947– : in
Observer 11 March 2007

Work and Leisure

66 *Work is always so much more fun than fun.* 99

Noël Coward

1 I will undoubtedly have to seek what is happily known as gainful employment, which I am glad to say does not describe holding public office.

Dean Acheson 1893–1971: in *Time* 22 December 1952

2 A professional is a man who can do his job when he doesn't feel like it. An amateur is a man who can't do his job when he does feel like it.

James Agate 1877–1947: diary, 19 July 1945

3 Ninety-nine per cent of the work of the professional bodyguard consisted of one activity: frowning.

Martin Amis 1949– : *Yellow Dog* (2003)

4 It has more strings than a philharmonic orchestra.
the Communication Workers' Union rejecting a pay deal

Anonymous: in *Mail on Sunday* 31 August 2003

5 If I am doing nothing, I like to be doing nothing to some purpose. That is what leisure means.

Alan Bennett 1934– : *A Question of Attribution* (1989)

6 I realized I could have written two songs and made myself some money in that time.
after taking two days of piano lessons

Irving Berlin 1888–1989: Caryl Brahms and Ned Sherrin *Song by Song* (1984)

7 *when criticized for continually arriving late for work:*
But think how early I go.

Lord Castlerosse 1891–1943: while working in the City in 1919 for his uncle Lord Revelstoke; Leonard Mosley *Castlerosse* (1956); remark also claimed by Howard Dietz at MGM

8 I do nothing, granted. But I see the hours pass—which is better than trying to fill them.

E. M. Cioran 1911– : in *Guardian* 11 May 1993

9 Work is always so much more fun than fun.

Noël Coward 1899–1973: Sheridan Morley *The Quotable Noël Coward* (1999)

10 I never work. Work does age you so.

Quentin Crisp 1908–99: in *Observer* 10 January 1999 'Sayings of the Week'

11 People who are lonely are those who do not know what to do with the time when they are alone.

Quentin Crisp 1908–99: in *Sunday Telegraph* 28 September 1999

12 My life is one demd horrid grind!

Charles Dickens 1812–70: *Nicholas Nickleby* (1839)

13 Anythin' for a quiet life, as the man said wen he took the sitivation at the lighthouse.

Charles Dickens 1812–70: *Pickwick Papers* (1837)

14 I have long been of the opinion that if work were such a splendid thing the rich would have kept more of it for themselves.

Bruce Grocott 1940– : in *Observer* 22 May 1988 'Sayings of the Week'

15 The three little sentences that will get you through life. Number 1: Cover for me. Number 2: Oh, good idea, Boss! Number 3: It was like that when I got here.

Matt Groening 1954– : *The Simpsons* 'One Fish, Two Fish, Blowfish, Blue Fish' (1991) written by Nell Scovell

16 I think some of the union rules are a little strict. I used to sing in the bath tub at home, now I've got to have another guy in there with me as a stand-by.
on trade unions

Bob Hope 1903–2003: attributed; in *Times* 29 July 2003

17 It is impossible to enjoy idling thoroughly unless one has plenty of work to do.

Jerome K. Jerome 1859–1927: *Idle Thoughts of an Idle Fellow* (1886) 'On Being Idle'

18 Being a specialist is one thing, getting a job is another.

Stephen Leacock 1869–1944: *The Boy I Left Behind Me* (1947)

19 A secretary is not a toy.

Frank Loesser 1910–69: song title (1961)

20 I can think of few nobler callings for elderly persons with leisure than to provide unindexed books with indexes.

E. V. Lucas 1868–1938: *365 Days and One More* (1926)

21 Why do men delight in work? Fundamentally, I suppose, because there is a sense of relief and pleasure in getting something done—a kind of satisfaction not unlike that which a hen enjoys on laying an egg.

H. L. Mencken 1880–1956: *Minority Report* (1956)

22 Work expands so as to fill the time available for its completion.

C. Northcote Parkinson 1909–93: *Parkinson's Law* (1958)

23 It's true hard work never killed anybody, but I figure why take the chance?

Ronald Reagan 1911–2004: interview; in *Guardian* 31 March 1987

24 I understand. You work very hard two days a week and you need a five-day weekend. That's normal.

Neil Simon 1927– : *Come Blow Your Horn* (1961)

25 It's dogged as does it. It ain't thinking about it.

Anthony Trollope 1815–82: *The Last Chronicle of Barset* (1867)

26 How to be an effective secretary is to develop the kind of lonely self-abnegating sacrificial instincts usually possessed only by the early saints on their way to martyrdom.

Jill Tweedie 1936–93: *It's Only Me* (1980)

27 Work is the curse of the drinking classes.

Oscar Wilde 1854–1900: Hesketh Pearson *Life of Oscar Wilde* (1946)

Writers

See also **Books, Literature, Poetry, Poets, Reading, Writing**

❝ *Let Shakespeare do it his way, I'll do it mine.* ❞
Mae West

1 *of the Bloomsbury Group:*
They lived in squares and loved in triangles.

Anonymous: unattributed saying

2 Wanting to know an author because you like his work is like wanting to know a duck because you like pâté.

Margaret Atwood 1939– : in *Globe and Mail* 7 September 1996

3 *on being telephoned by the* Evening News *to ask if he had any comment to offer on the occasion of Harold Pinter's fiftieth birthday:*
I don't; it's only later I realize I could have suggested two minutes' silence.

Alan Bennett 1934– : *Writing Home* (1994)

4 *of Dr Johnson and her husband James Boswell:*
I have seen many a bear led by a man: but I never before saw a man led by a bear.

Margaret Boswell 1738?–89: James Boswell *Life of Samuel Johnson* (1791) 27 November 1773

5 In general I do not draw well with literary men—not that I dislike them but—I never know what to say to them after I have praised their last publication.

Lord Byron 1788–1824: 'Detached Thoughts' 15 October 1821

6 *his Intourist guide had protested that Shakespeare's plays could never have been written by a grocer from Stratford-upon-Avon:*
They are exactly the sort of plays I would expect a grocer to write.

Robert Byron 1905–41: *The Road to Oxiana* (1980 ed.); introduction

7 The compulsion to make rhymes was born in me. For those sated readers of my work who wish ardently that I would stop, the future looks dark indeed.

Noël Coward 1899–1973: foreword to the *The Lyrics of Noel Coward* (1965)

8 HANNEN SWAFFER: I have always said that you act much better than you write.
NOËL COWARD: How odd, I'm always saying the same about you.

Noël Coward 1899–1973: Sheridan Morley *A Talent to Amuse* (1969)

9 There are three reasons for becoming a writer. The first is that you need the money; the second, that you have something to say that you think the world should know; and the third is that you can't think what to do with the long winter evenings.

Quentin Crisp 1908–99: *The Naked Civil Servant* (1968)

10 Most people are vain, so I try to ensure that any author who comes to stay will find at least one of their books in their room.

Duke of Devonshire 1920–2004: in *The Spectator* 22 January 1994

11 I love being a writer. What I can't stand is the paperwork.

Peter de Vries 1910–93: Laurence J. Peter (ed.) *Quotations for our Time* (1977)

12 An author who speaks about his own books is almost as bad as a mother who talks about her own children.

Benjamin Disraeli 1804–81: at a banquet given in Glasgow on his installation as Lord Rector, 19 November 1873

13 The nicest old lady I ever met.
of Henry James

William Faulkner 1897–1962: Edward Stone *The Battle and the Books* (1964)

14 A New Jersey Nero who mistakes his pinafore for a toga.
of Alexander Woollcott

Edna Ferber 1887–1968: R. E. Drennan *Wit's End* (1973)

15 It is splendid to be a great writer, to put men into the frying pan of your words and make them pop like chestnuts.

Gustave Flaubert 1821–80: letter to Louise Colet, 3 November 1851

16 The defendant, Mr. Haddock, is, among other things, an author, which fact should alone dispose you in the plaintiff's favour.

A. P. Herbert 1890–1971: *Misleading Cases* (1935)

17 The book of my enemy has been remaindered
And I rejoice . . .
What avail him now his awards and prizes,
The praise expended upon his meticulous technique,
His individual new voice?

Clive James 1939– : 'The Book of My Enemy has been Remaindered' (1986)

18 *a young admirer had asked if he might kiss the hand that wrote Ulysses:*
No, it did lots of other things too.

James Joyce 1882–1941: Richard Ellmann *James Joyce* (1959)

19 Tell them the author giveth and the author taketh away.
to a playwright afraid to tell the cast of cuts he had made

George S. Kaufman 1889–1961:
Howard Teichmann *George S.
Kaufman* (1973)

20 *objecting to having been appointed a Companion of Honour
without his consent:*
How would you like it if you woke up and found yourself
Archbishop of Canterbury?

Rudyard Kipling 1865–1936: letter
to Bonar Law, 1917; Charles
Carrington *Rudyard Kipling* (1978)

21 Mr. Ruskin, whose distinction it was to express in prose of
incomparable grandeur thought of an unparalleled
confusion.

Osbert Lancaster 1908–86: *Pillar to
Post* (1938)

22 The writer is to the real world what Esperanto is to the
language world—funny, maybe, but not *that* funny.

Fran Lebowitz 1946– : *Metropolitan
Life* (1978)

23 E. M. Forster never gets any further than warming the
teapot. He's a rare fine hand at that. Feel this teapot. Is it
not beautifully warm? Yes, but there ain't going to be no
tea.

Katherine Mansfield 1888–1923:
diary, May 1917

24 Dear Willie, you may well be right in thinking you write
like Shakespeare. Certainly I have noticed during these last
few months an adulation of your name in the more vulgar
portions of the popular press. And one word of brotherly
advice. *Do Not Attempt the Sonnets.*

Viscount Maugham d. 1958: letter to
his brother Somerset Maugham, in
Ned Sherrin in his Anecdotage (1993)

25 The humour of Dostoievsky is the humour of a bar-loafer
who ties a kettle to a dog's tail.

W. Somerset Maugham 1874–1965:
A Writer's Notebook (1949) written in
1917

26 There is no need for the writer to eat a whole sheep to be
able to tell you what mutton tastes like. It is enough if he
eats a cutlet. But he should do that.

W. Somerset Maugham 1874–1965:
A Writer's Notebook (1949) written in
1941

27 Poor Henry [James], he's spending eternity wandering
round and round a stately park and the fence is just too
high for him to peep over and they're having tea just too
far away for him to hear what the countess is saying.

W. Somerset Maugham 1874–1965:
Cakes and Ale (1930)

28 What obsesses a writer starting out on a lifetime's work is
the panic-stricken search for a voice of his own.

John Mortimer 1923–2009: *Clinging
to the Wreckage* (1982)

29 I am the kind of writer that people think other people are
reading.

V. S. Naipaul 1932– : in *Radio Times*
14 March 1979

30 THE EDITOR: We can't have much more of this, space must
also be found for my stuff.
MYSELF: All right, never hesitate to say so. I can turn off
the tap at will.

Flann O'Brien 1911–66: *The Best of
Myles* (1968)

31 [David Merrick] liked writers in the way that a snake likes
live rabbits.

John Osborne 1929–94: *Almost a
Gentleman* (1991)

32 He's a writer for the ages—for the ages of four to eight.

Dorothy Parker 1893–1967: R. E.
Drennan *Wit's End* (1973)

33 Those of us who had a perfectly happy childhood should
be able to sue for deprivation of literary royalties.

Chris Patten 1944– : in *Times 2*
February 2006

34 Authors are judged by strange capricious rules
The great ones are thought mad, the small ones fools.

Alexander Pope 1688–1744:
prologue to *Three Hours after
Marriage* (1717)

35 *on being asked to appear in a charity programme in support of imprisoned writers:*
No, on the whole I think all writers should be in prison.

Ralph Richardson 1902–83: in *Ned Sherrin in his Anecdotage* (1993)

36 A confessional passage has probably never been written that didn't stink a little bit of the writer's pride in having given up his pride.

J. D. Salinger 1919– : *Catcher in the Rye* (1951)

37 Virginia Woolf, I enjoyed talking to her, but thought *nothing* of her writing. I considered her 'a beautiful little knitter'.

Edith Sitwell 1887–1964: letter to Geoffrey Singleton, 11 July 1955

38 *the critic Moon's assessment of a dramatist:*
An uncanny ear that might have belonged to a Van Gogh.

Tom Stoppard 1937– : *The Real Inspector Hound* (1968)

39 The shelf life of the modern hardback writer is somewhere between the milk and the yoghurt.

Calvin Trillin 1935– : in *Sunday Times* 9 June 1991; attributed

40 He never leaves off . . . and he always has two packages of manuscript in his desk, besides the one he's working on, and the one that's being published.
on her husband Anthony Trollope

Rose Trollope 1820–1917: Julian Hawthorne *Shapes that Pass: Memories of Old Days* (1928)

41 What other culture could have produced someone like Hemingway and *not* seen the joke?

Gore Vidal 1925– : *Pink Triangle and Yellow Star* (1982)

42 To see him [Stephen Spender] fumbling with our rich and delicate language is to experience all the horror of seeing a Sèvres vase in the hands of a chimpanzee.

Evelyn Waugh 1903–66: in *The Tablet* 5 May 1951

43 Let Shakespeare do it his way, I'll do it mine. We'll see who comes out better.

Mae West 1892–1980: G. Eells and S. Musgrove *Mae West* (1989)

44 Just as Voltaire attributed everything good to a China he had never seen, so La Fayette idealised an America he had forgotten.

Edmund White 1940– : *Fanny, a fiction* (2003)

45 Mr. [Henry] James writes fiction as if it were a painful duty.

Oscar Wilde 1854–1900: 'The Decay of Lying' (1891)

46 Meredith! Who can define him? His style is chaos illuminated by flashes of lightning. As a writer he has mastered everything except language: as a novelist he can do everything except tell a story. As an artist he is everything, except articulate.

Oscar Wilde 1854–1900: 'The Decay of Lying' (1891)

47 I know no person so perfectly disagreeable and even dangerous as an author.

William IV 1765–1837: Philip Ziegler *King William IV* (1971)

48 Every author really wants to have letters printed in the papers. Unable to make the grade, he drops down a rung of the ladder and writes novels.

P. G. Wodehouse 1881–1975: *Louder and Funnier* (1932)

49 *A. A. Milne had written a hostile letter to the* Daily Telegraph *on the report of Wodehouse's broadcasting from Germany:*
My personal animosity against a writer never affects my opinion of what he writes. Nobody could be more anxious than myself, for instance, that Alan Alexander Milne should trip over a loose bootlace and break his bloody neck, yet I re-read his early stuff at regular intervals with all the old enjoyment.

P. G. Wodehouse 1881–1975: letter 27 November 1945

Writing

See also **Books, Literature, Poetry, Poets, Reading, Writers**

❝ *As to the Adjective: when in doubt, strike it out.* ❞

Mark Twain

1 If you can't annoy somebody with what you write, I think there's little point in writing.

Kingsley Amis 1922–95: in *Radio Times* 1 May 1971

2 The biggest obstacle to professional writing is the necessity for changing a typewriter ribbon.

Robert Benchley 1889–1945: *Chips off the old Benchley* (1949)

3 The only thing that goes missing in Nature is a pencil.

Robert Benchley 1889–1945: attributed, perhaps apocryphal

4 In the mind, as in the body, there is the necessity of getting rid of waste, and a man of active literary habits will write for the fire as well as for the press.

Jerome Cardan 1501–76: William Osler *Aequanimites* (1904); epigraph

5 Authors with a mortgage never get writer's block.

Mavis Cheek 1948– : in *Bookseller* 19 September 2003

6 You just have to work with what God sends, and if God doesn't seem to understand the concept of commercial success, then that's your bad luck.

Michael Frayn 1933– : in *Sunday Times* 3 February 2002

7 No plagiarist can excuse the wrong by showing how much of his work he did not pirate.

Learned Hand 1872–1961: *Sheldon v. Metro-Goldwyn Pictures Corp.* 1936

8 I had my fill of this dreamy abstract thing called business and I decided to face reality by writing lyrics . . . the capitalists saved me in 1929 . . . I was left with a pencil and finally had to write for a living.

E. Y. Harburg 1898–1981: lecture given at the New York YMCA in 1970

9 *explaining why he wrote opinions while standing:* Nothing conduces to brevity like a caving in of the knees.

Oliver Wendell Holmes Jr. 1841–1935: Catherine Drinker Bowen *Yankee from Olympus* (1944); attributed

10 Whence came the intrusive comma on p. 4? It did not fall from the sky.

A. E. Housman 1859–1936: letter to the Richards Press, 3 July 1930

11 Read over your compositions, and where ever you meet with a passage which you think is particularly fine, strike it out.

Samuel Johnson 1709–84: quoting a college tutor; James Boswell *Life of Samuel Johnson* (1791) 30 April 1773

12 No man but a blockhead ever wrote, except for money.

Samuel Johnson 1709–84: James Boswell *Life of Samuel Johnson* (1791) 5 April 1776

13 If you want to get rich from writing, write the sort of thing that's read by persons who move their lips when reading.

Don Marquis 1878–1937: attributed; Peter Kemp (ed.) *Oxford Dictionary of Literary Quotations* (1997)

14 The art of writing, like the art of love, runs all the way from a kind of routine hard to distinguish from piling bricks to a kind of frenzy closely related to delirium tremens.

H. L. Mencken 1880–1956: *Minority Report* (1956)

15 If you steal from one author, it's plagiarism; if you steal from many, it's research.

Wilson Mizner 1876–1933: Alva Johnston *The Legendary Mizners* (1953)

16 I'm glad you'll write,
You'll furnish paper when I shite.

Lady Mary Wortley Montagu
1689–1762: 'Reasons that Induced Dr
S— to write a Poem called the Lady's
Dressing Room'

17 It is our national joy to mistake for the first-rate, the
fecund rate.

Dorothy Parker 1893–1967: review
of Sinclair Lewis *Dodsworth*; in *New
Yorker* 16 March 1929

18 As to the Adjective: when in doubt, strike it out.

Mark Twain 1835–1910: *Pudd'nhead
Wilson* (1894)

19 Anyone could write a novel given six weeks, pen, paper,
and no telephone or wife.

Evelyn Waugh 1903–66: Chips
Channon diary 16 December 1934

Youth

See also **Children, Middle Age, Old Age**

66 *Be on the alert to recognize your prime at
whatever time of your life it may occur.* 99
Muriel Spark

1 It is better to waste one's youth than to do nothing with it
at all.

Georges Courteline 1858–1929: *La
Philosophie de Georges Courteline*
(1948)

2 I am just an ingénue
And shall be till I'm eighty-two.

Noël Coward 1899–1973: 'Little
Women' (1928)

3 Everybody my age should be issued with a 2lb fresh
salmon. If you see someone young, beautiful and happy,
you should slap them as hard as you can with it.

Richard Griffiths 1947– : in
Independent 11 October 2006

4 Remember that as a teenager you are at the last stage in
your life when you will be happy to hear that the phone is
for you.

Fran Lebowitz 1946– : *Social Studies*
(1981)

5 If you had seen me in my teens you would have bolted for
the door without picking up your coat.

Joanna Lumley 1946– : in *Sunday
Times* 24 February 2002

6 Youth is wasted on the young. I'm 52 now and I just can't
stay up all night like I did.

Camille Paglia 1947– : interview in
Sunday Times 6 June 1999

7 It's all that the young can do for the old, to shock them
and keep them up to date.

George Bernard Shaw 1856–1950:
Fanny's First Play (1914) 'Induction'

8 What music is more enchanting than the voices of young
people, when you can't hear what they say?

Logan Pearsall Smith 1865–1946:
Afterthoughts (1931)

9 Give me a girl at an impressionable age, and she is mine
for life.

Muriel Spark 1918–2006: *The Prime
of Miss Jean Brodie* (1961)

10 One's prime is elusive. You little girls, when you grow up,
must be on the alert to recognize your prime at whatever
time of your life it may occur.

Muriel Spark 1918–2006: *The Prime
of Miss Jean Brodie* (1961)

11 The only way to stay young is to avoid old people.

James D. Watson 1928– : in *Times* 9
March 2002

12 Being young is not having any money; being young is not
minding not having any money.

Katharine Whitehorn 1928– :
Observations (1970)

13 I have been in a youth hostel. I know what they're like.
You are put in a kitchen with seventeen venture scouts
with behavioural difficulties and made to wash swedes.

Victoria Wood 1953– : *Mens Sana in
Thingummy Doodah* (1990)

Buerk, Michael (1946–)
  Smoking 2
Buffett, Warren (1930–)
  Business 3
  Wealth 6
Buller, Arthur (1874–1944)
  Science 8
Bulmer-Thomas, Ivor (1905–93)
  Prime Ministers 7
Buñuel, Luis (1900–83)
  Religion 14
Burchfield, Robert (1923–2004)
  Sex 26
Burchill, Julie (1960–)
  Books 2
  Indexes 2
  Insults 6
Burgess, Anthony (1917–93)
  Politics 15
  Reading 3
  Sex 27, 28
  Technology 3
Burgess, Gelett (1866–1951)
  Quotations 2
Burke, Edmund (1729–97)
  Prime Ministers 8
Burke, Johnny (1908–64)
  Dictionaries 4
Burney, Fanny (1752–1840)
  Literature 7
Burns, George (1896–1996)
  Comedy 15
  Family 6
  Nature 1
Burt, Benjamin Hapgood
  (1880–1950)
  Drink 10
Busby, Matt (1909–94)
  Football 5
Bush, George (1924–)
  Bores 3
  Food 13
  Security 2
Bush, George W. (1946–)
  Languages 6
  People 12
  Self-Knowledge 5
Bush, Laura (1946–)
  Country 1
  Presidents 3
Butler, R. A. (1902–82)
  People 13
  Politics 16
  Speeches 2

Butler, Samuel (1835–1902)
  Birds 3
  Bores 4
  Food 14
  God 14
  Marriage 22
  Poets 1
  Progress 2
  Publishing 6
  Science 9
  Truth 1
  Women 4
Bygraves, Max (1922–) see
  Sykes, Eric and **Bygraves, Max**
Byron, Lord (1788–1824)
  America 4
  Body 7
  Certainty 8
  Children 6, 7
  Countries 4
  Critics 9
  Description 7
  Education 10
  England 6
  Epitaphs 8
  Family 7
  Gambling 1
  God 15
  Government 2
  Happiness 4
  Heaven 2
  Home 1
  Hypocrisy 2
  Intelligence 4
  Journalism 6
  Letters 3
  Literature 8
  Marriage 23, 24
  Mistakes 10
  Morality 2
  People 14
  Poetry 4
  Poets 2
  Publishing 7
  Religion 15, 16
  Self-Knowledge 6
  Sex 29, 30
  Truth 2
  Weather 4
  Weddings 4
  Writers 5
Byron, Robert (1905–41)
  Architecture 5
  Names 5

  Places 4
  War 5
  Wealth 7
  Writers 6

Cabrera Infante, Guillermo
  (1929–2005)
  Speeches 3
Caesar, Arthur (d. 1953)
  Snobbery 5
Caesar, Irving (1895–1996)
  Food 15
  Men and Women 5
Cahn, Sammy (1913–)
  America 5
  Marriage 25
Caillavet, Armand de
  (1869–1915) see **Flers, Robert,**
  Marquis de and **Caillavet,**
  Armand de
Caine, Michael (1933–)
  Awards 2
  Snobbery 6
Callaghan, James (1912–2005)
  Politicians 13
Camden, William (1551–1623)
  Names 6
Cameron, David (1966–)
  Conversation 3
Campbell, Alastair (1957–)
  Certainty 9
  God 16
  Success 4
Campbell, Mary
  Languages 7
Campbell, Mrs Patrick
  (1865–1940)
  Actors 9, 10
  Autobiography 3
  Bible 2
  Conversation 4
  Friends 5
  Home 2
  Insults 7
  Marriage 26
  Names 7
  People 15
  Science 10
  Sex 31
  Theatre 12
Campbell, Patrick (1913–80)
  Body 8
  Holidays 2

Comden, Betty (*cont.*):
Reading 4
Compton, Denis (1918–)
Cricket 9
Compton-Burnett, Ivy
(1884–1969)
Human Race 1
Condon, Eddie (1905–73)
Countries 9
Drink 14, 15, 16
Congreve, William (1670–1729)
Behaviour 7, 8
Class 7, 8
Gossip 1, 2
Letters 4
Love 7
Marriage 36, 37, 38, 39
Wit 7
Connery, Sean (1930–)
Retirement 2
Connolly, Billy (1942–)
Acting 4
Fishing 2
Marriage 40
Connolly, Cyril (1903–74)
Body 11
Generation Gap 4
Marriage 41
Names 10
Politics 22
Satisfaction 5
Success 6
Connolly, James (1868–1916)
Armed Forces 6
Connolly, Ray
Language 3
Connors, Jimmy (1952–)
Tennis 5
Conran, Shirley (1932–)
Housework 1
Time 9
Conran, Terence (1931–)
Marriage 42
Conybeare, Eliza (1820–1903)
Certainty 11
Cook, Dan
Opera 2
Cook, Peter (1937–95)
Books 4
Diplomacy 3
Judges 7
People 17
Cook, Robin (1946–2005)
War 7

Coolidge, Calvin (1872–1933)
Debt 2
Cooper, Diana (1892–1986)
Languages 9
Cooper, Duff (1890–1954)
Countries 10
Cooper, Gladys (1888–1971)
Housework 2
Cooper, Tommy (1921–84)
Comedy 31
Cope, Wendy (1945–)
Poetry 7
Poets 5
Corbett, Bobby (1940–99)
Debt 3
Description 10
Corbett, Ronnie (1930–) see
Barker, Ronnie and **Corbett,
Ronnie**
Coren, Alan (1938–2007)
Foolishness 3
Marriage 43
Television 3
Cornford, Francis M. (1874–1943)
Education 11
Lies 5
Costello, Lou (1906–59) see
Abbott, Bud and **Costello, Lou**
Courteline, Georges (1858–1929)
Youth 1
Coward, Noël (1899–1973)
Acting 5, 6, 7
Actors 12, 13
America 8
Appearance 7
Architecture 7
Aristocracy 3
Armed Forces 7, 8
Behaviour 9, 10
Body 12
Broadcasting 3
Children 11
Class 9
Clergy 4
Countries 11, 12
Crime 8, 9
Dance 6
Death 16, 17
Description 11
England 7
Fame 12
Family 9
Film Stars 4, 5
Food 19

France 2
God 20
Holidays 3
Hollywood 2
Home 5, 6
Hope 4
Letters 5, 6
Marriage 44, 45
Men 3
Men and Women 6
Mind 4
Mistakes 11
Murder 4
Music 11
Old Age 12
Opera 3
Parties 1
Past 6
Places 6
Quotations 3
Royalty 23
Science 12
Sex 33
Sickness 6
Society 8, 9
Speeches 5
Supernatural 3
Telegrams 7, 8, 9, 10, 11
Television 4
Theatre 14, 15, 16
Travel 6, 7
Universe 5
War 8
Weddings 5
Work 9
Writers 7, 8
Youth 2
Cowper, William (1731–1800)
Clergy 5
Country 2, 3
Crime 10
Foolishness 4
Journalism 13
Sickness 7
Smoking 3
Wit 8
Women 10
Crabbe, George (1754–1832)
Poverty 3
Secrecy 5
Cradock, Johnny (*c.*1904–87)
Cookery 7
Craigie, W. A. (1867–1967)
Dictionaries 6

Ebb, Fred
Life 9
Edelman, Maurice (1911–75)
Censorship 6
Eden, Anthony (1897–1977)
Self-Knowledge 9
Edgeworth, Maria (1767–1849)
Prejudice 3
Edison, Thomas Alva (1847–1931)
Intelligence 6
Edward IV (1442–83)
Royalty 26
Edward VII (1841–1910)
Dress 3, 4
Royalty 27, 28
Self-Knowledge 10
Edward VIII (1894–1972)
America 10
Edwards, Oliver (1711–91)
Philosophy 2
Edwards, Sherman
America 11
Ehrenreich, Barbara (1941–)
Health 5
Ehrlich, Paul Ralph (1932–)
Technology 4
Einstein, Albert (1879–1955)
Future 6
Lifestyle 4
Science 13
Eisenstaedt, Alfred (1898–1995)
Old Age 16
Ejogo, Carmen
Names 11
Eliot, George (1819–80)
Conversation 11
Humour 12
Women 15
Eliot, T. S. (1888–1965)
Poetry 10
Poets 6
Elizabeth I (1533–1603)
Body 18
Clergy 6
Elizabeth II (1926–)
Football 10
Honours 4
Old Age 17
Praise 3
Progress 6
Royalty 29
Elizabeth, Queen, the Queen Mother (1900–2002)
Animals 11
Countries 16

Poets 7
Royalty 30
Wine 4
Ellington, Duke (1899–1974)
Music 16
Elliott, Ted see **Rossio, Terry** and **Elliott, Ted**
Ellis, Alice Thomas (1932–2005)
Character 6
God 22
Virtue 8
Elson, Andy
Failure 4
Elton, Ben (1959–)
Fashion 7
Elton, Ben (1959–) see **Curtis, Richard** and **Elton, Ben**
Elyot, Thomas (1499–1546)
Football 11
Emerson, Ralph Waldo (1803–82)
Children 17
Hospitality 4
Music 17
Progress 7
Quotations 5
Virtue 9
Empson, William (1906–84)
Dictionaries 7
Enfield, Harry (1961–)
Comedy 29
England, Chris see **Smith, Arthur** and **England, Chris**
English, Mick
Names 12
Enniskillen, Lord (1918–89)
Poverty 4
Ephron, Nora (1941–)
Choice 4
Epstein, Julius J. (1909–2001) **et al.**
Crime 14
Erskine, Thomas (1750–1823)
Medicine 13
Eubank, Chris (1966–)
Success 8
Evangelista, Linda (1965–)
Money 11
Evans, Abel (1679–1737)
Epitaphs 12
Evershed, Lord (1899–1966)
Law 9
Ewart, Gavin (1916–95)
Actors 15

Ewer, William Norman (1885–1976)
God 23
War 11
Fadiman, Clifton (1904–99)
Food 24
Literature 15
Fadiman, William
Hollywood 4
Faith, Adam (1940–2002)
Last Words 3
Faithfull, Marianne (1946–)
Songs 10
Falkland, Lord (1935–)
Government 8
Faraday, Michael (1791–1867)
Technology 5
Farquhar, George (1678–1707)
Marriage 52
Religion 22
Women 16
Farrow, Mia (1945–)
Choice 5
Faulkner, William (1897–1962)
Drink 21
Film Producers 3
Writers 13
Feldman, Marty (1933–83)
Humour 13
Feldman, Marty (1933–83) see **Took, Barry** and **Feldman, Marty**
Fellowes, Julian (1949–)
Children 18
Fenwick, Millicent (1910–92)
Men and Women 10
Ferber, Edna (1887–1968)
Food 25
Old Age 18
Writers 14
Ferguson, Miriam A. 'Ma' (1875–1961)
Languages 10
Fermi, Enrico (1901–54)
Science 14
Feydeau, Georges (1862–1921)
Trust 4
Field, Eugene (1850–95)
Actors 16
Field, Frank (1942–)
Certainty 12
Fielding, Helen (1958–)
Body 19
Men and Women 11

Poets 12
Politics 36
Praise 5
Reading 10
Scotland 5, 6
Sports 19
Taxes 4
Theatre 27
Towns 18, 19
Travel 14
Trust 8
Virtue 10
Weather 12
Women 31
Writing 11, 12
Johnston, Brian (1912–94)
Names 17
Johnstone, John Benn (1803–91)
Marriage 77
Jones, Paul M. see de Leon,
Walter and Jones, Paul M.
Jones, Tom (1940–)
Songs 13
Jones, Vinnie (1965–)
Football 15
Jong, Erica (1942–)
Hollywood 9
Jonsson, Ulrika (1967–)
Marriage 78
Joplin, Janis (1943–70)
Death 38
Jopling, Michael (1930–)
Snobbery 8
Jordan, Mrs (1762–1816)
Royalty 42
Joseph, Jenny (1932–)
Old Age 27
Joseph, Michael (1897–1958)
Publishing 13
Josephson, Marvin
Publishing 14
Jowell, Tessa (1947–)
Names 18
Jowett, Benjamin (1817–93)
Books 7
God 28
Snobbery 9
Joya, Malalai (1978–)
Politicians 20
Joyce, James (1882–1941)
Art 18
Censorship 8
Drink 34
Failure 7
Food 37

Religion 32
Writers 18
Junor, John (1919–97)
Behaviour 16
Comedy 40
Junot, Marshal (1771–1813)
Aristocracy 11
Juvenal (*c.*AD 60–*c.*130)
Wit 16

Kahn, Gus (1886–1941)
Love 27
Kalmar, Bert (1884–1947) **et al.**
Dance 9
War 17
Women 32
Kanin, Garson (1912–99)
People 21
Kaufman, George S. (1889–1961)
Actors 24
Behaviour 17
Death 39
Family 22
Foolishness 8
Gambling 6
Government 17
Medicine 21
Music 26
Sickness 11
Sleep 4
Telegrams 15
Theatre 28, 29, 30, 31, 32,
33
War 18
Wealth 17
Wit 17, 18
Words 20
Writers 19
Kaufman, George S. (1889–1961)
and **Ryskind, Morrie**
(1895–1985)
Christmas 8
Kaufman, George S. (1889–1961)
and **Teichmann, Howard**
(1916–87)
Acting 17
Kavanagh, Patrick (1904–67)
Poverty 10
Kavanagh, Ted (1892–1958)
Comedy 1, 3, 22, 24, 27
Kavanagh, Trevor (1943–)
Politicians 21
Kay, Peter (1973–)
Food 38
War 19

Keane, Roy (1971–)
Football 16
Keating, Fred
Conversation 14
Keating, Paul (1944–)
Insults 23
Snobbery 10
Keats, John (1795–1821)
Conversation 15
Medicine 22
Names 19
Keats, John (1920–)
Transport 20
Keegan, William (1938–)
Wit 19
Keillor, Garrison (1942–)
Christmas 9
God 29
Men 10
Presidents 12
Kelly, Henry
Cookery 12
Kempton, Murray (1917–97)
Government 18
Kennedy, Florynce (1916–2001)
Men and Women 23
Kennedy, John F. (1917–63)
Family 23
Intelligence 9
Presidents 13
Kennedy, John F. Jnr. (1960–99)
Family 24
Kennedy-Martin, Troy (1932–)
Satisfaction 8
Kenny, Gerard (1947–)
New York 5
Kern, Jerome (1885–1945)
Music 27
Kerr, Jean (1923–2003)
Appearance 10
Diets 5
Kettle, Thomas (1880–1916)
Ireland 5
Keyes, Marian
Technology 9
Keynes, John Maynard
(1883–1946)
Economics 12
Examinations 4
Government 19
Past 7
Khrushchev, Nikita (1894–1971)
Music 28
Kilmuir, Lord (1900–67)
Politics 37

Llewelyn-Davies, Jack
(1894–1959)
Children 27
Lloyd, Elizabeth (1928–)
Men and Women 28
Lloyd, Jeremy see **Croft, David**
and **Lloyd, Jeremy**
Lloyd, Marie (1870–1922)
Censorship 11
Lloyd George, David (1863–1945)
Armed Forces 23
Death 41
Money 22
Politics 40
Prime Ministers 19, 20, 21,
22
Lock, Sean
Cinema 18
Loesser, Frank (1910–69)
Betting 5, 6
Birds 5
Business 9
Countries 24
Law 22
Men and Women 29, 30, 31
Sickness 12, 13
Theatre 34
Towns 21
Weather 14
Words 25
Work 19
Loewe, Frederick (1904–88)
Music 33
London, Jack (1876–1916)
Travel 18
Long, Huey (1893–1935)
Government 22
Longford, Lord (1905–2001)
Humility 3
Longworth, Alice Roosevelt
(1884–1980)
Children 28
Gossip 6
Insults 24
Trust 9
Loos, Anita (1893–1981)
America 20
Men and Women 32
Lopokova, Lydia (1892–1981)
Sex 54
Lord Massereene and Ferrard
(1914–93)
Country 12
Loren, Sophia (1934–)
Fashion 11

Food 43
Lorenz, Konrad (1903–89)
Science 20
Louis XIV (1638–1715)
Royalty 45
Lovelock, Terry
Drink 37
Lowry, Malcolm (1909–57)
Epitaphs 17
Lucas, E. V. (1868–1938)
Behaviour 20
England 19
Epitaphs 18
Work 20
Lucas, Matt (1974–) and
Walliams, David (1971–)
Body 29
Comedy 53
Computers 7
Luce, Clare Boothe (1903–87)
Censorship 12
Lumley, Joanna (1946–)
Youth 5
Lutyens, Edwin (1869–1944)
Food 44
Lynn, Jonathan (1943–) and **Jay,**
Antony (1930–)
Argument 13
Bureaucracy 10
Countries 25
Secrecy 9
Lyttelton, George (1883–1962)
Handwriting 4

McAliskey, Bernadette Devlin
(1947–)
Newspapers 8
Macaulay, Lord (1800–59)
Aristocracy 12
Behaviour 21
Critics 17
Description 20
Enemies 4
Names 23
Macaulay, Rose (1881–1958)
Love 31
Marriage 80
Newspapers 9
McCarthy, Cormac (1933–)
Mistakes 21
McCartney, Paul (1942–)
Old Age 31
McCord, David (1897–1997)
Critics 18
Epitaphs 20

McCourt, Frank (1930–)
Body 30
Weather 15
McCrum, Robert (1953–)
Sickness 14
MacDonald, George (1824–1905)
Epitaphs 19
Macdonald, John A. (1851–91)
Satisfaction 10
MacDonald, Ramsay (1866–1937)
Prime Ministers 23
McEnroe, John (1959–)
Tennis 7
McEwan, Ian (1948–)
Generation Gap 8
McGill, Donald (1875–1962)
Body 31
McGinley, Phyllis (1905–78)
Family 26
McGonagall, William
(c.1825–1902)
Death 42, 43
McGough, Roger (1937–)
Animals 22
People 23
Wit 23
Macgregor, Dr
Religion 36
McGregor, Jimmy
Football 19
McGuigan, Barry (1961–)
Boxing 11
Mackenzie, Compton (1883–1972)
Drink 38
Food 45
Women 36
Mackenzie, Kelvin (1946–)
Future 13
Politicians 22
Macleod, Iain (1913–70)
Political Parties 12
McLuhan, Marshall (1911–80)
Mind 9
Newspapers 10
McMahon, Ed
Comedy 17
McManus, Liz (1947–)
Food 46
Macmillan, Harold (1894–1986)
Birds 6
Clergy 14
Diplomacy 8
Government 23
Languages 16

Keyword *Index*

Adam all A.'s children — CLASS 14
made A. and Bruce — SEX 25
What a good thing A. had — QUOTATIONS 18
Adams John A. lies here — EPITAPHS 8
addicted a. to prayers — RELIGION 4
address lost my A. — BOOKS 20
addresses A. are given to us to conceal — PLACES 13
adjective a. currently used — WORDS 38
A.: when in doubt — WRITING 18
than one German a. — LANGUAGES 26
administrative a. won't — ARGUMENT 13
admiral not a doorman but a rear a. — TRANSPORT 5
admire cannot possibly a. them — POVERTY 23
admired more a. she was — POLITICIANS 13
admit Whenever you're wrong, a. it — MARRIAGE 88
adorable a. pancreas — APPEARANCE 10
nauseatingly a. — PEOPLE 34
adore a. those sort of people — BEHAVIOUR 30
need to a. me — FAME 20
ads watched the a. — EPITAPHS 22
adulterers I see some a. down there — SEX 42
adulterous would be a. — ARCHITECTURE 2
adultery a. out of the moral arena — SOCIETY 21
common as a. — AUTOBIOGRAPHY 8
Do not a. commit — SEX 32
gallantry, and gods a. — SEX 29
henceforward to the strictest a. — MORALITY 2
it's still a. — SEX 92
adults how I regarded a. — GENERATION GAP 8
only between consenting a. — SEX 94
advanced a. state of nudity — BODY 34
advancement useful for political a. — POLITICS 38
advantage A. rarely comes of it — SEX 32
take a mean a. — BEHAVIOUR 38
undertaking of Great A. — SECRECY 2
adversary mine a. had written — BOOKS 1
advertise eat what I a. — DRINK 17
advertisement one effective a. — ADVERTISING 4
advertisements column of a. by heart — QUOTATIONS 8
real estate a. — AUTOBIOGRAPHY 9
advertisers a. don't object to — NEWSPAPERS 24
advertising A. is the most — ADVERTISING 3
A. is the rattling — ADVERTISING 9
A. may be described — ADVERTISING 5
advise STREETS FLOODED. PLEASE A. — TELEGRAMS 3
advises It's my old girl that a. — MARRIAGE 47
advocate art of the a. — ARGUMENT 15
aesthete perfect a. — ART 26
aesthetic letting one's a. sense override — MORALITY 9

affair a. between Margot Asquith — INSULTS 30
a. with Ophelia — THEATRE 4
keep a measly a. secret — SECURITY 5
affairs religious a. *department* — BROADCASTING 2
afford Can't a. them, Governor — MORALITY 12
when he can't a. it — BETTING 9
afraid a. to die — DEATH 1
Africa more familiar with A. — WOMEN 46
African A. Primates Meeting — NAMES 31
after A. you, Claude — COMEDY 1
afternoon make love in the a. — FRANCE 1
nothing to do in the a. — THEATRE 3
against always vote *a.* — DEMOCRACY 5
life is 6 to 5 a. — GAMBLING 7
most people vote a. — DEMOCRACY 1
agapanthus Beware of the a. — COUNTRY 12
age A. before Beauty — INSULTS 29
being an enigma at Dylan's a. — SECRECY 10
can tell a woman's a. — WOMEN 21
lie about his a. — HUMOUR 20
Mozart was my a. — SUCCESS 14
not going to make a. an issue — OLD AGE 37
reached the a. to write — AUTOBIOGRAPHY 21
slam the door in the face of a. — OLD AGE 12
talk turns to a. — MIDDLE AGE 4
Thirty-five is a very attractive a. — MIDDLE AGE 16
What a. are you going to put — TRAVEL 21
whatever a. she is — FAME 5
when you've the a. — ACTING 23
woman who tells her real a. — WOMEN 70
Work does a. you so — WORK 10
aged I saw an a., aged man — OLD AGE 8
agenda a. will be in inverse proportion — TIME 13
agent a. to a publisher — PUBLISHING 14
good estate a. — HOME 8
literary a. was a grim, hard-bitten — PUBLISHING 19
much of a secret a. — SECURITY 1
agents and west by a. — HOLLYWOOD 4
ages He's a writer for the a. — WRITERS 32
agglomerated your a. lucubrations — PRAISE 4
aghast I'm a. — WIT 46
agnostic I have been an a. — GOD 11
You are not an a. — RELIGION 46
agnostics fans and a. — BASEBALL 4
agony a. is abated — BEHAVIOUR 21
it was a., Ivy — COMEDY 9
someone's screaming in a. — LANGUAGES 17
agreeable idea of an a. person — ARGUMENT 5
agreement public a. among doctors — MEDICINE 33
Too much a. — CONVERSATION 8
agrees person who a. with me — ARGUMENT 5
ahead a. in this world — LAW 20
aide-de-camp a. to General Brue — ARMED FORCES 3
ain't a. a fit night out for man — WEATHER 6

angel (*cont.*):

to the recording a.	MURDER 5
wrote like an a.	EPITAPHS 15

angels walk behind the a.   ROYALTY 28

anger A. and the gravest suspicions   SOCIETY 3

A. makes dull men witty	ANGER 1
designed to evoke incomprehension, a.	ART 22

Anglicans devoutly worshipped by A.

   RELIGION 48

angling 'a.' is the name given to fishing

	FISHING 5
a. or float fishing	FISHING 4

English A. is what we don' know   LANGUAGES 11

Anglo-Irishman He was an A.   IRELAND 1

angry always a. when I'm dying	LAST WORDS 7
when she's a. she is keen	WOMEN 54
when very a.	ANGER 10
when you get a.	ANGER 3
animal a. husbandry	SEX 53
a. lover	HUMAN RACE 9
Man is the Only A.	HUMAN RACE 11
animals All a. are equal	DEMOCRACY 13
A., I hope	SPORTS 29
distinguishes man from a.	MEDICINE 28
Men are a.	MEN 8
of Music Among A.	CRITICS 23
woollier a.	ART 20
animosity a. against a writer	WRITERS 49
a. towards	ACTORS 5
sisterly a.	FAMILY 42

ankles She had very thick a.   MURDER 15

annihilation A. ALL OF US PROBABLE	TELEGRAMS 10
A. of the Aberrant	TITLES 10
annoy A. 'im	GOD 6
a. somebody with what you write	WRITING 1

annoyance a. of a good example   CHARACTER 17

annuals a. are the ones   GARDENS 13

anomalies a. exist   GOVERNMENT 38

another A. bride, another June   LOVE 27

answer a. come out right	COMPUTERS 2
a. the phone	MISTAKES 28
believe that men were the a.	MEN 1
little English in that a.	GRAMMAR 3
love is the a.	LOVE 44
thought of the a.	FILM PRODUCERS 10
answering a. you in French	FRANCE 7
call my a. machine and sing	MUSICIANS 22

answers figure out the funny a.   HUMOUR 21

antagonistic a. governments	NEWSPAPERS 27
a. to the man	BASEBALL 6

antediluvian a. families   CLASS 7

anthologies employ to compile a.   QUOTATIONS 9

anthologist no a. lifts his leg   QUOTATIONS 1

anthology a. is like all the plums   QUOTATIONS 15

Anthony A. will make the speech   SPEECHES 2

anthrax a. bacillus   HUMAN RACE 6

anthropology familiar facts of a.   MARRIAGE 55

anticlimax kind of a.   FILM 16

ants social organization of a.   SCIENCE 10

anxious a. to tell the truth   TRUTH 5

anybody a.'s weddings	WEDDINGS 6
no one's a.	CLASS 18
anything A. goes	BEHAVIOUR 26
give you a. but love	POVERTY 5
Is there a. they *can't* do	FOOD 30

Anzac wear their medals on A. day   FACES 9

apart You mean a. from my own   MARRIAGE 59

apartment in the next a.   ARGUMENT 12

apathy stirring up a.   POLITICAL PARTIES 19

ape Is man an a. or an angel   RELIGION 19

apologize never to a.   BEHAVIOUR 38

apologizes a. to the truck   ENGLAND 20

apology a. for the Devil	GOD 14
God's a. for relations	FRIENDS 8

apostles A. would have done as they did

   RELIGION 15

apostrophe Aberrant A.   TITLES 10

appearance my external a.	SELF-KNOWLEDGE 14
person of very *epic* a.	PEOPLE 14

appearing Television is for a. on   TELEVISION 4

appendix Like an a.   CENSORSHIP 6

appendixes errors that lead to burst a.

   MEDICINE 24

appetite a. for lunch	DEATH 44
gratify the a.	GOSSIP 8
satisfying a voracious a.	LOVE 14

applause A., applause	THEATRE 21
A. is a receipt	MUSIC 45

apple greedy boy takes a. pie   CRITICS 17

apples a., cherries, hops, and women	PLACES 8
a. short of a picnic	FOOLISHNESS 9
begin to think of a.	CRICKET 10
what a. smell like	DESCRIPTION 25

applications filling out prize a.   JOURNALISM 1

appointment By a.: teddy bear	PEOPLE 1
making an a.	GOVERNMENT 26

appropriate in something a.   ACTORS 25

approved I a. of it   DEATH 70

April A. in Fairbanks   WEATHER 10

aqua all a., no vita   PEOPLE 6

Arabian A. *Nights* entertainment   SICKNESS 16

Arabs A. are only Jews	COUNTRIES 15
A. of means	ANIMALS 19

archaeologist marry an a.   MARRIAGE 32

archaeology Industrial a.   PAST 8

archangel A. Gabriel   DEMOCRACY 2

archbishop a. had come to see me	SEX 27
found yourself A. of Canterbury	WRITERS 20

archbishops get it from their a.   MORALITY 5

archdeacon (by way of turbot) an a.   CLERGY 17

astrology don't believe in a.   CERTAINTY 10
I don't believe in a.   SUPERNATURAL 2
asylum in an a.   DIPLOMACY 13
taken charge of the a.   CINEMA 24
asylums a. of this country are full   MIND 2
put people in a.   ACTING 10
ate Ms Fortier a. Mr Blunkett   FOOD 95
atheism a., breast-feeding   CHILDREN 31
atheist A. and a Vegetarian   POETS 18
a. is a man   RELIGION 13
He was an embittered a.   RELIGION 49
I am still an a.   RELIGION 14
remain a sound a.   CERTAINTY 17
very *chic* for an a.   RELIGION 57
atheistical 'Tis a damned a. age, wife
   MARRIAGE 120
atheists realise that they are a.   CLERGY 10
athletes All pro a. are bilingual   LANGUAGES 14
athletic only a. sport I ever mastered   SPORTS 17
athletics all a. as inferior forms   SPORTS 39
Atlantic cheaper to lower the A.   FILM 8
atom Leave the a. alone   PROGRESS 10
Rutherford was done with the a.   SCIENCE 18
atoms interchanging of the a.   TRANSPORT 26
attachment a. à la Plato   ART 12
attack a. from Mars   ARMED FORCES 24
a. the monkey   POLITICIANS 9
before you can have an a.   SICKNESS 22
by his plan of a.   ARMED FORCES 25
dared a. my Chesterton   LITERATURE 3
attendance a. at the House of Commons
   MARRIAGE 50
attendant lobster to a. shrimps   ROYALTY 50
attention compelled one's a.   FASHION 16
give their entire a. to it   MARRIAGE 15
paid constant a.   CHILDREN 11
Attlee [A. is] a modest man   INSULTS 9
attorney gentleman was an *a.*   LAW 17
office boy to an A.'s firm   LAW 11
rich a.'s Elderly ugly daughter   LOVE 20
attracted a. you to millionaire   MEN AND WOMEN 1
attractive grows increasingly a.   MARRIAGE 32
if they are a.   WOMEN 1
if they are in the least a.   MARRIAGE 27
audience arrival of *your* a.   SPEECHES 4
A. of Two   THEATRE 61
a. was a total failure   THEATRE 58
call the a. in tomorrow   THEATRE 31
get out of the a.   THEATRE 10
looks at the a.   MEDICINE 36
there is a kinder a.   TELEVISION 6
audiences English-speaking a.   LANGUAGES 27
I know two kinds of a.   MUSIC 46
August To recommence in A.   WEATHER 4

aunt A. in Yucatan   ANIMALS 7
A. is calling to Aunt   FAMILY 55
Charley's a.   FAMILY 47
have the Queen as their a.   ROYALTY 46
only woman who wasn't his a.   OPERA 8
when confronted by an a.   MEN 17
aunts bad a.   FAMILY 53
cousins and his a.   FAMILY 18
Australia A., *Inter alia*   AUSTRALIA 4
A. is a huge rest home   AUSTRALIA 1
A.'s original inhabitants   PREJUDICE 10
A.'s very own way   GAMBLING 5
emigrate to A.   AUSTRALIA 3
last year in A.   TRAVEL 26
authentic a. self into a letter   LETTERS 10
author among other things, an a.   WRITERS 16
at great personal risk by the a.
   MEN AND WOMEN 46
a. giveth   WRITERS 19
a. of this valentine   SECRECY 8
a. that wrote it was   READING 14
a. was executed   PUBLISHING 3
a. who comes to stay   WRITERS 10
a. who speaks about   WRITERS 12
dangerous as an a.   WRITERS 47
don't know who the a. is   THEATRE 48
Every a. really wants   WRITERS 48
Wanting to know an a. because   WRITERS 2
authority Distrust of a.   GOVERNMENT 7
talk with more a.   OLD AGE 43
authors A. are judged   WRITERS 34
A. with a mortgage   WRITING 5
Good a., too   WORDS 30
towards noble a.   ARISTOCRACY 12
try not to argue with a.   PUBLISHING 13
We a., Ma'am   PRAISE 1
autobiographer a. is the most   AUTOBIOGRAPHY 9
autobiographies in later life to a.
   AUTOBIOGRAPHY 17
autobiography An a. is an obituary
   AUTOBIOGRAPHY 6
A. comes out   AUTOBIOGRAPHY 1
a. is a sin   AUTOBIOGRAPHY 13
A. is now as common   AUTOBIOGRAPHY 8
a. is the most   AUTOBIOGRAPHY 20
a. should give   AUTOBIOGRAPHY 5
Every a.   AUTOBIOGRAPHY 16
you've read his a.   INSULTS 28
autocrat I shall be an a.   ROYALTY 18
autograph next day you're an a.   FAME 25
Autolycus named me A.   CHARACTER 11
automobile a. changed our dress   TRANSPORT 20
available a. men in their thirties   NEW YORK 6
time I've been a.   AWARDS 2

band b. is always playing   CHARACTER 3
  not even the best drummer in the b.
                      MUSICIANS 15
  prison b. was there   CRIME 17
  Silver B. so nonplussed   DESCRIPTION 31
  what the B. has just played   MUSIC 18
Band Aid B. was diabolical   SONGS 16
bands pursue Culture in b.   ART 42
bang standing there, going 'B.'   MURDER 9
bank All we want is a b. balance   SATISFACTION 11
  b. is a place   MONEY 20
  b. is a place where they lend you   MONEY 13
  robbing a b.   CRIME 5
banker as a Scotch b.   CANADA 3
banks b. went bust   ECONOMICS 9
banquet Judging from the b.   THEATRE 59
  Life is a b.   LIFE 8
Banquo as B.'s ghost   POLITICAL PARTIES 1
  unnerved by B.'s valet   ACTING 3
baptismal water b.   DEATH 26
Baptists B. are only funny underwater
                      RELIGION 65
bar b. on the Piccola Marina   COUNTRIES 11
  Did a stunt at the b.   PARTIES 1
  wrong b. or bed   MISTAKES 7
Barabbas B. was a much misunderstood
                      PUBLISHING 12
  B. was a publisher   PUBLISHING 9
barb b. that makes it stick   WIT 39
barbecue Sue wants a b.   FOOD 53
barbed like a b. wire fence   FASHION 11
Barbie Ken and B.   PARTIES 7
  Ken and B.'s romance   MEN AND WOMEN 2
  talk like B.   LIFESTYLE 8
Barbirolli wrath of Sir John B.   MUSICIANS 3
bards Phoney-rustic b.   BIRDS 10
barged b. down the Nile   ACTORS 6
bark heard a seal b.   CERTAINTY 23
barking b. up the wrong tree   CRITICS 11
Barkis B. is willin'   LOVE 11
bar-mitzvah idea for a b.   HOLLYWOOD 11
baronet half mad b.   PEOPLE 13
Baronetage any book but the B.   SNOBBERY 2
baronetcy b. a b.   HONOURS 10
barracuda Man he eat the b.   NATURE 5
barrels slurp into the b.   MONEY 12
barrenness In b., at any rate   POETS 10
Barrie Sir James B.'s cans   LITERATURE 19
barring B. that natural expression   VIRTUE 18
bars parallel b.   HEALTH 14
  research in b.   JOURNALISM 17
barter finding b. cumbersome   BUSINESS 7
baseball b. fans   BASEBALL 4
  b. goes for pay   BASEBALL 5
  b. in Italian   OPERA 5

  B. is very big   BASEBALL 7
  b. on valium   CRICKET 21
bashful b. young potato   ART 12
bashfulness in England a particular b.
                      RELIGION 1
Basingstoke hidden meaning—like B.   WORDS 15
basket eggs in one b.   BUSINESS 18
Basque more difficult to master than B.
                      LANGUAGES 3
bass Slap that b.   MUSIC 19
bastard all my eggs in one b.   SEX 71
  alternatives to 'b.'   CENSORSHIP 2
  b.! He doesn't exist   GOD 9
  Happy as a b.   HAPPINESS 2
  we knocked the b. off   SUCCESS 13
bat b. for the length of time   CRICKET 9
  gentleman holding the b.   BASEBALL 6
  Neither from owl or b.   ANIMALS 36
  see Dr Grace b.   CRICKET 4
  shake a b. at a white man   BASEBALL 7
  Twinkle, twinkle, little b.   UNIVERSE 4
bath b. every year   BEHAVIOUR 2
  coal in the b.   CLASS 24
  cold b. and a religious exercise   NEWSPAPERS 5
  Commander of the B.   ROYALTY 5
  Dizzy in his b.   BODY 16
  every morning, like a hot b.   NEWSPAPERS 10
  I'll take a b.   FAME 15
  in the b. overnight   FILM STARS 12
  I test my b. before I sit   SATISFACTION 12
  Only when you don't take a b.   SEX 55
  soaking in a hot b.   BUSINESS 1
  stepping from his b.   PRIDE 2
  used to sing in the b. tub   WORK 16
bathing caught the Whigs b.   POLITICAL PARTIES 6
  From the b. machine   DRINK 28
  surprised when b.   DESCRIPTION 8
bathroom as he goes to the b.   CLERGY 2
  Castro couldn't even go to the b.   POWER 7
baths five 'b.' on Christmas Day   CHRISTMAS 6
  Noble deeds and hot b.   MIND 12
bathtub drown it in the b.   GOVERNMENT 27
  in bed and in the b.   NAMES 26
bats their b. have been broken   TRUST 5
batsman b.'s Holding   NAMES 17
battle b. for the mind   PRESIDENTS 16
  history of a b.   WAR 30
battlefield rent on the b.   WAR 17
baying b. for broken glass   ENGLAND 39
BBC goad the B.   BROADCASTING 7
beak takes in his b.   BIRDS 7
bean Boston, the home of the b.   TOWNS 8
  not too French French b.   ART 12
beans in with the boy b.   SEX 64

bear b. led by a man   WRITERS 4
B. of Very Little Brain   ANIMALS 27
embrace the Russian b.   RUSSIA 1
Exit, pursued by a b.   THEATRE 47
beard thin vague b.   APPEARANCE 3
beast *B.* stands for   NEWSPAPERS 27
fit night out for man or b.   WEATHER 6
beastly b. to the Germans   COUNTRIES 12
beat guys I'd like to b. up   BODY 32
Beatles B., how did the name arrive   NAMES 20
B.' first L.P.   SEX 51
beats If anyone b. it   CRICKET 18
beaut it's a b.   MISTAKES 20
beautiful better to be b.   APPEARANCE 22
When a woman isn't b.   WOMEN 8
beauty Age before B.   INSULTS 29
b. am faded   APPEARANCE 14
b. being only skin-deep   APPEARANCE 10
b. is only sin deep   APPEARANCE 16
B. school report   EDUCATION 18
If b. is truth   APPEARANCE 19
No woman can be a b.   WOMEN 16
Beaverbrook B. is so pleased   POLITICIANS 5
existence of Lord B.   PEOPLE 43
becquerel All I know about the b.   SCIENCE 1
bed about his b.   SCIENCE 9
and a good b.   SHOPPING 2
And so to b.   SLEEP 6
any place but it were to his b.   ROYALTY 26
b. fell on my father   FAMILY 48
b. people   CLASS 6
fell out of b.   PRESIDENTS 2
gooseberried double b.   SEX 90
I go to b. early   SLEEP 10
in b. and in the bathtub   NAMES 26
in b. at the same time   SEX 76
in b. with my catamite   SEX 27
never good in b.   APPEARANCE 5
obliged to go to b.   PARENTS 5
Only about thirteen in a b.   SUPERNATURAL 3
quick dip in b.   HEALTH 15
should of stood in b.   BASEBALL 8
sinners are still in b.   RELIGION 56
stay in b. all day   MISTAKES 4
what she wore in b.   DRESS 13
Who goes to b. with whom   OLD AGE 38
wrong bar or b.   MISTAKES 7
bedpost b. overnight   FOOD 70
bedroom French widow in every b.   HOTELS 4
have one in their b.   TRANSPORT 34
take care of the b. bit   MARRIAGE 69
what you do in the b.   SEX 31
beds lush pastrami b.   PLACES 12
make the b.   HOUSEWORK 4
bedstead that b. would   SLEEP 1

bee hero is a b.   ANIMALS 13
Beecham's Pills B. are just the thing   MEDICINE 5
beef b.-faced boys   CHILDREN 15
love British b.   DIETS 2
Roast B., Medium   FOOD 25
beer B. and Britannia   ENGLAND 33
b. teetotaller   WINE 8
b. to cry into   DRINK 39
desire small b.   DRINK 52
really like b. commercials   FILM 9
beers other b. cannot reach   DRINK 37
bees Birds do it, b. do it   SEX 73
Honey b. are amazing creatures   ANIMALS 17
Beethoven Anything but B.   FILM 14
conducted a B. performance   MUSIC 40
playing B. on the kazoo   LITERATURE 32
What do you think of B.   MUSICIANS 23
where is B.   MUSIC 47
would like to thank B.   MUSIC 57
begin B. at the beginning   ROYALTY 17
should b. at home   CENSORSHIP 12
beginner She's a b.   FAME 5
beginning b., a middle   CINEMA 8
b., a muddle   LITERATURE 22
begot were about when they b. me   PARENTS 16
behave b. like gentlemen   WOMEN 36
behaving b. in this extraordinary manner
   THEATRE 53
behaviour b. everywhere   COUNTRIES 33
mitigate b.   GOLF 5
beheaded they had you b.   ROYALTY 67
behind it will be b. me   LETTERS 13
no bosom and no b.   ENGLAND 32
no more b. your scenes   THEATRE 27
travel broadens the b.   TRAVEL 10
walk b. the angels   ROYALTY 28
beige just my colour: it's *b.*   COLOURS 6
Belgium must be B.   TRAVEL 24
Belgrave beat in B. Square   ARISTOCRACY 6
believe b. all you read in the newspapers
   NEWSPAPERS 9
b. almost anything provided   INTELLIGENCE 13
b. I am between both   ARGUMENT 16
can't b. what isn't happening   SPORTS 10
Corrected *I b.*   RELIGION 33
don't b. in God   GOD 21
don't b. in it   CERTAINTY 7
I cannot quite b. in God   RELIGION 27
I don't *b.* it   COMEDY 38
If you b. that   PEOPLE 44
believed b. of any man   DRINK 58
I should not be b.   MARRIAGE 120
believers b. in Clough   EPITAPHS 26

bell Alexander Graham B. had been run over

TECHNOLOGY 10

sexton tolled the b. DEATH 32

bellman B., perplexed and distressed TRAVEL 3

belly-tension b. between a man and a woman

MARRIAGE 65

Belmarsh like B.'s version FOOD 2

belong B. TO ANY CLUB SOCIETY 16

below b.-stairs class CLASS 6

belt without hitting b. it PRIME MINISTERS 2

belt b. without hitting below it PRIME MINISTERS 2

belted b. you and flayed you ARMED FORCES 20

bench he fancied he was on the b. JUDGES 12

benches asleep on the same b. POLITICS 52

bend he can b. spoons SUPERNATURAL 5

beneath married b. him ACTING 7

benign b. form of house arrest CHILDREN 36

It's b. WORDS 2

Benn B. grabs child HEADLINES 8

Benois B. . . . If 'e come DANCE 4

bent b. her contraceptive LAW 10

bereaved would be b. HUMOUR 38

Berlin people of B. TOWNS 13

Bernstein B. has been disclosing MUSICIANS 16

berth lying in the upper b. MARRIAGE 20

best all your b. work go unnoticed SECRECY 3

in the b. of things HAPPINESS 13

Reagan for his b. friend FILM STARS 15

trouble with being b. man WEDDINGS 8

was the b. manager SELF-KNOWLEDGE 8

besticles testicles is b. WIT 30

best-seller b. is the gilded tomb BOOKS 15

bet that's the way to b. BETTING 7

Betjeman poems of Sir John B. CRITICS 16

betrayed He deserves to be b. TRUST 4

better areas do you think Middlesbrough were b.

FOOTBALL 30

b. in France FRANCE 9

b.-looking than oneself WORDS 38

b. man than I am ARMED FORCES 20

b. than we thought FOOTBALL 23

b. to be looked over SATISFACTION 17

B. to hang somebody PUNISHMENT 10

Discretion is not the b. BIOGRAPHY 13

don't know b. CHILDREN 37

expected b. manners BEHAVIOUR 9

further reaches of 'for b.' MARRIAGE 8

Gad! she'd b. UNIVERSE 3

He is not b. TELEGRAMS 1

if they had been any b. LITERATURE 11

rich is b. WEALTH 30

things I'd been b. without LOVE 36

Wagner's music is b. MUSIC 38

when I'm bad, I'm better VIRTUE 20

better-class b. people get it apparently

MEDICINE 7

betting keeps horse from b. BETTING 3

pass a b. shop FOOTBALL 9

Betty B. Fjord Clinic DRINK 60

between believe I am b. both ARGUMENT 16

I would try to get b. them SEX 87

something b. us BODY 24

Beulah B., peel me a grape FOOD 87

Beverly Hills in B. grows old OLD AGE 25

beware B. of men bearing flowers

MEN AND WOMEN 53

B. of the agapanthus COUNTRY 12

b. of the dog CERTAINTY 6

bewildered Bewitched, bothered and b.

MEN AND WOMEN 18

bewitched B., bothered and bewildered

MEN AND WOMEN 18

Bexhill buried quickly at B. FUNERALS 1

bible B. in the other POLITICAL PARTIES 20

we had the B. RELIGION 71

bibles here to Broken Hill with B. TRUST 7

bicycle cannot even use a b. COMPUTERS 4

fish needs a b. WOMEN 14

king rides a b. COUNTRIES 2

so is a b. repair kit MARRIAGE 40

bicycles half people and half b. TRANSPORT 26

bicyclists trouser-clip for b. TECHNOLOGY 12

bidet b.-fixe PARENTS 10

keep it in the b. CLASS 24

UNABLE OBTAIN B. TELEGRAMS 22

biennials b. are the ones GARDENS 13

big b. game hunting BIOGRAPHY 6

Hey! b. spender MEN AND WOMEN 12

I am b. FILM STARS 3

New York is b. TOWNS 2

too b. for them PRIME MINISTERS 7

bigamy b., Sir, is a crime MARRIAGE 85

B. is having one husband MARRIAGE 6

maximum punishment for b. MARRIAGE 102

Biggar this is B. TOWNS 2

bigger b. they are BOXING 5

little girls get b. WOMEN 35

need a b. boat TRANSPORT 4

bike Mind my b. COMEDY 32

bikers one-word nickname for b. MEDICINE 14

bikini decided to get a b. wax POLITICIANS 29

bilingual All pro athletes are b. LANGUAGES 14

bill paying the electricity b. MEDICINE 2

so far down the b. FAME 9

very large b. DEBT 7

billboard b. lovely as a tree ADVERTISING 7

bills I have the b. to prove it MEN AND WOMEN 25

two things about b. DEBT 5

Billy poke poor B. DEATH 28

catholic C. and sensual — COUNTRIES 5
  C. school children — RELIGION 12
  C. woman to avoid pregnancy — RELIGION 42
  C. women must keep taking — RELIGION 69
  I am a C. — RELIGION 6
  lapsed C. and a failed musician — READING 3
  Roman C. Church — POLITICS 44
Catholics pigeons, or C. — SEX 5
  Why did the C. invent — RELIGION 72
cats C. look down on us — ANIMALS 10
  count the c. in Zanzibar — TRAVEL 28
  has two c. — JOURNALISM 16
  to my dogs and c. — HOME 21
catsup c. bottle — FOOD 3
caught c. him at it — SEX 53
cauliflower C. is nothing — FOOD 85
cause c. of dullness — BORES 6
cautious c. letter-writer — LETTERS 3
cavalry Navy, and the Household C. — SEX 48
caviare c. is running out — WEALTH 7
  Open up the c. — FOOD 19
cavity fills wrong c. — WIT 14
Cecil after you, C. — COMEDY 1
ceiling shape of a patch on the c. — BORES 10
celebrity c. is a person — FAME 1
  modern c. is an adulterer — INSULTS 28
celibacy c. is almost always a muddy — MARRIAGE 92
celibate happy undersexed c. — SUCCESS 5
cellar born in a c. — CLASS 8
Celtic meaningless C. noises — SCOTLAND 4
censor c. is a man — CENSORSHIP 17
censorship by the c. laws — CENSORSHIP 15
  C., like charity — CENSORSHIP 12
  extreme form of c. — CENSORSHIP 18
centre c. of your script — CINEMA 23
  dead c. of middle age — MIDDLE AGE 1
cents metropolis for seven c. — WORDS 37
centuries All c. but this — FOOLISHNESS 5
century Albert Memorial C. — PAST 6
  get a c. there — CRICKET 7
Cerberus Womble taking C. — DESCRIPTION 9
cerise éminence c. — ROYALTY 58
certain not so c. — CERTAINTY 1
certainties rapid succession of opposing c. — CERTAINTY 25
certainty not the test of c. — CERTAINTY 16
certitude C. is not the test — CERTAINTY 16
Cézanne convince C. of anything — CERTAINTY 26
  learned as much from C. — SONGS 8
chaff see that the c. is printed — NEWSPAPERS 6
chaffeur AIRMAIL PHOTOGRAPH OF C. — TELEGRAMS 17
chainsaw imagination and a c. — ART 16
  joinery with a c. — DIPLOMACY 4

chair I am not a c. — WORDS 40
  voted into the c. — EDUCATION 11
chaise-longue hurly-burly of the c. — MARRIAGE 26
chalet I've a silly little c. — WEALTH 22
chalice c. from the palace — WIT 28
Cham great C. of literature — PEOPLE 37
chamber C. selected by the Whips — POLITICS 27
Chamberlain speech by C. — PRIME MINISTERS 5
chambermaid c. is very kind — HOTELS 3
chamberpot fortune empties her c. — SATISFACTION 10
chameleons Words are c. — WORDS 17
chamois dress up in c. leather — HAPPINESS 9
champ c. for about ten years — BOXING 1
champagne C. certainly gives — WINE 11
  C. for my real friends — FRIENDS 2
  c. teetotaller — WINE 8
  I get no kick from c. — LOVE 38
champion c. of the world — PHILOSOPHY 1
chance give someone a second c. — TRUST 11
  give war a c. — WAR 22
  Is this a game of c. — GAMBLING 4
  why take the c. — WORK 23
chancellor without a Lord C. — GOVERNMENT 8
Chanel C. No. 5 — DRESS 13
change c. from talking — CONVERSATION 7
  c. my plan — FASHION 6
  First you c. me schmall scheque — MONEY 6
  one thing to do with loose c. — MONEY 23
changed If voting c. anything — POLITICS 39
changes c. it more often — MEN AND WOMEN 21
changing c. a typewriter ribbon — WRITING 2
  not c. one's mind — CERTAINTY 18
channel C. 5 is all shit — LAST WORDS 3
  you are crossing the C. — TRANSPORT 11
chaos emotional c. — HUMOUR 36
  His style is c. — WRITERS 46
  primordial c. — BODY 45
chaps Biography is about C. — BIOGRAPHY 4
chapters no Previous C. — BOOKS 9
character about a fellow's c. — CHARACTER 10
  any great strength of c. — TRAVEL 23
  any other stain upon your c. — LAW 1
  c. dead — GOSSIP 11
  c. is to be abused — FAMILY 44
  enormous lack of c. — SELF-KNOWLEDGE 18
  have the strength of c. — HONOURS 5
  I knows an undesirable c. — SELF-KNOWLEDGE 11
  leave my c. behind — GOSSIP 10
characters too many c. — CINEMA 20
charge in c. of others — ARMED FORCES 1
  in c. of the Intelligence — SECURITY 5
charged asked me what I c. — MISTAKES 16
  c. straight through — ART 41
  he has been c. — SECRECY 9

charging c. like the Light Brigade	FOOD 82
Charing Cross human existence is at C.	
	TOWNS 19
charity C., dear Miss Prism	HUMILITY 6
Charles C. II was always very merry	ROYALTY 61
In good King C.'s golden days	POLITICIANS 3
used by C. the First	HOME 5
Charlotte Werther had a love for C.	
	MEN AND WOMEN 56
charm all of their c.	BODY 5
By my c.	BEHAVIOUR 10
know what c. is	BEHAVIOUR 4
Prince Umberto is c. itself	SELF-KNOWLEDGE 7
charmer Were t'other dear c. away	LOVE 16
charming c. face	ANIMALS 3
Farming is so c.	COUNTRY 16
Chartreuse C. can never really die	RELIGION 58
chasing always c. Rimbauds	LITERATURE 26
nobody's c. me	MEN AND WOMEN 43
chaste c. whore	HUMOUR 25
chastity c. and continency	SEX 14
chat kills a c.	CONVERSATION 8
chateau I've a c. in Touraine	WEALTH 22
Chatterley end of the C. ban	SEX 51
Chaucer C., who had geneyus	WORDS 39
cheap good actors—c.	THEATRE 7
handy and c.	FAMILY 1
how c. potent music	MUSIC 60
how potent c. music is	MUSIC 11
in c. shoes	FASHION 1
cheaper c. to lower the Atlantic	FILM 8
in the c. seats	CLASS 22
cheapish C., reddish	WINE 10
cheat lucrative to c.	CRIME 7
cheek blush into the c.	ENGLAND 9
C. to Cheek	DANCE 10
tongue being in your c.	WIT 3
cheekbones high c.	ACTORS 1
cheerful being so c.	COMEDY 27
cheerfulness c. was always breaking in	
	PHILOSOPHY 2
cheerio c. my deario	HOPE 6
cheese Botticelli's a c.	FOOD 67
c.eating surrender monkeys	FRANCE 5
C. it is a peevish elf	FOOD 69
chinks with c.	FOOD 81
dreamed of c.	SLEEP 8
silent on the subject of c.	FOOD 17
soft c. will kill you	FOOD 49
varieties of c.	FRANCE 3
very new c.	FOOD 74
cheesed humanity soon had me c. off	
	LITERATURE 4
cheesemakers Blessed are the c.	RELIGION 18
cheetah like a c.	HUMOUR 10

chef c. and a cook	COOKERY 9
chefs c. screaming risotto recipes	OPERA 6
chemicals found more dangerous c.	WAR 7
chemotherapy sessions of c.	MEDICINE 32
cheque be done with a c.	RELIGION 34
mail that c. to the Judge	JUDGES 6
schange me schmall c.	MONEY 6
written a bad c.	DEBT 6
cheques publisher has to do is write c.	
	PUBLISHING 18
cherries c., hops, and women	PLACES 8
cherry c. blossom is quite nice	POETS 19
cherub c.'s face, a reptile all	INSULTS 33
chest c. to slip down	FOOD 92
Chesterton dared attack my C.	LITERATURE 3
chestnuts pop like c.	WRITERS 15
chew fart and c. gum	INSULTS 20
chewing drops c. gum	PUNISHMENT 8
chianti bottles of C.	COUNTRIES 31
nice c.	FOOD 33
chic Radical C.	SOCIETY 25
very c. for an atheist	RELIGION 57
Chicago I'd expect to be robbed in C.	TOWNS 22
Chicagowards COCKBURN C.	TELEGRAMS 2
chicken c. and gravy	FOOD 54
c. whose head has been	ARISTOCRACY 13
frozen c.	COOKERY 3
I know c. shit	SPEECHES 12
chickened I promptly c. out	WAR 22
child Benn grabs c.	HEADLINES 8
I am to have his c.	SEX 28
knows his own c.	FAMILY 38
never was a c.	CHILDREN 17
preparing your c.	EDUCATION 23
produce the most perfect c.	MEN AND WOMEN 49
simpering, whimpering c. again	
	MEN AND WOMEN 18
childbirth Death and taxes and c.	DEATH 47
childhood C. is Last Chance	CHILDREN 39
had a perfectly happy c.	WRITERS 33
lousy c.	AUTOBIOGRAPHY 19
childminder underpaid as a c.	EDUCATION 30
children as the c. grow up	CHILDREN 42
C. and zip fasteners	POWER 12
C. are given us	CHILDREN 38
C. can be	CHILDREN 41
c. must be extra polite	BEHAVIOUR 13
C. of the Ritz	SOCIETY 8
c. only scream	CHILDREN 7
C. you destroy together	MARRIAGE 113
contempt—and c.	FAMILY 50
evacuated c.	CHRISTMAS 2
except his own c.	CLERGY 1
first class, and with c.	TRAVEL 1
fond of c. (except boys)	CHILDREN 9

children (*cont.*):
get it from your c. MIND 8
hold yourself up to your c. PARENTS 15
I disliked but c. CHILDREN 24
interest of the c. FAMILY 39
in touch with our c. PARENTS 1
made c. laugh EPITAPHS 6
make your c. carry BUSINESS 2
My c. are doing me in history now OLD AGE 42
our defenceless c. EDUCATION 17
parents obey their c. AMERICA 10
talks about her own c. WRITERS 12
teach their c. how to speak LANGUAGES 15
that I liked c. CHILDREN 6
tiresome for c. GENERATION GAP 5
Too many are like c. PUBLISHING 13
waiting till the c. are settled LOVE 49
with small c. CHILDREN 26
Chile Small earthquake in C. HEADLINES 9
chilli c. to Paul's jam PEOPLE 23
chimerical truth is c. TRUTH 1
chimney port is on the c. piece SEX 92
sixty horses wedged in a c. HEADLINES 11
chimpanzee vase in the hands of a c. WRITERS 42
chin had a c. on which APPEARANCE 3
china C. he had never seen WRITERS 44
slow boat to C. COUNTRIES 24
wouldn't mind seeing C. TRAVEL 17
wrong about where C. was TRAVEL 22
Chinese C. dinner FOOD 27
difficult to trust the C. TRUST 3
chinks fill hup the c. FOOD 81
chip c. of the old block PRIME MINISTERS 8
chipolata acorns and a c. BODY 12
Chipperfield C. commode WIT 44
Chirac C. would have been happy GRAMMAR 3
chocolate Dip me in c. SEX 91
It's called c. FOOD 94
choice not a c. LOVE 41
choosers buggers can't be c. SEX 23
chop when we c. a tree NATURE 4
You can't c. your poppa up MURDER 3
Chopin gap between Dorothy and C. MUSICIANS 1
chopper cheap and chippy c. PUNISHMENT 5
chorous knees of the c. girls THEATRE 23
Christ C. or Faust BOOKS 21
christened want Brooklyn to be c. RELIGION 5
Christian C. Dior me FAME 20
hadn't *got* a C. ANIMALS 35
Christianity between England and C. RELIGION 60
C. never got any grip RELIGION 62
delusions of C. RELIGION 64
Christians C. have burnt each other RELIGION 15

Christmas belong on a C. tree HONOURS 1
C., that time CHRISTMAS 12
C. begins CHRISTMAS 11
C. Eve can be hell CHRISTMAS 3
C. present from POETS 13
C. should fall out CHRISTMAS 1
five 'baths' on C. Day CHRISTMAS 6
from them for C. CHRISTMAS 2
insulting C. card CHRISTMAS 7
lovely thing about C. CHRISTMAS 9
Merry C. CHRISTMAS 5
nice to yu turkeys dis c. CHRISTMAS 13
they are C. decorations TRANSPORT 23
walking backwards for C. CHRISTMAS 10
chuck Queen to skip C. nups HEADLINES 3
chucked I've been c. MEN AND WOMEN 58
You're c. MEN AND WOMEN 37
Chudleigh Kiss me, C. MISTAKES 31
chumps C. always make the best husbands MARRIAGE 129
chundered c. in the old Pacific FOOD 35
church beset the C. of England RELIGION 17
Best Buy—C. of England RELIGION 25
bit like the c. MEDICINE 3
Broad of C. RELIGION 8
C. of England begins ENGLAND 26
C. of England is the only RELIGION 60
C.'s Restoration RELIGION 10
c. to God ARCHITECTURE 5
crisis of the C. of England CLERGY 10
get me to the c. on time WEDDINGS 7
get out of the c. lightly ROYALTY 26
he goes to c. CLERGY 2
pray that the c. WEDDINGS 11
Railways and the C. TRANSPORT 2
run the C. on Hail Marys RELIGION 38
what happened to Charlotte C. FUTURE 5
Churchill never was a C. ARISTOCRACY 7
Randolph C. went into hospital MEDICINE 37
churchman British c. CLERGY 2
Modern C. CLERGY 19
chutney do earwigs make c. ANIMALS 17
chutzpah C. is that quality FAMILY 36
cigarette c. into the lake COUNTRIES 19
c. is the perfect type HAPPINESS 17
I smoked my first c. SMOKING 6
Put that bloody c. out LAST WORDS 9
cigarettes c., whisky and wild LIFESTYLE 2
c. are the only product SMOKING 2
more c. than most SMOKING 1
Cinderella If I made C. FILM PRODUCERS 9
cinemas called after London c. TRAVEL 20
screens at c. CINEMA 5
circumcision breast-feeding, c. CHILDREN 31
circumlocution C. Office BUREAUCRACY 4

circumstance bitter, bitter c.   WOMEN 69

circumstantial c. evidence is very strong   LAW 35

circus celebrated Barnum's c.   PRIME MINISTERS 11

    c. it deserves   HOLLYWOOD 9

cistern loud the c.   OLD AGE 5

cities c. on the hill   AMERICA 26

    shape of our c.   TRANSPORT 20

city big hard-boiled c.   TOWNS 9

    family—in another c.   FAMILY 6

    I can get the same money for c.   WORDS 37

    is an Oriental c.   HOLLYWOOD 3

    stay in the c.   COUNTRY 15

civil Always be c. to the girls   WOMEN 39

    c. To everyone   CIVIL SERVANTS 7

    Pray good people, be c.   RELIGION 26

civilisation collapse of c.   NEW YORK 1

civilities groundless c.   BEHAVIOUR 14

civilization can't say c. don't advance

         PROGRESS 12

    menace to c.   PROGRESS 5

    thought of modern c.   PROGRESS 8

civilizations build c.   SHOPPING 1

civilized become genuinely c.   SCOTLAND 7

    c. man has built a coach   PROGRESS 7

civil servant c. doesn't make jokes

         CIVIL SERVANTS 4

    Give a c. a good case   CIVIL SERVANTS 3

    Here lies a c.   CIVIL SERVANTS 7

civil servants c. are human beings

         CIVIL SERVANTS 5

    C. by the clock   SEX 33

    novel about c.   READING 2

    persecuting c.   CIVIL SERVANTS 1

civil service c. has finished   CIVIL SERVANTS 6

claiming each c. to be   ARGUMENT 22

clan Not for C. Campbell   SUCCESS 4

clap c. your hands   CLASS 22

    Don't c. too hard   THEATRE 37

    gave Lancelot Gobbo c.   THEATRE 25

claret C. is the liquor for boys   DRINK 33

class c. distinctions   CLASS 23

    c.-ridden society   CLASS 21

    fourth c. people   SNOBBERY 7

    Infants' Bible C.   EDUCATION 48

    merciless c. distinction   APPEARANCE 12

    teaching c. consciousness   PREJUDICE 5

classes Clashing of C.   POLITICS 22

    three c. which need sanctuary   POLITICS 8

    two great c.   CLASS 3

classic 'C.' A book   READING 16

    C. music is th'kind   MUSIC 23

classics great homicidal c.   LITERATURE 31

classroom in every c.   COMPUTERS 6

    walks in the c.   EDUCATION 25

clatter c. of Sir James Barrie's cans   LITERATURE 19

Claude After you, C.   COMEDY 1

Claus ain't no Sanity C.   CHRISTMAS 8

claws panes of glass with its c.   MUSIC 4

clay Feet of c. everywhere   BIOGRAPHY 1

clean c., verb active   EDUCATION 12

    have to be c.   HUMOUR 40

    one more thing to keep c.   RELIGION 24

    when the air was c.   NATURE 1

    you get if you c. the toilets   HONOURS 14

cleaner c. than a man's   MEN AND WOMEN 21

cleanliness c. everywhere   COUNTRIES 19

Cleopatra C.—and sank   ACTORS 6

clergyman beneficed c.   CLERGY 19

    take a reference from a c.   TRUST 11

clergymen men, women, and c.   CLERGY 16

clever brains to be that c.   INTELLIGENCE 2

    c. men at Oxford   EDUCATION 15

    provided he is c. enough   INTELLIGENCE 13

cleverest c. people went into politics

         POLITICIANS 22

cliché c. and an indiscretion   DIPLOMACY 8

clichés C. make the best songs   SONGS 15

    dictionary of c.   DICTIONARIES 1

    have some new c.   CINEMA 14

    wreck it with c.   CIVIL SERVANTS 3

client c. moans and sighs   ADVERTISING 10

    [My] c.—God—is in no hurry   ARCHITECTURE 8

climax end a sentence with a c.   SPEECHES 14

    works its way up to a c.   CINEMA 16

climb c. every Mountie   CANADA 9

clinic Betty Fjord C.   DRINK 60

Clive like about C.   DEATH 12

close c. your eyes   SEX 16

    ON ICE TILL C. OF PLAY   TELEGRAMS 13

closed Philadelphia, but it was c.   TOWNS 12

    with a c. door   FILM PRODUCERS 20

closes Satire is what c. Saturday   THEATRE 32

closet walk-in c.   SECRECY 4

clothes C. by a man   FASHION 4

    had no c.   FASHION 2

    not quite enough c.   DRESS 20

    poured into his c.   APPEARANCE 23

    walked away with their c.   POLITICAL PARTIES 6

    wears her c.   DRESS 19

    with your c. on   ADVERTISING 3

         FAME 22

clothing sheep in sheep's c.   INSULTS 10

clouds I've found more c. of grey   LOVE 18

cloven pops the c. hoof   FAMILY 53

club C. THAT WILL ACCEPT ME   SOCIETY 16

    most exclusive c.   ENGLAND 23

    this place is a c.   INSULTS 38

coach civilized man has built a c.   PROGRESS 7

coachman c.'s a privileged indiwidual

         MEN AND WOMEN 8

coal c. in the bath — CLASS 24
made mainly of c. — BUREAUCRACY 3
price of c. going up too — LIFE 17
coalition c. of the willing — COUNTRIES 36
coals No more c. to Newcastle — ROYALTY 35
coarse In a c., rather Corsican way — MARRIAGE 45
is rather c. — ANIMALS 37
coast travel from c. to coast — TRAVEL 16
coat I hung on to his c. tails — PARENTS 14
picking up your c. — YOUTH 5
coca c. bushes — PAST 9
Coca-Cola C.'s Dasani mineral water — WAR 7
cocaine C. habit-forming — DRUGS 2
cock C. and a Bull — CONVERSATION 28
runt, and 11olb of c. — MEN 5
cockatoo natural to a c. — HOME 14
Cocklecarrot C. began the hearing — JUDGES 11
cocksure c. of anything — CERTAINTY 19
c. of many things — CERTAINTY 16
cocktail are the c. parties — DEATH 59
I don't want to go to a c. party — PARTIES 9
cocoa C. is a vulgar beast — DRINK 12
nice cup of c. — HOLLYWOOD 2
cocotte busted, disgusted c. — WOMEN 51
cod But not in the land of the c. — TOWNS 22
home of the bean and the c. — TOWNS 8
photographer is like the c. — TECHNOLOGY 14
piece of c. — FOOD 44
codeword 'recluse' is a c. — JOURNALISM 20
coffee if this is c. — DRINK 49
put poison in your c. — INSULTS 4
coffers money into the c. — ACTING 16
coffin becomes his c. — DEATH 25
C. Makers and Pickpockets — LITERATURE 24
silver plate on a c. — DESCRIPTION 12
Y-shaped c. — SEX 67
coffins c. of friends — HEALTH 10
coil bent her contraceptive c. — LAW 10
coins c. still read — ECONOMICS 9
front seat on the c. — GOD 43
cojones swinging your c. — BODY 50
cold any c. of yours — SICKNESS 1
baby, it's c. outside — WEATHER 14
c. as yesterday's mashed — MEN AND WOMEN 13
c. professional Germanic exterior — SPORTS 15
except for a slight c. — SICKNESS 11
Isn't it c. — WEATHER 18
person . . . can develop a c. — SICKNESS 13
straight past the common c. — MEDICINE 4
Colin C. is the sort of name — NAMES 13
coliseum Munich Beer Festival and the C. — SPORTS 38
You're the C. — PRAISE 6

collapse c. of civilisation — NEW YORK 1
C. of Stout Party — COMEDY 4
on the point of c. — BUREAUCRACY 11
collar hand of history on his c. — HISTORY 1
collarbone my silly old c.'s bust — SPORTS 5
colleague execution of a senior c. — POLITICS 20
college endow a c. — DEATH 57
or leave this c. — GOD 28
with a c. education — FOOD 85
cologne truths wearing diplomatic c. — WORDS 11
colonel C.'s Lady an' Judy O'Grady — WOMEN 33
colonies c. in your wife's name — WAR 15
colony I live in a c. — ANIMALS 16
colour Any c. — COLOURS 5
effective c. schemes — MORALITY 9
her c. is natural — SOCIETY 20
It's just my c. — COLOURS 6
There's been a c. clash — SPORTS 26
unreceptive to c. — DRESS 10
walk by the c. purple — COLOURS 10
coloured c., one-eyed — GOLF 3
colours nailing his c. — CERTAINTY 12
wholesome taste for bright c. — HONOURS 8
Columbus before you doubt C. — TRAVEL 12
C. discovered Caribbean vacations — TRAVEL 22
'I quite realized,' said C. — UNIVERSE 2
laughed at Christopher C. — PROGRESS 9
columnist at a newspaper c. — JOURNALISM 14
columnists When the political c. say — POLITICS 2
coma c. without the worry — TELEVISION 2
resentful c. — EDUCATION 21
combine c. Mumbo with Jumbo — RELIGION 11
come C., friendly bombs — TOWNS 7
c. out long before it is over — MUSIC 52
c. out to the ball park — BASEBALL 3
c. up and see me sometime — SEX 97
delighted to see them c. — CHILDREN 45
give a war and nobody will c. — WAR 24
I c. back — COMEDY 24
it needn't c. to that — POETRY 5
comedian c., a singer or an entertainer — PEOPLE 38
going to be a c. — HUMOUR 23
comedians accountants are c. — BUSINESS 4
comedies c. are not to be — CINEMA 11
comedy aspect of c. — HUMOUR 15
behind my c. — HUMOUR 16
C., like sodomy — HUMOUR 13
c. tonight — THEATRE 50
c. to those that think — HUMAN RACE 13
most lamentable c. — THEATRE 46
rules for great c. — HUMOUR 33
wouldn't give up an hour of c. — HUMOUR 32
comes c. again in the morning — SOCIETY 20
nobody c. — SEX 61

comfort not ecstasy but it was c.   MARRIAGE 48
comfortable c. estate of widowhood
    MARRIAGE 61
comfortably lived c. so long together
    MARRIAGE 62
comic c. with the cosmic   UNIVERSE 11
comma Whence came the intrusive c.
    WRITING 10
command give a single c.   POWER 9
commander C. of Milton Keynes   HONOURS 7
    C. of the Bath   ROYALTY 5
commandments first nine c.   FILM PRODUCERS 21
    Five C.   FILM 3
    only ten c.   BIBLE 2
    satisfied with Ten C.   PRESIDENTS 4
    Ten C.   BIBLE 7
    ten c.   HANDWRITING 7
    Ten C. would have looked like   RELIGION 54
commences long enough after it c.   MUSIC 52
comment C. is free   JOURNALISM 21
    couldn't possibly c.   COMEDY 57
commentators learned c.   CRITICS 27
commerce obstructed interstate c.   SEX 46
commercial concept of c. success   WRITING 6
    you're labelled c.   MUSIC 35
commercialism [C.] is doing well   BUSINESS 20
commercials really like beer c.   FILM 9
commit refusing to c. oneself   BEHAVIOUR 19
committed c. breakfast with it   VIRTUE 11
committee c. discussions   BUREAUCRACY 10
    c.'s idea   DESCRIPTION 25
    horse designed by a c.   BUREAUCRACY 8
    written by a c.   BIBLE 6
commode Chipperfield c.   WIT 44
common c. murderer   COOKERY 18
    c. where the climate's sultry   SEX 29
    Horseguards and still be c.   SOCIETY 17
commonplace loop on a c.   WIT 24
commons C. must bray   ARISTOCRACY 9
common sense defiance of c.   ARCHITECTURE 9
    likes sports hates c.   SPORTS 24
    little more c.   INTELLIGENCE 12
    never ascribe c.   GOD 32
    Nothing but c.   LAW 27
commotion she likes lights and c.   SOCIETY 10
communicate trying to c. with me   DRUGS 1
communist C. Party   ACTING 16
    Is he a C.   PREJUDICE 4
commuter C.—one who spends his life
    TRAVEL 30
companies c. an idiot could run   BUSINESS 3
company C. for carrying on   SECRECY 2
    c. he chooses   DRINK 10
    C. of Four   THEATRE 61
    play it the c. way   BUSINESS 9

Running a c.   BUSINESS 13
    steal out of your c.   CRIME 20
comparisons C. are odorous   WIT 32
compassion c. in the very name   CLERGY 18
compensate c. people for the damage
    LITERATURE 33
competition home c.   HUMOUR 3
competitive Sex was a c. event   SEX 40
    squash is a c. activity   SPORTS 4
complain hardly knows to whom to c.
    UNIVERSE 7
    little to c. o'   MARRIAGE 21
complaints c. about the pauses   SPEECHES 8
complexion convictions and her c.   COLOURS 7
    My c. owes little   BODY 22
compliance by a timely c.   SEX 38
compos non c. penis   CRITICS 19
composed c. for the retreat   ARMED FORCES 21
composer blind c.   FILM 14
    c. and *not* homosexual   MUSICIANS 7
    c. did not leave directions   SONGS 2
    c. is to be dead   MUSICIANS 12
composers I don't like c. who think   MUSIC 13
composing Is he still c.   MUSICIANS 9
compromise c. with being swallowed   CHOICE 11
compromising so busy c.   MURDER 2
compulsion What c. compels them   TRAVEL 6
compulsory Blood is c.   THEATRE 52
    c., like a thunderstorm   CHRISTMAS 9
computer c. in every   COMPUTERS 6
    C. says No   COMPUTERS 7
    modern c.   COMPUTERS 3
    requires a c.   COMPUTERS 1
Conan C. the Grammarians   EDUCATION 26
conceal c. our whereabouts   PLACES 13
conceited It makes me far too c.
    SELF-KNOWLEDGE 30
conceived c. three times   PRESIDENTS 6
concentrates c. his mind   DEATH 37
concert definition for C.   MUSIC 42
concertina Rum, Bum and C.   TITLES 6
concerts c. you enjoy together   MARRIAGE 113
concession only c. to gaiety   WALES 6
concrete scored for bagpipes and c. mixer
    MUSICIANS 14
concubine c. to an opium addict   WOMEN 62
concubines I had three c.   ROYALTY 26
    Twenty-two acknowledged c.   ROYALTY 39
condemned c. veal   ACTORS 7
conditions if you have the c.   SUCCESS 26
condom c. full of walnuts   DESCRIPTION 17
conducted c. a Beethoven performance
    MUSIC 40
conducting c. an orchestra   DIPLOMACY 16
conductor affair with a c.   MEN AND WOMEN 57

curate albino c.	FRIENDS 16
bland country c.	FACES 4
I feel like a shabby c.	SCIENCE 3
like a Protestant c.	DANCE 11
pale young c.	CLERGY 8
remember the average c.	CLERGY 7
very name of a C.	CLERGY 18
curates preached to death by wild c.	RELIGION 67
curbed must be c.	EDUCATION 1
cure c. for sea sickness	TRAVEL 19
in the twentieth, it's a c.	SEX 88
no C. for this Disease	MEDICINE 6
once-bitten there is no c.	FISHING 3
cured C. yesterday of my disease	MEDICINE 31
curiosity lost all c.	AUTOBIOGRAPHY 21
Love, c., freckles, and doubt	LOVE 36
curiouser C. and curiouser	WIT 6
curls c. up like carbon paper	MEN 17
current c. is turned on	WORDS 7
curry lampshade in a c. house	FASHION 12
curse c. of the drinking classes	WORK 27
Fathers don't c.	PARENTS 9
journalistic c. of Eve	JOURNALISM 25
curtain after the c. has risen	ROYALTY 42
c. was up	THEATRE 35
her c. calls	ACTORS 12
remove the c. rings	DRESS 7
curtains c. looked like duvets	HOTELS 2
sew rings on the new c.	INSULTS 7
curtsey C. while you're thinking	BEHAVIOUR 6
Curzon second Lady C.	DEATH 18
cushions c. had cushions	HOTELS 2
custard bathed us like warm c.	DESCRIPTION 5
custom aid of prejudice and c.	PREJUDICE 8
cut BETTER AFTER IT'S BEEN C.	TELEGRAMS 5
c. my conscience to fit	POLITICS 32
c. you down to my size	MEN AND WOMEN 20
keep having my hair c.	BODY 10
right of final c.	FILM PRODUCERS 21
cuter When I was c.	MIDDLE AGE 12
cutlet enough if he eats a c.	WRITERS 26
cutting damned c. and slashing	PUBLISHING 7
cuttings press c. to prove it	ACTORS 26
cyclists C. see motorists	TRANSPORT 19
cymbal like an ill-tuned c.	JUDGES 14
cynic What is a c.	CHARACTER 19
cynical c. about politicians	POLITICS 69
cynics composed of c.	GOVERNMENT 25
d I mean Big D.	TOWNS 21
I never use a big, big D.	LANGUAGE 7
dad d.'s name all over his underwear	FASHION 9
They fuck you up, your mum and d.	
	PARENTS 11

dada art belongs to D.	ART 28
mama of d.	LITERATURE 15
daddy D. sat up very late	DRINK 8
English teacher D.-o	EDUCATION 25
keep D. off her	FAMILY 32
dagger d. in one hand	POLITICAL PARTIES 20
daintily must have things d. served	SOCIETY 4
Dalai horns of a D. Lama	WIT 47
Dali D. is the only painter of LSD	ART 23
Dallas that spells D.	TOWNS 21
damage compensate people for the d.	
	LITERATURE 33
dammed saved by being d.	COUNTRIES 21
damn don't give a d.	SATISFACTION 7
no general idea is worth a d.	IDEAS 4
old man who said 'D.'	TRANSPORT 16
damnations Twenty-nine distinct d.	BIBLE 1
damned lies, d. lies and statistics	LIES 6
Life is just one d. thing	LIFE 10
music is the brandy of the d.	MUSIC 50
public be d.	BUSINESS 19
those d. dots	ECONOMICS 5
written a d. play	THEATRE 44
damp like a d. mackintosh	DESCRIPTION 11
dance d. on pinheads	CERTAINTY 9
I'm giving a d.	SATISFACTION 13
join the d.	DANCE 5
no d. on Sunday	DANCE 16
Paralysed Girl Determined to D.	HEADLINES 10
rather d. with the cows	DANCE 9
towers of Notre Dame to d.	CERTAINTY 26
dances Also d.	FILM STARS 1
dandy Candy is d.	DRINK 43
Dane if you've got a great D.	THEATRE 34
play a D.	ACTING 2
danger be in less d.	FAMILY 29
But only when in d.	RELIGION 51
dangerous d. as an author	WRITERS 47
d. when active	CENSORSHIP 6
found more d. chemicals	WAR 7
Science becomes d.	SCIENCE 24
Daniel lionized was D.	HUMAN RACE 10
Daniels den of D.	FRIENDS 18
dank d. rock pools	FOOD 46
dare It wouldn't d.	TRANSPORT 6
dark Isn't it d.	WEATHER 18
those d. glasses	FILM STARS 11
too d. to read	ANIMALS 24
darken Never d. my Dior	FASHION 10
darling oh, he's a d. man	MEN 12
date keep them up to d.	YOUTH 7
dates broken d.	LOVE 24
question of d.	TRUST 12

daughter Don't put your d.   ACTING 5
Elderly ugly d.   LOVE 20
happens to my d.   PARENTS 3
I'm your d.   SONGS 11
I trust Bush with my d.   PRESIDENTS 17
daughter-in-law her own d.   FAMILY 21
daughters D. are best   FAMILY 4
David D. wrote the Psalms   RELIGION 44
Davy D. Abominated gravy   SCIENCE 5
day Another d. gone   HUMOUR 26
d. away from Tallulah   DESCRIPTION 13
D. will break   FOOD 15
During the d.   MARRIAGE 111
I knew Doris D.   SEX 57
no matter what happens in one d.   NEWSPAPERS 20
when people write every other d.   LETTERS 8
daylight skulk in broad d.   PEOPLE 20
days five or six d.   POLITICS 17
dead all our best men are d.   LITERATURE 28
blooming well d.   DEATH 63
character d.   GOSSIP 11
composer is to be d.   MUSICIANS 12
contact I ever made with the d.   SUPERNATURAL 4
d., and buried at last   DEATH 42
d., or my watch has stopped   DEATH 45
d. bird   OLD AGE 11
d. for a year   SUCCESS 14
d. for the next two months   LETTERS 14
d. or deported   TELEVISION 8
d. sinner revised   VIRTUE 3
For being d.   DEATH 12
hopes of dropping d.   DEATH 33
if I am d.   DEATH 31
in hopes of dropping d. at the top   OLD AGE 26
Lord Jones D.   JOURNALISM 10
Mayfair of the d.   DEATH 60
must be d.   DEATH 7
Not many d.   HEADLINES 9
Once you're d.   DEATH 30
rot the d. talk   SUPERNATURAL 1
seen d. with   DEATH 73
think that Ned Sherrin is d.   BROADCASTING 6
was alive and is d.   EPITAPHS 5
wealthy and d.   DEATH 67
deaded told you I'd be d.   DEATH 46
deadlier email of the species is d.   COMPUTERS 5
deadline met his own d.   EPITAPHS 1
deadlines I love d.   TIME 2
deadlock Holy d.   MARRIAGE 73
deadly d. in the long run   EDUCATION 42
deaf d. man to a blind woman   MARRIAGE 33
longing to be absolutely d.   MUSIC 59
old man's getting d. as well   OLD AGE 10

deafness Her d. is a great privation   RELIGION 74
To my d. I'm accustomed   OLD AGE 24
dean I am the D. of Christ Church   PRIDE 7
To our queer old d.   WIT 42
dear D. 338171   LETTERS 6
dearth d. of bad pictures   CINEMA 10
death between wife and d.   DEATH 50
Cake or d.   RELIGION 31
d., sex and jewels   ART 37
d., which happened   DEATH 32
d. and taxes   DEATH 23
D. and taxes and childbirth   DEATH 47
D. has got something   DEATH 4
D. is always a great pity   DEATH 66
D. is the most convenient   DEATH 41
d. is unreliable   DEATH 8
d. of a political economist   ECONOMICS 1
D. to anyone who drops   PUNISHMENT 8
improved by d.   DEATH 62
makes d. a long-felt want   INSULTS 43
my d. duties   DEATH 68
no drinking after d.   DRINK 25
old maid is like d. by drowning   OLD AGE 18
preached to d.   RELIGION 67
quality of d.   COUNTRIES 7
Reports of my d.   DEATH 69
terror to d.   BIOGRAPHY 16
thought of d.   DEATH 64
debating It is the Lords d.   ROYALTY 16
debauchery Drink and d.   GOLF 2
debt National D.   DEBT 8
debts get caught up on your d.   HOLLYWOOD 17
If I hadn't my d.   DEBT 9
début never make one's d. with a scandal   OLD AGE 44
decadence Everywhere one looks, d.   PROGRESS 1
decay one argues a d. of parts   WIT 7
deceiving nearly d. your friends   LIES 5
decency D. is Indecency's conspiracy   VIRTUE 15
d. is sort of secret   CHARACTER 15
decent d. people live beyond   SOCIETY 18
decide d. I was right   FOOTBALL 6
decipherable was d.   HANDWRITING 6
deciphering only hope of d.   HANDWRITING 2
decision difficult d. I've ever made   POLITICIANS 29
decisions d. he is allowed to take   MANAGEMENT 7
declare nothing to d. except my genius   INTELLIGENCE 15
decline d. two drinks   LANGUAGES 26
I went into a bit of a d.   PAST 1
decompose d. in a barrel   DEATH 22
decomposing Baytch is d.   MUSICIANS 9
decorative be d. and to do right   WOMEN 17
decoyed see these poor fools d.   MARRIAGE 93

dedicated d. follower .... FASHION 5
  d. himself so many times .... PRESIDENTS 22
deduct teach him to d. .... EDUCATION 23
deep d. peace of the double-bed .. MARRIAGE 26
  treading water in the d. end ..... TAXES 1
deeper shown a d. sense .... DEATH 24
defeat *d. a law of God* .... FOOLISHNESS 18
  In d. unbeatable .... WAR 6
defectors D. are like grapes ..... TRUST 10
defendant d., Mr Haddock .... WRITERS 16
  d. became insane .... MURDER 14
defining d. what is unknown ...... DICTIONARIES 11
definite d. maybe .... CERTAINTY 13
deflowered At last you are d. .... TELEGRAMS 7
defoliant aerosol d. .... GARDENS 8
degenerated Newspapers, even, have d.
.... NEWSPAPERS 28
degree I know I've got a d. ...... INTELLIGENCE 18
deity between the D. and the Drains . PEOPLE 39
delayed d. till I am indifferent . INSULTS 21
delight English D. .... TRAVEL 7
delighted You have d. us long enough
.... SATISFACTION 1
delightful It's d., it's delicious . WEDDINGS 10
  Liverpool, though not very d. ... TOWNS 16
delinquents Three juvenile d. .... CRIME 9
delusion Love is the d. .... LOVE 33
delusions d. of Christianity ..... RELIGION 64
demand not a note of d. .... MUSIC 45
  some less delightful d. .... MARRIAGE 20
demented d. refrigerator .... THEATRE 45
de Mille Cecil B. d. .... FILM PRODUCERS 1
demi-tasses With your villainous d. . POVERTY 17
democracy D. is the name .... DEMOCRACY 6
  D. is the recurrent .... DEMOCRACY 16
  D. is the theory .... DEMOCRACY 10
  D. means .... DEMOCRACY 3
.... GOVERNMENT 17
  D. means simply .... DEMOCRACY 17
  less d. to save .... WAR 3
  not the voting that's d. .... DEMOCRACY 15
  triumph for d. .... DEMOCRACY 9
  Try parliamentary d. .... DEMOCRACY 7
  Under d. .... DEMOCRACY 11
democrat Santa Claus is a D. ..... POLITICAL PARTIES 15
democrats stop telling lies about D. . POLITICS 66
demonstrator obligation of the d. . ARGUMENT 14
dentist consulting a d. regularly . MEDICINE 29
  D. fills .... WIT 14
  I'd sooner go to my d. .... SEX 95
  talk like a d. .... BEHAVIOUR 36
dentists on a level with d. ...... ECONOMICS 12
dentures To my d. I'm resigned ... OLD AGE 24
denunciation d. of the young ..... GENERATION GAP 11

deny d. nothing .... CERTAINTY 8
  I never d. .... ROYALTY 25
denying not d. anything .... CERTAINTY 20
department outpatient's d. .... OLD AGE 9
deported dead or d. .... TELEVISION 8
  they would be d. .... CHRISTMAS 4
deposit d. in my name .... GOD 2
depressing d. the keys of the machine . MUSIC 9
depression best cures for d. ..... MIND 12
  d. when you lose .... BUSINESS 17
  got him on tablets for d. ...... MEDICINE 7
  source of d. .... FACES 10
depths Down in the d. .... HOPE 10
derangement nice d. of epitaphs .. WIT 35
descendants your d. Outnumber your friends
.... OLD AGE 33
description Damn d. .... DESCRIPTION 7
desert Zuleika on a d. island .... WOMEN 2
deserve d. a crown .... ROYALTY 3
  d. to get it .... DEMOCRACY 10
desiccated d. calculating machine . POLITICIANS 10
design there is a d. .... BORES 14
designer d. jeans .... FASHION 13
designs His d. were strictly honourable
.... MARRIAGE 53
desire d. should so many years ... SEX 80
  get your heart's d. .... HAPPINESS 12
  horizontal d. .... DANCE 15
  provokes the d. .... DRINK 53
desk manuscript in his d. .... WRITERS 40
  subservience to the d. .... BUREAUCRACY 5
desks Stick close to your d. ..... ARMED FORCES 11
despair form of d. .... HOPE 2
  leads to d. .... CHOICE 1
  sign of d. .... DRESS 20
  upgrades d. .... MONEY 18
desperately D. accustomed .... SPEECHES 5
despised I always d. Mr Tattle ... MARRIAGE 37
destination getting man to his ultimate d.
.... TRANSPORT 2
destined d. to bloom late .... APPEARANCE 11
destiny d. of bores .... BORES 7
destroy Whom the gods wish to d. . SUCCESS 6
detective borrows a d. story ..... READING 11
  doesn't want to look like a d. . LAW 38
detest both d. you .... GENERATION GAP 2
  d. him more .... ENEMIES 4
detested d. him for 23 years ..... BEHAVIOUR 34
detrimental d. to keep it .... ANGER 5
devil apology for the D. .... GOD 14
  d. and the Holy See .... CENSORSHIP 14
  D. sends cooks .... COOKERY 8
  d. understands Welsh .... WALES 4
  I believe in the D. .... PEOPLE 43
  taken over by the D. .... SUCCESS 16

devil (*cont.*):
to God of the d.'s leavings — OLD AGE 35
vote for the d. — DEMOCRACY 18
Devon started that morning from D. — TRAVEL 13
devout One cannot be d. in dishabilly
— RELIGION 22
dey as the d. was long — SEX 65
diabetes known to cause d. — PEOPLE 34
triumph of sugar over d. — PEOPLE 28
diagonally lie d. in his bed again — MARRIAGE 114
dialect d. I understand very little — SPORTS 28
dialogue 19th-century d. — FILM 5
diameter organ of prodigious d. — POETRY 1
diamond d. and safire bracelet — AMERICA 20
diamonds D. are a girl's best friend — WEALTH 24
put d. on the floor — HEALTH 13
Real d. — WEALTH 32
diaries d. of men who enjoy — DIARIES 3
diary keep a d. — DIARIES 6
more dull than a discreet d. — DIARIES 2
without my d. — DIARIES 7
write a d. every day — DIARIES 4
DiCanio You've got D. — FOOTBALL 1
Dick Any Tom, D. or Harry — MARRIAGE 97
At Dirty D.'s — DRINK 4
Dickens put to D. as children — LITERATURE 4
dictation told at d. speed what he knew — LIFE 2
dictionaries Big d. — DICTIONARIES 2
opening d. — DICTIONARIES 10
Short d. — DICTIONARIES 7
will publish d. — DICTIONARIES 11
dictionary D. has not attempted — DICTIONARIES 6
d. out of order — DICTIONARIES 5
ever made the d. — DICTIONARIES 13
'Ex's' in this bloody d. — WORDS 5
Like Webster's D. — DICTIONARIES 4
Oxford D. of Quotations — NEWSPAPERS 7
die afraid to d. — DEATH 1
all must d. — EPITAPHS 25
At first, you fear you will d. — TRAVEL 18
back to America . . . to d. — AMERICA 16
choose to d. — MEDICINE 13
D., and endow — DEATH 57
D., my dear Doctor — LAST WORDS 8
d. before they sing — DEATH 15
d. beyond my means — DEATH 74
d. in *The Times,* — FAME 2
done my best to d. — BIOGRAPHY 10
had to d. in my week — DEATH 38
I'll d. young — DRUGS 3
I shall some day d. — DEATH 40
remain so until *they* d. — PARENTS 13
tomorrow we shall d. — DEATH 52
You d. thin — DIETS 3

died crustaceans d. in vain — POLITICS 33
d. last night of my physician — MEDICINE 31
nearly d. laughing — HUMOUR 3
dies little something in me d. — SUCCESS 24
One d. only once — DEATH 49
diets feel about d. — DIETS 5
difference d. of taste — HUMOUR 12
different arguing from d. premises — ARGUMENT 18
d. from the home life — ROYALTY 10
d. kinds of herring — FOOD 11
how d. it was from Venice — TOWNS 4
on d. subjects — IGNORANCE 6
difficult can be very d. — FUTURE 3
D. do you call it — MUSIC 25
Luckily, this is not d. — MEN AND WOMEN 63
That would be d. — POLITICAL PARTIES 10
difficulties little local d. — POLITICS 42
digest wholesome to d. — FOOD 7
digesting D. it — BEHAVIOUR 17
digests It d. all things — FOOD 69
dignity Elizabeth Windsor has maintained her d.
— ROYALTY 49
I left the room with silent d. — MISTAKES 15
Official d. — BUREAUCRACY 7
digressions D., incontestably — BOOKS 18
dildos wooden d. are made — BUSINESS 14
dilly Don't d.-dally — HOME 3
dime Of a shiny new d. — POVERTY 15
dine d. with some men — ARCHITECTURE 3
dined d. in every house — SOCIETY 24
I d. last night with the Borgias — SOCIETY 2
I have d. today — FOOD 75
more d. against than dining — SOCIETY 6
diner without hitting a d. — BUSINESS 10
dining more dined against than d. — SOCIETY 6
dinner All gong and no d. — TENNIS 9
better than the d. — MARRIAGE 35
doing for d. — BEHAVIOUR 17
eating a hearty d. — RELIGION 39
had a better d. — COOKERY 10
having an old friend for d. — SOCIETY 13
hungry for d. — BEHAVIOUR 15
inviting us to d. — HANDWRITING 4
number for a d. — FOOD 31
served the sort of d. — HOTELS 5
sherry before d. — DRINK 45
Dior Christian D. me — FAME 20
Never darken my D. — FASHION 10
dip quick d. in bed — HEALTH 15
diplomacy D.—lying in state — DIPLOMACY 6
diplomat D. these days — DIPLOMACY 18
distinction of a d. — DIPLOMACY 15
diplomatic truths wearing d. cologne — WORDS 11
diplomats D. tell lies — GOVERNMENT 20
direct d. this play the way you — THEATRE 17

do (*cont.*):

how to d. what I want to do — LAW 26
I can d. that — AMERICA 19
I'll d. him for you — ACTING 32
Let's d. it — COUNTRIES 28
way I d. it — FILM STARS 16
what to d. with the time — WORK 11
when you don't want to d. anything

MANAGEMENT 4

doctor d. anybody's literature — HONOURS 12
d. being always in the right — MEDICINE 33
d. gets the credit — SICKNESS 19
d. whispers in the hospital — MEDICINE 35
d. will see you now — WORDS 7
God and the d. we alike adore — RELIGION 51
kind of d. I want — MEDICINE 21
not love thee, D. Fell — ENEMIES 2
regimental d. — DRESS 6
doctored I knew he'd been d. — INSULTS 5
doffed d. their lids — SNOBBERY 10
dog d. ate my homework — DIPLOMACY 11
d. chooses to run after — SPORTS 2
d. eat dog — CINEMA 13
d. for a nurse — CHILDREN 2
d. is to the Greenlander — ANIMALS 18
d. walking on his hinder legs — WOMEN 31
door is what a d. — DOGS 3
good fer a d. — DOGS 7
hard d. to keep — PRESIDENTS 5
Inside of a d. — ANIMALS 24
man bites a d. — JOURNALISM 3
nothin' but a hound d. — LOVE 29
pollution, the d. — DOGS 5
Whose d. are you — DOGS 4
without having a d. — CERTAINTY 6
your d. comes back to life — MUSIC 53
doge D. of Venice gave Lancelot Gobbo

THEATRE 25

dogged It's d. as does it — WORK 25
dogma serve to beat a d. — ARGUMENT 9
dogs bachelors love d. — CHILDREN 30
bitch that d. me — FOOD 84
D. look up to us — ANIMALS 10
D. who earn their living — DOGS 2
Don't let's go to the d. — BETTING 4
feels about d. — CRITICS 12
go to the d. or the Radicals — POLITICIANS 34
hates d. and babies — PEOPLE 33
Mad d. — ENGLAND 7
our d. when well — MEDICINE 9
Tom and the other d. — EPITAPHS 9
to my d. and cats — HOME 21
values d. — DOGS 6
D'oh D.! — COMEDY 5

doing D. well — BUSINESS 8
don't know what I am d. — SCIENCE 6
see what she's d. — CHILDREN 34
doll only doing it for some d. — MEN AND WOMEN 31
vast d.'s house — DESCRIPTION 26
dollars looks like a million d. — MARRIAGE 79
owes me ninety-seven d. — DEBT 1
thirty-seven d. and a Jap guitar — MUSICIANS 8
you leave him with two d. — MEN AND WOMEN 59
dolls Shirley Temple d. — MEN AND WOMEN 14
dome D. gigantic — ARCHITECTURE 9
domestic d. work — HOUSEWORK 5
except in his d. life — ARMED FORCES 31
dominant looks like the d. male — MEN 17
don Remote and ineffectual D. — LITERATURE 3
donate d. his face to the US Bureau — FACES 1
done Apostles would have d. — RELIGION 15
D. the elephants — TRAVEL 29
d. the old woman in — SICKNESS 20
d. very well out of the war — POLITICIANS 4
pleasure in getting something d. — WORK 21
should not be d. at all — BUSINESS 20
what has he d. for Wales — WALES 2
donkey d. that carries a load — POLITICIANS 20
old grey D. — ANIMALS 26
woman who runs a d. sanctuary — WOMEN 62
Donne D.'s verses are like — POETS 11
donors nickname for bikers: D. — MEDICINE 14
don't D. — MARRIAGE 99
d. call me Shirley — COMEDY 47
donuts D.. Is there anything — FOOD 30
door bolted for the d. — YOUTH 5
d. is what a dog — DOGS 3
found my way out the d. — BUSINESS 12
handle of the big front d. — LAW 11
slam the d. in the face of age — OLD AGE 12
doorbell continually ringing the d. — JUDGES 11
doormat d. in a world of boots

SELF-KNOWLEDGE 21

d. or a prostitute — WOMEN 68
doors blow the bloody d. off — SATISFACTION 8
both d. open — FILM STARS 9
doorstep do this on the d. — BEHAVIOUR 16
loitered of old on many a d. — JOURNALISM 23
dope he was a d. — CHARACTER 7
sex, smoking d. — EDUCATION 9
Dotheboys D. Hall — EDUCATION 13
dots those damned d. — ECONOMICS 5
double d.-breasted suit — FAME 3
d. the crowd — SPEECHES 17
leading a d. life — HYPOCRISY 9
safest way to d. your money — ECONOMICS 10
with a d. meaning — HUMOUR 2
double-bed deep peace of the d. — MARRIAGE 26
doubles d. your chances for a date — SEX 7

drunk (*cont.*):
  not so think as you d.   DRINK 57
  stand around at a bar and get d.   SPORTS 27
  Winston, you're d.   INSULTS 11
  You're not d.   DRINK 40
drunken convictions for d. driving   DRINK 9
  d. porter   GOVERNMENT 28
drunks two miniature d.   CHILDREN 13
dry Drink Canada D.   DRINK 5
  d. she ain't   FILM STARS 13
  I am on d. land   HOPE 12
  into a d. Martini   DRINK 2
  Those d. Martinis   DRINK 1
dryness morbid d. is a Whig vice   VIRTUE 2
Dubliners real D. lead   IRELAND 9
duchess every D. in London   PRIME MINISTERS 23
  married to a d.   PUBLISHING 20
duchesses four bereaved D.   ARISTOCRACY 2
duck After that everything's a d.   BIRDS 9
  know a d. because you like pâté   WRITERS 2
ducking like d. questions   PEOPLE 12
ducks stick to d.   BIRDS 4
duke avoided either d.   BIRDS 6
  D. of Fife   BEHAVIOUR 3
  enough who knows a d.   CLERGY 5
  palace of the D. of Ferrara   ARISTOCRACY 16
dukes drawing room full of d.   SCIENCE 3
  d. were three a penny   GOVERNMENT 9
dull after-sales service, and is very d.   TENNIS 6
  always d.   ENGLAND 41
  Anger makes d. men witty   ANGER 1
  d. in a new way   BORES 8
  d. in himself   BORES 6
  land of the d.   AMERICA 25
  more d. than a discreet diary   DIARIES 2
  Only d. people   BORES 18
  paper appears d.   BORES 14
  Telford is so d.   TOWNS 20
  that he be d.   GOVERNMENT 1
dullness cardinal sin is d.   CINEMA 2
  cause of d.   BORES 6
  D. is so much stronger   BORES 4
dum wrote d.-dum-*dee*-dum   SONGS 12
dumb d. at the very moment when   MUSIC 59
  not a d. blonde   INSULTS 31
  Our D. Friends   DRINK 46
  so d. he can't fart   INSULTS 20
dum-dums NICHI NICHI'S D.   HEADLINES 2
dumping eternal d. ground   FAME 8
dunce d. with wits   INSULTS 34
  How much a d.   FOOLISHNESS 4
Dunkremlin We call it D.   SECURITY 8
Dunn Miss Joan Hunter D.   MEN AND WOMEN 4
Durham Heaven and the Earl of D.   ENGLAND 27

dusk d. was performing   WIT 26
  d. with a light behind   WOMEN 20
dust d. on a Venetian blind   CRITICS 8
  Excuse My D.   EPITAPHS 23
dustbin d. upset in a high wind   SLEEP 3
Dutchmen wearing the shield of the D.   SPORTS 23
duties my death d.   DEATH 68
  smaller d. of life   PRAISE 9
duty as if it were a painful d.   WRITERS 45
  declares that it is his d.   MORALITY 11
  do things from a sense of d.   MORALITY 8
  D. is what one expects   BEHAVIOUR 37
  d. of an Opposition   POLITICS 24
  d. to speak one's mind   MORALITY 16
  one d. we owe   HISTORY 18
duvets curtains looked like d.   HOTELS 2
dwarfs dozen red-bearded d.   JUDGES 11
dying always angry when I'm d.   LAST WORDS 7
  d. with the help of too many physicians   MEDICINE 1
  Here I am, d.   DEATH 55
  If this is d.   LAST WORDS 11
  I'm fucking d.   SICKNESS 4
  stay d. here all night   ACTING 31
  through not d.   DEATH 3
  unconscionable time d.   ROYALTY 20
  unmoved see thee d.   DEATH 20
Dylan being an enigma at D.'s age   SECRECY 10
dynamite Several tons of d.   FILM 1
dysfunctional head of a d. family   ROYALTY 51
  synonyms for d.   NEW YORK 7
dyslexic I'm a d. Satanist   RELIGION 66

eagle soar like an e.   SUCCESS 20
  speak to Mr S. P. E.   NAMES 1
ear cut his e. off   ART 24
  out of your wife's e.   ANIMALS 28
  uncanny e. that might have   WRITERS 38
  wouldn't piss in his e.   ENEMIES 1
earl fourteenth e. is concerned   ARISTOCRACY 10
early came out too e.   RELIGION 56
  E. to rise   DEATH 67
  Rise e.   SUCCESS 10
  think how e. I go   WORK 7
earned you've e. your wrinkles   APPEARANCE 20
earrings e. probably won't last   BUSINESS 11
ears E. like bombs   CHILDREN 10
  No, with my e.   MUSICIANS 11
  That man's e.   FILM STARS 9
earth E. is here so kind   AUSTRALIA 2
  E. was not a rhombus   UNIVERSE 2
  heavy on him, E.   EPITAPHS 12
  meek shall inherit the e.   WEALTH 14

eldest not the e. son   FAMILY 15
elected e. a President, not a Pope   PRESIDENTS 23
  e. to lead, not to read   PRESIDENTS 8
elections E. are won   DEMOCRACY 1
electric biggest e. train set   HOLLYWOOD 20
  e. typewriters keep going   TECHNOLOGY 3
  little e. chairs   RELIGION 12
  mend the E. Light   DEATH 10
electricity e. was dripping invisibly   SCIENCE 26
  paying the e. bill   MEDICINE 2
  usefulness of e.   TECHNOLOGY 1
elegant Economy was always 'e.'   MONEY 14
  e. simplicity   MONEY 26
elementary E., my dear Watson   CRIME 13
elephant e. seal   ANIMALS 33
  life an e.'s   BODY 8
  They couldn't hit an e.   LAST WORDS 10
elephantiasis e. and other dread diseases
        PLACES 10
elephants done the e.   TRAVEL 29
eleven e. at night   DRINK 54
  less than e.-and-a-half days   TIME 7
elf Cheese it is a peevish e.   FOOD 69
  Oh fuck, not another e.!   LITERATURE 14
Elginbrodde Martin E.   EPITAPHS 19
Eliot E.'s standby was Worry   POETS 3
  I'd not read E.   POETS 17
élitist well-known é.   ARISTOCRACY 8
Elizabeth E. Windsor has maintained her dignity
        ROYALTY 49
elms Behind the e. last night   SEX 75
elopement e. would be preferable WEDDINGS 1
else happening to Somebody E.   HUMOUR 30
elsewhere something that happens e.   LIFE 5
elusive One's prime is e.   YOUTH 10
email e. of the species is deadlier COMPUTERS 5
emasculated has not been e. AUTOBIOGRAPHY 15
embalm get some fluid and e. each other
        PARTIES 6
embalmer triumph of the e.'s art   PEOPLE 42
embarrass begins to e. other people
        MIDDLE AGE 3
embarrassing e. pause   MARRIAGE 46
emblem e. of mortality   DEATH 21
embody e. the Law   LAW 12
embrace e. your Lordship's principles INSULTS 47
embracing change the world by e.
      SELF-KNOWLEDGE 12
eminence e. by sheer gravitation SUCCESS 21
éminence cerise é. cerise   ROYALTY 58
emotion poetry is an e.   POETRY 7
emotions gamut of the e.   ACTORS 28
emperor Canadian out of the German E.
        TRANSPORT 37
empire founded the British E.   POLITICS 34

employment known as gainful e.   WORK 1
empresses I don't think much of E. SNOBBERY 9
empty Bring on the e. horses   CINEMA 3
emulate most wanted to e.   WINE 1
encoded e. adjective   TENNIS 1
encouragement sympathy and e. FAMILY 54
end go on till you come to the e. ROYALTY 17
  ignorance that it can ever e.   LOVE 13
  noise at one e.   CHILDREN 23
  Where it will all e., knows God NEWSPAPERS 4
  where's it all going to e.   TIME 16
endangered even as an e. species   LAW 16
  they were an e. species   LOVE 9
ending quickest way of e. a war   WAR 23
ends e. I think criminal   GOVERNMENT 19
  see how it e.   EXAMINATIONS 8
  similar sounds at their e.   POETRY 15
enemies choice of his e.   ENEMIES 9
  conciliates e.   FRIENDS 1
  forgiving one's e.   ENEMIES 8
  hundred e.   HUMOUR 34
  no time for making new e. LAST WORDS 13
  pain it brings to your e.   HONOURS 2
  turning one's e. into money JOURNALISM 5
  wish their e. dead   ENEMIES 5
enemy acute e.   BIOGRAPHY 2
  better class of e.   FRIENDS 9
  book of my e.   WRITERS 17
  e. of good art   MARRIAGE 41
  hasn't an e.   FRIENDS 17
  men will have upon the e.   WAR 29
  Morrison was his own worst e. POLITICIANS 11
  sleeps with the e.   MARRIAGE 5
  your e. and your friend   FRIENDS 15
engaged now I'm e.   MEN AND WOMEN 4
engagement e. should come MARRIAGE 124
  sort of eternal e.   MARRIAGE 10
engine e. [a watch] to our ears TECHNOLOGY 15
  e. in boots   SPORTS 14
  e. of pollution   DOGS 5
  e. that moves   TRANSPORT 16
England amusements in E.   ENGLAND 34
  between E. and Christianity RELIGION 60
  dowdiness in E.   ENGLAND 29
  E. and America   COUNTRIES 34
  E. did for cricket   CRICKET 8
  expect to convert E.   RELIGION 53
  Good evening, E.   ENGLAND 25
  he bored for E.   BORES 13
  I left E. when I was four   ROYALTY 41
  in E. a particular bashfulness RELIGION 1
  road that leads him to E.   SCOTLAND 5
  stately homos of E.   SEX 34
  summer in E.   WEATHER 22

essential e. ingredient — MARRIAGE 94
  only item of e. equipment — MARRIAGE 89
esses so many e. in it — NAMES 15
establishment forelock to the British e. — SNOBBERY 10
estate dealing with e. workers — CLASS 12
  good e. agent — HOME 8
eternal concept of an e. mother — ROYALTY 27
eternity equation is something for e. — SCIENCE 13
  E.'s a terrible thought — TIME 16
  some conception of e. — CRICKET 12
ethics yob e. — FOOTBALL 28
Ethiopia concern for the people of E. — SONGS 16
etiquette E., sacred subject — BEHAVIOUR 22
  E. (and quiet, well-cut clothes) — RELIGION 48
  It isn't e. — BEHAVIOUR 5
Eton hoidays from E. — EDUCATION 38
Etonians Hail him like E. — SOCIETY 15
eunuch e. and a snigger — CLERGY 7
eunuchs Critics are like e. — CRITICS 6
  seraglio of e. — POLITICS 27
euphemism keep the . . . e. — WORDS 1
  lateral e. — TENNIS 1
euphemisms E. are unpleasant truths — WORDS 11
Euripides Mr E. was guilty — PREJUDICE 5
Europe In E., when a rich woman — MEN AND WOMEN 57
  length and breadth of E. — TRAVEL 2
evacuated e. children — CHRISTMAS 2
even e. terror of their lives — PREJUDICE 14
evenings do with the long winter e. — WRITERS 9
  exciting e. — HOLIDAYS 7
  Shouting in the e. — ACTING 35
eventide perfect e. home — OLD AGE 40
ever Well, did you e. — MARRIAGE 96
every Climb e. Mountie — CANADA 9
  E. thinking man — POLITICS 2
everybody e. is ignorant — IGNORANCE 6
everyone e. else has — ACTORS 13
everything get e. — MARRIAGE 119
  Macaulay is of e. — CERTAINTY 19
evidence abstains from giving us wordy e. — CONVERSATION 11
  circumstantial e. is very strong — LAW 35
  e. of life after death — POLITICS 64
  it's not e. — LAW 6
evil don't think that he's e. — GOD 1
  e. reptilian kitten-eater — POLITICIANS 1
  we must return good for e. — MORALITY 14
evils Between two e. — VIRTUE 22
  greatest of e. — POVERTY 16
exaggerated greatly e. — DEATH 69
examination at issue in an e. — EXAMINATIONS 1
  like an e. — BIBLE 7
examined needs to have his hod e. — ART 21

examiners than my e. — EXAMINATIONS 4
example annoyance of a good e. — CHARACTER 17
  don't set a good e. — CLASS 33
  not as an e. — PARENTS 15
  pretty e. — EDUCATION 48
  vivid e. — GENERATION GAP 14
exams rigorous judging e. — JUDGES 7
exception glad to make an e. — INSULTS 26
excess Nothing succeeds like e. — SUCCESS 25
excise e.. A hateful tax — TAXES 4
exclusive not mutually e. — MANAGEMENT 5
  put e. on the weather — NEWSPAPERS 14
excuse E. My Dust — EPITAPHS 23
excuses Several e. — ARGUMENT 11
execution e. of a senior colleague — POLITICS 20
exercise don't take enough e. — HEALTH 17
  E. is the yuppie version — HEALTH 5
  who took e. — HEALTH 10
exercises two best e. — HEALTH 3
exertion e. is too much — HUMOUR 29
exhausted e. all other alternatives — HISTORY 7
  e. volcanoes — DESCRIPTION 14
exhaustion pudding of e. — OLD AGE 32
exist God does e. — GOD 22
  He doesn't e. — GOD 9
  right to e. — AMERICA 2
  that He doesn't e. — GOD 38
existed if he e. — GOD 35
existence all e. in an epigram — WIT 52
  e. of Lord Beaverbrook — PEOPLE 43
exit E., *pursued by a bear* — THEATRE 47
  graceful e. — BEHAVIOUR 16
expands Work e. to fill the time — WORK 22
expected e. better manners — BEHAVIOUR 9
expects e. nothing — HOPE 9
  e. the Spanish Inquisition — COMEDY 34
  what one e. from others — BEHAVIOUR 37
expenditure annual e., nineteen nineteen six — MONEY 9
  E. rises to meet income — ECONOMICS 13
expense e. of two — GOD 19
expenses all e. paid — HOLIDAYS 1
  facts are on e. — JOURNALISM 21
expensive court is just an e. habit — LAW 31
  e. it is to be poor — POVERTY 2
expensively e. humiliated — MIND 4
experience e. has taught me — SELF-KNOWLEDGE 9
  e. will be a lesson — MARRIAGE 3
  some legal e. — FAMILY 23
  triumph of hope over e. — MARRIAGE 76
  we need not e. it — TECHNOLOGY 6
experimented e. with marijuana — DRUGS 4
expert against the educated e. — LAW 36

explain e. why it didn't happen — POLITICIANS 14
explaining e. things — GENERATION GAP 5
  lot of e. to do — MURDER 5
explanation e. of everything — CERTAINTY 24
  tons of e. — LIES 10
exploded immediately e. — TRAVEL 8
explored e. the further reaches — MARRIAGE 8
exposed his intellect is improperly e. — MIND 13
express caught the down e. — DESCRIPTION 32
expression brain and his e. — HUMOUR 6
  inarticulate human e. — SPORTS 21
extensive delightfully e. — HOME 1
exterior this flabby e. — SELF-KNOWLEDGE 18
exterminator your e. called — ADVERTISING 1
extinct I am e. — OLD AGE 39
extinction total e. — CHOICE 1
extremity gone to the other e. — WIT 15
exuberance e. of his own verbosity — INSULTS 13
eye already lost one e. — CRIME 2
  anywhere if you have the e. — QUOTATIONS 8
  close one e. — FRIENDS 7
  e. that can open an oyster — DESCRIPTION 34
  God caught his e. — EPITAPHS 20
  had but one e. — BODY 13
  less in this than meets the e. — THEATRE 5
  one's e. for the high birds — POLITICIANS 18
  painter's e. — ART 10
  spoils one's e. — CRICKET 11
  unforgiving e. — CHARACTER 12
eyeballs two e. — FOOD 86
eyebrow Left e. raised — ACTING 22
eyebrows Kipling's e. — DESCRIPTION 23
  tried to shave off my e. once — FACES 7
eyes close your e. — SEX 16
  e. are like the prairie — AMERICA 5
  e. wide open before marriage — MARRIAGE 54
  in some people's e. — MORALITY 3
  those blue e. — FILM STARS 11
eyesight man with exceptionally good e.
— SONGS 21

face can't think of your f. — NAMES 29
  especially my f. — FACES 10
  f. looks like a wedding cake — FACES 3
  f. of a Venus — ACTORS 2
  f. was that wrinkled — FACES 8
  had the sort of f. — FACES 5
  hear my Thisby's f. — WIT 31
  I never forget a f. — INSULTS 26
  My advice is to keep your f. — MIDDLE AGE 5
  take care of your f. — FOOTBALL 15
faces everybody's f. — ART 11
  older f. — HOSPITALITY 5

fact any f., no matter how suspect — PAST 13
  F. — COMEDY 11
  terrifying f. about old people — OLD AGE 34
  trifling investment of f. — SCIENCE 27
factories f. would close down — CLASS 34
factory pubic hair f. — DESCRIPTION 21
facts f. are on expenses — JOURNALISM 21
  Get your f. first — TRUTH 10
  politics consists in ignoring f. — POLITICS 3
factual truthful than f. — HUMOUR 28
faded beauty am f. — APPEARANCE 14
fag want a f. with a pussy — MARRIAGE 60
fail try to f. better — FAILURE 1
failed f. his practical — EXAMINATIONS 3
  I don't think we have f. — FAILURE 4
  men who have f. — CRITICS 10
  possibilities had f. — CHARACTER 1
  you f. miserably — FAILURE 6
failure been a f. in life — FAILURE 8
  f. he is one of God's children — SUCCESS 16
  f. may be your style — FAILURE 3
  twentieth-century f. — SUCCESS 5
faint when you're f. — FOOD 16
fair If it prove f. weather — LOVE 42
  set f. — PRIDE 1
  short-legged sex the f. sex — MEN AND WOMEN 47
Fairbanks April in F. — WEATHER 10
fairy loves a f. when she's forty — MIDDLE AGE 7
faith great act of f. — GOD 27
  It's a jolly friendly f. — RELIGION 25
  lost his f. again — CERTAINTY 11
faithful seldom strictly f. — MARRIAGE 27
fake yours is a f. — HAPPINESS 8
fall chance that you will f. out — MISTAKES 4
  Did he f. or was he pushed — DEATH 35
  further they have to f. — BOXING 5
  Let's f. in love — COUNTRIES 28
  walk brusquely away I f. over — BODY 17
falls F. with the leaf — DRINK 26
false produces a f. impression — BEHAVIOUR 36
falsehoods furbish f. — JOURNALISM 6
falter moment that you f. — POLITICS 16
fame best f. — FAME 16
  F. is like V.D. — FAME 23
  f.'s eternal — FAME 8
  Physicians of the Utmost F. — MEDICINE 6
familiar f. surroundings — HOLIDAYS 4
familiarity F. breeds contempt — FAMILY 50
families antediluvian f. — CLASS 7
  best-regulated f. — FAMILY 12
  happy f. — FAMILY 49
  mothers of large f. — ANIMALS 6
family bunker of the f. — CHRISTMAS 12
  decencies of f. life — FAMILY 52
  f. can join in — FAMILY 20

family (*cont.*):

head of a dysfunctional f.	ROYALTY 51
his f. was not unworthy	PRIDE 3
little less intellect in the f.	INTELLIGENCE 12
loving, caring, close-knit f.	FAMILY 6
man who left his f.	BOOKS 19
spend more time with my f.	FAMILY 33
Starting a f. tree together	MARRIAGE 64
very large f.	FAMILY 30
when anyone left the Royal f.	ROYALTY 67

famine Geldof is such an expert on f.

	MUSICIANS 6

famous he'll be rich, or f.	JOURNALISM 14
I'll be f.	NAMES 21
world f.	CANADA 8
fan duties of the f.	BASEBALL 1
no greater f. than I	MEN AND WOMEN 25
president of his own f. club	ARGUMENT 2
state of the football f.	FOOTBALL 14
fanatics f. are on top	GOVERNMENT 25
fancy young man's f.	LOVE 22
Fanny doughnuts like F.'s	COOKERY 7
fans baseball f.	BASEBALL 4
fantastics grittiness of *The F.*	SONGS 20
fantasy possesses himself of a f.	JOURNALISM 24
far took it all too f.	MUSICIANS 19
You can see as f. as Marlow	MISTAKES 11
you're never f. from home	WEALTH 22
farce nothing about f.	HUMOUR 24
wine was a f.	FOOD 66
farces Ridiculous f.	THEATRE 19
farm f. is an irregular patch	COUNTRY 15
Nixon's f. policy is vague	SPEECHES 19
farmer being a f.	BODY 19
F. will never be happy	COUNTRY 9
finding a f.'s daughter	WORDS 6
farming F. is so charming	COUNTRY 16
fart can't f. and chew gum	INSULTS 20
Love is the f.	LOVE 43
fashion follower of f.	FASHION 5
in and out of f.	FAME 3
fashions fit this year's f.	POLITICS 32
fast f.-forward button	HISTORY 16
Isn't it a little f.	ARMED FORCES 21
None so f. as stroke	SPORTS 9
Stealing too f.	BUSINESS 16
will not f. in peace	POVERTY 3
faster run far f. than the rest	BETTING 1
fastest f. time ever run	SPORTS 11
fastidiousness f. a quality useful	POLITICS 38
fat addicted to f.	DIETS 2
cheerful, f. missionary	SECURITY 7
f. and proud to be fat	DIETS 4
f. greedy owl	CHILDREN 35
if you're f., is a minefield	DIETS 6

in every f. man	BODY 11
in which their f. was fried	WEDDINGS 3
Is Elizabeth Taylor f.	DIETS 7
'til the f. lady sings	OPERA 2
fatal deal of it is absolutely f.	VIRTUE 25
I am a f. man	MEN AND WOMEN 55
fate f. became a cert	BIRDS 6
F. cannot harm me	FOOD 75
F. was quietly slipping the lead	MISTAKES 32
f. worse than marriage	MARRIAGE 10
F. wrote her a most tremendous	ROYALTY 14
I have a bone to pick with f.	MIDDLE AGE 10
father as a rapper than you are as a f.	PARENTS 6
bastard on F.'s Day	HAPPINESS 2
bed fell on my f.	FAMILY 48
called F. by everyone	CLERGY 1
either my f. or my mother	PARENTS 16
f. had an accident	ANIMALS 34
f.'s an actor	BEHAVIOUR 13
f. told me all about	SEX 47
f. was a dragon	FAMILY 35
f. was so ignorant	GENERATION GAP 13
gave her f. forty-one	MURDER 1
poor f. used to say	ART 15
whistle your f.	FAMILY 3
wise f.	FAMILY 38
You are old, F. William	OLD AGE 7
your f. whom you love, dies	THEATRE 53
fathers F. don't curse	PARENTS 9
My f. can have it	WALES 5
fathom f. the inscrutable	ARGUMENT 17
fattening immoral, or f.	HAPPINESS 18
fault anybody's f.	EDUCATION 29
no f. or flaw	LAW 12
faute *F. de* what	LANGUAGES 29
fava with some f. beans	FOOD 33
favour count in their f.	MISTAKES 21
in f. iv dhrink	DRINK 20
favourite second f. organ	BODY 1
fax fox from a f.-machine	COUNTRY 4
faxed proposal which my secretary f.	LOVE 15
FBI F. and the CIA	BIOGRAPHY 3
F. are powerless	SEX 46
fear At first, you f. you will die	TRAVEL 18
constipation is the big f.	SICKNESS 14
f. of the Law	RELIGION 32
feast Marriage is a f.	MARRIAGE 35
feather writes with a f.	THEATRE 22
feather-footed F. through the plashy fen	
	LANGUAGE 10
feathers three white f.	CLASS 9
February not Puritanism but F.	WEATHER 13
fecund first-rate, the f. rate	WRITING 17
fee small f. in America	AMERICA 21
feed F. the brute	MARRIAGE 98

finer for the f. folk   CLASS 20
finest f. bloody fast bowler   CRICKET 19
  f. wines available to humanity   DRINK 51
  this is our f. shower   SEX 70
finger I lift up my f.   SONGS 18
  little f. to become longer   MUSIC 48
  looking at your f.   FAME 24
  what chills the f. not a bit   SATISFACTION 12
fingernails biting your f.   MISTAKES 25
  finished the f.   FILM 11
finish draw right to the f.   DEATH 34
  start together and f. together   MUSIC 8
  until I f. talking   MANAGEMENT 10
finished f. in half the time   FAMILY 54
  Then he's f.   MARRIAGE 58
Finland worst food after F.   COOKERY 6
fire f., a little food   HOSPITALITY 4
  f. has gone out   OLD AGE 14
  other irons in the f.   PUBLISHING 1
  shouted 'F.'   LIES 4
  supplied the f. themselves   WEDDINGS 4
  write for the f.   WRITING 4
Firenze COUGHING MYSELF INTO A F.   TELEGRAMS 8
fireside by his own f.   HOME 15
firing faced the f. squad   CHARACTER 16
first f. class, and with children   TRAVEL 1
  f. one's the hardest   MARRIAGE 116
  f. ten million years   PAST 1
  never been born the f. time   RELIGION 73
  to mistake for the f.-rate   WRITING 17
fish came up with the f.   FOOD 47
  f. are having their revenge   ANIMALS 11
  f. needs a bicycle   WOMEN 14
  He eats a lot of f.   INTELLIGENCE 16
  like f. into a letterbox   FILM PRODUCERS 12
  no self-respecting f.   NEWSPAPERS 18
  Not a fatter f. than he   ROYALTY 43
  surrounded by f.   BUREAUCRACY 3
  throw her a f.   ACTORS 31
fishes Luca Brasi sleeps with the f.   DEATH 58
fishing 'angling' is the name given to f.
                                          FISHING 5
  angling or float f.   FISHING 4
  F. is a form of madness   FISHING 3
  f. is a religion   FISHING 1
fish-knives Phone for the f., Norman   SOCIETY 4
fishy f. about the French   FRANCE 2
fit It isn't f. for humans now   TOWNS 7
five breakfast every f. minutes   OLD AGE 19
  count to f.   ANGER 3
  f.-day weekend   WORK 24
  I have wedded f.   MARRIAGE 29
fiver No woman is worth more than a f.   LOVE 32
fix coming to f. the show   WIT 17
  only sport you can't f.   SPORTS 22

fjord Betty F. Clinic   DRINK 60
flag High as a f.   AMERICA 13
flakes long streamy f. of music   DESCRIPTION 20
flamingo very large f.   DEBT 7
flared copiously f.   DRESS 1
flashes f. of silence   CONVERSATION 27
flat Fell half so f.   CRITICS 2
  how f. he really did want it   SONGS 2
  just how f. and empty   PLACES 3
  Very f., Norfolk   PLACES 6
flats can't walk in f.   FASHION 8
flatter they'd be rather f.   COUNTRIES 37
flattered f. by the censorship   CENSORSHIP 15
flattering you think him worth f.   PRAISE 8
flattery Everyone likes f.   ROYALTY 24
  f. hurts no one   PRAISE 10
  give them f.   ART 35
  what your f. is worth   PRAISE 5
flaunt f. it   COMEDY 23
flavour spearmint lose its f.   FOOD 70
flaw f. in any argument   ARGUMENT 15
  no fault or f.   LAW 12
flea between a louse and a f.   POETS 12
fleas Even educated f. do it   SEX 73
  reasonable amount o' f.   DOGS 7
  smaller f. to bite 'em   ANIMALS 38
fleet F.'s lit up   DRINK 64
Fleet-street F. has a very animated appearance
                                          TOWNS 19
flesh delicate white human f.   LOVE 14
  have more f.   BODY 40
  makes man and wife one f.   MARRIAGE 38
flies you leave our f. alone   CRICKET 1
flood f. could not wash away   CLASS 7
flooded STREETS F. PLEASE ADVISE   TELEGRAMS 3
floor lie on the f.   DRINK 40
  put f. on the floor   HEALTH 13
  table near the f.   FOOD 48
floozie f. in the jacuzzi   ARCHITECTURE 1
flopping f. yourself down   FAMILY 10
floppy weak, f. thing in the chair
                                          PRIME MINISTERS 25
flower try f. arrangement   SPORTS 4
flowers Beware of men bearing f.
                                          MEN AND WOMEN 53
  silk suit who sends f.   FILM PRODUCERS 8
  smelling f.   HEALTH 7
  wild f., and Prime Ministers   POLITICS 8
flu Beware of f.   THEATRE 33
fluid get some f. and embalm each other
                                          PARTIES 6
fly f. to attempt to cross it   FACES 6
  f. which had been trained   HANDWRITING 1
  made the f.   ANIMALS 29

show the f. the way out — PHILOSOPHY 11
with an open f. — FILM PRODUCERS 20
foal f. and broodmare — WEATHER 1
foam amber f. — FOOD 26
focus f. on my salad — COOKERY 20
foe find a f. — FRIENDS 10
fogs insular country subject to f. — POLITICS 26
foible omniscience is his f. — INSULTS 41
fold f. it over and put it — ECONOMICS 10
Folies-Bergère goes to the F. — MEDICINE 36
folk All music is f. music — MUSIC 2
incest and f.-dancing — SEX 9
you know 600 f. songs — MUSICIANS 26
folks W'en f. git ole — OLD AGE 23
follies author's f. — AUTOBIOGRAPHY 5
f. which a man regrets most — MEN 13
My f. are intact — OLD AGE 22
follow F. the van — HOME 3
follower f. of fashion — FASHION 5
follows lie f. — BEHAVIOUR 27
folly f. of 'Woman's Rights' — WOMEN 65
f.'s all they've taught me — WOMEN 42
woman stoops to f. — WOMEN 22
Fondas Henry F. lay on the evening — DESCRIPTION 11
font be done with a f. — RELIGION 34
portable, second-hand f. — CLERGY 12
food aftertaste of foreign f. — DRINK 14
alcohol was a f. — DRINK 63
favourite f. is seconds — DIETS 7
f. a tragedy — FOOD 66
f. enough for a week — BIRDS 7
f. I ate and not the show — SLEEP 4
f. is more dangerous — FOOD 49
It was the f. — DEATH 29
problem is f. — MONEY 10
worst f. after Finland — COOKERY 6
fool every f. is not a poet — POETS 16
f. and his money — GAMBLING 5
f. and his wife — COUNTRY 15
f. at the other — FISHING 4
f.'s paradise — FOOLISHNESS 8
f. with booze — DRINK 21
I'm just a f. — WOMEN 27
let a kiss f. you — FOOLISHNESS 6
Prove to me that you're no f. — RELIGION 55
that does not marry a f. — MARRIAGE 131
without being a f. — FOOLISHNESS 15
foolish He never said a f. thing — ROYALTY 56
most f. people — NEW YORK 3
saying a f. thing — FOOLISHNESS 14
foolproof f. items — FOOLISHNESS 3
fools all the f. in town — FOOLISHNESS 17
f. of gardeners — GARDENS 9
leaves 'em still two f. — MARRIAGE 38

see these poor f. decoyed — MARRIAGE 93
the small ones f. — WRITERS 34
tolerate f. — FOOLISHNESS 1
foot caught my f. in the mat — MISTAKES 15
F.-in-the-grave — MEN 7
Forty-second F. — ARMED FORCES 16
One square f. less — ARCHITECTURE 2
silver f. in his mouth — PRESIDENTS 18
football become a f. referee — FOOTBALL 13
F., wherein is — FOOTBALL 11
F. and cookery — FOOTBALL 27
f. crazy — FOOTBALL 19
F. is a simple game — FOOTBALL 18
F.'s football — FOOTBALL 7
go to the f. — MEN 4
like he does a f. — FOOTBALL 9
Never mind f. — DEMOCRACY 7
no longer be a f. — FOOTBALL 8
playing f. is a lot easier — FOOTBALL 31
Queen Mother of f. — FOOTBALL 25
spell f., never mind understand it — FOOTBALL 16
state of the f. fan — FOOTBALL 14
think f. is a matter — FOOTBALL 24
when I played f. — FOOTBALL 15
footballers professional f. — FOOTBALL 28
footnotes f. to Plato — PHILOSOPHY 10
footprint looking for a man's f. — WOMEN 2
forbids if the law f. it — LAW 23
force fasteners do not respond to f. — POWER 12
Other nations use f. — ENGLAND 40
ford I mean John F. — FILM PRODUCERS 16
fore shout 'F.' when — GOLF 4
foreign aftertaste of f. food — DRINK 14
contempt for every thing f. — COUNTRIES 4
f. conductors — MUSIC 6
f. picture award — FILM PRODUCERS 17
in a f. language — PARENTS 12
foreigner lost on the f. — HUMOUR 37
foreigners f. always spell better — LANGUAGES 25
f. are fiends — COUNTRIES 27
forelock tugged the f. — SNOBBERY 10
foreseen no doubt have f. — FUTURE 13
forest f. laments — PRIME MINISTERS 10
foretell f. what is going to happen — POLITICIANS 14
forever safire bracelet lasts f. — AMERICA 20
forget f. about it in the morning — RETIREMENT 4
I never f. a face — INSULTS 26
I sometimes f. — ROYALTY 25
forgetting f. you've slept with — SEX 84
forgive do they f. them — CHILDREN 46
F., O Lord — GOD 24
good Lord will f. me — ROYALTY 18
never quite f. the British — COUNTRIES 16
forgiving f. one's enemies — ENEMIES 8
forgot f. to tell us why — ANIMALS 29

forgotten America he had f.   WRITERS 44
Byron!—he would be all f.   PEOPLE 8
when you have f.   EDUCATION 4
fork using a f.   BEHAVIOUR 3
formula destroy 'the f.'   IGNORANCE 4
Forster F. never gets any further   WRITERS 23
forte Science is his f.   INSULTS 41
Fortier Ms F. ate Mr Blunkett   FOOD 95
fortissimo F. at last   MUSIC 34
fortunate should have been more f.   NAMES 19
fortune beauty without a f.   WOMEN 16
f. empties her chamberpot   SATISFACTION 10
good f. to others   MISTAKES 8
in possession of a good f.   MARRIAGE 9
little value of f.   WEALTH 29
rob a lady of her f.   MARRIAGE 53
forty 20 to f. is the fillet steak   MIDDLE AGE 8
At f. I lost my illusions   OLD AGE 22
f.-nine plus VAT   MIDDLE AGE 4
loves a fairy when she's f.   MIDDLE AGE 7
one passes f.   MIDDLE AGE 11
forty-three pass for f.   WOMEN 20
forward looking f. to the past   PAST 10
foul really f. things up   COMPUTERS 1
founding f. a bank   CRIME 5
fountain f.-pen filler   GOSSIP 7
four at the age of f.   ARMED FORCES 30
Company of F.   THEATRE 61
count f.   ANGER 10
F. legs good   ANIMALS 32
f.-letter words   WORDS 30
fourteen Wilson requires F. Points   PRESIDENTS 4
fourteenth f. Mr Wilson   ARISTOCRACY 10
fourth full of f.-rate writers   READING 1
third and f. class   SNOBBERY 7
fowl liver-wing of a f.   HONOURS 9
fowls f. for dissenters   FOOD 76
fox Brer F., he lay low   ANIMALS 15
f. from a fax-machine   COUNTRY 4
gentlemen galloping after a f.   SPORTS 41
I loves the f. less   SPORTS 35
metaphysical f.   CONVERSATION 29
They've shot our f.   POLITICS 13
foxed was even almost f.   WINE 5
fox-hunting inferior forms of f.   SPORTS 39
prefer f.   POLITICAL PARTIES 9
fragrant would be very f.   ARISTOCRACY 8
frailty therefore more f.   BODY 40
framed f. and glazed   WEATHER 22
France better in F.   FRANCE 9
Everything is easier in F.   BUREAUCRACY 12
F. is a country   FRANCE 11
F. is the only place   FRANCE 1
Francesca di Rimini F., miminy, piminy   MEN 6
Francis Like dear St F.   POVERTY 24

frank many f. words   DIPLOMACY 3
Frankenstein F. get married   EDUCATION 47
frankly F., my dear   SATISFACTION 7
frappé now completely f.   CHILDREN 20
Frazier F. is so ugly   FACES 1
freckles Love, curiosity, f., and doubt   LOVE 36
Fred Here lies F.   EPITAPHS 5
free bring it to you, f.   DEATH 4
favours f. speech   CENSORSHIP 4
f. in America   AMERICA 21
F. your mind   DIETS 8
I'd as soon write f. verse   POETRY 11
I'm f.   COMEDY 26
in favour of f. expression   CENSORSHIP 3
This is a f. country   BEHAVIOUR 31
freedom achieve fuller f.   CENSORSHIP 16
as f. fries   WORDS 3
fight for f.   DRESS 8
F. of the press   CENSORSHIP 9
F. of the press in Britain   NEWSPAPERS 24
I gave my life for f.   WAR 11
vacant f.   PROGRESS 13
freemasonry have a kind of bitter f.   LOVE 3
freeway f. is . . . the place   TRANSPORT 3
French answering you in F.   FRANCE 7
Englishman is about to talk F.   LANGUAGES 28
fishy about the F.   FRANCE 2
F., they say, live to eat   FOOD 1
F. are always too wordy   FRANCE 6
F. are awful   FRANCE 10
F. are masters   DIPLOMACY 11
F./British relationship   DIPLOMACY 9
F. for bullshit   WORDS 23
F. fry potatoes   WORDS 3
F. of Parys   WOMEN 7
F. Revolution   FAMILY 52
F. went in   COUNTRIES 25
F. widow in every bedroom   HOTELS 4
hate the F.   FRANCE 4
how it's improved her F.   LANGUAGES 13
much more in F.   CENSORSHIP 5
not too F. French bean   ART 12
reading a F. novel   CRITICS 21
serve the F.   FOOD 8
Speak in F.   LANGUAGES 8
speaking F. fluently   LANGUAGES 9
trouble with the F.   LANGUAGES 6
Frenchmen fifty million F.   FOOD 65
What asses these F. are   LANGUAGES 29
frenzy f. closely related to delirium   WRITING 14
Freud investigations of Herr F.   ART 19
trouble with F.   HUMOUR 11
Freudian F. nightmare   FAMILY 31
friction f. threatening   WAR 33
fridge in the f.   AWARDS 4

furniture (*cont.*):
rearrange the f.   POLITICS 49
twice as much f.   HOME 17
furs f. the jewels, the glamour   WEALTH 16
further explored the f. reaches   MARRIAGE 8
f. they have to fall   BOXING 5
f. you got from Britain   POLITICIANS 13
furtive look of f. shame   LANGUAGES 28
fury beastly f.   FOOTBALL 11
fuss insufficient f.   SATISFACTION 15
fustian whose f.'s so sublimely bad   POETRY 20
future about the f.   AUTOBIOGRAPHY 21
bridge to the f.   FUTURE 11
especially about the f.   FUTURE 3
f. for Russian humorists   RUSSIA 5
f. looks dark indeed   WRITERS 7
f. refusing   FUTURE 1
Garlic bread—it's the f.   FOOD 38
never think of the f.   FUTURE 6

Gabriel Archangel G.   DEMOCRACY 2
enough for the Archangel G.   PRIME MINISTERS 13
So blow, G., blow   RELIGION 52
Gaelic something under its breath in G.   DOGS 8
gaffe terrible social g.   PARTIES 7
gaiety g. is a striped shroud   WALES 6
gaily G. into Ruislip Gardens   SOCIETY 5
gainful happily known as g. employment   WORK 1
gaining Something may be g.   BASEBALL 11
Galatians text in G.   BIBLE 1
galaxy smart alecksy, With the g.   PROGRESS 10
gallant Stop being g.   THEATRE 15
gallantry What men call g.   SEX 29
galleon Stately as a g.   DANCE 7
galloping g. consumption you had   SICKNESS 3
gallows upon the g. or of the pox   INSULTS 47
galoshes vest and g.   CHARACTER 14
gamble Life is a g.   LIFE 16
gamblers g. are as happy   GAMBLING 1
game Anarchism is a g.   POLITICS 61
g. at which only one   EDUCATION 28
g. which takes less   BASEBALL 13
latest popular g.   FAMILY 20
no g. from bridge to cricket   SPORTS 20
only a g.   BASEBALL 14
parody is a g.   WIT 25
Take me out to the ball g.   BASEBALL 10
wouldn't be the g. it is   FOOTBALL 7
gamekeeper life of an English g.   CRITICS 3
gamut g. of the emotions   ACTORS 28
Gandhi [G.] knew the cost   POVERTY 12
gap g. between Dorothy and Chopin   MUSICIANS 1
garbage week of the g. strike   APPEARANCE 17
garbled Rather g.   MARRIAGE 44

Garbo unwelcoming Greta G.   MEN AND WOMEN 33
garden g., however small   GARDENS 2
led up the g. path   DIPLOMACY 1
man and a woman in a g.   BIBLE 8
gardener not a dirt g.   GARDENS 1
gardeners fools of g.   GARDENS 9
grim g.   GARDENS 11
garlic clove of g. round my neck   POLITICIANS 25
G. bread—it's the future   FOOD 38
gas as if I had g. on the stomach   MUSIC 28
G. smells awful   DEATH 54
Had silicon been a g.   EXAMINATIONS 7
gate A-sitting on a g.   OLD AGE 8
gathering intransitive operation of g.   WIT 26
gauze shoot her through g.   FILM STARS 2
gay g. or not   FOOTBALL 21
Glitter and be g.   WOMEN 69
I think that g. marriage   MARRIAGE 103
support g. marriage   MARRIAGE 56
gazelle love a dear g.   MONEY 7
geeks Beware g. bearing scripts   FILM 2
geisha Get yourself a G.   COUNTRIES 14
Geldof G. is such an expert on famine   MUSICIANS 6
gender get My g. right   GOD 7
general g. called Anthea   MEN AND WOMEN 34
G. was essentially   ARMED FORCES 31
host is like a g.   HOSPITALITY 6
generals my other g.   ARMED FORCES 10
we're all G.   ARMED FORCES 30
generation g. of English   DRUGS 6
Poland to polo in one g.   SNOBBERY 5
generations g. of inbreeding   BEHAVIOUR 18
Genghis map of the world to G. Khan   ECONOMICS 11
geniality g. of the politician   POLITICIANS 24
genitals actresses do make my g. quiver   THEATRE 27
breaking my g.   HAPPINESS 3
G. are a great distraction   SEX 24
genius G. is one percent inspiration   INTELLIGENCE 6
g. with the IQ of a moron   ART 39
Men of g. are so few   INTELLIGENCE 3
nothing to declare except my g.   INTELLIGENCE 15
stronger than g.   BORES 4
talent and g.   INTELLIGENCE 9
geniuses g. are devoid of humour   SPEECHES 18
gentiles big meetings with important g.   FILM PRODUCERS 2
gentleman being a g.   CLASS 30
Every other inch a g.   INSULTS 45
g. falls in love   COUNTRY 13
g. never eats   CLASS 1
He's a g.   CLASS 27

government (*cont.*):

g. get out of war	WAR 14
G. I despise	GOVERNMENT 19
g. of laws	GOVERNMENT 18
man who understands g.	POLITICIANS 32
no g. in history	JOURNALISM 18
no law or g.	GOVERNMENT 2
Overthrow the G.	AMERICA 15
they want Irish g.	IRELAND 6
weather is like the G.	WEATHER 11

governor *Stewart* for g. — FILM STARS 15
goyim g. Annoy 'im — GOD 6
grabs Benn g. child — HEADLINES 8
grace does it with a better g. — FOOLISHNESS 12
  g. is sometimes better — MARRIAGE 35
  There but for the g. of God — POLITICIANS 15
graceful g. exit — BEHAVIOUR 16
Gracie goodnight, G. — COMEDY 15
gracious Goodness g. me — TITLES 5
grades into four g. — EDUCATION 43
graffiti No g. — COUNTRIES 19
grammar don't want to talk g. — CLASS 26
  self-made g. school lass — POLITICAL PARTIES 14
  talking bad g. — LAST WORDS 1
Grammarians Conan the G. — EDUCATION 26
grammatical seven g. errors — EPITAPHS 10
grand Ain't it g. — DEATH 63
  doing a g. job — COMEDY 44
  g. enough to be asked there — ROYALTY 30
Grand Canyon rose petal down the G. — POETRY 16
grandchild fourteenth g. — CHILDREN 43
granddaughter seventh g. — CHILDREN 43
grandeur prose of incomparable g. — WRITERS 21
grandiose taste for the g. — ARCHITECTURE 10
grandma It was good enough for G. — WOMEN 28
grandmother g. took a bath — BEHAVIOUR 2
  We have become a g. — FAMILY 45
granite breasts like g. — FILM STARS 18
grape how to jump on a g. — COUNTRIES 9
  peel me a g. — FOOD 87
grapes Defectors are like g. — TRUST 10
  man who has lost his g. — SELF-KNOWLEDGE 23
grass Keep off the g. — EPITAPHS 27
  shit on g. — FOOTBALL 26
grassed I just g. on him — TELEVISION 11
gratitude G. is not a normal feature — POLITICS 37
gratuitous is the most g. — AUTOBIOGRAPHY 20
grave g. in a Y-shaped coffin — SEX 67
  g. yawns for him — BORES 17
  kind of healthy g. — COUNTRY 18
graves g. of little magazines — POETRY 21
  look at the g. — BUSINESS 15
gravitation eminence by sheer g. — SUCCESS 21
gravy chicken and g. — FOOD 54
  It's the rich wot gets the g. — POVERTY 1

greasy toad in an equally g. hole — FOOD 57
great All my shows are g. — SELF-KNOWLEDGE 13
  feeling that he is g. — JUDGES 4
  g. being a priest — CLERGY 13
  Leonard, we know you're g. — SONGS 23
  some men are born g. — PRIDE 5
  think him *g.* — BORES 8
  Whenever he met a g. man — SNOBBERY 13
greater G. love — FRIENDS 14
greatly g. to his credit — ENGLAND 12
greatness g. thrust upon them — PRIDE 5
greed G. is right — ECONOMICS 15
  swallow with g. — COUNTRIES 10
greedy like a g. shark — CONVERSATION 15
Greek half G., half Latin — TELEVISION 10
  is G. for 'men'. — WORDS 24
  No G.; as much Latin — QUOTATIONS 6
  only G. Tragedy I know — PEOPLE 45
  original G. — CRITICS 31
green big g. one out there — FOOTBALL 30
  dyeing their hair g. — GENERATION GAP 7
  g. about the gills — DRUGS 5
  g. belt was a labour idea — NATURE 8
  G. with lust — ROYALTY 15
  just as g. — GARDENS 5
greenery mountain g. — COUNTRY 7
greenery-yallery g., Grosvenor Gallery — MEN 7
greenfly dosing the g. — GARDENS 8
greenroom hang about the g. — POLITICS 43
grew when I g. up — GENERATION GAP 14
grey seemed a g. crew — GENERATION GAP 8
grief used for augmenting g. — SONGS 1
grievance Scotsman with a g. — SCOTLAND 12
grieve will g. a month — EPITAPHS 25
grind My life is one demd horrid g. — WORK 12
grittiness g. of the Fantastics — SONGS 20
grocer expect a g. to write — WRITERS 6
  photograph of the G. — DIPLOMACY 16
groom abrupt disappearance of the g. — WEDDINGS 12
  Including the bride and g. — WEDDINGS 9
  She made the g. — ROYALTY 55
grooves In predestinate g. — TRANSPORT 16
groovy g. baby, yeah — COMEDY 37
gross reconciling my g. habits — POVERTY 6
grosser your g. reminiscences — LETTERS 16
Grosvenor violence in G. Square — EDUCATION 46
Grosvenor Gallery greenery-yallery, G. — MEN 7
grotesque meaning of the word g. — WIT 41
Groucho Marxist—of the G. tendency — POLITICS 5
ground worship the g. you walk on — MARRIAGE 127
grounds walks round the g. — GARDENS 10
grouse g. do it — BIRDS 8
grovelled g. before him — SNOBBERY 13

grow never g. out of it .... ARMED FORCES 30
growed s'pect I g. .... CHILDREN 40
growing hard price to pay for g. up
                                      MIDDLE AGE 14
  keeps on g. again .... BODY 10
grown-ups G. never understand
                               GENERATION GAP 5
grunt guttural g. .... BEHAVIOUR 19
gruntled he was far from being g.
                               SATISFACTION 19
guaranteed g. only to those .... CENSORSHIP 9
guardian reading *The G.* .... FOOTBALL 21
guess In disease Medical Men g. ...... MEDICINE 22
  Let me g. .... DEATH 61
guests hosts and g. .... CLASS 3
guile squat, and packed with g. .... PLACES 2
guilt easy the assumption of g. .... VIRTUE 7
  sign of g. .... BEHAVIOUR 7
guilty g. never escape unscathed .... LAW 2
guineas two hundred g. .... ART 44
Guinness G., sarcasm and late nights .... IRELAND 9
  G. makes you drunk .... DRINK 6
guitar he couldn't play g. .... MUSICIANS 19
  play the g. with your teeth .... MUSICIANS 11
  thirty-seven dollars and a Jap g. ...... MUSICIANS 8
gum chew g. at the same time .... INSULTS 20
gun Buy a big g. .... HAPPINESS 15
  g. across the Savoy Grill .... BUSINESS 10
  Is that a g. in your pocket .... MEN AND WOMEN 60
  we have got The Maxim G. .... POWER 1
  wrong end of a g. .... SPORTS 42
Gunga G. Din .... ARMED FORCES 20
guns G. aren't lawful .... DEATH 54
  g. don't kill people .... MURDER 9
  loaded g. with boys .... SECRECY 5
Guthrie as I have from Woody G. .... SONGS 8
guts Spill your g. at Wimbledon .... TENNIS 5
guy g.'s only doing it .... MEN AND WOMEN 31
  straight sort of g. .... SELF-KNOWLEDGE 4

h even *without the h.'s* .... THEATRE 12
ha funny h.-ha .... HUMOUR 19
habit court is just an expensive h. .... LAW 31
habit-forming Cocaine h. .... DRUGS 2
habits Inhibit their h. .... ANIMALS 14
  reconciling my gross h. .... POVERTY 6
hack some government h. .... GOVERNMENT 18
Hackensack I took a trip to H. .... TOWNS 24
hacks Efficient h. are very rare ...... JOURNALISM 2
had been h. by all .... CHARACTER 18
  WE ALL KNEW YOU H. IT IN YOU ...... TELEGRAMS 18
haddock *Quotations* and a very large h.
                                      NEWSPAPERS 7
  sausage and h. .... COOKERY 22

hail H., Fellatio .... WIT 45
  H. him like Etonians .... SOCIETY 15
Hail Marys run the Church on H. .... RELIGION 38
hair anything with long h. .... MUSICIANS 17
  At fifty I lost my h. .... OLD AGE 22
  beat hell out of h. curlers .... SEX 83
  does her h. with Bovril .... FRIENDS 5
  h. of the horse .... HYPOCRISY 6
  h. straight from his left armpit .... TRUST 9
  have their h. done .... APPEARANCE 19
  keep having my h. cut .... BODY 10
  like the h. we breathe .... SPORTS 36
  pin up my h. with prose .... LETTERS 4
  Presbyterian h. .... BODY 30
  pubic h. factory .... DESCRIPTION 21
  You have lovely h. .... WOMEN 8
  your h. has become very white .... OLD AGE 7
haircut h. will be crew .... FAMILY 17
hairpiece not his own h. .... APPEARANCE 21
hairpieces reliable as his h. .... AUTOBIOGRAPHY 17
hairs h. weakly curled .... APPEARANCE 3
hairstyle sense of duty, and her h. ...... ROYALTY 49
half are cut in h. .... ART 2
  h. mad baronet .... PEOPLE 13
  need cutting by h. before .... FRANCE 6
hallelujah H.! Was the only .... LAST WORDS 5
hallucinogenic h. icing .... PEOPLE 23
halo For a h. up in heaven .... RELIGION 28
  jealousy with a h. .... MORALITY 15
  What after all Is a h. .... RELIGION 24
ham when there's h. .... MEDICINE 12
Hamburg slipped on a hamburger in H.
                                       MISTAKES 24
hamburger slipped on a h. in Hamburg
                                       MISTAKES 24
Hamlet Did H. actually .... THEATRE 4
  H. himself longed .... THEATRE 49
  H. sure did enjoy .... THEATRE 34
  I'm doing H. .... ACTING 32
  want to play H. and Macbeth .... ACTORS 22
hand h. of history on his collar .... HISTORY 1
  h. that lays .... FILM PRODUCERS 6
  H. that rocked the cradle .... DEATH 5
  kiss on the h. .... WEALTH 24
  'Tes the h. of Nature .... NATURE 3
handbag bred in a h. .... FAMILY 52
  hitting it with her h. .... POWER 3
handclasp Where the h.'s firm .... FAMILY 26
Handel For either of them, or for H.
                                       MUSICIANS 13
handicap terrible a h. .... ENGLAND 17
  What is your h. .... GOLF 2
  What's your h. .... GOLF 3

handicapper h. is spoken of most respectfully

SPORTS 32

handkerchief like a damp h.

FOOD 45

scent on a pocket h.

PRIME MINISTERS 19

handle doesn't h. very well

HUMAN RACE 12

hands has the most beautiful h.

ART 14

Holding h. at midnight

LOVE 17

ice on your h.

DRESS 2

into the wrong h.

CENSORSHIP 7

prize-fighters shaking h.

WOMEN 37

handstand H. IN SHOWER

TELEGRAMS 22

handwriting exquisite h.

HANDWRITING 1

in his h.

HANDWRITING 3

your own h.

HANDWRITING 8

handy h. and cheap

FAMILY 1

hang Better to h. somebody

PUNISHMENT 10

they h. a man first

LAW 25

hangdog shifty, h. look

LANGUAGES 28

hanged h. in a fortnight

DEATH 37

hanging H. is too good

PUNISHMENT 4

h. prevents a bad marriage

MARRIAGE 106

happen accidents which started to h.

MISTAKES 22

foretell what is going to h.

POLITICIANS 14

to whom things h.

MISTAKES 21

happened after they have h.

FUTURE 9

what h. to Charlotte Church

FUTURE 5

what h. to him

ARMED FORCES 7

happening believe what isn't h.

SPORTS 10

happens no matter what h. in one day

NEWSPAPERS 20

nothing h., twice

THEATRE 36

there when it h.

DEATH 1

happily h. a woman may be married

MARRIAGE 83

happiness h. is assured

FUTURE 2

H. is having a large, loving

FAMILY 6

Last Chance Gulch for h.

CHILDREN 39

lifetime of h.

HAPPINESS 11

man in pursuit of h.

WEDDINGS 4

Money won't buy h.

MONEY 27

result h.

MONEY 9

happy conspiracy to make you h.

AMERICA 24

H. as a bastard

HAPPINESS 2

h. as most people

GAMBLING 1

h. as the dey

SEX 65

h. families

FAMILY 49

h. New Year

INSULTS 44

haven't been so h.

BOOKS 20

How h. I could be with either

LOVE 16

not a h. one

HAPPINESS 6

someone, somewhere, may be h.

RELIGION 41

very h. life

FAMILY 9

will never be h.

COUNTRY 9

harbour God made the h.

TOWNS 1

hard doing it the h. way

SUPERNATURAL 5

h. dog to keep

PRESIDENTS 5

h.-faced men

POLITICIANS 4

h. man is good to find

MEN 16

h. to be funny

HUMOUR 40

very h. guy

BETTING 8

hardback modern h. writer

WRITERS 39

hard-boiled big h. city

TOWNS 9

h. eggs

CHARACTER 21

hardest first one's the h.

MARRIAGE 116

hare h. of the bitch

FOOD 84

harem eunuchs in a h.

CRITICS 6

hark H.! the herald angels sing

MEDICINE 5

harlot holiest h. in my realm

ROYALTY 26

prerogative of the h.

JOURNALISM 15

harmless h. drudge

DICTIONARIES 8

harp pianoforte is a h. in a box

MUSIC 24

Harpic As I read the H. tin

OLD AGE 5

Harrow H. man, I expect

EDUCATION 47

I wish Shelley had been at H.

POETS 9

Harry Any Tom, Dick or H.

MARRIAGE 97

Uncle H.'s not a missionary

CLERGY 4

Harvard He was from H.

TOWNS 15

harvest laughs with a h.

AUSTRALIA 2

harvesting h. and crop spraying

BODY 19

Harwich steamer from H.

TRANSPORT 11

has-been word for washed-up h.

SUCCESS 7

haste repent in h.

MARRIAGE 39

hat brim of her floppy h.

MEN AND WOMEN 33

exactly the right h.

FASHION 21

means a Paris h.

SEX 74

hate h. for queers

EPITAPHS 11

h. the French

FRANCE 4

I h. all Boets and Bainters

ROYALTY 31

I h. men

MEN AND WOMEN 42

I h. music

MUSIC 15

I h. you

COMEDY 20

players who h. your guts

BASEBALL 12

teach them to h. the things you hate

CHILDREN 21

hated I h. it

ARMED FORCES 17

hates hateful h.

LOVE 24

h. dogs and babies

PEOPLE 33

h. them for it

HOPE 11

man who h. his mother

MARRIAGE 16

hating h., my boy

ENEMIES 7

hatred h. of domestic work

HOUSEWORK 5

spoil the purity of my h.

POLITICIANS 31

hats so many shocking bad h.

POLITICIANS 33

Haughey H. buried at midnight

POLITICIANS 25

haunt certain to h. her

FAMILY 7

have already h. it

GOVERNMENT 38

having have what she's h.

CHOICE 4

h. an old friend for dinner

SOCIETY 13

helped can't be h.   PUNISHMENT 2
Hemingway H. and *not* seen the joke   WRITERS 41
hen gentle useful h.   FOOD 20
   h. is only an egg's way   BIRDS 3
   h. you ran over the other day   MARRIAGE 90
   this is Mr C. O. H.   NAMES 1
Henery I'm H. the Eighth, I am   MARRIAGE 87
hen-pecked have they not h. you all

                                            INTELLIGENCE 4
herald Hark! the h. angels sing   MEDICINE 5
herbaceous h. border   LIES 7
herbs intolerance to h.   DRINK 62
herds H. of wildebeeste   PLACES 5
here H. at last is Asia   PLACES 4
   H. lies Spike Milligan   EPITAPHS 21
   H.'s . . . Johnny   COMEDY 17
   I'm still h.   MISTAKES 18
   want you to be h. and sexy   MARRIAGE 111
hereditary Insanity is h.   MIND 8
heresy Englishman believes be h.   RELIGION 63
hero aspires to be a h.   DRINK 33
   h. is a bee   ANIMALS 13
   h. is the author   BOOKS 21
Herod character of H.   CHILDREN 6
   hour of H.   CHILDREN 22
heroine when a h. goes mad   MIND 11
heron h.'s eggs   FOOD 26
herring different kinds of h.   FOOD 11
   these pickle h.   FOOD 72
Herzog thought Moses H.   MIND 1
heterodox It would have been less h.   LETTERS 2
heterodoxy another man's h.   BEHAVIOUR 32
hick Sticks nix h. pix   HEADLINES 4
hidden h. in each other's hearts   CHARACTER 5
                                                SECRECY 7
   teems with h. meaning   WORDS 15
hide Minister has nothing to h.   PRIDE 2
hideous horrid, h. notes of woe   MISTAKES 10
high fly fishing is h. church   FISHING 1
   her h. days and low days   MEDICINE 3
   h. altar on the move   DESCRIPTION 6
   h. cheekbones   ACTORS 1
   h. road that leads   SCOTLAND 5
   h.-water mark   FAMILY 48
   I'm getting h.   DRINK 15
   She's the Broad and I'm the H.   PRIDE 7
   walk along H. Holborn   HOPE 8
highballs Three h. and I think   DRINK 46
highbrow What is a h.   INTELLIGENCE 14
higher capable of h. things   LITERATURE 16
high-tech h. is that you always end up
                                            TECHNOLOGY 8
highway Thanks to the interstate h.   TRAVEL 16
himself more interested in h.   SELF-KNOWLEDGE 2
hindquarters h. ought to be   ARMED FORCES 22

hindsight H. is always twenty-twenty   PAST 15
hinges more h. in it   GOLF 1
hip never let his left h. know   DANCE 17
hippopotami like hell-bound h.   WOMEN 51
hippopotamus shoot the H.   ANIMALS 5
hips Mae West's h.   ACTORS 15
   tight about the h.   DESCRIPTION 33
   when your h. stick   MEN AND WOMEN 35
hire h. someone to read for me   WEALTH 15
hired h. the money   DEBT 2
hireling Pay given to a state h.   TRUST 8
historian still a medieval h.   HISTORY 3
historians H. repeat one another   HISTORY 5
history disasters of English h.   WALES 7
   hand of h. on his collar   HISTORY 1
   H. came to a stop   HISTORY 10
   h. comes equipped   HISTORY 16
   H. gets thicker   HISTORY 14
   H. is more or less   HISTORY 8
   H. is not what you thought   HISTORY 9
   H. is women following   HISTORY 2
   H. repeats itself   HISTORY 5
   H. started badly   HISTORY 19
   H. teaches us   HISTORY 7
   make more h.   COUNTRIES 30
   My children are doing me in h. now

                                                OLD AGE 42
   owe to h.   HISTORY 18
   People who make h.   HISTORY 6
   takes a great deal of h.   LITERATURE 21
   What will h. say   HISTORY 11
   write the h. of a battle   WAR 30
hit h. 'em in the body   BOXING 4
   H. me with   TITLES 2
   think and h.   BASEBALL 2
Hitler H.'s Eagle's Nest   HOLLYWOOD 11
   H. swore an oath on every one   TRUST 7
   kissing H.   FILM STARS 6
   Springtime for H.   WEATHER 3
hitter poor h.   BASEBALL 9
hitting h. people in the head   BOXING 10
ho What h.   CONVERSATION 34
Hoare H.-Laval pact   DIPLOMACY 10
Hoares No more H. to Paris   ROYALTY 35
hockey play h. properly   PARTIES 2
hod needs to have his h. examined   ART 21
Hoffa H.'s most valuable   DEATH 48
hog disadvantage of being a h.   ANIMALS 28
hogamus H., higamous   MARRIAGE 75
hokum Of all the h.   CLASS 23
holding batsman's H.   NAMES 17
   h. his bloody hyphen   NAMES 12
   without h. on   DRINK 40
holds she h. herself very well   ROYALTY 1

horrible awe-inspiringly h. CHILDREN 41
divided up into the h. and the miserable LIFE 1
horror bristling with h. HOLIDAYS 6
h. and struck FILM 7
horse about the h. ANIMALS 37
By putting money on a h. BETTING 1
does not make him a h. IRELAND 12
got a h. right here BETTING 5
hair of the h. HYPOCRISY 6
heard no h. sing a song MUSIC 2
h. designed by a committee BUREAUCRACY 8
h. is at least *human* TRANSPORT 32
h. is to the Arab ANIMALS 18
H. sense is a good judgement BETTING 3
like a h. and carriage MARRIAGE 25
phone, a h. or a broad PEOPLE 25
tail of the noble h. MUSIC 30
to the h. dentist ANIMALS 21
tried to milk the h. COUNTRY 1
where's the bloody h. LITERATURE 9
horseback Jews upon h. COUNTRIES 15
Horseguards You can be in the H. SOCIETY 17
horses Bring on the empty h. CINEMA 3
don't spare the h. TRANSPORT 18
frighten the h. SEX 31
given to h. SCOTLAND 6
'h.' should have read 'cows' MISTAKES 23
sixty h. wedged in a chimney HEADLINES 11
They eat h. FOOD 65
Wild h. on their bended knees WIT 2
horseshoe h. hanging over CERTAINTY 7
horticulture lead a h. WOMEN 50
hospital doctor whispers in the h. MEDICINE 35
is his h. ENGLAND 14
patient in any h. in Ireland MEDICINE 27
visited in h. by Margaret Thatcher HEALTH 16
hospitality H. consists HOSPITALITY 4
shrink from acts of h. PARTIES 5
hospitals big fear in h. SICKNESS 14
pay more taxes, but the h. don't kill BUREAUCRACY 12
host have been under the h. DRINK 47
h. is like a general HOSPITALITY 6
hostility based on h. HUMOUR 31
fosters international h. SPORTS 25
hosts h. and guests CLASS 3
hot It's Rome, it's h. CINEMA 1
never been cool, we're h. IRELAND 2
red h., mate CENSORSHIP 7
hot dog h. and vintage wine FOOD 39
hotel back to the h. SELF-KNOWLEDGE 17
great advantage of a h. HOTELS 6
It used to be a good h. PAST 12
hound I loves the h. more SPORTS 35
nothin' but a h. dog LOVE 29

hour h. of Herod CHILDREN 22
Some people can stay longer in an h. HOSPITALITY 7
hourglass Egghead weds h. WEDDINGS 2
hours But I see the h. pass WORK 8
in for ten h. MEDICINE 8
it has been going three h. OPERA 7
most rewarding h. TRANSPORT 3
house called a woman in my own h. WOMEN 67
COULDN'T DRAW IN THIS H. TELEGRAMS 15
Englishman's h. ENGLAND 14
every h. in London SOCIETY 24
give her a h. MARRIAGE 68
H. at Pooh Corner CRITICS 20
H. Beautiful is play lousy THEATRE 39
H. of Peers GOVERNMENT 11
in the way in the h. FAMILY 16
I want a h. HOME 11
leaving her present h. CLASS 25
sell his h. HOME 18
Spinks will come to your h. BOXING 12
swell h. PROGRESS 15
when I divorce I keep the h. MARRIAGE 57
you lose your h. MARRIAGE 7
household Navy, and the H. Cavalry SEX 48
householder housekeeper think she's a h. MARRIAGE 128
housekeeper h. think she's a householder MARRIAGE 128
seems an economical h. THEATRE 59
housekeeping He taught me h. MARRIAGE 57
house-keepings jining of hearts and h. LOVE 12
House of Commons advice for H. quotations QUOTATIONS 6
attendance at the H. MARRIAGE 50
H. en bloc do it SEX 33
H. is trying GOVERNMENT 39
libraries of the H. LIBRARIES 4
untrue in the H. LIES 11
House of Lords H. is a perfect eventide home OLD AGE 40
H. is sitting DRINK 29
houses books in their h. BOOKS 12
people like that to our h. MARRIAGE 31
housework I hate h.! HOUSEWORK 4
law of H. HOUSEWORK 1
no need to do any h. HOUSEWORK 3
how H. can they tell DEATH 53
say why and h. AUTOBIOGRAPHY 22
hucksters h.' shops DICTIONARIES 10
hugged h. by Diana Rigg MEDICINE 32
human bona fide h. being HUMAN RACE 8
civil servants are h. beings CIVIL SERVANTS 5
contempt for h. nature SELF-KNOWLEDGE 26
disappointed in h. nature HUMAN RACE 3

Kipling K.'s eyebrows — DESCRIPTION 23
kippers country smells of k. — COUNTRIES 39
kiss Before I k. the world goodbye — OLD AGE 15
  dollars for a k. — HOLLYWOOD 14
  K. me, Chudleigh — MISTAKES 31
  k. my ass in Macy's window — POWER 5
  k. on the hand — WEALTH 24
  k. the hand that wrote Ulysses — WRITERS 18
  let a k. fool you — FOOLISHNESS 6
  wanting to k. me — PRIME MINISTERS 23
  When women k. — WOMEN 37
  you get when you k. a guy — LOVE 8
kissable thought of women as k. — MEN AND WOMEN 10
kissed k. by a man who *didn't* wax — MEN AND WOMEN 24
  never k. her again — SEX 89
kisses fine romance with no k. — MEN AND WOMEN 13
kissing K. don't last: cookery do — MARRIAGE 84
  k. Hitler — FILM STARS 6
  like k. God — DRUGS 3
kitchen threw the k. sink — TENNIS 8
  wasn't even in the k. — CONVERSATION 24
Kitchener K. is a great poster — WAR 2
kitten evil reptilian k.-eater — POLITICIANS 1
Klee Kandinsky had feet of K. — ART 40
knack k. of so arranging the world — TECHNOLOGY 6
knee Rita's k. got the better of him — SICKNESS 2
knees don't really like k. — BODY 38
  k. of the chorous girls — THEATRE 23
  K. to Knees — DANCE 10
  like a caving in of the k. — WRITING 9
  up to her k. — PREJUDICE 12
  Wild horses on their bended k. — WIT 2
knew WE ALL K. YOU HAD IT IN YOU — TELEGRAMS 18
knickers just counted how many k. — SONGS 13
knife k. to a throat — PUBLISHING 14
  using a k. — BEHAVIOUR 3
knighted I didn't know he'd been k. — INSULTS 5
knitter beautiful little k. — WRITERS 37
knitting opened a k. shop — WOMEN 11
knock K. as you please — WIT 29
  k. it never is at home — WIT 8
  nice k.-down argument — WORDS 9
knocked k. everything but the knees — THEATRE 23
  we k. the bastard off — SUCCESS 13
knocking just k. it through — TOWNS 13
knocks k. you down with the butt — ARGUMENT 8
knot there's no k. for me — LOVE 18
know do not wish to k. — EXAMINATIONS 5
  don't k. what I am doing — SCIENCE 6
  don't k. what I said — IDEAS 9
  How do you k. — GOD 8

I Don't K. — COMEDY 49
  merely k. more — CHILDREN 37
  say I don't k. — OLD AGE 43
  things we k. nothing about — BOOKS 14
  You lie and you k. it — SPORTS 33
  You should bl-bloody well k. — ROYALTY 37
knowable nothing empirical is K. — PHILOSOPHY 8
knowledge k. of a lifetime — ART 44
  quite a fair show of k. — QUOTATIONS 4
known apart from the k. and the unknown — PHILOSOPHY 6
  k., and do not want it — INSULTS 21
  there are k. unknowns — IGNORANCE 7
knows He k. nothing — POLITICS 60
  if you k. of a better 'ole — WAR 4
  man who k. more — CENSORSHIP 17
Knox see John K. in Paradise — HEAVEN 4
knuckle k.-end of England — SCOTLAND 10
  k. to his duste — PEOPLE 23
knuckles biting my k. — FILM 11
Krakatoa K. number — ANGER 4
Kruschev married Mrs K. — HISTORY 15

labels l. served up — FOOD 96
laboratory used to be a l. — DRUGS 7
labour green belt was a L. idea — NATURE 8
  L. is led by an upper class — POLITICAL PARTIES 14
  L. Party is going round stirring — POLITICAL PARTIES 19
  L.-voting Scotland — DIPLOMACY 17
  leader for the L. Party — POLITICIANS 10
  two days' l. — ART 44
Labrador badly-informed l. — SEX 66
  wrong drop of blood should get into their L. — FAMILY 28
lack no time have I suffered a l. thereof — INSULTS 8
ladder I never climbed any l. — SUCCESS 21
ladies Here's to the l. who lunch — WOMEN 57
  L., just a little more — ACTING 34
  l. apparently rolled along — MEN AND WOMEN 22
  l. in love with buggers — LIFE 17
  lords of l. intellectual — INTELLIGENCE 4
  than leading l. — ACTORS 27
  when l. declare war on me — ROYALTY 45
lads We are l. — MEN 4
lady I'm no l. — SONGS 11
  l. doth protest too much — WOMEN 55
  l. is a tramp — BEHAVIOUR 15
  l. might think — MEN AND WOMEN 54
  l.'s conversation — COUNTRY 13
  nicest old l. — WRITERS 13
  talk like a l. — CLASS 26
  tattooed l. — BODY 26
  writing for an elderly l. — JOURNALISM 16
  young l. named Bright — SCIENCE 8

letterbox like fish into a l.   FILM PRODUCERS 12
letters able l. to *The Times*   PEOPLE 8
Any further l.   DEBT 3
l. get in the wrong places   LANGUAGE 9
l. printed in the papers   WRITERS 48
like women's l.   LETTERS 9
man of l.   FOOLISHNESS 14
my name in such large l.   PRIDE 9
leveller great l.   INDEXES 5
lexicographer L. A writer   DICTIONARIES 8
lexicographers these l.   DICTIONARIES 3
lexicon Two men wrote a l.   DICTIONARIES 12
liaisons L.! What's happened   ARISTOCRACY 16
liar answered 'Little L.'   LIES 4
exceptionally good l.   TRUTH 6
ignorant, uncultivated l.   LAW 36
liars Income Tax has made more L.   TAXES 7
liberal ineffectual l.'s problem   MORALITY 4
Is either a little L.   POLITICAL PARTIES 8
l. education   EDUCATION 2
l. is a man who leaves the room
    POLITICAL PARTIES 4
particular L. Party   POLITICAL PARTIES 11
liberals L. have invented   EDUCATION 29
L. offer a mixture   POLITICS 41
liberation pie-eaters' l. front   DIETS 4
liberties my belief in civil l.   PREJUDICE 17
liberty consistent with the l.   MARRIAGE 52
libraries l. of the House of Commons   LIBRARIES 4
library Another corpse in the l.   LIBRARIES 10
go to the l.   APPEARANCE 19
l. must be full of them   IDEAS 2
l. of sixty-two thousand volumes   ROYALTY 39
Majesty's l. in every county   LIBRARIES 3
sit in a l.   LIBRARIES 6
thing to have in a l. is a shelf   LIBRARIES 5
you have a public l.   LIBRARIES 2
licence temporary l.   DRUGS 9
lid Don't slam the l.   MEDICINE 39
Liddell right part wrote L.   DICTIONARIES 12
lie Here l. I   EPITAPHS 19
l. diagonally in his bed again   MARRIAGE 114
l. follows   BEHAVIOUR 27
L. heavy on him   EPITAPHS 12
l. is an abomination   LIES 1
l. less convincingly   JOURNALISM 17
sent to l. abroad   DIPLOMACY 19
You l. and you know it   SPORTS 33
lies Diplomats tell l.   GOVERNMENT 20
enough white l.   LIES 2
John Adams l. here   EPITAPHS 8
l., damned lies and statistics   LIES 6
l. he has been telling   CONVERSATION 10
Matilda told such Dreadful L.   LIES 3
spring of endless l.   JOURNALISM 13

stop telling l. about Democrats   POLITICS 66
tell l. as usual   HISTORY 11
life been a part of l.   WOMEN 11
Book of L. begins   BIBLE 8
crushed l. is what I lead   MARRIAGE 90
evidence of l. after death   POLITICS 64
function well in l.   ART 1
get a l.   TELEVISION 12
goes through l.   CHARACTER 6
If l. was a party   CONVERSATION 24
I gave my l. for freedom   WAR 11
isn't l. a terrible thing   LIFE 19
it's the l. in my men   SEX 98
let a woman in your l.   MEN AND WOMEN 27
l. for ourselves at the Ritz   ROYALTY 12
l. had been ruined by literature   LITERATURE 6
L. imitates Art   ART 46
l.-insurance agents   DEATH 40
L. in the movies   CINEMA 19
l. is 6 to 5 against   GAMBLING 7
L. is a banquet   LIFE 8
L. is a Cabaret   LIFE 9
L. is a gamble at terrible odds   LIFE 16
L. is a glorious cycle of song   LOVE 35
L. is a sexually transmitted   LIFE 3
L. is a shit sandwich   LIFE 14
l. is generally something   LIFE 5
L. is just one damned thing   LIFE 10
L. isn't like coursework   EDUCATION 19
L. is something to do   LIFE 11
l. is the thing   READING 15
L. is too short   TIME 9
l.-saving certificate   INTELLIGENCE 18
l.'s rich pageant   LIFE 12
l.'s story   AUTOBIOGRAPHY 2
l. was coming to consist   LIFE 2
l. will perhaps seem   DIARIES 5
L. would be very pleasant   HAPPINESS 14
made for l.   DEATH 30
malevolent l. of their own   TECHNOLOGY 13
matter of l. and death   FOOTBALL 24
My l. was simply hellish   SATISFACTION 13
new terror to l.   INSULTS 43
no quality of l.   COUNTRIES 7
Not too much of l.   LIFE 13
on a l.-support machine   APPEARANCE 6
précis of l.   WORDS 13
read the l.   BIOGRAPHY 9
real l. escapes   BIOGRAPHY 11
some problems with my l.   LIFE 15
stretch your l. out   MEDICINE 23
think there's intelligent l.   UNIVERSE 12
third of my l.   MIDDLE AGE 2
tired of l.   TOWNS 18
University of L.   EDUCATION 7

literature (*cont.*):

L.'s always a good card to play	LITERATURE 5
locks of l.	CRITICS 28
performed for German l.	LITERATURE 17

litigant l. drawn to the United States   LAW 5

little I ask very l.   SATISFACTION 5

l. local difficulties	POLITICS 42
Thank heaven for l. girls	WOMEN 35
though she be but l.	WOMEN 54
very l. one	CHILDREN 29

live all you have to do is to l. long enough

	OLD AGE 17
didn't l. there all the time	POLITICIANS 21
French, they say, l. to eat	FOOD 1
gonna l. this long	OLD AGE 6
l. in *Who's Who*	FAME 2
l. to be over ninety	OLD AGE 1
l. well on nothing a year	POVERTY 21
never to l.	AMERICA 16
way I l., once is enough	LIFESTYLE 7
you have to l. with rich people	WEALTH 27
You might as well l.	DEATH 54

lived l., nightly, and drank, daily   EPITAPHS 17

where Gettysburg l.   READING 4

liver ate his l.   FOOD 33

l. is on the right	MEDICINE 25
l.-wing of a fowl	HONOURS 9

Liverpool L., though not very delightful

   TOWNS 16

living books about l. men   BIOGRAPHY 7

But who calls dat l.	OLD AGE 20
Dogs who earn their l.	DOGS 2
had to write for a l.	WRITING 8
I *love* l.	LIFE 15
Lady Disdain, are you yet l.	INSULTS 36
work for a l.	ACTING 21

Lizzie Borden L. took an axe   MURDER 1

llama female l.   DESCRIPTION 8

Lloyd George L. did not seem to care

   PRIME MINISTERS 4

loaded I practise when I'm l.   MUSICIANS 21

loafing organized l.   CRICKET 16

lobster l. to attendant shrimps   ROYALTY 50

small l.	FOOD 62
world is your l.	SUCCESS 12

local little l. difficulties   POLITICS 42

lock key still in the l.   SEX 8

l., stock and iceberg   CANADA 6

locks louse in the l.   CRITICS 28

lodgings pent up in a frowzy l.   POVERTY 19

log On a l.   DEATH 20

log hut piano gets into a l.   MUSIC 17

logic L. and taxation   TAXES 5

Professor of L.   PHILOSOPHY 1

logical l. positivists   LOVE 2

Well, that's l.   PHILOSOPHY 9

logo l. twice the size   ADVERTISING 10

loitered l. of old on many a doorstep

   JOURNALISM 23

London in L. only is a trade   POETRY 9

L. at night	CRIME 8
L. Transport Diesel-engined	TRANSPORT 9
tired of L.	TOWNS 18
wear brown in L.	COLOURS 4

loneliness If you are afraid of l.   MARRIAGE 30

lonely l. eating spaghetti   FOOD 55

People who are l.   WORK 11

long all you have to do is to live l. enough

	OLD AGE 17
anything with l. hair	MUSICIANS 17
As l. as I could walk	TRANSPORT 36
as the dey was l.	SEX 65
But it's so l.	THEATRE 12
gonna live this l.	OLD AGE 6
It often lasts too l.	LIFE 13
Like German opera, too l.	WAR 27
little study you'll go a l. way	EDUCATION 32
l., long time	BROADCASTING 3
l. as the real thing	THEATRE 14

longer little finger to become l.   MUSIC 48

longest l.-lived animal in the world   HEALTH 17

longevity attribute my l.   OLD AGE 13

longing focus of l.   RELIGION 43

longitude l. with no platitude   LANGUAGE 4

look I never l. up   TRAVEL 2

l. another	BODY 27
l. at me that way	MORALITY 7
l. like the second week	APPEARANCE 17

looked better to be l. over   SATISFACTION 17

looking she was l. all the time   SEX 89

looking-glass cracked l.   ART 18

looks One of those l.   MARRIAGE 43

she needs good l.   MIDDLE AGE 15

looney-bin janitor to the l.   MEDICINE 38

loop l. on a commonplace   WIT 24

loose one thing to do with l. change   MONEY 23

lord L. above made liquor   DRINK 35

L. designed the Universe	UNIVERSE 10
L. says	DEBT 4
representation of Our L.	ART 3
to a point, L. Copper	JOURNALISM 22

lords it is the L. debating   ROYALTY 16

only a wit among L.	INSULTS 22
sleeps with the L.	ROYALTY 6
to be said for the L.	ARISTOCRACY 9

lordships good enough for their l.   POLITICS 4

Los Angeles Versailles of L.   HOLLYWOOD 15

marriage (*cont.*):

M. is very difficult	MARRIAGE 11
m. . . . it resembles a pair of shears	
	MARRIAGE 112
m. makes man and wife one flesh	MARRIAGE 38
M. may often be a stormy lake	MARRIAGE 92
m. 'tis good for nothing	MARRIAGE 104
She broke her m. vows	SEX 36
support gay m.	MARRIAGE 56
twenty years of m.	MARRIAGE 125
What are your views on m.	MARRIAGE 44

marriages unhappy m. come from   MARRIAGE 129

married amoebae getting m.   MARRIAGE 80

best thing about being m.	MARRIAGE 78
don't get m.	MARRIAGE 30
happily a woman may be m.	MARRIAGE 83
if ever we had been m.	MARRIAGE 62
I m. beneath me	INSULTS 3
I'm getting m. in the morning	WEDDINGS 7
incomplete until he has m.	MARRIAGE 58
kids when they got m.	PARENTS 4
m. beneath him	ACTING 7
M. in haste	MARRIAGE 39
most m. man I ever saw	MARRIAGE 122
never being m. to anyone	WOMEN 40
not if he is m.	FOOLISHNESS 10
not m. at all	BEHAVIOUR 8
result of being unhappily m.	POLITICS 54
Sorry, girls—he's m.	PEOPLE 2
thankfu' ye're no m. to her	MARRIAGE 21
usually m. to each other	PARTIES 3
very old m. couple	DIPLOMACY 9
We can't get m. at all	MARRIAGE 126
we had never m. at all	MARRIAGE 24
wench who is just m.	MARRIAGE 63
what delight we m. people have	MARRIAGE 93
woman's business to get m.	MARRIAGE 107
would not have m.	HISTORY 15
young man m.	MARRIAGE 105

marry Advice to persons about to m.

	MARRIAGE 99
don't m. them	MARRIAGE 31
every woman should m.	MARRIAGE 49
How can a bishop m.	SEX 85
if you never m.	MARRIAGE 81
let Carlyle and Mrs Carlyle m.	MARRIAGE 22
m. a man who hates his mother	MARRIAGE 16
means to m. any vun among them	
	MEN AND WOMEN 8
men we wanted to m.	WOMEN 59
never know who they may m.	WOMEN 39
never meant to m.	LOVE 21
not to m. ladies	MARRIAGE 3
that does not m. a fool	MARRIAGE 131
When you m. your mistress	MARRIAGE 66

Mars attack from M.	ARMED FORCES 24
Gordon Brown is from M.	POLITICIANS 27
Martha had enough of M.	CLERGY 14
martinet I am more than a m.	MUSICIANS 24
martinetissimo I am a m.	MUSICIANS 24
Martini into a dry M.	DRINK 2
martini finding two olives in your m.	
	HAPPINESS 5
Martinis Those dry M.	DRINK 1
martyrdom saints on their way to m.	WORK 26
Marx M is for M.	POLITICS 22
Marxist M.—of the Groucho tendency	POLITICS 5
Mary time for some M.	CLERGY 14
Mary Jane Lieutenant-General M.	LAST WORDS 5
marzipan made out of pink m.	FACES 4
Masefield To M. something more	LITERATURE 1
mask m. like Castlereagh	MURDER 13
mass too lazy to go to M.	RELIGION 46
Massachusetts chop your poppa up in M.	
	MURDER 3
masses Movement of M.	POLITICS 22
master m. of the multipurpose metaphor	
	POLITICIANS 6
masters like the old m.	FILM PRODUCERS 16
m. came and went	EDUCATION 45
mastodons like m.	FAMILY 55
masturbation Don't knock m.	SEX 1
M. is the thinking man's	SEX 43
M.: the primary sexual activity	SEX 88
mate should m. for life	SEX 5
mathematics resort to m.	RELIGION 42
maths see your m. master	RELIGION 7
Matilda M. told such Dreadful Lies	LIES 3
Matisse hanging a M. together	MARRIAGE 64
matrimony critical period in m.	MARRIAGE 72
m. at its lowest	MARRIAGE 115
m. consistent with the liberty	MARRIAGE 52
safest in m. to begin	MARRIAGE 109
mature m. poets steal	POETRY 10
maturing my mind is m. late	MIDDLE AGE 10
maturity M. is a hard price to pay	MIDDLE AGE 14
maudit hard to be a poet m.	POETS 4
mausoleum built like a brick m.	INSULTS 37
mauve offending orange and m.	COLOURS 1
mauver mauve and m.	WEATHER 1
maxim we have got The M. Gun	POWER 1
maximum m. of temptation	MARRIAGE 108
may at least the seventh of M.	WEATHER 20
maybe definite m.	CERTAINTY 13
Mayfair M. of the dead	DEATH 60
mayonnaise on m.	FOOD 8
mayor married the M.	POLITICIANS 5
m. gave no other	BEHAVIOUR 19
M. of Birmingham in a lean year	
	PRIME MINISTERS 21

MCC M. ends   ENGLAND 26
me interested in himself than in m.
                                              SELF-KNOWLEDGE 2
   m. is the most used two-letter word   WORDS 14
   M. Tarzan   FILM 15
meal building a m.   FOOD 52
   m. was never found   COOKERY 21
   of a good m.   FOOD 50
mealy M. boys   CHILDREN 15
mean only m. one thing   HUMOUR 2
   say what you m.   CONVERSATION 5
meaning m. of 'is'   WORDS 10
   teems with hidden m.   WORDS 15
meanings two m. packed up into one word
                                                     WORDS 8
means die beyond my m.   DEATH 74
   live within our m.   HAPPINESS 16
   m. just what I choose   WORDS 9
measles Love's like the m.   LOVE 26
measured m. malice of music   MUSIC 29
meat If you give him m.   PEOPLE 15
   sends us good m.   COOKERY 8
   very old m.   FOOD 74
mechanics M. not microbes   PROGRESS 5
medals wear their m. on Anzac day   FACES 9
media I'll alert the m.   FAME 15
   m.. It sounds like   BROADCASTING 8
medical advance of m. thought   DRINK 63
medicinal M. discovery   MEDICINE 4
medicinally m. salutary   CRITICS 24
medicine desire to take m.   MEDICINE 28
   home studying m.   MEDICINE 21
   m. by a completely new method   MEDICINE 25
   m. never gets anywhere near   SICKNESS 12
   professor of rotational m.   POLITICS 48
mediocre it's m.   FILM 6
mediocrities M. Think   AUSTRALIA 4
mediocrity m. thrust upon them   INSULTS 18
meditation transcendental m. with a punch-line
                                                  FISHING 2
Mediterranean from the M.   COUNTRIES 31
medium m. because nothing's well done
                                               TELEVISION 1
   Roast Beef, M.   FOOD 25
medley m. of extemporanea   LOVE 35
meek m. shall inherit the earth   WEALTH 14
meekness Ever heard of m. stopping   CLERGY 3
meet never seem to m.   HOME 8
meeting hearing, or m.   HOME 1
meetings big m. with important gentiles
                                          FILM PRODUCERS 2
   M. are a great trap   MANAGEMENT 4
melancholy surprisingly m.   MEN AND WOMEN 54
melodies I play his m.   MUSIC 32

melody My music without m.   INTELLIGENCE 5
   When I think of a m.   MUSICIANS 22
member ACCEPT ME AS A M.   SOCIETY 16
   elected m.   HONOURS 10
memoirs Like all good m.   AUTOBIOGRAPHY 15
   M. of the frivolous   AUTOBIOGRAPHY 4
   write one's m.   AUTOBIOGRAPHY 18
memoranda read these m.   GOVERNMENT 29
memorandum m. is written   BUREAUCRACY 1
men all our best m. are dead   LITERATURE 28
   believe that m. were the answer   MEN 1
   gets to know of m.   DOGS 6
   If m. could get pregnant   MEN AND WOMEN 23
   I hate m.   MEN AND WOMEN 42
   is Greek for 'm.'   WORDS 24
   I swear by m.   MEDICINE 10
   It's not the m. in my life   SEX 98
   manners out of m.   MEN AND WOMEN 9
   m. had to have babies   CHILDREN 14
   m. have got love well weighed up   LOVE 1
   M. seldom make passes   MEN AND WOMEN 39
   m. we wanted to marry   WOMEN 59
   on account of them being m.   SCIENCE 12
   Some m. are born mediocre   INSULTS 18
   too late that m. betray   WOMEN 22
   You m. are unaccountable things   MEN 15
mendicant you're a m.   POVERTY 14
mending ways of m. a broken heart   LOVE 39
mental It's not m.   MEDICINE 7
mention Don't m. the war   COUNTRIES 8
   resolved not to m.   CONVERSATION 6
menu waiters discussing the m.   FOOD 10
   when the Christians were on the m.   SPORTS 38
mercury littered under M.   CHARACTER 11
mercy leaving m. to heaven   PUNISHMENT 3
   like God's infinite m.   POLITICS 53
   m. o' my soul   EPITAPHS 19
Meredith M.'s a prose Browning   LITERATURE 34
meretricious m. and a happy   INSULTS 44
merger trying to pull off a m.   HEAVEN 8
meringue m.-utan   PEOPLE 10
merit *m.* for a bishopric   CLERGY 20
merriment m. of parsons   CLERGY 11
merry M. Christmas   CHRISTMAS 5
mesh Biography is the m.   BIOGRAPHY 11
mess By man what a m.   AUSTRALIA 5
   m. left over from other people   TOWNS 23
   why I'm a m.   FAMILY 40
message if there is a m.   JOURNALISM 18
   M.? What the hell do you think I am   THEATRE 9
   take a m. to Albert   LAST WORDS 2
messages M. should be delivered   CINEMA 12
messenger as the m.   ACTING 13
Messiah He's not the M.   GOD 17
   When M. comes   RELIGION 29

money (*cont.*):

German shepherd and no m.	TRAVEL 9
get m. from it	ADVERTISING 5
hain't the m., but th' principle	MONEY 21
he's a bum with m.	WEALTH 8
hired the m.	DEBT 2
Hollywood m.	HOLLYWOOD 18
interested in m.	CINEMA 25
I really love having m.	WEALTH 9
just sit and count m.	MUSIC 36
lend you m.	MONEY 20
lost m. by underestimating	INTELLIGENCE 11
made myself some m.	WORK 6
make a little m.	HOLLYWOOD 17
M., wife, is the true fuller's earth	MONEY 15
M. couldn't buy	FRIENDS 9
m. falls apart	FRANCE 11
M. gives me pleasure	MONEY 4
M. is better than poverty	MONEY 1
M. is what you'd get on	MONEY 19
m. or your life	MONEY 5
M.— the one thing	PARENTS 1
M. was exactly like sex	MONEY 2
m. was handed out	EDUCATION 16
M. won't buy happiness	MONEY 27
no m. refunded	ROYALTY 42
NO M. TILL YOU LEARN TO SPELL	TELEGRAMS 16
poor man with m.	WEALTH 13
rich man without m.	WEALTH 31
safest way to double your m.	ECONOMICS 10
suddenly get loads of m.	WEALTH 1
That's the way the m. goes	POVERTY 11
try to rub up against m.	MONEY 24
turning one's enemies into m.	JOURNALISM 5
what the Lord God thinks of m.	WEALTH 3
When you have m.	MONEY 10
wrote, except for m.	WRITING 12
you need the m.	WRITERS 9

monkey m. looking for fleas — SPEECHES 14
no reason to attack the m. — POLITICIANS 9
monkeys cheese-eating surrender m. — FRANCE 5
million m. — COMPUTERS 8
monogamous Woman m. — MARRIAGE 75
monogamy M. is the same — MARRIAGE 6
monotony long m. of marriage — MARRIAGE 65
monster many-headed m. of the pit — THEATRE 40
monstrous m. carbuncle — ARCHITECTURE 6
month Arrival of Book of the M. — READING 5
if they wait for a m. — LETTERS 8
m. of honey — MARRIAGE 18
months Eleven m.' hard work — GARDENS 7
monument m. to modern man's — BUREAUCRACY 5
monumental I had a m. idea — IDEAS 3
moo One end is m. — ANIMALS 31
mood improves the m. of the Party — POLITICS 20

moon pointing at the m.	FAME 24
moonlight in the wasted m.	MARRIAGE 14
moral adultery out of the m. arena	SOCIETY 21
Arthur is wicked and m.	VIRTUE 6
m. or an immoral book	BOOKS 22
often the most m.	GOVERNMENT 25
override one's m. sense	MORALITY 9
thinks he is m.	ENGLAND 30
morality Goodbye, m.	ART 15
suburbs of m.	VIRTUE 8
morals either m. or principles	ARISTOCRACY 7
Have you no m., man	MORALITY 12
m. make you dreary	MORALITY 13
m. of a Methodist	HYPOCRISY 4
morbid m. dryness is a Whig vice	VIRTUE 2
most m.	FAMILY 43
more m. equal than others	DEMOCRACY 13
m. than nothing	DRINK 11
m. than one woman	MEDICINE 26
m. than she ever did	WOMEN 32
There's m. of you	ECONOMICS 2
want some m.	FOOD 23
you've made a lot m.	GOD 39
Morgan J. P. M. bows	AMERICA 12
Morley Road Company Robert M.	DESCRIPTION 27
morning dawn of the m. after	DRINK 1
forget about it in the m.	RETIREMENT 4
Good m.	COMEDY 14
I'm getting married in the m.	WEDDINGS 7
started that m. from Devon	TRAVEL 13
Mornington present of M. Crescent	ACTING 14
Morocco we're M. bound	DICTIONARIES 4
moron consumer isn't a m.	ADVERTISING 8
IQ of a m.	ART 39
morphia taste for m.	ARCHITECTURE 10
mortality emblem of m.	DEATH 21
mortals M. use 'um'	SPEECHES 11
mortgage Authors with a m.	WRITING 5
mortgaged m. to the hilt	HOME 6
Mortimer Are you Edmund M.	ROYALTY 59
Moses leave M. out of	FILM PRODUCERS 1
M. had run them through the US Congress	
	RELIGION 54

mosquitoes Vietnam without the m. — WAR 16
moss Kate M. would be used as — ART 9
mother And her m. came too — PARENTS 17
behave like Whistler's M. — DESCRIPTION 3
concept of an eternal m. — ROYALTY 27
done with your m. — FAMILY 37
either my father or my m. — PARENTS 16
gave her m. forty whacks — MURDER 1
Gin was m.'s milk — DRINK 55
having killed his m. — FAMILY 36
I threw my m. into it — PARENTS 14
man who hates his m. — MARRIAGE 16

murderers mass m. ART 17
upset some m. MURDER 2
murdering executed for m. his publisher PUBLISHING 3
Murdoch wrapped in a M. newspaper NEWSPAPERS 18
museum shelf of an anatomical m. WORDS 19
mushroom too short to stuff a m. TIME 9
music all his m. accepts it MUSICIANS 20
All m. is folk music MUSIC 2
all the better for m. MUSICIANS 18
Appreciation of M. CRITICS 23
But the m. that excels MONEY 12
Classic m. is th'kind MUSIC 23
good m. and bad preaching RELIGION 17
how potent cheap m. is MUSIC 11
I don't like my m. MUSIC 33
I hate m. MUSIC 15
It'll be good Jewish m. MUSIC 27
long streamy flakes of m. DESCRIPTION 20
may not like m. ENGLAND 3
measured malice of m. MUSIC 29
m. had finished DANCE 8
M. helps not the toothache MUSIC 22
m. is the brandy of the damned MUSIC 50
M. makes you feel a feeling WORDS 18
m. of our own opinions LAW 34
m. one must hear several times MUSIC 43
m. was more important than sex SEX 58
My m. without melody INTELLIGENCE 5
People never talked about my m. SONGS 13
play American m. COUNTRIES 9
plays good m. CONVERSATION 32
potent m. can be MUSIC 60
reasonable good ear in m. MUSIC 49
What m. is more enchanting YOUTH 8
with its own verbal m. MUSIC 51
musical disclosing m. secrets MUSICIANS 16
M. comedy is the Irish stew of drama THEATRE 62
M. people are so absurdly unreasonable MUSIC 59
not unduly m. WEDDINGS 5
musicologist m. is a man who MUSICIANS 5
mustard Pass the m. HUMOUR 17
mutton make them into m.-pies COOKERY 5
what m. tastes like WRITERS 26
mutual m. knowledge FRIENDS 16
my M. arse COMEDY 33
my-lorded m. him SNOBBERY 13
myopia all we got was Dev's m. IRELAND 4
myself He reminds me of m. SELF-KNOWLEDGE 7
mystery hissed my m. lectures WIT 43

nags N. away from arsehole to PEOPLE 29

nailing n. his colours CERTAINTY 12
nails have our n. done SOCIETY 8
relatively clean finger n. LAW 27
naive n. domestic Burgundy WINE 12
naïve both a little n. FOOLISHNESS 7
naked I had never seen a n. woman WOMEN 61
n. and not be upstaged BODY 39
n. women TRAVEL 27
name alien, distasteful n. NAMES 16
Beatles, how did the n. arrive NAMES 20
colonies in your wife's n. WAR 15
dad's n. all over his underwear FASHION 9
halfway through her n. NAMES 4
I don't wish to sign my n. LETTERS 15
If my n. had been Edmund NAMES 19
if my n. occurs AUTOBIOGRAPHY 1
I write my n. BOOKS 11
my n. in such large letters PRIDE 9
n. is neither one thing NAMES 8
n. is not in the obits DEATH 17
n. *not* suggest COUNTRIES 1
n. we give the people DEMOCRACY 6
remember your n. NAMES 29
Under an assumed n. GAMBLING 6
named n. a country FILM 4
so good they n. it twice NEW YORK 5
why the department was so n. BROADCASTING 2
names American n. as Cathcart NAMES 16
n. of all these particles SCIENCE 14
new n. NAMES 6
Napoleon Jesus Christ and N. PRIME MINISTERS 22
N.'s armies ARMED FORCES 27
Napoleons worship the Caesars and N. POWER 4
narcissistic defining 'n.' WORDS 38
narrow n. waist MIDDLE AGE 6
notions should be so n. CLERGY 6
nasty n. as himself HOPE 11
Something n. in the woodshed MISTAKES 14
when we turn n. CHARACTER 8
Natchez young belle of old N. WOMEN 44
nation let alone a n. HUMOUR 7
Our N. stands for ENGLAND 5
teddy bear to the n. PEOPLE 1
top n. HISTORY 10
national N. Debt DEBT 8
nations n. behave wisely HISTORY 7
Other n. use force ENGLAND 40
native Esperanto like a n. LANGUAGES 18
natural her colour is n. SOCIETY 20
I do it more n. FOOLISHNESS 12
n. animosity ACTORS 5
On the stage he was n. ACTORS 21
twice as n. LIFE 6

nature collected directly from n.

MEN AND WOMEN 46

missing in N. is a pencil WRITING 3
n. has anticipated me THEATRE 23
N. has no cure POLITICS 62
N. is creeping up ART 45
N.'s way of telling you DEATH 6
phenomenon of n. FILM STARS 10
position in n. HUMAN RACE 5
seeing n. as cuddlesome NATURE 7
stuff that n. replaces it with NATURE 11
'Tes the hand of N. NATURE 3
natures terribly weak n. CHARACTER 20
naughty He's a very n. boy! GOD 17
Oh wasn't it n. of Smudges SPORTS 5
Navaho than Basque or N. LANGUAGES 3
naval n. tradition ARMED FORCES 5
navy joined the N. ARMED FORCES 4
n. blue of India COLOURS 9
No n., I suppose SCIENCE 10
of the Queen's N. ARMED FORCES 11
Ruler of the Queen's N. LAW 11
Nazi join the N. Party POLITICAL PARTIES 3
Neanderthal N. A glowering thug MEN 9
near When I'm not n. the girl I love LOVE 23
necessarily It ain't n. so BIBLE 5
necessity nasty old invention—N. POVERTY 7
neck break his bloody n. WRITERS 49
why I should break my n. SPORTS 2
need n. a bigger boat TRANSPORT 4
whenever we n. them DEMOCRACY 6
needle n. in a haystack WORDS 6
neglect die of n. IDEAS 8
perfectly understandable n. MEN AND WOMEN 30
Negro N. could never *hope* PREJUDICE 2
one drop of N. blood PREJUDICE 9
Negroes culture of the N. MUSIC 39
neigh people expect me to n. ROYALTY 2
neighbour Our Good N. TITLES 3
neighbourhood if you only lived in a better n.

MARRIAGE 127

neighbours N. you annoy together

MARRIAGE 113

neither N. am I BOOKS 4
Nell death of Little N. CRITICS 37
Little N. and Lady Macbeth PEOPLE 46
nephews erring n. FAMILY 56
Nero New Jersey N. WRITERS 14
nerve after the n. has been extracted

MARRIAGE 101

always called a n. specialist MEDICINE 38
nervous disease, they call it n. MEDICINE 22
n. to kill himself CHARACTER 13
Nescafé N. society SOCIETY 9
nest does not leave the n. OLD AGE 11

net habits with my n. income POVERTY 6
surfed the N. PROGRESS 6
tennis with the n. down POETRY 11
too old to rush up to the n. MIDDLE AGE 1
neurosis n. is a secret MIND 15
neurotic For I'm a n. erratic MEN AND WOMEN 17
never I n. use a big, big D LANGUAGE 7
n. can tell CERTAINTY 22
N. give a sucker GAMBLING 3
n. to be played again MUSIC 18
new all the n. boys GOVERNMENT 16
happy N. Year INSULTS 44
have some n. clichés CINEMA 14
kill you in a n. way PROGRESS 12
make n. friends FRIENDS 3
making n. enemies LAST WORDS 13
n. names NAMES 6
WHAT'S N. TELEGRAMS 19
Newcastle No more coals to N. ROYALTY 35
New England N. is not Puritanism WEATHER 13
news Good n. rarely comes MONEY 17
President who never told bad n. PRESIDENTS 12
that is n. JOURNALISM 3
wonderful how much n. there is LETTERS 8
New South Wales Go out and govern N.

POLITICIANS 8

newspaper Accuracy to a n. NEWSPAPERS 22
exactly fits in the n. NEWSPAPERS 20
n., humdrum ENGLAND 6
n. which weighs as much NEWSPAPERS 7
rule never to look into a n. NEWSPAPERS 21
Whenever I see a n. NEWSPAPERS 13
wrapped in a Murdoch n. NEWSPAPERS 18
newspapers believe all you read in the n.

NEWSPAPERS 9

I read the n. avidly NEWSPAPERS 1
It's the n. I can't stand NEWSPAPERS 23
N., even, have degenerated NEWSPAPERS 28
nothing in the n. is ever true NEWSPAPERS 3
People don't actually read n. NEWSPAPERS 10
When n. became solvent NEWSPAPERS 12
worst n. AUSTRALIA 1
New York back in N. NEW YORK 8
goes to N. NEW YORK 3
I happen to like N. TOWNS 24
kind of N. TOWNS 27
New York, N. NEW YORK 2
N. is Big TOWNS 2
N. is new and phoney NEW YORK 4
N. makes one think NEW YORK 1
N.'s Bohemian and artistic ART 48
writing about N. NEW YORK 7
New Zealanders When N. emigrate AUSTRALIA 3
NHS N. is quite like heaven SICKNESS 10

Niagara On seeing N. Falls — MUSIC 34
nice be a n. boy — MEN 2
  Be n. to people — SUCCESS 17
  cherry blossom is quite n. — POETS 19
  hurt us to be n. — FAMILY 22
  lots of n. guys — HOLLYWOOD 8
  n. girl's ambition — HOPE 1
  N. guys — CHARACTER 8
  N. guys are a dime a dozen — MUSIC 14
  N. work if you can get it — LOVE 17
  such a n. woman — ACTORS 10
nicest n. old lady — WRITERS 13
nicety n. of terminology — CONVERSATION 20
nicked we've n. your stereo — FOOTBALL 1
nickel put the n. in the toilet — POWER 7
nickname really needed a n. at school — NAMES 3
niece I have a n. called Smith — SNOBBERY 11
Nietzsche would not like N. — PHILOSOPHY 12
night ain't a fit n. out for man — WEATHER 6
  At n. I want you to be here — MARRIAGE 111
  Baby, I went to n. school — MEN AND WOMEN 62
  It goes of a n. — SOCIETY 20
  It was a n. — SATISFACTION 2
  London at n. — CRIME 8
  only for a n. and away — MEN AND WOMEN 67
  returned on the previous n. — SCIENCE 8
nightgowns tweed n. — ENGLAND 13
nightingale She sings as sweetly as a n.
— MEN AND WOMEN 48
Nile allegory on the banks of the N. — WIT 37
Nina keener than little N. — DANCE 6
nine are there two n. o'clocks — TIME 3
  We met at n. — OLD AGE 28
nineteenth snappy n.-century — FILM 5
ninetieth on the n. floor — HOPE 10
ninety live to be over n. — OLD AGE 1
  n.-minute patriots — SCOTLAND 9
  n. minutes — BROADCASTING 3
nipples upstaged by your n. — BODY 39
nix Sticks n. hick pix — HEADLINES 4
Nixon N. impeached himself — PRESIDENTS 1
no can say n. — DIPLOMACY 15
  can't say N. in any of them — WOMEN 48
  Computer says N. — COMPUTERS 7
  I cain't say n. — WOMEN 27
  It's n. go the Yogi Man — SATISFACTION 11
  simple N. will suffice — SEX 79
  Yeah but n. but yeah — COMEDY 53
Noah N. he often said — WINE 3
Nobel dinner for N. Prizewinners — INTELLIGENCE 9
  you deserve the N. prize — OLD AGE 4
noble N. deeds and hot baths — MIND 12
  towards n. authors — ARISTOCRACY 12
nobleman as a n. should do — ARISTOCRACY 15
noblest n. prospect — SCOTLAND 5

nobly Spurn not the n. born — ARISTOCRACY 4
nobody give a war and n. will come — WAR 24
  n. knew what was going on — MUSIC 31
  n. knows De stubble I've seen — FACES 2
  n.'s chasing me — MEN AND WOMEN 43
  Well, n.'s perfect — MARRIAGE 126
nod I just n. — AMERICA 12
noise love the n. — ENGLAND 3
  n., my dear! And the people — WAR 1
  n. at one end — CHILDREN 23
  n. like that of a water-mill — TECHNOLOGY 15
  valued till they make a n. — SECRECY 5
noises meaningless Celtic n. — SCOTLAND 4
noisy twice as n. — THEATRE 14
Nollekens picture to remain as by N. — ROYALTY 47
non is a n.-starter — COMPUTERS 4
  n. compos penis — CRITICS 19
none If Nun, write N. — FAMILY 37
  I have n. — ENEMIES 6
nonentity n. who resents — BORES 11
nonexistent obsolescent and the n. — COMPUTERS 3
Norfolk Very flat, N. — PLACES 6
normal Thank God we're n. — SEX 70
north came from the N. — ENGLAND 27
  Good Neighbour to the N. — TITLES 3
  Lots of planets have a n. — SPEECHES 6
Norway male brothel in N. — BIOGRAPHY 5
Norwegian N. language — LANGUAGES 1
  N. television — TELEVISION 2
Norwegians don't like the N. — COUNTRIES 39
nose Entuned in hir n. — WOMEN 7
  insinuated n. — EPITAPHS 29
  lifts his n. — FOOLISHNESS 16
  man who could not make up his n. — THEATRE 54
  not a n. at all — BODY 45
  wipe a bloody n. — ARGUMENT 7
nostalgia N. isn't what it used to be — PAST 2
not N. while I'm alive he ain't — POLITICIANS 11
note Wobbly top n. — SONGS 22
notebook wrote it down herself in a n.
— PEOPLE 22
nothing doing n. to some purpose — WORK 5
  going to do n. — EPITAPHS 4
  I do n., granted — WORK 8
  live well on n. a year — POVERTY 21
  man who, having n. to say — CONVERSATION 11
  not enough to do n. — WEALTH 6
  n. a-year, paid quarterly — POVERTY 20
  N. for nothink — ECONOMICS 14
  n. happens, twice — THEATRE 36
  n. *like* it — FOOD 16
  n. on in the photograph — PEOPLE 27
  of you with n. on — HOPE 8
  Worked myself up from n. — POVERTY 13

notice hand-painted n. — DANCE 16
taken no n. of — TELEVISION 7
notices I got pretty good n. — MUSIC 31
Mixed n. — THEATRE 28
notions n. should be so narrow — CLERGY 6
Notre Dame towers of N. to dance — CERTAINTY 26
novel Anyone could write a n. — WRITING 19
In every first n. — BOOKS 21
n. about civil servants — READING 2
reading a French n. — CRITICS 21
novels ideal reader of my n. — READING 3
novelty n. of sleeping with a queen — ROYALTY 66
now If they could see me n. — CLASS 13
nudity advanced state of n. — BODY 34
enjoy their own n. — DIARIES 3
nuisance really rather a n. — ARISTOCRACY 17
null N. an' Void — LAW 29
number called the wrong n. — MISTAKES 28
n. for a dinner — FOOD 31
numbers lisped in n. — CHILDREN 32
nun extremely rowdy N. — MURDER 4
If N., write *None* — FAMILY 37
nice to have a n. around — RELIGION 35
nuns n. in a rugger scrum — ARCHITECTURE 11
recreation for dedicated n. — SPORTS 3
nups Queen to skip Chuck n. — HEADLINES 3
nurse dog for a n. — CHILDREN 2
keep a-hold of N. — CHILDREN 4
n. sleeps sweetly — SICKNESS 7
N. UNUPBLOWN — TELEGRAMS 20
nut N. SCREWS WASHERS — HEADLINES 6
nuts where the n. come from — FAMILY 47

oatcakes Calvin, o., and sulphur — SCOTLAND 10
oath Hitler swore an o. on every one — TRUST 7
oats feeds the horse enough o. — ECONOMICS 6
O.. A grain, which in England — SCOTLAND 6
Obadiah O. Bind-their-kings — NAMES 23
OBE O. goes on for ever — HONOURS 13
O. is what you get if you clean — HONOURS 14
obedient now totally o. — GARDENS 1
obey people would immediately o. — POWER 9
obeyed She who must be o. — WOMEN 24
obits name is not in the o. — DEATH 17
obituaries read the o. — DEATH 64
obituary autobiography is an o. — AUTOBIOGRAPHY 6
just read o. — DEATH 51
to the o. page — MIDDLE AGE 11
oblate o. spheroid — UNIVERSE 2
oblivion O. (noun) — FAME 8
obscurity snatches a man from o. — THEATRE 44
observation faculty for o. — BOOKS 12
only o. — LAST WORDS 5

observations universe is a totality of o. — UNIVERSE 13
observer keen o. of life — INTELLIGENCE 1
obsolescence With built in o. — UNIVERSE 10
obsolescent o. and the nonexistent — COMPUTERS 3
obstacle o. racing — HOME 20
obstacles incredible lack of o. — SUCCESS 22
obstructing without o. the view — FASHION 11
occasional o. heart attack — HEALTH 1
occupation o. for an idle hour — SNOBBERY 2
some sort of o. — DEBT 9
occupations worse o. in the world — WOMEN 60
occurred Ought never to have o. — MISTAKES 5
o'clocks are there two nine o. — TIME 3
odd astonishment's o. — GOD 5
exceedingly o. — GOD 31
It's an o. job — HUMOUR 22
Not o. of God — GOD 6
not so o. — GOD 13
o. of God — GOD 23
odds gamble at terrible o. — LIFE 16
odium He lived in the o. — SCIENCE 5
odorous Comparisons are o. — WIT 32
Oedipus It could be O. Rex — THEATRE 18
off o.-the-record briefing — GOD 30
offal don't do o. — COOKERY 13
feel like discarded o. — BROADCASTING 5
offence ended up taking o. — HUMOUR 35
offensive You are extremely o. — INSULTS 39
offer o. he can't refuse — POWER 8
office By office boys for o. boys — NEWSPAPERS 19
except public o. — POLITICAL PARTIES 18
in which the o. is held — BUREAUCRACY 7
o. boy to an Attorney's firm — LAW 11
O. hours — GOVERNMENT 17
o. party — CHRISTMAS 11
o. party is not — PARTIES 8
ready for a woman in the Oval O. — PRESIDENTS 14
official O. Secrets Act — SECRECY 9
This high o. — GOVERNMENT 14
officials public o. — BUREAUCRACY 9
officiously O. to keep alive — DEATH 14
oil boiling o. — PUNISHMENT 7
like an o. painting — APPEARANCE 8
sound of o. wells — MONEY 12
Strike o. — SUCCESS 10
oilcloth o. pockets — FILM PRODUCERS 11
old another o.-fashioned — DRINK 48
Anyone can get o. — OLD AGE 17
avoid o. people — YOUTH 11
conservative when o. — POLITICAL PARTIES 7
from ingenue to o. bag — THEATRE 56
give an interest to one's o. age — OLD AGE 44
Growing o. is like being — OLD AGE 36
HOW O. CARY GRANT — TELEGRAMS 14

old (*cont.*):

in Beverly Hills grows o.	OLD AGE 25
It means I'm growing o.	ROYALTY 45
like the o. masters	FILM PRODUCERS 16
nicest old o.	WRITERS 13
o. age is always fifteen years older	OLD AGE 3
o.-fashioned house	MONEY 12
o. have reminiscences	GENERATION GAP 10
o. maid is like death by drowning	OLD AGE 18
outrageous o. fellow	GENERATION GAP 6
putting o. heads	EDUCATION 41
staff to my father's o. age	PARENTS 14
terrifying fact about o. people	OLD AGE 34
thing about getting o.	OLD AGE 30
too o. to rush up to the net	MIDDLE AGE 1
virtuous in their o. age	OLD AGE 35
What a sad o. age	OLD AGE 41
What's the point in growing o.	GENERATION GAP 3
When I am an o. woman	OLD AGE 27
when o. age crept over them	RELIGION 44
You are o., Father William	OLD AGE 7
You dirty o. man	COMEDY 56
young can do for the o.	YOUTH 7
you're too o.	ACTING 23

older As I grow o. OLD AGE 38
ask somebody o. than me	SEX 22
fifteen years o. than I am	OLD AGE 3
o. faces	HOSPITALITY 5

oldest o. established BETTING 6
olive in an o. grove HOLIDAYS 2
olives finding two o. in your martini HAPPINESS 5
ombibulous I'm o. DRINK 41
omelette like a savoury o. GOSSIP 8
o. all over our suits	MISTAKES 9

omelettes make o. properly COOKERY 2
omnibus Ninety-seven horse power O. TRANSPORT 9
omniscience o. is his foible INSULTS 41
on things that Chico was always o. PEOPLE 25
Onan named her canary 'O.' NAMES 25
onanism O. of poetry POETS 2
Onassis O. would not HISTORY 15
once every house in London, o. SOCIETY 24
only be killed o.	POLITICS 18
same mistake o.	MISTAKES 3
way I live, o. is enough	LIFESTYLE 7

once-bitten o. there is no cure FISHING 3
one contract is so o.-sided LAW 9
number o. book	BIBLE 6
registered as—o. two three	TRANSPORT 31

onion ate o. soup DIETS 1
half an o. left over	COOKERY 15

only o. a hole BASEBALL 14
O. connect	BOXING 9

oozed brain has o. out TRAVEL 15
open eyes wide o. before marriage MARRIAGE 54
it was an o. cow	LAW 14
o. in two weeks	ACTING 11
o. pickle jars	MEN AND WOMEN 15
o. that Pandora's Box	DIPLOMACY 2
We o. in Venice	THEATRE 42
with an o. fly	FILM PRODUCERS 20

opened o. a pier FAME 14
opening Another o. of another show THEATRE 41
opera language an o. is sung in OPERA 1
Like German o., too long	WAR 27
o. ain't over	OPERA 2
O. in English	OPERA 5
o. isn't what it used to be	OPERA 3
O. is when a guy gets stabbed	OPERA 4
Parsifal is the kind of o.	OPERA 7

operas French o. sung by Swedish artists LANGUAGES 27
operation o. to get a joke SCOTLAND 11
Ophelia affair with O. THEATRE 4
much worse for my sister O.	NAMES 3
she is not O.	INSULTS 7

opinion His o. of himself PRIDE 1
never had a humble o.	HUMILITY 1
o. against that of millions	MUSIC 33

opinions high quality of early o. BOOKS 6
music of our own o.	LAW 34

opium concubine to an o. addict WOMEN 62
He smoked o.	DRUGS 5

opportunity commit when he had the o. MEN 13
manhood was an o.	MEN 10
maximum of o.	MARRIAGE 108
o. of saying a good thing	WIT 13

oppose o. everything POLITICS 24
opposing rapid succession of o. certainties CERTAINTY 25
opposite o. of people ACTORS 30
o. of talking	CONVERSATION 17

opposites O., opposites MARRIAGE 13
opposition duty of an O. is very simple POLITICS 24
oppressed I don't do o. HUMILITY 2
oppression injustice and o. DIPLOMACY 12
oracular use of my o. tongue WIT 35
oral word about o. contraception SEX 6
oral-genital cases of o. intimacy SEX 46
orange happen to be an o. AMERICA 1
offending o. and mauve	COLOURS 1

oratorio more disgusting than an o. MUSIC 54
oratorios o. being sung in the costume MUSIC 37
orchard Trees in the o. COUNTRY 5

pagan something p. in me | CERTAINTY 8
page allowed P. 3 to develop | NEWSPAPERS 15
  first mistake on p. 850 | AUTOBIOGRAPHY 12
  secret p. | BOOKS 11
pageant life's rich p. | LIFE 12
pages thirty-five p. | AUTOBIOGRAPHY 2
paid if not p. *before* | LAW 21
pain p. in my head is wracking | SICKNESS 8
  p. it brings to your enemies | HONOURS 2
  seek to ease his p. | ECONOMICS 7
  teach you the meaning of p. | FASHION 14
  threshold of p. | FAMILY 22
paint He would fain p. a picture | SATISFACTION 4
painted unreality of p. people | THEATRE 55
painter Our p. | ART 13
  p. of LSD without LSD | ART 23
  p.'s eye | ART 10
painting like my p. muddy | INTELLIGENCE 5
palace chalice from the p. | WIT 28
palaces live in p. | HOME 12
pale p. green man | BIOGRAPHY 8
  p. young curate | CLERGY 8
palsy stricken wid de p. | OLD AGE 23
pancreas adorable p. | APPEARANCE 10
Pandora open that P.'s box | DIPLOMACY 2
panegyric write *A P.* | AUTOBIOGRAPHY 11
panics only p. in a crisis | POLITICAL PARTIES 12
pants lower limbs in p. | APPEARANCE 13
  Uncle Bud's p. | DESCRIPTION 30
paper as p. all they provide is rubbish | NEWSPAPERS 13
  brilliant on p. | FOOTBALL 26
  files in the p. | BIOGRAPHY 3
  furnish p. | WRITING 16
  more personality than a p. cup | TOWNS 9
  p. appears dull | BORES 14
  p. it is written on | CINEMA 15
  p. sagged open | MIDDLE AGE 11
  p. work down to a minimum | READING 13
  sides of the p. | EXAMINATIONS 6
  Wonderful on p. but disappointing | PEOPLE 16
  written on both sides of the p. | LAW 9
papers Anything in the P. | WAR 33
  go to the p. | CLASS 6
  letters printed in the p. | WRITERS 48
  P. are power | GOVERNMENT 34
paperwork What I can't stand is the p. | WRITERS 11
paradise Bournemouth in lieu of P. | RETIREMENT 1
  fool's p. | FOOLISHNESS 8
  passport to P. | HEAVEN 2
  see John Knox in P. | HEAVEN 4
  squeeze into P. | BODY 7
parallel p. bars | HEALTH 14

paralysed P. Girl Determined to Dance | HEADLINES 10
paranoid p. survive | MANAGEMENT 6
pardon God will p. me | GOD 26
  With a thousand Ta's and P.'s | SOCIETY 5
parent look at yourself as a p. | PARENTS 6
  lose one p. | FAMILY 51
  p. who could see his boy | CHILDREN 25
  primitive Irish p. | PARENTS 2
parentage P. is a very important | FAMILY 39
parents especially step-p. | CHILDREN 33
  girl needs good p. | MIDDLE AGE 15
  Jewish man with p. alive | PARENTS 13
  job all working-class p. want | POLITICS 1
  loving their p. | CHILDREN 46
  our p. won | GENERATION GAP 9
  p. did for me | GENERATION GAP 14
  p. finally realize | FAMILY 2
  p. have done it for you | MONEY 8
  p. obey their children | AMERICA 10
  p. warned us about | PARENTS 8
  p. were English | ENGLAND 16
  p. were very pleased | ARMED FORCES 17
  what their p. do not wish | CHILDREN 42
Paris built in P. | FASHION 17
  means a P. hat | SEX 74
  No more Hoares to P. | ROYALTY 35
  People don't talk in P. | TOWNS 10
  they go to P. | AMERICA 27
parish six children on the p. | ROYALTY 3
park come out to the ball p. | BASEBALL 3
  To poison a pigeon in the p. | MURDER 10
parliament available in P. | HEALTH 7
  enables P. to do | DRINK 54
  [p.] are a lot of hard-faced men | POLITICIANS 4
  p. of whores | DEMOCRACY 12
parliamentarian pleasure for a p. | POLITICS 23
parliamentary Try p. democracy | DEMOCRACY 7
parody p. is a game | WIT 25
Parsifal as long as *P.* | THEATRE 16
parsley P. Is gharsley | FOOD 56
parson p. knows enough | CLERGY 5
parsons merriment of p. | CLERGY 11
part I read p. of it | READING 8
  p. the Red Sea | APPEARANCE 21
  p. to tear a cat in | ACTING 30
participants p. and not the accoutrements | LOVE 40
particles names of all these p. | SCIENCE 14
parts good as his p. | ACTORS 35
  P. of it are excellent | FOOD 68
  private p. have become | BODY 4
  save all the p. | TECHNOLOGY 4

party at my p.'s call · DEMOCRACY 8
  Collapse of Stout P. · COMEDY 4
  each p. is worse than the other · POLITICS 57
  hell is a very large p. · PARTIES 2
  If life was a p. · CONVERSATION 24
  improves the mood of the P. · POLITICS 20
  I've been to a marvellous p. · PARTIES 1
  Join the Nazi P. · POLITICAL PARTIES 3
  prove the other p. · DEMOCRACY 11
  tried to make the p. go · HOSPITALITY 9
  What a swell p. this is · MARRIAGE 96
party-going interferes with p. · THEATRE 26
pass let him p. for a man · MEN 14
  p. a betting shop · FOOTBALL 9
  p. for forty-three · WOMEN 20
  p. the blame · BUREAUCRACY 13
  P. the mustard · HUMOUR 17
  P. the sick bag · COMEDY 40
passage p. which you think is · WRITING 11
passed p. a lot of water since then · TIME 12
  That p. the time · TIME 5
passengers one of its p. · ART 36
passes Men seldom make p. · MEN AND WOMEN 39
passeth p. all understanding · FOOD 44
passion speak with more p. · SPEECHES 16
  To inspire hopeless p. · MEN AND WOMEN 55
  vows his p. is infinite · LIES 8
passionless more interesting than the p. creep
· BORES 10
Passover is called P. · AWARDS 3
passport put warmonger on my p. · WAR 5
past looking forward to the p. · PAST 10
  Many a woman has a p. · WOMEN 71
  nothing but the p. · PAST 7
  old man's getting a bit p. it · OLD AGE 10
  prejudge the p. · PAST 14
pastoral historical-p. · ACTING 29
pastrami lush p. beds · PLACES 12
pat P. is the last straw · NAMES 7
patches garments were always in p. · WOMEN 44
pâté know a duck because you like p. · WRITERS 2
  p. de foie gras · HEAVEN 6
path about God's p. · SCIENCE 9
pathetic 'P.', he said · ANIMALS 26
patience P., stamina and good luck
· PRIME MINISTERS 16
patient I am extraordinarily p.
· SELF-KNOWLEDGE 27
patients Whenever p. come to I · MEDICINE 13
patriarch bearded p. · GOD 44
patriotism P. is the last refuge · ART 27
patriots ninety-minute p. · SCOTLAND 9
patron Is not a P., my Lord · INSULTS 21
pattable she is p. · MEN AND WOMEN 36
paucity p. of human pleasures · SPORTS 19

Pauli marvellous working for P. · SCIENCE 28
pause embarrassing p. · MARRIAGE 46
  p., and puff—and speak · SMOKING 3
  p. just long enough for an angel · TIME 10
pauses Actors use p. · SPEECHES 11
  complaints about the p. · SPEECHES 8
Pavarotti P. is not vain · SELF-KNOWLEDGE 28
paved streets are p. · CINEMA 22
pavilion P. Cost a million · ARCHITECTURE 7
paw accept its p. · RUSSIA 1
pay Kindly adjust p. · DEATH 51
  never p. till you · DEBT 5
  p. for my American Express · ADVERTISING 11
  P. given to a state hireling · TRUST 8
  p. is good · PRESIDENTS 13
  p. me twice my usual roylties · THEATRE 60
  p. to see my Aunt Minnie · FILM STARS 17
  to p. Paul · GOVERNMENT 33
paycheck month that has no p. · FOOD 58
paying p. the electricity bill · MEDICINE 2
payments missing a couple of car p. · HOPE 13
pea once ate a p. · FOOD 12
peace brought P. to Vietnam · DIPLOMACY 5
  deep p. of the double-bed · MARRIAGE 26
  democracy and p. · COUNTRIES 40
  essentially a man of p. · ARMED FORCES 31
  good war, or a bad p. · WAR 12
  like the p. of God · POETS 11
  Now she's at p. · MARRIAGE 51
peaceful p. solution · CHARACTER 1
peacock mornin' till night like a p.
· MEN AND WOMEN 38
pearls having a string of p. · FAME 17
  P. at Random Strung · POETRY 8
  P. before swine · INSULTS 29
pears no need for Peter P. · MUSICIANS 2
peasant For Pheasant *read* P. · MISTAKES 26
peccavi P.—I have Sindh · WAR 32
pecked just there to be p. · FILM PRODUCERS 7
pecker I want his p. in my pocket · POWER 5
peculiar Funny-p. · HUMOUR 19
pedagogue Ev'ry p. · EDUCATION 14
pedantry smells of p. · BOOKS 3
pedestal Mommy on a p. · FAMILY 32
  place my wife under a p. · MARRIAGE 1
pedestrian have you been a p. · TRANSPORT 36
  Red Sea p. · COUNTRIES 6
peel p. me a grape · FOOD 87
  plums and orange p. · QUOTATIONS 15
  stuff you had to p. · SEX 35
peerage study the P. · ENGLAND 42
  When I want a p. · WEALTH 19
peers do not create p. · GOVERNMENT 6
  House of P. · GOVERNMENT 11
peke supply of books, and a P. · LIFESTYLE 9

pelican wondrous bird is the p.   BIRDS 7
pellet p. with the poison   WIT 28
pen every stroke of the p.   HANDWRITING 7
  pleasure with his p.   SECURITY 1
  prevents his holding a p.   LETTERS 7
  tool Is mightier far than the p.   CRITICS 34
penchant p. for something romantic
    LITERATURE 30
pencil I was left with a p.   WRITING 8
  missing in Nature is a p.   WRITING 3
  throw down his p.   ANGER 8
penis non compos p.   CRITICS 19
  You're King Kong's p.   SEX 11
pension P. Pay given to a state   TRUST 8
  spend my p. on brandy   OLD AGE 27
pentagon P., that immense monument
    BUREAUCRACY 5
pentameter 'Twas his rhythm—Iambic P.
    POETRY 1
people betting on p.   BETTING 3
  bludgeoning of the p.   DEMOCRACY 17
  half p. and half bicycles   TRANSPORT 26
  Let my p. go   CRITICS 22
  noise, my dear! And the p.   WAR 1
  opposite of p.   ACTORS 30
  p. are only human   HUMAN RACE 1
  P. he don't like   HUMAN RACE 9
  p. is first what it eats   ENGLAND 8
  p. know what they want   DEMOCRACY 10
  p. standing in corners   TELEVISION 3
  p. who do things   SUCCESS 18
  protect the p. from the press   NEWSPAPERS 26
  supports the p.   SCOTLAND 6
peppered Shepherd's pie p.   FOOD 77
perennials P. are the ones   GARDENS 13
perfect everyone has p. teeth   APPEARANCE 15
  It's not p.   PAST 4
  None of us are p.   HUMILITY 6
  Well, nobody's p.   MARRIAGE 126
perfection P. of planned layout   BUREAUCRACY 11
  very pink of p.   SOCIETY 11
perform p. in a role hundreds of times
    THEATRE 45
performance ELSIE FERGUSON'S P.   TELEGRAMS 24
  so many years outlive p.   SEX 80
  takes away the p.   DRINK 53
performances some of my best p.   SONGS 6
performed p. for twelve presidents   PRESIDENTS 10
performing faint aroma of p. seals   LOVE 25
  thing wrong with p.   ACTING 20
Peron Eva P. as either a saint   PEOPLE 24
perpendicular out of the p.   HANDWRITING 5
  p. expression   DANCE 15
perpetual p. middle age   MIDDLE AGE 9
Perrier P. or Malvern water   CHOICE 2

persecute hound and p. the young
    GENERATION GAP 3
persecuting p. civil servants   CIVIL SERVANTS 1
persistence p. of public officials   BUREAUCRACY 9
person I am a most superior p.   PEOPLE 4
  not to be the kind of p.   CHARACTER 3
  one p. at a time   GOSSIP 3
  p. . . . can develop a cold   SICKNESS 13
  p. . . . can develop a cough   SICKNESS 12
  p. you and I took me for   MARRIAGE 28
personality come to the end of my p.
    CHARACTER 4
  From 35 to 55, good p.   MIDDLE AGE 15
  no more p. than a paper cup   TOWNS 9
  where p. is concerned   AMERICA 3
perspiration ninety-nine percent p.
    INTELLIGENCE 6
perspire Gladstone may p.   PRIME MINISTERS 10
perspiring City of p. dreams   TOWNS 25
Peru young man from P.   POETRY 2
pessimist p. waiting for rain   HOPE 3
  what a p. is   HOPE 11
pet p. is a cow   ANIMALS 9
petal p. down the Grand Canyon   POETRY 16
Peter Pan wholly in P. ever since   PEOPLE 41
phagocytes stimulate the p.   MEDICINE 34
phallus is the p.   FUTURE 11
pharynx wild about my p.   MEDICINE 30
phase Puberty is a p.   LIFESTYLE 6
pheasant For P. read Peasant   MISTAKES 26
  p., the pheasant   FOOD 76
phenomenon infant p.   ACTORS 14
  p. of nature   FILM STARS 10
Philadelphia I went to P.   TOWNS 12
  living in P.   EPITAPHS 13
philharmonic Keep your P.   MUSIC 19
  than a p. orchestra   WORK 4
philosopher one p. arguing   PHILOSOPHY 4
  p. is like a mountaineer   PHILOSOPHY 3
  to be a p.   PHILOSOPHY 2
philosophy did p.   PHILOSOPHY 9
  faced with p.   WOMEN 15
  What is your aim in p.   PHILOSOPHY 11
phlegm two new seams of p.   SICKNESS 5
phone answer the p.   MISTAKES 28
  couldn't p. it in   ACTING 20
  p., a horse or a broad   PEOPLE 25
  P. for the fish-knives, Norman   SOCIETY 4
  p. is for you   YOUTH 4
  p. whenever you felt like it   READING 14
  Stand on two p. books   PLACES 3
  What is that but a p. box   RELIGION 72
phone bill itemised p. ranks up there
    TECHNOLOGY 7
phoney P.-rustic bards   BIRDS 10

photograph AIRMAIL P. OF CHAUFFEUR
	TELEGRAMS 17
p. is not quite true	SELF-KNOWLEDGE 14
p. of the Grocer	DIPLOMACY 16

photographed next war will be p. WAR 8
photographer p. is like the cod TECHNOLOGY 14
photographers don't trust p. APPEARANCE 9
phrase all systems in a p. WIT 52
  p. becomes current LANGUAGE 8
physical chiefly from p. conditions POETRY 13
  For p. pleasure SEX 95
physically p. desirable APPEARANCE 12
physician died last might of my p. MEDICINE 31
  p. can bury ARCHITECTURE 16
physicians help of too many p. MEDICINE 1
  P. of the Utmost Fame MEDICINE 6
pianist Please do not shoot the p. MUSICIANS 4
piano p. gets into a log hut MUSIC 17
  p. is a parlour utensil MUSIC 9
  p. when played by a sister MUSIC 58
  push a grand p. CHILDREN 28
  teach the drummer to play p. MUSIC 36
pianoforte p. is a harp in a box MUSIC 24
Picasso P., sunbathing and jazz SATISFACTION 16
piccola bar on the P. Marina COUNTRIES 11
picket It's not cricket to p. POLITICS 58
pickle open p. jars MEN AND WOMEN 15
  weaned on a p. DESCRIPTION 1
pickpockets Coffin Makers and P. LITERATURE 24
picnic apples short of a p. FOOLISHNESS 9
picture It was a cute p. FILM 13
  p. to remain as by Nollekens ROYALTY 47
  set off in this p. FILM 1
pictures behind all the p. SECURITY 2
  dearth of bad p. CINEMA 10
  know which p. are yours FILM PRODUCERS 3
  P. are for entertainment CINEMA 12
  p. that got small FILM STARS 3
  without p. or conversations LITERATURE 10
pie man appeared on a flaming p. NAMES 20
  p.-eaters' liberation front DIETS 4
  put into a p. ANIMALS 34
piece p. of cod FOOD 44
pier only seaside p. on which NAMES 27
  opened a p. FAME 14
piety reputation for p. WEATHER 15
pig p. got up and slowly walked DRINK 10
  p. in a silk suit FILM PRODUCERS 8
  p. is to the Irishman ANIMALS 18
  shrewd, levelheaded p. INTELLIGENCE 17
  silk stockings on a p. BOXING 7
  When not, a p. CHILDREN 11
pigeon crooning like a bilious p. LANGUAGES 23
  To poison a p. in the park MURDER 10
pigeons p., or Catholics SEX 5

pigs fond of p. ANIMALS 10
Pilate since Pontius P. JUDGES 8
piles Awards are like p. AWARDS 5
Pilgrim 'P.'s Progress' BOOKS 19
pill not even going on the p. BODY 29
  Protestant women may take the p. RELIGION 69
  something of a p. LOVE 47
pillow like the feather p. INSULTS 15
pills don't believe in vitamin p. MEDICINE 10
piminy miminy, p. MEN 6
pimples scratching of p. BOOKS 24
pin p. up my hair with prose LETTERS 4
pinafore mistakes his p. for a toga WRITERS 14
pineapple p. of politeness WIT 34
pinheads dance on p. CERTAINTY 9
pink all this wonderful p. COLOURS 2
  made out of p. marzipan FACES 4
  P. is the navy blue COLOURS 9
  p. was her favourite colour COLOURS 1
  very p. of perfection SOCIETY 11
pint p. . . . . why that's very nearly MEDICINE 15
pints had 40 p. MEDICINE 8
pious he was rarther p. RELIGION 4
pipe p. with solemn interposing puff SMOKING 3
  three-p. problem CRIME 12
Pippa P. passes THEATRE 8
piss pitcher of warm p. PRESIDENTS 7
  pour p. out of a boot STUPIDITY 3
  wouldn't p. in his ear ENEMIES 1
pissed you p. in our soup TRUST 1
pissing inside the tent p. out POWER 6
  like p. down your leg SPEECHES 13
pistol Is that a p. in your pocket
    MEN AND WOMEN 60
  p. misses fire ARGUMENT 8
pit many-headed monster of the p. THEATRE 40
pitchfork thrown on her with a p. DRESS 19
pith p. is in the postscript LETTERS 9
pitied more to be p. than censured
    LANGUAGES 29
Pitt P. is to Addington PRIME MINISTERS 9
Pittsburgh guy I knew in P. MEN AND WOMEN 33
pity it was a p. to get up WEATHER 16
pix Sticks nix hick p. HEADLINES 4
pizza stopped with the p. oven SCIENCE 7
place good p. to have them BEHAVIOUR 35
  know your p. CLASS 21
  our only dry p. WEATHER 15
  to keep in the same p. PROGRESS 3
place mats coming home with Rembrandt p.
    SOCIETY 21
places friends in both p. HEAVEN 7
plagiarism gets in the way of their p. MUSIC 13
  is p. HOLLYWOOD 16
  steal from one author, it's p. WRITING 15

prize as a Pulitzer P.   JOURNALISM 11
  filling out p. applications   JOURNALISM 1
prize-fighters p. shaking hands   WOMEN 37
prizes P. are like sashes   AWARDS 1
probabilities based on p.   HANDWRITING 6
problem p. is food   MONEY 10
  p. to be overcome   MEN 10
  research staff to study the p.   MONEY 27
  three-pipe p.   CRIME 12
proceeds on the p.   HYPOCRISY 7
prodigal p.'s return   RELIGION 59
produced If any play has been p.   THEATRE 24
producer associate with a p.   FILM PRODUCERS 19
producers film p.   CINEMA 21
product fitting the p.   BUSINESS 6
production ON YOUR LATEST P.   TELEGRAMS 5
profanity speak English and p.   LANGUAGES 14
profession have a second p. in reserve

                                                 POLITICS 51
  head of the literary p.   PRAISE 2
  isn't a p.   FAME 4
  p. with a high sexual strike rate   HISTORY 3
  second oldest p.   POLITICS 56
  successful in your p.   CRIME 11
  very important p.   FAMILY 39
professional p. courtesy   INSULTS 25
  p. is a man who can   WORK 2
professor P. of Logic   PHILOSOPHY 1
  p. of rotational medicine   POLITICS 48
profitable p. to its possessor   VIRTUE 12
programme dreadful, off-colour p.

                                             BROADCASTING 6
  ideal p.   HUMOUR 21
progress illusion of p.   MANAGEMENT 2
  indeterminate p.   PROGRESS 13
  Scotland has made enormous p.   SCOTLAND 7
prohibition P. makes you want   DRINK 39
prologue witty p. to a very dull play

                                               MARRIAGE 36
prologues P. precede the piece   THEATRE 20
Prometheus P., with the vultures   ANGER 11
promise don't fulfil the p.   CHILDREN 33
  p. of a man   CHILDREN 16
  Whose p. none relies on   ROYALTY 56
promises man who p. least   POLITICS 9
promising p. little war   WAR 28
  they first call p.   SUCCESS 6
pronounce spell better than they p.

                                              LANGUAGES 25
Prooshans may be P.   COUNTRIES 13
propaganda on p.   LIES 5
proper I'll be p. and prim   NAMES 21
property Thieves respect p.   CRIME 6
proposal p. which my secretary faxed   LOVE 15
propose p. nothing   POLITICS 24

proposed President p.   PRESIDENTS 2
proprietor death of a p.   HYPOCRISY 1
prose All that is not p. is verse   POETRY 18
  Meredith's a p. Browning   LITERATURE 34
  murderer for a fancy p. style   MURDER 11
  pin up my hair with p.   LETTERS 4
  p. in ribands   POETRY 14
  p. of incomparable grandeur   WRITERS 21
  p. run mad   POETRY 20
  speaking p. without knowing it   POETRY 19
prospect noblest p.   SCOTLAND 5
prospects affording delightful p.   HOTELS 4
prosper affairs p.   FUTURE 2
prostitute doormat or a p.   WOMEN 68
  mistaken for a p.   MISTAKES 16
  p. all their powers   LITERATURE 16
prostitution field of p.   HOLLYWOOD 5
protect Heaven will p. a working-girl

                                                POVERTY 17
  p. the Government of the day   SECURITY 6
  p. the people from the press   NEWSPAPERS 26
  p. the writer   BUREAUCRACY 1
protected squirrels, must be p.   LAW 30
protest lady doth p. too much   WOMEN 55
  p. against golf   CRICKET 6
Protestant I am the P. whore   RELIGION 26
  like a P. curate   DANCE 11
  P., if he wants aid   RELIGION 20
  P. with a horse   IRELAND 1
Protestantism contribution of P.   GOD 33
proud always p. of the fact   SLEEP 7
  Everyone was poor and p.   POVERTY 10
prove p. that you don't need it   MONEY 20
  to p. it I'm here   COMEDY 13
                                               COMEDY 30
proverbs Solomon wrote the P.   RELIGION 44
proves p. that he is one himself   PHILOSOPHY 4
providence workings of P.   ARGUMENT 17
provinces peddles in the p.   WIT 51
provocations intolerable p.   GOLF 5
provoker Drink, sir, is a great p.   DRINK 53
prudence effect of p. on rascality   VIRTUE 16
Prussians may be P.   COUNTRIES 13
psalms David wrote the P.   RELIGION 44
psychiatrist Any man who goes to a p.

                                              MEDICINE 16
  p. is a man who goes   MEDICINE 36
  p.'s couch   MIND 9
psychiatry P. is a waste   MIND 7
psychical For P. Research   MURDER 4
puberty P. is a phase   LIFESTYLE 6
pubic p. hair factory   DESCRIPTION 21
public as if I was a p. meeting   ROYALTY 64
  become p. property   BODY 4
  describe holding p. office   WORK 1

English p. school | EDUCATION 44
give the p. something | DEATH 65
in a p. place | BEHAVIOUR 31
It's not a p. conveyance | MARRIAGE 86
one to mislead the p. | POLITICS 6
p. be damned | BUSINESS 19
p. relations | JOURNALISM 18
p. think you are either dead | TELEVISION 8
to p. speaking | SPEECHES 5
uncritical buying p. | ADVERTISING 4
went to p. school | EDUCATION 6
publication praised their last p. | WRITERS 5
publicity it's a p. stunt | TRANSPORT 24
now called p. | FAME 18
publicly not insult his wife p. | MARRIAGE 117
published before this book is p. | BIOGRAPHY 10
publisher agent to a p. | PUBLISHING 14
Barabbas was a p. | PUBLISHING 9
murdering his p. | PUBLISHING 3
p. has to do is write cheques | PUBLISHING 18
p. who writes is like a cow | PUBLISHING 15
publishers Easier to change p. | PUBLISHING 11
p. and printers | CENSORSHIP 8
p. are untrustworthy | PUBLISHING 17
publishing easier job like p. | PUBLISHING 2
pubs all the p. in Dublin | DEATH 22
pudding plums for the p. | WIT 51
p. of exhaustion | OLD AGE 32
Take away that p. | FOOD 18
puff friends all united to p. | EPITAPHS 26
solemn interposing p. | SMOKING 3
pug O most charming p. | WIT 10
Pulitzer as a P. Prize | JOURNALISM 11
Pulitzers apply for the P. | JOURNALISM 1
pull had to p. him out | PEOPLE 17
pulls p. a lady through | HOPE 6
pulse feeling a woman's p. | WOMEN 60
pun suspecting me of a p. | ARMED FORCES 2
punch start a p.-up | CRITICS 16
want to p. its light out | SELF-KNOWLEDGE 12
punch-line transcendental meditation with a p. | FISHING 2
punctual would always be p. | FILM STARS 17
punctuation p. vigilante | GRAMMAR 7
punishing p. anyone who comes between them | MARRIAGE 112
punishment My fees are sufficient p. | LAW 2
punster inveterate p. | WIT 21
pupped come down and p. | ARCHITECTURE 14
pure has not a p. heart | COOKERY 1
p. as the driven slush | VIRTUE 1
truth is rarely p. | TRUTH 11
purée p. of white kid gloves | FOOD 71
purgatory department of P. | OLD AGE 9
purge p., and leave sack | ARISTOCRACY 15

Puritanism not P. but February | WEATHER 13
puritanism P. The haunting fear | RELIGION 41
purity spoil the p. of my hatred | POLITICIANS 31
purple I shall wear p. | OLD AGE 27
story of a p. man | BIOGRAPHY 8
walk by the colour p. | COLOURS 10
purpose happy sense of p. | CERTAINTY 21
If people want a sense of p. | MORALITY 5
purposive such a word as p. | WORDS 19
purrs stroke a platitude until it p. | NEWSPAPERS 11
pursue p. Culture in bands | ART 42
pursued it is you who are the p. | MEN AND WOMEN 50
pursuit full p. of the uneatable | SPORTS 41
man in p. of happiness | WEDDINGS 4
p. of truth is chimerical | TRUTH 1
push didn't p. him in | PEOPLE 17
P. de button | PROGRESS 11
pushed Did he fall or was he p. | DEATH 35
pussy want a fag with a p. | MARRIAGE 60
pustule p. on the rump of the body politic | ARISTOCRACY 14
put up with which I will not p. | LANGUAGE 2
putts missed short p. | GOLF 12
when he p. | GOLF 4
puzzle Don't p. me | ARGUMENT 19
Pygmalion P. is not good enough | MUSIC 51
pyjamas buy those blue p. | FASHION 6
cardigan over his p. | MEN AND WOMEN 28
p. look nice on him | MEN AND WOMEN 19
Pyramus death of P. and Thisby | THEATRE 46

quack went, with a q. | BIRDS 5
quad no one about in the Q. | GOD 31
quails how we want our q. done | SOCIETY 8
qualifications q. to detain them | SUCCESS 23
qualities such q. as would wear well | MARRIAGE 67
quantum q. solar energy | HOSPITALITY 1
quarrels in q. interpose | ARGUMENT 7
q. that were hapless | TOWNS 14
q. with one's husband | MARRIAGE 19
quarries q. to be used at will | QUOTATIONS 9
quarry marked down q. | MEN AND WOMEN 50
quarterly nothing a-year, paid q. | POVERTY 20
queen being a drag q. | FASHION 8
God save the Q. | ROYALTY 65
have the Q. as their aunt | ROYALTY 46
home life of our own dear Q. | ROYALTY 10
love of a Q. | CINEMA 4
Q. has the quality | MARRIAGE 94
Q. is most anxious | WOMEN 65
Q. Mary looking like | ROYALTY 19
Q. Mother of football | FOOTBALL 25
Q. to skip Chuck nups | HEADLINES 3

regal make someone that height look r.

ROYALTY 1

regimental r. doctor

DRESS 6

regret living to r. it

POLITICAL PARTIES 16

  perfunctory r.

SATISFACTION 14

  r. in the theatre

ACTORS 3

regrets r. she's unable

BEHAVIOUR 25

regular brought r.

DRINK 18

rehearsal ten o'clock r.

THEATRE 31

reigned if only he had not r.

POWER 11

reincarnation believe in r.

DEATH 13

  'Thank you, no r.'

UNIVERSE 9

reindeer Red-Nosed R.

ANIMALS 23

reinvented r. unsliced bread

WIT 19

reiterate I r.

CONVERSATION 31

rejection Fifteen years of r.

LIFESTYLE 6

rejoice not much reason to r.

LOVE 41

  R., rejoice

ENEMIES 3

relation nobody like a r.

FAMILY 44

relations apology for r.

FRIENDS 8

  company are all r.

DANCE 3

relationship have a working r.

GOD 20

  r. that goes bad

SONGS 10

relative in a r. way

SCIENCE 8

reliable r. as his hairpieces

AUTOBIOGRAPHY 17

reliance firm r.

CRITICS 14

relied now be absolutely r. relied upon

NEWSPAPERS 28

religion all of the same r.

RELIGION 21

  don't know into what r.

RELIGION 5

  every thing that regards r.

RELIGION 1

  fishing is a r.

FISHING 1

  fox-hunting—the wisest r.

POLITICAL PARTIES 9

  Millionaire. That is my r.

WEALTH 26

  no reason to bring r. in to it

RELIGION 47

  r. is allowed to invade

RELIGION 40

  state r.

FOOD 8

  vice and r.

ENGLAND 34

religious any r. belief

CLERGY 19

  cold bath and a r. exercise

NEWSPAPERS 5

  manners can replace r. beliefs

RELIGION 48

  r. affairs department

BROADCASTING 2

  r. system that produced

RELIGION 58

  r. upon a sunshiny day

RELIGION 16

  though a r. man

RELIGION 70

remaindered my enemy has been r.

WRITERS 17

remarkable very r. man

FUTURE 8

Rembrandt right at the R.

HOSPITALITY 3

remedy have no r.

HAPPINESS 8

remember Ah yes! I r. it well

OLD AGE 28

  no-one can r.

HUMOUR 33

  not difficult to r.

TITLES 4

  r. your name

NAMES 29

  what you can r.

HISTORY 9

remembered like to be r.

BEHAVIOUR 10

reminiscence best-selling r.

AUTOBIOGRAPHY 10

reminiscences r. of Mrs Humphrey Ward

AUTOBIOGRAPHY 13

  some of your grosser r.

LETTERS 16

remorse R. Those dry Martinis

DRINK 1

remote R. and ineffectual Don

LITERATURE 3

remove not malignant and r. it

MEDICINE 37

  owl of the R.

CHILDREN 35

  r. my overdraft

DEBT 3

renaissance R. was just something

PROGRESS 4

Reno King's Moll R.'d

ROYALTY 4

rent paid a month's r.

WAR 17

  r. ain't paid

DEBT 4

  r. out my room

FAMILY 2

reorganized we would be r.

MANAGEMENT 2

repainting anything that eats or needs r.

WEALTH 25

repartee best r.

DEMOCRACY 4

  fear r. in a wife

MARRIAGE 130

repeats History r. itself

HISTORY 5

repent r. at leisure

MARRIAGE 39

repented she strove, and much r.

SEX 30

replied r. to your letter

LETTERS 12

report Beauty school r.

EDUCATION 18

reporters doesn't like to talk to r.

JOURNALISM 20

reports R. of my death

DEATH 69

repose r. is taboo'd by anxiety

LANGUAGE 6

represent don't r. anybody

ARISTOCRACY 9

representative indignity of being your r.

RELIGION 6

reproduction pretty good r.

BODY 9

reproductive modern r. processes

BODY 48

reptile r. all the rest

INSULTS 33

reptilian evil r. kitten-eater

POLITICIANS 1

republic aristocracy in a r.

ARISTOCRACY 13

republican God is a R.

POLITICAL PARTIES 15

Republicans like a lot of R.

POLITICAL PARTIES 18

  make a bargain with the R.

POLITICS 66

repulsive Right but R.

DESCRIPTION 29

reputation girl who lost her r.

SELF-KNOWLEDGE 29

reputations murdered r.

GOSSIP 2

  true fuller's earth for r.

MONEY 15

re-read r. all his early stuff

WRITERS 49

rescuers firing on the r.

ACTORS 36

research Basic r. is what I am doing

SCIENCE 6

  name of r.

EDUCATION 21

  r. in bars

JOURNALISM 17

  salaries of a large r. staff

MONEY 27

  steal from many, it's r.

WRITING 15

resemblance another's r. to ourselves

SELF-KNOWLEDGE 3

Richard unjustly reckoned A R. the Third
POLITICIANS 2

riches that of the titled for r.
TITLES 7

ricicles r. are twicicles
WIT 30

rid before getting r. of it
BUREAUCRACY 6

ridiculous R. farces
THEATRE 19

Sublime To the R.
TRANSPORT 13

riding Are you fond of r., dear
SPORTS 30

Riga young lady of R.
ANIMALS 4

Rigg hugged by Diana R.
MEDICINE 32

right almost always in the r.
POLITICS 63

be decorative and to do r.
WOMEN 17

being the r. way up
ARGUMENT 4

brains are in the r. place
DESCRIPTION 2

decide I was r.
FOOTBALL 6

doctor being always in the r.
MEDICINE 33

give my r. arm
ART 4

half of the people are r.
DEMOCRACY 16

having to be r.
POLITICS 67

In boxing the r. cross-counter
BOXING 14

it's all r. with me
MIND 1

men go r. after them
MEN AND WOMEN 61

r. at the Rembrandt
HOSPITALITY 3

R. but Repulsive
DESCRIPTION 29

R. Now is a lot better
PAST 4

should be on my r.
POLITICAL PARTIES 10

Whenever you're r., shut up
MARRIAGE 88

Where did we go r.
SUCCESS 3

rights folly of 'Woman's r.'
WOMEN 65

rigorous what a r. exam
JUDGES 7

Rimbauds always chasing R.
LITERATURE 26

rings read the r.
MARRIAGE 82

Too many r. around Rosie
MEN AND WOMEN 5

riot Blamelessness runs r.
BIOGRAPHY 15

rioting r. and learning
EDUCATION 9

rip R.-Van-With-It
NAMES 10

rise carcases, which are to r.
BODY 7

risen Frost has r. without trace
SUCCESS 19

rising from r. hope
SUCCESS 9

risk at great personal r. by the author
MEN AND WOMEN 46

risks one of the r.
AMERICA 23

risotto screaming r. recipes
OPERA 6

Ritz Children of the R.
SOCIETY 8

life for ourselves at the R.
ROYALTY 12

sits At the R.
CLASS 29

river didn't write 'Ol' Man R.'
SONGS 12

road and not the r.
EPITAPHS 22

middle of the r.
LIFESTYLE 5

r. that leads him to England
SCOTLAND 5

roam sent to r.
FOOLISHNESS 4

roar I storm and I r.
ANGER 6

r. their ribs out
HUMOUR 17

roareth What is this that r. thus
TRANSPORT 12

roast learned r.
COOKERY 14

no politics in boiled and r.
POLITICAL PARTIES 17

R. Beef, Medium
FOOD 25

r. beef and rain
ENGLAND 8

rob meant to r. her
LOVE 21

r. a lady of her fortune
MARRIAGE 53

robbed I'd expect to be r. in Chicago
TOWNS 22

We was r.
BOXING 8

robbing r. a bank
CRIME 5

robin little r.
COUNTRY 20

Robin Hood modern-day R.
FILM PRODUCERS 18

robs r. Peter
GOVERNMENT 33

rock cast the first r.
MEN AND WOMEN 32

dank r. pools
FOOD 46

dealing in r.'n'roll
HUMAN RACE 8

R. Journalism
JOURNALISM 28

Rockefeller rich as R.
WEALTH 12

Rockefellers Where would the R. be today
WEALTH 21

rocking-horse in love with my r.
MIND 4

mad r. and a rawhide suitcase
FILM STARS 5

rodeoing R. is about the only sport
SPORTS 22

rogue this r. and whore together
RELIGION 3

rogues couple of r.
ART 11

role perform in a r.
THEATRE 45

roll Assistant heads must r.
MANAGEMENT 1

rolled r. along on wheels
MEN AND WOMEN 22

rollers glanced at her Carmen r.
NAMES 11

roller skates up hill in r.
BORES 1

Roman no R. ever was able to say
SOCIETY 2

rhyme for r.
WIT 10

R. Conquest
ENGLAND 28

Roman Catholic is a R.
FRIENDS 6

romance fine r. with no kisses
MEN AND WOMEN 13

lifelong r.
LOVE 46

r. has come to an end
MEN AND WOMEN 2

Twenty years of r.
MARRIAGE 125

romances torrid r.
CENSORSHIP 1

romantic her penchant For something r.
LITERATURE 30

most r. signature
TITLES 1

R.? In your mother's clean
LOVE 40

Rome all the sights in R. were called
TRAVEL 20

It's R., it's hot
CINEMA 1

room All I need is r.
HOME 13

find my way across the r.
PREJUDICE 8

lighten a r.
PEOPLE 3

not a rhinoceros in the r.
PHILOSOPHY 8

sitting in the smallest r.
LETTERS 13

Roosevelt Once we had a R.
AMERICA 14

Rooshans may be R.
COUNTRIES 13

Roosian might have been a R.
COUNTRIES 20

said (*cont.*):

nobody had s. it before   QUOTATIONS 18

s. what she thought   VIRTUE 19

what the soldier s.   LAW 6

Saigon S. is like all the other   TOWNS 23

sailing failing occurred in the s.   TRAVEL 3

sailor No man will be a s.   ARMED FORCES 18

sailors three young s.   COUNTRIES 11

saint make of me a s.   LOVE 7

s. or the incarnation of Satan   PEOPLE 24

saints overrun by a Wave of S.   RELIGION 61

s. on their way to martyrdom   WORK 26

salad focus on my s.   COOKERY 20

s. lies in a group   TRAVEL 25

shit from a chicken s.   SPEECHES 12

salary s. depends on not understanding

     MANAGEMENT 8

sale last day of a great white s.   MIND 16

sales would halve the s.   SCIENCE 15

salmon issued with a 2lb fresh s.   YOUTH 3

s. over his shoulder   ART 34

s. standing on it's tail   PEOPLE 40

short stout s.   CHILDREN 44

salon s. for his agents   ARCHITECTURE 5

salt Not enough s.   FOOD 9

s. left in my shaker   OLD AGE 15

Salteena Mr S. was an elderly man of 42

     OLD AGE 2

S. was not very addicted   RELIGION 4

salutary medicinally s.   CRITICS 24

Sam think of me as S.   NAMES 26

wouldn't have a Willie or a S.   MARRIAGE 87

same come back the s. day   TRAVEL 17

He is much the s.   TELEGRAMS 1

make all the s. mistakes   LIFE 4

saying the s. about you   WRITERS 8

sample If this planet is a s.   UNIVERSE 9

sampled sort of s.   MEN AND WOMEN 58

sanctions Baldwin denouncing s.   CERTAINTY 2

sanctuary three classes which need s.   POLITICS 8

sand s. in the porridge   HOLIDAYS 3

sandals wearing s. but never with socks

     DRESS 18

sandwich cheaper than a prawn s.   BUSINESS 11

Life is a shit s.   LIFE 14

s. named after me   FAME 21

watercress s.   FOOD 90

sandwiches green s.   FOOD 74

Sandy my friend, S.   COMEDY 18

sanitary glorified s. engineer   PEOPLE 39

sanity ain't no S. Claus   CHRISTMAS 8

Santa Claus S. is a Democrat   POLITICAL PARTIES 15

sapphire s. bracelet   AMERICA 20

sarcasm Guinness, s. and late nights   IRELAND 9

sardine than a s. tin   GOLF 1

sardines s. will be thrown   JOURNALISM 9

sashes nice new s.   DEATH 28

Prizes are like s.   AWARDS 1

sat arse upon which everyone has s.

     POLITICIANS 16

no one has ever s. on me   WORDS 40

Satan incarnation of S.   PEOPLE 24

S. made Sydney   TOWNS 1

S. probably wouldn't   GOD 36

satanist I'm a dyslexic S.   RELIGION 66

satire It's hard not to write s.   WIT 16

it was s.   HUMOUR 39

s. is a lesson   WIT 25

S. is a sort of glass   SELF-KNOWLEDGE 25

S. is what closes Saturday   THEATRE 32

S. or sense, alas   INSULTS 32

satirical any s. programme   HUMOUR 35

satirist bounding past the s.   HUMOUR 10

satisfaction I can't get no s.   SEX 49

satisfied Massey won't be s.   ACTORS 24

S. great success   MUSIC 56

satisfying s. a voracious appetite   LOVE 14

Saturday date on a S. night   SEX 7

on a S. night   HUMOUR 11

on S. nights   TELEVISION 6

Satire is what closes S. night   THEATRE 32

S. morning, although recurring   TRANSPORT 10

sauce pouring tinned s.   COOKERY 3

sausage s. and haddock   COOKERY 22

savage s. nobility   CRITICS 14

untutored s.   MARRIAGE 55

savaged s. by a dead sheep   INSULTS 17

save less democracy to s.   WAR 3

s. all the parts   TECHNOLOGY 4

saved Are you s.   RELIGION 37

s. by being dammed   COUNTRIES 21

saving S. is a very fine thing   MONEY 8

Savoy gun cross the S. Grill   BUSINESS 10

saw I s. you do it   ACTORS 30

say did not s. them things   CERTAINTY 15

don't s. much   ACTING 36

do what I s.   GOVERNMENT 36

I did not s.   CERTAINTY 20

man who, having nothing to s.

     CONVERSATION 11

s. a few words   SPEECHES 10

s. a thing, it's true   PRIME MINISTERS 18

s. of me behind my back   SELF-KNOWLEDGE 30

s. the perfectly correct   BEHAVIOUR 28

s. what you mean   CONVERSATION 5

someone else has got to s.   ARGUMENT 6

way I s. it   FILM STARS 16

you have something to s.   WRITERS 9

second for a s. time   GARDENS 10
  like a s. home   POLITICIANS 21
  s. oldest profession   POLITICS 56
  s.-rate ones   MUSIC 6
seconds favourite food is s.   DIETS 7
secret bother with s. signals   SEX 15
  decency is sort of s.   CHARACTER 15
  discovered the s.   MIDDLE AGE 9
  keep a measly affair s.   SECURITY 5
  keep your s.   ACTORS 33
  much of a s. agent   SECURITY 1
  neurosis is a s.   MIND 15
  one of my most s. vices   SECRECY 6
  s. dies with me   LIBRARIES 1
  s. in the Oxford sense   GOSSIP 3
  that's a s.   GOSSIP 1
secretary s. is not a toy   WORK 19
  to be an effective s.   WORK 26
secrets disclosing musical s.   MUSICIANS 16
  heard some s.   SECRECY 1
  s. with girls   SECRECY 5
seduction In s., the rapist   SEX 37
see come up and s. me sometime   SEX 97
  I can hardly s.   SEX 19
  If they could s. me now   CLASS 13
  I'll come and s. you   ACTING 25
  I s. a voice   WIT 31
  I shall never s.   ADVERTISING 7
  not worth going to s.   TRAVEL 14
  s. the world   ARMED FORCES 4
  You can s. as far as Marlow   MISTAKES 11
seed spills his s.   NAMES 25
seeing without s. anything   TRAVEL 16
seen s. dead with   DEATH 73
  s. one Western   CINEMA 26
sees s. and hears all we do   MARRIAGE 100
self devoted s.-sacrifice   BUREAUCRACY 2
  For s.-revelation   SELF-KNOWLEDGE 16
  low s.-esteem   SELF-KNOWLEDGE 20
  s.-assertion abroad   NEWSPAPERS 27
  s.-cleaning oven   HOUSEWORK 6
  S.-denial is not a virtue   VIRTUE 16
  s.-limiting revolution   PROGRESS 14
  s.-made man   ENGLAND 2
  s.-sufficiency at home   NEWSPAPERS 27
  starves your s.-respect   POLITICS 55
self-control s. in cabinet   ANGER 8
sell I'll s. him   CHILDREN 25
  s. his house   HOME 18
sells she s.   CINEMA 17
semi s.-house-trained polecat   POLITICIANS 17
semicolon telephoned a s.   JOURNALISM 4
senators look at the s.   GOVERNMENT 12
senescence S. begins   OLD AGE 33
senna dutiful boy takes s.-tea   CRITICS 17

sense Satire or s., alas   INSULTS 32
  s. beneath is rarely found   WORDS 29
  s. of humour   ENGLAND 19
senses should they come to their s.
                           POLITICIANS 26
sensibilité word equivalent to s.   LANGUAGES 20
sensible S. men are all of the same   RELIGION 21
sensitively lie to them s.   MEN AND WOMEN 37
sensitivity extraordinary s.   HYPOCRISY 1
sensual Catholic and s.   COUNTRIES 5
sentence end a s. with a climax   SPEECHES 14
  half a s. at a time   SMOKING 3
  let her husband finish a s.   MARRIAGE 91
  Marriage isn't a word . . . it's a s.   MARRIAGE 121
  originator of a good s.   QUOTATIONS 5
  perfect s. construction   EDUCATION 26
  S. structure is innate   GRAMMAR 1
  simple declarative s.   EPITAPHS 10
sentences Backward ran s.   LANGUAGE 5
sentencing s. a man   PUNISHMENT 9
sentimental s. crap of it   AMERICA 8
  s. value   BODY 20
separated so joined that they cannot be s.
                           MARRIAGE 112
seraglio s. of eunuchs   POLITICS 27
serendipity s. means   WORDS 6
serial s. killer   APPEARANCE 9
serious joke's a very s. thing   HUMOUR 9
  more s. than that   FOOTBALL 24
  s. and the smirk   ART 8
  s. thing as a joke   HUMOUR 27
  You cannot be s.   TENNIS 7
seriously S., though   COMEDY 44
seriousness S. is stupidity   STUPIDITY 4
sermons look for s. in stones   NATURE 2
  S. and soda-water   HAPPINESS 4
  She can't even hear my s.   RELIGION 74
servant answer to the s. problem   SCIENCE 19
  lookingglass of a s.   ART 18
  s.'s cut in half   DEATH 27
  s. to the devil   CIVIL SERVANTS 7
servants English s.   COUNTRIES 4
  in the s.' hall   CLASS 2
serve s. both God and Mammon   GOD 40
service soong the s. dyvyne   WOMEN 7
  unfit for military s.   ARMED FORCES 14
serviette say 's.'   TITLES 8
sesquippledan 'S. verboojuice'   WIT 49
set he had a complete s.   LIBRARIES 7
  s. fair   PRIDE 1
settled waiting till the children are s.   LOVE 49
seven Even the Almighty took s.   POLITICS 17
  learned in s. years   GENERATION GAP 13
  lowly air Of S. Dials   ARISTOCRACY 6
  talk about the s. inches   BODY 46

side don't care which s. wins | SPORTS 8
I am on the s. of the angels | RELIGION 19
Yo! Turkey I'm on your s. | CHRISTMAS 13
sides both s. of the paper | EXAMINATIONS 6
everyone changes s. | GENERATION GAP 4
holding on to the s. | CHARACTER 6
said on both s. | ARGUMENT 1
sidestep I never s. skunks | INSULTS 12
sideways tried walking s. | TRANSPORT 24
walk s. towards them | CRICKET 15
We think s. | IRELAND 7
Siegfried listen to the last scene of S. | SECRECY 6
sight at first s. | FRIENDS 12
sights few more impressive s. | SCOTLAND 1
sign I don't wish to s. my name | LETTERS 15
s. on the door | CERTAINTY 6
some clear s. | GOD 2
signalling wildly s. | BODY 11
signature official s. | TITLES 1
One day you are a s. | FAME 25
one's style is one's s. | LETTERS 15
signed he never s. off | POLITICIANS 7
significance song of social s. | POLITICS 59
silence easy step to s. | POLITICS 7
flashes of s. | CONVERSATION 27
Indecency's conspiracy of s. | VIRTUE 15
two minutes' s. | WRITERS 3
silent Absolutely s. | SOCIETY 15
'g' is s. | INSULTS 6
God is s. | GOD 3
Poets have been mysteriously s. | FOOD 17
t is s. as in *Harlow* | INSULTS 2
silhouette impressive in s. | ACTORS 32
silicon Had s. been a gas | EXAMINATIONS 7
silk make a s. purse | ANIMALS 28
pig in a s. suit | FILM PRODUCERS 8
s. makes the difference | CLASS 14
s. stockings of your actresses | THEATRE 27
worn with a s. hat | DRESS 3
silly getting s. | BIBLE 2
silver Georgian s. goes | POLITICAL PARTIES 13
s. foot in his mouth | PRESIDENTS 18
s. lining in the sky-ee | WAR 31
s. plate on a coffin | DESCRIPTION 12
thirty pieces of s. | POLITICS 10
simple beautiful and s. | CRIME 15
rarely pure, and never s. | TRUTH 11
S. tastes, you will agree | SATISFACTION 5
What do the s. folk do | ROYALTY 44
simplicity s. of the three per cents | MONEY 26
sin autobiography is a s. | AUTOBIOGRAPHY 13
beauty is only s. deep | APPEARANCE 16
cardinal s. is dullness | CINEMA 2
Excepting Original S. | VIRTUE 5
go away and s. no more | ROYALTY 7

not generally a social s. | HYPOCRISY 5
one unpardonable s. | SUCCESS 1
researches in original s. | SEX 72
s. with Elinor Glyn | SEX 10
sincere wit should be no more s. | WIT 7
sincerity s. is a dangerous thing | VIRTUE 25
Sindh I have s. | WAR 32
sing call my answering machine and s. | MUSICIANS 22
die before they s. | DEATH 15
heard no horse s. a song | MUSIC 2
people s. it | SONGS 5
s. my best in this position | SONGS 6
they could s. | PREJUDICE 10
used to s. in the bath tub | WORK 16
singer comedian, a s. or an entertainer | PEOPLE 38
singing don't want you s. | FUNERALS 2
in spite of the s. | OPERA 9
single s. man in possession | MARRIAGE 9
singles What strenuous s. we played | TENNIS 2
sings instead of bleeding, he s. | OPERA 4
With every word it s. | DESCRIPTION 16
sinister went around looking s. | SECURITY 7
sink s. my boats | MARRIAGE 2
threw the kitchen s. | TENNIS 8
sinking desert a s. ship | CERTAINTY 3
like a s. ship | ACTORS 36
swimming *towards* a s. ship | TRUST 2
sinner I've been a s. | RELIGION 52
Or I of her a s. | LOVE 7
s. revised and edited | VIRTUE 3
sinning in good shape for more s. | RELIGION 56
sins She s. not with courtiers | ROYALTY 6
s. were scarlet | DEATH 11
sissy rose-red s. | DESCRIPTION 28
s. stuff that rhymes | POETRY 24
sister bury my s. | FUNERALS 3
trying to violate your s. | SEX 87
sisterly s. animosity | FAMILY 42
sisters s. and his cousins | FAMILY 18
s. under their skins | WOMEN 33
sit allowed to s. down | DIPLOMACY 18
come and s. by me | GOSSIP 6
Here I s., alone and sixty | OLD AGE 5
sitcom s. in America | TELEVISION 13
site By God what a s. | AUSTRALIA 5
sits s. down before he stands up | SPEECHES 15
Sometimes I s. and thinks | PHILOSOPHY 7
sitter ask the s. | ART 35
sitting keep your face, and stay s. down | MIDDLE AGE 5
unsportsmanlike to hit a s. ball | GOLF 7
you're s. on it | FILM STARS 8
Sitwells friend of the S. | SOCIETY 1

six forget the s. feet   BODY 46
sixpence precious little for s.   ECONOMICS 14
   shot at for s.   ARMED FORCES 9
sixty alone and s.   OLD AGE 5
   recently turned s.   MIDDLE AGE 2
sixty-five s. you get social security   SEX 82
size cut you down to my s.   MEN AND WOMEN 20
   s. of the onion, the dish   COOKERY 15
   they're s. ten   BODY 8
skate I could s. on them   DRESS 2
skating s. on thin ice   ACTORS 9
skay s. is only seen   ACTING 33
skeleton s. in their closet   SECRECY 4
ski s. are the most capricious   TRANSPORT 8
ski-ing s. consists of wearing   SPORTS 27
skin taxidermist takes only your s.   TAXES 8
   what a white s. was   BODY 16
skinhead s. big brother   DESCRIPTION 26
skins had such white s.   CLASS 10
   sisters under their s.   WOMEN 33
skit I think you're full of s.   WIT 27
Skugg S. Lies snug   EPITAPHS 14
skulk s. in broad daylight   PEOPLE 20
skunks I never sidestep s.   INSULTS 12
sky s. falls on my head   FILM PRODUCERS 14
slab Beneath this s.   EPITAPHS 22
slain swain getting s.   CINEMA 4
slam Don't s. the lid   MEDICINE 39
   s. the door in the face of age   OLD AGE 12
slamming s. Doors   CHILDREN 3
slap S. that bass   MUSIC 19
   s. them as hard as you can   YOUTH 3
slapped s. my mother   APPEARANCE 24
slashed s.-wrist shot   FILM PRODUCERS 17
slashing damned cutting and s.   PUBLISHING 7
slate thoughts upon a s.   POETS 8
slaves never will be s.   ENGLAND 31
   Rum to S.   AMERICA 11
   s. . . . are so cordial   FILM 12
sleep been to s. for over a year   SLEEP 10
   I love s.   SLEEP 5
   I s. easier now   MIDDLE AGE 12
   like men who s. badly   SLEEP 7
   make anyone go to s.   SLEEP 1
   she tried to s. with me   SEX 36
   s. is so deep   LIBRARIES 4
   suffer nobody to s. in it   RELIGION 2
   when you can't get to s.   LIFE 11
   won't get much s.   ANIMALS 1
sleeping s. with a queen   ROYALTY 66
sleepless S. themselves   POETS 15
sleeps Homer sometimes s.   LITERATURE 8
   Luca Brasi s. with the fishes   DEATH 58
   s. alone at last   EPITAPHS 7

   s. with the enemy   MARRIAGE 5
   s. with the Lords   ROYALTY 6
sleeve lacy s. with a bottle of vitriol   PEOPLE 46
sleigh overtaken a s.   DESCRIPTION 31
slept forgetting you've s. with   SEX 84
   hearing that a judge had s.   JUDGES 12
   s. more than any other   GOVERNMENT 24
   s. with mice   FAME 12
   s. with your Auntie Phyllis   SEX 20
slice S. him where you like   CHARACTER 22
sliding home s. down Coldwater   WEALTH 16
slightly he was S. in *Peter Pan*   PEOPLE 41
slime doin' 'The S.'   DANCE 10
slipped s. on a hamburger in Hamburg

                                                  MISTAKES 24
slipping career must be s.   AWARDS 2
slob You are just a fat s.   RELIGION 46
slogged s. up to Arras   ARMED FORCES 25
slopes butler's upper s.   SATISFACTION 18
Slough fall on S.   TOWNS 7
slow s. boat to China   COUNTRIES 24
   Talk s.   ACTING 36
   telling you to s. down   DEATH 6
   was s. poison   DRINK 7
slower Reading it s.   TECHNOLOGY 16
slowly angel to pass, flying s.   TIME 10
sluicing browsing and s.   FOOD 93
slum swear-word in a rustic s.   LITERATURE 1
slums intimacy of the s.   EDUCATION 44
slurp s., slurp, slurp into the barrels   MONEY 12
slush pure as the driven s.   VIRTUE 1
sluts *Divorced Lesbian S.*   BOOKS 2
smacked s. in the mouth   BOXING 11
small as a s. whisky   DRINK 27
   desire s. beer   DRINK 52
   It's a s. word   TITLES 4
   Microbe is so very s.   SCIENCE 4
   pictures that got s.   FILM STARS 3
   schange me s. scheque   MONEY 6
   s. and full of holes   SMOKING 1
   s. of the back   DESCRIPTION 32
   s.-talking world   LANGUAGE 4
smaller s. fleas to bite 'em   ANIMALS 38
smallest s. room of my house   LETTERS 13
smart Don't get s. alecksy   PROGRESS 10
   versus S. Alec   CHOICE 6
smarter many who thought themselves s.

                                          PRIME MINISTERS 3
smarty be a s.   POLITICAL PARTIES 3
smell run after a nasty s.   SPORTS 2
smelt Are you s.   FOOD 6
smile Cambridge people rarely s.   PLACES 2
   Colman's s.   ACTORS 15
   faint fleeting s.   CHARACTER 16

something it actually tells you s.   POETRY 17
   S. for everyone   THEATRE 50
   S. may be gaining   BASEBALL 11
   was there s.   COMEDY 14
somewhat tough joints more than s.   WOMEN 53
somewhere If you want to get s. else   PROGRESS 3
son bring my 11-year-old s. Bilak here   FAMILY 8
   our s. of a bitch   POLITICIANS 28
   s. asleep on the same benches   POLITICS 52
song I tune my latent s.   SONGS 4
   s. makes you feel thought   WORDS 18
   s. of social significance   POLITICS 59
   think this s.   SELF-KNOWLEDGE 22
   two men to write one s.   SONGS 17
songdom used two-letter word in S.   WORDS 14
songs Clichés make the best s.   SONGS 15
   few good s.   SONGS 10
   know what my s. are about   SONGS 9
   written two s.   WORK 6
   you know 600 folk s.   MUSICIANS 26
songwriters s. should worry about Art   ART 32
son-in-law My s.   FAMILY 17
sonnets *Do Not Attempt the S.*   WRITERS 24
   passibly effective s.   ADVERTISING 4
   written s. all his life   MARRIAGE 23
sons have four s.   PARENTS 18
sooner same mistakes—only s.   LIFE 4
soprano town-and-country s.   SONGS 1
sorrows all my s. are at an end   MARRIAGE 63
   s. of the world   HAPPINESS 8
sorry I'm s., now, I wrote it   QUOTATIONS 2
   S., girls—he's married   PEOPLE 2
   S., I don't   COOKERY 13
   s. for the poor browns   COLOURS 3
soul cents for your s.   HOLLYWOOD 14
   give his s. for the whole world   WALES 3
   improving the s.   BUREAUCRACY 2
souls sell their s.   HYPOCRISY 7
sound none of the s. ideas is original   POLITICS 41
   other not very s.   ENGLAND 35
   something direful in the s.   TOWNS 5
sounds music is better than it s.   MUSIC 38
   similar s. at their ends   POETRY 15
soup cake of portable s.   DIARIES 1
   cannot make a good s.   COOKERY 1
   can steal s.   FILM PRODUCERS 11
   consume like s.   POETRY 3
   Gentlemen do not take s.   CLASS 11
   s. and love   FOOD 28
   s. was fanned   BEHAVIOUR 12
   you pissed in our s.   TRUST 1
south Reykjavik of the S.   TOWNS 26
South African S. police would leave no stone   PREJUDICE 14
soybeans tilling s.   SEX 64

space s. between their cartoons   NEWSPAPERS 8
   S. is almost infinite   UNIVERSE 14
   s. must also be found   WRITERS 30
   s. where nobody is   AMERICA 22
spade call a s. a thpade   SPEECHES 9
   I have never seen a s.   INSULTS 46
spaghetti Everything I have I owe to s.   FOOD 43
   lonely eating s.   FOOD 55
Spain give S. a miss   HOLIDAYS 10
   Go to S. and get killed   POETS 14
   Rain in S.   COUNTRIES 23
Spanglish S. is langlish we know   LANGUAGES 11
Spanish expects the S. Inquisition   COMEDY 34
   reddish and S.   WINE 10
   S. is seldom spoken   LANGUAGES 12
spanking s. black girls   PREJUDICE 17
spare don't s. the horses   TRANSPORT 18
   s. a rope   AMERICA 14
   S. us your thoughts   BIRDS 10
sparerib s. that I can spare   FOOD 78
sparrow wings of a s.   FOOTBALL 3
sparrows know s. from starlings   BIRDS 9
   to the road for the s.   ECONOMICS 6
speak Say she be mute and will not s.   MEN AND WOMEN 48
   s. Esperanto   LANGUAGES 18
   s. ill of everybody   AUTOBIOGRAPHY 18
   s. it fluently   LANGUAGES 17
   teach their children how to s.   LANGUAGES 15
speaker most popular s.   SPEECHES 15
   Not see the S.   WIT 38
speaking have no s. voice   DESCRIPTION 16
   Is he s. to you   BROADCASTING 4
   when I am s.   SPEECHES 1
speaks s. to Me as if I was   ROYALTY 64
spearmint s. lose its flavour   FOOD 70
special those 's. searches'   TRAVEL 5
specialist Being a s. is one thing   WORK 18
species they were an endangered s.   LOVE 9
   Wonderful theory, wrong s.   POLITICS 70
spectacle intimate s.   FILM PRODUCERS 5
speculate when he should not s.   BETTING 9
speculator raised by a s.   FAMILY 41
speech Anthony will make the s.   SPEECHES 2
   aspersion upon my parts of s.   WIT 33
   make a speech on s.   NATURE 9
   Reading a s. with his usual   SPEECHES 21
   s. by Chamberlain   PRIME MINISTERS 5
   s. on economics   SPEECHES 13
   s. to finish being invented   LANGUAGE 3
speeches corn surplus by his s.   SPEECHES 19
speed what good is s.   TRAVEL 15
spell anybody who can s. TUESDAY   WORDS 28
   couldn't s. *Indescribable*   NAMES 2
   Do you s. it with a "V"   WORDS 12

foreigners always s. better — LANGUAGES 25
How do you s. 'accelerator' — WORDS 5
inability to s. — HANDWRITING 3
NO MONEY TILL YOU LEARN TO S. — TELEGRAMS 16
s. football, never mind understand it — FOOTBALL 16
speller He's the wuss s. I know — WORDS 39
taste and fancy of the s. — WORDS 12
spelling My s. is Wobbly — LANGUAGE 9
spellings revised s. — ADVERTISING 2
spend s. more time with me — FAMILY 33
spender real big s. — MEN AND WOMEN 12
spending money-s. always vulgar — MONEY 14
spent realize what you s. — CHRISTMAS 11
spheroid oblate s. — UNIVERSE 2
spill S. your guts at Wimbledon — TENNIS 5
spills s. his seed — NAMES 25
spinach I say it's s. — FOOD 88
spine shiver looking for a s. — INSULTS 23
spinster saved many an English s. — WOMEN 39
spiritual his s. home — DRINK 42
not being a s. people — CRICKET 12
skip his s. struggles — MUSIC 32
spiritualists convention of s. — BROADCASTING 8
spirituality sense of s. — RELIGION 5
s. of man — RELIGION 39
spitter He was a poor s. — TRUST 13
splat can't do s. — WORDS 21
split I s. it so it will stay split. — GRAMMAR 2
spoil s. our own — DRINK 32
s. the purity of my hatred — POLITICIANS 31
spoiled good walk s. — GOLF 10
spoken s. word is repeated — DEBT 6
spoons faster we counted our s. — VIRTUE 9
he can bend s. — SUPERNATURAL 5
let us count our s. — VIRTUE 10
locks up its s. — ARMED FORCES 29
sport only s. can be — BIOGRAPHY 6
s., any sport — SPORTS 13
S., as I have discovered — SPORTS 25
s. of kings — SPORTS 36
s. with ambulances at the bottom — SPORTS 6
sports person who likes s. — SPORTS 24
sportsman man described as a 's.' — SPORTS 7
sports writers craft of s. — JOURNALISM 8
Let's face it, s. — JOURNALISM 7
propose a toast to the s. — SPORTS 37
spot It was a sumpshous s. — WEALTH 2
spout killed when they s. — SPEECHES 20
spring In the s. a young man's fancy — LOVE 22
S., Spring, Spring — ANIMALS 25
s. of endless lies — JOURNALISM 13
springs like Jell-O on s. — BODY 47
springtime S. for Hitler — WEATHER 3
spurn S. not the nobly born — ARISTOCRACY 4

spy s. for or against my country — TRUST 5
s. who came in for a cardie — SECURITY 4
spying s. out all his ways — SCIENCE 9
squandering under a s. Tsar — RUSSIA 4
square country so s. — CANADA 1
so thoroughly s. — MEN AND WOMEN 26
squares lived in s. — WRITERS 1
squash s. is a competitive activity — SPORTS 4
squeak s.'s heard in the orchestra — MUSIC 30
such a narrow s. — RELIGION 37
squeezing with you in the s. of a lemon — TIME 11
squirrels like red s., must be protected — LAW 30
stabbed guy gets s. in the back — OPERA 4
stable Because a man is born in a s. — IRELAND 12
s. or a zoo is better — POLITICIANS 20
stableboy s. among gentlemen — CLASS 28
staff s. to my father's old age — PARENTS 14
stage daughter on the s. — ACTING 5
go on s. — THEATRE 10
On the s. he was natural — ACTORS 21
She comes on s. as if — INSULTS 7
stain any other s. upon your character — LAW 1
stained hole in a s. glass window — WOMEN 5
staircase S. wit — WIT 9
stairs go up my 44 s. — DEATH 33
still go up my 44 s. two at a time — OLD AGE 26
wife down a flight of s. — MISTAKES 1
stake s. driven through his heart — POLITICIANS 25
stamina Patience, s. and good luck — PRIME MINISTERS 16
stamps collect s. — FASHION 7
stand he intended to s. — PRIME MINISTERS 15
s. up to anything — ARMED FORCES 28
up to you whether you s. — SPORTS 37
standing s. on the corner — MEN AND WOMEN 29
stands sits down before he s. up — SPEECHES 15
star Being a s. has made it possible — PREJUDICE 2
discovery of a new s. — COOKERY 4
not exactly a big s. — FAME 21
Suddenly he was a big pop s. — MUSICIANS 19
Wet, she was a s. — FILM STARS 13
stardom S. isn't a profession — FAME 4
stark s. insensibility — EDUCATION 20
starlet S. is the name — WOMEN 29
starlings know sparrows from s. — BIRDS 9
stars fading s. — FAME 7
mistake each other for s. — HOLLYWOOD 1
start s. together and finish together — MUSIC 8
s. without me — SEX 17
When does it s. — CRICKET 13
started get s. with you — AMERICA 12
s. that morning from Devon — TRAVEL 13
starter Few thought he was even a s. — PRIME MINISTERS 3
starving some poor suckers are s. — LIFE 8

state lying in s.   DIPLOMACY 6
stately round a s. park   WRITERS 27
   S. as a galleon   DANCE 7
   S. Homes   ARISTOCRACY 3
   S. Homes of England   MURDER 4
   s. homos of England   SEX 34
statesman requirement of a s.   GOVERNMENT 1
   s. is a politician who's   POLITICIANS 32
statesmen requires grave s.   POLITICS 26
static used to think it was s.   MUSIC 28
station ideas above her s.   LANGUAGES 22
stationmaster where she was s.   CHARACTER 2
statistics lies, damned lies and s.   LIES 6
statue s. has never been set up   CRITICS 25
   S. of Liberty   SEX 3
stay Some people can s. longer in an hour
     HOSPITALITY 7
   S.away from the neighbourhood   FILM 10
   s. up all night   CHILDREN 5
steak they'll have s. too   FOOD 83
steal can s. soup   FILM PRODUCERS 11
   mature poets s.   POETRY 10
   preferred to s.   BUSINESS 7
   s. from many, it's research   WRITING 15
   s. out of your company   CRIME 20
   Thou shalt not s.   CRIME 7
stealing S. too fast   BUSINESS 16
steals s. from the poor   FILM PRODUCERS 18
steam ran out of s.   WIT 18
steam-engine s. in trousers   PEOPLE 36
steamer s. from Harwich   TRANSPORT 11
steel hand of s.   PEOPLE 46
step especially s.-parents   CHILDREN 33
   s. is short from the Sublime   TRANSPORT 13
stepsons and three s.   PARENTS 18
stereo we've nicked your s.   FOOTBALL 1
sterilized thoroughly s.   SATISFACTION 14
stew Musical comedy is the Irish s. of drama
     THEATRE 62
stick barb that makes it s.   WIT 39
   S. close to your desks   ARMED FORCES 11
   s. to ducks   BIRDS 4
   with your Rhythm S.   TITLES 2
sticks S. nix hick pix   HEADLINES 4
stiff S. upper lip   ENGLAND 11
stigma Any s., as the old saying   ARGUMENT 9
still If you s. have to ask   MUSIC 3
   I'm s. here   MISTAKES 18
stimulant supply of the s.   DRINK 23
stimulate s. the phagocytes   MEDICINE 34
stings what s. is justice   LAW 24
stock lock, s. and iceberg   CANADA 6
stockholders working for my s.   BUSINESS 19
stolen had I s. the whole   PRIDE 8

stomach have a s. ache   MEDICINE 18
   healthy s.   FOOD 14
   s. must digest   FOOD 73
stomachs march on their s.   ARMED FORCES 27
stone beats a heart of s.   SPORTS 15
   give them the s.   ENEMIES 5
   heart of s.   CRITICS 37
   spectacular s. in his kidney   SICKNESS 6
   underneath this s.   EPITAPHS 2
stones look for sermons in s.   NATURE 2
stood should of s. in bed   BASEBALL 8
stop come to the end: then s.   ROYALTY 17
   Must s.   BIBLE 1
   nobody's going to s. 'em   BASEBALL 3
   s. everyone from doing it   LAW 13
   S. messing about   COMEDY 46
   S. shooting   FILM 3
storerooms nothing but s.   DICTIONARIES 2
storm I s. and I roar   ANGER 6
story life's s.   AUTOBIOGRAPHY 2
   s. because it is true   TRUTH 7
   s. of a purple man   BIOGRAPHY 8
   used the basic s.   FILM 13
stout Collapse of S. Party   COMEDY 4
   one glass of s.   DRINK 42
   usually short, s. men   SONGS 19
St Pancras Towers of S. Station   MUSIC 7
St Paul's designing S.   ARCHITECTURE 3
   S. had come down   ARCHITECTURE 14
Strabismus Dr S.   TECHNOLOGY 12
straight pretty s. sort of a guy   SELF-KNOWLEDGE 4
   try and get this s.   HONOURS 4
strain sense of s.   ARGUMENT 22
   s. of having to be right   POLITICS 67
Strand I walk down the S.   SOCIETY 12
strange very s. and well bred   BEHAVIOUR 8
stranger S. than fiction   TRUTH 2
   wiles of the s.   FAMILY 29
strangle s. bad persons   MURDER 7
Stratford S. atte Bowe   WOMEN 7
Strauss S.'s car   TRANSPORT 31
straw Pat is the last s.   NAMES 7
strawberry I'm not a s.   SELF-KNOWLEDGE 10
straws start drawing s.   CRICKET 17
streamy long s. flakes of music   DESCRIPTION 20
street don't do it in the s.   SEX 31
   sunny side of the s.   WEALTH 12
streets s. are paved   CINEMA 22
   S. FLOODED. PLEASE ADVISE   TELEGRAMS 3
streetwalking in the s. scene   ACTING 28
strength When you've the s. for it   ACTING 23
streptococci you figure the s. lurk   SICKNESS 13
stretched There was things which he s.   TRUTH 9
stricken entry into many a s. home
     JOURNALISM 23

strike s. it out   WRITING 11
   week of the garbage s.   APPEARANCE 17
   when in doubt, s. it out   WRITING 18
string too much s.   POETRY 8
strings more s. than a philharmonic   WORK 4
striped gaiety is a s. shroud   WALES 6
striptease fashion at a s.   EXAMINATIONS 1
strive need'st not s.   DEATH 14
stroke None so fast as s.   SPORTS 9
   s. a platitude until it purrs   NEWSPAPERS 11
strong two s. men stand   ARGUMENT 22
strove little still she s.   SEX 30
struck not s. by lightning   WEDDINGS 11
   women should be s. regularly   MEN AND WOMEN 6
struggling still s.   SUCCESS 27
strumpet Enter the s. voluntary   SEX 93
Stuart Do you know S. Hampshire   BOOKS 17
stubble nobody knows De s. I've seen   FACES 2
student for every s.   TRANSPORT 34
study Criticism is a s.   CRITICS 15
   little s. you'll go a long way   EDUCATION 32
   s. is the last pursuit   EDUCATION 10
   s. of mankind is *black*   PREJUDICE 16
   s. of wit   WIT 40
stuff our s. can get by without it   LOVE 1
   too short to s. a mushroom   TIME 9
stumbled occasionally s. over the truth   TRUTH 3
stump mount the s. and make a speech   NATURE 9
stunt Did a s. at the bar   PARTIES 1
stunted s. his growth   BODY 49
stupid all questions were s.   SCIENCE 28
   appear s.   STUPIDITY 5
   interesting . . . but s.   COMEDY 51
   It's the economy, s.   ECONOMICS 4
   s. auld bitch   STUPIDITY 1
   s. man is doing something   MORALITY 11
   You s. boy   COMEDY 59
stupidity Seriousness is s.   STUPIDITY 4
Stygian horrible S. smoke   SMOKING 4
style failure may be your s.   FAILURE 3
   make it a matter of s.   SOCIETY 21
   one's s. is one's signature   LETTERS 15
   taste, and s.   BEHAVIOUR 23
subject Etiquette, sacred s.   BEHAVIOUR 22
   one s. you must stay away from   POLITICS 68
subjects elementary s.   EDUCATION 17
   embarked on all five s.   CONVERSATION 6
subjunctive s. mood is in its death throes   GRAMMAR 5
sublime step is short from the S.   TRANSPORT 13
submarines worked with more s.   ACTORS 27
subordinate quaint old s.   GOD 37

subtract don't teach him to s.   EDUCATION 23
subtraction two dollars, that's s.   MEN AND WOMEN 59
suburbs s. of morality   VIRTUE 8
subversive It just had to be s.   NAMES 15
succeed How to s. in business   SUCCESS 15
   If at first you don't s.   FAILURE 3
   If at first you don't s.   FAILURE 5
   if at first you don't s.   FAMILY 15
   want to s. in politics   POLITICS 40
succeeds Nothing s. like excess   SUCCESS 25
   s. he is taken over   SUCCESS 16
   Whenever a friend s.   SUCCESS 24
succès S. *d'estime*   WIT 18
success If *A* is a s. in life   LIFESTYLE 4
   obstacles to achieve his s.   SUCCESS 22
   Satisfied great s.   MUSIC 56
   S. is a science   SUCCESS 26
   S. is the one unpardonable sin   SUCCESS 1
   s. that ran out of   WIT 18
successful s. in your profession   CRIME 11
succession rapid s. of opposing certainties   CERTAINTY 25
suck s. on a boiled sweet   SEX 96
sucker Never give a s.   GAMBLING 3
sucking all that s. and blowing   MARRIAGE 7
sudden s. cuckoo   COUNTRIES 41
sue S. me, sue me   LAW 22
suffice No will s.   SEX 79
suffragettes s. were triumphant   WOMEN 3
sugar can't rhyme 's.'   WORDS 25
   shower you with s. lumps   ANIMALS 21
   S. Replacement Therapy   FOOD 94
   triumph of s. over diabetes   PEOPLE 28
suggest name *not* s.   COUNTRIES 1
suggestions In Rome, they are s.   TRANSPORT 23
suicide committed political s.   POLITICAL PARTIES 16
   committed s.   MARRIAGE 11
   where they commit s.   COUNTRIES 2
suit double-breasted s.   FAME 3
   lugubrious man in a s.   POETS 7
   point his s.   FILM STARS 7
   second-hand s.   QUOTATIONS 11
suitcase mad rocking-horse and a rawhide s.   FILM STARS 5
suitor Each night meant another s.   MIDDLE AGE 12
   You think you are Ann's s.   MEN AND WOMEN 50
suits omelette all over our s.   MISTAKES 9
sukebind s. hangs heavy   NATURE 3
sulk I will not . . . s.   MEN AND WOMEN 11
sulphur Calvin, oat-cakes, and s.   SCOTLAND 10
sultry where the climate's s.   SEX 29
sum six-figure s.   AUTOBIOGRAPHY 23
   To s. up   THEATRE 53

tastes His strongest t. were negative

	SATISFACTION 16
Simple t., you will agree	SATISFACTION 5
t. were exactly like mine	SEX 56

tattooed t. lady — BODY 26

taut who t. it — BODY 36

tax *Excise*. A hateful t. — TAXES 4

lunatic and inequitable t. — TAXES 3

soon be able to t. it — TECHNOLOGY 5

T. collectors who'll never know — TAXES 1

taxidermist and a t. collector — TAXES 8

t. rich people — DEATH 41

taxation Logic and t. — TAXES 5

taxes death and t. — DEATH 23

Death and t. and childbirth — DEATH 47

pay more t., but the hospitals don't kill — BUREAUCRACY 12

They pay less t. — WEALTH 10

true . . . as t. is — TAXES 2

your Queen has to pay t. — ROYALTY 38

taxi I am going in a t. — TRANSPORT 33

look like a t.-cab — FILM STARS 9

taxidermist t. takes only your skin — TAXES 8

Tay Bridge of the Silv'ry T. — DEATH 43

Tchaikovsky If I play T. — MUSIC 32

tea counsel take—and sometimes t. — ROYALTY 53

if this is t. — DRINK 49

large cup of t. — FOOD 62

no Latin word for T. — LANGUAGES 5

Take some more t. — DRINK 11

T., although an Oriental — DRINK 12

t.'s out of the way — DRINK 50

there ain't going to be no t. — WRITERS 23

When I makes t. — DRINK 34

teach wants to t. — EDUCATION 34

teacher asked my t. — WORDS 33

calls his English t. — EDUCATION 25

music t. came twice a week — MUSICIANS 1

t. I most wanted to emulate — WINE 1

teaches He who cannot, t. — EDUCATION 37

tea-girl t.'s chance to kiss — PARTIES 8

team breeding our own t. — FOOTBALL 29

simple t. talk — FOOTBALL 5

teams both t. are wearing white — SPORTS 26

West Country t. — CRICKET 10

teapot covering a t. — APPEARANCE 7

further than warming the t. — WRITERS 23

tear Wipe the t., baby dear — WAR 31

teases knows it t. — CHILDREN 8

teatray like a t. in the sky — UNIVERSE 4

technical few t. details — SEX 66

technological Italians' t. contribution — SCIENCE 7

technology modern t. — HISTORY 16

T. . . . the knack — TECHNOLOGY 6

teddy t. bear to the nation — PEOPLE 1

teems t. with hidden meaning — WORDS 15

teenager as a t. you are at — YOUTH 4

t. in San Francisco — GENERATION GAP 7

teens seen me in my t. — YOUTH 5

teeth Americans wear their t. — FACES 9

everyone has perfect t. — APPEARANCE 15

is his front t. — BETTING 8

play the guitar with your t. — MUSICIANS 11

take the bull between your t. — WIT 11

two back t. — BODY 43

we lose t. — SPORTS 18

women have fewer t. — SCIENCE 23

teetotaller beer t. — WINE 8

telephone hear his t. ring without — TECHNOLOGY 10

no t. or wife — WRITING 19

teapot or a t. — APPEARANCE 7

under the table with the t. — WAR 9

telephoned t. a semicolon — JOURNALISM 4

t. by the *Sunday Express* — NEWSPAPERS 16

telephones Tudor monarchy with t. — POLITICS 15

television be on t. — TELEVISION 14

first law of t. — BROADCASTING 1

intelligent enough to watch t. — SPORTS 43

movie out of for t. — BOOKS 10

Norwegian t. — TELEVISION 2

rich person on t. — POLITICS 14

sex in Ireland before t. — TELEVISION 5

switch on the t. — BROADCASTING 6

t. commercials — DOGS 2

T. has brought back murder — MURDER 6

T. is for appearing on — TELEVISION 4

T. is more — TELEVISION 3

T. is simultaneously blamed — TELEVISION 9

T.? The word is half Greek — TELEVISION 10

thinking man's t. — SEX 43

Telford T. is so dull — TOWNS 20

tell Don't t. me — DEATH 61

For this was T. a hero — COUNTRIES 41

How can they t. — DEATH 53

I'll t. thee everything I can — OLD AGE 8

never can t. — CERTAINTY 22

t. her she mustn't — CHILDREN 34

those who cannot t. — EXAMINATIONS 5

tells it actually t. you something — POETRY 17

t. you — BORES 15

temper never to lose me t. — ANGER 5

temple Shirley T. dolls — MEN AND WOMEN 14

temporary only a t. solution — DEATH 2

temptation made liquor for t. — DRINK 35

maximum of t. — MARRIAGE 108

resist everything except t. — VIRTUE 24

yield to t. — CHOICE 8

tempting nothing very t. — HEAVEN 2

temptress buxom t. — ACTORS 32

thought (*cont.*):
t. of an unparalleled confusion   WRITERS 21
t. of the answer   FILM PRODUCERS 10
thoughts Dr Tayler's t. are very white   MIND 16
t. are seldom   INSULTS 16
thousand If I had five t. a year   VIRTUE 17
t.; too much   ROYALTY 33
threat Cameron's actually a serious t.   POLITICIANS 12
t. of a woman   CHILDREN 16
three breakfast t. times   FOOD 51
T. in one, one in three   RELIGION 7
t.-pipe problem   CRIME 12
t. white feathers   CLASS 9
T. Wise Men   CHRISTMAS 4
threw She t. me in front of the judges   SPORTS 5
thriller t., a chilla, and a killa   BOXING 2
throat knife to a t.   PUBLISHING 14
rustle in your dying t.   DEATH 72
sore t. during my most prolific   POETRY 13
throne bolster behind the t.   ROYALTY 58
through do *you* read books t.   READING 10
thrown should be t.   BOOKS 13
then t. out   COOKERY 11
thumb stood out like a sore t.   MISTAKES 19
thunderstorm compulsory, like a t.   CHRISTMAS 9
tickle t. her with a hoe   AUSTRALIA 2
tickled I'll be t. to death to go   WAR 31
tide incoming t.   DRINK 28
tie discouraging t.   DRESS 14
little rebellion was to have my t. loose   DRESS 11
ties buys his t.   DRESS 5
tiger On a t.   SEX 10
one poor t.   ANIMALS 35
smile on the face of the t.   ANIMALS 4
T. fierce   EPITAPHS 3
T. well repay   ANIMALS 6
tighten T. it   MONEY 23
tights she played it in t.   ROYALTY 14
tile it's white t.   EDUCATION 31
Timbuctoo On the plains of T.   BIRDS 11
time expands to fill the t.   HOUSEWORK 1
get me to the church on t.   WEDDINGS 7
It saves t.   BEHAVIOUR 6
I was on t.   OLD AGE 28
no t. in reading   READING 6
original good t.   CHARACTER 18
rapid flight of t.   HOLIDAYS 4
spend more t. with me   FAMILY 33
That passed the t.   TIME 5
this t. of year   WEATHER 9
T. is an illusion   TIME 1
T. is the one thing   GENERATION GAP 1
T. shall moult away his wings   LOVE 42

T. spent on any item   TIME 13
t. to cultivate modesty   PRIDE 6
unconscionable t. dying   ROYALTY 20
What's the bleeding t.   MEDICINE 17
what to do with the t.   WORK 11
will be on t.   ARMED FORCES 6
wrong bar or bed at the wrong t.   MISTAKES 7
timely by a t. compliance   SEX 38
times able letters to T.   PEOPLE 8
bad times just t.   HOPE 4
timetables Europe by railway t.   WAR 26
timid capital is always t.   NEWSPAPERS 12
Timothy T. Winters   CHILDREN 10
tinge t. of disgrace   GOSSIP 9
tinkering first rule of intelligent t.   TECHNOLOGY 4
tinkling t. silvery laugh   HUMOUR 41
tinned pouring t. sauce   COOKERY 3
tins dine out of t.   FOOD 96
tinsel Behind the phoney t.   HOLLYWOOD 10
tip straight t. from a business   PUBLISHING 6
they're t. mad   FRANCE 10
tiptoe stand on t.   HEALTH 3
tire t. of a lecture   EDUCATION 22
tired always was t.   EPITAPHS 4
go home when you're t.   LIFESTYLE 1
has always t. me   ART 6
I'm t. of Love   MONEY 4
they'll be bloody t.   CRICKET 18
t. of London   TOWNS 18
tiring Shakespeare is so t.   ACTING 17
Titanic furniture on the deck of the T.   POLITICS 49
title editions and t.-pages   BOOKS 3
No need to change t.   PUBLISHING 11
t. from a better man   PRIDE 8
t. is really rather   ARISTOCRACY 17
unlikely you've got a t.   TITLES 8
titles 'Oxford Book of . . . ' t.   PUBLISHING 5
that of the rich for t.   TITLES 7
titter t. ye not   COMEDY 39
toad intelligent Mr T.   EDUCATION 15
t. in an equally greasy hole   FOOD 57
toast eating bits of cold t.   PARTIES 9
had a piece of t.   FOOD 60
propose a t. to the sports writers   SPORTS 37
tobacco good t.   HONOURS 3
leave off t.   SMOKING 5
no time for t. since   SMOKING 6
Toby seen T.'s willy   BODY 42
today get where I am t.   COMEDY 21
toenail suffering from an ingrowing t.   CHILDREN 47
toes lick your lacquered t.   ROYALTY 15
makes sensitive t.   DRESS 16
toff I saunter along like t.   SOCIETY 12
toga mistakes his pinafore for a t.   WRITERS 14

train (*cont.*):

to read in the t. DIARIES 7

t. going into a tunnel HUMOUR 42

trained We t. hard MANAGEMENT 2

trainers pair of t. ARISTOCRACY 8

trains t. in last year's Bradshaw GOVERNMENT 23

tram I'm a t. TRANSPORT 16

tramp lady is a t. BEHAVIOUR 15

tranquillity remembered in t. HUMOUR 36

transcendental t. meditation with a punch-line

FISHING 2

transition t. from Who's Who RETIREMENT 3

translate It doesn't t. WORDS 21

translated t. into Italian LANGUAGES 27

translation Browning's t. CRITICS 31

mistake in the t. MORALITY 14

Perhaps we could have a t. LANGUAGES 16

translations T. (like wives) MARRIAGE 27

transplanted When our organs have been t.

MEDICINE 19

transvestite t. potter won AWARDS 6

trap Meetings are a great t. MANAGEMENT 4

t. in a trap DANCE 12

trapped t. or shot MEN 8

trashman t. and the policeman INSULTS 24

travel award for t.-writing AWARDS 7

Englishman does not t. ENGLAND 36

never t. without DIARIES 7

rapid and convenient t. TRAVEL 23

real way to t. TRANSPORT 14

ship would *not* t. due West TRAVEL 3

thirty years of t. together MARRIAGE 89

t. broadens the behind TRAVEL 10

t. broadens the mind TRAVEL 4

t. I'm too late TIME 14

t. light BODY 20

two classes of t. TRAVEL 1

Why do the wrong people t. TRAVEL 6

travelled which way he t. PRIME MINISTERS 4

travelling T. Swede COUNTRIES 10

trawler When seagulls follow a t. JOURNALISM 9

tread t. most neatly EPITAPHS 2

treason [T.], Sire, is a question TRUST 12

t. to his country TRUST 8

word t. to me means nothing TRUST 1

treated t. me very well UNIVERSE 5

treatment scientific t. for all diseases

MEDICINE 34

tree barking up the wrong t. CRITICS 11

billboard lovely as a t. ADVERTISING 7

cut down a redwood t. NATURE 9

sit under a t. TRAVEL 19

when we chop a t. NATURE 4

trees birds coughing in the t. HOLLYWOOD 6

I think of the poor t. NEWSPAPERS 13

naturally felled t. BUSINESS 14

T. in the orchard COUNTRY 5

trembles list of their names, he t. WAR 29

trench like t. warfare PRESIDENTS 16

triangle idea for a new t. IDEAS 1

triangles loved in t. WRITERS 1

trickle T.-down theory ECONOMICS 6

tried pick the one I never t. VIRTUE 22

trinity also is a T. man GOD 10

hazy about the T. RELIGION 7

trip t. through a sewer HOLLYWOOD 13

triple Lazarus with a t. bypass POLITICIANS 19

trisexual I am t. SEX 48

I'm a t. SEX 21

triste jamais t. HOPE 7

triumph t. of hope over experience MARRIAGE 76

t. of modern science MEDICINE 37

t. of the embalmer's art PEOPLE 42

trivial diversion of t. men POLITICS 50

Nothing t., I hope SICKNESS 15

Trojan T. 'orses will jump out DIPLOMACY 2

trooping t. in companies HUMAN RACE 4

trophy he wants a t. MEN AND WOMEN 16

trot Slowed down to a t. SICKNESS 3

trouble asking for t. NAMES 22

my *business* to get him in t. BOXING 13

t. with being best man WEDDINGS 8

t. with the French LANGUAGES 6

t. with words WORDS 31

when you're in t. HOLLYWOOD 7

women and care and t. WOMEN 66

troubles over all its t. HOME 11

trouser illluminated t.-clip TECHNOLOGY 12

trousers best t. on DRESS 8

ironing a pair of t. SUCCESS 8

I wear the t. HOME 19

my t. fell down FACES 7

steam-engine in t. PEOPLE 36

t. so copiously flared DRESS 1

trout find a t. in the milk LAW 35

trowel lay it on with a t. ROYALTY 24

reach of a t. ARCHITECTURE 15

truck apologizes to the t. ENGLAND 20

truckman t., the trashman INSULTS 24

Trudeau T., Canada has at last produced

CANADA 4

true entirely t. GOSSIP 12

no matter how t. PAST 13

nothing in the newspapers is ever t.

NEWSPAPERS 3

story because it is t. TRUTH 7

truer nothing's t. than that TAXES 2

trumpet creep of a Miles Davis t. solo BORES 10

trumpets to the sound of t.   HEAVEN 6
trust difficult to t. the Chinese   TRUST 3
   t. with anything   POLITICAL PARTIES 18
trusted is not to be t.   POWER 2
   t. neither of them as far   TRUST 13
   t. two persons whom I knew   PEOPLE 26
truth anxious to tell the t.   TRUTH 5
   ask for t.   ART 35
   best policy to speak the t.   TRUTH 6
   I just tell the t.   TRUTH 8
   lures the t.   JOURNALISM 24
   mainly he told the t.   TRUTH 9
   stumbled over the t.   TRUTH 3
   telling the t. about them   POLITICS 66
   t. at last   EPITAPHS 18
   t. is always strange   TRUTH 2
   t. is chimerical   TRUTH 1
   T. is no more at issue   EXAMINATIONS 1
   t. is rarely pure   TRUTH 11
   T. is suppressed   SECURITY 6
   t. was like a second home   POLITICIANS 21
   wedded to the t.   GOVERNMENT 30
truthful t. than factual   HUMOUR 28
try lesson is, never t.   FAILURE 6
   t. again. Then quit   FAILURE 5
   t. anything once   SEX 21
   t. him afterwards   LAW 25
trying business without really t.   SUCCESS 15
   I am t. to be   INSULTS 39
tsar T. of all the rushes   FILM PRODUCERS 13
   under a squandering T.   RUSSIA 4
tub got his t.   TENNIS 8
tuba t. is certainly the most   MUSIC 12
tube toothpaste is out of the t.   POLITICS 30
Tudor do you know T. Cornwall   BOOKS 17
   US presidency is a t. monarchy   POLITICS 15
Tuesday If it's T.   TRAVEL 24
   T. simply doesn't count   WORDS 28
tummy he'll get a t. ache   FOOD 53
tune I t. my latent song   SONGS 4
   keep thinkin'll turn into a t.   MUSIC 23
tunes I only know two t.   MUSIC 21
tunnel at the end of the t.   GAMBLING 2
   train going into a t.   HUMOUR 42
turbot by way of t.   CLERGY 17
   T., Sir   FOOD 86
turd rhyming is nat worth a t.   POETRY 6
turkeys nice to yu t. dis christmas   CHRISTMAS 13
   surrounded by t.   SUCCESS 20
turned anything t. up   HOPE 5
Turner resembled a T. sunset   DESCRIPTION 15
   won the T. Prize   AWARDS 6
turnip candle in that great t.   STUPIDITY 2
turnstones T. were turning   DESCRIPTION 24

turtle t. Enormously fert'le   ANIMALS 25
   t. lives   ANIMALS 30
Tutankhamun T.'s tomb   COLOURS 2
TV T. —a clever contraption   TELEVISION 1
tweed t. nightgowns   ENGLAND 13
tweet I say 't. tweet'   SONGS 18
twentieth-century t. failure   SUCCESS 5
twenty T. years of romance   MARRIAGE 125
   you're t. minutes   CHARACTER 21
twenty-twenty Hindsight is always t.   PAST 15
twice must do t. as well as men   MEN AND WOMEN 63
   nothing happens, t.   THEATRE 36
   so good they named it t.   NEW YORK 5
   t. as much as your last   THEATRE 60
twinkle Twinkle, t., little bat   UNIVERSE 4
twins Clara threw the t.   CHILDREN 19
twisted t. imagination   ART 16
two are there t. nine o'clocks   TIME 3
   Audience of T.   THEATRE 61
   Between t. evils   VIRTUE 22
   make only t. people miserable   MARRIAGE 22
   since he was about t.   BODY 42
   starts with the number t.   WINE 9
   there are t. meanings   WORDS 8
   T. for a woman   MEDICINE 5
   t. men to write one song   SONGS 17
   t. of them   PEOPLE 5
   t. people with a German shepherd   TRAVEL 9
   t. things about   ANIMALS 37
   t. things that will be   DRINK 58
   wanna go for t.   CRIME 2
   Why I see t.   WIT 38
typewriter changing a t. ribbon   WRITING 2
typewriters electric t. keep going mmmmmmm   TECHNOLOGY 3
   million t.   COMPUTERS 8
typewriting t. machine, when played   MUSIC 58
tyrannical t. and uncaring   TRANSPORT 19
tyranny if you really want to end t.   PRESIDENTS 3
   t. of the razor   CRICKET 14

ubiquitous by being at any rate u.   INTELLIGENCE 3
uglier u. a man's legs are   GOLF 11
ugliness u. was destined   APPEARANCE 11
ugly Bessie, you're u.   INSULTS 11
   Frazier is so u.   FACES 1
   I was so u.   APPEARANCE 24
   knowing that he is u.   JUDGES 4
   than to be u.   APPEARANCE 22
ukelele died playing the u.   EPITAPHS 17
ulsterior look for the U. motive   PREJUDICE 15
Ulysses Joist wrote U.   WORDS 4
   kiss the hand that wrote U.   WRITERS 18
um Mortals use 'u.'   SPEECHES 11

umble so very 'u. HYPOCRISY 3
umbrella lend you an u. in fair weather MONEY 13
   unjust steals the just's u. VIRTUE 4
unattractive most u. old thing OLD AGE 21
unawareness u. of the world of ideas IDEAS 6
unbearable in victory u. WAR 6
unbeatable In defeat u. WAR 6
unbends nothing u. the mind WOMEN 19
unbribed man will do u. JOURNALISM 27
uncanny u. ear that might have WRITERS 38
uncivilized unconquered, and u. ENGLAND 24
uncle Call U. Teddy FAMILY 24
   obliged to call him U. CLERGY 1
   U. Bud's pants DESCRIPTION 30
   u. who lives there FAMILY 46
uncles wronged u. FAMILY 56
uncomfortable he is only u. ENGLAND 30
unconquered kept u. ENGLAND 24
unconscionable u. time dying ROYALTY 20
uncool U. people FASHION 7
undecided five who are u. BASEBALL 12
under have been u. the host DRINK 47
   talk u. their feet PRESIDENTS 21
underachiever he's an u. GOD 1
undercover queen of u. loves SECRECY 8
underdeveloped u. the country WOMEN 18
underestimate u. them FOOTBALL 23
underestimating u. the intelligence INTELLIGENCE 11
undergraduates of the u. EDUCATION 10
undersexed happy u. celibate SUCCESS 5
undersized could call the u. MEN AND WOMEN 47
understand don't u. too hot SEX 78
   God doesn't seem to u. WRITING 6
   u. English LANGUAGES 2
   u. what you're saying ACTING 19
understanding pass all u. POETS 11
   salary depends on not u. MANAGEMENT 8
   u. all the ins BODY 48
undertakers As u. walk before the hearse THEATRE 20
   nothing against u. FUNERALS 3
undertaking u. of Great Advantage SECRECY 2
underwater Baptists are only funny u. RELIGION 65
   German spoken u. LANGUAGES 1
underwear dad's name all over his u. FASHION 9
undesirable I knows an u. character SELF-KNOWLEDGE 11
undone Anne Donne, U. FAMILY 14
unearned no better example of unearned u. MONEY 22
uneatable pursuit of the u. SPORTS 41

uneducated government by the u. GOVERNMENT 3
unemployment long stretch of u. THEATRE 56
un-English so very u. ART 3
   u. dislike of taxation TAXES 3
unexpectedness I call *u.* GARDENS 10
unfair It's *sooo* u. COMEDY 29
unfit u. for military service ARMED FORCES 14
   u. for public business DIPLOMACY 10
unfurnished write u. FOOLISHNESS 13
ungrammatical invariably u. GRAMMAR 8
unhappily result of being u. married POLITICS 54
unhappy instinct for being u. HAPPINESS 10
   Men who are u. SLEEP 7
   u. anywhere CANADA 7
   u. family FAMILY 49
uniform u. 'e wore ARMED FORCES 19
   u. must work its way WOMEN 12
uninspiring I may be u. ROYALTY 36
union u. of a deaf man MARRIAGE 33
   u. rules are a little strict WORK 16
unique conscious of being u. SELF-KNOWLEDGE 28
United States Can the U. ever become SCOTLAND 7
   litigant drawn to the U. LAW 5
universe better ordering of the u. UNIVERSE 1
   Fuller 'accepted the u.' UNIVERSE 3
   good u. next door UNIVERSE 6
   imagine the u. run GOD 34
   Lord designed the U. UNIVERSE 10
   u. is a totality of observations UNIVERSE 13
   u. is not only queerer UNIVERSE 8
university call it the U. EDUCATION 10
   Jimmy's u. EDUCATION 31
   U. of Life EDUCATION 7
   We are the U. PRIDE 7
unjust u. steals the just's umbrella VIRTUE 4
unkind witty, u. things FOOLISHNESS 1
unknowable decide the u. LAW 39
unknown apart from the known and the u. PHILOSOPHY 6
   buried the U. Prime Minister PRIME MINISTERS 1
   something equally u. DICTIONARIES 11
unknowns also unknown u. IGNORANCE 7
unlike So u. anything else LIFE 20
unloaded Luggage left alone u. TRAVEL 8
unlucky u. that he runs into accidents MISTAKES 22
unmarried keep u. as long as he can MARRIAGE 107
unnatural u. act HUMOUR 13
unnoticed all your best work go u. SECRECY 3
unpardonable Success is the one u. sin SUCCESS 1
unplayable another u. work MUSIC 48

widow French w. in every bedroom   HOTELS 4
like an Indian w.   WOMEN 39
widower inconsolable w.   GENERATION GAP 15
widowhood comfortable estate of w.
   MARRIAGE 61
wife And nobody's w.   WOMEN 30
between w. and death   DEATH 50
colonies in your w.'s name   WAR 15
due to their w.   INDEXES 4
fear repartee in a w.   MARRIAGE 130
Here lies my w.   MARRIAGE 51
his w. has to help him   TRUST 4
hope that keeps up a w.'s spirits   MARRIAGE 61
How's the w.   CRICKET 3
if God had been his w.   GOD 36
in want of a w.   MARRIAGE 9
joined me as my w.   MARRIAGE 71
kicking his w. down a flight of stairs
   MISTAKES 1
look out for a w.   BEHAVIOUR 29
marry my second w.   LOVE 21
mistook ye for my w.   STUPIDITY 1
My w.'s gone to the country   MARRIAGE 17
no telephone or w.   WRITING 19
place my w. under a pedestal   MARRIAGE 1
riding to and from his w.   TRAVEL 30
rug-making or w.-swapping   BIRDS 2
she is your w.   ADVERTISING 8
Take my w.   COMEDY 48
That's my first w. up there   MARRIAGE 118
untrue to his w.   INTELLIGENCE 1
virtuous w. of mine has left me   MORALITY 2
What I need is a w.   MARRIAGE 34
Why does my w. like young men   CRITICS 34
w. and a prostitute   COOKERY 9
w. came home from work   FAMILY 5
w. has ever taken   COUNTRIES 31
w. ran off with the fellow next door
   MEN AND WOMEN 7
w. turning the pages   SPEECHES 7
your w. I would put poison   INSULTS 4
wig resemble a w.   GOVERNMENT 5
resplendent in his wig   GOVERNMENT 8
Wigan mothers-in-law and W. Pier
   CIVIL SERVANTS 2
wild I'm w. again   MEN AND WOMEN 18
lurking like w. beasts   HOSPITALITY 2
w. as pension plans   POETS 5
wildebeeste Herds of w.   PLACES 5
will I'm in his w.   FAMILY 46
My w. is strong   MORALITY 7
political w.   ARGUMENT 13
W. you, won't you   DANCE 5
You w., Oscar, you will   WIT 50

Willie needs a W.   PRIME MINISTERS 24
wouldn't have a W. or a Sam   MARRIAGE 87
willing Barkis is w.   LOVE 11
coalition of the w.   COUNTRIES 36
willy Can't see my little W.   BODY 31
seen Toby's w.   BODY 42
Wilson fourteenth Mr W.   ARISTOCRACY 10
Wimbledon Spill your guts at W.   TENNIS 5
wimps Lunch is for w.   MANAGEMENT 9
win finally w. something   TENNIS 9
You w. some, you lose some   SUCCESS 11
wind how the w. doth ramm   WEATHER 17
upset in a high w.   SLEEP 3
when the w. blew due East   TRAVEL 3
w. that swept down from the Urals   PLACES 9
window appears for a moment at a w.   THEATRE 8
hole in a stained glass w.   WOMEN 5
look out of the w.   THEATRE 3
out of the w.   BODY 3
w., a casement   EDUCATION 12
windows if we had glass w.   SECRECY 7
wine buy a bottle of w.   SEX 37
get into the w.   WINE 3
Good w. needs no bush   ADVERTISING 6
Marquis's Son Unused to W.   HEADLINES 12
red w. of Shiraz   BODY 15
so much w.   WINE 5
take a glass of w.   HOME 15
white w. came up   FOOD 47
w. and whoopee   GOD 29
w. and women   HAPPINESS 4
w. was a farce   FOOD 66
wines finest w. available to humanity   DRINK 51
wing I've got to take under my w.   OLD AGE 21
winner next to Michael W.   CHOICE 12
winning as important as w.   SUCCESS 4
winter bad being homeless in the w.   POVERTY 8
English w.—ending in July   WEATHER 4
It's the middle of w.   WEATHER 18
Middle of W.   CHRISTMAS 1
through the perils of w.   WEATHER 20
W. for Poland and France   WEATHER 3
W. is icummen in   WEATHER 17
wipe Gives it a w.—and all is gone   POETS 8
wire Along the electric w.   TELEGRAMS 1
wisdom w. on the Queen's Ministers   RELIGION 36
wise Do you think it's w.   WINE 4
Nor ever did a w. one   ROYALTY 56
Three W. Men   CHRISTMAS 4
w. father   FAMILY 38
wisecrack w. that played Carnegie   WIT 22
wiser no w. now than I was   JUDGES 13
wisest many iv th' wisest   NEW YORK 3

won never w. an argument	ARGUMENT 3
Sun Wot W. It	HEADLINES 5
we'd have w. the war	WAR 21
wonder One can only w.	MISTAKES 5
see the boneless w.	PRIME MINISTERS 11
wonderland Malice in W.	NAMES 9
won't administrative w.	ARGUMENT 13
wood can't get the w.	COMEDY 55
woodcock w., by a happy fluke	BIRDS 6
w.'s leg	FOOD 5
wooden APPROPRIATE W. GIFT	TELEGRAMS 24
literary man—*with* a w. leg	LITERATURE 12
w. dildoes are made	BUSINESS 14
woodland few acres of w.	GARDENS 2
woodpecker went steady with a w.	SEX 47
woods Whose w. these are	COUNTRY 14
woodshed Something nasty in the w.	
	MISTAKES 14
wool If I send her the w.	SEX 12
woollier w. animals	ART 20
woolsack W. without a Lord	GOVERNMENT 8
Woolworth paying a visit to W.'s	
	PRIME MINISTERS 5
word beauty of the written w.	ADVERTISING 2
for the wrong w.	CRITICS 32
having a cross w.	ARGUMENT 10
It's a small w.	TITLES 4
know only one w.	HOLLYWOOD 19
most used two-letter w.	WORDS 14
no individual w.	HANDWRITING 6
no w. in the Irish language	SEX 68
packed up into one w.	WORDS 8
spoken w. is repeated	DEBT 6
"waiter" is such a funny w.	FOOD 79
When I use a w.	WORDS 9
w. about oral contraception	SEX 6
w. for doing things tomorrow	WORDS 32
w. is half Greek	TELEVISION 10
w. shows up instead	WORDS 16
words borrow the w.	DICTIONARIES 9
changed the w. of the song	OLD AGE 31
combination of w.	WORDS 7
four-letter w.	WORDS 30
frying pan of your w.	WRITERS 15
get your w.' worth from a poet	WIT 23
knows a hundred and twenty w.	MARRIAGE 79
lost for w.	CRITICS 33
Man does not live by w.	WORDS 35
many frank w.	DIPLOMACY 3
most beautiful w.	WORDS 2
my w. are my own	ROYALTY 22
Ordinary w. cannot express	BIRDS 1
say a few w.	SPEECHES 10
trouble with w.	WORDS 31
W. are chameleons	WORDS 17

W. are like leaves	WORDS 29
W. make you think a thought	WORDS 18
w. of tongue and pen	SATISFACTION 6
Wordsworth Fancy a symphony by W.	POETS 1
W. sometimes wakes	LITERATURE 8
wordy French are always too w.	FRANCE 6
work another way that doesn't w.	FAILURE 4
can walk to w.	PRESIDENTS 13
domestic w.	HOUSEWORK 5
Eleven months' hard w.	GARDENS 7
hard w. never killed anybody	WORK 23
immortality through my w.	DEATH 3
never have to w. again	TELEVISION 13
Nice w. if you can get it	LOVE 17
plenty of w. to do	WORK 17
thing that doesn't w. any more	PAST 8
those that don't w.	TECHNOLOGY 2
used to w.	ACTING 21
waist is my own w.	BODY 22
Why do men delight in w.	WORK 21
w. at it	GOLF 6
W. does age you so	WORK 10
W. expands to fill the time	WORK 22
W. is always much more	WORK 9
W. is the curse	WORK 27
W. is *x*	LIFESTYLE 4
W. late	SUCCESS 10
w. terribly hard	EDUCATION 27
w. very hard	WORK 24
w. were such a splendid thing	WORK 14
worked W. myself up from nothing	POVERTY 13
workhouses w. and Coffin Makers	LITERATURE 24
working besides the one he's w. on	WRITERS 40
have a w. relationship	GOD 20
Heaven will protect a w.-girl	POVERTY 17
I killin' meself w.	MEN AND WOMEN 38
W. in Hollywood	HOLLYWOOD 5
w. on a case of Scotch	DRINK 8
working-class if it wasn't for w. people	CLASS 34
job all w. parents want	POLITICS 1
workings w. of Providence	ARGUMENT 17
works Greed w.	ECONOMICS 15
world around the w. to count the cats	TRAVEL 28
arranging the w.	TECHNOLOGY 6
makes the w. go round	DRINK 38
not as fast as the w. record	SPORTS 11
only one girl in the w.	MEN AND WOMEN 66
small-talking w.	LANGUAGE 4
upstairs into the w.	CLASS 8
w. doesn't read its books	READING 11
w. famous	CANADA 8
w. has treated me	UNIVERSE 5
w. has turned upside down	PAST 3
w. is a comedy	HUMAN RACE 13
w. is disgracefully managed	UNIVERSE 7